The

Bessie Parmet Kannerstein '32

𝔐emorial 𝔉und

Established by

MR. JOSEPH PARMET

for the purchase of

REFERENCE BOOKS

for the

CEDAR CREST COLLEGE

LIBRARY

American Directors

Volume II

American Directors

Volume II

Jean-Pierre Coursodon
with Pierre Sauvage

McGRAW-HILL BOOK COMPANY
New York   St. Louis   San Francisco   Bogotá   Guatemala
Hamburg   Lisbon   Madrid   Mexico   Montreal   Panama
Paris   San Juan   São Paulo   Tokyo   Toronto

840086

The essays in this volume appear in print for the first time, with the following exceptions:

Michael Henry's *Brian DePalma* originally appeared as "L'Oeil du malin" in *Positif,* no. 193, May 1977. Copyright © 1977 by Michael Henry and Editions Opta. All rights reserved. Translated by permission (article updated by the author).

Richard Thompson and Tim Hunter's *Clint Eastwood* originally appeared as "Clint Eastwood: Auteur" in *Film Comment,* Vol. 14, no. 1, January-February 1978. Copyright © 1978 by Richard Thompson and Tim Hunter. All rights reserved. Reprinted by permission (article updated by Richard Thompson).

Jean-Pierre Coursodon's *Jerry Lewis* originally appeared in slightly different form as "Jerry Lewis's Films: No Laughing Matter?" in *Film Comment,* Vol. 11, no. 4, July-August 1975. Copyright © 1975 by the Film Society of Lincoln Center. All rights reserved. Reprinted by permission.

Ronnie Scheib's *Ida Lupino* originally appeared in somewhat different form as "Ida Lupino, Auteuress" in *Film Comment,* Vol. 16, no. 1, January-February 1980. Copyright © 1980 by Ronnie Scheib. All rights reserved. Reprinted by permission.

Mark LeFanu's *Bob Rafelson* originally appeared, in a longer and somewhat different version, in *Positif,* no. 206, May 1978. Copyright © 1977 by Mark LeFanu and Nouvelles Editions Opta. All rights reserved. Translated by permission.

1 2 3 4 5 6 7 8 9 0 D O C D O C 8 7 6 5 4 3

ISBN 0-07-013264-X {H.C.}
     0-07-013262-3 {PBK}

LIBRARY OF CONGRESS CATALOGING IN PUBLICATION DATA

Coursodon, Jean Pierre.
American directors.
Includes filmographies.
1. Moving-picture producers and directors—United
States—Dictionaries. I. Sauvage, Pierre. II. Title.
PN1998.A2C657   791.43'0233'0922   82-15199
ISBN 0-07-013263-1 (v. 1)   AACR2
ISBN 0-07-013261-5 (pbk.: v. 1)
ISBN 0-07-013264-X (v. 2)
ISBN 0-07-013262-3 (pbk.: v. 2)

Book designed by Judy Allan

Contents

Preface

The idea of a book presenting original, comprehensive essays on virtually every American film director of recognized'(and, in quite a few instances, underrecognized) stature goes back to the early 1970s, although most of the entries in these two volumes of *American Directors* were written later, in the mid and late seventies, or even, in some cases, as late as 1982. The project went through numerous phases and changes over the years, but the final product is not too wide of the original mark. Within certain self-imposed limitations, all but a very few of the filmmakers with a claim to the serious film student's attention have been included; and although a few articles have been reprinted from magazines, 95 percent of all the essays have been written specifically for the book, and appear in print for the first time.

It is safe to say that the endeavor is the first of its kind in any language. There have been precedents of sorts, of course: Andrew Sarris's classic *The American Cinema* (1968), and my own "Dictionary of Directors" in *Trente ans de cinéma américain* (1970, co-authored by Bertrand Tavernier); but entries in both books were quite short—sometimes a few hundred words, or even less. They were capsule evaluations rather than the full-length essays devoted to most of the directors included in these two volumes.

American Directors is a collaborative effort. I have written 66 of the 118 essays in the two volumes. Twenty contributors wrote between 1 and 3 (in one case 4) essays each, for a total of 42, while Pierre Sauvage, who was involved with the project from the very beginning, took care of the balance.

When I first met Pierre Sauvage in 1970, he had worked in Paris as an assistant to the French Cinémathèque's legendary director Henri Langlois and was then involved in film production as an assistant to producer-director Otto Preminger. He had very high praise for the recently published *Trente ans de cinéma américain* and urged me to attempt an American equivalent, offering to collaborate with me on it. When I took him up on his offer some time later, it did not take us long to realize that the format of the French book did not lend itself to an effective American adaptation, and that we should think in terms of writing a brand new book. The project went through a series of evolutions in the decade after we embarked upon it, and so did our respective roles in it. My own texts, mostly on major directors, got longer and more ambitious, squeezing out, by mutual consent, a number of Pierre's excellent essays on lesser directors (he also compiled the filmographies and did considerable initial research).

At the same time, Pierre's own directorial activities increasingly took precedence over his interest in film criticism, and his involvement in the book decreased. But overall, his role has been an important one throughout the history of this book; his advice and moral support have been invaluable.

By early 1977, about 50 percent of the essays on a list by then pared down from about 350 to a little over a hundred names was completed—an already imposing manuscript of some 400,000 words. It became clear that outside help would be needed if the project was ever to reach completion. A list of some 25 names to be "farmed out" was drawn up, and we started scouting about for the best specialists we could find on each director.

The response to our quest was highly encouraging. The roster of contributors includes both established film scholars and less familiar ones, but all have in common their enthusiasm for film and dedication to film studies, as well as considerable expertise on the directors they agreed to deal with. I am pleased that the essays they contributed are very much in the general spirit of the book as I envisioned it and do not clash in tone or content with my own, or with each other (even though, of course, I do not necessarily agree with every opinion expressed in them, just as their authors probably do not agree with all the opinions expressed in mine).

This unity may be attributed not only to the competence and seriousness of the contributors, but also to the fact that we all share, albeit to varying degrees, a somewhat "auteurist" approach to film criticism. While we are well aware that a film is always a collective effort (and that filmmaking is, of course, an art that is also a business, and vice versa), we would all agree not only that virtually all worthwhile directors have the preponderant responsibility for what appears on the screen but also that the most interesting among them tend to be those whose personalities unmistakably shape their work, whether intentionally or not. The consequence can be a stylistic, thematic, and structural consistency, which the critic should make apparent through his analysis of a director's films.

This concept, which was considered somewhat revolutionary 20 years ago in the United States, except when applied to a handful of (mostly foreign) prestigious filmmakers, has now become the basic tenet of mainstream American criticism—that of the two major news weeklies as well as of the more specialized film journals—so that our critical approach can hardly be called daring. One of our goals has been to apply this approach not only to major directors (many of whom, incidentally, were until recently, or still are, sorely underrated by the general public and many critics) but also to many comparatively obscure, yet highly personal and creative filmmakers—some of whom never had an article devoted to their work as a whole before. Should there still be some diehards who take a dim view of auteurism (an American coinage, by the way) as a Gallic aberration, they may be comforted by the thought that neither I nor any of the other contributors to this book take a dogmatic stance; indeed, berating the excesses of auteurism is a recurring theme throughout the book.

Although *American Directors* is broad in its coverage, it makes no claim to exhaustiveness. No attempt has been made to encompass the whole of American film history through its directors. Because the focus is primarily—though by no means exclusively—upon the sound era, those directors whose careers belonged entirely or predominantly to the silent period were not considered for inclusion. It was decided at the outset to exclude directors who had been dead or otherwise inactive after 1940, which eliminated some major names (Murnau, Stroheim, Griffith, Keaton) and some lesser but not negligible ones. A few borderline cases (James Whale and Dorothy Arzner, for example) were also left out because their careers were practically over by 1940. Since the original intention was to deal only with directors whose careers were sufficiently advanced at the time of writing to allow for critical perspective, people who began directing in the late sixties or later were not originally considered for inclusion. However, a number of directors who were newcomers, or had not even directed anything yet when the book was started, had already built up a respectable body of work by the time it reached completion. The publisher felt that at least the most prominent among them should be added (although we decided not to include directors with only a few features to their credit at the time).* A tentative list of names was prepared, and since I could only handle a few of these additional essays myself, a quest for new contributors was launched. While the additions were kept down to about a dozen names, well over twice as many would have been worthy of inclusion. Thus, the coverage of "new" directors is much more selective than that of their seniors. Moreover, the selection, while it includes the obvious top names—e.g., Allen, Altman, Coppola, Scorsese, Spielberg—was somewhat dependent upon the contributors' willingness—or lack thereof—to write about specific directors. The result was the exclusion of some names which I was quite anxious to see included (e.g., Jim McBride, Alan J. Pakula, Jerry Schatzberg), while a couple about whom I felt somewhat less than enthusiastic did find their way into the book. In any event, this book is not intended as an up-to-the-minute survey of the "new Hollywood"; the essays on the new directors should be considered an "extra, added attraction" rather than the main feature.

We have also excluded those foreign directors who have occasionally made films in the United States but whose output remains predominantly non-American (e.g., John Boorman, Alexander Mackendrick, Roman Polanski), as well as the peculiar case of American-born Richard Lester, most of whose films are British. Also excluded are René Clair, Max Ophuls, and Jean Renoir, who fled from Europe to the United States during World War II and worked for a number of years in Hollywood before resuming their careers in France. The latter exclusions may seem regrettable to some readers, especially in the case of Ophuls, whose Hollywood films are among his very best, but to the extent that the essays in the book attempt to deal with the whole of each director's career, such exceptional cases would have been difficult to handle. The best rationale for keeping them out, however, is that they were not and never became "American" directors in any conceivable sense of the term.

Also excluded were some interesting directorial "careers" that consisted of only one, two, or three pictures, such as those of Howard Hughes, Leslie Stevens, George Axelrod, or Jack Garfein, and of actors John Wayne, Marlon Brando, and Charles Laughton (even though the latter's *Night of the Hunter* is a unique masterpiece, and Brando's *One-Eyed Jacks* is a superb, highly original western). Finally, it must be kept in mind that the book limits itself to the field of feature-length, live-action film, so that directors working in such areas as the documentary, animation, and short films, as well as experimental and "underground" filmmakers, are not included.

Within these admittedly important limitations, the book's coverage is quite thorough, although certainly not as complete as one might ideally wish. Each reader will have his or her personal list of deplorable omissions. I myself particularly regret the absence of André de Toth, William K. Howard, Phil Karlson, Monte Hellman, Albert

---

* This exclusion ruled out consideration of some of the most interesting (if not always the most popular or critically appreciated) American films of the seventies: the works of one-shot directors like Leonard Kastle (*The Honeymoon Killers*) or Barbara Loden (*Wanda*); the occasional and sometimes remarkable forays into directing by such performers as Peter Fonda, Dennis Hopper, Paul Newman, Elaine May, Jack Nicholson, and Gene Wilder; the sporadic efforts of highly original but commercially unsuccessful filmmakers (e.g., John Byrum's *Inserts,* James B. Harris's *Some Call It Loving*); and the work of more recent newcomers such as Philip Kaufman, Terrence Malick, Alan Rudolph, Joan Micklin Silver, Claudia Weill, and writer-turned-director Paul Schrader—as well as the hits of director-turned-producer George Lucas. The most regrettable exclusion, to this writer, was that of Michael Cimino, whose much maligned *Heaven's Gate* I consider, despite its flaws, one of the most personal and fascinating American films in many years.

Lewin, Paul Mazursky, Robert Montgomery, Gert Oswald, Ted Post, Martin Ritt, Franklin Schaffner, and Charles Vidor.

The writing of such a book involves viewing literally thousands of films, and we are of course grateful to the institutions and individuals that made such viewings possible. I am most indebted, as are all New York film enthusiasts, to the following: The Museum of Modern Art and its film staff, whose superbly mounted homages to individual directors, genres, or motion picture companies have been perhaps my one single most important source of film viewing throughout the decade; William K. Everson's New School and Huff Society screenings, for which this tireless and most generous film scholar has unearthed, over the past 20 years or so, countless long-forgotten or presumed lost gems from the thirties and the silent era; the long defunct Gallery of Modern Art and its film series, especially during the tenure of auteurist programmer Martin Rubin; Howard Mandelbaum and Roger McNiven, who, throughout most of the 1970s, operated their "Thousand Eyes"—later Cine Club—in a variety of locations around town, including their own apartments, and who were instrumental in turning the Carnegie Hall Theatre into one of the best repertory houses in New York during their too brief stint as programmers there.

Pierre, our collaborators and/or myself are also grateful to the staffs of the Library of the Performing Arts at Lincoln Center, the Museum of Modern Art Film Study Center, the Margaret Herrick Library of the Academy of Motion Picture Arts and Sciences, the Charles K. Feldman Library of the American Film Institute, and the Library of Congress's Motion Pictures Division; and to Peter Meyer, Michel Ciment, Ann Kuhn, and Jane Jordan Browne. Pierre wishes to make public his deep appreciation for the supportive endurance of his wife, Barbara M. Rubin. Our special thanks go to Tim Yohn and John Fitzpatrick, who are not only outstanding editors but also knowledgeable film buffs in their own right (the latter contributed two essays to the book in addition to his editing chores), and whose help in getting the manuscript into shape was invaluable. Finally, I want to express my gratitude to all the collaborators who manifested their faith in the project by contributing first-rate essays, then patiently bearing with me over the protracted gestating period.

Although *American Directors* is totally different from *Trente ans de cinéma américain,* the fact that the latter included entries on most of the directors about whom I have written here makes it inevitable that some opinions expressed in the 1970 book should reappear in this one. Actual borrowings, however, are very few. I have used my short *Trente ans* entries on Jerry Lewis and Sam Peckinpah as introductions to my new essays on the two directors; the opening of the Welles essay is very similar to that in the earlier book; and the first third or so of the essay on Joseph Losey is freely adapted from the *Trente ans* entry. Bertrand Tavernier, my partner on *Trente ans,* is probably to be credited for some scattered bits and pieces, which I can't identify, as some of our texts were written in close collaboration, and it is difficult, more than a dozen years later, to remember who contributed what. I also wish to thank Bertrand for the input and encouragement he provided, especially in the early stages of the enterprise.

Paul Valéry said that a poem is never finished, only abandoned, an observation that certainly holds true for other aesthetic endeavors, as well as for any remotely creative efforts, including essays on film directors! I do not know how sincere Samuel Johnson was when he wrote that he viewed the publication of his celebrated Dictionary—a project that took about as much time to complete as this book—with "frigid tranquility"; I assume that this stance is the wisest an author can adopt to inure himself to adverse criticism, but such equanimity is beyond me. One may get weary of, even exasperated at, a labor of love with which one has lived for so long, but indifferent? Over the years, I developed considerable empathy for those retentive directors who keep reediting their films until minutes before the opening, or whose "works in progress" (as Welles's or Nicholas Ray's in their late period) are periodically announced to be "nearly completed" but somehow never see the light of day. If I had my way, I would probably want to tinker with the book for some more months, which might quite conceivably turn into years. Therefore, the publisher's no-nonsense insistence on my "abandoning" it is undoubtedly a blessing in disguise, as it allows the more rational part of me to heave a sigh of relief.

JEAN-PIERRE COURSODON

Notes on the Filmographies

We have listed for each director whose work is analyzed in this book the titles of all the feature films on which he or she received a screen credit as director, as well as some additional relevant information.

Since any compiler of such data must rely largely on often inaccurate and contradictory secondary source materials—the primary sources are, of course, the actual screen credits—there are bound to be some errors in these filmographies. However, we are confident that they are more accurate and more complete than any such lists published to date. We have not simply cribbed from what has already been compiled elsewhere—the established practice in this field—but have engaged in extensive, tedious checking and double-checking, going through trade publications, specialized magazines, and every American (and many foreign) reference work, as well as combing the invaluable files of the library of the Academy of Motion Picture Arts and Sciences. The objective was not only to list the right titles for each director but also to list them as they probably appeared on the screen.

Our working definition of a feature was borrowed from the American Film Institute's catalogue of feature films of the 1920s: a film that is "4,000 ft. or more in length or, in cases where exact or approximate footage is unknown, of 4 or more reels." The films are listed in chronological order of release (not production), and in ascertaining those dates we relied heavily on the Motion Picture Almanacs, the Film Daily Yearbooks, the A.F.I. catalogues for the 1920s and 1960s, and trade reviews.

When we happen to be aware that a film was made at least two years before it went into release, we have included in parentheses the year when production was completed, e.g., Frank Capra's 1944 (1941) *Arsenic and Old Lace.* If a film was not released, the year listed is the year production was completed.

On films that we consider to be foreign productions—an arbitrary judgment call in some cases, and one we didn't do any deep research to arrive at—the initial date given aims to be the year of release in the country most involved in the production. Whenever we determined that such a film was also released in the United States, the date of that release is included in parentheses, preceded by the American title if it is different from the foreign one, e.g., 1955—*Les carnets du Major Thompson* (France; U.S., *The French They Are a Funny Race,* 1957).

We chose to adopt a restrictive definition of a silent film and a correspondingly extensive one for a sound feature, the latter being considered to be any feature released with any stretch of synchronized sound track, even if that track contained only music and sound effects. Thus, some of the early sound films listed are not talkies. It should also be mentioned that we have indicated alternate titles for films only when those other titles were used to some significant degree.

While we have sought to be exhaustive and consistent regarding credited feature film work, much of the additional information included in the filmographies is selective and even arbitrary. Under the catchall heading of *television movies* we have listed some feature-length (1½ hours or more minus commercials) series episodes and have even included as "compilations" a few syndicated telefeatures put together from series episodes, particularly when these hybrid movies received some theatrical release (usually abroad).

The most erratically supplied information is that which indicates uncredited work by a director (the reference being to footage specifically shot for and used in a film on which this footage's director was not credited as a director or a second-unit director). It is also our most arguable bit of shorthand in that it does not distinguish between a comparatively meaningless few retakes at one extreme and a major role in the film at the other. But the research that would have been required simply to characterize that contribution with some degree of accuracy was beyond our resources, and we can only hope that film historians will increasingly ferret out the relevant details. In the meantime, it appeared desirable to underscore that the directing credit does not always tell the whole story.

PIERRE SAUVAGE

American Directors

Volume II

1. Robert Aldrich (1918)

1953—*Big Leaguer;* 1954—*World for Ransom; Apache; Vera Cruz;* 1955—*Kiss Me Deadly; The Big Knife;* 1956—*Autumn Leaves; Attack!;* 1959—*The Angry Hills; Ten Seconds to Hell;* 1961—*The Last Sunset;* 1962—*What Ever Happened to Baby Jane?; Sodoma e Gomorra* (Italy; U.S., *Sodom and Gomorrah,* 1963, credited codirector in Italy: Sergio Leone); 1963—*4 for Texas;* 1965—*Hush . . . Hush, Sweet Charlotte;* 1966—*The Flight of the Phoenix;* 1967—*The Dirty Dozen;* 1968—*The Legend of Lylah Clare;* 1969—*The Killing of Sister George;* 1970—*Too Late the Hero;* 1971—*The Grissom Gang;* 1972—*Ulzana's Raid;* 1973—*Emperor of the North* aka *Emperor of the North Pole;* 1974—*The Longest Yard;* 1975—*Hustle;* 1976—*Twilight's Last Gleaming;* 1977—*The Choirboys;* 1979—*The Frisco Kid;* 1981—. . . *All the Marbles*

Uncredited
1957—*The Garment Jungle* (Vincent Sherman)

Uncompleted
1969—*The Greatest Mother of Them All*

For if the darkness and corruption leave
A vestige of the thoughts that once I had . . .

The lines of Christina Rossetti's sonnet—which ran through *Kiss Me Deadly* like an Ariadne's thread leading to a Pandora's Box—come teasingly to mind when the vexing subject of Robert Aldrich's evolution is brought up. While Aldrich has not gone away into Rossetti's "silent land," he has strayed into an artistic no man's land whose darkness and corruption certainly took their toll on the thoughts he once had. Early in the game, ignoring the symbolical warning of his masterpiece, he threw open his own Pandora's Box and has been struggling with the contents ever since.

Few directorial careers have risen and plummeted so sharply and so many times as Aldrich's—both artistically and commercially. This bulldozer of a man does everything in a big way, failing included. Somehow, he always managed to bounce back. His determination to—in his own words—"stay at the table" is indomitable. He has always viewed power as a condition of creativity, and his career has been an uninterrupted struggle to grasp power, increase, maintain, or regain it. Were he not at heart an artist, he might have become one of the most resourceful producers around. Indeed, being his own producer was his aim since his earliest directing days (he coproduced *World for Ransom*), and at one time he was the only film director in the country to head his own producing outfit and also own an actual studio. (The venture foundered after a series of commercial failures in the late sixties and early seventies.) Aldrich has the astute producer's knack of coming up with box-office "concepts," propositions that click with audiences and launch trends (*Whatever Happened to Baby Jane?, The Dirty Dozen*). At the same time, there is a dangerous recklessness about his enterprises, an overconfidence in his ability to predict and cater to the public's tastes, an ability that has proved far from infallible.

It seems undeniable that Aldrich's work has been undergoing a steady process of deterioration, although it is not easy to determine exactly when the process began. His decline was more than once offset and obfuscated by the appearance of some powerful and *honest* picture that would revive one's flagging esteem. Thus, the arduous and thankless task of "reevaluating" Aldrich has presented itself again and again with awesome regularity for the past two-and-a-half decades.

When Aldrich first burst upon the scene, turning out six films, four of them outstanding, in hardly more than two years, he appeared to many (in Europe at least) as the most exciting new American director since Welles. The release, in quick succession, of *Apache, Vera Cruz,* and *Kiss Me Deadly* was perhaps the single most exciting cinematic event of the mid-fifties. Aldrich seemed to provide the ideal and much needed link between the old and the new, demonstrating an ability to function within a tradition (the "craftsmanlike" practice of the genres) while at the same time transcending it through *enhancement,* be it lyrical (*Apache*), humorous (*Vera Cruz*), or paroxysmal (*Kiss Me Deadly*).

His early efforts displayed an amazing vitality, an absorption in the sheer exhilaration of movie making that irresistibly brought Welles to mind. Aldrich brought to the medium an innate sense of pace, an instinctive flair for camera placement and spatial arrangements. These qualities were incipient in *World for Ransom,* but the material was too flimsy for Aldrich's work to come through as more than a stylistic exercise verging on parody. It was with *Apache* that he really came into his own. The film is often neglected, even by admirers of Aldrich's early period (who tend to consider *Kiss Me Deadly* his first really important film) perhaps for no more substantial reason than the fact that many people find it difficult to take the casting of Burt Lancaster and Jean Peters as Apache Indians seriously. (In fact, Lancaster's performance is one of his most underrated, and the credibility of both stars is remarkably high.)

A film of many moods, full of humor and sadness, excitement and pathos, *Apache* is an intensely romantic work that blends tenderness and despair with a delicacy Aldrich was seldom able or willing to summon again in later years. It is perhaps the most convincing of all the "pro-Indian" Westerns, because it is one of the very few that focuses on the Indian as an individual rather than just the emblem of a race. Yet, it would be misleading to describe it as an antiracist Western in the tradition of Delmer Daves's *Broken Arrow.* It is, first and foremost, a love story—which, incidentally, gives the film a rather unusual position within a genre that traditionally keeps romance subservient to action. (Aldrich's genre films, even when successful as such, are always somehow untypical of the genre.) Not only is the developing relationship between Massai and Nalinle central to the story, but it is closely related to the major themes of the film; it is through his love for the woman that Massai finds a new way of life (crop growing) and a renewed sense of dignity. Thus, in the climactic sequence, the juxtaposition of fertility (Massai's corn field) and childbirth (his and Nalinle's child) takes on high symbolical value and imparts tremendous dramatic impact to the scene.

Although it is one of Aldrich's most entertaining films, *Vera Cruz* may seem at first glance a comparatively minor effort beside *Apache* and *Kiss Me Deadly.* For one thing, the Scope format (SuperScope, to be exact), which Aldrich was using for the first time—and which he managed to avoid for the rest of his career—tended to subdue his visual style. An adept of tight framing and crowded setups, he worked best in more traditional aspect ratios, and the vast expanses of the 2.35:1 screen dwarfed rather than enhanced his sense of space. Noting that Aldrich seems somewhat uneasy out-of-doors and that "nature doesn't inspire him at all," French critic Gérard Legrand argued that "the itineraries of his few 'Mexican' films lead to an enclosed space for a climax, such as the ruins in *Vera Cruz.*" Although the remark hardly applies to *The Last Sunset,* a "Mexican" Western whose final shootout is filmed predominantly in extreme long shots and high-low angles encompassing a great deal of open space, it is true that, on a purely quantitative basis, indoor scenes vastly outnumber outdoor scenes in Aldrich's cinema; more importantly, his interiors are often oppressive, either literally or metaphorically entrapping the characters who inhabit them. *Vera Cruz* makes better use of the format than many early—and later—Scope films; yet the one visual motif the viewer probably best recalls from it is Lancaster flashing his ubiquitous grin to which only the wide screen seemed able to do justice.

The major strength of *Vera Cruz,* aside from Lancaster's infectious energy and the unique opportunity of watching him and Gary Cooper playing off each other, is the wry humor of a craftily engineered script that smoothly moves from one plot twist to another without ever becoming repetitious or predictable. The *Vera Cruz* script is one of Hollywood's small wonders, a collaborative concoction that must have gone through many hands and many changes but eventually came out a homogeneous entity and a constructionist's dream. Borden Chase, who received credit for original story, also wrote a first draft. ("That was the Cooper I knew and the Lancaster I knew," he told Jim Kitses.) The final script was by James R. Webb (whose other notable credits are *Apache* and *Cheyenne Autumn,* both based on strong novels) and Roland Kibbee; Lancaster's input as producer and costar must have been important. (He probably hired Kibbee, who had scripted *The Crimson Pirate* for him a few years earlier, to recapture the tongue-in-cheek spirit of that boisterous swashbuckler.)

Thematically, *Vera Cruz* is much closer to *Kiss Me Deadly* and later Aldrich films than to *Apache.* Greed is its characters' sole motivation, treachery their only modus operandi. Historically, it is one of the very first Westerns to substitute a largely cynical, amoral attitude for the Manichaean moralism that had characterized the genre. The film has two heroes, neither of them a "good" guy, or even a "good/bad guy" in the traditional sense of the phrase. Both are larcenous and different only in the extremes to which they are prepared to go get what they want. Thus Aldrich was unwittingly paving the way for a later type of Western, best represented perhaps by the films of Sergio Leone. Ironically, Leone, with whom Aldrich was to clash on the set of *Sodom and Gomorrah,* received sole directorial credit for that film's Italian release.

Aldrich's masterpiece, and one of the key films of the fifties, *Kiss Me Deadly* displays his early style at its most flamboyant, yet most functional. No other American director since Welles had exhibited such sustained visual-aural inventiveness or such obvious delight in manipulating the film-making apparatus. Yet this dazzlingly brilliant work eschews formal overindulgence; it relentlessly strives for effect, but its effects (barring an occasional quirk, such as the credit titles unreeling backwards) are by no means gratuitous. It is one of those rare films whose every shot and cut seems as completely apposite as it is startling, so that ultimately—and this is one of Aldrich's major paradoxes—it comes through as more classical than baroque (whereas Welles's *Touch of Evil,* which otherwise has so much in common with Aldrich's film, decidedly leans toward the opposite direction.)

Aldrich's films often deal with the plight of individuals trapped in a changing world, victims of shifting conditions. In *Apache,* the Indian warrior, faced with deportation to an ignominious reservation, made his escape and in time singlehandedly recycled

tion to an ignominous reservation, made his escape and in time singlehandedly recycled himself into a corn farmer—the first Apache ever to do so. One might say that all the characters in Kiss Me Deadly—including its brash but seedy hero—need recycling into the nuclear age. They scurry about, driven by petty greed, utterly unaware of the nature or magnitude of what they are getting involved with. There is something almost medieval about the atmosphere of ignorance that pervades their pathetically stubborn quest and the obscure fears that attend it. With the Rossetti sonnet as his sole, improbable lead (the poem's opening words, "Remember me," are the film's "Rosebud," its eleventh and twelfth lines the clue concealed by its very visibility, like Poe's purloined letter), a stolid Mike Hammer goes around looking up a nightmarish gallery of frightened—or frightening—people, trying to put together the pieces of a puzzle literally too hot for him or anybody else to handle. When at last he secures the fateful box—as lethal a McGuffin as ever was devised—it promptly burns and contaminates him with radiation. Hammer's obstinacy is like a caricature of the scientific spirit trudging its way to Promethean power through countless obstacles. The theme of the hidden secret—all the more valuable and coveted because it is inaccessible—is expressed through the motif of enclosures, containers within containers, answers buried away in the deepest recesses of the mind, or body; the box is found enclosed within another box—a locker—the key to which has been retrieved from the bowels of a dead girl after she left the cryptic words "remember me" as a clue (so that words, memory, then the text of a poem—which thus is turned into a palimpsest—become more sealed boxes to be pried open.) When the box is finally opened in an apocalyptic final sequence, it sets a whole house—metonymically, perhaps, the whole world—ablaze, while a stunned Hammer and his girl stagger out and into the Pacific, an image of mankind returning to the primal sea after nuclear holocaust.

Aldrich doesn't waste one foot of film on the kind of straight exposition that slows up and dulls parts of even the snappiest thrillers. The bombardment of weird images and essential—although undecipherable—messages begins with the opening frames and never lets up for 105 minutes. Even in scenes whose sole purpose in the narrative scheme is to convey information (e.g., Hammer visiting his secretary while she practices ballet), camera work, the use of sets and props, unexpected bits of business, peculiarly worded dialogue, or unusual delivery keep the spectator stimulated and the atmosphere of strangeness intact. What makes the film extraordinary is not only the high level of cinematic excitement it produces, but the fact that this production is uninterrupted, as though to belie the principle that audiences must be provided with periods of rest in between the more intense moments. (In this respect, only Touch of Evil can compare with Kiss Me Deadly, although Welles's film, unlike Aldrich's, is slightly marred by a few brief "unproductive" moments, the flat, bland scenes the producers insisted should be added for clarification, which Welles did not direct.)

Aldrich's attitude to Kiss Me Deadly has always been ambivalent. On the one hand, he has often stated that he liked the film very much, that he was "very proud" of it; on the other, he sometimes sounds more annoyed by the kind of reputation it gained in Europe than by the almost total lack of recognition with which it was met in this country at the time of its release. The reasons for his reservations (". . . it wasn't as profound as many of the French thought it was") testify to his lack of pretentiousness but are largely irrelevant, for it is not necessary to read anything into the film to be convinced of its extraordinary excellence. Kiss Me Deadly does deal, metaphorically, with McCarthyism, but a hypothetical spectator who had never heard of McCarthy still wouldn't miss any of the film's greatness, even though he might miss some of its or third level of analysis; it has little to do with whatever social or political comment Aldrich and Bezzerides sneaked into the script or even with the fact that the film provides a subtle metaphor for the mental state of the country at a certain time. It lies, in a much simpler and more essential way, at the very surface of the film, in its cinematic texture. Its quasi-surrealistic juxtaposition of disconnected, constantly renewed items—people, places, objects, motions, and occurrences—has the compelling power of a successful collage in which balance and harmony are born of seemingly arbitrary arrangements, and the esthetic achievement lies in the arranging itself rather than in the nature of the manipulated material.

Kiss Me Deadly was ignored or dismissed as trash by most people at the time, and Aldrich was too ambitious not to realize that being involved with this type of film would lead him nowhere, no matter how brilliantly he directed.

The Big Knife was the first turning point in his career, a "respectable" vehicle with a message. The message—an indictment of fascistic behavior in a corrupted world—was not substantially different from the one that could be detected in *Kiss Me Deadly,* but it was put across in a more strident, while at the same time culturally more acceptable fashion, spelled out in the flowery idiom of a famous playwright, Clifford Odets. The Stanley Hoff character, a composite of some of the most powerful and most hated Hollywood producers (principally Louis B. Mayer and Harry Cohn), also bore a striking resemblance, both in his methods and some psychological traits, to Senator Joseph McCarthy. Thus *The Big Knife,* unlike most films on the subject, deals with Hollywood not as a self-contained epiphenomenon insulated from the rest of the world but on the contrary as a microcosm of American society. (Twenty years later, in *The Longest Yard,* Aldrich was to use Richard Nixon as a model for a Hoff-like character, the State Penitentiary director who cajoles and manipulates a prestigious inmate in much the same way Hoff did Charlie Castle.)

Esthetically, Odets's theatricality, his taste for verbal flourish, and relentless dramatic tension were attuned to Aldrich's own leanings, so that far from feeling uncomfortable with the play's hysterical overtones, he found in them a classy alibi to indulge himself. The same applies, to a certain extent, to *Attack!,* his first war picture, which was also adapted from a play and focused on conflicts between high-strung individuals rather than on physical action. Like Hoff, Captain Cooney (played by Eddie Albert, who Aldrich was to use again in similar roles in *Hustle* and *The Longest Yard*) is a power-wielding villain cynically manipulating the men under him, and Jack Palance was cast again as the victim. *Attack!* was Aldrich's first film with an all-male cast, and, coming after *Autumn Leaves,* his first film with a woman as the protagonist, established the pattern of alternation between "male" and "female" pictures that was to characterize his cinema for the next decades.

Autumn Leaves, a Joan Crawford tearjerker, is not without its charm, which is largely the charm of the perverse—a perversity more subtle, but for that very reason more effective, perhaps, than that of *What Ever Happened to Baby Jane?* to which *Autumn Leaves* is in some ways a forerunner. Aldrich once said that "self-survival" made him do *Autumn Leaves.* He went on to explain that "people were getting collective in their criticism of the violence and anger and wrath in my pictures . . . and I thought it was about time I made a soap opera" (quoted in Higham and Greenberg, *The Celluloid Muse*). The irony is that the film turned out to be, in its way, just as vicious as any of his earlier ones. Aldrich plunged into the task with a relish verging on sadism, clearly delighting in the tribulations of his lonely, middle-aged heroine. Even in a genre dedicated to female suffering, few characters have been subjected to so in a genre dedicated to female suffering, few characters have been subjected to so much undeserved mental anguish, not to mention physical abuse. (Joan Crawford's mentally disturbed husband beats her up and even crushes her hand with her typewriter—he was aiming at her head but she ducked—after which *she* has to hug and comfort *him*, because he is upset at what he did.) Aldrich relentlessly focuses on the heroine's cringings as embarrassment and feelings of insecurity and inadequacy overcome her when a younger man courts her and then on her agonized hand wringing as she goes through ordeal after ordeal after marrying the man and discovering, first that he is a pathological liar and a petty thief, then that he is still married to another woman, and finally as she has to confront his engulfing, murderous schizophrenia. Aldrich's direction makes up for the visual drabness built into the script (most of the action takes place in Crawford's two-room bungalow, with a couple of walks down the block to the bus stop and one outing to the beach providing the "opening out") by indulging in some of the weirdest camera angles in the history of the genre: extreme high and low angles (such as the camera being placed on the kitchen floor, looking up at Crawford's nervous pacing up and down), tilted setups, extreme close-ups, and one truly bizarre camera placement when he cuts from a shot of Cliff Robertson trying to open a locked closet door, his back to the camera, to the reverse angle *from inside the closet,* as though the wooden door were a plain glass panel. Aside from these occasional flourishes, however, Aldrich keeps the film as minimal looking as a television soap opera (which is where its plot really belongs) as though intent upon eschewing any possible distraction from the plight of the long-suffering heroine.

No matter how impressive the series that comprises Aldrich's third to eighth pictures may appear, it brought him only modest recognition from the industry and mediocre financial rewards. ("I think I made three very good movies: *The Big Knife, Attack!* and *Kiss Me Deadly.* I worked almost for nothing, economically, on those movies.") When his Columbia period—which had just started with *Autumn Leaves*—ended with his being fired a few days before *The Garment Jungle* finished shooting, a career that had started with a resounding bang seemed to be petering out with a barely audible whimper.

But Aldrich still had to live through his worst period, the wretched "European experience." He became the typical Hollywood expatriate, a victim of the so-called runaway production with its waste of talent, its illusions of freedom, the lure of "meaningful" stories, and the realities of compromise and commerce (only, in his case and at that time, there was nothing much to be lured away from). Too strong a fighter to allow himself to be destroyed, Aldrich left the runaway production to its sorry state after three dismal experiences (*The Angry Hills, Ten Seconds to Hell, Sodom and Gomorrah*) and ran home.

The home front, however, had changed. Hollywood, the perennial phoenix, was waiting for the next rebirth. It was no longer possible to make something like *Kiss Me Deadly* in three weeks on a shoestring. Besides, Aldrich was not interested in shoestring ventures any more. He had a vision of Aldrich and Associates becoming a major independent, and he needed money to revive the concern. So he aimed below the belt and pulled no punches with *Whatever Happened to Baby Jane?,* working on the gamble—which turned out to be correct—that audiences would be titillated by the degradation of Bette Davis into a demented, vicious old hag with a ravaged face and the deportment of a drunken female impersonator. Partly, but not only, because it was so superior to the countless imitations that attempted to cash in on its success, the film, far from having aged badly, looks rather better a decade and a half later than it did when it came out. Its nastiness and magnified ugliness turn out to possess more stylistic coherence than was generally acknowledged at the time. It may have been Aldrich's cynical answer to commercial demand, but it was nevertheless a thoroughly personal effort.

Underneath its amazing surface versatility, Aldrich's work conceals a strong, almost obsessive thematic consistency. Since the pivotal *Baby Jane*, most of his films have echoed in some way or other his major achievements of the fifties. There is an obvious relationship between *The Dirty Dozen* and *Attack!*; *The Legend of Lylah Clare* or *The Longest Yard* and *The Big Knife*; *The Grissom Gang* or *Hustle* and *Kiss Me Deadly*; *Ulzana's Raid* and *Apache*. The later films are, with few exceptions, overblown offshoots of the early ones, with the same basic characteristics in evidence: deliberate theatricality, dramatic and visual grandiloquence, a taste for violence and unpleasantness, a fascination with moronic characters and physical or psychological monstrosity.

Comparing the early films and the late variations, some critics have been dismayed by what they interpret as ideological apostasy. According to them, Aldrich renounced his liberalism in favor, if not of a downright reactionary attitude, at least of ambiguous positions suggesting a shift toward conservatism. That an evolution took place is undeniable. However, identifying Aldrich—as was often done early in his career—with the leftist directors for whom he had worked during his days of assistantship (Joseph Losey, Abraham Polonsky, Robert Rossen) was probably a mistake in the first place. Although he considers himself a liberal (which he may very well be in his private life), Aldrich as a director functions best when dealing with politically uncommitted material. While such early pictures as *Kiss Me Deadly, The Big Knife* and *Attack!* may be read as veiled political metaphors, their cinematic excellence owes little to whatever topical message they may carry.

In later years, Aldrich demonstrated that, given the opportunity, he could easily fall prey to ideological irresponsibility, but that can hardly be equated with creeping fascism. Aldrich is, first and foremost, a craftsman and entertainer. His primary concern is always to turn out as efficient a piece of work as he possibly can. He won't allow ideological niceties to stand in the way of performance. His natural tendency is toward bombast, excess, distortion, vulgarity; the new permissiveness of the late sixties enabled him to indulge this proclivity to an extent that would have been previously unthinkable. With so many shock techniques and cynical twists becoming permissible, Aldrich's dedication to effect could only run wild; as a result, ideologically dubious material became welcome provided that it *worked*.

Thus, *The Dirty Dozen*, with its casting of a bunch of murderers and degenerates as superheroes, may or may not have been intended at the outset as an ironic comment on the ambiguities of war heroism. What matters is that Aldrich's concentration on sensation and shock value turns the film into a paean to violence for violence's sake. The constant jocularity, the sustained sporting metaphor (the men being coached for their suicide mission pretty much like a football team) perpetuate the comic-strip vision of war as a game, full of thrills and fun. In *The Longest Yard*, an actual football game in which both teams play dirty becomes a metaphor for the game of life. One might say that Aldrich veered from liberalism to a kind of nihilism; or, more accurately, that he is a romantic who, in the face of "darkness and corruption," shuns realistic exposés and takes refuge in a heightened, operatic vision of reality that turns evil into pure spectacle.

This theatrical detachment (which should not be mistaken for "distancing") is stylistically expressed, among other things, by Aldrich's habit of pulling the camera and *Baby Jane,* for example, all end with a receding camera abandoning the hero and/or heroine on the brink of, respectively, genocidal extinction (for even if one is willing to accept *Apache*'s tacked on happy ending, the "happiness" it promises is, at best, a precarious one), nuclear destruction, and insanity. In the closing shot of *Emperor of the North Pole,* the hero, not the camera, recedes in the distance, but the effect is similar. As Lee Marvin, standing on top of the conquered freight train, shouts his flamboyant farewell address to a dumped and bewildered Keith Carradine, the breathtaking grandeur of the landscape engulfs his dwindling figure, and his voice gradually dies away in an ironic undercutting of the harangue's content. Similarly, the long shot of Catherine Deneuve walking away through the airport crowd at the end of *Hustle* is like an absurdist's shrug acknowledging the inevitability, not to say the banality, of evil.

The bizarre tag-end of *The Legend of Lylah Clare,* the most striking instance of these last-minute defusings of what was supposed to be the film's message, is also the most paradoxical, inasmuch as it screams for symbolic interpretation. It is a daring conceit (it takes guts to wrap up a melodrama with a dog food commercial), but although its cheap, aggressive boldness somehow befits the pretentious trashiness of the script (based on a teleplay that all but plagiarized Hitchcock's *Vertigo*), it fails to make sense on any level, precisely because of its obviousness; it could mean anything at all and is therefore superfluous, not to say obnoxious. (Discussing the film in *Interview* magazine, Aldrich stated that the commercial "was not a joke" but conveyed the idea that "it's all dog meat, and you're all going to get destroyed." To which cryptic elucidation he added, unwittingly giving away the clue to the scene's weakness, "If you haven't figured that out by now, here's the commercial that's going to let you know that." Clearly, if the spectator hasn't figured out the message by the end of the movie, either he is very obtuse or the director has failed to make his point, in which case it is too late to do anything about it.)

In the decade following *The Dirty Dozen,* Aldrich directed a melodrama of Hollywood mores, an adaptation of a stage play about a lesbian couple, a World War II picture, a thirties gangster saga, a Western, an uncategorizable "Wild Boys of the Railroad" epic, a crime thriller, a disaster film of sorts, and a slapstick chronicle of police life. His eclecticism in selecting material is almost matched by the diversity of stylistic approaches he has brought to these projects. The breadth of his expressive range is well illustrated by a comparison between the two films he made back to back between 1972 and 1973: *Ulzana's Raid* and *Emperor of the North Pole* (which was shortened to *Emperor of the North* for some obscure reason).

Ulzana's Raid, one of the few important Westerns of the seventies, and one of Aldrich's major works, is formally as restrained and unadorned as one would expect a William Wellman Western to be. *Emperor of the North Pole,* on the other hand, is Aldrich at his most operatic, a festival of bigger-than-life set pieces. *Ulzana's Raid* is evenly paced and tightly controlled throughout but somewhat lacking in visual impact (although one brief scene, in which a soldier shoots a woman, then himself to avoid capture by a group of Indians, is one of the most cinematically stunning moments Aldrich ever put on film), while *Emperor of the North Pole* is uneven and sometimes hesitant as to what it is trying to achieve. The attempt at suggesting a musical-comedy feeling through stylized dialogue, exaggerated posturing, and theatrical groupings (at times the cast does seem to be about to break into song) does not always work as intended; but the look of the entire production is unlike any other, and such scenes as the fire in the freight yard at dawn, the city dump sequence or the climactic Marvin-Borgnine fight stay as vividly in one's mind as anything Aldrich ever did.

Ulzana's Raid provides the most impressive instance of Aldrich's ability to take up the general theme of an earlier film and to approach it in an entirely renewed fashion. (Alan Sharp's ground-breaking script deserves much credit for it.) Some critics blamed Aldrich for reverting to a racist ideology, because the film depicts Indian atrocities, and does so, moreover, with more graphic realism than had ever been dared in any Western; but *Ulzana's Raid* is actually neither racist nor antiracist, neither "pro" or "anti" Indian. Its originality lies in the fact that it substitutes an all but ethnographic objectivity for the Manichaean conceptions that have always been the rule of the genre. Foregoing the romantic approach to the Indian question, which had been the one adopted by practically all pro-Indian Westerns, *Apache* included, Aldrich and Sharp make the point that the Indians' savagery (e.g., torturing captured enemies to death) is a natural consequence of their world view and modes of thinking, a cultural condition quite alien to the European's moral and humanistic responses. Ulzana and his braves are a far cry from the noble savage depicted in *Apache* and probably a great deal closer to historical reality. The film may be called pessimistic in that it views cultural patterns of behavior as ineradicable and cultural differences as irreconcilable, but this is hardly racist. Whites are in no way reinstated to the status of a superior race. Most whites in the film are decent enough people, but their helpless rage when confronted with the Apaches' incomprehensible cruelty is compounded by the realization that, under certain circumstances, their own kind (and they themselves as individuals) can behave just as savagely despite the benefits of civilization.

The film does not take sides and thus makes it difficult for the spectator to do so. It is not so much that one side is equated with the other; rather, both the Indians' and the whites' endeavors seem so hopelessly erratic and meaningless that one can't really care who wins. And, as it turns out, nobody does. Rampaging Indians, settlers, and soldiers are all equally losers in the end. Every single strategy fails, although not without considerable loss of human life each time. It is almost as though the lack of understanding between the two races were so total as to make them unable even to fight each other in any coherent manner. This bleak outlook is typical of late Aldrich; the film's ending, for example, strikes the same sad note as that of *Hustle.* In both films, the protagonist dies meaninglessly, alone. We are left with a feeling that "life goes on" (Deneuve walking away through the airport; the survivors riding back to the fort), but there isn't much left to live for.

Interestingly, though, the relationship of failure to the absence of human understanding is also a dominant theme in Arthur Penn's *Night Moves,* another Alan Sharp script (Gene Hackman's symbolically gloomy observation as he watches a football game on TV—"Nobody's winning, one side is just losing slower than the other"— could epitomize the situation in *Ulzana's Raid*). Although Sharp's screen credits are too few to allow for a serious appraisal of his work, the fact that he has written two of the best (and most underrated) American films of the decade—both originals— can hardly be a coincidence. Both scripts are complex but tightly constructed and functional. Aldrich works best, perhaps, with writers whose sense of structure can counterbalance his own tendency to looseness and excess. Sharp's collaboration must have something to do with the fact that *Ulzana's Raid* is one of Aldrich's soberest, most controlled pictures. Such collaborations have been rare in Aldrich's career, especially in the seventies.

Despite such bright interludes as *Ulzana's Raid* or *Emperor of the North Pole,* Aldrich's more recent films tend to be rambling, bloated efforts with verbose, disjointed scripts. The neat, sharp look of earlier pictures has given way to a general air of messiness. Setups are cluttered, without any meaningful or visually suggestive arrangement being imparted to the clutter. Familiar stylistic devices (e.g., the low-angle shot) are repeated ad nauseam. (In the football sequences of *The Longest Yard,* every other shot or so is a worm's eye view of the action, filmed with a buried camera.) Editing is jagged and desultory, juggling many different angles of one scene without apparent necessity. (Aldrich always shoots with two cameras, thus ending up with a considerable mass of material to choose from in the cutting room.)

Typical of this formal decomposition is *The Longest Yard,* a noisy, untidy and protracted—although intermittently enjoyable—allegory that drags the moral conflicts of *The Big Knife* out of the living room onto the football field (even substituting an actual penitentiary for the metaphorical prison in which Odets' Charlie Castle was entrapped). Physical ugliness matches formal messiness here, as Aldrich assembled a collection of gargoylelike types to surround glamourous Burt Reynolds. The ugly look is extended to the only woman in the cast outside of the opening sequence, a secretary played by Bernadette Peters. Aldrich perversely photographed her from angles and through lenses that make her appear all but anamorphic, and her bleached beehive hairdo and carefully mismatched lipstick and nail polish are as indicative of the director's penchant for "degrading" women as any indignity suffered by females in *Baby Jane* or *Sister George.* But whereas, in *Emperor of the North Pole,* Ernest Borgnine's plain looks were exalted into a kind of epic, truly glorious ugliness (one has to agree with Aldrich that Borgnine's performance is "probably the best job he's ever done"), the ugliness in *The Longest Yard,* no matter how insistent, remains down-to-earth and never becomes transfigured into style.

Although *Hustle* has a look and pace of its own, quite different from *The Longest Yard* (its messiness is less visual than structural), its major problem is also excess and redundancy. Material for at least two or three movies was crammed into one, and, indeed, it takes several viewings to sort out and take stock of all its contents. Practically every single theme ever touched upon in an Aldrich movie comes up at one time or another. This, however, doesn't make *Hustle* the archetypical Aldrich film, since it is also overloaded with writer Steve Shagan's own idiosyncrasies, which do not necessarily jibe with the director's. In John G. Avildsen's *Save the Tiger,* another film written by Shagan, the hero spent a great deal of time wallowing in nostalgia; the same is true, although to a much lesser degree, of the hero of *Hustle,* which is based on Shagan's own novel. Nostalgia, however, is hardly a dominant ingredient of Aldrich's cinema, even though he pioneered a particular form of it in *What Ever Happened to Baby Jane?* Moreover, Burt Reynolds as a cop getting misty eyed over old Bogart movies is a proposition that puts a heavy strain on one's willingness to suspend disbelief.

Whereas *Kiss Me Deadly* could be experienced—and thoroughly enjoyed—as a straight thriller without any aspiration toward redeeming social value, *Hustle* loudly advertises the film makers' commitment to "making points" about as many aspects of our society as possible. What would pass as social comment is so mechanically injected into every scene that its perfunctoriness soon becomes painfully obvious. Aldrich has remarked that the material, as far as the crime story was concerned, was "second-rate TV stuff," and although his direction, no matter how flawed, surpasses anything of the kind, the film is indeed reminiscent of the slick shallowness of the police series ground out by the networks. One might wonder, incidentally, why Aldrich decided to buy, coproduce, and direct a property for which he had so little respect. His only reason for doing it, he claims, was the "love story"; and it is a measure of his faltering judgment that this turned out to be the film's weakest element. One has to go all the way back to *Apache* for a successful love story in Aldrich's work.

When dealing with Aldrich's evolution, it is difficult to eschew moralizing entirely and equally difficult to prevent the moralizing from drifting into weltschmerz. After all, Aldrich's films of the seventies present a fairly accurate reflection of the cynicism and callous indifference that seemed to become the prevalent mood of the country during the decade. How critical Aldrich really is of the "moods" he reflects has always been hard to tell. The disjointedness of films like *The Longest Yard, Hustle,* or *The Choirboys* might be construed as the formal correlative of an increasing fuzziness in Aldrich's moral outlook. Yet he is still able to come up with as major a surprise as . . . *All the Marbles,* his most personal and controlled film since *Ulzana's Raid* and *Emperor of the North Pole,* whose almost antithetical qualities it manages to reconcile. (It could also be described as a successful female version of *The Longest Yard.*) Coming after the disturbingly lowbrow escapade of *The Choirboys,* in which we were told in effect that nothing matters and anything can be turned into a joke—the dirtier the better—. . . *All the Marbles* is yet another one of those "powerful and *honest*" films that periodically restore our faith in the integrity of the most Phoenix-like of American directors.

2. *Woody Allen* (1935)

1969—*Take the Money and Run;* 1971—*Bananas;* 1972—*Everything You Always Wanted to Know About Sex** (**But Were Afraid to Ask);* 1973—*Sleeper;* 1975—*Love and Death;* 1977—*Annie Hall;* 1978—*Interiors;* 1979—*Manhattan;* 1980—*Stardust Memories;* 1982—*A Midsummer Night's Sex Comedy;* 1983—*Broadway Danny Rose*

Miscellaneous
1966—*What's Up, Tiger Lily?* Credited as writer and associate producer, Allen was responsible for this reedited, English-language version of *Kagi no kagi* (Senkichi Taniguchi, 1964, Japan).

The critic endeavoring to write anything short of a book-length study on Woody Allen, the film maker, from the vantage point of the early 1980s is naturally tempted to focus his attention on the loose trilogy formed by *Annie Hall, Manhattan,* and *Stardust Memories* (and also, probably, on the peculiar case of *Interiors*) at the expense of the earlier—and, according to the consensus, cruder—comedies, which run the risk of finding themselves relegated to footnotes and incidental references. Moreover, the contrast between the two groups of films is so sharp and Allen's growth in what could be called his postslapstick period so striking that one finds it difficult to deal with the early efforts without comparing them—unfairly—with the masterful works that were to follow.

Whatever their flaws, however, Allen's early films were unique, highly personal comic statements of a kind he most probably will never indulge in again, which is a stiff if not unreasonable price to pay for the maturing of his talent. One may view the pre-*Annie Hall* period as one of apprenticeship; yet, because the Allen-directed films of that period are such fine examples of a brand of humor that was to become subdued in *Annie Hall* before being almost entirely banished from *Manhattan*—and, of course, *Interiors*—(although it did resurface sporadically in *Stardust Memories*), they deserve to be discussed for themselves and the way they were perceived before Allen became a more "serious" artist.

The first part of the following essay does exactly that. It was written in 1973, before and immediately after the release of *Sleeper*. Only the footnotes have been added.

Woody Allen's movies are plotless, chaotic, uneven, self-indulgent, and—at least for his first two as writer-director-star—shoddily produced and clumsily directed. They also happen to be the funniest comedies filmed in this country or anywhere else since the heyday of the Marx Brothers, and who wouldn't be willing to settle for that? With the exception of Jerry Lewis—who, unlike Allen, took an awful lot of time coming into his own—Allen was the only American comedian in four decades to wrench complete control from producers and make his own films his own way. No matter how much influence the Marx Brothers or W. C. Fields may have exercised on their film material, they were not, ultimately, in charge of their own movies. The latter were usually directed by hacks, and look it. Allen's movies, no matter how flawed, *look*—and not just sound—like Allen movies and nothing else. To that extent, and no matter how far removed from classic silent comedy his style may be, he is the true heir of Chaplin and Keaton and Langdon, whose tradition of personally evolved and controlled comedy he has brilliantly picked up and revived from apparent extinction.

Allen's comic inspiration thrives—almost exclusively it sometimes seems—on various forms of parody and mimicry. Most of his pieces for *The New Yorker* or other magazines are takeoffs on some style or genre of fiction or nonfiction writing, and his pictures constantly spoof film genres and individual movies. But while this approach is implicitly—and often explicitly—critical, parody per se is not Allen's exclusive, or even primary, interest. The forms, literary or cinematic, which he takes on are conducive to his imagination, and he *works* with them as much as he laughs at them. Thus, the narrative structure of *Take the Money and Run* is a parody of the semidocumentary style of crime movies that became popular in the mid-forties, but it is also an ideal format for what Allen is trying to do. The pseudoscientific case-history approach, the not very illuminating interviews, the pompous drone of the voice-over narration are funny parody in themselves, but, quite as importantly, they hold together the loosely constructed script, bridge the gaps between disconnected episodes, and distract from the repetitiousness of the situations. Allen has an uncanny gift for reproducing with perfect accuracy the structural patterns and stylistic devices that characterize particular genres and subgenres; his true originality, however, lies not in this talent for mimicry but in the wild contrast between the familiar forms and style he manipulates and the outrageous new content he injects into them, a content that is deeply rooted in the tradition of nonsense humor and yet comes across as thoroughly idiosyncratic.

Nonsense and parody have always had a natural affinity (most of Lewis Carroll's poems, for example, were spoofs of well-known Victorian works), and Allen developed his own blend even before he started making his own movies. The formula can best be seen at work in the pieces he started publishing around 1966, chiefly in *The New Yorker*, and, interestingly, in his second and most unusual film effort, the palimpsestic dubbing of the Japanese thriller that was to emerge on American screens in 1966, after Allen was finished with it, as *What's Up, Tiger Lily?* The comic principle is very much the same in both the film and the magazine stories. Just as, in the latter, Allen removes the content from some literary genre and stuffs the empty shell with his own crazy conceits, in *Tiger Lily* he eradicated the dramatic content of the original film by discarding the soundtrack and replacing it with narration and dialogue that tell a different and gloriously zany story in which groups of spies and gangsters vie for the possession of a coded egg salad recipe (the first indication on film of Allen's irresistible attraction to food as comic material). This outlandish effort has generally been dismissed as a one-joke experiment that soon exhausts itself through repetitiousness, but aside from the fact that its ability to amuse is remarkably sustained, considering the obvious limitations of such an endeavor, *Tiger Lily* also constitutes a fascinating instance of the consistency of Allen's comic strategy.

Tampering with a finished product may seem like an overcautious first step into film making, but the experiment, while allowing Allen to remain in the familiar realm of verbal humor, also gave him the opportunity—which no other medium could afford— to combine parody and its own object into one. The object, to be sure, was too easy a target; the grade-Z Japanese thriller is pretty much its own parody, and Allen's jokes often sound almost redundant, when they should blast the material up on to a different level. But again, parody is not, here or elsewhere, Allen's major concern. The purpose is to make us laugh not at the silly Japanese movie but at the contrast between its images (and the straight plot we can easily reconstruct underneath) and Allen's outpouring of verbal nonsense in the narration and substituted dialogue. Much in the same way, a Lewis Carroll would use a solemn piece by Tennyson less as a target for parody or satire than as a mold in which to pour his nonsensical inventions.

Although Allen would probably be the first to deny the presence of any serious intention in *Tiger Lily,* the film is, in some ways, thought-provoking. It is a rare—not to say unique—instance of the extent to which the word can deflate, distort, and pervert the image. And, whether intentionally or not, it makes a perfect case against the monstrous, although universally accepted, practice of dubbing foreign-language films. The ludicrousness that results from the Japanese actors exchanging Woody Allen lines in New York-accented American is merely a comic exaggeration of the ludicrousness inherent in any dubbing job. In that sense, *Tiger Lily* is something like Allen's *Modest Proposal.*

Allen's humor, like all humor that relies heavily on nonsense, usually eschews cleverness and wit and seems to make it a point not to make any point. Instead, he draws upon the repertoire of comic effects common to all nonsense writers and comedians since Lewis Carroll and Edward Lear: the non sequitur, the ridiculously bland or obvious observation, the mind-boggling understatement, the sudden skidding into meaninglessness after an initial gesture toward making sense. Allen's own favorite variation on the latter device is a dizzying leap from the heights of speculative thought down to the lower depths of triviality; his aphorism on God's existence and the availability of plumbers on weekends (which the *New York Times* has singled out as "the basic Woody Allen joke") being one among almost countless examples, which include, "Eternal nothingness is OK if you're dressed for it"; "If man were immortal, do you know what his meat bills would be?"; or, even better, "Art, all art, is merely an expression of something," which is reminiscent of the maddeningly minimal Lear of such limericks as "The Old Person of China."

Similarly, witticisms, plays on words, or double entendres are rare in Allen's film dialogue. His approach is far removed from a Bob Hope's nonstop flow of wisecracks.* Bright repartees are not at all his cup of tea, although he could probably turn them out (and occasionally does) with as much ease as the next smart fellow. For a typical Allen line—funny in a deliberately dumb, nonwitty way—consider, in *Bananas,* Fielding Mellish's reaction upon learning that the girl he has just met takes courses at CCNY: "You're a student at City College?" he exclaims in awed excitement, "It's a great school, I ate in the cafeteria there once." The technique here again is a brutal plunge from the lofty (the connotations of "great school") to the down-to-earth (Fielding's actual experience of the college). The character, it is important to note, is not being facetious, which would give the line a completely different quality; he is quite sincere, and the joke is Allen's, not his. This kind of anticlimax is such a basic fixture of Allen's stock in trade that it often tends to become mechanical; here, however, the line, which would be funny in any context, is also in character (we learn later that Fielding never finished college, was, indeed, expelled—like Allen himself—after a few days' attendance from an institution of higher learning that may very well have been CCNY), as well as befitting the general tenor of a conversation throughout which our hero has tried very hard to impress the girl with his less than staggering background and sophistication.

For a man who is primarily a writer, Allen is unusually impervious to the religion of dialogue. "I only care that the idea of a scene gets across," he stated in an interview. "It doesn't matter at all to me if nobody does any of my dialogue." The evidence of the films bears him out. Much of the dialogue seems improvised or semi-improvised (see, for instance, his fine breaking-up scene with Louise Lasser in *Bananas*), and there is no attempt at keeping the lines funny all the time. Thus, most of the interviews in *Take the Money and Run* are almost straight, very understated dialogue. They are funny only indirectly, that is, not because of what is being said but in relation to what we already know about the person being discussed.

Although his humor is essentially verbal, Allen thinks his movies as much in visual as in verbal terms, and much of their comic impact derives from the interaction between the image and the word. The best instances of this interaction are found in *Take the Money and Run,* because the film makes extensive use of the voice-over narration. True, Allen cannot resist sneaking in many throwaway lines that are pure verbal play and have no visual correlative, as when the narrator, going through the criminal records of Virgil's associates, enumerates such unlikely offenses as "marrying a horse, exposing oneself to one's in-laws, and dancing with a mailman." Clearly, such eminently Allenish incongruities would gain nothing from being acted out in front of the camera (although a similar conceit, Virgil's temporary transformation into a rabbi after being inoculated with a new vaccine, is not merely mentioned but also shown.)

On the other hand, the scene in which Virgil is seen attempting to play his cello with a marching band, dragging a chair after him and sitting down every hundred yards or so for a few hasty scratches of his bow, then running off again in pursuit of the other musicians is considerably funnier visually than its mere verbal description. When Virgil plans a bank robbery and cases the joint by filming the premises with

---

* When writing this, I was unaware of Allen's now well-publicized admiration for Bob Hope, whom he has called his favorite comedian, and in whose honor he compiled and narrated an anthology of film clips for a 1979 benefit at Lincoln Center in New York. Although Allen insists that Hope's influence on him is pervasive in his films, it is mostly indirect and remains submerged underneath crucial differences. The one film in which it becomes perceptible—indeed striking—is *Love and Death,* the last of the early comedies, after which Allen's evolution was to take such a sharp turn as to make any Hope influence even less discernible than before.

what the narrator describes as "a cleverly concealed camera," the picture simultaneously reveals Virgil's "clever" ploy as a hilariously self-defeating device: the camera is hidden inside a loaf of bread, which our master criminal carries around and through which he is seen peering not too inconspicuously. The gag is funny not only because of the nonsensical inadequacy of the stratagem but also because of the contradiction between what we see and the deadpan commentary of the voice-over. One entire scene in *Take the Money and Run,* and one of Allen's funniest—the bank robbery that founders because of the bank's employees' inability to decipher Virgil's scrawled stick-up note (many of them make out the key sentence to read: "I have a bun pointed at you")— seems to have originated in a single one-liner, which Virgil himself uses post facto as he matter-of-factly accounts for his failure: "I misspelled the stick-up note."

Paradoxically, for a comedian whose inspiration is the most bizarre and outlandish in the history of screen comedy, Allen's movies display a remarkable flair for realistic detail. (*Take the Money and Run* was one of the films screened as part of a 1973 New School film course on "American Realism.") People and places in his films look real, his characters sound natural. The interviewees in *Take the Money and Run* speak in the language of their social class and profession. (Allen's refraining from placing wisecracks in their mouths is part of his realism.) The character played by Louise Lasser in *Bananas* is not a caricature but a straight, everyday type, a girl we all might know, and Lasser's performance is at times painfully true to life. The dinner-party chatter of the middle-class Jewish couples in the transvestism sketch of *Everything You Always Wanted to Know About Sex* could have been taken verbatim from an actual social encounter in suburbia. Allen likes to use media celebrities (Howard Cosell in *Bananas,* Jack Barry and the panelists of "What's My Line?" in *Everything You Always Wanted to Know About Sex*) and make them perform with a straight face (although with outrageous material) exactly as they do on television; Cosell comments on the hero's wedding night as he would a sports event, and the quiz show panelists have to guess a contestant's sex perversion rather than his occupation. (The comic device, incidentally, is the same in both cases, involving a shift in the socially accepted status of sexual activity from private to public.) In such scenes—in which Allen does not satirize sportcasting or game shows but uses them straight, merely changing their object—the realism of the treatment is the condition for the comedy to be effective.

But the personality of Allen himself is what contributes most to this curiously convincing quality in his film work. Of all film comedians past and present, Allen is the one with whom it is easiest to identify; indeed, he is probably the first with whom identification other than of the most rudimentary nature (e.g., feeling dizzy with Harold Lloyd as he climbs up the front of that skyscraper) is at all possible. As Richard Schickel has said, "All of us . . . harbor a Woody Allen inside ourselves just waiting to jump forth. . . . He is a walking compendium of a generation's concerns, comically stated." However, the originality of Allen's relationship to his comic persona, and, through it, to his audience, cannot be overestimated.

All comedians keep a distance—often considerable—between their private and performing selves, but in Allen's case, the distance is, or is made to seem, minimal. He steps out of our everyday world. For one thing, he manages to look funny and ordinary at the same time, which distinguishes him from practically every other comedian. Of course, there have been other comedians in film (mostly minor ones) who looked ordinary, but they had to do or say something funny before we started laughing. Allen's, moreover, is not the bland ordinariness of a Bob Hope, who could be Mr. Average American. He is a New York Jew, a fact audiences are seldom allowed to forget. This, in itself, is unheard of among film comedians. Traditionally, they have always cultivated an outlandish, rootless persona. The comic hero on screen is from everywhere and nowhere. Jewish comedians, even the most identifiable of them (Chaplin, Groucho Marx) always played down or even ignored their Jewishness; a Chico Marx even submerged his underneath a vaudeville Italian immigrant costume and accent. But Allen, unlike most of his elders, does not strive for "universal" appeal. He is the perfect film comedian for an era in which the movies have ceased being mass entertainment. His audience, which is still comparatively limited, is largely made up of people with the same background as Allen himself—middle-class intellectuals or semi-intellectuals (not necessarily Jewish and/or New Yorkers, although it helps), who pretty much share the same values and attitudes and are sophisticated enough to identify the targets of Allen's humor—many of which are probably above the heads of a truly popular audience.

Allen's steadfast identification with both his Jewish background and the city of New York make for heightened realism, although it may limit his appeal. It is impossible to think of him as anything but a New Yorker, and some of his jokes must be lost on strangers to the city (see, for instance, the glazed, vacant stare Virgil adopts the moment he steps into a subway car). There is something disturbing about the film version of Play It Again, Sam taking place in Los Angeles. Woody simply is not a West Coast type, and his humor seems as uprooted as he himself does in the California sunshine. Far from trying to play down this aspect of his persona, Allen uses it for comic effect by remaining exactly the same in whatever exotic surroundings and situations he places his character. Thus, in Bananas, Fielding goes about securing food for an entire army of guerrillas as if he were ordering a quick snack "to go" from the corner delicatessen (with all the usual fastidious specification as to kinds of bread, side orders, etc. . . . .), a fine example of Allen's realism and his deliriousness on a collision course.

Allen's dedication to realism sometimes goes beyond the call of duty. The first part of the chain-gang sequence in Take the Money and Run, with the warden's warning speech to the new inmates, is done entirely straight and comes across as convincingly as any of the similar scenes from dramatic movies Allen is imitating (again, not spoofing) here. James Anderson's craggy face, slitlike, steely blue eyes and menacingly level drawl are archetypally apposite to the part and without a hint of comic exaggeration about them. Our only reason for not responding to the scene as we would—or would be expected to—in a "serious" movie is our awareness of the fact that we are watching a Woody Allen comedy; but it is somehow not quite sufficient a reason, and uneasiness creeps in as Allen slowly builds up the scene to its climax—or rather anticlimax— and only comic moment, Virgil's inquiring from the warden, after the latter has rhetorically asked if there were any questions, "Do you think it's right for a girl to pet on the first date?"

The line, incidentally, is derived—indeed, borrowed almost verbatim—from a scene in the Marx Brothers' Monkey Business in which Groucho is threatened by a big-shot gangster who has just found him hiding in a closet in his girlfriend's cabin. The comic hero's situation is thus much the same in both scenes (he is at the mercy of a threatening bully), but the difference in contest and treatment points to the essential difference between Allen's world and the Marx Brothers' (although the Brothers are an obvious influence on Allen). Groucho's crack in Monkey Business is only one in a series of derisive remarks, and we know that the gangster, like all the other foils in the Brothers' movies, will obligingly, albeit seethingly, bear with Groucho until he difference between Allen's world and the Marx Brothers' (although the Brothers are an obvious influence on Allen). Groucho's crack in *Monkey Business* is only one in a series of derisive remarks, and we know that the gangster, like all the other foils in the Brothers' movies, will obligingly, albeit seethingly, bear with Groucho until he has exhausted his quota of jokes and insults for the particular scene. He is no more a menace to Groucho than Margaret Dumont is when she occasionally gets wise to the comedian's putdowns and innuendos. In *Take the Money and Run,* on the other hand, the situation is so real and the warden so convincing that Virgil's absurd question comes as a total shock, and Allen has no choice but to fade out on it, for the context allows for no tolerance on the warden's part beyond his initial, slow-burning stare of disbelief.

The Marx Brothers may have been the most iconoclastic of film comedians, but their anarchism was aimed at a cardboard world that offered little or no resistance to their assaults. Allen's world is a recognizable one, solid and three-dimensional, with the consequence that his madness comes out as much more outrageous and lethal than theirs. When the Brothers wage war, for example (*Duck Soup*), their war is a clean one; when Allen does (*Bananas*), he doesn't hesitate to joke about the most gruesome realities of war, as in the scene in which political prisoners stand in line and take numbers to be shot, as though they were waiting for ice cream at Baskin-Robbins. One might argue that the very outrageousness of the gag defuses the realism of the situation, but does it? Reality has been known to be just as outrageous in its ironies. Allen stays rather close to the realm of the real; at times a little too close for comfort.

In a largely negative review of *Everything You Always Wanted to Know About Sex* (*But Were Afraid to Ask)*—hereafter referred to as *Sex**—a *Sight and Sound* critic wrote: "Allen's new film undoubtedly has an advantage over his two previous features in that it lacks the inconvenience of a plot." There is more to the remark than mere sarcasm, for plots do seem to be a hindrance to a comic mind of Allen's breed. Or perhaps it is more a matter of format than of plot. As a film maker, Allen feels comfortable with the ten- to fifteen-minute sketch format, just as, as a writer, he feels comfortable with the short pieces he has been publishing in various magazines. To expect him to be as comfortable and successful with a feature-length comedy may be as unfair as to expect him to write a successful novel. In a much earlier era, when the two-reeler was a commercially viable and artistically reputable format for film comedy, he would undoubtedly have used it, as did all the great silent comedians in the first stage of their development.

As a feature film made up of a series of sketches, *Sex** is an interesting compromise, and, on the whole, a highly successful one. Paradoxically, because of its very episodic format, it turns out to be Allen's most cohesive picture to date. To the obvious thematic unity provided by its topic, it adds the structural and stylistic unity of each segment being patterned after a specific film genre or style (television also provides the format for one skit).

Sex was the ideal topic for a Woody Allen comedy, for sex, to him, is not just an obsession, it is also (like food, with which it is constantly combined in his jokes) intrinsically funny. The character he plays in the "Mad Sex Researcher" section of the film has written a book whose title, *Advanced Sex Positions; How to Achieve Them Without Laughing,* epitomizes the predicament of *homo eroticus* according to Allen. Departure from the sexual norm is even funnier than normal intercourse, so, not surprisingly, rabbi gets whipped by a woman while his wife is made to eat pork at his feet. There is no way, however, Allen can make kinky sex more ludicrous than it is in reality. In *Masochism in Sex and Society*, Theodor Reik mentions the case of a man who became sexually aroused at the sight of a chicken leg. This sounds like a typical Allenism, except that it is case history.*

While sexual perversions are a choice target for Allen's wild imagination, the more "normal" forms of erotic behavior do not escape his pitiless scrutiny either. The very concept of "foreplay," for example, seems to collapse when Allen, trying to arouse a phenomenally lethargic Louise Lasser, hilariously demonstrates that you can take a woman to bed but you can't make her come. The vexing paradox of the male erection, a state often most difficult to achieve when most desired, is graphically demonstrated in the closing segment (in which Woody plays a sperm with second thoughts about its calling when ejaculation threatens) as are some of the curious mating rituals (such as the sharing of food in public places) that prevail in our culture.

Allen sees all sexual activity, one might say, as its own caricature. Making such a film must have been quite a challenge, to the extent that it is extraordinarily difficult to caricature a caricature. At times, he fails to overcome the difficulty; thus, the transvestite episode is totally unfunny. Perhaps Allen is too matter-of-fact, too direct—too realistic—in his handling of the whole thing. He creates a ludicrous situation and quietly develops it against a background of total ordinariness (middle-class, middle-aged couples making dull, predictable conversation about vacation spots, travels abroad, purchases, etc.), purposefully refraining from injecting any joke. The transvestite himself (played by the decidedly unfeminine-looking Lou Jacobi) is a totally bland, nondescript person—even his name, Sam, is ordinary. When Sam sneaks into a bedroom, puts on a dress, and minces about delightedly, he does not look funny but simply ludicrous— which indeed seems to be Allen's point; he takes a cold, objective, almost scientific look at this particular quirk and seems to be telling us: "Here is how your average closet queen looks; don't blame me if it's silly and sad." We are a far cry from *Charley's Aunt, Some Like It Hot,* or *La Cage aux folles.*

Within minutes, poor Sam finds himself trapped in a situation so nightmarishly embarrassing and humiliating (he is discovered in his ridiculous drag by a group of people consisting of his wife, his daughter, her fiancé, and the young man's parents, in addition to a couple of lady neighbors and a police officer) that we can only cringe

---

* An even better instance of nature imitating Allen's art: A man wrote to a sex magazine about his lifelong attraction to wet fish, describing how he liked to "purchase a large fillet of fish," take it to the bathroom and rub it against his body. Once he sneaked one into bed while his wife was asleep, and that turned out to be "one of the most rewarding experiences" in his life. "My wife," the man added, "knows about my fetish for fish and understands it, although she doesn't care for fish herself." Both in style and content, this wonderful letter reads uncannily like a Woody Allen piece. The word "fish" and the names of various fish are among Allen's vast repertoire of words he finds naturally funny and always good for a laugh. Moreover, he often associates fish with sex. In *Conversations with Helmholtz,* for example, he describes an ex-rapist whom therapy had cured by inducing "a more socially acceptable habit" in him; "when he chanced upon an unsuspecting female, instead of assaulting her he would produce a large halibut from his jacket and show it to her." (Note the use of "large" by both the letter writer and Allen; the latter often resorts to this adjective for comic enhancement.) In *Love and Death,* the character played by Diane Keaton marries a fishmonger, who at one point is seen surreptitiously carrying a large (naturally) fish upstairs. The letter even reproduces one of Allen's most personal and frequent stylistic devices, the use of "although" introducing a comic qualification or understatement. One almost suspects Allen himself, or at least some gifted imitator, to have written the letter. You can't tell an honest to goodness sex fantasy from one cooked up by Allen for laughs.

at his predicament. The only escape from this unbearable situation is through total breakdown. In a delirious fit, Sam tears off his borrowed clothes, which he throws screaming at the bewildered and dismayed little group. That is definitely not funny, and it is doubtful that Allen intended it to be. What he did, rather, was take an innocuous (and, we are told, quite widespread) sexual quirk, place it in a credible, everyday context, then imagine the worst consequences that could possibly result from the "pervert's" indulgence in it. Allen's insertion of Sam's farcical ordeal in a matter-of-factly realistic context invites us to respond to the character as a real human being rather than a mere comic puppet, and our only possible reaction is to be appalled at what happened; clearly, the man's life has just been destroyed. Allen must have realized that he had gone too far, for he ended the skit on a contrived lighter touch, as if to minimize the magnitude of Sam's humiliation. Back home, Sam's wife tells him: "You should have told me . . . If you had said, 'I'm sick, I have a diseased mind, I am not fit to live with decent human beings' I would have understood." Then she reminisces about the afternoon's adventure and giggles at the thought of "their faces when they saw you"—which is totally out of character and probably Allen's weakest excuse for a punch line in his entire career.

The bleakness of the episode is typical of Allen's approach to sex throughout this film (as well as in others; in *Sleeper,* his vision of sex in the future is one of orgasm machines replacing intercourse; everyone is frigid anyway, which certainly simplifies matters). What makes *Sex** ultimately sad, even depressing despite its many hilarious moments, is his view of sexuality as a degrading force. The most extreme example of the destructiveness of sex in the film, along with the transvestism skit, is the one called "What Is Sodomy?", in which a psychiatrist, when his fatal infatuation with a sheep is discovered, is socially disgraced, loses everything, and sinks first to menial jobs, then to skid row, where he is last seen drinking from a half-pint bottle of Woolite, an indication of his continuing obsession. One may take the simple view that Allen is just having his fun with some dramatic stereotypes—which of course he is (the obvious reference here is *The Blue Angel,* that archetypal tale of degradation through infatuation). But Allen is quite capable of having his fun while still making an earnest statement. The parody is only a thin layer, through which the underlying, raw dramatic content occasionally shows. When the fallen psychiatrist (played by Gene Wilder with hardly a trace of comic exaggeration) breaks down in the middle of his work in a crowded coffee house and screams at patrons: "I'm not a waiter, I am a doctor!", the scene is chillingly realistic and, like Sam's breakdown in the transvestism episode, not played for laughs. The premise of this droll cautionary tale may be far-fetched, but reality can be even more so. If a man can be aroused by a chicken leg, the oddness of being aroused by a sheep becomes comparatively mild. (Moreover, the sheep is no ordinary animal but a beautiful, exotic specimen "from the hills of Armenia"; the man may be a pervert, but he has taste.) And who is to tell where sexual attraction turns to love or decide what a proper love object is? The sheep stands metonymically for any love object, reminding us that beauty is in the eye of the beholder, and that the object's adequacy or inadequacy is never an issue for the lover, since love is a private fantasy that bears little if any relation to whom or what the loved one really is. Allen may never make a serious dramatic film about the folly of human desires and relationships, but one suspects he has the wherewithal to do so if he ever chooses to.

If nothing else, straight drama would solve Allen's continuing problem with plots. One reason why drama is easier to do than comedy is the narrative's tendency to interfere with comic invention in the latter. Allen's approach to his films has been to ignore plot as much as possible. The "plot-versus-gag" dilemma, however, has been central to film comedy ever since it outgrew the two-reeler format, and one may assume that, like all creative film comedians before him, Allen will eventually come to rely on stronger scripts.

Sleeper, in which he saddled himself with a semblance of story, seems to point in that direction. It has not much of a plot, to be sure, but what little it has is still more than in any previous Allen movie. It is reassuring to find that this evolution has not resulted, as often was the case with other comedians, in a downplaying of visual comedy. On the contrary, *Sleeper* has more sight gags than any other previous Allen movie. Indeed, the film suggests, if anything, that *too much* visual comedy could prove Allen's undoing. Knockabout pantomime, chases, pratfalls, and such are exercises he proves adequate at, but one gets the impression that he is demonstrating his versatility with an eye to broadening his audience. The very incongruity of Allen doing out-and-out slapstick routines is what makes them funny, rather than any true visual inspiration. It is unlikely that traditional slapstick can ever be revitalized and used creatively in film comedy, but if anyone one does it, it probably won't be Allen. His uniqueness lies in his manipulation of concepts and the language that expresses them. He has proved equally unique in his ability to translate these verbal skills into filmic terms.

At the time of *Sleeper,* Allen's film career was approaching a major turn. His next picture, *Love and Death,* was to be the last one in his "early" style. However, there is little justification for isolating *Sleeper* and *Love and Death* in a second "period" all of their own. They may be transitional pictures, but even with the benefit of hindsight, it is difficult to find much in them that announces what was to come. In fact, *Love and Death* is, in some ways, a regressive film. What it does have that earlier efforts did not is production values—scenic locations, period costuming, crowds of extras, camera work by Ghislain Cloquet, a cinematographer of international reputation. As far as the comedy itself is concerned, however, the film is traditional Allen. It shows no evolution toward the comedy of character later to emerge in *Annie Hall* and *Manhattan;* on the contrary, it chiefly relies on a near nonstop flow of one-liners—both in the dialogue (or monologues) and the voice-over narration, with only occasional bits of visual business thrown in.

At times, the performance bogs down into an actual stand-up routine, with Allen facing the camera and reeling off jokes. In typical fashion, he acknowledges the fact and turns it into a gag at one point, during the jail scene, when a spotlight falls on him, then is turned off before he is through with his monologue, and he calls for it to be turned on again. The film ends, rather limply, with yet another series of one-liners delivered in close-up before the closing shot of Allen dancing away with Death in mock early-Bergman style. The verbal overkill yields some gems but also many cheap shots, strained conceits, and tired rehashes of old, familiar Allenisms. The aphorisms on death, in particular, become quite tiresome, as we have heard or read so many of them before, and all of Allen's jokes on the subject are basically the same, using comic understatement as a common underlying principle. The trick is to compare death—being dead—with some mildly annoying experience of everyday life and to remark that death either is worse or, on the contrary, not so bad after all, since it eliminates the annoyance. In *Sleeper,* the hero remarks, "At least after death you're not nauseous." In *Love and Death,* it is, "Think of it as a way of cutting down on your expenses." The latter is the film's closing statement (but then, Allen has always had a weakness for weak endings—another heritage from the tradition of nonsense).

Love and Death is the one Woody Allen movie in which his debt to Bob Hope is clearly acknowledged. As in practically all of Hope's films, most of the jokes in *Love and Death* deal either with the hero's lechery or with his cowardice. (He even spells out the word *flee,* f-l-e-a, like Hope in *Road to Morocco,* the movie Allen says inspired him to become a comedian when he first saw it at age seven.) In his view of himself as a lover, Allen's Boris practices much the same alternation of boasting and self-deprecation as the characters played by Hope. He even manages to combine the two in a line that could be called typical Bob Hope except for the fact that it would not have passed the censors at the time Hope made most of his movies. (When praised by a lady for his sexual prowess, Boris modestly replies, "I practice a lot when I'm alone at home.") As in Hope's movies, especially the *Road* series, there are asides to the audience, as well as a sprinkling of deliberately "impossible" gags, e.g., Allen turned into a human cannonball. Even Allen's weakness for visual quotations from other films is reminiscent of the *Road* pictures, which were probably the first comedies to introduce such in-jokes.

Allen's admiration for Hope is understandable, even though one may not choose to share it. Hope is a comedian's comedian, and his peers like to praise the perfection and ease of his delivery, his mastery of the ad-lib, the quick repartee. Beyond the technical expertise, however, Hope's comedy is shallow, mechanical, and often unpleasantly leering. That its influence is felt at all in *Love and Death* militates against the claim that Allen is doing anything really original or ground breaking in this film.

Curiously, however, *Love and Death* is Allen's own favorite among his films—he said so, at least, in an interview recorded after he completed *Manhattan* (*Positif,* September 1979). One can understand his satisfaction in successfully handling an elaborate, costly production with a large cast, a period setting, location shooting in Europe, etc. As far as craftsmanship is concerned, *Love and Death* was undoubtedly his most polished film to that date. But it is difficult to believe that a man of Allen's intelligence and subtlety really thinks that the film achieves (as Robert Benayoun, *Positif*'s interviewer, suggests, along with some other critics) some kind of profundity or even seriousness. Calling a comedy *Love and Death* and cramming it with pseudophilosophical jargon may be something only a Woody Allen could get away with, but it doesn't qualify him as a deep thinker—which he knows he isn't. (He is interested in intellectual speculation, which is not the same.) Certainly, Allen's ontological preoccupations are genuine, and his constant mockery of the language of metaphysics is a way of concealing his earnestness behind laughter, as well, probably, as of keeping anguish at bay. Yet, it seems highly exaggerated to write, as does Foster Hirsch, that *Love and Death* is "a comedy about ideas, about intellect." The film is as much about ideas and the intellect as *Bananas* is about politics and revolution or *Take the Money and Run* about crime and the penal system. The philosophical jargon the Diane Keaton character spouts throughout the film may be an anticipation of the same Keaton's glib, affected patter in *Manhattan* but no more so than any number of earlier Allen pieces in which he mocked various kinds of intellectual cant.

As film comedy, *Love and Death* is at its best in some thoroughly unpretentious, old-fashioned routines, such as the ones in which Boris keeps goosing ladies with his sword sheath as he bows to others or repeatedly bops Diane Keaton over the head with a vase in a desperate attempt at simulating playfulness. (The original intention was to knock out the personage—a member of Napoleon's entourage—with whom Keaton was talking and who unfortunately turned around as Boris was about to hit him.) Indeed, the whole sequence dealing with the attempt to assassinate Napoleon is perhaps the most successful, as well as the most traditional, portion of the film, because Allen, rather than doing solo work or mere dialogue, is actually going through visual routines with Keaton, and they come across (much better than in *Sleeper*) as a wonderful male-female comedy team, a rarity in film. (Burns and Allen were strictly stand-up; Allen and Keaton *do* funny things. One might have to go back to Mabel Normand and Fatty Arbuckle in the Keystone comedies to find such a felicitous pairing.) If there is an intimation of things to come in *Love and Death*, it is Allen's growing awareness of the possibilities of team work and of Diane Keaton's comic potential. That potential was to be fully realized in *Annie Hall*. From then on, Allen, without relinquishing the spotlight, was to prove increasingly willing to share it with other characters—not puppets or foils but realistically drawn individuals—thus developing a more serious type of comedy, based on the study of relationships in a socially and emotionally plausible context.

The praise heaped upon *Annie Hall* and *Manhattan*—unquestionably Allen's masterpieces to date—has been nothing short of phenomenal. These must be the two most acclaimed American films of the seventies, even though there exists a tiny subculture of naysayers who, having probably reflected that such unanimity *had* to be suspicious, proceeded to announce that the Emperor was naked.

The response to *Interiors* was only slightly less enthusiastic, although some of the excitement may have been motivated by Allen's chutzpah in venturing into straight drama territory, rather than by his actual achievement. Only *Stardust Memories* has been met with mixed reactions; indeed, it is the only Woody Allen movie that seems to be disliked, even hated, by a sizeable segment of the public (including many Allen fans) and the critical establishment—not so surprisingly, perhaps, since it is the one film in which Allen seems to have gone out of his way to antagonize audiences—especially critics and fans.

Leaving aside *Stardust Memories*, then, it is clear that Allen, in at least two films to date, has achieved what is usually in the sole province of genius: reaching universality through a genuinely individualistic, even unique, vision. The word *universality* may need some qualification; there are large sections of the American population (to limit oneself to this country) that probably find little to identify with and relate to in Allen's self-centered small world of beautiful, talented New York neurotics. Yet, when a film gathers all the top Oscars, as *Annie Hall* did, it can be said to have struck a responsive chord in the American mainstream.

Allen's most conspicuous contribution to the evolution of screen comedy since *Annie Hall* has been to redefine the very concept of comic persona. By divesting the comic hero of his traditionally alien, other-worldly status and turning him into an ordinary mortal (and one as close as possible to the real-life Woody Allen, who, of course, is not all that ordinary), he allowed his movies to straddle levels of expression never before united in film comedy, the presence of the "new" Woody Allen as the focus of the films, guaranteeing a unique, serio-comic point of view that eschews the temptations of both slapstick and straight drama.

The paradox of the comedian, as exemplified with remarkable clarity by Allen's evolution, is that the more ambitious he grows, the further away from comedy he feels compelled to move. This is a peculiar, yet natural process. The difference between comic and dramatic action is one of attitude (the author's, as well as his audience's) more than of content. Extra energy is required to maintain such an attitude—comedy is drama *plus.* Comedy's natural tendency to gravitate toward seriousness might be called, loosely, a form of entropy; the laughter-producing energy inevitably diminishes. As the comic graduates from "low" to "high" comedy (the reverse evolution—or is it regression?—hardly ever occurs), there are fewer and fewer "laughs" in his work, until he eventually breaks into the exalted realm of pure drama, where there are no laughs at all.

Comic creators often feel ambivalent about their ability to make people laugh. For years Allen expressed his dissatisfaction with being a "mere" provider of laughs.* In his case, moreover, the comedian makes us laugh about things that he actually takes very seriously. It is clear that, for a long time, he viewed his practice of comedy as an escape from the responsibility of dealing properly with his obsessions and preoccupations, perhaps as an indication of his inability to do so. A film like *Interiors,* therefore, is not an oddity, but the result of a natural evolution, Allen's attempt to prove to himself and his audience that he could indeed tackle serious concerns adequately.

In *Interiors,* Allen dealt with his usual preoccupations without, as he puts it himself "hiding behind gags." Deriding the film, as Foster Hirsch does, because in it "preoccupations and affectations previously lanced by his wit are now set up as worthy of the most sober scrutiny," is not only unfair but missing the point entirely; the "preoccupations and affectations" in question were worthy of his wit in the first place precisely because they are worthy of sober scrutiny. Taking exception to *Interiors'* "solemn, portentous style" with its "nods to Ingmar Bergman, O'Neill, Ibsen, Strindberg and Chekhov" (Hirsch again) is to misunderstand the nature, and unity, of Allen's style, which is and has always been fundamentally *imitative.* When Hirsch posits that "Woody can't have it both ways . . . he can't treat being a neurotic as a subject of comedy in one film and as the stuff of domestic tragedy in another," he seems to assume, rather naively, that there is no common ground between comedy and tragedy. If we see the difference between the two as one of attitude, however, Allen's shift in attitude becomes perfectly legitimate and logical. There is no reason on earth—except a critic's insistence on pigeonholing every artist—why Allen, or anybody else for that matter, couldn't "have it both ways." The proof of the pudding, after all, is in the eating. *Interiors* may not be on a par with the best of Allen's models (especially Bergman), but why should it be? Would anyone expect Ingmar Bergman to come up with a comic masterpiece if he tackled the genre? (He did once, with disastrous results.) *Interiors* may be seen as an exercise, not that it is more superficial or less personal than Allen's comedies, quite the contrary, but in the sense that the straight rendition of a classical composition constitutes an exercise for a jazz musician (which Allen also happens to be) accustomed to expressing himself through improvisation. Pursuing the analogy, one might say that drama concerns itself with the melody line, while comedy, like jazz, focuses on the chord structure as a springboard for variations—verbal or visual gags.

The lure of high comedy, and eventually serious drama, for the funny man is well documented. Molière grew from slapstick farces performed in market places to such dramatically charged psychological comedies as *Tartuffe, Don Juan,* and *Le Misan-*

---

* In the already mentioned *Positif* interview, Allen stated, "I have always had a feeling that I was making superficial films . . . slapstick to me has become a dead end. . . . It's interesting to know you can keep people laughing for an hour and a half, but I know I can. . . . One soon gets tired of making people laugh continually, it's like eating only ice cream, you start longing for something more substantial. There are things that can be said only in a serious picture."

thrope and wrote one tragedy, which flopped, to his bitter disappointment. Chaplin went from the slapstick of the early Keystone comedies to the pathos of *Gold Rush, The Kid,* and *City Lights* and then on to the philosophical musings of *Monsieur Verdoux* and *Limelight.* There are clear indications that Harry Langdon, had his career not suddenly foundered, would have followed a similar course; after his first hits, he reportedly started screaming to his writers and directors for "more pathos" à la Chaplin. Chaplin felt ready for the dramatic film as early as 1923; indeed, *A Woman of Paris* was his first real feature-length film. *The Day the Clown Cried* was Jerry Lewis's own stab at a tearjerker.

Both Chaplin and Allen chose not to appear in their first dramatic effort, realizing that the funny man is cursed with being (or at least looking) funny all the time and therefore does not physically belong in the realm of drama. Lewis solved the problem by casting himself as a clown in his dramatic film—which is what Chaplin himself had done in *Limelight.* Paradoxically, it is by playing the part of a clown that the comedian can himself cease to be one and become an actor like any other. Allen's strategy has been pretty much the same as theirs. In *Annie Hall, Manhattan,* and *Stardust Memories* he has cast himself as the comic performer and/or auteur he actually is, but we see him mostly off the job, busy living his own personal life. Moreover, the hero's (Allen's) dissatisfaction with his old, crude style of comedy becomes a major theme. In *Manhattan,* Isaac Davis quits his lucrative job as a television comedy writer because he can no longer stand what he considers mechanical, inferior writing. Disclaimers are issued again and again. In *Stardust Memories,* comedy routines are supposed to be clips from the hero's old movies—which he despises, although fans and critics love them. Allen makes it very clear that he has left all that behind him and now wants to concentrate on dramatic material.

The hero's relationship to his work is, indeed, one of the two main themes that vie for the spotlight in the three films. (In *Interiors,* too, most of the characters are writers with creativity problems.) The other theme, of course, is his relationship to women. As far as the latter is concerned, Allen seems to be playing a game of oneupmanship with himself as he moves from film to film. While *Annie Hall* focuses on the hero's affair with the title character from first meeting to last goodbye, Isaac Davis in *Manhattan* shuttles between two lovers, and Sandy Bates in *Stardust Memories* engages in no fewer than three love affairs (two of them overlapping), not counting a one-night stand with a persistent groupie. The films, especially *Manhattan,* are all about falling in and out of love, about lovers fighting and making up or breaking up, about rejection and jealousy, about changes of heart and uncertainties as to one's true feelings—the stuff of most fiction and drama, good or bad. One only has to sit down and try to write a synopsis of *Manhattan* to realize how conventional the bare plot outline is.

Always quick to preempt criticism by pointing out his own weaknesses (real or imagined), Allen has Isaac remark at one point, "We're beginning to sound like a Noel Coward play, we should be drinking Martinis." In Allen's code of esthetic values, Coward is no doubt synonymous with clever, superficial playwrighting about the smart set and their love affairs, but one could make a case for Allen's becoming (in *Manhattan,* at least) a modern-day, American equivalent of Coward. He, too, deals with the amorous life of fashionable people, not the idle rich of yesteryear, to be sure, but their contemporary counterparts, the glamorously employed, well-off New York artists-intellectuals.

Allen's compulsive sincerity is what makes him scoff at the analogy; he takes his material much too seriously to accept being identified with a purveyor of superficial entertainment, no matter how brilliant. And indeed, Allen's dogged earnestness is what salvages the anecdote from banality—not the sprinkling of witty remarks (about which Allen has become almost apologetic anyway). This seriousness is what distinguishes Allen from a Coward, whose attitude always suggests that nothing is worth being taken very seriously. When Isaac discards his first draft of an opening chapter ("He adored New York City; to him, it was a metaphor for the decay of contemporary culture") as "too preachy," Allen's conviction is unmistakable underneath the distancing putdown, and when Allen tells an interviewer, *"Manhattan* isn't a film that merely says, 'clean up Central Park,' it says, 'Clean up your emotional lives, or else you'll never be able to clean Central Park,' " one couldn't be more preachy—or sincere.

Annie Hall and *Stardust Memories* are intricately constructed collages dislocated by flashbacks that juxtapose various levels of reality and fantasy in surreal fashion. *Manhattan,* on the other hand, is linear, streamlined, and uncluttered, without any of the jumps in time or wild outbursts of fantasy of the other two films. Its basic situation is a chain of unrequited loves—A loves B who loves C who loves D who loves E—as trimly classical as that of a Racine tragedy. (It is precisely the same chain Racine used in *Andromaque.*) The Aristotelian unity of action is respected; there are no subplots, and each character's actions have an impact on all the others. The unity of place is provided by the island of Manhattan, a locale that really *encloses* the characters, although not as claustrophobically as the antechambers imposed by obsessive dramatic theorists upon Racine and his contemporaries.

Manhattan is also (like *Annie Hall,* but to a much greater extent, and unlike *Stardust Memories*) a craftily mounted operation in seduction that, from the opening frame, conditions the audience to love the film and the film maker. The beautiful wide-screen shots of the city in daringly artistic black-and-white, the voice-over reading of Isaac's successive drafts of his ode to New York, and the strains of Gershwin's *Rhapsody in Blue* (it is difficult not to feel ambivalent about it, and ambivalence is, precisely, the keynote of this opening sequence) all blend to compose a compelling, multilayered statement that has been known to draw applause from audiences by the time the credit titles start unfolding. This is Allen at his most manipulative and efficient.

Isaac Davis has been fashioned into the most attractively likable character ever played by Allen, who, whether deliberately or not, now seems to set himself up as an example and model for us to admire and emulate. Isaac is a good father (despite the interference of a vindictive ex-wife), a loyal friend (who wouldn't dream of making a pass at his pal's girlfriend until he knows they have broken up), a charming, considerate lover (terrific in bed, as he smugly keeps reminding us), and an artist with the integrity to quit a writing job he has come to despise, even though it means an immediate and drastic reduction in his standard of living. The people who surround Isaac—with the exception of Tracy, Allen's fantasy of uncorrupted juvenile innocence and wisdom— all exhibit various forms and degrees of intellectual and moral phoniness. He alone comes across as thoughtful and sincere, effortlessly striking the balance between shrewdness and sensitivity, intelligence and common sense, earnestness and humor that seems to elude everybody else. Whether he tries to convince Tracy—for her own good— that he is too old for her, talks sense to the emotionally unstable Mary, or lectures his friend Yale (in a classroom) on the necessity of moral integrity, his is always the voice of reason and righteousness. Allen was careful to suggest that Isaac has weaknesses and foibles too, but these, by making him more human, also make him more endearing. Isaac Davis is clearly intended to stand out as a tower of honesty and decency in a world of corrupted values. The misanthropy and self-righteousness implicit in the attitude were to be unleashed, to the dismay of countless fans, in Allen's next effort.

The relationship of the creator to his work and to his audience is brought to the forefront in *Stardust Memories,* although the film also deals, abundantly, with the hero's love life. As a matter of fact, the title, with its double, or even triple, meaning (it refers to the Stardust Hotel, where Sandy Bates is trapped for a weekend of screenings of his films but also to the Hoagy Carmichael song—a song about memories of lost loves—and more specifically to the classic 1932 Louis Armstrong recording, which Bates identifies with a rare moment of perfect happiness in a past love affair) manages to fuse the two themes, better perhaps than the film itself does. *Stardust Memories* is Allen's most complex, most ambitious and most daring film to date; if it is a failure, as so many have said, then it is a magnificent one. Relinquishing the relatively safe confines of the microcosms he had explored in his earlier films, Allen ventures into the most private recesses of his mind, making an entire film out of a plotless but infinitely intricate stream-of-consciousness meditation on Woody Allen's life and work, his countless obsessions, fears and phobias, his incurable weltschmerz, and occasional epiphanies.

Although Sandy Bates in an interview ironically denies being narcissistic ("The mythological character I identify with is Zeus") *Stardust Memories is* one of the most self-centered movies ever made. As one commentator (Laura J. Ross in *New York Arts Journal*) put it, the film asks the question: "What is it like to be Woody Allen?" According to the same writer, such a question can only be of interest to "rabid fans, close friends, and the director himself," and as a result, Allen "lost the universality" he had achieved with *Annie Hall* and *Manhattan.* It is excessively naive, however, to suggest that the universality of a work of art is merely a function of the topics it deals with. In a sense, the question "What is it like to be me?" is always at the core of a creator's preoccupation, no matter what his material may be; the creative process is largely an effort to deal with the issue. It is difficult to understand how one could be interested at all in Woody Allen and not find *Stardust Memories* fascinating.

Most of the adverse reaction to the film has consisted either of irrelevant moralizing (Allen as a misanthropic megalomaniac who bites the hand that feeds him) or equally irrelevant comparisons of Allen's achievement with his "sources' " and influences' (e.g., Bergman and Fellini). The moralizing is irrelevant not only because an artist owes his public no special gratitude for buying his product, or even admiring him, but also because it is simplistic to take *Stardust Memories* as a straight, accurate expression of what Allen actually thinks and feels. After all, the film is a work of fiction, and Sandy Bates, no matter how reminiscent of Woody Allen, is a fictional character. Allen himself has said that it would be a mistake to confuse him with his hero. Although such disclaimers are standard procedure whenever a character becomes too uncomfortably close to a real-life model, they help remind us that fiction is not life and that the two cannot be approached in the same manner. In Allen's case, the rearrangement of life's raw data into an artistic statement involves a great deal of exaggeration and distortion. Sandy Bates is a fantasy projection of the real Woody Allen, just as his trials and tribulations are fantasy projections of Allen's perception of his own life.

As for the criticism concerning Allen's alleged attempt to emulate foreign directors he admires (no reviewer failed to describe *Stardust Memories* as his *8½,* although the relationship is mostly superficial), it is also irrelevant because, as stated before, Allen's art is essentially imitative, and the distinction between borrowing, influence, parody, and plagiarism is so blurred in his case as to become meaningless. Allen's relationship to his influences has become so fluid and free that in *Stardust Memories* he can acknowledge them and use them in ways that transcend categories (comedy/ drama), just as they transcend the concept of parody. What makes audiences uneasy is what makes the film original—Allen's evolving of his own genre beyond genres. Thus, although in some ways even gloomier than *Interiors, Stardust Memories* at the same time recaptures the wild nonsensical energy of the early comedies.

The gloom now is never far underneath the laughter, however. In an uncollected piece published by *The New York Times* in the early seventies, Allen mused about the nature of comedy, astutely remarking, "Laughter usually occurs when something funny has happened; that is why the death of a friend seldom evokes a chuckle, but a funny hat does." Not only has Allen largely done away with funny hats in recent years, but he has become ready to tackle such subjects as the death of a friend; at the beginning of *Stardust Memories,* the hero is brooding about just that. Intimations of mortality and of the absurdity of all things. What's the use of doing anything in this world anyway? Sandy Bates whines as his producers and associates rather disgustedly file out of the room; science tells us that the universe is slowly decaying, heading for ultimate, ineluctable nothingness. This thought, in earlier days, would have triggered a familiar Allenian anticlimax. Now, however, Allen no longer needs punch lines and reassuringly deflating quips. Instead, he proposes a visual correlative to the character's anguish. Bates walks out of the frame, and we are left gazing at a blank white wall, as empty as the future universe he has just evoked. Many may think that Allen has come a long way in the wrong direction, but his itinerary is trailblazing of the most excitingly adventurous kind.

3. *Robert Altman* (1925)

by DAVID STERRITT

1957—*The Delinquents; The James Dean Story* (documentary), codirector: George W. George; 1968—*Countdown* (uncredited codirector: William Conrad); 1969—*That Cold Day in the Park;* 1970—*M*A*S*H; Brewster McCloud;* 1971—*McCabe and Mrs. Miller;* 1972—*Images; The Long Goodbye;* 1974—*Thieves Like Us; California Split;* 1975—*Nashville;* 1976—*Buffalo Bill and the Indians, or, Sitting Bull's History Lesson;* 1977—*3 Women;* 1978—*A Wedding;* 1979—*Quintet; A Perfect Couple; Health;* 1980—*Popeye;* 1982—*Come Back to the Five & Dime Jimmy Dean, Jimmy Dean*

Television Movie
1964—*Nightmare in Chicago* (TV compilation, *Kraft Suspense Theater*)

In the summer of 1981, Robert Altman sold his production company—Lion's Gate Films—for $2.3 million. The buyer was Jonathan Taplin, producer of two Martin Scorsese movies. As reported by Aljean Harmetz of the *New York Times,* the company had been on the market for months "in the wake of financial claims and counterclaims with Paramount Pictures over the budget of *Popeye* and the collapse of [Altman's] next project, *Lone Star,* at United Artists." Altman was quoted as saying, "I feel my time has run out. . . . The movies I want to make are movies the studios don't want." According to Harmetz, "He thinks he will return to film directing through making films for cable and videodisks, more specialized markets that might find his personal style of film making attractive."

The end, yet not the end. A pullback from the wide theatrical screen, with vague talk about the home-video market and its ability to target "select" audiences of any size. A retreat from the Monopoly-board world of mass-market features, yet a determination to dig in *somewhere* and keep the good fight going. In the meantime, Altman scurried to the stage, directing one-act plays for Los Angeles and Off-Broadway theaters, and publicly setting his sights on Broadway.

For the legion of Altman fans, the sale of Lion's Gate—and its message about Altman's position on the Monopoly board—was more sad than surprising. In almost a quarter-century of feature film making, he has rarely played it safe, though some of his risks have been bolder than others. His willingness to push beyond "normal" narrative conventions—coupled with a compulsively busy production schedule, especially during the climactic stage of his career—has resulted in a long string of films that challenge their audience as deliberately and directly as they challenge the Hollywood genres they superficially seem to fit. This is stimulating for critics and diverting for culture-conscious movie buffs. But provocation is not what big hits are made of. And while you can survive in Hollywood without making blockbusters, it would be a rare director who could outlast such a string of box-office disappointments as *Quintet, A Perfect Couple,* and the just-barely-released *Health.* It isn't just that these films failed; they didn't try hard enough to "succeed" in the first place—to please a wide audience at all costs, with the film maker's druthers and sensibilities either channeled wholeheartedly into this task or trailing unobtrusively behind. Clearly, at least one of Altman's eyes was fixed somewhere other than on the bottom line. And that seems to be more than the system can stomach at a time when even the bravest young directors keep their big-budget experiments carefully hedged in by structural and referential tradition.

It is ironic that Altman began the major phase of his career, in 1969, with a film that ingeniously combined audience appeal with a proud flurry of expressive innovations. *M*A*S*H* introduced numerous gestures that were to become hallmarks of the Altman method: overlapping dialogue, eccentric camera movements, quirky characterizations, and a general refusal to travel in a straight line. Conditioned by current film trends to a certain degree of experimentalism, audiences sensed the unity between the director's apparently anarchic style and his definitely anarchic subject, to wit, the state of spiritual slap-happiness that can render bearable the physical horror and mental chaos that are the aftermath of combat.

By thus identifying style and subject, however, Altman took the heat off the potentially fiery issues he was dealing with. His heroes, army doctors near the front lines, used hysterical humor as a release. Altman and his audiences did just the same, by gearing their attention and responses to the zany main characters rather than to their sickening surroundings. In an interview five years later, Altman castigated the hit *M*A*S*H* television series for the immorality of depicting "war without blood." Yet his own version was a war of greatly reduced anguish, for all its references to corporeal misery and shots of blood-stained surgery rooms. Anyway, this wasn't the current conflict in Vietnam; it was the Korean war, safely removed in time. Playing it safe in a few key areas, Altman shaped *M*A*S*H* into a reasonably commercial product, as unsurprising in its success as it was promising in its hints of further experimentation to come. The climax is a football game, drenched in good old Hollywood humor, albeit with a raunchy twist. It's also a letdown for any viewer who's been duly stimulated by the cinematic hijinx that precede it and who hopes Altman has a payoff up his sleeve that's equal to his visual audacity. He didn't, at least not in 1969. But he did prove that he had an eye and a mind of his own and a sense of how to soothe his audience's expectations even as he toyed with new possibilities for the venerable war-movie framework and pushed his own message that war is a hilarious kind of hell.

*M*A*S*H* was a debut film, of sorts, after the comparative flatness of *That Cold Day in the Park* and the apparent insignificance of *The Delinquents, The James Dean Story, Countdown,* and *Nightmare in Chicago* (originally made for TV). It remained to be seen whether Altman would pursue the avant-garde or the reactionary aspects of *M*A*S*H,* its confidently self-inventing visual style or the self-conscious cuteness of its football finale.

Altman moved decisively. *Brewster McCloud* was surreal enough to alienate a multitude of critics, an army of spectators, and even the author of the original screenplay. The flamboyance of *M*A*S*H* was seen as an unusual but legitimate response to a notoriously intractable subject matter. By contrast, *Brewster McCloud* wasn't rooted in reality at all. Its whimsy seemed gratuitous; there was no *excuse* for it. The bird-boy Brewster was cuddly enough, as played by Bud Cort, but he was driven by obsessions as fantastic as his own personality. Worse, he wasn't alone. A full array of characters revolved in bizarre orbits around his peculiar persona, each performing some baroque variation on traditional movie characterizations. It wasn't the radical stuff of a Luis Buñuel, a Jacques Rivette, or a David Lynch. But it was a self-contained universe that operated according to its own laws and principles, and that was enough to turn a passel of viewers against it.

Even though its development is less than coherent at times and its performances are uneven, *Brewster McCloud* is nonetheless a fascinating mixture of comedy, mystery, and dream; and it gives a tantalizing glimpse of the fantastical concerns Altman was to probe more deeply in more exploratory films to follow. The main character is a young man whose ambition is to fly under his own power and who practices with an elaborate pair of wings in the Houston Astrodome, where he also lives. His protector is evidently a fallen angel of some kind, played by Sally Kellerman; other women in his life are an adoring fan (Jennifer Salt, busily building an off-beat career in early films by Brian De Palma and Paul Williams) and his first sexual partner (Shelley Duvall, newly discovered by mentor-to-be Altman). Among many other characters are the detective (Michael Murphy) who investigates the murders that are piling up around Brewster and an ornithological lecturer (René Auberjonois) who becomes increasingly birdlike as the film proceeds. The plot is less important than the other-worldly atmosphere built by these people. The ending is self-referential, like that of *M*A*S*H,* with the fiction of the story suddenly giving way to the fact of the film *qua* film.

The gratuitous nature of *Brewster McCloud* is the movie's most telling quality. Though it takes pot shots at various cultural artifacts, from health foods to cops, this is no satire or protest or "statement" film, as *M*A*S*H* was on some of its levels. It's a fantasy, daft and dark at the same time, and clearly not plugged into Hollywood's standard fantasy formats. As a piece of sustained whimsy, it invites audiences to enter its world, to "escape." Then that world turns chilly, leaving many viewers to feel trapped in somebody else's—well, certainly not nightmare but not exactly rollicking high spirits, either.

In filming *Brewster McCloud,* Altman gambled on his imagination to a degree that had few precedents (especially recent precedents) in commercial American film. While shooting *M*A*S*H* he had told Sally Kellerman (according to Judith M. Kass's book, *Robert Altman: American Innovator*) not to worry about how her role would develop, explaining, "I plan to make up this movie as we go along." Bold beginnings. Yet this war film was still grounded in a familiar framework despite the liberties it so cavalierly took. The more radical *Brewster,* like its own hero, took off on wings of its own conceiving. Years later, Altman still regarded it as his favorite among his works, noting with a sad smile that "you always love the sick child the most."

Still, he came back to earth for his next outing. *McCabe and Mrs. Miller* doesn't toy with genres like its war and fantasy predecessors; it's an unequivocal Western complete with heroes, villains, horses, and guns. Yet it marks a return to an important part of the *M*A*S*H* sensibility: Again the director takes a stock movie situation—not a war this time but the building of a frontier town, which can also be a violent process—and probes into its peculiarities with the zeal of a termite inspector who's so determined to find every last bug that it's okay with him if the entire structure nearly collapses from the holes he's drilling.

And he knows where the trouble lies: business. As befits a young town like Presbyterian Church in a young country like the U.S.A., everyone is in it for the money, and the economy is expanding nicely. Only the main male character, hapless McCabe, doesn't quite understand how big bucks swallow little ones. He tries to hang onto his dignity, and the natural order of things can't accommodate such an unlikely gesture. Hence his demise.

The story of *McCabe and Mrs. Miller* revolves around capital. McCabe comes to town and sets up a brothel. Mrs. Miller arrives and shows him how to do it better. She fancies McCabe but charges the usual fee for fornication, because business comes first. When outside interests decide to buy him out, McCabe refuses on the preposterous ground that he enjoys his enterprise and wants to keep enjoying it. He is doomed from here on. And where is Mrs. Miller as he meets his end? Drifting through an opium daze in the Chinese quarter in silent company with the most wretched of her fellow pioneers.

As usual in an Altman film, plot is the least interesting aspect of *McCabe and Mrs. Miller.* The characters are compelling in themselves, almost regardless of what happens to them. McCabe comes first in the title and the story, cutting a handsome figure (in the person of Warren Beatty) yet proving to be surprisingly and amusingly vacuous. In his celebrated first encounter with Mrs. Miller, she instantly takes over the situation, brandishing a cigar and criticizing his "cheap Jockey Club cologne," as if he were the whore and she the customer. As the film proceeds, McCabe becomes ever more encrusted by macho manifestations that have little to do with the inner him; everything about him rings a little—not false, but hollow. From his first appearance in town, it's hard to credit his tough-guy reputation for having killed someone named Bill Roundtree (in typical Altman fashion, we hear that name again and again, buzzing in the air) or even his nickname, the obviously ill-fitting "Pudgy." Maybe it's his very identity that's empty at the core, since he doesn't bother refuting any of these things. No wonder he winds up dead in the snow, vanquished by the villains of the piece, his body as frozen by the elements as his soul was frozen (so he said) by Mrs. Miller.

She, meanwhile, is a more fascinating character yet, the nexus of a moral equation that becomes more complex as the film unwinds. A woman, she nonetheless holds her own with men, at least the men who matter in her business. A capitalist, she operates nonetheless according to principle, insisting on hygiene and professionalism in her operation. A vigorous exploiter—this strong frontierswoman is, after all, basically a pioneer pimp—she nonetheless finds her ultimate solace in the most primitive of proletarian pleasures, the opium pipe.

The town of Presbyterian Church plays a part in defining these characters, as well as developing its own collective personality. In an article for *Cinéaste,* Judith Gustafson points out the town's complicity in McCabe's self-delusions and his own acquiescence in the (ultimately fatal) falsity that grows around him. When mistaken for the gunfighter who killed Bill Roundtree, he doesn't say no. When flattered by a lawyer who has personal ambitions to fulfill, he listens. Most crucially, when confronted by a Goliath he has no chance of besting, he seems to take the challenge as a testament to his own importance. The fact is, though, he's not a survivor. By contrast, Mrs. Miller keeps going by realizing that (in Gustafson's words) "her society views all women as a commodity," up to and including whores and mail-order brides. Staying free of illusions is her key to staying alive.

Illusions are part and parcel of Americana, though, and these fascinate Altman; it's not surprising that McCabe is the more involving and more deeply explored of his two title characters. The town of Presbyterian Church is itself a rich web of incipient American illusions—wistful visions of order and decency and wealth that seem to be waiting in the wings but haven't quite arrived yet, either. The lawyer, who insists that McCabe is the prototypical American businessman, is a clear forerunner of the politician, Hal Phillip Walker, in *Nashville* and perhaps of the Glenda Jackson character in *Health.* He believes what he says. But lots of people believe what they say in Altman films, and it doesn't make things any better. Or more real. Or, in McCabe's case, more alive.

Stylistically, the film reflects the fractured growth of the town and its denizens. In color and composition, the images have a strong period quality. But cinematic nostalgia is largely offset by the soundtrack, which provides an elaborate counterpoint to the story's visual level—proceeding in fits and starts, building precise layers of meaning through fragmentary phrases often picked out of a crowded conversational din. It seems muddled at first, but it isn't; Altman has done our work for us, like any conscientious craftsman, and the important words are always the ones that leap out, regardless of their sonic surroundings.

In his manipulation of sound, Altman makes a major leap forward here, pointing the way toward the masterfully layered soundtrack of *Nashville.* Yet for all its boldness— and despite its crystallization of the rapidly emerging Altman style—the manipulation of sound and image in *McCabe and Mrs. Miller* never quite pulls the plot or characters free of their rather cold genre moorings. Mrs. Miller freezes our soul a little, too, and McCabe isn't quite lovable enough to be excused for his folly. *McCabe and Mrs. Miller* is a provocative but rarely exciting movie, more to be respected than thrilled to. Audiences responded appropriately, often clinging to the affecting death of the Keith Carradine character as a needed emotional straw, though it's a minor event in the fabric of the film as a whole.

It is generally agreed that the next Altman work, *Images,* is a failure. Yet it was a significant step in the director's development, allowing him to float largely genre-free again (as in *Brewster McCloud*) and to play with the medium for its own sake. For 101 minutes, Susannah York goes mad, surrounded by an international cast that anticipates the more interesting *Quintet* of years later. Through it all, a recurring Altman problem reveals itself: a fey quality (the heroine is writing a book on unicorns; the

actors and characters have the same first names, though reshuffled; the film ends with
the image of a puzzle) that veers over into mere mystification. It is obvious that Altman
is deeply moved by his dreams and fantasies, but at times he seems to find them
cute; and that's a combination that doesn't easily translate into grown-up film. Ultimately,
it's doubtful that the artist understands the mental dynamics he's dealing with in *Images*.
And as soon as we sense this, the center cannot hold. The film falls apart—remaining
lovely to look at, though, and dispelling any lingering doubt about Altman's willingness
to soar beyond ready-made conventions of subject, style, and psychology.

After the failure of *Images*, Altman again scampered back to the more-or-less
real world, making another genre picture. By now, however, it was clear that Altman
never looked his projects in the eye and took them on their own terms. *The Long
Goodbye* is a detective movie with a lot of big twists, including some that seem deliberately
perverse. "The camera is always looking in the wrong place," Altman enthused some
time later, relishing this visual correlative of his gnarled whodunit plot borrowed from
a Raymond Chandler novel. Reflexivity also plays a major part in the movie's construction, though it takes a more campy, movie-fan shape here (recalling the dowager in
Brewster McCloud who dies wearing the red shoes from *The Wizard of Oz*) than in,
say, the finale of *M*A*S*H*. In part, *The Long Goodbye* is a movie about the fun of
movies, with a death scene borrowed from *A Star Is Born* and an ending right out of
The Third Man, not to mention a rendition of "Hooray for Hollywood" at the very
beginning.

Careful choices all, and thoroughly Altmanesque. Yet these flourishes don't manage to deepen a film that remains more plotty than inspired, despite the director's
decision to simplify the original novel and use the storyline merely as a launching
pad for a series of cinematic studies and observations. Genre plots have a way of
intruding, even when film makers consider them secondary and try to work around
them. (Critics praise Howard Hawks for transcending the plot of *The Big Sleep*, yet
the plot casts its shadow everywhere, clouding the otherwise clean lines of the picture.)
In such works as *The Long Goodbye*, *McCabe and Mrs. Miller*, and *Thieves Like Us*, Altman
can be seen yearning toward his chosen role as "essayist in film" without quite having
the courage to dispense with traditional story structures. That brave gesture, approached
in *Brewster McCloud* and the unfortunate *Images*, wasn't to be accomplished until the
heroic *Nashville* and (even more so) *A Wedding* some years later.

In the meantime, Altman moved to the Depression crime format in *Thieves Like
Us*, extending his camera-in-the-wrong-place maneuver to a general avoidance of "obligatory" scenes, such as the death of a major character and most of the bank robberies
that are central to the action. "Film audiences have been trained," he said in an interview
for the *Christian Science Monitor*, "or they've come to expect, that they have this great
privilege of violating all points of view. They're able to see everything because they're
shown everything, especially when it comes to violence or that sort of thing—in fact,
that's usually the reason subjects are picked, so you can show that 'action.' But in
Thieves Like Us we purposely tried to keep things on an emotional level, rather than
on that 'motion-picture' level. . . ."

Always fascinated with sound, Altman uses the soundtrack of *Thieves Like Us*
to fill in many of his self-imposed visual gaps or to provide an ironic counterpoint: a
banal radio narration about Romeo and Juliet as two young characters go to bed together; a "Gangbusters" broadcast as the thieves make their getaway from a bank.
This is a heavy-handed technique, even under Altman's careful guidance. Yet there
are moments when words assume a triumphantly meaningful place in this movie about

largely inarticulate people, particularly at the very end when the survivor of the story, played by Shelley Duvall, offers an enigmatic epilogue through her speech (to a character played by screenwriter Joan Tewkesbury) about how her late husband "crossed me up one time too many lyin'." Indeed, the dialogue is frequently more subtle than the performances—Bert Remsen comes on too strong as the elder criminal, T-Dub, for example, but his character gets to the heart of cynical American folk wisdom when he realizes (echoing a famous observation by Woody Guthrie) that "I should have robbed people with my brain instead of with a gun."

For the rest, *Thieves Like Us* is an enormously atmospheric, unevenly acted drama that advanced Altman's reputation as a capable craftsman while it abandoned the kind of wholly idiosyncratic exploration that made some of his earlier flawed works more distinctive. In any case, audiences were not impressed—Altman was convinced that Pauline Kael's critical overpraise had scared viewers away—and he returned to more personal territory.

Personal in subject as well as style, *California Split* is about Altman's hobby, gambling. It's also a buddy movie of sorts, with Elliott Gould and George Segal as complementary personalities all wrapped up in a world where winning and losing are always big but happen for no particular reason. The film marvelously mirrors its subject, with a loose and improvisatory feel and few genre conventions to distract the director from following his cinematic nose in whatever directions seem most fruitful. Though there are few moments of great inspiration in the picture, its soundtrack is consistently strong—Lion's Gate's eight-track sound further enhancing Altman's sound practices used in earlier films—and the ending is devastating, demonstrating (in the words of one critic) that for a born loser, winning can be the ultimate down.

On the release of *Nashville* soon after, it was widely agreed that Altman had found the film he was born to make. The secret of its success was simple: It was all structure and characterization, with plot relegated to a distinctly subsidiary position. True, what plot there was—the thread of action leading to the climax—was weak. But this hardly mattered with so many cinematic and behavioral riches to release us and the film maker from bothering too much about mere story.

Though the film's promotion cheated a bit by proclaiming twenty-four major characters—some were so minor they hardly counted—there are still more people to get involved with here than in three or four ordinary movies combined. And some are important despite their elusive qualities. Consider the "tricycle man" played by Jeff Goldblum, for example. He shows up infrequently to perform whimsical magic tricks. Yet these suggest a key to the deeper resonances of Altman films, which are ultimately about the mystery, the unsolvability of human existence. Who is this "tricycle man"? Where does he come from? What does he think he's doing? That's precisely the enigma, not only about him but about the obviously "major" characters as well.

There is no need to belabor the consummate technical achievement represented by *Nashville,* with its extraordinarily textured soundtrack, its restlessly roving camera, its allusive images, and its energetically eccentric performances by a large and diverse cast. It's too bad Altman didn't devote more attention to the young character who precipitates the climax by gunning down a pop star, to be dragged away in one of the most wooden—or is it mythic?—images Altman has ever shaped. But the long and lavish *Nashville* careens past its lapses on the strength of sheer filmic exuberance. It's the culmination of all Altman's previous work, and it clearly points the way to future explorations.

Yet the follow-up, *Buffalo Bill and the Indians, or, Sitting Bull's History Lesson,* was resoundingly unpopular. Altman admitted he was "very nervous about this film" shortly before it opened, acknowledging that its construction was not easy, fluctuating as it did between parody and seriousness. "But that's my style," he said at a press conference. "I wanted to disarm the audience with humor, then let them find their own meanings."

And there's the clue. Once again, Altman is more interested in mystery and manifestation than in any single "meaning" the audience can "take home with it," to echo Thornton Wilder. He has spoken wistfully of a film so purely cinematic that it couldn't be talked about, only watched and responded to and *felt*. This is not anti-intellectualism; it is a sincere protest against the dictatorship of the film maker over the audience. The movies are his department, the interpretation is ours. "I have no message, nothing to say, no statements to make to anybody about anything," he said apropos of *Buffalo Bill*. But then he added, asserting himself as an artist, "In my films I try to reflect my view. It's what I *see*, not the way I think things should be."

The mixed results of *Buffalo Bill* reflect the difficulty of combining this intensely personal viewpoint with history, which is presumably a commodity we all share. Altman considered the film to be "very historical," populated with figures "all based on actual characters." Yet he freely stated that "nothing on the screen is a fact in itself," since the facts of the past are mostly buried beyond recovery, anyway. "We present history on an emotional level," Altman said. "The history is correct philosophically, if not actually."

To a degree, this is gibberish. But the point is that *Buffalo Bill* is less a history lesson than a meditation on the meaning of history—a staunchly subjective exercise with multiple points of view, a legendary old fraud for a main character, and a culmination wherein Paul Newman rambles at length to an ephemeral figure who isn't really there. Audiences didn't much like it despite its colorful characters and its impressive cast. Both the material and the approach were too rarefied. "By the time a culture is willing to look at its past," said Altman, "and try to find out the truths of its origins, the tracks have been so covered up that it's impossible to find them. . . ." Apparently he was more right than he wanted to be.

Altman turned in a drastically different direction next, devising one of his most intimate and ingenious films. *3 Women* started as a dream (literally) and grew to a thirty-three-page outline, which Altman discussed for ten minutes with Twentieth Century-Fox before launching into production. An unlikely origin, perhaps, but enough to result in an extraordinarily evocative 125-minute movie.

3 Women moves at a glacial pace; there are times when one thinks the story will disintegrate right off the screen. There are only two main characters, though others poke around the edges of the plot. The action has a distinctly dreamlike logic: Two young misfits become friends; one undergoes a personality change after a (suicidal?) accident; a third woman gives birth to a stillborn child; the personalities of all three merge into a single, collective psychology. The ending is one of Altman's most enigmatic moments, which he has explained in (among other places) a *Sight and Sound* interview: "One sees seals, or sea-lions, basking on rocks, just kind of lying around. And I see *3 Women* as if those three female seals had kicked the last male off that rock and are much more comfortable . . . but at the same time you know it means the end of the species."

With its total immersion in Altmanesque imaginings, *3 Women* is an unprecedented film; even the somewhat similar *Images* had a thriller plot (sort of) and a fair amount of violence (physical and emotional) to serve as conventional pegs for audience involvement. *3 Women* eschews sensationalism, relying entirely on its own dreamish dynamics and superbly delirious performances by Shelley Duvall and Sissy Spacek, among others. The dialogue has an uncanny precision, as if it were carefully scripted, though in fact the film was constructed entirely through improvisation, with monologues and conversations developed shortly (hours or days) before the cameras rolled.

The film has serious flaws, particularly its tendency to go overboard on self-consciously exotic effects, such as Bodhi Wind's background murals and Gerald Busby's pretentious music. Yet on the whole it works startlingly well, drawing the viewer into its unique world with surprising consistency and conviction. Asked how he dared plunge into such a strange and risky venture, Altman answered, "I always think my new one is going to be a big hit. I thought *3 Women* would be as big as *Annie Hall.*" It wasn't, and it never had a chance. On its own terms, though, it stands as a stunning achievement.

Altman's next film, *A Wedding,* is his masterpiece. It isn't the eye-opener *Nashville* was, because it picks up where *Nashville* leaves off. But it carries Altman's explorations further than ever into the crannies of contemporary behavior. And it weaves the twin threads of his oeuvre into a seamless pattern for the first time.

Previously, Altman's films had fallen roughly into two categories: intense probes of private fantasy (*Images, 3 Women*) and broad social canvases (*M*A*S*H, McCabe and Mrs. Miller, Nashville*). While these categories seem separate, they are closely related (like the sides of a coin), since social interaction is the product of personal thought and behavior, manifested in collective situations. It remained for Altman to combine these perspectives—to depict the workings of the private psyche through and within the social ritual.

For the central ritual of *A Wedding,* Altman chose a phenomenon that is even more universal than the war of *M*A*S*H,* the community-building of *McCabe,* the gambling of *California Split,* or the pop culture of *Nashville.* Further, he resurrected the classical unities of time (one day) and space (one location, except for a few early scenes) and crammed forty-eight characters (twice as many as in *Nashville*) into this amazingly concentrated milieu. Despite the complexity of this undertaking, *A Wedding* was assembled in the patented Altman manner, with the structure emerging as the shooting proceeded.

According to the director, the movie had "a very detailed, three-act construction." Its main ideas and incidents were written on cards "and shuffled around a big board, until we got the order we thought we wanted." Altman described the rest of his method in this way: "When we're ready to shoot a particular scene, we write it— maybe the night before, maybe during rehearsal, or maybe a week ahead—with changes made to reflect what's happened since. It's like a football game. You come out with a game plan, and some things don't work, and some things need changing, and other things work so well you want to continue them. It's like an architect's blueprint, in a way."

The blueprint worked. *A Wedding* has a striking visual scheme that helps all kinds of elements to cohere, while expressing some of the film's largest general truths. The opening scenes begin elegantly, with smoothly zooming shots that establish a dignified, properly ritualistic pace, while affording quick access to large amounts of visual information. As the movie proceeds, this orderly structuring method deliberately breaks down, leading us further into the chaos that lurks just beneath the all-too-human facade of this rigorously socialized occasion and preparing us for the strange events that lie in store. "To relinquish the pattern," Altman has said, "was part of the control" he exercised as director. He likens the overall plan of the film to an immaculately dressed woman who steps onto an elegant dance floor and finds that her string of pearls has suddenly broken. The film becomes (studiedly) more scattered. Yet each careening fragment of action or emotion is under precise, if hidden, control every moment. This method has its payoff when the apparent cinematic decontrol meshes with the increasingly frazzled psyches of the characters, who reveal themselves more and more openly (even helplessly) as the strain of the occasion, mirrored by the film's visual style, gets to them. The climax occurs not in the car accident that demolishes two of the characters, nor in the resulting mental stress among the wedding guests, but in two quick shots of fierce-eyed statues that stand guard on the lawn of the wedding estate—darkly brooding spirits that hover over the occasion. The stuff of madness and even of evil lurks within each of the cavorting guests at the ceremony, and it is this melancholy circumstance (somehow caught in the eyes of those statues) that fascinates Altman most—far more than the jokes and romances and petty rivalries that form the surface of the show. Indeed, he tries to implicate his audience in the same mad mentality. When two characters die in an accident, most of the wedding guests are less upset than relieved that it wasn't them or their nearest and dearest. Spectators of the film, Altman points out, are likely to feel just the same, even as they condemn this attitude in the on-screen figures.

The main charge leveled against *A Wedding* by hostile critics was its purported cruelty to its characters, a charge Altman refuted by saying, "I don't dislike any of the people. . . . I have counterparts of every one of those characters in myself, and even more so in my family." For that matter, his acuity in developing so many characters in so much detail indicates a basic, if skeptical, humanism on Altman's part. "I'm looking for an arena in which to mix people up together and disclose things about them," he said in a 1978 conversation. "I try to make things cohesive, and I try to make them exciting, but I don't give much of a hoot about plots." Part of the glory of *A Wedding* is its willingness to dispense with plot more than any previous Altman film, reveling in behavior for its own sake. Instead of making up a story, Altman gives us a unity based on attention to detail and on the presiding spirit of the occasion— a mixture of benign looniness and threatening darkness that seems unerringly true.

In describing *3 Women,* Altman likened the last scene to a situation in which "the species ends," and in at least one published interview, he added that this "might not be bad." But he didn't get around to ending the human species himself until *Quintet* in 1979. Though this film excited Altman very much—he talked about it eagerly before *A Wedding* had even opened—he knew it would be a tricky film to present. He wished audiences could see it with no advance preparation of any kind, just walking in and encountering it like a sudden vision materializing out of nowhere. (Stan Brakhage has used similar words to describe an ideal first encounter with some of his work.) Naturally, such conditions were not to be; and generally scathing reviews paved the way to overwhelming audience rejection.

Yet *Quintet* is a provocative work despite its flaws, and Altman doesn't seem to have given up on it: More than two years later he talked about it in a *Sight and Sound* interview, comparing it to the later *Popeye* in its attempt to create "a culture that has its own restrictions and boundaries." Though he recognizes the failure of *Quintet* to communicate with critics or audiences, he defends it as an allegorical adventure with a deliberately outlandish setting and a sourly humanistic message in which hope springs eternal even when it's pointless. Recognizing that some aspects of the film were confusing for many viewers, Altman admits that "maybe it's my own arrogance that says you don't have to understand them." Still, he asserts what seems to be a key ingredient in his artistic personality and in his critical attitude toward conventional film form: "We accept everything in our own lives, yet we want order in our fantasies." For Altman, fantasies and life are too close to separate so easily. Like a few other creators who don't always insist on explicating what they have come up with—Stanley Kubrick, say, in *2001: A Space Odyssey*—he is content at times to manifest a cinematic form without bothering too much over its meanings. *Quintet* is such an occasion, when Altman manages to throw "the nerves in patterns on a screen" without necessarily fathoming his own achievement.

This is not to tag *Quintet* as a ragingly successful film. Some of its conceits are labored, some of its images are arch, and its performances seem as cold as the Ice Age (the film was shot above the Arctic Circle) that surrounds them. Yet it often shines with a dark and dangerous beauty, offering some of the richest visual textures of the director's career. If admiration for it must be tempered, respect—if only for the pure audacity of the attempt—is entirely in order.

Some critics who didn't like any of Altman's films from *3 Women* to *Quintet* flocked to *A Perfect Couple*, a minor and much more conservative work. The main characters struggle to establish a romance despite their different backgrounds—he's an old-world classical-music type; she's a hip rock'n'roll person—and the music of the movie parallels their ups and downs. As Diane Jacobs states in *Hollywood Renaissance*, the film "is as much about the mating of symphony and rock music as of boy and girl." Trouble is, the music is often uninspired—the band called Keepin' 'Em Off the Streets was not an energizing choice—and Altman lazily substitutes long moments of mooning about for the kind of genuine atmosphere-building he handled so well in earlier movies. It's a mild little film, no more.

The same goes for *Popeye*, an amiable but forgettable romp. Based on the classic Max Fleischer cartoons, which Altman has admitted were not favorites of his, the movie follows its hero through a Freudian frolic wherein he and Olive Oyl are drawn together by affection for the mysterious orphan Swee'pea, while Popeye searches for his own long-lost pappy. It is a somewhat unsettling film, considering its supposedly carefree ambience of cartoon characters and slapstick action: The setting, Sweethaven, is indeed a "doll's village of a child's dreams" as Tom Milne suggests, but it is also rather ugly; and the characters often seem ill-at-ease with their caricaturish attributes, which are intermittently commented upon—in violation of the unspoken rule of ortho-dox cartoonery, to take absurdity for granted. But then, this isn't a cartoon, even if its elements seem rooted in a precariously early phase of personality development (probably the oral stage, which positively howls for attention through the very names of Sweethaven, Swee'pea, and Olive Oyl, not to mention Wimpy's hamburgers; there's more appeal to the mouth than to the eye in this movie). It's a live-action musical, which works very hard but fails to find a balance between the demands of the great musical tradition (toward which it strives) and Altman's own idiosyncratic leanings (which are only fitfully expressed). The result is little more than a momentary diversion.

Health seems to have been the film that rang the death knell for Altman as a studio director and, for a time at least, as a practicing film maker. It languished on the shelf for months after completion, finally going into limited and cautious release through Films Inc., which considered it worth a limited and cautious gamble. Reports on the film indicate that Altman's alleged "cruelty to the characters" is again a problem; in any case, the film failed in previews, where audiences refused to respond to its quirky characters gathered at a health-foods convention.

Altman's premature, forced, and surely temporary retirement from the wide screen in 1981 was an abrupt turnaround from the situation in 1978, when he was introduced on opening night of the New York Film Festival—prior to a gala screening of *A Wedding*—as the greatest working director in American cinema. Ironically, he has garnered a reputation for laboring uncommonly hard and generating an uncommon number of movies; sloth or carelessness are surely not among his shortcomings. "Everybody's supposed to take two years for a film," he said in 1978, "but I find I work better with more things to do. I don't know any painter who works on just one canvas at a time. Also, I go from little films to big ones, which gives me a kind of vacation— like going to the beach. You relax some muscles and use some others. I think our brains work best when used a lot."

The trouble is, he continued, "painters all have stacks of canvases they don't show anyone. But movies are expensive, and we have to toss 'em out to the public, whether we want to or not. Knowing this, we try to protect them a little more, so we probably end up hurting them—making them less experimental than they should be. We temper them so they'll make money, or be successful on *some* level, because otherwise we're stopped."

In 1981, Altman was stopped, at least where feature films are concerned. Yet his optimism about the video market and his enthusiasm for "honing his talent" in the theater augured more experiments still to come. "I always want to entertain," he once remarked, "but I'm always dealing with impressions, abstractions." His films were a bit too abstract and impressionistic for Hollywood to tolerate indefinitely, as it happens. Nevertheless, his most committed admirers saw his departure from the studio scene as an annoying interruption, at worst, and possibly the beginning of a new creative phase that would invent its own form as it proceeded, much like Altman's own best works.

4. Laslo Benedek (1907)

1949—*The Kissing Bandit; Port of New York;* 1952—*Death of a Salesman;* 1954—*The Wild One; Bengal Brigade;* 1955—*Kinder, Mütter und ein General* (Fed. Rep. of Germany); 1957—*Affair in Havana;* 1960—*Moment of Danger* (Great Britain; U.S., *Malaga,* 1962); *Recours en grâce* (France); 1966—*Namu the Killer Whale;* 1968—*Daring Game;* 1971—*The Night Visitor;* 1976—*Assault on Agathon*

To most people, Benedek is the typical one-shot director, with *The Wild One* his only claim to fame. In all fairness, however, he would deserve to make the two-shot (or at least the one-and-a-half-shot) category, for *Death of a Salesman* is better than most critics suggested. Otherwise, Benedek's Hollywood movies *are* inconsequential, and the seven films he made in various countries between the mid-fifties and the early seventies are so obscure that only a Benedek scholar would be able to account for them.

The Hungarian-born director was a photographer, writer, and editor before he was signed up as a director by MGM in 1948, but his only notable work was done for independent Stanley Kramer who produced both *Death of a Salesman* and *The Wild One*. Benedek was blamed for his adaptation of the former as if he had desecrated some immortal material, but the truth is that the play, although affecting in many ways and a minor masterpiece of sorts, was marred by Arthur Miller's usual lack of subtlety and heavy reliance upon simplistic psychoanalytical devices. Although the film itself is no masterpiece, Benedek should be praised for his acceptance—more courageous than slavish—of the play as a piece of theatrical contrivance, an acceptance that did not prevent him from getting convincing and moving performances from the cast, notably Fredric March and Mildred Dunnock.

There is something strange about Benedek's career (he says he was "greylisted" because of his friendship with witchhunt victims) and something even stranger about the career of his most famous movie. In spite of Brando's fame at the time, *The Wild One* was all but ignored when it came out, and its critical reputation slowly grew through the late fifties and early sixties while, simultaneously but in a curiously unrelated way, it also became a sort of mythological item, slowly impregnating the American consciousness through television exposure and such commercial spinoffs as the famous poster of leather-jacketed Brando slouching on his bike. By the time *The Wild One* had reached that Olympus of popular acceptance, where the good, the bad, and the worse blissfully cohabit, the weird and unfamiliar subject of motorcycle gangs had become commonplace, and critics who had liked the film for its offbeat quality started dropping it from their lists. Although Europeans were intrigued, and sometimes shocked, by its exotic theme and puzzling violence (the film was banned in England, and one French critic captioned his review, "The Martians Have Arrived"), *The Wild One* was really quite tame when compared to what was to follow in the next decade. It now looks like a typical product of the fifties, with crew cuts instead of long hair, beer instead of pot, minor vandalism instead of sex, and clean West Coast jazz instead of sloppy rock. Still, it remains the granddaddy of all motorcycle flicks and possibly the best of them all. In spite of the fifties aura, it does not seem to suffer much from the generation gap. The best instance of the younger crowd's allegiance to the film is to be found in Kenneth Anger's *Scorpio Rising* in which a motorcycle freak watches *The Wild One* on television while getting ready for an outing.

Fashion aside, *The Wild One* endures as an unforgettable movie. Unforgettable not because it was great or even outstanding but simply because it is difficult to forget. Benedek's direction, while not overly original, was in the best Hollywood tradition of efficiency. It has a sense of place (the drowsy little California town, Bleeker's Café, the empty, tree-shaded roads at night), of objects (the gleaming, roaring, swerving bikes, the trophy), of attitudes and postures (Brando's sulky inarticulateness, Lee Marvin's flamboyance). It sticks in one's mind as a purely audio-visual affair, a film that makes its point through sounds and images and the taut editing that binds them and drives them on. *The Wild One* may not be great cinema, but it is only cinema, pure and undiluted. That is a lot, and for it Benedek must be remembered, no matter how indifferent the rest of his career may have been.

5. Budd Boetticher (1916)

by BARRY GILLAM

Credited as Oscar Boetticher, Jr. through 1945 and as Oscar Boetticher from 1948 through 1950.

1944—*One Mysterious Night; The Missing Juror;* 1945—*Youth on Trial; A Guy, a Gal and a Pal; Escape in the Fog;* 1948—*Assigned to Danger; Behind Locked Doors;* 1949—*Black Midnight; Wolf Hunters;* 1950—*Killer Shark;* 1951—*The Bullfighter and the Lady;* 1952—*The Cimarron Kid; Bronco Buster; Red Ball Express; Horizons West;* 1953—*City Beneath the Sea; Seminole; The Man From the Alamo; Wings of the Hawk; East of Sumatra;* 1955—*The Magnificent Matador;* 1956—*The Killer Is Loose; Seven Men From Now;* 1957—*The Tall T; Decision at Sundown;* 1958—*Buchanan Rides Alone;* 1959—*Ride Lonesome; Westbound;* 1960—*The Rise and Fall of Legs Diamond; Comanche Station;* 1968—(1958-1968) *Arruza;* 1969—*A Time for Dying*

Uncredited
1944—*The Girl in the Case* (William Berke); *U-Boat Prisoner* (Lew Landers)

It is tempting to read Budd Boetticher's career in the terms of his own fictional world. He fits the role easily: a Randolph Scott character, resourceful, taciturn, alone. A professional who, working under the cover of his professionalism, is on a personal, moral quest in treacherous territory. A man who accomplishes his task superbly again and again but finds the rewards unsatisfactory and, while still fit and in possession of his talents, quits the scene.

A man, moreover, to whom appreciation comes late if at all. At the height of his career (1955–1960), a single notice stands out: André Bazin's immediate recognition of *Seven Men From Now*. Some further attention followed in the early sixties (notably from Andrew Sarris in 1963 and *Cahiers du Cinéma* in 1964), climaxing in a chapter in Jim Kitses's study of authorship within the Western, *Horizons West* (1969). Kitses's piece on Boetticher is among the best film criticism in the language, but Boetticher is still known to few, and his films are still seldom shown.

A romantic interpretation of his career is fostered by critics' comparisons with Hemingway and by the mystique surrounding Boetticher's own early career in bullfighting. One might even see a touch of Fitzgerald in Boetticher's celebration on film of his own youthful adventures. And in truth, the period on which his reputation rests is so brief (six years), productive (nine films), and brilliant that it should have been followed by glory, not the torturous decade Boetticher spent making the documentary *Arruza*. An autobiographical novel dealing with those years is entitled *When in Disgrace* and the crowning indignity was that *Arruza*, his artistic testament, quickly disappeared, and the book describing its making was not published. One last Western made in 1969 (*A Time for Dying*) has yet to receive American distribution. Boetticher has since withdrawn from film making to a ranch in Mexico, where he raises horses.

These highly dramatic final scenes distinguish a career that otherwise describes a familiar trajectory: assistant director in the early forties; director of "B"s or programmers by the mid-forties; first notable films (often dubbed "sleepers") in the early or mid-fifties; and thereafter greater directorial control while still on medium- and low-budget films (these generally unnoticed by critics, many never opening in New York); television in the late fifties and early sixties; and a falling off in production in the sixties. With a few changes, this outline could also apply to Phil Karlson, Don Siegel, or Joseph H. Lewis. The recent spectacular success of the first two has not affected the relative unavailability of their early work.

Many of Boetticher's early films are unknown quantities, some literally so: of his several movies for the Armed Forces, only one title has been identified. His commercial work, though more extensively catalogued, is almost as obscure. This is particularly true of his first ten fiction features (1944–1950): "B"s and programmers for Columbia, Eagle Lion, and Monogram.

His second film, *The Missing Juror,* is a none too logical investigating reporter yarn, embellished with bizarre details (Mike Mazurki reciting "The Ballad of Reading Gaol" as he gives a massage to George Macready) and expressionist shadows, symbols, and omens. These tend to aggrevate the unreality and archness of the script at the same time that they enliven it. What seems Boetticher's main contribution is the film's chief distinction: a headlong narrative movement that stresses how over why and what over how. The film jumps forward into new situations with a minimum of verbal explanation or established link. These unsettling leaps in the narrative have perhaps more to do with the film's partial success as a thriller than its panoply of nooses, black cats, and disappearing bodies.

A Guy, A Gal and A Pal, Boetticher's fourth, is a hectic comedy that again moves speedily from situation to situation as the characters form an improvised family to get cross country under wartime restrictions and other difficulties. This vague foreshadowing of Boetticher's later "journey" films is the only point of interest, though. Other early films include the two Eagle Lion productions from 1948: *Assigned to Danger* and *Behind Locked Doors.* The first is a mediocre crime drama that bottles its characters up in a mountain lodge à la Tod Browning as they wait to make their getaway. The second, however, uses the same strategy with greater success.

Behind Locked Doors has an investigator-in-an-asylum plot that looks forward to *Shock Corridor* (1963), even if Boetticher's conventional thriller hardly approaches Samuel Fuller's American nightmare in its scope or style. Boetticher does manage, nevertheless, to invigorate the script's assembly of stock elements by heightening the contrasts in mood and character. This also helps to vary the pace from scene to scene, thereby aiding in Boetticher's control of tempo throughout the film. The sanitarium, for instance, is first introduced when the detective hero and reporter heroine meet outside its side entrance one night—each there on a different trail. The detective is cocky, self-assured, so unaffected by the locale that he comes on to the reporter. This playful mood is restrained when the detective enters as a mock patient, chagrined by the dullness of the institution's daylight aspect. By night, however, screams ring out, and the corridors are patrolled by a sadistic guard who uses his jangling keys to beat the uncooperative.

The detective's control and authority erode throughout the film. His frivolous gesture of gallantry and sexual aggrandizement in taking the woman's place as infiltrator of the asylum leads first to the constraint of earnest role playing and then to actual incarceration. Later, as he seeks the room of the judge in hiding, who is the object of their search, he will be locked into a cell with a homicidal wrestler. It is the girl who rescues him. This descent into terror and claustrophobia is paralleled by the growing ties of affection and respect between man and woman. The detective's early protestations against any higher motive than the reward money gradually change as he and the reporter together work out the problems confronting them.

This scheme of descent and redemption is also present in *The Bullfighter and the Lady*, which Boetticher indicated was the first film he took responsibility for by signing it "Budd Boetticher" instead of the formal "Oscar Boetticher, Jr." that appeared on his previous movies. Drawn from his own experiences as an American matador in Mexico, *The Bullfighter and the Lady* is a rite of passage on three levels: the discipline and traditions of bullfighting, the customs and language of Mexico, and the courtship of a woman. In each, Chuck Regan (Robert Stack) makes humiliating mistakes and transgressions. But Regan's gaffes are transformed by the visual style in which they are portrayed: the long shot of destiny. This is the fourth level of the film: its reference to a world of legend recalling Fritz Lang's *Nibelungen* movies. And ultimately it is this last dimension that distinguishes the film and leads one back to consider such other aspects as the moral and social.

Bullfighter is stronger visually than dramatically. The things that stay with the viewer are not scenes but images: a pan down from the stadium's statues of bulls and matadors to Regan as he enters for his first lesson; Regan emerging from the white mist of the steam room as a blonde Apollo; Regan going into a forest after his beloved, seen in extralong shot so that he is physically dwarfed by the size of the country and the problems it presents.

The next stage in Boetticher's career is a series of nine low- or medium-budget action films for Universal that seem a retreat from the personal commitment one feels in *Bullfighter*. These tend to be less interesting in themselves than for the elements of style and theme, which hindsight tells us will later be developed more fully: the antagonists as doubles in *Seminole;* the circular motion of *Red Ball Express;* the varying claims of money and friendship in *City Beneath the Sea;* the staging of action along the contours of the landscape in *Wings of the Hawk;* in *Horizons West*, the ironic treatment of the action-hero who finds himself in a situation he cannot control—sometimes shot from above to give a Walshian sense of his now diminutive figure and position; the characters, also in *Horizons West*, who live in the past or who try to recreate or avenge that ever-present past. Some of these films are meretricious, and some are well crafted, but while all might profitably be revived for reassessment, none succeeds as a whole— even a flawed whole such as *Bullfighter*.

The most interesting of the series is the first, *The Cimarron Kid*. Within the confines of the action formula, it is more expressionist and eccentric than the others, which seems a carryover from *Bullfighter*. The action is the most clear-cut, vivid, and imaginative in any of these early films: tactical ploys over a given terrain with certain obstacles and opposing forces. There is one sequence in particular—a battle in and through a railroad roundhouse—that is cleverly staged in a play between superior force and superior wit, mechanical and human movement, entrapment and escape: the town with its posse and laws on one side and the open countryside on the other. A moral, aphoristic quality infuses the violence: a bank robber shot, bleeding to death as his clutched loot also spills out into the street.

The Cimarron Kid is also remarkable for its overall design, its sympathetic but stoic treatment of the characters and their fates. The band of robbers, several of the same family, are decimated as the film progresses from one holdup to the next. One dead here, a few there, they are immediately forgotten as the gang hurtles forward toward ever greater visions of gold. At the end only the eponymous Kid is left alive, and he doesn't get the gold, either. In fact, he goes straight: all his friends have died in vain. The film begins as he is released from prison. It ends as he is brought back to jail. There is a hint here of something Chaucerian in the way that Boetticher clothes the bones of this ironic parable with the muscles of narrative and the flesh of human foibles, wishes, and desires.

Boetticher's second bullfight movie is everything the first wasn't: a brassy Hollywood treatment that obscures and trivializes its subject. Again based on a story by Boetticher, *The Magnificent Matador* is different from *Bullfighter* in ways that reflect the casting. Instead of grim, repressed, nailbitingly moral Robert Stack, the matador this time is Anthony Quinn, exuberant, vulgar, self-indulgent. Boetticher's responsiveness to actors has not been stressed nearly enough.

The Killer Is Loose is the first of Boetticher's films to begin to fulfill the promise shown in his earlier work. Concerned once more with opposed strategies, it deals not only with law versus outlaw but also with the procedural versus the psychotic. Policeman Sam Wagner (Joseph Cotten) is trying to protect his wife from bank robber Leon Poole (Wendell Corey), who holds Wagner responsible for the death of Poole's wife. Here, for the first time, Boetticher makes something of the identification of antagonists: their shared devotion to, and loss of, their wives, their conviction that they are victims of circumstance, their frustration and feelings of futility and failure, and, at the same time, their sense of having a mission that overrides other concerns: "I've got a job to do." The division of audience loyalties gives added bite to the crosscutting between the efficient police preparations, with their maps and patrols and Poole's eccentric movements, impromptu evasions, and improvised disguises. This is followed right down to the final one-on-one confrontation between Wagner's experience and intuition and Poole's crazy cunning.

The narrative complicates this cat-and-mouse game with its teasing, elusive progress. Verbal statements are followed by visual contradictions. Visual ellipses of action as it moves toward violence are later confirmed or denied by verbal reports. Each of the several leading characters moves at a different, inconstant speed of comprehension and action, thereby varying and adding texture to the overall pace and narrative of the film. These moves and feints are also practiced upon the viewer, who is invited to participate in putting action and tactics together: key pieces are deliberately missing.

In comparison with the characters' urgency and desperation, the film has a laconic, flat, unrelenting pace. This is to some extent a reflection of Poole's inhuman aspect as deranged avenger. And as such it is the cage of time within which Wagner must try to maneuver and outmaneuver Poole. Scenes of character exposition, though, are just as terse as scenes of action. The opening section of robbery, apprehension, trial, and incarceration has the brevity of images from a dream, detached and sketchy. The rest of the film seems to be scenes from a nightmare in its concentration on details, objects, weariness, inexplicable loss, and unraveled plans.

If the characters in *The Killer Is Loose* are ultimately somewhat impersonal, this has much to do with Boetticher's lack of control over the casting: Cotten and Rhonda Fleming are both miscast, and their disinterest shows. As a footnote, it should be noted that the screenwriter of *The Killer Is Loose*, Harold Medford, also cowrote Gerd Oswald's *Brainwashed*, which uses some of the same techniques as well, if not better.

In the five years following *The Killer Is Loose*, from 1956 to 1960, Boetticher shot the seven Westerns starring Randolph Scott that are usually known as the Ranown series (for the Randolph Scott/Harry Joe Brown production company that backed five of them). One critic notes that Boetticher did not seem hampered by his "B"-picture budgets. This is undeniably true but rather condescending. The best of the series are *Ride Lonesome, The Tall T,* and *Comanche Station.* The four remaining titles—*Seven Men From Now, Decision at Sundown, Buchanan Rides Alone,* and *Westbound*—are minor films made notable by the application of Boetticher's mature style to uneven or inadequate material.

Although the unity of the series has sometimes been overstated, the films share so many elements (and bear such interchangeable titles) that it is easy, on first acquaintance, to confuse one with another. (This is especially true at their core: the four scripts by Burt Kennedy, for *Seven Men, The Tall T, Ride Lonesome,* and *Comanche Station.*) *Ride Lonesome* seems both representative and exemplary and thus may serve as the primary subject for discussion.

The first element the viewer sees, generally under the credits, is the landscape: hills, rocks, an abstract stopping just this side of Tanguy. It is the wasteland between small towns, almost bereft of natural reference points. The only inhabitants are the managers of the stage-line way stations—Conradian outposts of progress. Distances are measured from one to another, as if the land itself were just empty miles. The meaning of this land is improvised by the few men who ride it. This is no Monument Valley but a nearly featureless, landmark-less expanse whose significance is temporary and changing. The Indians are the mobile aspect of the land, one of the harsh conditions of existence that makes white habitation untenable.

During the credits, the viewer notices something moving, a dark spot that emerges from behind or within the jumbled rockstrewn maze. The rider follows the horizons and declivities, the natural contours of the land. This is the Randolph Scott character. He is equated visually with the Indians who will later make their appearance in the same manner: suddenly *there*—a new speck on the horizon that is neither rock nor tree. He is also identified with the Indians by his stance: the stoic's straight back, the lean, weathered face and frame, the watchfulness, like an animal sniffing the air, the sense of ceremony and the aversion to all but the most necessary speech. More than any other character, Scott knows the Indians and, like them, he knows the land. Like them, again, in their raids of revenge, he is policing the land. He is often a lawman once removed, retired or somewhat disreputable, a comanchero in *Comanche Station,* a bounty hunter in *Ride Lonesome.* Underneath this formal activity there is something else, a personal odyssey of vengeance. Its origin is in something that happened to his wife. She was captured by the Indians or killed in a holdup. Scott's search to find her or avenge her has gone on so long, perhaps ten years, that the goal has grown chimerical. The odyssey itself now gives structure and meaning to his life.

If Scott is a kind of knight errant on a quest of honor, his counterpart, the villain, is one of the more earthy, lustful knights, one who will never see the Grail. (He would, for that matter, have little interest in such an ineffable property; gold is more in his line.) He is also a different physical type from Scott. A few years younger, he is shorter, springier, more relaxed yet more excitable, more muscular, more "of the flesh." Actors cast in this role include Richard Boone, Pernell Roberts, Lee Marvin, and Claude Akins. While Scott is "all the time alone," the villain travels with friends or at least accomplices. He is more talkative, more gregarious. For all his range lore, he would rather be in a town or city. At that, his range lore is sketchier than Scott's, particularly in its geography and knowledge of the Indians. Where Scott respects them as a natural force, the villain reacts with fear: he wants to kill them.

As both hero and villain move outside normal areas of white habitation and travel, so they are also outside ordinary society, its values, and its structured routine of family and occupation. Where Scott's quest supersedes any job, the villain's activities constitute an evasion of work, an attempted shortcut to money. Thus, although the villain momentarily takes up Scott's profession of comanchero or bounty hunter to secure the reward, it is only a temporary arrangement between other, more larcenous, schemes. In this sense *Ride Lonesome* is an important variant, for here the admitted outlaw does not want the money but the bonus that comes with it: amnesty and the chance for a new life. He would still, however, kill Scott to obtain that legal purification. For all this, hero and villain like and respect each other, and each will save the other's life from the Indians when it would be easier and safer to let his opponent die. The villain, then, has a code, however flexible, of his own.

Several of Boetticher's earlier films deal in opposing strategies. This pattern is sublimated in the Ranown films into what Kitses calls a dialogue between hero and villain. Its subject is not tactics now but ethics. The stakes in the struggle are dollars, but the essential question is elsewhere: what will a man do for the money, and what will he do with it? Because the money is only a pretext for Scott and because he has, in any case, withdrawn from such earthly pursuits, he has a detached, philosophical attitude toward the younger man's very human interests and endeavors.

The other characters are variously bewildered and intrigued by this wide-ranging, often nonverbal discourse. The woman in the party resembles Conrad's women in her ignorance of the conditions of life in the wilderness. Naturally, she is shocked by the pragmatic attitude to death and the quixotic attitude to money she finds there. She reacts to events but seldom acts herself. Far from superfluous, though, she represents in many ways what the men are fighting for: Scott to justify the sanctity of marriage and the home, the outlaw to achieve the financial, if not social, status that will enable him to establish his own menage. The woman appeals to both men, her sensuality held in check by a strong sense of propriety and purpose. Scott suppresses his feelings, remarking at most that she reminds him of his wife. The outlaw, though, openly offers his "protection," which she declines, insisting on her self-reliance.

The woman is also important as the one outsider in this group of men. She becomes the viewer's voice, eyes, and ears. The motives underlying the mens' actions are often hidden and only revealed when this outsider asks an impertinent question. Thus the audience's view of and understanding of the main characters are in some ways tied to the woman's.

She is, however, only a temporary inhabitant of the wilderness. The villain's "young guns" have a greater stake in the "dialogue" between hero and villain for their future lies somewhere within that spectrum. Barely experienced, they still talk of parents and childhood, and they still have dreams of "amounting to something." Though they are effectively hired killers, they are invariably more courteous to the woman than gruff Scott is. When one young gun considers going straight, Scott tells him: "A man can cross over any time he's a mind."

This is true of all the characters, though. Most of the Ranown films take the form of journeys, episodes between stations in life. Change is immediately available to all. Their choice of options marks their characters, and the rejection of change by Scott and the villain puts a special doom on them—Scott endlessly repeating his noble, empty gesture of quest, while the outlaw loses his life by insisting once too often that he *will* have the money.

The paradox is that to realize their rigid goals the two men must be extremely flexible and resourceful in all practical matters. Much of the charm and the very structure of the films derive from this play between a single, obsessive end and its various, circuitous means. Andrew Sarris's description was particularly apt. The series was, he wrote, "constructed partly as allegorical odysseys and partly as floating poker games where every character took turns at bluffing about his hand until the final showdown."

The poker metaphor underlies the first scene of *Ride Lonesome*. Bounty hunter Ben Brigade (Randolph Scott) has just caught up with his quarry, outlaw Billy John (James Best). Brigade seems to be in control (his gun on Billy John), but Billy John has in fact been waiting for him, casually making coffee over an open fire. Billy John springs his trap (he has four men up in the hills with their guns on Brigade), but Brigade bluffs ("Before I hit the ground I'll blow you half in two"). Billy John prevaricates, quavers, then crumbles into a whine, sending his men off to get his older, tougher brother Frank.

The two shots early in the sequence contrast the two characters: Brigade wary yet ramrod stiff, while Billy John lounges on the ground. Like Hawks and Ford, Boetticher often equates physical stance with moral stance. The characters are revealed in action: Brigade cautiously evaluating the situation but rapidly reacting as it changes; Billy John swaggering verbally, putting everything on one ploy and then falling apart when *it* does.

The standard staging would be as a one-on-one standoff. Boetticher and Kennedy introduce the mountain as a wild card, its threat combining with a vague preposterousness. The central confrontation is then photographed as a three-handed poker game among Brigade, Billy John, and the mountain, the last boasting the blankest of poker faces. This reorganization of what might have been a showdown is crucial to Boetticher's method. Brigade is not a gunfighter, and this is not a contest of skill but a confrontation of wit, nerve, and character.

All will be tested as Brigade takes Billy John in. Two outlaws, Sam Boone (Pernell Roberts) and Wid (James Coburn), join Brigade's traveling party with the stated purpose of taking Billy John from Brigade and trading him for the government-offered amnesty. Newly widowed Carrie Lane (Karen Steele) comes along for protection from the Indians menacing and attacking the group. And, finally, Billy John's brother, Frank (Lee Van Cleef), is rapidly gaining on Brigade.

Although the action of *Ride Lonesome* creates this traveling party with a single thing in common (the Indian threat), all the characters remain individuals. In fact, every person Brigade meets will try or plot to kill him or at least pull a gun on him. Brigade's responses are various, but they seldom involve his own weapons. Boetticher tends to place Brigade in situations where weapons are unavailable or action itself is impossible: standing alone before many Indians or caught by Billy John's rifle already leveled at him.

This last situation finds all five members of the traveling party in close proximity, and the editing pattern, cutting rapidly from one face to another around and around the whole circle, not just between Brigade and Billy John, informs us that this is a game in which everyone has a stake, even if a divided one. Brigade is saved only by Boone's counterbluff that the rifle is not cocked and ready to fire. As in the opening sequence, Billy John's bravado shatters easily, and the progress of the scene is toward character revelation: Mrs. Lane had felt sorry for young Billy John, but now she comes to realize his murderousness. Boone and Wid would gain by having Brigade dead, but Boone saves his life.

The one thing that all the confrontations have in common is freedom and captivity. Here Billy John tries to escape; earlier the Indians bargained to buy Mrs. Lane. Most of these confrontations are interrupted or stalemated before they reach a point of violence, and by means of a comic or pastoral anticlimax, some reconciliation or postponement is effected. The one sequence that must end in violence is the climactic face-off between Brigade and Frank, his real quarry. Reversing the opening scene, Billy John is once more the bait, but Brigade has set the trap, and Frank and his men ride into it. Even this has a comic coda, as Boone calls Brigade out for what would be the one, traditional showdown of the film. When Boone demands Billy John or else, Brigade surprises Boone by readily acceding—Brigade having no more use for him.

The film covers four days with distinct camp scenes each night and much dialogue devoted to destinations and rates of progress. The effect of the film, though, is not one of careful structure but of effortless flow from one event and place to another. This results in part from the pacing and the generally unchanging landscape. Then again, we do not see the characters ride from A to B but simply across the landscape, and the composition and editing are such that we see an almost continuous band of movement. Shots in riding sequences often take their length from the pace of the horses, the time it takes them to cover the ground in the shot. This Griffithian respect for natural rhythms creates a feeling of ease and leisure which, with the graceful composition of a string of riders in the Scope frame, produces a pleasurable relaxation from the rapid editing of the dramatic scenes. This is also aided by the viewer's realization that the narrative progresses as much through character development (or revelation— no one changes) as through physical acts.

Those characters, and the acting creating them, are one of the joys of the best Boetticher films. While Scott's stiffness and William S. Hart-like rectitude are the central elements of the Scott characters, Boetticher humanizes Scott, often by playing against those qualities, so that Scott will bump his head or be caught in situations where his qualities are superfluous. The casting of the films is impeccable and reminds us of the incredible pool of low-budget acting talent in the fifties, which so few directors knew how to use. *Ride Lonesome,* for instance, was James Coburn's first film. Boetticher's warmth toward his characters is such that in *Ride Lonesome* one understands their reprieve from the usual decimation of a revenger's tragedy: by the end of the film we love them all.

On better acquaintance, the other films in the Ranown series tend to become ever more individual. The visual strategies of *Ride Lonesome* could apply to no other film. Where *Ride Lonesome* and *Comanche Station,* the only two in CinemaScope, stress the expansiveness of the landscape, *The Tall T* deals in constriction. Here Scott and the woman are captives (the original title) and despite ransom demands, know they will soon be killed. The recurrent framing devices and the confines of a small cabin with low roof and pillars further dividing that small space are echoed in the repeated discussions of limited time, of how the money will be spent, of how many men have been killed or will be killed. The film opens with unusually bright blue skies and green trees which yield, on the villains' arrival, in stark contrast, to silhouettes and dark interiors.

Comanche Station, on the other hand, is a study in the use of CinemaScope, especially in its many two-shots. Mutual trust is a major concern of the film, and the two-shots are varied with considerable nuance so that relative position within the frame tells us much about the characters' feelings. Beyond the expected separation to opposite ends of the image and proximity near the center, a diagonal two-shot suggests tension, and differences in height of ground mix moral and strategic superiority in interesting ways. Crane shots are early identified with the menace of the Indians, and their unobtrusive use during later pastoral riding sequences introduces an element of vulnerability to the traveling party as a whole.

The other notable film in the series is *Buchanan Rides Alone,* which is distinguished not by its visual style but by its narrative technique. The tone is farcical, the villain having been divided into a family of fat men, variously comic, mean, and urbane, who rule a small border town. The action of the film follows Scott's circular progress or lack of progress in this maze of greed and self-interest. Halfway through the film, after various escapes and battles, he is back in jail, where he began, still under threat of death. The absurdist elements present in the Ranown series take over this film, as the characters' movements into and out of captivity are shadowed and parodied by the movement through different hands and safes of the money either stolen from them or being offered to ransom them. Money is constantly being counted and recounted, and monetary values are assigned arbitrarily to everything and everyone in sight.

That sense of detached "play" is also present in *The Rise and Fall of Legs Diamond,* Boetticher's last film before leaving Hollywood to make *Arruza.* In narrative style, *Legs Diamond* is closest to *The Killer Is Loose,* and where the earlier film's cold, relentless, elliptical progress seemed to describe its eponymous madman, so the elegant, cool, dancing motion of *Legs Diamond* is the image of its hero. Heel might be a better word, for Legs (Ray Danton) is an opportunist of the first order, using then discarding everyone he encounters. Boetticher's stylistic control is so assured that in *Legs Diamond,* perhaps alone of his films, the character's wit and economy and grace are totally externalized into the editing, camera movement, and narrative. The grace that Diamond possesses, though, is entirely physical and manipulative, unlike the Randolph Scott character, so the film has something of the quality of an object lesson. Early on, he plays and preys upon his victims with cool efficiency, obtaining exactly the service or reward he wants. But each person he victimizes becomes another closed door when he needs their help later. Legs has no interior resources and hardly any character. Our lack of sympathy at first becomes lack of remorse when his fortunes turn.

This is, interestingly, one of the more curious aspects of *Arruza,* Boetticher's documentary about his friend Carlos Arruza, the great bullfighter. Staged scenes with Arruza's wife are more awkward than affecting, and we never get any sense of Arruza the man. Arruza is subsumed totally in his professional role, performing against the bulls with courage and style. Arruza, as Kitses says, reminds us of Scott both physically and in his role. But where Scott is granted wit and character interplay, Arruza stands entirely alone. The scenes in the stadium, photographed in long, unmoving takes, present a man whose interior calm and certainty are expressed in his smallest motions and gestures as he stands still and alone before a charging bull. This unique spectacle, ritualized and in some ways purest for its very uselessness, rewards Arruza with glory and fame, which he seeks but which do not seem to satisfy him.

Boetticher's reputation will continue to grow even though it is unlikely that it will ever be quite as wide as it deserves to be. It seems likely that the very source of the intense pleasure of his films, their simplicity of means and their complexity of subject, their uncritical love for genre materials and their subtle nuances and variations, will be lost on most viewers. It is a pure shame, as one of his villains says, dying. Pure.

6. Peter Bogdanovich (1939)

by BARRY PUTTERMAN

1968—*Targets;* 1971—*The Last Picture Show;* 1972—*What's Up, Doc?;* 1973—*Paper Moon;* 1974— *Daisy Miller;* 1975—*At Long Last Love;* 1976—*Nickelodeon;* 1979—*Saint Jack;* 1981—*They All Laughed*

Television Movie
1971—*Directed by John Ford*

Miscellaneous
1966 (possibly unreleased theatrically)—*Voyage to the Planet of Prehistoric Women,* pseudonym: Derek Thomas. Credited as narrator only, Bogdanovich directed additional footage for this re-edited, English-language version of one or more Russian films.

Peter Bogdanovich broke spectacularly onto the film scene in the early seventies with three successive commercial blockbusters that made him the hottest director in Hollywood at the age of thirty-three. Although his star burned out just as spectacularly over the next few years, he had, in that short time, signaled a shift away from the technically eclectic, antiauthoritarian "youth" films made in the wake of the Vietnam war and became the vanguard of the current generation of directors whose work self-consciously reflects the films and film makers they grew up watching and admiring. Further, despite his ups and downs in the marketplace, his films as a group can be seen as chapters in an artistically coherent career, a career that seems to have now righted itself, after his fall from grace, onto a steadier, if less grandiose, course.

He is the first American director to come from the world of film criticism, beginning at the tender age of twenty by writing program notes for Dan Talbot's famous New Yorker revival house. In 1961 he was asked by the Museum of Modern Art to write a monograph on Orson Welles as part of their retrospective of his films. During the next two years Bogdanovich was able to persuade the Museum to sponsor similar monographs for retrospectives on Howard Hawks and Alfred Hitchcock to tie in with studio releases of the former's *Hatari* and the latter's *The Birds.*

His critical approach placed him within the emerging group of American writers who were in consent with the fifties French *Cahiers du Cinéma* critics, popularizing what became known in this country as "the auteur theory."

Over the next few years Bogdanovich's writing career expanded. He wrote regular celebrity profiles for *Esquire,* was pretty much the American correspondent for *Movie,* the British auteurist film magazine, and wrote pieces for various other film publications, such as *Film Culture.* He even turned his hand to producing and directing off-Broadway productions of two Hollywood-themed plays of earlier eras, Odets's *The Big Knife* and Kaufman and Hart's *Once in a Lifetime.*

In 1964 he moved to California, and in 1965 he went to work as Roger Corman's general assistant on *The Wild Angels* (1966). Around the same time he also did the American re-editing and dubbing for one of Corman's foreign pickups, which became known here as *Voyage to the Planet of Prehistoric Women.* An early indication of Bogdanovich's tendency to structure his films in relation to film history can be seen in his almost verbatim lifting of Michael O'Hara's closing monologue in Welles's *The Lady From Shanghai* to end this film.

Corman was sufficiently impressed with his work to give him a directorial assignment. Bogdanovich was allowed a small production budget and told he could make whatever he wanted as long as there was a part in the film for Boris Karloff, who owed Corman two days work on his contract, and the film could accommodate the inclusion of footage from *The Terror,* a 1963 Corman effort made under similar circumstances, which had additional footage by then Corman assistants Francis Ford Coppola and Monte Hellman. The film that emerged, *Targets,* told the parallel stories of an aging horror-film star (Karloff) trying to come to terms with his career while preparing to attend the premiere of his latest film at a Los Angeles drive-in and a "typical" clean-cut suburban young man (Tim O'Kelly), who suddenly goes berserk, killing his family and then, à la Charles Whitman, sniping at passersby from high distances until he eventually winds up at the drive-in premiere. The actor's successful disarming of the sniper serves as the catharsis for his personal problems and the beginning of Bogdanovich's exploration of the role movies play in shaping our dreams and values. The film shows Bogdanovich's appreciation of and affinity with Frank Tashlin's sense of social satire in characterizing the sniper and his family through the decor of their house and the anarchic spirit of Raoul Walsh by staging the sniper's psychotic liberation at the drive-in much in the manner of the climax to *White Heat.* Although *Targets* shows degrees of ingenuity, ambition, and creativity, it was a bit too awkward in all of its components to really come together properly. Yet despite its obscurity, the film has received a kind of retroactive cult following, particularly in the wake of later Bogdanovich films that were deemed to be more commercial than creative.

During this time Bogdanovich continued his career in criticism, mainly with career-spanning interviews with directors John Ford, Fritz Lang, and Allan Dwan, which were released as books in 1968, 1969, and 1971 respectively. He also made a television film version of the Ford book, a documentary combining a Ford interview with illustrative clips, called *Directed by John Ford* and released in 1971. However, it was with his second narrative film, *The Last Picture Show,* also released in 1971, that Bogdanovich made a significant impact on the industry and made some film history of his own.

Based on a novel by Larry McMurtry and adapted by the author and the director, *The Last Picture Show* told the story of a group of high-school seniors coming of age in the small, dying town of Anarene, Texas, during the early fifties. Bogdanovich set the yearnings of the naive, uncertain young generation searching for values and ideals in the mythic, historic mold of the Western film genre, thus organizing the material self-consciously along defined aesthetic and ideological lines. The traditionalist conservative social structure of the John Ford Western, with each generation handing down rituals and values for the new generation to use as its social and moral guide, becomes framed as the necessary resolution for the confused teenagers, and the death of the town, i.e., the death of the land becomes the death of the dreams and hopes of the older generation who have nothing to offer the youngsters.

Bogdanovich further extended this by having Ben Johnson, long identified with Ford, play the positive, paternal moral figure who dies, as the land dies, before he can complete his task of molding the new generation. Also, by extension, Bogdanovich implies that it is the classical Hollywood films of the studio system that exert this moral force for the generations of the twentieth century. The movie theater closes down with the land, and the last picture show of the title is Hawks's *Red River,* a film very much about the expansion of the land and a generation coming of age with positive values. It is only in this sense that Bogdanovich's explanation that the film is about the coming of television can be understood.

Coming in the midst of a long cycle of films that challenged the forms and values of traditional American movies, both in reaction to imported techniques and domestic political unrest, the enormous critical and commercial success of *The Last Picture Show,* the first major American narrative film to be shot in black and white for four years, signaled the end of that cycle. Moreover, Bogdanovich and his film were taken up by many of the veteran directors he admired and used as a club to beat out their long, deep-seated resentment over the recent course of American film making. The ironic part of the tug of war that developed over *The Last Picture Show* was the fact that it was produced by BBS Productions, the outfit that was responsible for such key films of the previous cycle as Dennis Hopper's *Easy Rider* and Bob Rafelson's *Five Easy Pieces.*

Bogdanovich solidified his foothold on the commercial highground with his next two films, *What's Up, Doc?* and *Paper Moon.* Both reiterated his predeliction for couching his films in terms of established Hollywood genres, screwball comedy in the former case and the outcast adult/orphan child team in the latter. Both films continued the development and expansion of a generalized stock company of players, including Ryan O'Neal, Eileen Brennan, Madeleine Kahn, John Hillerman, and others who worked comfortably in Bogdanovich's rhythm of overlapping dialogue, a rhythm that wavered between Hawksian and Wellesian. And both films in their own ways continued the main Bogdanovich theme of gentle, dreamy characters confronting and defining their identities while meeting another character's set of values.

What's Up, Doc? was, in many ways, a reversal of *The Last Picture Show.* In *Picture Show*'s tragic vision the passive, dreamy male, Sonny (Timothy Bottoms) finds that Jacy, the woman he marries (Cybill Sheperd), is part of the harsh and unfeeling world that defeats all of the hopes for a rebirth of the land and of positive values. The comic reversal in *What's Up, Doc?* allows the woman (Barbra Streisand) to redeem the passive, dreamy male (Ryan O'Neal) from a narrow, dead world for a more spontaneous, romantic vision of life. Indeed, as the picture show closed down on the characters' search for values in the first film, the union of the happy couple in *What's Up, Doc?* is intercut with a song-and-dance sequence from Bob McKimson's cartoon of the same name, implying that this is the improbable but joyous mating of Bugs Bunny with Elmer Fudd.

On the other hand, while *What's Up, Doc?* looked back to *The Last Picture Show,* *Paper Moon* represented the first, hesitant steps toward the more distanced, ironic approach to the characters that Bogdanovich would take in his later films.

In 1973 Peter Bogdanovich seemed to be on top of the world. With three successive smash-hit films, he was considered to have the magic touch. He had recently formed a production company called The Directors Company with colleagues Francis Ford Coppola and William Friedkin, of which *Paper Moon* was the first release. And a collection of his *Esquire* pieces had just been published in book form as *Pieces of Dreams.* Yet there were rumblings of discontent surrounding the man. Some resented the successes of *What's Up, Doc?* and *Paper Moon,* feeling that they were the commercialized work of a director who had "sold out," a not uncommon reaction when a critical hit like *The Last Picture Show* also leads to commercial popularity. He was also personally disliked by many in the Hollywood community for what was seen as his arrogance and egotistical self-promotion, as well as the promotion of his live-in protegee, Cybill Sheperd. For someone who admired the work of Orson Welles so much, Bogdanovich might even have appreciated the kind of Georgie Minafer reputation he was getting.

Indeed, Bogdanovich's next film, an adaption of the Henry James novella *Daisy Miller,* almost seemed like ironic commentary on his situation. Not only did the film cast Sheperd as the gauchely coquettish nouveau riche American destroyed by the Old World set of ritualized manners but for some time Bogdanovich considered casting himself as Winterbourne before finally settling on Barry Brown. While the film owes much of its structure to James and much of its dialogue to screenwriter Frederic Raphael, it emerges as the clearest distillation of Bogdanovich's concerns and is regarded by many to be his finest work.

Here the ironic distance hinted at in *Paper Moon* seems to have found its proper tone and consistency. Whereas in past films the gentle dreamers either found their mates to be part of the hard reality of the defeating environment (*Picture Show*) or the triumphant topography of a higher level of humanity (*Doc* and *Moon*), here Bogdanovich was showing us characters who combined aspects of dreamers and realists. The socially untutored but emotionally incisive Daisy and the socially mature but emotionally naive Winterbourne are shown in all their foolishness but as essentially good people who could have helped each other fill in the gaps in their personalities had not their mismatched failings made them tragically vulnerable to the surrounding society. Further, as the characters are more complex, so is the style of the film.

Each Bogdanovich film seems to find its correlative in the work of a past director he admires. *The Last Picture Show* and *Paper Moon* are to a greater and lesser degree successfully Fordian, and *What's Up, Doc?* may have underrated the subtlety of the seemingly "functional" Howard Hawks style, but none seemed to have much dimension beyond finding the proper style to suit the material. *Daisy Miller,* done in Wellesian deep focus with overlapping dialogue, on the other hand, found its style enhancing the tensions in the material and helping to put a layer of modern commentary upon the nineteenth-century story, which neither condescended to nor disengaged the viewer from the film.

Daisy Miller was not a commercial success, but that fact was not held against its director. It was accepted as a noble attempt at difficult material and even admired by some who didn't like it for being an artistic gamble after such commercial success. It was the total failure of his next two films, *At Long Last Love* and *Nickelodeon* that almost ended his career as spectacularly as it began.

At Long Last Love was particularly damaging to the director's reputation, since it was considered to be an inept, expensive personal indulgence without any sense of audience participation. In fact it is a very curious film that has some very interesting admirers, particularly among those who don't like Bogdanovich's work in general. It is an attempt to do a romantically cynical film along the lines of Ophuls's *La Ronde* and *Le Plasir* in the context of an early thirties Lubitsch musical, using the music of Cole Porter as the expressive correlative of that romantic cynicism. With Burt Reynolds replacing Elliott Gould in the lead and with Bogdanovich regulars Sheperd, Brennan, Kahn, and Hillerman rounding out the cast, there was very little musical talent on hand to make the material acceptable to the audience. Indeed, with sixteen songs and only one dance, the picture took on a lopsided and claustrophobic feel for the genre's fans.

Also, the ironic distancing of *Daisy Miller* was extended to an extremely icy detachment. One can identify this as the means to approximate the harsh, puppet-in-a-side-show view of the characters that one gets from a Lubitsch or an Ophuls, but the bawdiness that Lubitsch used and the romanticism that Ophuls used to package this view were beyond Bogdanovich's reach, and the conventions of the early thirties musicals that he tried to use in their place were too remote.

Remote also was the word for *Nickelodeon,* which, in the wake of the initial fiasco, died a quieter but just as immediate death. Based mainly on anecdotes Bogdanovich garnered from his interviews with Leo McCarey, Raoul Walsh, and especially Allan Dwan, the film told the story of a bumbling lawyer who accidentally becomes the director for a movie troupe making Westerns in the early teens.

Although Bogdanovich had blazed the trail and signaled the dawn of the generation of directors whose films built on the work of previous film makers, tastes were shifting so rapidly in the volatile seventies that by the time of *At Long Last Love* and *Nickelodeon* Bogdanovich was already considered remotely out of touch with the spirit of the times. Whereas his films reflected the more classical traditions of the thirties, the newer directors like Lucas and Scorsese derived their inspiration from the more idiosyncratic postwar people such as Minnelli, Fuller, and Michael Powell.

Also damaging was the director's own kind of eerie remoteness from the blatantly emotional connections built into the earlier films. It was as if Bogdanovich had taken the analytical distancing to its logical conclusion in *At Long Last Love* and given the public nothing but the analysis yet still in the form of thirties entertainment, thus being judged anachronistic and incompetent at the same time. That film was probably too much of a personal project to have ever found an audience, but *Nickelodeon* is in many ways similar to *What's Up, Doc?,* with the acting troupe standing in for Barbra Streisand and Griffith's *Birth of a Nation* representing the Bugs Bunny film for the Ryan O'Neal character. However, there seemed to be little of the drive and cohesion that gave life to the earlier film's old genre form; it looked like the work of a very tired man.

Bogdanovich dropped out of sight after *Nickelodeon,* reemerging three years later in 1979 with *Saint Jack,* an adaptation of the Paul Theroux novel. He was almost self-consciously returning to his own roots by making this film for Roger Corman's low-budget New World Pictures, and although he went well over budget, it remained a very modest-sized film.

The film was back in familiar Bogdanovich territory, with Ben Gazzara as the title character who builds his own little kingdom of commerce and nonexploitational vice in an almost make-believe Asian outpost, only to have it invaded and destroyed by the cold-eyed reality of the organized outside world. But the film had a new look to it. The correlation of the dreamer's ideals and values with old movies was gone. The film was photographed with his customary icy clarity by German New Wave cameraman Robby Muller, and the overlapping dialogue was no longer Hawksian or Wellesian but in the more contemporary style of Robert Altman.

Indeed, one could parallel *Saint Jack* with Altman's *McCabe and Mrs. Miller* and make the case that ultimately both directors are primarily concerned with an ambivalent affirmation of foolish dreamers in a cold, unfeeling, alien world. Perhaps this accounts for the bad blood between both men, particularly on Altman's side. For while they are conceptually compatible, they use completely opposite methods of reaching their goal. Whereas Altman uses traditional Hollywood genres in order to explode them from within as dead social structures that defeat his dreamers, Bogdanovich sees them as positive social forces that give direction and vision to his characters. Altman and

Bogdanovich are perhaps the archetypical examples of contemporary Hollywood liberals and conservatives.

While it was not a major success, *Saint Jack* brought Bogdanovich back into the mainstream of Hollywood film making with a critically respected product. But curiously, after the production of his latest film, *They All Laughed,* brought him all the way into the Hollywood establishment, the distribution of the film has taken him completely back out again.

The film itself is one of Bogdanovich's major achievements, prehaps his finest. Using the looser, more modern approach first explored in *Saint Jack,* this film reworks the basic ideas of *At Long Last Love* into a more complex, ambitious, and entertaining framework. The direct correlation of the movie metaphor is extended to the more encompassing concept of the males as private detectives following the activities of the females, much as the movie viewer follows the characters on the screen. By having the men/private eyes/movie viewers break cover and engage in romantic interaction with the women/suspects/movie icons, Bogdanovich is able to adjust the structure of Keaton's *Sherlock Jr.* to his own vision of the romantic merry-go-round through the use of Lubitschian point-of-view editing that reveals to his male observers only selective empirical evidence that usually leads to false conclusions.

The multitude of musical numbers that served as foreground expressions of and commentary on the characters' feelings in *At Long Last Love* is now a continuous background sound track that adds another layer of expression to the proceedings. Taking its place at the center is the Bogdanovich overlapping dialogue structured on repeated phrases and thoughts to the point where it ultimately becomes a kind of spoken song lyric. Most impressive in this regard is the performance of singer-actress Colleen Camp who is able to sustain this style not only in the ensemble but also within the rhythm of her own speech in extended monologue. She is scheduled to star in Bogdanovich's next project called *I'll Remember April,* and one can only hope that they will sustain and extend what promises to be an exciting collaboration.

They All Laughed was made for the fledgling Time-Life Films division to be distributed by Fox, but before the film was released Time-Life went out of the film business, and Fox lost faith in the film's commercial possibilities. Dissatisfied with Fox's handling of the film, Bogdanovich bought back the rights and set up his own production/distribution company called Moon Pictures, which he hopes to build into a steady producer of modest-budget films, much as his early mentor Roger Corman did with New World. For a historian as concerned as Bogdanovich is with the product of the Hollywood studio system, it will be interesting to see how he goes about building his own studio. Indeed, while Bogdanovich's place in film history is yet to be fully determined, his emergence as Hollywood's first neoclassicist assures him of a spot that will be more than a footnote.

7. Richard Brooks (1912)

by JOHN FITZPATRICK

1950—*Crisis; The Light Touch;* 1952—*Deadline U.S.A.;* 1953—*Battle Circus; Take the High Ground;* 1954—*The Flame and the Flesh; The Last Time I Saw Paris;* 1955—*Blackboard Jungle;* 1956—*The Last Hunt; The Catered Affair;* 1957—*Something of Value;* 1958—*The Brothers Karamazov; Cat on a Hot Tin Roof;* 1960—*Elmer Gantry;* 1962—*Sweet Bird of Youth;* 1965—*Lord Jim* (Great Britain; U.S., 1965); 1966—*The Professionals;* 1968—*In Cold Blood;* 1969—*The Happy Ending;* 1971—*$;* 1975—*Bite the Bullet;* 1977—*Looking for Mr. Goodbar;* 1981—*Wrong Is Right*

A successful novelist and screenwriter, Richard Brooks began directing for MGM in 1950. His rise was rapid: he directed his own script for his very first film, and since 1955 has worked from his own screenplays (often original) almost exclusively. From 1965 he has also functioned as independent producer, though never taking screen credit in this capacity.

Brooks's career thus seems to be the epitome of personal cinema authorship. No Hollywood director has operated so independently for so long; even today, studios and stars do not get to see a Brooks script in advance. But independence is no guarantee of originality, and the quality of Brooks's work has varied wildly. Some of his most personal films have been embarrassments, and some of his studio work still holds up. His slickest commercial success (*The Professionals*) is one of his most revealing works. Brooks's career is the ideal demonstration of how, for a film maker who is a better director than a writer and who is fatally prone to bursts of liberal rhetoric, the "Old Hollywood" system could discipline and support, as well as hinder, artistic expression.

Brooks was born in Philadelphia in 1912. His knockabout youth typifies American writers of his generation: freight trains, soup kitchens, some journalism, some radio scripts (for Orson Welles), and a hitch in the Marines. Out of this last experience came his first novel, *The Brick Foxhole* (1945), about the boredom and pressures of barracks life and the consequent murder of a homosexual victim. It was later filmed by RKO as *Crossfire* (directed by Edward Dmytryk).

By this time Brooks had become a successful screenwriter, rising from such things as *Cobra Woman* to collaboration with John Huston on *Key Largo* and to extensive work on Mark Hellinger's crime dramas, *Brute Force, The Killers,* and *The Naked City.* (*The Producer* [1951], Brooks's third and final novel, is an incisive portrait of Hellinger and the pressures confronting the independent film maker, a subject that is not without relevance to Brooks's later career.)

An MGM contract promised Brooks the opportunity to direct, and his first feature was *Crisis,* about a doctor forced to save the life of a Latin American dictator he personally despises. Apart from a post-*noir* (one might almost call it *gris*) ambiance it shares with Huston's vastly superior *Asphalt Jungle* and a typical concern with professionalism under pressure, the film is not distinguished. MGM, concerned to protect Cary

Grant's popularity against this uncharacteristic role, did little to help the picture and in general hampered Brooks for the next five years. Tough, masculine subjects (always Brooks's forte) were regularly undermined, as when Humphrey Bogart's MASH surgeon was saddled with a love interest in *Battle Circus* and the basic training story of *Take the High Ground* was turned partly comic. (*Deadline U.S.A.,* Brooks's most successful early picture, was made for Fox.)

The film that made Brooks's reputation was *Blackboard Jungle,* a "message" picture about classroom violence, in which several typical concerns are already apparent: male groups, rhythmical and often extreme violence, and a tough-guy liberal hero equally prone to speechmaking or fistfighting in the service of his basically humane ideology. In fact, the degree to which the verbal rhetoric is controlled and the action allowed to speak for itself is a fair index of the success of a Brooks film.

Blackboard Jungle does succeed, in spite of the inevitable prologue that tells us how *most* American schools are really fine places and in spite of the soap-operatic problems of the teacher's wife. Chief among the film's merits is the multileveled expression of the students' rage, demonstrated not only by the taut, mostly nonprofessional cast (another Brooks strength) but also by the musical score. Brooks was perspicacious enough to realize that a pop song he had heard earlier would be the perfect accompaniment for teenage mayhem, and it was through his efforts that "Rock Around the Clock" was allowed to drive its rhythms into the American psyche and vivify the film's title metaphor in an altogether unexpected manner.

Rhythm is also the means by which one teacher tries to impress upon his students the mathematical principles of jazz, but this weak and ineffectual character is predictably made to suffer for his efforts a savage beating to a rock and roll beat. It is the crew-cut veteran Glenn Ford who finally "reaches" the students through the machine shop and above all through the use of his own two fists in disarming the most vicious of the lot. It is a simplistic close, not untypical of Brooks, yet it does not deny the genuine power of the earlier scenes.

Brooks's wayward and violent ways continued to alienate the studio in *The Last Hunt,* which with its uncharacteristic use of Robert Taylor as a psychopathic killer of buffalo and men, managed to put off audiences as well. But *Something of Value* demonstrates a firm control over medium as well as message. A drama of the Mau Mau uprising, it benefits immensely from its black-and-white location photography in Kenya. One suspects that escape from studio restrictions, as well as a desire for authenticity, underlies the large amount of location shooting in all Brooks's later films. The plot, in which blood brothers Rock Hudson and Sidney Poitier are divided by the revolt, offers pitfalls enough for facile rhetoric, but these are mostly avoided. Even a scene in which Hudson carries the injured Poitier (the "white man's burden") on his back is well integrated into the plot. Poitier, whose career had been sparked by his classroom role in *Blackboard Jungle,* here becomes a commanding presence. The scenes of his initiation into the Mau Mau, the meeting with the suited intellectual leader by day, the sickening blood-oath by night, and above all the terrible raid on his friend's plantation—all these are filmed with a brutally heightened realism of exaggerated camera angles and grim performances.

Set against this violence, the rather cool romance between Hudson and Dana Wynter, both in love with the land as well as with each other, seems for once a germane element. Miklós Rózsa's score, elsewhere given over to fierce African chants, is here restricted to harp and flute and together with the lovingly detailed photography of farm and jungle and town makes for an audibly as well as visibly authentic backdrop.

In the film's final scene, the two protagonists fight in a jungle clearing while the Kikuyu's naked child crawls near the gaping pit of an animal trap. Poitier, finally impaled on the stakes, asks that the child join him in death, but even this consolation is denied as Hudson takes the baby off to be raised with his own newborn nephew: "Maybe for them it will be better." Despite this mildly optimistic finale, *Something of Value* was too grim for most viewers in 1957. It deserves reconsideration as one of Hollywood's toughest examinations of revolutionary violence and its consequences.

As a "prestige" director, Brooks began to receive larger budgets from MGM in the late fifties, but his freedom and creativity did not always increase in equal measure. *The Brothers Karamazov* fails inevitably, but it is surprising how little Dostoevskian energy the author of *The Brick Foxhole* was able to capture. Aside from some vigorous performances, most notably Albert Salmi's Smerdyakov, the film's one real strength is the expressionistic color lighting scheme that Brooks and cinematographer John Alton began to experiment with here.

Alton, unfortunately, did not work on the two Tennessee Williams adaptations, which in consequence are drowned in a warm bath of Metrocolor. *Cat on a Hot Tin Roof,* though not a very personal film, survives as one of the screen's best Williams adaptations on the strength of its exciting performances. But *Sweet Bird of Youth* is a travesty, its castration climax modified to a mere beating so that Chance Wayne can drive off with Heavenly Finley in an absurd soft-focus finale. Unable to achieve script freedom even in 1962, Brooks left MGM for good.

Two years earlier, however, he had made his first independent production for United Artists: *Elmer Gantry,* a masterpiece. Brooks had received Sinclair Lewis's own blessing for the project many years before, and it had long been his goal to film the book whenever the public climate would allow. Whether the years of thought or the restraining influence of the vestigial Production Code were responsible, the resulting film is very different from, and much superior to, the original novel.

What started out as a sour attack on organized religion per se turned into something far more subtle. Still unable to defame any recognized church, Brooks made sure to establish early that neither the hell-and-damnation preacher Gantry nor the revivalist leader Sister Sharon Falconer were ordained ministers at all. What seems even more of a compromise is that neither is even a charlatan. Sister Sharon, as played by Jean Simmons, is passionately sincere in her preaching, able not only to inspire the rural masses but to tame the cynical big-city journalist (Arthur Kennedy) with a humble prayer.

It is Sharon who inspires Elmer Gantry as well, raising his animal lust at least to the level of a romantic passion. Gantry, though still an unbeliever, is "redeemed" in the film by Burt Lancaster's irresistably boyish charm and by his obviously genuine love for Sharon, which allows him to fall naturally—if falsely—into preaching that "old-time religion" for her benefit. The tragedy really springs from Sharon's hubris, her use of Gantry's sermons and sexual services for what she perceives as higher ends. It is through this near-megalomania that she allows herself to be taken by Gantry under a revolving electric cross in one of the oddest seductions ever filmed. And it is soon afterward in this very same "tabernacle" that she performs an apparent miracle and finally perishes, trampled in a very literal hellfire by a congregation with whom she has finally lost all human contact.

It is impossible in limited space to convey all the felicities of style in this powerful film: Alton's photography, subtler than in *Karamazov,* catches the Dust Bowl reds and browns by day and casts them against blue-black voids at night; Andre Previn's music helps gain sympathy by leavening its nervous rhythms with sweetly American modal lyricism. Above all, the film is charged with Brooks's affection for his principals, whose preaching tendencies for once seem germane. Sharon, as tough a revival leader as Gantry is with his fists, has the "professionalism" of a true Brooks hero, even though her pride makes her a tragic one. For Richard Brooks, his first freedom, still stabilized by Code restrictions, was his finest moment.

Brooks's career as an independent film maker began in earnest after 1962 and may be characterized by two quotations: "I'm an independent producer," says the compromised hero of *The Producer*, "I can't afford to take chances." Also: "All films talk too much—especially mine" (Brooks in a 1965 interview).

In the matter of taking chances Brooks has acquitted himself admirably. Discovering that the commercial pressures from which the studios had sheltered him were now his own, he has, since the ambitious failure of *Lord Jim*, hewn to small projects over which he could continue to maintain total control. His development of new talent, like cinematographer Conrad Hall and the then unknown leads of *In Cold Blood*, plus his recognized mastery of fast, efficient, low-budget location shooting, have given Brooks an enviable record of freedom to make personal projects—and to fail at them. At the same time, his rhetorical tendencies have gone unchecked to such a degree that one sometimes longs to see a restraining studio hand on his work.

The Professionals perfectly illustrates the paradoxes of Brooks's late films. Ostensibly a slick, safe, commercial project designed to recover some of the losses on *Lord Jim*, it is also a taut expression of Brooksian themes. Four mercenaries are commissioned to cross into Pancho Villa's Mexico and rescue a millionaire's wife from the revolutionary leader who has kidnapped her. The men are professionals, loyal only to each other and to their hope of reward. Two of them, the cheerfully amoral Burt Lancaster character and the businesslike Lee Marvin, are even riding against the revolutionary leader with whom they had once served. The professional loyalty of these men, to each other and even to their horses, is the film's great constant, beautifully dramatized against the red desert images of Conrad Hall that mark this film as Brooks's first successful use of the wide screen.

But all is not as it seems. When it develops that the woman has actually *chosen* to forsake her American husband, the professionals set her free, thus abandoning reward and "betraying" their employer in the interest of a higher personal code. Unfortunately, even in an action picture (one of Hollywood's last successful Westerns), Brooks cannot let the story speak for itself. Thus in the climactic gunfight between revolutionary comrades turned antagonists, Jack Palance and Burt Lancaster seem intent on talking each other to death. In what one hopes is a burst of self-parody, Brooks even makes Palance's Mexican begin, "The *revolución* eez like a woman . . ."!

Similarly outlandish strands of excess "meaning" entangle all of Brooks's later films. Thus while *In Cold Blood*, much the best of them, examines its lost criminal protagonists in an icy black-and-white light that nevertheless generates more Dostoevskian heat than the earlier *Karamazov*, it also bears the burden of a reporter-commentator who follows them around wondering about the wisdom of capital punishment. *$*, an already convoluted "heist" picture, is further saddled with Brooks's editorializing on the nature of greed. And *Bite the Bullet*, about a cross-country horse race, collapses under the weight of plot twists.

Among the most confused of the later films are the two on women's subjects. *Looking for Mr. Goodbar* seems as out of control as the modern sexuality it seeks to portray. Where Judith Rossner's novel offered a secretive young schoolteacher whose night life sinks through a succession of singles bars to her own murder, Brooks consistently interjects irrelevancies—overemphasizing, for example, her work with deaf schoolchildren, which echoes *Blackboard Jungle* but does little to explain Theresa Dunn. Brooks's Theresa is a flaming seductress from the start, which leaves little room for character development. Instead the narrative moves via fantasies and flashbacks to such dubious explanations as a hidden birth defect and the "repression" of a grotesquely caricatured Catholic background. (Theresa's father does little but rant through the entire film, often costumed in a Notre Dame jacket.) Even Brooks's technical flair is counterproductive here. Despite the low budget (against which he mortgaged his own home), Brooks succeeds in lighting the difficult Chicago locations so well that *Goodbar* achieves precisely the studio-slick look he was trying to avoid. Only a range-stretching performance from Diane Keaton and even more vivid work from the young men in her life save the picture from total absurdity.

The Happy Ending, made eight years earlier, is the most personal—and therefore the most wildly compromised—of all Brooks's films. It stars Jean Simmons, Brooks's own wife since *Elmer Gantry,* in an examination of marriage in modern America from the woman's point of view. The film is a flabbergasting mixture of slickness and insight. There are clips from *Casablanca,* an escape to Bermuda, a seductive gigolo whose attentions put the heroine to sleep, and a mother-daughter reunion staged (to a syrupy Michel Legrand score) in a manner more appropriate to *Tristan and Isolde.* Brooks even inserts a speech about how the American economy depends on marriage.

Against such nonsense is set the complexly moving portrait of a wife rebelling against an outwardly happy marriage for reasons she herself does not fully understand. Her alcohol-inspired flight from a comfortable Denver home to a series of adventures in Bermuda brings no real satisfaction, and in the perfectly poised ending we are forced to stand with her husband and confront the woman's ultimate mystery. Her last line is a question—If you had it to do over again, would you still marry me?— and John Forsythe's answer, an obvious look of bewilderment (achieved in part by Brooks's customary withholding of scripts from actors), is also the inevitable response to this film and to Brooks's entire career.

Indeed, Brooks himself, now seventy, divorced from Simmons, and still very much the Hollywood maverick, acknowledges this bewilderment with the modern world in his most recent film. *Wrong Is Right,* an apparent satire on everything from television "news" to Palestinian terrorism, consists of almost nothing but conflicting testimonies on the problems of a world gone out of control. Unfortunately, nothing said by any of the contrived characters is as pertinent as the film maker's own confession in a prerelease interview: "We're living in a vacuum and everybody's crazy. . . . We're all bats. Including me."

8. John Cassavetes (1929)

by MYRON MEISEL

1961—*Shadows* (16-mm); 1962—*Too Late Blues;* 1963—*A Child Is Waiting;* 1968—*Faces;* 1970—*Husbands;* 1971—*Minnie and Moskowitz;* 1974—*A Woman Under the Influence;* 1976—*The Killing of a Chinese Bookie;* 1977—*Opening Night;* 1980—*Gloria*

From his first feature, *Shadows* (made between 1959 and 1961), John Cassavetes' movies have inspired poles of violent reaction, creating a controversy that tended to linger almost obsessively off the mark. Since the critical debate was cast largely in the irrelevant terms of his supposed "realism," Cassavetes' attackers tended to score better points than his defenders. Critical comments devolved largely upon the crude edges of his technique, the affected artiness of the one-word titles and the limited production values, and Cassavetes was taken to task for glaring gaffes in his accumulation of naturalistic details. Similarly, because of the extreme improvisatory veneer to his staging, it was assumed that he was not a careful screenwriter, although all of his later pictures were scrupulously scripted even when their genesis was in improvisatory exercises. No one seemed to account for the master scenes that went on and on, with the actors clearly engaging in a style of performance far more self-conscious than the traditionally "invisible" customs of screen acting.

Few noticed that, as with all good film directors, Cassavetes' expressive talent resided fundamentally in the cumulative power of his images, partly since in his case, the images happened to be almost exclusively dominated by actors. The exceptions to the bromide that emotions in movies are expressed through, rather than by, actors are generally the solipsistic director-actors such as Chaplin or Jerry Lewis. Yet Cassavetes almost alone among directors manages to obliterate that distinction. The emotional support he bestows upon his players allows them to express their deepest feelings, and what his directorial method accomplishes is to unify his expressive objectives with those of the actors themselves.

Typically, with Cassavetes, this unity has been accomplished through his basic theme—the strain for self-definition—as well as through the particular mode of comedy; all his films skirt the tragedy implicit in their hysteric plots, as much because as in spite of their intensity and melodramatic gesturing.

That the underlying strategy of Cassavetes is comic in nature was not self-evident in the subterranean flourishes of the earlier pictures. *Shadows,* that vanguard independent film, parlayed the beat atmosphere of one style of urban living in the late fifties into a model for low-budget narrative films dedicated to personal expression. *Shadows* unified the cultural imperative for self-expression with the traditions of narrative film making and thereby altered both in the process. His humor utterly lacking in sardonicism, despite a wise-guy manner, Cassavetes examined imperfect relationships—tentative, fervent, and cruel—with skeptical compassion. He also set the rudiments of what came to be recognized as the Cassavetes style: long scenes, frequently shot in master takes (a cinema aware of its theatrical origins); raw edges; home-movie tics and emotional extravagance—all lurching toward an elaboration of the beauties of his own truth. But that truth was not a naturalistic one, however it may have appeared, but rather lay in directness of apprehension of the elaborate emotional circuitry of his modern characters.

The two "Hollywood" films, *Too Late Blues* and *A Child is Waiting*, represent uneasy compromises between Cassavetes' independent approach to film making and the norms of commercial production. Both are respectable, fascinating artistic failures. *Too Late Blues* deals with a jazz musician who scorns commercial prosperity to play in his own way, only to find himself undone in the most humiliating fashion: playing for the squares. In *A Child Is Waiting*, a new teacher at a school for mentally disturbed children follows the dictates of her heart in contravention of the disciplinary methods of the headmaster. In these films, as in *Shadows*, Cassavetes shows questing, idealistic characters who avoid disaster only through the realization that the best possible approach to an imperfect world is through an uneasy synthesis of temperaments, a willingness to harbor the strengths of the individual heart through finding effective ways to communicate emotion to others. The crux of Cassavetes' view of human relationships is character, without which emotions become difficult things to live with.

Returning to his home-movie production methods, Cassavetes shot *Faces* piecemeal over a period of four years, using many actors with whom he had previously worked. *Faces* is flat-out Cassavetes: a raw, nervy comedy of marital breakup, it finally launched him on the main course of his career. If it seemed more emotionally valid over its long haul than any other of his films until *A Woman Under the Influence*, it was in part because Cassavetes chose suddenly to explode his novel vision on a surprised audience via the communicated agony of skilled yet mostly unknown performers (much as Rossellini had fooled some American critics into believing that the Anna Magnani of *Open City* was a nonprofessional). Also, the quantity of his actors' expressiveness became as much to the point as the quality of that expressiveness. The characters in *Faces* laugh hollowly at their own jokes, even as their world collapses about them. They continually confront one another in the name of honesty and truth, but it is not until the very end, when the consequences of their actions have been made plain by the unraveling of events, that any real honesty or awareness becomes evident. Not coincidentally, it is the first moment of stasis and of silence in the picture.

Faces combined highly individualized epiphanies along with undeniable longueurs, and it was primarily redeemed by unflagging thematic and stylistic intensity. The camera obsessively watches its subjects crowded in the frame as they hassle out their existences, straining to escape from the bondage of social mannerisms on which they have always depended for their own survival. Yet only Cassavetes could have taken the despairing final shot of the exhausted couple collapsed together on the stairs at the conclusion of *Faces* and then elaborated it into a comedy of destiny desperately delayed. For that is exactly what *Husbands* is.

Where John Marley and Lynn Carlin were convincing as the couple down the block, so that the audience forgot about their presence as actors, in *Husbands* the three stars are evidently enjoying their sterile laughter much more. Even more than laugh, however, these characters talk and talk and talk, generally in a state of low dudgeon and at high volume. They have to make themselves heard, after all, and on the emotional battleground, they seem to know instinctively that they must hold the floor or be wiped up on it. In *Husbands*, talk is a means of putting off the consequences that they feel approaching and encroaching, without ever acknowledging them. The three husbands simply cannot bring themselves to go home to their wives. For all their demands for honesty in their group-therapy-style hijinks, that honesty is exactly what they never manage to achieve in their relationships. Once again, Cassavetes examines what people feel about their relationships and how they act at cross-purposes to those feelings, an examination so intense that it demands the tight focal lengths, the discomfort of his compositions, and the rambling, almost associative, structure of his long, long scenes.

The theatricality of people's posturings is emphasized by the pacing of *Husbands:* essentially, there are twelve master scenes. When the camera is not placed in close-up, its position tends to be oblique and in medium long shot, insistently anchored in its eccentric viewpoint. What camera movements there are, as in *Faces,* serve only to underline the actions of the actors, to bolster the sense of performance, and to further isolate those actions essential to Cassavetes' preoccupations with human behavior. The result is a dramatic method that is highly stylized and utterly at odds with the supposedly realistic thrust of the pictures. With *Faces,* the self-conscious stylization that was latent in the earlier pictures becomes increasingly evident. The pop-Pirandello mechanisms, such as the opening movie-within-a-movie sequence in *Faces* or the intruding sound boom in the penultimate scene of *Husbands,* are only the most obvious manifestations.

Yet much of what is most stimulating and teasing about the films strikes one initially as gratuitous. One of the most subtly tantalizing of all is the barroom scene in *Husbands,* where the three men ruthlessly direct a rather cowed barfly as to the appropriate inflections she ought to give an old-fashioned torch song. What really matters is the bullying sadism and furtive longing in the men's unyielding insistence that she do it over and over until she gets it right and beyond that, the inescapable awareness of the performance on the part of every bit and lead in the scene. The three buddies have pounced on some worn lyric and, for them, it begins to represent an isolated particle of very intense personal meaning, so they try to bully the old lady lush into making it sound the way they want to hear it. The men never know when to stop, when to slow up, when to go home, since their dissatisfaction cannot be relieved. Limited, somewhat unpleasant people, they take a certain delight in their petty cruelties.

The point is that people's actions don't show what is really bothering them; instead, their actions grow out from those problems. Thus Harry and Archie feel the need to press one another with every minute detail that may come into their heads and always feel compelled to act out and display their personal crises. *Husbands* is vulgar, crude, and sometimes smug, and, in an occasional close-up, unforgivable. The film plainly relates to notions of machismo and the emptiness of bourgeois existence, but it also resists any extended analysis as a thesis film. *Husbands* is maddeningly indifferent about scoring points; instead, it takes common denominators of the contemporary experience and struggles to create gestures, both behavioral and stylistic, to express Cassavetes' private view of manners in a changing society.

Minnie and Moskowitz is perhaps the most direct avatar of the Cassavetes style: an unmistakable comedy with strong elements of fantasy in which the lovers have nothing in common and connect by shouting at one another incessantly. It's noisy, but nice. Like the other films, it is based on notions of liberation without really being about liberation (the converse, shall we say, of Buñuel). It prefers instead to be about the glories of characters gleefully at contradictory purposes. Something of a rough draft for the masterpiece to come, it blows up behavioral detail into extravagant gesture, the better to make plain the accommodations of the heart to the necessities of human intractability.

With *A Woman Under the Influence,* which he distributed, Cassavetes consolidated his artistic method into a work of unqualified success that validated all that had gone before. Mabel Longhetti is a lower-middle-class wife and mother, devoted to her family, loving, tender, funny, perceptive, sensitive. She is also mad as a loon. In the din of noisy verbal battles that rage in the Longhetti family living room, Mabel has developed the horrible, delightful talent for being just the woman everyone else needs. She has given up her sanity to the family to preserve its rationality as a living unit. They love her deeply for it, only now, as the film begins, she is *nuts* and too desperately in need of their love for anyone to respond in kind. Her family is like the audience, sympathetic, but they don't understand. They couldn't. Instead, Cassavetes demonstrates that people do try to love the very best they can and that while it may never be enough, it has to go a long way, because it may be all they've got.

A Woman Under the Influence was originally conceived as a series of plays that proved too strenuous to perform. Formally, then, the film was organized in a manner most appropriate to Cassavetes' established shooting style. The tight focal lengths and discomfiting compositions sustain cadenza-length master scenes that achieve an intensity that is both theatrical and cinematic, as in the films of Orson Welles.

This unity is reinforced by Gena Rowlands's performance. She plays Mabel as crazy, not simply neurotic, employing a lexicon of memorably outlandish gestures. Like Cassavetes' direction, her performance is both hyper- and self-conscious, yet it manages to be harrowingly convincing. Where such gestures in another context would alienate the audience into incredulity, here it actually encourages involvement in Mabel's situation. The keynote is involvement, not identification, and Cassavetes understands the way to accomplish this is to implicate the audience in the feelings of the characters.

This is why Cassavetes' great expressive talent resides in the cumulative power of his images of actors. The first principle in a Cassavetes film is acting—not the actor, but acting itself—and his preoccupation with human behavior as performance. Rowlands uses her considerable technical skills as an actress to make a nigh unbelievable connection between her lexicon of personal psychological experience on the one hand and the emotional circumstances of the dramatic moment on the other. She is not alone. Everyone in the film *performs.* At an early morning breakfast-supper for her husband and his work buddies after an all-night overtime stint, Mabel coaxes some of the shy men into song and into a sudden, unaccustomed, unabashed spate of emotion. It works better than the parallel scene with the barfly in *Husbands,* because here there is no cruelty in the manipulation. Instead, we see limited people doing the best they can, and when the men turn against Mabel for drawing too deeply from them, we experience the pain that goes with the joy of any liberation, however partial, since these bursts of freedom are ever limited by their own range, our own powers, and by their own temporary, evanescent nature. You can't be free with your feelings all of the time, Cassavetes is saying. That may be wonderful, but it would be crazy.

The scene is one of Cassavetes' finest and it illustrates how closely akin his dramatic sense is to the comedy of manners. He is attentive to how people are expected to behave and how they get punished for violations, and he doesn't challenge conventions and social strictures even as he exposes them, because he is sensitive to how deep they cut in his characters' emotional lives. Manners are no less than the way we organize our awareness of behavior. Cassavetes astutely sees that the culmination of the ongoing daily agonized reappraisal of our lives is best described in terms of how one sits at a table or appears to the children or whether guests know when to leave. One of the sublime ironic touches of the film is that Peter Falk's coworkers know that the time has come to split, while the relatives remain hopelessly insensitive to the needs of their hosts.

Improbable as it may seem, Cassavetes might best be described as a middle-class Lubitsch embolded with a dash of the show-off. Jerry Lewis and Chaplin spring to mind. Chaplin is often quoted to the effect that tragedy is close-up and comedy long-shot, but Cassavetes' compassion, like that of Chaplin, explodes the truism. The most objective of directors in his close-ups, he is also the most passionately committed to the feelings of his characters. The closeness of the camera in key moments registers sympathy by its proximity yet also enforces hard observation by its concentrated revelation of facial detail. Cassavetes himself recognizes the influence of Frank Capra, which is noticeable in his upfront confrontations with his own feelings and a palpable way with scenes of humiliation.

Cassavetes' camera obsessively watches the subjects crowded into the frame as they hassle out their existences, either straining to escape (Rowlands) or at least survive (Falk) the awful bondage of the social restrictions that they must cling to for their lives. The profound point is that the comedy of manners, when played for keeps, isn't funny. I know of no instance more appalling, more shocking, than the scene where Mabel has returned home from a mental institution, subdued, cautious, tired, and happy, only to have Falk take her aside in frustration to ask why she doesn't act "natural" like the Mabel he had loved. The very cuckoo gesticulations that had been symptoms of her madness were also what her family had come to associate with her warmth and tenderness. "Why don't you do *this*—and *this?*" he pleads with her, contorting his face and throwing about his hands. For an instant it is perplexing to watch his deep sensitivity to Mabel so distorted into an egregious insensitivity; the next instant the insight is close to a cathartic horror.

Yet we never lose our sympathy for Falk or Rowlands or even for the unpardonable neighbors and in-laws. Cassavetes understands his people too well ever to condemn them. While the feminist overtones of the work are undeniable, they never are explicitly raised. At the end, the power of life seems to have triumphed for the moment, the future as uncertain as it was in the exhausted staircase conclusion of *Faces* (here, too, the staircase forms an important dramatic arena). But it is certain that no happiness can exist for either character outside of their relationship, home, and family. This emotional respect for the characters' needs is the final glory of the film.

Cassavetes' subsequent production, *The Killing of a Chinese Bookie,* plays rather like a collage of Cassavetes materials unmelded into any artistic whole. The superficial trappings of gangster melodrama do not command much attention from Cassavetes, but the diffidence of their execution seriously undermines any emotional thrust to the work, especially when compared with *Gloria,* which undercuts conventions with concentrated purpose. Ben Gazzara remains the best exemplar of the emotionally constipated protagonist—nostalgic, jokey, hard-boiled—who Cassavetes likes to explore for untapped lodes of feeling. While thematically of a piece with the remainder of his work, the picture's novel dramatic strategies sidetrack the narrative from its thematic path. It's anticlimax without a point. Probably the most desperate of his films, it fails to vindicate its low-keyed approach by ending up a tragedy so muffled as to be indistinct. It is perhaps the only Cassavetes film that cannot be classed as a comedy, having tragic overtones instead (like all serious gangster films, save *Scarface*), and it has a dour patina that robs his character insights of their customary complexity. The attitude toward the characters in the story revels more in squalor than contradiction, depriving the film of the emotional tension so important to Cassavetes' social observations. Instead, the consciously affectionate absurdities of the film are most reminiscent of the failed later scenes in *Husbands,* when the boys wander off to London, in which the plot of the film takes on the appearance of becoming the fantasy of its own characters.

This germ of an idea becomes more prominent in *Opening Night* and *Gloria.* Unfortunately, *Opening Night,* while a better film than *Bookie,* compounded the flaws of that picture, neither succeeding as narrative nor coherent as drama. One odd paradox of this story of a star-calibre Broadway actress trying out her first character-lead vehicle out of town is that the play-within-a-film has dialogue seemingly straight out of a John Cassavetes movie, so one can never tell when the performers are speaking their lines from the playscript or when they are instead breaking out of character to talk out their problems: the loss of such texture is fatal to such a semiformal exercise. The Gothic flourishes of Rowlands being haunted by the ghost of a dead teenage fan are a startling departure, as if Cassavetes were out to scotch the "realism" rap once and for all, but they are not convincingly integrated into the lead character's progress toward breakdown. It's apparent that Cassavetes is seeking directions in which to grow as an artist, but what was dispiriting after two such false starts was how his considerable virtues tended to recede in the face of his disorganized plotting. On the other hand, he remained resolutely true to his own idiosyncratic rhythms, to his esthetic, and to himself. Even so, *Opening Night* reveled less in theatricality than in flamboyant love, compassion and irony about performers, their insecurities exultant. Cassavetes set up a happy ending only to snatch it harshly from under his characters. It's no accident that by that point either possible ending would have been discomfitingly absurd. So, generous to a fault, he gave us both of them.

It seemed then that discipline was less essential than the need for him to formulate an attitude toward what discipline meant and either accept, reject, or confront the implications of his cool yet strung-out character analysis. Compassion and objectivity clearly weren't enough in themselves; what *Bookie* and *Opening Night* lacked was a command of the consequences of style, which had been astute even in a misfire like *Husbands.* While his talent may have been too prodigious to regulate, it was also too powerful to scatter.

This command is present in *Gloria* and makes that film a revelation as well as a delight, synthesizing so many loose elements from his previous experiments. The film played with conventional expectations of genre payoffs, even unto an editing style that denied us the angle we most needed, out of force of narrative habit. The savvy location shooting counterpoints the calculated fantasies of the plot, so that when the film entered the mind of the young boy at the end, many people were uncomfortably jolted, but the contrivance was a logical culmination of the sly reversals of perception that peppered the picture. It was *Bachelor Mother* flees *The Godfather,* and Cassavetes snatched only what he needed in genre terms to lend some urgency to his series of vaudeville turns on hastily assembled alliances. He's at such pains to avoid conventional sentimentality that his own brand of disavowed sentiment shows through. We don't pick our responsibilities; they choose us. The film's complex kitchen-sink approach to fashioning a universe of Cassavetes' own devising seems richer when viewed in the light of the previous films: what might have seemed determined eccentricity becomes instead the integrated collage of movie memories and nurtured themes.

What makes the absurdities in Cassavetes endearing is the contradiction between his ability to share the consciousness of his characters, even on their own shabby terms, without sacrificing his awareness of their sore limitations. Much like John Ford, Cassavetes approaches his social criticism from the inside, and the agony of realization is consequently rich and deeply felt. Also like the Ford of the sixties films, he lurches increasingly into fantasy as the one possible refuge in which to express lyrical feelings about harsh realities. His great achievement has been his ability to meld compassion with criticism, without ever compromising his unique ability to link his own artistic concerns in a direct relationship with the very different, yet highly relevant, feelings of his characters. He applies his gestures to a canvas of observed behavior, painting with character.

9. William Castle (1914–1977)

1943—*The Chance of a Lifetime; Klondike Kate;* 1944—*The Whistler; She's a Soldier, Too; The Mark of the Whistler; When Strangers Marry;* 1945—*The Crime Doctor's Warning; Voice of the Whistler;* 1946—*Just Before Dawn; Mysterious Intruder; The Return of Rusty; The Crime Doctor's Manhunt;* 1947—*The Crime Doctor's Gamble;* 1948—*Texas, Brooklyn and Heaven; The Gentleman From Nowhere;* 1949—*Johnny Stool Pigeon; Undertow;* 1950—*It's a Small World;* 1951—*The Fat Man; Hollywood Story; Cave of Outlaws;* 1953—*Serpent of the Nile; Fort Ti; Conquest of Cochise; Slaves of Babylon;* 1954—*Drums of Tahiti; Charge of the Lancers; Battle of Rogue River; Jesse James vs. the Daltons; The Iron Glove; The Saracen Blade; The Law vs. Billy the Kid;* 1955—*Masterson of Kansas; The Americano; New Orleans Uncensored; The Gun That Won the West; Duel on the Mississippi;* 1956—*The Houston Story; Uranium Boom;* 1958—*Macabre;* 1959—*House on Haunted Hill; The Tingler;* 1960—*13 Ghosts;* 1961—*Homicidal; Mr. Sardonicus;* 1962—*Zotz!;* 1963—*The Old Dark House* (Great Britain; U.S., 1963); *13 Frightened Girls;* 1964—*Strait Jacket;* 1965—*The Night Walker; I Saw What You Did;* 1966—*Let's Kill Uncle;* 1967—*The Busy Body; The Spirit Is Willing;* 1968—*Project X;* 1974—*Shanks*

To call William Castle a poor man's Hitchcock would not only be insulting to both poor men and Hitchcock but also unfair to Castle himself, whose statements make it clear that he suffered from no delusion of artistic grandeur. "I have modeled my career on Barnum rather than Hitchcock," he once told an interviewer. He was referring of course to the later, horrific part of his career, which started in the late fifties after a decade of cheap Western and adventure programmers, that followed upon nearly a decade of "B" thrillers.

In 1957 the success of *Diabolique* inspired him to sell out two television series ("Men of Annapolis" and "Meet McGraw"), mortgage his house, and invest the money in an independent production, *Macabre*. "When I had finished I looked at it and recognized that a Clouzot I ain't," he told a *Los Angeles Times* reporter with unusual candor. "I had to have a gimmick to sell that movie." The gimmick he came up with was to have the spectators' lives insured by Lloyd's of London in case anyone died of fright (nobody did). The movie did good business and was followed by a dozen others in the same vein, Castle apparently devoting more ingeniousness to the devising of promotional stunts than to the direction of the movies themselves.

Castle had been involved with horror long before he launched his blood-and-scream series, since he had directed the second runs of such plays as *Dracula* (with Bela Lugosi), *The Last Warning,* and *The Cat and the Canary.* (As the manager of a summer stock company in Stony Creek, Connecticut, he had also produced a play of his, *This Little Piggy Had None,* reportedly about a bank clerk who becomes insane and turns into—or at least behaves like—a pig when his advances to the opposite sex are rejected.) He also wrote and acted in radio soap operas ("The Romance of Helen Trent," for one) before being signed by Columbia in 1939. He worked as a dramatic coach, dialogue director, and cutter until 1943, when he was given a chance to direct. His first twelve films were made for Columbia, with the exception of Monogram's *When Strangers Marry,* which happens to be the most renowned. The film gave Robert Mitchum his first important part and cast newcomer Kim Hunter as a convincingly confused small-town girl coming to New York to meet her husband and discovering that he might be a murderer. The character was not unlike the one she had played the year before for Val Lewton in *The Seventh Victim,* and indeed Castle's direction cleverly made use of some of Lewton's principles (the scene of Hunter walking across Central Park at night was obviously suggested by the similar scene in the Lewton-produced *Cat People*). Wrote James Agee: "I have seldom, for years now, seen one hour so energetically and sensibly used in film. Bits of it, indeed, gave me a heart-lifted sense of delight in real performance and perception and ambition which I have rarely known in any film context. . . ."

Most of Castle's Columbia assignments were either in the *Whistler* or the *Crime Doctor* series. He directed Richard Dix in the first *Whistler* film and in three subsequent installments. The series, based on a radio show, was an unusual one in that the title "character" was not the hero, not even a character at all but rather an introductory device (a mysterious, whistling personage), while the protagonist played by Dix changed with every film. *Crime Doctor,* also from a radio show, starred Warner Baxter in ten episodes, of which Castle directed four (*Just Before Dawn* was one of them).

In the late forties and early fifties, Castle made a few pictures at Universal before returning to Columbia for a number of exotic and pseudo-historical programmers, moving swiftly from Cleopatra's Egypt (*Serpent of the Nile,* with an unexpected Rhonda Fleming as Cleopatra) to Nebuchadnezzar's Babylon (*Slaves of Babylon*), to nineteenth-century Tahiti (*Drums of Tahiti*), to eighteenth-century England (*The Iron Glove*), to the Crimean War (*Charge of the Lancers*). His other assignments during this very prolific period (seventeen films in four years) were grade-"B" Westerns, mostly of the "name-dropping" type (the title character in *Masterson of Kansas* met two other famous gunmen, Doc Holliday and Wyatt Earp, and the Clantons-James confrontation was effected through giving the latter a son) and a couple of "exposé" pictures. As the market for programmers dwindled in the mid-fifties, he turned to television for a couple of years before making his *Macabre* comeback in 1958.

When he decided to ballyhoo his own product, Castle tied in promotion and exhibition to such an extent that the gimmicks meant to sell the movies practically became part of the movies. For *House on Haunted Hill* (which had a "screamiere" rather than a premiere), after the villain was reduced to a skeleton in a vat of acid, an inflatable plastic skeleton would be dropped into the audience from the theatre's ceiling. During the showing of *The Tingler,* seats were buzzed with low-voltage electricity, which supported the publicity blurb claiming, "You actually feel real physical sensation as you shiver to its flesh-crawling action." Special glasses were distributed to audiences so that they could screen out the ghosts in *13 Ghosts* at will, and it seems that spectators were actually guaranteed their money back if they walked out of *Homicidal* a few minutes before the end (whether because *Homicidal* was one of the best of the batch or simply because of audience apathy, the movie's career was apparently not hurt at all by this unusual offer). For practical reasons, those stunts could be used only during first runs, so that any evaluation of the films based upon subsequent or small-screen viewing can only take into account the material on film, which is probably just as well. Castle's promotional inventiveness started to dry up after *Homicidal*. (A late instance of his peculiar sense of humor was his own, whimsically Hitchcockian appearance as a stand-in for the Columbia logo at the opening of *Zotz!*, an otherwise feeble attempt at horror in a comic vein.)

After Bette Davis and Joan Crawford clicked in Aldrich's *What Ever Happened to Baby Jane?*, Castle decided to use name stars (instead of his usual "B" performers) as his only gimmick, and he promptly signed Joan Crawford and Barbara Stanwyck, the former to star as a retired ax murderess in *Strait Jacket*, the latter as a widow harassed by constant nightmares about her dead husband in *The Night Walker*. Both films were based on novels by Robert Bloch, the author of *Psycho*. Joan Crawford starred again (with John Ireland) in *I Saw What You Did*, whose plot was somewhat reminiscent of Ted Tetzlaff's *The Window*. All three films were above-average Castle, but the balance of his production since the mid-sixties was anticlimactic, and his last effort, *Project X*, was as anonymous as its title. Castle's smartest move in a long time was his purchasing of the rights to *Rosemary's Baby* (from the galley proofs) and his entrusting the picture's direction to Roman Polanski.

---

10. *Francis Ford Coppola* (1939)

by DIANE JACOBS

1963—*Dementia 13* (uncredited codirector: Jack Hill); 1966—*You're a Big Boy Now;* 1968—*Finian's Rainbow;* 1969—*The Rain People;* 1972—*The Godfather;* 1974—*The Conversation; The Godfather, Part II;* 1979—*Apocalypse Now;* 1981—*One From the Heart;* 1982—*The Outsiders;* 1983—*Rumble Fish*

Miscellaneous
Sixties nudie films that Coppola directed segments of include: 1961—*Tonight for Sure* aka *The Wide Open Spaces;* 1962—*The Playgirls and the Bellboy,* re-edited, English-language version of *Mit Eva fing die Sünde an* (Fritz Umgelter, 1958, Fed. Rep. of Germany); 1962?—*Come On Out*

Uncredited
1963—*The Terror* (Roger Corman; uncredited codirectors: Monte Hellman, Jack Nicholson, Jonathan Haze, Dennis Jacob)

Television Movie
1977—*The Godfather Saga* (re-edited version of *The Godfather, The Godfather, Part II,* and outtakes from the two theatrical features)

Francis Ford Coppola remains something of an anomaly in the "new" Hollywood that he, more than any film maker of his generation, helped shape. As an artist he possesses neither the unmistakable personal style of an Altman or a Scorsese nor Lucas's and Spielberg's passion for special effects nor the modern satirical vision of Allen, Mazursky, and Ritchie. No single genre or authorial voice compels Coppola, whose films are as notable for their range as for their depth. From *You're a Big Boy Now* through *Apocalypse Now*, his greatest strengths have been the conventional, literary ones of strong characters and engrossing plot; and, like the studio director of yore, he bends style to subject matter: thus, there are few *visual* connections between a leisurely, intimate road picture like *The Rain People* and the majestic *Godfather* saga. Still, Coppola's increasingly provocative body of work *is,* thematically, very much of a piece; and the conflicts he grapples with today have been with him from the beginning, in his life as well as his art.

Like his most notorious protagonists, Coppola was born into a close-knit (though, one hastens to add, non-Mafia) New York Italian family. His mother was an actress, his father flautist Carmine Coppola, who shared an Academy Award with Nino Rota for the score of *The Godfather, Part II.* (Coppola's sister, Talia Shire, was also nominated for her *Godfather* performance that year.) As a child, Coppola was a gifted musician and a gadget fanatic: he quickly mastered the tuba and, by the age of ten, began experimenting with the use of sound in home movies. The crisis in Coppola's youth, as in Harry Caul's in *The Conversation,* was a severe case of polio which, happily, left him physically unscarred.

As a theater major at Hofstra University, Coppola wrote the book and lyrics for *A Delicate Touch.* And in 1959 he entered the UCLA film school, where his career began with a vengeance. By the mid-sixties, he had won the Samuel Goldwyn Award for his (never produced) screenplay *Pilma, Pilma;* had directed the low-budget horror film *Dementia 13* for Roger Corman; and had written or collaborated on nearly a dozen screenplays (among them the script for *Patton*) for Seven Arts. In 1967 he made his first "personal" feature, the low-budget *You're a Big Boy Now,* and in 1968 directed the more lavish, less interesting *Finian's Rainbow* for Warner Brothers. In 1969, while completing *The Rain People,* he founded his own production company, American Zoetrope.

As these early ventures indicate, Coppola wasted no time establishing his dual role as personal film maker and businessman/patron. With its goal of launching new talent (most spectacularly that of George Lucas), American Zoetrope was a business venture that also reflected Coppola's deepest personal commitments. (This is true of his support for *Our Hitler, Napoleon,* and the work of Jean-Luc Godard and Wim Wenders in the eighties as well.) But, for the most part, Coppola describes his work as either/ or. His stockholder's interest in Cinema V, for instance, was strictly professional; just as *Finian's Rainbow* and, much later, *The Godfather* were envisioned as commercial films. *The Rain People* and *The Conversation,* on the other hand, were self-initiated "personal" movies, while *Apocalypse Now* began as a studio project and wound up, in all respects, Coppola's most "personal" endeavor to date.

These labels are, of course, a bit too easy. As *The Conversation* and *The Godfather* so vividly demonstrate, there is no firm line between business and "personal": inevitably, the two entwine; and it's not a coincidence that the *Godfather* films are at once Coppola's best and his most popular. Still, the conflict between art and commerce, between private and professional is thematically vital for Coppola, particularly in his mature work. It is the conflict of Harry Caul, the cipher whose wiretapping business ultimately destroys his privacy. It is the conflict acknowledged by Vito Corleone when he warns his son never to take his Mafia business more seriously than his family life.

Interestingly, Vito Corleone's words also suggest the other major conflict in Coppola's work: between the family as a positive, nourishing force and the family (or a familylike unit) as enemy to personal growth and fulfillment. Would Michael Corleone have been better or worse (indeed, would he even have survived?) without "family" protection? Questions such as these are at the root of all Coppola's work; and, more than the "personal" versus business dilemma, distinguish his first two "personal" films, *You're a Big Boy Now* and *The Rain People.*

Coppola's debut feature is the promising, but decidedly lightweight, story of a young Long Island innocent—"Big Boy" Bernard Chanticleer—set loose in the Big City. Here the family is represented by Bernard's parodistically jealous, overprotective mother, whose fears of city life initially seem as ridiculous as her lengthy harangues. Why shouldn't Bernard enjoy the thrills, primarily sexual, of independence and anonymity in New York? By the end of the film—when Bernard finds himself homeless, impotent, romantically rejected and, as the coup de grâce, in jail—Coppola has supplied answers aplenty. And significantly, the "happy ending" epilogue finds Bernard committed to a "nice" Long Island girl and a dog: thus, the family triumphs over more intriguing but far riskier alternatives.

While its tone and situations are derivative of the French New Wave, *You're a Big Boy Now* introduces a pleasingly lusty, beleaguered young protagonist and several memorable sequences. In one, an ebullient Lovin' Spoonful score accompanies a blissful Bernard-in-love on a romp down the street; in another, half the film's cast courses through the New York Public Library on roller skates. Although most of the characters are stereotyped, Bernard's unattainable idol, "Barbara Darling," anticipates the women of Coppola's later work. Unlike them, Barbara Darling is clinically disturbed. Yet many of her predilections—notably, a tendency to vacillate between affection and disgust, greed and generosity—will be shared by the "normal" protagonists in *The Conversation* and *The Rain People.*

The latter film is Coppola's favorite "personal" vehicle, and with good reason. One of the first road pictures and a woman's film in the best sense of the word, *The Rain People,* like *You're a Big Boy Now,* charts an innocent's escape from the predictability of family life into the more precarious unknown. Coppola's mise en scène is more graceful and assured here, balancing realism (we hear authentic traffic noises, feel time passing as it does in real life) with spectacular rural landscapes and telling close-up details.

The Rain People opens in the languor of early morning, with garbage trucks passing almost noiselessly through the light rain of cloistered, suburban streets. In bed, Vinny adjusts a sleeping arm to embrace—and constrain—his very much awake wife, Natalie (Shirley Knight). This is the last we see of Vinny. Within moments, Natalie has showered and headed off for her childhood home, a matter of blocks away. "I just said I wanted to be free for five minutes," she explains to her parents, "for half an hour, half a day." Having discovered that she's pregnant, Natalie panics and leaves family—husband *and* parents—to see if she might just possibly have made something different of herself; if she can manage to unshackle her grocery-list's worth of responsibilities that add up to life with a husband she loves.

She can't, of course. Like Bernard before and Michael Corleone after her, Natalie finds the dangers *out there* more daunting than security is boring. More important for *The Rain People,* Natalie also finds chance responsibilities confusing and no less compelling than parenthood. This point is eloquently conveyed through her evolving relationship with a retarded young hitchhiker named Killer (sensitively portrayed by James Caan). "I only picked you up in the first place because I thought I wanted to make it with someone new, and I end up with a freak!" moans Natalie when she first finds herself saddled with this helpless man. Yet, finally, irrevocably, she accepts his need for her—and thereby embraces parenthood and the ritual of family obligations.

Although its message is direct, *The Rain People* is filled with gentle ambiguities: How much of Killer's helplessness is knowingly self-serving? Might a smarter woman than Natalie have avoided her succession of mishaps? In her finest performance to date, Shirley Knight gives Natalie an intriguing inconsistency. She's spoiled, selfish, petulant but also caring, funny and, at times, glowingly sensuous. Just how responsible is Natalie for Killer's melodramatic death in the film's last scene?

Coppola's title here is actually misleading. In a rather forced expository statement, Killer tells Natalie, "The rain people are made of rain, and when they cry, they disappear altogether." But Coppola's protagonists don't disappear—even Michael Corleone in *Godfather II* is denied the release of death. Natalie must live on, with her guilt and dilemma of choice.

With its outlaw protagonists, *The Godfather* at once complicates and branches out from the dilemmas of Coppola's earlier films. Again, the function of the family is a prominent concern. As in *The Rain People* and *You're a Big Boy Now,* the outside world is remote and unpredictable, the family a buffer between one lonely Italian immigrant and the chaos and subjugation of American life. Don Vito renounces the American government, which would make him a mere "puppet." Shortly before his death, Vito tells Michael, "I refused to be a fool, dancing on a string for all those big guys." Within the context of the film, the "Godfather's" choice makes sense. And yet, even if we accept its purpose, the Mafia families and, by implication, all families work very much like tiny governments. Employing the subtle enticement of love and the less sentimental inducement of gunpoint, the Mafia demands loyalty of its godchildren. Thus, even Michael, who might well have flourished in the world at large, is rendered "puppet" to his father's designs.

The Godfather also introduces the conflict between "personal" and "business," which was to be more scrupulously engaged in the subsequent *The Conversation.* Unlike cipher Harry Caul, Don Vito appraises the personal (in this case nuclear-family) life as every bit as important as business dealings. Repeatedly, he tells Michael that a man is not a man unless he spends time with his wife and children, and Vito is himself incapable of killing his son-in-law Carlo, although Carlo has killed the Don's own child, Sonny. By carefully dividing his two functions, Vito manages to thrive both in business and in domestic life. Sonny, on the other hand, suffers from an inability to differentiate between these two realms. He brings his personal grudges into business dealings and thus is doomed from the outset.

The Godfather is the richest of Coppola's films, offering provocative themes, a compulsively engrossing story, and wonderful character portraits. It has been argued that Richard Castellano (Clemenza) or Abe Vigoda (Tessio) could have played Don Vito without giving a thought to Method Acting. Perhaps. But Marlon Brando lends unmatchable dignity to this role, and his death scene (misconstrued by his grandson as playacting) is almost otherworldly in its grace and understatement.

Al Pacino is also superb as Michael, and Coppola develops this favored son's gravitation toward the Family with utmost subtlety. In the movie, as in Mario Puzo's book, it is a scene by his father's hospital bed that turns the tide; and Pacino skillfully displays how the yen for power and authority, as much as loyalty, draws Michael magnetically into the clan.

The Conversation pursues many of *The Godfather*'s themes in rarer air. The protagonist here, Coppola's most transparently symbolic to date, is Harry Caul—professional wiretapper and personal loner. As with Sonny in *The Godfather* and Natalie in *The Rain People*, Harry's tragic weakness is an inability to discover the balance between business and personal. Sensing that his client is planning to murder two young people whose activities he is paid to record, Harry begins to assume "personal" responsibility for the repercussions of his "business" ventures. Like Antonioni's *Blow-Up*, *The Conversation* pieces together the puzzle of a crime through editing. But here the conclusions drawn are misleading. And Coppola gleans irony from a final narrative twist where Harry discovers that the victims in his "private" melodrama were, in fact, the perpetrators of a real-life crime. Furthermore, by abandoning objectivity, Harry has left himself prey to other wiretappers—his privacy, like his autonomy, irrevocably violated.

Some of *The Conversation*'s most stunning details are a function of Coppola's lifelong fascination with electronics. With the help of sound expert Walter Murch, he stages some breathtaking sound effects (the most outstanding are found in a hotel sequence where a crime is, literally, committed before our ears); and the film-within-a-film idea is deftly conveyed. Coppola said that he decided not to use a long lens to suggest directorial eavesdropping, because it was a hackneyed convention: "Then I thought of doing it with a static camera which gave the impression that it didn't have an operator." Thus, at one point, the camera continues to focus, ominously, on a small section of Harry's apartment, even after Harry himself has moved out of the frame. Taken to a metaphysical extreme, which Coppola intends, this type of shot conveys the irony of free will.

Where *The Godfather* is warm and compelling, *The Conversation* cool and detached, *Godfather II* is a powerful mixture of both approaches. To compare *Godfather II* to its predecessor is to compare Tintoretto's *Last Supper* with Da Vinci's. In the later Godfather film, the basic elements of the earlier work are uncannily, almost parodistically, reshaped. Michael is now established as Godfather, with a somewhat dowdier Kay as wife and mother of his two children. Robert De Niro has replaced Brando as the young Vito Corleone; and the central "Family" members seem pinched variations of their full-bodied counterparts in the earlier work.

Godfather II, much of which is told in flashbacks, is both more visually voluptuous and more literary than *The Godfather*, and family and religion are painstakingly connected here. Michael's weakling brother Fredo is killed while saying a Hail Mary; and the water, instrument of baptism, serves as premonition of death: it is while sitting in a boathouse, looking out over the snow-covered lake, that Michael tells Fredo, "You're nothing to me now. You're not a brother, you're not a friend."

Thus, family loyalty, the most sympathetic chord in *The Godfather*, is more than a little off pitch. In the flashbacks to Vito Corleone's activities, we sense that intelligence as well as ruthlessness were at work in the genesis of the "Family" network. Vito grew up to avenge the deaths of his Sicilian parents and his older brother, but he also used his wits to devise a system that would permit fellow Italians to prosper in the New World. Michael himself is aware that neither business nor family will be as straightforward for him as for his pioneer father. For a start, his business is, in the words of partner Hyman Roth, "bigger than U.S. Steel." And Michael is puzzled by changing times and policies. To his mother, he poses the ultimate question of leadership: by being strong for his family, could he *lose* it? Indeed, this is Coppola's theme.

And it is a theme he carries into the murkier, more kaleidoscopic world of *Apocalypse Now* as well. Here the "family" is America, the outside world the vast, teeming continent of Asia. Marlon Brando, playing Kurtz, is now the Italian Godfather gone to demonic extreme, while personal and business everywhere collide. As a village goes up in flames behind him, an American colonel (superbly played by Robert Duvall) casually suggests that his men might do a little surfing. And the "personal" matter of how Coppola conceived this film uncannily mirrors the business of America's approach to the Vietnam War. Coppola has said, "We went about shooting this movie the way the Americans went into Vietnam: we were in the jungle, and we had too much equipment, too much money . . . little by little we went crazy."

Apocalypse Now is as visually dense and virtuosic as *The Conversation* is spare. In the film's brilliant opening sequence, "The End" by the Doors blasts on the soundtrack while palm trees, fire, and the image of an upsidedown head are superimposed over one another so fluidly they might be adrift in a fishbowl. The time is the late sixties, and American intelligence is still confident that the Vietnam War will be won. Coppola's narration explains that a dissipated-looking Captain Willard (Martin Sheen), unhappily idle in Saigon, is shaking himself from a three-day drunk to receive orders for an intelligence mission. As they consume a sumptuous meal, Willard's commanding officers inform him that he will be asked to travel into Cambodia to ferret out and murder a certain Colonel Kurtz. Once an exemplary soldier, Kurtz has apparently gone mad, setting himself up as a god/king and ordering executions at whim. One officer suggests that, "What Lincoln calls 'the better angle of our nature' has lost out in the battle for Kurtz's soul." He is to be eliminated swiftly and with discretion.

Apocalypse Now has almost no story and little suspense. We know that Willard will survive the various challenges to his intelligence, cunning, and physical well-being, because we know he must live to confront Kurtz. Coppola has called *Apocalypse Now* an "experience" rather than a movie, and experience is an apt description of the film's first ninety minutes. The genius of Coppola's mise en scène here is that it at once batters and soothes. While the stereophonic sound whooshes at us from speakers all over the theatre, the limpid images attract us with their sensuous beauty and repel us with their violent content. Similarly, the cinematography renders us both victim and perpetrator of Coppola's interpretation of Conrad's "the horror." In the film's most spectacular scene, we first watch fire-spitting helicopters swoop down from the skies as if we were the bewildered Vietnamese on the ground. In the next shot, the camera places us behind the helicopter's steering wheel, affording us the arrogant, shameful exhilaration of power.

The ultimate confrontation between Willard and Kurtz is at once the film's most provocative and most troubled aspect. By showing Kurtz/Brando only in profile and in half-light, Coppola renders him almost without substance, as far from the realm of the body as from sanity. And Brando delivers his pivotal speech, a rumination on the frightening good sense of severing the arms of children, with a power that rivals any of his earlier performances. Yet, because we have been insufficiently prepared for Kurtz's rendezvous with Willard—indeed, we scarcely know who Willard, much less Kurtz, is—there's a hollowness to this demon's extraordinary presence and ideas. A comparison between Vito Corleone and Kurtz finds the latter not only more heinous but vaguer. Thus, while Coppola's stylistically conveyed message on the thrill and terror of war comes across loud and clear, his subtler Kurtz-related themes remain elusive.

Still, *Apocalypse Now* is an extraordinary work which, along with *Godfather II,* shows Coppola's powers as a stylist as well as a superb storyteller. And yet the sheer cinematic lushness of these recent films and their fascination with style, often for its own sake, raise a question about Coppola's future: will he retain the range and narrative density of his earlier work or grow ever more self-consciously fascinated with the power of his medium?

11. Roger Corman (1926)

by JOHN H. DORR

1955—*Five Guns West; Apache Woman;* 1956—*The Day the World Ended; Swamp Women; The Oklahoma Woman; Gunslinger; It Conquered the World;* 1957—*Naked Paradise* aka *Thunder Over Hawaii; The Undead; Not of This Earth; Attack of the Crab Monsters; Rock All Night; Carnival Rock; Teenage Doll; Sorority Girl; The Saga of the Viking Women and Their Voyage to the Waters of the Great Sea Serpent;* 1958—*War of the Satellites; Machine Gun Kelly; Teenage Caveman; She Gods of Shark Reef;* 1959—*I, Mobster; A Bucket of Blood; The Wasp Woman;* 1960—*Ski Troop Attack; House of Usher; The Last Woman on Earth; The Little Shop of Horrors;* 1961—*Atlas; Creature From the Haunted Sea,* codirector (pretitle sequence): Monte Hellman; *The Pit and the Pendulum;* 1962—*Premature Burial; The Intruder; Tales of Terror; Tower of London;* 1963—*The Raven; The Young Racers; The Terror,* uncredited codirectors: Francis Ford Coppola, Monte Hellman, Jack Nicholson, Jonathan Haze, Dennis Jacob; *The Haunted Palace; X—The Man with X-Ray Eyes;* 1964—*The Masque of the Red Death; The Secret Invasion; The Tomb of Ligeia* (Great Britain; U.S., 1965); 1966—*The Wild Angels;* 1967—*The St. Valentine's Day Massacre; The Trip;* 1970—*Bloody Mama; Gas-s-s-s . . . or It Became Necessary to Destroy the World in Order to Save It!;* 1971—*Von Richthofen and Brown;* 1980—(1968) *Target: Harry* aka *What's in It for Harry?* aka *How To Make It* (originally made for television but not broadcast; released under the pseudonym Henry Neill)

Uncredited
1967—*A Time for Killing* (Phil Karlson); 1969—*De Sade* (Cy Endfield; uncredited codirector: Gordon Hessler)

Between 1955 and 1971, Roger Corman directed, and usually also produced, some forty-nine features, mostly on very low budgets and very short shooting schedules and usually aimed at a young audience. Working exclusively in the "exploitation" genres—Westerns, science fiction, horror, gangsters, war, rock and roll, teenage gangs, beatniks, motorcycle gangs, and LSD—these films were fast, fun, and fanciful. In addition, since entering the motion-picture business in 1953, he has produced, financed, or overseen a large number of films that he did not himself direct but for many of which he provided the original impetus, storyline, or idea.

Since the early seventies, Corman has devoted himself to the running of his own production and distribution company, New World Pictures—a family operation in which his wife, Julie Corman, and his brother, Gene Corman, are also involved as producers. Throughout his career, and particularly through New World, Corman has employed talented young film makers and given them their initial breaks in the industry. Alumni of the Corman school include Francis Ford Coppola, Peter Bogdanovich, Curtis Harrington, Jack Nicholson, Bruce Dern, Robert Towne, Martin Scorsese, Monte Hellman, Jonathan Demme, and Jonathan Kaplan. New World has also gained respectability as the American distributor of such prestigious European directors as Bergman, Fellini, and Truffaut.

An immensely practical and successful businessman, Corman has always chosen to remain independent, functioning largely outside the major studios. As producer-director he worked most frequently with distribution deals from American-International Pictures and Allied Artists, pairing his very brief films in exploitation double bills for quick saturation playoffs. He prides himself on the fact that while the margin of profit on his style of low-budget film making was small, very few of his films ever lost money. He stood as a solitary example of the small-is-good philosophy during a period when the rest of the industry was reeling from the excesses of an overconsuming culture. He stopped directing at the beginning of the culturally barren seventies when industry retrenchment proved unfavorable to his off-the-cuff style of film making. Increasing distributor interference, the higher stakes of bigger budgets, and the self-consciousness that came with critical recognition seemed to take the fun out of directing for Corman.

Corman's work was never meant to be taken too seriously. But his fantastic melodramas, with their visionary and apocalyptic overtones, seemed better focused on the crises of modern existence than most of the cold, despairing realist films of the sixties and seventies. Corman's films were never as mindless or as exploitative as their lurid sex-and-violence ad campaigns presented them as being. Within the genre conventions and often ludicrous low-budget devices, Corman dealt with serious themes, the silliness of their form mitigating the pretensions of their content.

Many of his films take the form of moral lessons—cautionary tales warning of humanity's willful urge toward self-destruction, be it in the form of nuclear holocaust (*The Day the World Ended, Teenage Caveman, The Last Woman on Earth*), neurotic morbidity (*Machine Gun Kelly, A Bucket of Blood, House of Usher, Premature Burial, The Young Racers, The Tomb of Ligeia, Bloody Mama*), through the hubris of an overreaching challenge of the gods (*The Undead, The Wasp Woman, X—The Man with X-Ray Eyes, The Masque of the Red Death*), or as a result of purely evil intentions (*It Conquered the World, The Intruder, The Haunted Palace*).

As a moralist, Corman was concerned with the opposition of good and evil, the latter of which was the more colorfully depicted. That his characters were so frequently unsavory bastards, two-dimensionally drawn and locked in ruthless struggles for survival, hints at a certain misanthropy in the director. He was always pessimistic about humankind, at times justifiably cynical. The time of judgment seemed always near. The gods were angry, and thunder and lightning inevitably punctuated the climaxes.

The trademark formalism of Corman's images and staging is a function of a deterministic point of view. It is the unrelenting progression of events that carries his short stories swiftly to their inevitable conclusions. His characters cannot escape their fates, and it is on how they struggle that they are judged. The actors have no freedom of movement within the camera frame but move in strict chalk-marked courses. Corman often used a fireplace point-of-view shot, observing the machinations of his characters through the flames, suggesting that fate will see them roast in hell. From the simple, utilitarian staging, mono-images, and straightforward parallel intercutting of his fifties' films, Corman evolved his visual style (as time and budget allowed) into a sophisticatedly fluid use of fatalistic tracking shots, wide screen, and symbolic color in his adaptations of Edgar Allan Poe stories in the sixties.

Like the exploratory Biograph period of another determinist film maker, D. W. Griffith, Corman's fifties' films have a spontaneous freshness and a fast, sketchy charm. In his initial outburst of activity (twenty-one little films, some hardly over an hour long, between 1955 and 1958), Corman tried out a wide range of subject matter, executed with the game cooperation of his repertory company of resourceful technicians and largely naive actors.

Cinematographer Floyd Crosby, whose career dates back to Murnau's *Tabu,* photographed some twenty of Corman's films; and it is to Crosby that Corman credits his developments in wide screen, color, and camera movement. Crosby's shadowy lighting was crucial to sustaining the creepy mood of Corman's science-fiction and horror films. The tinny orchestrations of another frequent Corman collaborator, Ronald Stein, gave those films an eerie, off-kilter feel. Corman's editors, Ronald Sinclair, Charles Gross, Jr., and Anthony Carras, kept the pace ruthlessly fast but were not above repeating the same shot twice to keep an action sequence alive. Corman's very resourceful art director was Daniel Haller, whose cumulatively expanded castle interiors became a trademark of the Poe series.

Throughout his career, Corman repeatedly used a stable of screenwriters on whom he could rely to expand his story ideas within genre conventions and with the limitations of budget always in mind. Writers R. Wright Campbell, Richard Matheson, Charles Beaumont, Robert Towne, and Lou Rusoff all have four or more Corman pictures to their credit. Foremost among Corman's writers was Charles B. Griffith, a master of the cliché as comedy, who led Corman to explore the self-parodying ridiculousness that his low-budget techniques and reliance on genre conventions cried out for. Griffith's horror spoofs (*A Bucket of Blood, The Little Shop of Horrors, Creature From the Haunted Sea*) make a surreal virtue of what passes for unintentional humor in other films. Like other members of the Corman company, Griffith could also turn up in the cast or as assistant director or in whatever other capacity might be handy. Corman himself turns up as an actor in *War of the Satellites* and *Ski Troop Attack.*

Corman loyally and affectionately made repertory use of certain players, sometimes in the leads, sometimes in bit parts. They constituted a family of very willing (if not overly talented in a conventional sense) familiar faces who specialized in straight-faced readings of hilariously clichéd lines and a lowest-common-denominator point of view. Corman loved to take apparently naive actors and actresses and have them deliver his often portentous dialogue with an innocence that was sometimes disarmingly direct, sometimes high camp. "I won't love a monster! I won't" insists Beverly Garland in *It Conquered the World.* Garland, along with Richard Denning, "Touch" Connors, Paul Birch, Barboura Morris, and Susan Cabot, were the top "stars" of Corman's fifties' films.

Two favorite Corman family members, who seemed to turn up in everything, were Jonathan Haze and Dick Miller. Haze's specialty was psychotic young troublemakers. Miller frequently was the cynical wise guy or bartender, delivering such philosophical lines as "The secret of life is not to be too involved." In *Apache Woman,* Miller recalls playing both a posse member and the Indian he shoots. Haze and Miller did comic routines together as two dumb army guards in *It Conquered the World.* Each had his moment of glory in a starring role in a Chuck Griffith horror parody. *The Little Shop of Horrors,* made on a legendary two-day shooting schedule, features Jonathan Haze as the keeper of a talking carnivorous plant that demands human victims for dinner. In *A Bucket of Blood,* an hilarious exposé of the pretensions of the fifties' beatnik scene, Dick Miller is the demented bus boy who murders people and makes plaster casts of their death throes as sculpture.

Throughout the fifties, women played a central role in many of Corman's movies where reversal of the usual sexual stereotypes was deemed a good exploitation device. If the actresses who played these roles were not always convincing in their ascribed heroic physical capabilities, the gesture of equality still plays as quite advanced. In *The Saga of the Viking Women and Their Voyage to the Waters of the Great Sea Serpent,* for example, the women are fully the equal of the men in both heroics and physical strength. In an arm-wrestling contest between a Viking woman and a barbarian man, the man wins the first round, the woman the second, and the third is called off by the male barbarian ruler lest the chance be taken that the woman would win.

There would often be a good woman and a bad woman to oppose each other. Inevitably the bad woman had the leading role, while the good woman, often played by Barboura Morris, was subsidiary. A favorite "bad girl" starring in six of the fifties' films was the dark-haired, voluptuous, and always conniving Susan Cabot. In *Sorority Girl,* as a neurotic, compulsively destructive college girl, she was a tortured Machiavellian whose cynical grasp of the dark realities behind affluent fifties' culture placed her distinctly at odds with the naive sorority-house existence. Like a female counterpart of the James Dean character in *East of Eden,* she was condemned as bad; yet her sado-masochistic spanking of a pledge/slave and her blackmail of other girls served the function of cutting through the moral flabbiness and hypocrisy of her victims.

In the sixties, however, Corman's treatment of women became more stereotyped. In subsidiary roles, they functioned as sex objects—either passive victims or more often, as with Hazel Court in the Poe pictures, as dangerous, slutty handmaidens to their evil male masters.

Some of Corman's most enjoyable work of the fifties was in science fiction. Here his ideas, though often derivative of other popular sci-fi hits of the time, were clearly on a higher plane than his budgets. Yet much of their delight came from the audacious and patently silly ways he would get around spending money on special effects: disembodied voices, monsters seen by characters but not shown, girls screaming in terror, gruesome sound effects. The monsters themselves were often delightfully absurd and unconvincing men in monster suits or creepy things flying on strings that plop down on people's heads or just a claw reaching in from the side of the screen.

In *The Day the World Ended,* after the nuclear holocaust, atomic mutants lurk about an isolated ranch house where a few desperate characters kill each other off for the last uncontaminated provisions. *The Last Woman on Earth* is an even cheaper version on this *huit clos* theme, sans monsters, where two male survivors fight it out for the last woman while wandering around an island where the streets are cluttered with dead bodies. In *Teenage Caveman,* what appears to be a prehistoric setting turns out to be a postholocaust reversion, and the monster turns out to be a survivor of "the atomic age"—a theme much later exploited in the *Planet of the Apes* series. In *The Undead,* which has a prologue delivered by Satan himself, a mad scientist travels back into the earlier lives of a woman whose present incarnation is as a streetwalker and thus sets up the intriguing situation of tampering with the whole of history by changing one fate in medieval times.

It Conquered the World, using themes from both *The Day the Earth Stood Still* and *Invasion of the Body Snatchers*, imagines a mad scientist who makes radio contact with an alien monster intent on "rescuing mankind from itself"—but in fact it intends to enslave the planet for its own uses via brain control. In the midst of these horrific events, the characters never cease their clever, sarcastic dialogue and continuously philosophize on the nature of human freedom. The conclusion: Man is a feeling creature and because of it the greatest in the universe. Perfection (as promised by the alien) cannot be given to man; it has to be achieved. Whenever man strives for perfection, it ends in disaster. There is hope, but it has to come from inside—from man himself.

If in the fifties Corman seemed to be saying: watch out or you might blow it; in the sixties there was the feeling that it was already too late. The characters of the fifties functioned merely as pawns in the struggle between good and evil, and Corman rarely elaborated on their psychologies. But beginning with the Poe series in the early sixties, Corman began to focus on the haunted conscience of the individual, exploring the doomed psyches of men of extraordinary power who were not satisfied living within the natural limits of mankind. These antihero protagonists shared common traits: an obsession with their eyes (as symbols of their visionary insight); a morbid fear of, and attraction to, death; and a decadent indulgence in the self. The Poe series, dominated by the possessed characterizations of Vincent Price, became ritualistic *danses macabres* paralleling the cancerous decadence of willful sixties excess.

The very successful Poe series brought Corman to critical attention. While repetitious and formularized, the series was a remarkable set of variations on the theme of decadence. *House of Usher* set the tone and formula for the whole series. Atmosphere was all: the endless somnambulist walkings through chambers and corridors and catacombs of the decaying castle; the strangely slamming doors and screams in the night; the enveloping fog; the ornate decor; the blood-red candles in chandeliers looming threateningly above the characters; the cobwebs and the rats; the bloody hand raising the lid of a casket; the colored-filter nightmares; the obligatory accompaniment of thunder and lightning; the apocalyptic ending in flames.

Vincent Price established himself as the definitive Poe tormented soul, afflicted with a painful acuteness of the senses that motivated his archly florid acting. The stories invariably concerned a dashing young man who came to an isolated castle in search of a girl who had fallen under the power of Price. Despite repeatedly being told that he must leave, the young man remains and is the catalyst of the ensuing holocaust. No match for Price, the young men were played by a succession of handsome, but bland, male ingenues (including Jack Nicholson) who gave the young audience someone to identify with.

The Pit and the Pendulum was a lurid sado-masochistic fantasy in which narrative decayed into a ritual formula of scare-show devices. The razor blade of the "pendulum of fate" swung relentlessly through the Panavision frame, inching toward man-as-victim bound hand and foot on his last island, surrounded by the pit, which was Hell. In *Premature Burial*, for variety, Ray Milland replaced Price. With one episode of *Tales of Terror* and *The Raven*, Corman played his grand-gesture melodrama for comedy. *The Terror*, a minor effort starring Boris Karloff, was made famous by its reuse in Peter Bogdanovich's *Targets*.

In *The Haunted Palace*, Price is purely evil, a Satan-worshipper with a fiery pit in his dungeon that connects directly to Hell. Price lures the local virgins here to wed with monsters, and the girls subsequently give birth to a race of mutants who become the curse of the nearby town generations after the townspeople have burnt

Price at the stake as a warlock. Based more on a story by H. P. Lovecraft than on Poe, the second part of the story concerns a descendant of this satanist, also played by Price, who is hypnotized by the eyes of his ancestor's portrait in order to reactivate the work of the devil. History repeats itself, and we are left to believe it will repeat itself again, in one of the best incarnations of a favorite Corman theme—the cyclical damnation of the human race.

The Masque of the Red Death is Corman at his most deterministic—an allegory in which Death, the great leveler, is personified in solemn, hooded figures who walk a ravaged landscape bringing plague to the oppressor and the oppressed alike. "Each man creates his own heaven and his own hell," Death tells Price, who had hoped, in vain, that an alliance with the Devil would save him. The last of the Poe series, *The Tomb of Ligeia,* is the most lavish and delirious summation of the Poe formula. The story is almost immaterial. What matters are the endless wide-screen tracking shots and the symbolic color schemes—an abstract exercise in style shot not on the usual castle sets but on natural locations in England.

Buoyed by the success of the Poe pictures, and perhaps in reaction to their artificiality, Corman began making more ambitious pictures on more overtly serious, contemporary subjects. His liberal identification with sixties activism led him to invest his own money in *The Intruder,* a strange, hysteria-ridden melodrama in which an ingratiating outsider (William Shatner) arrives in a small Southern town and stirs up racial fears and hatred against forced integration. While the outsider supposedly represents some right-wing organization in Washington, Corman emphasizes a decidedly demonic gleam as he dollies into close shots of Shatner's eyes. A "Thrifty-Cut Rate" neon sign blinks in the foreground while crosses burn in the background, as Corman explores what he terms "the contradictions and absurdities of modern society." It ends, like *The Haunted Palace,* with the intimation that this evil will live on. *The Intruder,* the film of which Corman is most proud, remains in obscurity, never having found proper distribution.

The Young Racers spends less time on Grand Prix action footage than on philosophical probings into the motivations driving a prize-winning racer. The racer is described as "arrogant, ruthless, crude and altogether a hateful human being" who treats women and cars alike, controlling and using both out of contempt and fear. Like the Poe characters, he is haunted by fatalistic dreams, and we are led to expect an ending in flames. But through the questioning of a journalist writing a book on "a man who wants the world," the racer becomes self-aware and sympathetic. While the tragedy must play itself out on the race track, the racer survives—a better man. Corman pits corrupt civilization against vital barbarism and suggests that in a jungle (the modern world), only the cruel and the passionate survive.

Corman's investigation into inner vision culminates in *X—The Man with X-Ray Eyes,* which is a closer representation of an LSD-type experience than Corman was later to achieve in *The Trip.* Here, a mad scientist (Ray Milland) discovers a serum that gives him the power to see through material objects. Absorbed in the wonder of "flesh dissolved in the acid of light," he wants to see ever more and keeps increasing the dosage. What does he ultimately see? "There are great darknesses, and beyond the darkness a light in the center of the universe—the eye that sees us all." This is a modern lesson, in Old Testament parable form, of the fate of those who challenge the gods—who seek to see too much.

In 1966 Corman found the perfect metaphor for the anger and alienation of the time in the exploits of an outlaw motorcycle gang, the Hell's Angels of Venice,

California. The resultant film, *The Wild Angels,* started a whole new genre of the late sixties. It exploited the fears of safe and secure Middle America with the threat of terrorization at the hands of these modern barbarians on wheels. The Angels were the dark, guilt-spawned furies that would wreak horrible vengeances for our mass sins in Vietnam. They took glee in tearing down all that America held sacrosanct. Corman sided with these forces of anarchy, romanticizing their outlaw existence. As assistant director, Peter Bogdanovich added a sense of Hawksian camaraderie, realizing that this new genre had much in common with the classical Western. Morally, in embracing self-destruction, the film was a dead end, which Corman was well aware of. Yet the idealistic subtext of the film made it a sympathetic rallying archetype for the disillusioned young who agreed with its antihero protagonist, Peter Fonda, in concluding that there was "nowhere to go."

But for Corman too, *The Wild Angels* seemed to leave him with nowhere to go. The late sixties was a period of crisis for Corman. *The St. Valentine's Day Massacre* and *Bloody Mama* were both sturdy genre pieces, cynically played for violence, that had little to say. *The Trip,* inflated with arbitrary fantasy sequences, was disappointingly unfocused and pat, its frenetic visual effects dating badly. Two projects that Corman began, *A Time for Killing* and *De Sade,* were completed and signed by other directors. Another film, *What's in It for Harry,* shot in 1967 in Monaco and Turkey for ABC, was completed but hardly released at all. His last two features were major accomplishments; but *Gas-s-s* was re-edited and poorly distributed by American International, and *Von Richthofen and Brown* received bad reviews and did little business. It was at this point that Corman withdrew from directing.

Gas-s-s-s . . . or It Became Necessary to Destroy the World in Order to Save It is a giddy, scatter-shot parody of American culture, celebrating a postcatastrophe youth-cult anarchy. It is Corman's totally self-conscious summation of his careerlong obsession with humanity's recurring urge toward self-destruction. "Those who fail history are destined to repeat the course" is the moral of the story. A highly experimental orgy of creation and destruction, this chaotic group undertaking is a perfect reflection of the idealistic sixties youth movement at that apogee of hysteria, ready to leap off the edge into the disillusionment of Altamont, that set the tone for the early seventies. In a wildly improvised, free-form narrative, layered with throwaway humor and hippie wisdom subtexts, a band of young survivors crosses the American Southwest in an Edsel, encountering a series of metaphorical adventures, in search of "the Answer." Corman seems to give himself over to his young collaborators, unable himself to make sense of all the diverse forces in play yet with an open confidence that in the way of anarchy would coalesce a future. This swan-song picture at once looks backward in a catalogue of his careerlong preoccupations and forward to his commitment to the young film makers to whom he would subsequently turn over the reins of directing at New World Pictures.

Corman's last film to date is *Von Richthofen and Brown.* Turning determinist historian, Corman analytically stages a morality play in which Von Richthofen stands for human nobility, a dying nineteenth-century concept, and Brown for cold cynicism, the conquering twentieth-century point of view. Asked if he expects to live forever, Von Richthofen explains that every moment in his plane is forever. Faced with the suggestion that everyone has to die sometime, Brown retorts "We're dead already." Von Richthofen prefers to die with a tradition that has been his life. Brown realizes that he must live with a reality which, lacking humanism, is as empty as death. In Corman's career, Von Richthofen parallels the death of a director and Brown the survival of a producer.

12. Jules Dassin (1911)

1942—*Nazi Agent; The Affairs of Martha; Reunion in France;* 1943—*Young Ideas;* 1944—*The Canterville Ghost;* 1946—*A Letter for Evie; Two Smart People;* 1947—*Brute Force;* 1948—*The Naked City;* 1949—*Thieves' Highway;* 1950—*Night and the City;* 1955—*Du Rififi chez les hommes* (France; U.S., *Rififi,* 1956); 1957—*Celui qui doit mourir* (France; U.S., *He Who Must Die,* 1958); 1959—*La Legge* (Italy; U.S., *Where the Hot Wind Blows,* 1960); 1960—*Pote tin kyriaki* (Greece; U.S., *Never on Sunday,* 1960); 1962—*Phaedra;* 1964—*Topkapi;* 1966—*10:30 P.M. Summer;* 1968—*La guerre amère* (U.S., *Survival 1967,* documentary); *Uptight;* 1970—*Promise at Dawn;* 1974—(unreleased) *The Rehearsal* (documentary); 1978—*A Dream of Passion;* 1981—*Circle of Two*

Some admirers of Dassin's Hollywood films felt betrayed when he went to Europe and have never forgiven him. The feeling is understandable. His two-part career perfectly illustrates the proposition that the more interesting an American director has proved to be when working in his own country, the more disappointing he will turn out to be when exiled, even (or rather especially) if exile provides him with the "artistic" freedom Hollywood had denied him. Yet, one should not be overly selfish; it is not, after all, a negligible achievement to make one's life a total success against initially severe odds, and it is not all that afflicting if film buffs have to lose in the bargain.

Dassin has achieved not only what he wanted but probably more than he had ever dreamed of in his early career. He broke loose from Hollywood and the U.S. at a particularly stifling time in the history of the country, he adopted the European life-style he was attracted to, became famous, met the woman of his life and made *her* famous, and was even called back to his own country to direct Broadway shows and a film. Against such personal achievement, what can we enter on the Hollywood side of the ledger? Little more than a couple of good movies and one unquestionable masterpiece—*Night and the City,* which, ironically, was filmed entirely in London.

Dassin was born of Russian immigrant parents who had settled in Connecticut early in the century. The family later moved to New York City (Harlem), where the boy went to high school. The Dassins's means were modest, and Jules's schooling never went further than high school. Very early he developed a passion for the stage and joined the ARTEF players collective, where he played about seventy-five parts in six years, also taking turns in directing and various other chores, usually for little or no compensation. In 1936 he went briefly to Europe, where he studied drama. Upon his return he was again involved with ARTEF and played the lead in *Revolt of the Beavers,* a Marxist-oriented musical for children produced by the then very active and highly controversial Federal Theatre Project. The play offended not only Brooks Atkinson but also the New York police commissioner, who closed it down after a three-week run. Early in 1940 Dassin wrote a radio adaptation of Gogol's *The Overcoat* and sold it to a New York radio station, which led to an offer from Martin Gabel to direct *Medicine Show,* a Federal Theatre project that had been rescued by independent backers after the FTP foundered in 1939. *Medicine Show,* which had a score by Hanns

Eisler, used the "living newspaper technique," an FTP creation, to dramatize the problems of inadequate medical care in the United States and to make a plea for socialized medicine. According to the *New York Times* it was "a completely absorbing presentation of a public problem," while the *New York Post* noted that the show was "directed with uncommon felicity." All these activities probably contributed to cast suspicion upon Dassin (who had been a member of the Communist party for a few months in 1939) when the red-baiting madness swept Hollywood a dozen years later.

The success of *Medicine Show* brought Dassin a Hollywood contract as an apprentice director for RKO. He later told an interviewer, "I sat and observed for six months, and then they said, 'That's all, you're fired.'" (During his stay on the RKO lot he had attended the filmings of Garson Kanin's *They Knew What They Wanted* and Hitchcock's *Mr. and Mrs. Smith*.) He started making the rounds of the other studios and recalls that the executive who interviewed him at MGM was at the same time conducting a telephone conversation about plans to produce a two-reel adaptation of Poe's *The Tell-Tale Heart*. Dassin started interjecting suggestions, and the executive offered him to direct the short, which he did. According to Dassin, "They looked at it after I finished and loathed it," and the film was released only because of a shortage of short subjects at the time. *The Tell-Tale Heart*, which starred Joseph Schildkraut, was highly praised, received several awards, and resulted in Dassin's promotion to feature director. In the next few years he made seven pictures for MGM, most of them low-budget comedies and melodramas. In 1947 he moved to Universal, there to direct his two best-known pictures, *Brute Force* and *The Naked City*, which were to be Mark Hellinger's last two productions. Dassin's last two pictures before exile, and his best (*The Naked City* and *Thieves' Highway*), were made for Fox, and the second of them was filmed in England. When he returned to the States, he found the political situation worse than when he had left, and several film projects fell through. The blacklist was taking its toll.

In April of 1951 Edward Dmytryk, appearing before the House Committee on Un-American Activities, testified that Jules Dassin had been one of seven Screen Directors Guild members he had known to be members of the Communist party. HUAC subpoenaed Dassin in the fall of 1952, at which time he was in New York directing the rehearsals of *Two's Company*, a musical revue starring Bette Davis. Dassin asked for and obtained a postponement for the purpose of completing his directing task.

Early in 1953 Dassin's appearance before HUAC was again postponed, this time "indefinitely," but although the committee was willing to let him off the hook, he had been "compromised" enough to find it impossible to get any job either in New York or Hollywood. Like many other blacklistees, he moved to Europe and settled in France where film producers were at first reluctant to employ him. (He says that he supported himself and his family "by writing plays and poems," a rather unlikely source of income, and by "borrowing heavily," which sounds more probable.)

In 1954 Dassin got a chance to direct *Du Rififi chez les hommes*, a cheaply produced thriller based upon a novel by Auguste Le Breton, a specialist of French underworld mores and parlance (the slang word *rififi* was so unfamiliar to the average French audience that a song explaining its meaning was written into the plot). Dassin coscripted the film and cast himself in an important part, using the pseudonym Perlo Vita. *Du Rififi chez les hommes* (known in the U.S. as plain *Rififi*) was a critical and box-office hit, perhaps the most popular and talked-about French film of the year 1954, and

Dassin was suddenly in a position to write his own ticket. However, he did not make another film until more than two years later, being dissatisfied with the projects offered him, most of them gangster stories trying to capitalize on the success of *Rififi*.

In 1956 Dassin met Greek actress Melina Mercouri, and their enduring relationship (they were married ten years later) was to prove a major influence not only in his private life but also on his evolution as a film maker. He first featured, then starred, Mercouri in all his subsequent pictures with the exception of the American-made *Uptight*, and Greece became his major source of inspiration. With the help of her father, a representative in the Greek Parliament, Dassin arranged to film his next picture on the island of Crete.

He Who Must Die, based on Nikos Kazantzakis's novel, was the kind of ambitious endeavor Dassin had been dreaming of, and it was selected as the official French entry at the Cannes Festival of 1957. There followed *Where the Hot Wind Blows,* a French-Italian coproduction made in Italy with an all-star cast (Gina Lollobrigida, Marcello Mastroianni, Yves Montand, Pierre Brasseur) and the enormously successful *Pote tin kyriaki* (*Never on Sunday*), Dassin's own script, which he filmed in Athens and in which he costarred opposite Melina Mercouri. It is somewhat ironic that this Greek production got American exile Dassin some indirect recognition from the Motion Picture Academy when Melina Mercouri was nominated for best actress and Manos Hadjidakis received the best song award.

Early in 1962 Dassin came to the United States to direct a Broadway play, Robert L. Joseph's *Isle of Children,* starring Patty Duke. Most critics found it excessively bleak and depressing, and it closed after seven performances. It was back to Greece again for Dassin with another ambitious project, *Phaedra,* a modern transposition of Euripides' *Hippolytus.* His next picture, the caper-comedy *Topkapi,* based on an Eric Ambler mystery and filmed in Istanbul, turned out to be a major hit, which was not the case for *10:30 P.M. Summer,* an adaptation of Marguerite Duras's novel, which Dassin coproduced with Anatole Litvak and coscripted with Duras. Dassin has said that he made the film mainly to please his wife, who considered the part of Maria the most demanding and most important of her career. During the same year plans for a musical adaptation of *Never on Sunday* starring Mercouri materialized. The show, called "Illya Darling," was directed by Dassin himself, who also wrote the book, and opened on Broadway in April 1967. It ran for nearly a year.

As a consequence of Dassin's hostility to the new regime imposed upon Greece by the military junta in 1967, the director became unable, as well as unwilling, to work or live in the country. (In 1970 he was indicted in absentia by a military court for allegedly providing help to a democratic association accused of terrorist activities. Dassin denied the charges, which were dropped in 1973.) 1967 was also the year of the Arab-Israeli Six-Day War, which was the subject of a French-produced documentary Dassin directed with the collaboration of Irwin Shaw. *La guerre amère* (released here as *Survival*) took a deliberately pro-Israeli stand. The following year, Dassin made his first American film in almost two decades, the Paramount-produced *Uptight,* an adaptation of Liam O' Flaherty's *The Informer,* transposed from early twenties Dublin to New York City in 1968 and filmed on location in Harlem with a black cast including Raymond St. Jacques, Ruby Dee, and Julian Mayfield (the last two receiving cowriting credit with Dassin). The film was beset by tensions and various difficulties while in production and did not seem to strike a very responsive chord in the public, black or otherwise, when released. Dassin was soon back in Europe working on a new Mercouri vehicle, *Promise at Dawn,* which he adapted from the novel by Romain Gary.

Dassin's early MGM movies, although modestly budgeted, were not quite "B" pictures for, as Don Miller points out in *B Movies,* "What was considered a 'B' pic by MGM would grace the production schedules of other companies as important contributions." The first of these features, *Nazi Agent*—originally released as *Salute to Courage* and also known for some time as *House of Spies*—was a twin-brothers story with Conrad Veidt playing both the nice brother and the evil one. According to Miller, "the film had that costly MGM physical appearance and attention to detail that bespoke careful handling."

Dassin's next assignment was a comedy, whose title was also changed (from *Once Upon a Thursday* to *The Affairs of Martha*) shortly after its release. It starred Marsha Hunt—whom Dassin was to direct later in *A Letter for Evie,* and Richard Carlson in a cast featuring Spring Byington and Marjorie Main. Dassin was then handed two top stars (Joan Crawford and John Wayne) and a terrible script, and the result was the dismal *Reunion in France,* of which the director said later: "*Reunion* was bad. Everything it said was bad. It was an apology for collaboration with the Nazis." He made more comedies, but the only one that received—or deserved—any critical attention was the fairly entertaining *Canterville Ghost* with Margaret O'Brien and Charles Laughton in the title role.

Dassin's style underwent a drastic change when he moved to Universal and switched from comedy to crime melodrama with a "realistic" touch. Still, it is difficult today to account for the praise *Brute Force,* a routine prison film, received when first released. Its thoroughly conventional script and dialogue—by Richard Brooks—verge on the ludicrous in a series of clumsy flashbacks purporting to provide insight into each convict's past. James Agee wrote of the film: "There isn't a line in it, or a performance, or an idea, or an emotion, that belongs much later than 1915, and cheesy 1915 at that." Then came the vastly superior yet much overrated *The Naked City,* Dassin's first shot at a domestic brand of neorealism. After countless movies presenting New York City in a combination of blatant studio sets and equally obvious process shots, it was a definite plus for a crime film to be filmed almost entirely on location (Henry Hathaway's *The House on 92nd Street* and *Kiss of Death* had shown the way a couple of years before); on the other hand, the authenticity of the locale tended to emphasize the more conventional aspects of the script. Dassin's camera captured the atmosphere of a sweltering New York summer powerfully (William Daniels received an Academy Award for his photography), and some of the characterizations are memorable (Fitzgerald, Duff, De Corsia); but on the whole, the film's high reputation can only be understood in the context of a period when *The Bicycle Thief* made everybody's all-time ten-best list and critics were unconditionally sold on the notion of Hollywood's "artificiality" being intrinsically inferior to continental realism.

Dassin's move to Fox after *The Naked City* and Hellinger's death seemed to be a logical one, since the studio had launched the on-location, semidocumentary style of crime film *Naked City* belonged to. At Fox, Louis de Rochemont had produced the Hathaway films mentioned above as well as Elia Kazan's *Boomerang.* However, De Rochemont had left the studio when Dassin joined it, and Dassin's two Fox films, which turned out to be his best, though shot on location were far from adhering strictly to the principles of documentary realism. *Thieves' Highway,* a remake of Walsh's *They Drive by Night,* was written by A. I. Bezzerides, the author of the original novel. A minor but, in its kind, perfect achievement and a much tighter film than the Walsh (the two scripts are actually very dissimilar), *Thieves* focused on the entanglement of crime and labor, anatomizing the inside workings of the San Francisco market, the trucking business, and their infiltration by racketeers with a fair degree of clarity. Such fine set pieces as the accident on the road, with the truckload of apples rolling down the hill, or the final showdown between Richard Conte and Lee J. Cobb make *Thieves' Highway* memorable. But Dassin's masterpiece is unquestionably his next, and last, American film, *Night and the City.* The idea behind this filmed-on-location adaptation of Gerald Kersh's novel of the London underworld was obviously to do for London what *The Naked City* had done for New York and *Thieves' Highway* for San Francisco, but the picture actually confirmed the impression, already conveyed by *Thieves' Highway,* that Dassin's forte was not so much documentary realism as baroque lyricism in the tradition of the *film noir.* A visual poem of heightened reality, *Night and the City*—no title has ever been more apposite—is characterized by a sustained nightmarish atmosphere. The city's presence is more suggested than shown, as most of the film takes place indoors, in strange, oppressive sets: a night club whose manager's office is a glass cage from which huge Francis L. Sullivan rules over a microcosm of evil and corruption, a seedy gymnasium where two wrestlers grapple to death, a barge on the Thames. The pace of the film is keyed to the hectic activities of its pathetic hero— splendidly portrayed by Richard Widmark in what must be the best performance of his career—as he runs breathlessly from one con job to another, chasing rainbows in gutters, dreaming up crazy schemes that he almost succeeds in making sound convincing through the sheer power of his manic enthusiasm. Another moving—and prophetic— character in this unforgettable film is the aging champion who has remained faithful to the noble practice of Greco-Roman wrestling and bemoans the commercialization of his art. It was an unexpected clue to Dassin's future attraction to Greece and classicism, an attraction he might have done well to resist.

Unlike Joseph Losey's European films, which, while outwardly very different from his Hollywood efforts, still express attitudes that are distinctly traceable to the earlier period, Dassin's European films display very little relation, in subject matter, style, or outlook, to his American work. *Rififi,* an overpraised quickie, which Dassin himself dismisses ("I was ashamed of *Rififi,"* he told an interviewer in 1966. "I threw it together in a couple of days to make some quick money.") retained some connection to his former films and to the American thriller in general, if only by virtue of its story and treatment; it was, after all, deliberately patterned after Huston's *The Asphalt Jungle.* As for the rest—including *Uptight*—it boils down to an all too familiar case of inflated ambitions and depleted inspiration.

---

13. *Brian DePalma* (1940)

---

by MICHAEL HENRY *(translated from the French by Jean-Pierre Coursodon)*

1968—*Murder a la Mod; Greetings;* 1969—(1964–66) *The Wedding Party;* 1970—*Hi, Mom!;* 1972— *Get To Know Your Rabbit;* 1973—*Sisters;* 1974—*Phantom of the Paradise;* 1976—*Obsession; Carrie;* 1978—*The Fury;* 1979—*Home Movies;* 1980—*Dressed to Kill;* 1981—*Blow Out;* 1983—*Scarface*

Miscellaneous

1970—*Dionysus in '69;* DePalma shared the camera and editing credit (no director was specifically credited) on this film version of a stage production directed by Richard Schechner.

At the risk of bringing grist to the mill of those who dismiss him as a mere virtuoso given to empty stylistic exercises, Brian DePalma will readily admit that he selects material for its visual potential. Undeniably, constructing his trompe l'oeil, fitting their pieces together, polishing their mechanism sometimes engages his attention more than does credibility or the emotions of the characters caught up in their complex machinery. When discussing his early films, he is more anxious to justify their formal experiments than to comment on their relation to the troubled social and political context in which they were made and which they reflect. Is he too much of a tinkerer—no matter how clever and brilliant—to be taken seriously?

Unlike Martin Scorsese, DePalma belongs to a breed of artists who do not create to express themselves but express themselves to create. His primary interest lies in the handling of signs and figures, in subverting codes and their conventions, in the dialectics of objective and subjective shots, in the intricate alchemy through which fiction comes into existence. Deliberately opting for illusionism, he seems to have set out, from his earliest efforts on, to inventory all the resources of filmic rhetoric. From the juvenile patchwork of *The Wedding Party* to the elaborate architecture of *Carrie,* he has methodically investigated the expressive powers of the language. His direction shapes his material rather than serves it. Far from striving for invisibility, it keeps ostentatiously calling attention to itself, reminding us that there is no such thing as an innocent image. Each shot reveals the presence—the omnipresence—of the taskmaster. In that respect DePalma is, after Stanley Kubrick, one of the few American directors of his generation to carry on the demiurgic ambition of German expressionism. Indeed, the emphasis, throughout his work, on the theme of the double suggests the influence of the German school as much as that of the Anglo-Saxon gothic tradition. Lang, Murnau, and later Hitchcock taught him that the theme lent itself better than any other to specular games.

However, the critics' excessive attention to the referential aspect of DePalma's films—his avowed debt to Hitchcock—tends to obfuscate the fact that his work has a coherence all of its own. What his films deal with essentially, and systematically, is cinema itself. There lies their limitation, no doubt, but it would be unfair not to acknowledge their deliberately experimental purpose. Cinema is the stuff his fictions are made of. Voyeurism, magic, hypnotism, paramnesia, telekinesis, telepathy to mention a few of his dramatic devices, may be seen as so many manifestations of mise-en-scène, so many modes of the director's gaze upon himself as he relentlessly assesses, questions, and reflects his own personality. The medium is the film maker's double, his alter ego. Countless correspondences, exchanges, and metaphors link his eye and the camera's, the director's inner gaze and the camera's electronic gaze, the mental images that go through the clairvoyant's mind and the shams devised by the film maker's mise-en-scène.

DePalma's predilection for freaks—whether, in the literal sense, the monsters of *Sisters, Phantom of the Paradise,* and *Carrie,* or the dropouts and marginal types who people his early New York chronicles—is easy to account for; whether they inspire contempt, disgust, or mere curiosity, these norm-defying beings make a *spectacle* of themselves. Their very monstrosity condemns them to schizoid existence—which is just what Swan seems to be reminding Winslow in *Phantom of the Paradise* when he tears off his mask and forces him to look at his disfigured face in the Paradise's hall of mirrors. Miss Collins does exactly the same thing, though with the best intentions, when she pushes Carrie in front of a mirror to shame her with her pitiful appearance. In a dramatic world ruled by deception, *looking* is bound to occupy a central position. The heroine's bizarre fate in *Murder à la Mod,* DePalma's second feature, is hardly surprising. In a studio specializing in stag movies, her eye is stabbed, first "for fun," with a trick ice pick wielded by a prankster member of the cast, then for real after all the lights suddenly go out. The killing, which has thus been staged before being actually perpetrated, is then reenacted by three witnesses, each of whom gives his own version of the events. Although DePalma now disowns the eccentric excesses of his early works, the unlikely encounter of the eye and the ice pick on a movie set, with its combining of two obsessional motifs of the later films, cannot fail to take on a symbolic value.

One may see *Hi, Mom!* as the director's esthetic manifesto. Throughout this series of scenes of bohemian life in New York City, DePalma is less concerned with capturing the mood of the times or recording the aspirations of the counterculture, than with mocking the naive pretentions of cinema verité. Like Jim McBride in his *David Holzman's Diary,* he ridicules the fashion of "cameras stalking reality" as a degree zero of film language whose ultimate expression turns out to be pornography, preferably recorded by an invisible cinematographer. The hero (Robert De Niro), an inveterate voyeur, passes himself off as a film maker to a small-time porn producer but, failing miserably, is soon reduced to being his own star. He seduces a girl who lives in the apartment building next door, so that he can train his camera on her window and film their lovemaking. It is also tempting to see *Hi, Mom!* as an early version of *Taxi Driver.* Like De Niro's Travis Bickle in Scorsese's film, Jon Rubin is a Vietnam veteran, endlessly walks the streets of Manhattan, tries to forget his loneliness in movie houses and, after suffering all the frustrations of modern city life, "frees" himself in an outburst of terrorist violence. The two characters differ only in the nature of their obsession; Travis is into firearms, Jon into optical equipment.

Already, in the earlier *Greetings,* the same Jon Rubin, when interviewed by a television reporter in a Vietnam rice paddy, had hit upon the inspiration of attempting to rape a Vietnamese girl in order to attract attention. In *Hi, Mom!,* after blowing up his apartment building, he parades in combat uniform before TV cameras and decries the anarchy and violence that undermine the moral fiber of the country's youth, throwing in a totally irrelevant, "Hi, Mom!" In the ultimate turnabout, he poses as the all-American nice boy, in front of real cameras, at last paid attention to by a whole nation. To a nation of voyeurs, DePalma hands a grotesque mirror. It is to be noted that all the individuals De Niro snoops on are engaged in the same kind of activity as he; he catches them photographing, filming, or recording themselves, or watching television . . . From the zoom to the telephoto lens, *Hi, Mom!* reviews—and if need be demonstrates—all the gadgets intended to expand the scope of our vision. They were to be used again in later films, as we know, not only by DePalma, but by those of his creatures to whom he would occasionally delegate some of his privileges for the duration of a picture.

DePalma considerably broadened his range when he detached himself from his New York environment, but he never lost his taste for constructions *en abyme.** *Get*

* A French critical term, of heraldic origin (shield within a shield), used to designate such self-referential devices in works of art as a novel-within-a-novel, a film-within-a-film, etc. [Translator's note.]

to Know Your Rabbit, his initial, and unhappy, experience with a major studio, introduced the first of a series of manipulators with occult or parapsychological powers over other characters. An onlooker, rather than a voyeur, the manipulator now appears as the hero's nemesis. This paranoia found its definitive expression in the allegory of *Phantom of the Paradise,* in which Swan is implicitly introduced as a demiurge—his manager, when addressing him, looks straight into the camera; only Swan's white gloves are seen in the lower portion of the frame, and his voice comes to us from a space out of camera range. Swan is the Dr. Mabuse of rock concerts. Thanks to his closed-circuit video system, he enjoys the ubiquity and omnipotence of a demigod and toys with destinies the way one pulls puppets' strings. Through the ironclad contracts he forces upon composers and performers alike, he secures for himself the rights to all their work. The imagery of the vampire naturally imposes itself, as when the "Phantom," plugged into a console, breathes the notes of his cantata so that Swan can mix, filter, modulate, and rebuild his broken voice. When Winslow rebels, he turns the tables on his tormentor by using the very weapons that served the latter so well. He actually takes over the direction of the show by training the spotlights on Phoenix, then giving the audience an unexpected added attraction: Beef's transformation into a human torch. Swan at that point is revealed to be vulnerable, because he, too, is under contract. Winslow challenges his power at the precise moment when Swan comes on stage for the first time and thus can be unmasked and exposed by the Phantom. Equal at last in their monstrosity, the tormentor and his victim form an inseparable couple, and it is fitting that they should die side by side in the limelight, amidst the applause of mystified fans.

Phantom of the Paradise insistently suggested an identity between the record business and the film industry, and DePalma was probably settling some very personal accounts. *Sisters* and *Obsession,* less literal or explicit, carefully describe the progress of a mise-en-scène at the second degree. In *Sisters,* Grace, the newspaper reporter who investigates the murder she has witnessed, is herself not as innocent as it might seem. Her investigation becomes an obsession, and she closes in on the murderous Danielle and her psychiatrist-protector, Emil—another "monstrous" couple—with an increasingly morbid fascination, even imitating James Stewart in *Rear Window,* when she follows the search of the suspect apartment through binoculars from her own window. Taking justice in one's own hands and prying into the realm of madness both have their risks, however. Grace's snooping soon triggers a response from the psychiatrist, who manages to pass her off as one of his own patients and proceeds to brainwash her, removing the mental traces of the murder from her mind, just as he had earlier removed its tangible traces from the apartment. Like Swan, he will eventually be killed by the creature (Danielle/Dominique) he kept in his power, but his mise-en-scène will be perpetuated by Grace herself, the secret remaining forever buried in her subconscious.

In *Obsession,* Michael Courtland is twice the victim, over a fifteen-year period, of his partner's machinations to cheat him of his shares in their real-estate business. La Salle's scheme boils down to a sordid swindle, but it involves such a shrewd and meticulous reconstruction that it produces the illusion of déjà vu in the victim. As in *Vertigo,* the second act of the plot is a "remake" of the first, with Courtland's daughter Sandra taking over from her mother in the principal role. Whereas Danielle in *Sisters* seemed in more ways than one doomed to a split personality (as a Siamese twin but also as an advertising model), this doesn't at first appear to be the case for Courtland—although the point is made that he is regarded as a dreamer and artist in his trade.

He cares so little about his financial interests that his partner has no trouble securing the collaboration of a psychiatrist. In the opening scene, La Salle, in his toast to his "friend" remarks that Courtland combines the manners of the Old South and the dynamism of the New South. The hero is like New Orleans and Florence, those twin, dual cities in which past and present coexist without ever blending. He is also partly responsible for his own predicament. As a result of his willingness to go along with the police stratagem to deceive the kidnappers of his wife and daughter (a phony ransom payment), he will be constantly suspected of duplicity. Fifteen years after the wife dies in the misbegotten rescue attempt, he is also betrayed by the daughter he had lost on the same occasion.

It would be somewhat inaccurate to call *Carrie* a *"film fantastique."* DePalma's adaptation of Stephen King's novel deliberately stripped the story of its supernatural dimension, discarding the more bizarre manifestations of the fundamentalist mystique represented by the character of Carrie's mother, whom he pushed into the background to focus on the episode of the prom. There are no longer any apocalyptic prophecies but rather a fairy tale that turns to nightmare when Cinderella herself is revealed to be a monster. Two opposite but symmetrical mises-en-scène bring about Carrie's "mutation": Sue's—the good girl who talks her boyfriend into playing Prince Charming for a night—and Chris's—the bad girl whose perverse imagination dreams up a most loathsome hoax. These two mises-en-scène themselves reflect their victim's twofold attraction—toward heaven (the prom promises "love among the stars") and hell (the vengeful graffiti of the epilogue, "Carrie White burns in hell"). To defend herself, as well as to take revenge, Carrie only has her "powers"—the origin of which is deliberately left undisclosed. Ultimately, DePalma is only interested in the gaze through which those telekinetic powers are exercised. Whether Carrie upsets an ashtray, throws a brat off his bike, or literally blasts her mother, the camera always adopts her point of view, the lens substituting for her eye. On the other hand, the long sequence of the senior prom derives its dramatic impact from the multiplicity of points of view. The entire student body is involved, and everyone is part of a spectacle. We see the look in Carrie's tear-filled eyes as she poses for the photographers, the vicious look in Chris's eyes as she crouches under the stage, ready to pull on the string, the intent gaze of the gathered audience, anxiously awaiting something exceptional to happen. Then, after a series of shots that involve the spectator himself as the suspense is being stretched out—we discover the props set up for the practical joke—yet another point of view is introduced, Sue's, as she realizes what is afoot and is therefore in a position to do something to prevent the deed. This slow crescendo climaxes with an extreme close-up of Chris's flaming eye as she makes the fateful gesture. After the tragedy, Chris will again try to destroy Carrie, an attempt whose futility is suggested by a nice internal rhyme, the extreme close-up, of Carrie's eye, this time, occupying the screen for a split second before the car swerves off the road and crashes.

Every film maker instinctively knows that the integrity of the image is a guarantee of objectivity to the spectator. DePalma seems to enjoy questioning this illusion right after creating it. In *Carrie,* again, although this is the most linear of his narratives, he uses several minutes of split screen for the heroine's revenge. His predilection for the device is due to the fact that it allows him to include the gaze and its object in the same frame. As in *Phantom of the Paradise* (Winslow sabotaging the Beach Bums performance), a character who had been long deceived relishes her revenge and gloats over the destruction she has wrought. In *Sisters,* the split-screen sequence is a literal translation of the film's subject; it not only mirrors the identity transfer effected between the Siamese twins on the operating table but also anticipates Grace's later identification with them.

A related device regularly used by DePalma is the screen-within-the-screen, from *Greetings,* which opens and closes on a televised speech by President Johnson ("We never had it so good") to *Carrie,* in which the finale of *Duel at Diablo* can be glimpsed on a television screen. It is, again, in *Sisters,* that the relationships between the two levels of representation are most complex. The film opens with a television game show called "Peeping Toms," in which the two protagonists are contestants. The theme: Will the black publicist, coming upon a blind girl disrobing, look away or stare? At this point, the camera discloses that this is indeed a "show" by introducing the audience. As the story unfolds, after the game show, the game is reenacted in reality, but with its terms inverted; a seemingly willing Danielle allows her partner to undress her but stabs him blind after they have made love.

In *Hi, Mom!,* Jon auditions for and gets the part of a fascistic cop in a show called *Be Black, Baby!,* but it is on a black-and-white TV screen that we watch, as he does, the performance of the play, a confrontation of white liberals and black revolutionaries. DePalma in this case was able to dispense with split-screen techniques, as the high-rise's bay windows become so many miniscreens on which half a dozen different skits unfold. This trompe l'oeil set even allows him to repeat one of *Sherlock, Jr.'s* most famous gags: De Niro falls asleep while filming and dreams that he enters the field of the camera to give Jennifer Salt some flowers.

DePalma occasionally performs his manipulations on the very texture of the image. Adopting the collage techniques dear to pop art, he inserts heterogeneous elements that create a distancing effect. No fewer than three different types of film are used in *Hi, Mom!:* a 16-mm color home movie, the 16-mm black-and-white of the National Intellectual Television Journal, and the scraps of porn footage shot by Jon Rubin. The videotape the journalist finds in *Life* magazine's archives (*Sisters*) outwardly looks like a piece of scientific reporting, yet the actors of the primary fiction can briefly be glimpsed in it. Although Grace's nightmare is not given as "real," it is visualized in black-and-white shots whose grain and format are the same as those of said documentary. The unconscious so easily mixes "reality" and its representations that all the people Grace came across in the course of her investigation play a part in it, indeed a double part, since each of them is—inevitably—accompanied by a double. In *Phantom,* the videotape works even more explicitly as a *mise en abyme.* Swan's dialogue with his satanic double reveals that he owes his eternal youth to the film itself ("When it goes, you go"). All Winslow has to do is to destroy the film in order to return the demiurge to his mortal condition. Nothing could better suggest the vanity of the shadowplay master's sham.

These are only some of the more obvious, or more "perverse" devices of DePalma's style, but his directing calls our attention to itself through numerous other "manipulations"—wide-angle shots, tilted setups, slow motion, speeding up, kaleidoscopic effects, etc. DePalma's cinema is saturated with tropes that distinguish it from common film language—rhetoric is the basis of his poetics. Does this mean that technique and know-how are all there is to his style? On the contrary, he is trying to reach a perfect harmony of vision and expression. As for his borrowings from Hitchcock, one should note that the very theme of "borrowing" has provided DePalma with some of his most telling metaphors, from *Phantom,* in which Swan appropriates Winslow's cantata, to *Carrie,* in which Tommy Ross copies a poem and passes it off as his own—the theme is always associated with the concept of mise-en-scène. It is present again in

Obsession, in the exemplary form of a palimpsest. In San Miniato church, Genevieve Bujold explains that a flood led to the discovery of a primitive underneath a famous Renaissance fresco. Should the masterpiece be destroyed to restore the original? she asks, to which Cliff Robertson replies, "Beauty should be protected." In the emotional context of the scene, this may be taken as a warning; Courtland is about to fall in love with Sandra, but through her, it is his love for her mother, Elizabeth, that he will attempt to revive. Will he sacrifice Sandra to her double, which is a mere shadow? Let us venture another interpretation. Since the primitive work that *Obsession* reproduces is Hitchcock's *Vertigo,* DePalma is asking his critics to judge an artist on the evidence of his work. What counts is the text itself, the live, reincarnated text the film maker gives us today.

Unfortunately, DePalma's pictures since *Carrie* have tended to repeat themes and devices mechanically, rather than expand or enrich his vision. Thus, *The Fury* borrows all its motifs and tricks from earlier films but merely paraphrases them in an inflated manner. The telekinetic Robin and Gillian are "monsters," although innocent ones, isolated because of their difference, and doomed to become the victims of a "manipulator" who hopes to channel their untapped mental gifts to his own profit. Childress (John Cassavetes) is the new avatar of the evil figures played by John Astin (*Get to Know Your Rabbit*), Paul Williams (*Phantom*), William Finley (*Sisters*), and John Lithgow (*Obsession*). The narrative derives its dynamic from an eminently *visual* conflict, which opposes two modes of vision, the clairvoyant's and his master's, the latter based on audiovisual technology. Only the rebellion of the manipulated creature (a spectacularly destructive one) can foil the manipulator's mise-en-scène. Childress's crimes are logically sanctioned by his losing his eyesight; by kissing his eyes, Gillian draws tears of blood from them, thus keeping him under her power until she disintegrates him.

Onto this thoroughly familiar pattern, DePalma grafted equally familiar motifs, such as that of the "psychic twins," which he had so brilliantly handled in *Sisters.* The symmetrical destinies of the two "monsters" gradually converge, until Kirk Douglas has to exclaim: "like twins!" The two sister souls are so much in tune that one can mentally visualize fragments of the other's past, and Robin is even able to transfer his own powers to Gillian before dying—a transfer that takes place the first and only time they look at each other. The theme of paramnesia, on which the structure of *Obsession* relied, is also illustrated, when Robin, being used as a guinea pig, is forced to watch the commando film and to relive the traumatic scene he had actually once witnessed.

The coherence of DePalma's vision is undeniable, but these endless thematic variations can only lead to repetitiousness. He is so involved in his conjuring tricks that he forgets to impart some life to his characters; he grants them too little autonomy for us to become involved. This lack of sympathy is blatant in Kirk Douglas's scenes. The father's ordeal in his quest for his son should engage our emotions. Instead, DePalma ridicules him, putting him through wryly humorous skits that wouldn't have been out of place in *Hi, Mom!* or *Greetings* but are decidely unseemly in this dramatic context. Paradoxically, DePalma piles up "distancing" effects at the very moment he would have the audience identify with the character, and the result is numbing. DePalma's insensitivity, which partakes of the scientist's coldness, is apparent in the "biofeedback training" sequence, in which we are urged, through Gillian, to empty our minds: "Imagine that you are in front of a blank movie screen. . . ."

Home Movies is to the first part of DePalma's career what *Fury* is to the second part, a thematic and stylistic catalogue whose figures are essentially referential. By refurbishing an old, vaguely autobiographical project permeated with the oddball humor popular on campuses in the late sixties, he was probably attempting to free himself from the strictures of big production to which he had by then become committed. Although this collective workshop effort (made with DePalma's students at Sarah Lawrence, where he himself had made his film debut with *The Wedding Party*) is far from exhibiting the brilliance of DePalma's early films, the master's hand in it is unmistakeable. (He claims that only "one-twentieth" of the film was shot by his students.) As in *Greetings* and *Hi, Mom!*, various film sizes and types are mixed. The "star therapy" classes (16-mm) and the young protagonist's film diary (super-8) are inserted within a surrealistic comedy of manners that constitutes the body of the film (35-mm). As in the earlier films, the characters are defined in terms of their relationship to vision and its powers. Kirk Douglas, who is constantly directing himself, keeps cameras, microphones, and spotlights trained on his own person. Keith Gordon, his disciple, ashamed of being "an extra in his own life," records every detail of it in order to reach the higher status of filmic creature. The characters in the main narrative (all equipped with outrageous, ridiculous quirks) are placed in a voyeur's position when they don't make a spectacle of themselves.

"The camera never lies!" exclaims Kirk Douglas, the manipulator intruding upon his students' fictions (does he stand for the director himself, imposing his will upon inexperienced collaborators?).

In *Dressed to Kill*, it is the fiction itself that is the product of a collage, since it refers in turn to *Psycho* and to *Sisters* or even to *Psycho through Sisters*. The tribulations of Kate, the unfulfilled wife (Angie Dickinson) obviously borrow from Hitchcock, with the disciple spelling out what was merely suggested by the master: rape fantasies, the fascination of illicit affairs, the equating, through juxtaposition, of sexual pleasure and dying. The ironic use of the split screen emphasizes Kate's degradation as she goes from one Freudian bungled action to the next, losing first her glove, then her panties, and finally her wedding ring. Erotic transgression is twice sanctioned, first in a grotesque mode (Kate comes across a medical report revealing that her sex partner has VD), then tragically, when she is murdered with the very same object—a razor—which she had identified with the phallus in her earlier bathroom fantasy. On the other hand, the young prostitute's investigation, which constitutes the other portion of the narrative, borrows from the newspaper reporter's investigation in *Sisters*. Like Grace, Liz (Nancy Allen), first a passive witness to a murder, becomes the focus of the dramatic action; like her, she enters the realm of madness to bait and unmask a perverted psychiatrist. Also as in *Sisters*, there are uncanny correspondences between the two heroines. Kate's sexual frustration is echoed by Liz's nymphomania, and the latter becomes so identified with the former that she will eventually share her rape/murder fantasy in the shower.

Nothing much is new, then, in DePalma's theater of the unconscious, except that the theme of the double is justified this time by the "monster's" bisexuality; torn between two contradictory urges the psychiatrist, Dr. Elliott, has made up a fictitious patient, his murderous twin, who, as Bobby, leaves messages ("I feel like a woman in a man's body") on his answering machine and dresses up as a phallic mother to eradicate the feminity Elliott is unable to assume. These mirror effects culminate in the sequence in which Elliott watches a television program on transsexuals. The televised image simultaneously appears in both spaces brought together by the split-screen technique—the "masculine" space, represented by the doctor's office, and the "feminine" space in which Liz is seen applying makeup. As could be expected, DePalma uses yet another mirror effect to disclose the doctor's secret; when Liz comes to "consult" him and makes an even bolder pass than Kate had by starting to strip, the camera catches the reflection of Michael Caine's face in the mirror placed on his table—which foreshadows the final metamorphosis to take place in the next scene. Pushing the thematic overkill to the verge of caricature, DePalma does not hesitate to jazz up the episode even more with the introduction—for the sheer pleasure of confusing us—of a new "double," who turns out to be a providential lady cop with the same general appearance and blond hair as "Bobby."

Another familiar DePalma figure, the wiz kid—out of *Home Movies*—is used again, in a peripheral part, in *Dressed to Kill.* This time Keith Gordon, as Angie Dickinson's son, comes up with his own version of the candid camera to film Dr. Elliott's patients coming in and out of his building. This "positive" character takes center stage as John Travolta's Jack Terry in *Blow Out.* Terry, a sound technician, is of all of DePalma's protagonists the one most easy to identify with the director—which a number of autobiographical references encourage us to do. The action takes place in Philadelphia, DePalma's hometown. Like him, Jack has a background in cybernetics and has won several awards in scientific competitions. Jack's involvement with the narcotics division enables DePalma to put to use the preproduction work he had done on *Prince of the City* before the project was taken over by Sidney Lumet. Finally, Jack's activity in the story duplicates that of his creator, as he reconstructs, frame by frame, the film of the accident, synchronizing the photographs from *Newsweek* to the sounds he recorded on the bridge.

The prologue and epilogue suggest an even closer identification. Jack happens to work on the technical crew of an exploitation movie that owes much to DePalma's own films. The murderer's subjective-camera wanderings, the cavorting college girls caught in their intimacy, the murder in the shower are references to, respectively, *Phantom of the Paradise, Carrie,* and *Dressed to Kill.* While the producing company, Independence Pictures, is reminiscent of the sleazy outfit for which De Niro made porn films in *Hi, Mom!,* it also hints at DePalma's debuts in independent production. Should this deliberately parodistic opening be construed as a healthy questioning by DePalma of the very kind of cinema he has helped develop? And should the last scene, in which Jack delivers the first hardcore horror film, be seen as a condemnation of the tendency to overkill, which is the corollary of his taste for experiment? Doesn't the pursuit of effect for its own sake ultimately lead to precisely this extreme degree of the obscene?

The fact is, unfortunately, that the body of the narrative uses the same rhetoric and caters to the same crude instincts as the film-within-the-film. The political element, barely suggested, is immediately spirited away in favor of a preposterous plot that refurbishes the worst puritanical fantasies from *Dressed to Kill.* Again, the spectator is systematically encouraged to indulge his voyeurism, especially in the scenes that do not involve the hero; Burke's murders, for example, are described with an abundance of leering, misogynous details (a prostitute, expert at fellatio, is punished, with the same kind of "poetic" justice as Angie Dickinson, by strangulation). When it is not thwarted by these shifts in point of view, the emotion that the relationship between John Travolta and Nancy Allen might generate is destroyed by the excesses of DePalma's orchestration—thus such purely spectacular set pieces as the truck's race through a parade or the final fireworks. Jack's paranoia alone seems authentic. It is the paranoia of a man who sees his work threatened, then destroyed, by an unseen hand. The discovery of the ransacked auditorium in which all the tapes have been erased is filmed in one of those 360-degree panning shots that DePalma usually saves for emotional climaxes, such as Cliff Robertson's and Genevieve Bujold's reunion at the end of

Obsession or Sissy Spacek's lyrical waltz with William Katz in *Carrie*. To DePalma, there is no worse disaster than the destruction of one's work; it seems to affect him much more than his protagonists' fates or the future of his country. One could not be more unconcerned by the "humanistic" preoccupations expressed in such films as *The Parallax View* or *Three Days of the Condor*, which belong to a fairly similar type of fiction.

One must note, finally, DePalma's tendency to shift identification in mid-film. Does he want the spectator to recognize himself in the murderer, after being made to identify with the hero? Or is it for the sheer directorial excitement he derives from it that he projects himself first through Jack, the investigator attempting to find the truth, then through his opposite, the psychopath who betrays his backers to give free rein to his fantasies? Indeed, the two characters ultimately become one—literally (in the final struggle, Jack turns Burke's knife against him) and metaphorically (Sally dies a second time when Jack picks up her dying scream on the sound track). Jack's microphone and Burke's ice pick are the inseparable emblems of a work in which the compulsion to see and hear has always been associated with death. After this attempt at exorcism, which rehashes most of DePalma's obsessions, one would like to see him take a drastically new direction.

14. Edward Dmytryk (1908)

1935—*The Hawk;* 1939—*Television Spy;* 1940—*Emergency Squad; Golden Gloves; Mystery Sea Raider; Her First Romance;* 1941—*The Devil Commands; Under Age; Sweetheart of the Campus; The Blonde From Singapore; Secrets of the Lone Wolf; Confessions of Boston Blackie; Counter-Espionage;* 1943—*Seven Miles From Alcatraz; Hitler's Children; The Falcon Strikes Back; Captive Wild Woman; Behind the Rising Sun; Tender Comrade;* 1944—*Murder, My Sweet;* 1945—*Back to Bataan; Cornered;* 1946— *Till the End of Time;* 1947—*So Well Remembered* (Great Britain; U.S., 1947); *Crossfire;* 1949— *Obsession* (Great Britain; U.S., *The Hidden Room,* 1949); *Give Us This Day* (Great Britain; U.S., *Salt to the Devil,* 1950); 1952—*Mutiny; The Sniper; Eight Iron Men;* 1953—*The Juggler; Broken Lance;* 1954—*The Caine Mutiny;* 1955—*The End of the Affair* (Great Britain; U.S., 1955); *Soldier of Fortune; The Left Hand of God;* 1956—*The Mountain;* 1957—*Raintree County;* 1958—*The Young Lions;* 1959—*Warlock; The Blue Angel;* 1962—*Walk on the Wild Side; The Reluctant Saint;* 1964— *The Carpetbaggers; Where Love Has Gone;* 1965—*Mirage;* 1966—*Alvarez Kelly;* 1968—*Anzio; Shalako;* 1972—*Barbe-Bleue* (France; U.S., *Bluebeard,* 1972)

Uncredited
1939—*Million Dollar Legs* (Nick Grinde)

There is a gloomy, neurotic streak to most of Dmytryk's films, particularly his more personal and memorable ones. His characters are often misanthropes, misogynists, cynics and self-haters, bent upon destroying themselves as much as others, haunted by guilt feelings and obsessive memories. This latter trait seems to have grown in importance at the time of Dmytryk's clash with the House Un-American Activities Committee and his eventual recantation of his Communist past before them. Perhaps as a form of vicarious self-punishment, he introduced into his films scenes in which characters mutilated themselves to assuage their guilty consciences: the hero of *Give Us This Day* impales his hand on the spike of an iron railing; the psychopathic killer of *The Sniper* burns *his* hand on a stove; much later, others maimed hands were to turn up in *Warlock* and *Alvarez Kelly*. But it is safe to say that the HUAC trauma, if it did foster Dmytryk's neurotic dispositions, did not create them, as they can be traced almost to his earliest works. Sado-masochism, for instance, which is rampant in *The Hidden Room* and *The Sniper*, was already a dominant feature in *Murder, My Sweet* and *Cornered* and even in some of his earlier "B" movies.

Dmytryk did toil obscurely for quite some time in the late thirties and early forties before gaining recognition. Prior to becoming a director in 1939, he had worked his way up through various lowly studio jobs. The son of Ukrainian immigrants who had first settled in Canada but moved to Los Angeles when he was a young child, Dmytryk was employed as a messenger and projectionist at the Paramount studios while still in high school. He later dropped out of Cal Tech, where he had taken up physics as his major, to rejoin Paramount, this time as a full-time projectionist. He subsequently worked in the studio's editing department, became an assistant cutter, then, in 1930, chief editor, a position he retained through the thirties. (Among his assignments were *The Royal Family of Broadway, Ruggles of Red Gap,* and *Zaza*). His first crack at directing, *The Hawk,* was an independently produced, privately financed Western, but his directorial career was launched for good only four years later, when, after reportedly salvaging the floundering *Million Dollar Legs* (a college comedy starring Betty Grable, *not* a remake of the W. C. Fields classic), he was offered a contract as a "B" director by his Paramount employers. Of his four Paramount efforts, at least one, *The Golden Gloves,* enjoys a small reputation as a somewhat above-average prize-fighting yarn. Dmytryk went on to Columbia for more "B"s, then to RKO, where he got a chance to handle a subject both topical and unusual (although still on a "B" level) with *Hitler's Children,* a melodramatic but gripping account of the impact of nazism on German youth. (Dmytryk took over the film's direction from Irving Reis.) *Hitler's Children* attracted critical attention and proved an unexpected box-office success, which led to a seven-year contract and Dmytryk's promotion to "A" pictures. The first of these was *Tender Comrade,* a topical, girls-on-the-homefront tearjerker written by Dalton Trumbo, who disliked the film. (He has stated that he intended to polish the script and particularly whittle down a long, sentimental Ginger Rogers speech at the end; but the film was rushed into production.) After *Tender Comrade* was made, Dmytryk entered a fruitful association with writer-turned-producer Adrian Scott and screenwriter John Paxton, who were to be his collaborators on his best films of the forties.

The team's first venture was *Murder, My Sweet,* an adaptation of Raymond Chandler's Philip Marlowe mystery, *Farewell My Lovely,* which, curiously, had already been filmed by RKO two years earlier as an entry in the *Falcon* series starring George Sanders. Dmytryk's revamping of the vehicle was tantamount to a statement of rejection of the "B" esthetics and adoption of an "A" (for arty) style of directing. Certainly, *Murder, My Sweet* must qualify as the most chi-chi of all *films noirs*. It is a cinematographer's field day, a festival of shadows, weird angles, and nightmarish special effects for a sequence in which the hero—who gets roughed up every other reel or so—

hallucinates after being knocked down and drugged. Typical of Dmytryk's visual overindulgence is one scene at a beach house at night, in which he has Claire Trevor walk around the living room switching lights on and off (there is a profusion of low lamps with heavy shades, that unavoidable trademark of *film noir*) for no other purpose than showing off a variety of eerily lit setups. Much of this trickery is fairly enjoyable, but it never amounts to anything that could be called style, and whenever the straining for effect relaxes, we are left gazing at wooden acting made worse by unimaginative two-shots or over-the-shoulder setups.

Dmytryk's direction of *Cornered,* however, is straightforwardly nondescript from start to finish. A strangely unsuspenseful thriller about a Canadian airman tracking down the Nazi killer of his French wife, the film has the look and style of an average "B" (skimpy sets, flat lighting, stereotyped characterization, and poor acting, with the notable exception of Walter Slezak, who is also given the script's only good lines of dialogue), and its reputation as one of Dmytryk's best films is an absolute puzzle. The script's disregard for verisimilitude occasionally reaches surrealistic proportions. Thus Dick Powell, too restless to wait for a passport to France, rows across the English Channel in a tiny boat, sinks the skiff when in view of the French coast, swims ashore, and launches into a relentless investigation before his clothes are dry, immediately stumbling over clues and valuable information conveniently scattered all over the place. He subsequently travels to Marseilles, to Switzerland, and finally to Argentina without apparent difficulty. In Buenos Aires, he runs into an assortment of urbanely menacing characters, and it takes him and the audience the best part of the remaining footage to sort out the good guys from the bad guys in between a few well-meaning speeches about the threat of fascism.

Crossfire, although overrated by most critics (including James Agee, who himself wrote that the film was overrated), is easily the best of the Dmytryk-Paxton-Scott collaborations. The direction, while eschewing the fancy flourishes of *Murder, My Sweet* (except in the opening scene, a fight and murder filmed with low camera angles and weird shadows on the walls), is much more efficient and inventive than in *Cornered.* The pace of its rather complicated action (which takes place over a twenty-four-hour period) never falters. Paxton's dialogue is consistently crisp, sober, and to the point, and there are fine performances from the three Roberts (Young, Ryan, and Mitchum, the latter even more understated than usual) as well as from almost everybody in the cast (especially Paul Kelly in the brief part of Gloria Grahame's neurotic husband). Nevertheless, *Crossfire* would be little more than a well-made thriller whose plot might have been used for one of those "B" quickies Dmytryk had been turning out until a few years before were it not for the one element that earned the film its inflated reputation: the character played by Robert Ryan is anti-Semitic and kills a man for no other reason than that he is a Jew (he had been a homosexual in Richard Brooks's source novel). To say that the film is "about" anti-Semitism, however, is a gross exaggeration. The racist angle is used as a mere gimmick, and anti-Semitism is actually addressed in only one scene (the police captain's sober and quite moving indictment of prejudice). What the film is really concerned with is the machinery of the crime thriller, with its familiar components: the innocent man arrested for murder, his friends' (and wife's) attempts to clear him, the hard-nosed but fair-minded cop investigating the case, his cat-and-mouse playing with the real murderer, whom he suspects without conclusive evidence, and the clever trap he sets for him to expose his guilt. The film even ends with the obligatory scene of the murderer running away after betraying himself and being shot in the back by the detective, a gratuitous killing, incidentally, since the fugitive could easily have been picked up by police massed along the block for that purpose. (Apparently, the authors' liberalism did not extend to indicting such indiscriminate use of firearms by police, for the scene is treated with the same all's-well-that-ends-well lightheartedness as are countless other similar scenes in Hollywood cinema.)

By the time *Crossfire* was released, the country was in the throes of another kind of madness, which resulted in Dmytryk's estrangement from Hollywood for several years. In 1947 he was one of the ten witnesses subpoenaed by HUAC who refused to answer questions concerning their belonging to the Screen Writers Guild and/or the Communist party. The ten were cited for contempt pending trial. The Motion Picture Association then resolved to discharge them without compensation and "not to reemploy any of them until such time as he is acquitted or has purged himself of contempt and declares under oath that he is not a Communist." Dmytryk left for England together with his producer Adrian Scott, also one of the "Ten," and there they made *So Well Remembered* (again written by Paxton), a film about social unrest in a factory town. After the film was completed, Dmytryk returned to the United States and took part in various legal activities and public appearances of the "Hollywood Ten," but he went to England again in the summer of 1948 and stayed about one year, during which he directed *Give Us This Day* and *The Hidden Room*. The latter, also known as *Obsession*, detailed a jealous husband's preparations to trap his rival in a basement, wall him in, and watch him slowly die. *Give Us This Day*, a social-minded study of immigrant construction workers in England, was highly praised by European critics but has not been seen in a long time (it has apparently never been shown on television in the United States), and the dim memory of a couple of salient scenes (a man being buried alive in a concrete mixer and the already mentioned self-mutilation) is certainly not enough to allow one to judge the film.

In mid-1949 Dmytryk was back in the United States, still fighting alongside the other nine "unfriendly" witnesses. The next year, the Supreme Court refused to review their case, and they were subsequently tried, found guilty of contempt, and sentenced to one year or, in Dmytryk's case, six months' imprisonment. While serving his sentence, Dmytryk issued a formal statement denouncing the Communist party. Upon his release, he appeared before HUAC, testified that he had indeed been a party member between 1944 and 1945, and "named" a number of Hollywood people (including fellow directors Herbert Biberman, John Berry, and Jules Dassin) as having been Communists at the time. He thus became infamous among liberals as the only one of the "Ten" who submitted to pressure in order to be able to work again in Hollywood. Shortly after his testimony, he was signed by independent producer Stanley Kramer (who, ironically, had been under suspicion at the time) and for him made what is possibly Dmytryk's best film—and one of the finest Kramer productions—*The Sniper*.

A typical early Kramer, small-budget production with a message, *The Sniper* deals with a disturbed young man driven by a neurotic hatred of women and a compulsion to shoot them at the slightest hint of rejection. It is a brooding, gripping psychological thriller, tightly written by Harry Brown with an ear for everyday speech and a light touch in the handling of sociological overtones, ably acted by Arthur Franz (an actor Dmytryk has used several times) and the entire cast, filmed with efficient realism on San Francisco streets, and visually impressive without any of the *Murder, My Sweet* gimmickry (the shooting of a witness as he climbs a tall factory smokestack is a memorable image). Curiously, attitudes toward women expressed throughout the film by various characters are so matter-of-factly misogynous, or male chauvinistic, that the hero's murderous bent almost seems a logical, if distorted, outgrowth of the ambient ideology. In a grimly ironic scene, society itself provides him with an opportunity to safely act out his hostility as he very successfully tries his hand at a carnival game that consists in hitting a target with a baseball, thus causing a girl seated on a collapsible stool to fall into a pool of water below. As for the film's simple message, a plea for preventive psychiatric treatment of psychotics and sex offenders, it is put across convincingly, without didactic ponderousness; moreover, it appears less banal and more commendable in retrospect after the kind of mindless brutality condoned by Don Siegel in *Dirty Harry,* a much later film on a similar theme.

Dmytryk directed two more pictures for Kramer: *Eight Iron Men* (also written by Brown) and the famous *The Caine Mutiny,* which both esthetically and ideologically might be considered the beginning of the end for him. After appearing to make a case for rebellion against authority gone mad, it performed a neat turnabout and lashed out at the rebels as irresponsible opportunists. Thus Dmytryk could reaffirm his liberal convictions while paying allegiance to the powers that be, all with the excuse of adapting a best-selling novel. His ambition did not extend far beyond this feat of ideological tightrope walking; the film was routinely directed and is mostly remembered today for Humphrey Bogart's Captain Queeg, one of his few histrionic performances and consequently a highly praised one.

After the huge box-office success of *The Caine Mutiny,* Dmytryk found himself promoted to the status of big-time director, with major stars and expensive productions on his hands. Simultaneously, he seemed to relinquish all ambition aside from delivering the product. He directed Bogart (*The Left Hand of God*) and Gable (*Soldier of Fortune*) in some of the more forgettable of their late films and apparently felt no qualms about remaking *The Blue Angel,* a mindless endeavor if there ever was one (although, on a purely physical level, May Britt's frigidly statuesque allure is in a way more effective than Dietrich's still unrefined plumpness in Sternberg's classic), or about butchering Nelson Algren's superb *A Walk on the Wild Side* (the film has little to recommend it other than Saul Bass's credit titles). *Raintree County,* obviously intended by MGM as the *Gone With the Wind* of the fifties, is a rambling, ponderous would-be epic over which Dmytryk failed to exercise much directorial control. Montgomery Clift suffered serious injuries in a car accident during production and had to undergo facial plastic surgery, which may account for the unevenness of his performance, but Elizabeth Taylor's was quite as desultory.

In the mid-sixties, Dmytryk went through a brief Joseph E. Levine-Harold Robbins period that yielded *The Carpetbaggers,* a gallery of pulp-fiction stereotypes flittingly enlivened by some hijinks involving a drunken Carroll Baker, and *Where Love Has Gone,* a dismal tearjerker hardly up to daytime television standards. *Mirage* opened promisingly, but the script soon exhausted the possibilities of the well-worn amnesia gimmick (it also killed off the most interesting character, a private detective played with much verve by Walter Matthau). *Anzio* was one of those almost interchangeable World War II superspectacles of the sixties in which the director's job seemed to consist chiefly in regulating heavy traffic and making sure that explosions went off on cue, a not insignificant task but artistically a limited one (the film was shot simultaneously in an English and an Italian version, the latter directed by Duilio Coletti). Finally, Dmytryk hit rock bottom with *Shalako,* a ludicrous British-made Western bizarrely starring Sean Connery and Brigitte Bardot, which hardly seems to have been directed at all (an "action sequences director" was credited alongside Dmytryk, who may have been overwhelmed by the hopelessness of the project). He did not make another picture until four years later, when he came back with *Bluebeard,* a French-German-

Italian production starring Richard Burton as an Austrian World War I hero turned Nazi and woman killer. The film played down the political angle, grotesquely overdid the horror, and failed to work on any level.

From the shambles of Dmytryk's career since *The Sniper,* one can salvage only a very few titles, among which the flawed but often stirring *The Young Lions,* by far the best of his large-scale productions, expertly adapted from Irwin Shaw's novel by Edward Anhalt—a Kramer associate who had scripted *The Sniper*—with impressive black-and-white CinemaScope photography by Joe MacDonald and fine performances from most of the all-star cast. More surprisingly, a couple of Westerns stand out, although Dmytryk's Westerns always tend to be overlong, overwritten affairs ladden with psychological complications and superfluous plot twists (*Warlock,* for instance, has enough material for three ordinary scripts). *Broken Lance,* a remake of Joseph L. Mankiewicz's *House of Strangers,* worked at least as well as a Western as in its original version, and the brooding quality of *Warlock,* its complex relationships (especially between hired gunman Henry Fonda and Anthony Quinn as his crippled sidekick), and the tension it generates make *Warlock* easily the most satisfying of Dmytryk's pictures since the late fifties.

It is easy to gloat about the collapse of Dmytryk's career in the sixties and to make smug pronouncements about "selling one's soul," but the truth of the matter is that, whatever one may think of Dmytryk's attitude back in 1951, it has very little to do with the diminishing quality of his subsequent films, a decline more reasonably attributable to the normal wear and tear that age and changing times are liable to inflict upon modest talent.

15. Stanley Donen (1925)

1949—*On the Town* (codirector: Gene Kelly); 1951—*Royal Wedding;* 1952—*Love Is Better Than Ever; Singin' in the Rain* (codirector: Gene Kelly); *Fearless Fagan;* 1954—*Give a Girl a Break; Seven Brides for Seven Brothers; Deep in My Heart;* 1955—*It's Always Fair Weather* (codirector: Gene Kelly); 1957—*Funny Face; The Pajama Game* (codirector: George Abbott); *Kiss Them for Me;* 1958—*Indiscreet; Damn Yankees* (codirector: George Abbott); 1960—*Once More With Feeling; Surprise Package;* 1961—*The Grass Is Greener;* 1964—*Charade;* 1966—*Arabesque;* 1967—*Two for the Road; Bedazzled;* 1969—*Staircase;* 1974—*The Little Prince;* 1975—*Lucky Lady;* 1978—*Movie, Movie;* 1980—*Saturn 3*

Uncredited
1955—*Kismet* (Vincente Minnelli)

From the mystery partner in a unique directing team to the full-fledged solo director of a few brilliant musicals in the twilight period of the genre, Stanley Donen barely had the time to make his mark in the field before the field disappeared. But if, in the words of the French poet, he "came too late in too old a world," he showed a remarkable talent for making hay while the sun still shone. In the less than ten years that separate his first (codirected) from his last musical picture, his record outshines anybody else's, including Vincente Minnelli's. When left in the lurch by the demise of the genre, the still young Donen—he was only thirty-seven when he directed his last musical—went through an awkward period of readjustment (the dreary *Surprise Package, Once More With Feeling, The Grass Is Greener*) from which he emerged with a new formula and a couple of highly entertaining if superficial comedy-adventures (*Charade* and *Arabesque*), later followed by two offbeat comedies (*Two for the Road, Bedazzled*) in which he promisingly explored new territories. His output was noticeably dwindling, however, and in the seventies, a wealthy exile enjoying the gracious living of a jet-set environment, he has infrequently returned to the screen with disappointingly miscon-ceived and overproduced ventures. The musicals, however, would more than suffice to secure his reputation.

Any list of the ten best Hollywood musicals of the fifties would have to include *Singin' in the Rain, Seven Brides for Seven Brothers, It's Always Fair Weather, Funny Face,* and *The Pajama Game,* all of which were directed or codirected by Donen. It has been suggested by some critics—with little evidence to support the claim—that Donen was merely Gene Kelly's helping hand in their epoch-making MGM musicals. The next steps in this line of reasoning are to credit codirector George Abbott for the success of *The Pajama Game* (or *Damn Yankees,* if one happens to like the film), then to clinch the matter by dismissing Donen's solo efforts in the musical genre as mediocre. Unfortunately for the anti-Donen critic, a couple of these are generally recognized as outstanding, so that they have to be written off as unaccountable strokes of luck— as if great musicals somehow just happened—or else the skeptic falls back on the "collaboration" theory, dragging in the names of everybody involved in the film in an attempt to deflate the director's contribution. But granted that the Hollywood musical was the most collaborative genre in an essentially collaborative medium, and further granted that Donen is indeed greatly indebted to his various collaborators, it still seems both unfair and absurd to condemn his contribution to the genre for the sake of some dubious critical consistency.

The initial resistance to the notion of Stanley Donen as a major director may be accounted for, in part, by the curious circumstances of his early career. He was, as is well known, a dancer in the chorus of *Pal Joey* on Broadway when he became friendly with Gene Kelly, the star of the show, who was soon to make him his assistant for dance numbers, in which capacity Donen worked on such films as *Anchors Aweigh* and *Cover Girl.* The original idea of *Take Me Out to the Ball Game* was a joint effort by the two men, who staged and directed the film's dance numbers. It would have been excusable to think that Donen owed much, if not everything, to his mentor— which, in a sense, he did—although it should have been obvious, too, that the young man must be doing something right. Arthur Freed himself must have been hesitant about Donen's stature; even after the triumph of *On the Town,* it was only by a fluke that Donen got to direct *Royal Wedding,* his first solo assignment. Rehearsals had started with June Allyson as the female lead opposite Fred Astaire, and Charles Walters was directing; when Allyson became pregnant and bowed out, she was replaced by Judy Garland, and it was Walters' turn to bow out, as he didn't want to work with Garland again. Donen was assigned as his replacement (ironically, Garland was suspended before shooting started and replaced by Jane Powell). Whatever Freed may have thought of Donen's work on *Royal Wedding,* he never entrusted to him alone one of his unit's musicals. Donen directed two mild comedies and a small-budget musical (*Give a Girl a Break*) for other MGM producers, but he never again soloed on an Arthur Freed production. (Freed's was strictly a prestige unit by then, producing only expensive musicals.)

Both *Royal Wedding* and *Give a Girl a Break* are traditional, even retrogressive, musicals if compared to *On the Town* or *Singin' in the Rain,* but they exhibit the same brisk pacing, fluid, elegant camera work, and infectious sense of humor. In *Royal Wedding,* Astaire and Powell play a brother-and-sister act, and most of the song-and-dance numbers are quite unimaginatively set as on-stage performances. Indeed, the opening scene is a production number that could have been lifted from a Ziegfeld revue, with the stars dancing among an army of uniformed chorus boys on an opulent red and gold set, complete with carpeted staircases and candelabra. A Donen musical, however, couldn't help kidding this kind of material, and although the scene is done straight, the film's true spirit is revealed when, in a later sequence, the two give a demonstration of professional ballroom dancing aboard an ocean liner. A rough sea causes the boat to rock and the ballroom floor to tilt, whereupon Astaire starts adjusting to the situation with his customary resourcefulness, fitting the choreography to the weather conditions.

Although *Royal Wedding* contains two excellent solos in the Astaire idiom (a dance in a gym using all the props around and featuring a coat rack as his partner; and his famous dance on the walls and ceiling) as well as one hilarious Astaire-Powell duo, the score is largely forgettable (there is one memorable song, "Too Late Now"), the choreography routine, and the film as a whole more enjoyable for its straight comedy than for its musical material. The premise is gimmicky rather than really imaginative, and the plot is strictly cliché but peppered with gags and incongruous touches. Two lovers have to shout sweet nothings, because their words are drowned by a brass band marching past their window; Powell's suitors get into ritualistic fist fights every time they meet, while she pays no attention whatsoever; twins, one settled in Britain, the other in the States, illustrate the accuracy of the phrase "separated by a common language." It must have been a challenge for the man whose entire career until then had been associated with Gene Kelly to find himself working with Astaire on his first solo directing assignment, and while the result was modest, the collaboration was not an inauspicious forerunner to the two men's reunion seven years later for *Funny Face,* Donen's solo masterpiece.

Give a Girl a Break is the quintessential backstage musical done on a shoestring (an MGM shoestring, that is). Every situation and plot twist is predictable, but the film's unquestioning acceptance of convention is one of its charms. *Give* was one of three small musicals MGM rushed Debbie Reynolds into after the success of *Singin' in the Rain* but still hedging the bet by starring Marge and Gower Champion above her and throwing in Bob Fosse as an added attraction. The latter's duo with Reynolds on a Burton Lane–Ira Gershwin song called "State of Our Union" is one of the film's two highlights, the other being a rooftop dance by the Champions (Gower and Donen collaborated on the film's choreography).

The one failure among Donen's MGM musicals, *Deep in My Heart,* is not exactly a musical but falls into the hybrid and notoriously thankless subgenre of songwriters' life stories, the victim in this case being Sigmund Romberg, portrayed by Jose Ferrer. Donen belonged to the MGM postwar school of musicals that had imposed and generalized the principle of songs and dances integrated to the plot line, a principle that can rarely be applied in a composer's film biography, except at the most pedestrian and unenlightening level of the "and then he wrote" type of narration. Aside from one very funny comedy scene in which Ferrer mimes an entire operetta single-handedly for a group of friends, the only interesting moments in *Deep in My Heart* are numbers performed by guest stars with little or no part in the action proper. Within this limitation, some of them are quite enjoyable, as MGM was unstinting with the guest talent on this production (which may have proved in need of musical boosting at some point along the line). They include a fair solo by Cyd Charisse on "One Alone" (from *Desert Song*); an outstanding dance by Ann Miller to "It"; and a vaudeville-type number by Gene Kelly and his brother Fred (the latter's only screen credit) that is reminiscent of Kelly's and O'Connor's "Fit as a Fiddle" in *Singin' in the Rain.*

Whereas *Royal Wedding, Give a Girl a Break,* and *Deep in My Heart* had been straightforward explorations of genre conventions, *Seven Brides for Seven Brothers* was a highly original experiment—although its originality is quite different from that of the Kelly-Donen pictures. The book (based on Stephen Vincent Benèt's story, "The Sobbin' Women"), score, lyrics, as well as much of the choreography, are distinctly Broadway-ish, yet the film doesn't look or sound at all like a filmed stage play. It is as though screenwriters Albert Hackett and Frances Goodrich (a team whose experience in the genre was largely with traditional musicals, going back to Jeanette MacDonald operettas in the thirties) and composer Gene de Paul and lyricist Johnny Mercer had set out to write a Broadway musical—more or less in the *Oklahoma!* vein—and then switched media and fashioned the material directly for the screen instead. The end result is a picture quite unlike any other Hollywood musical, although it somehow *seems* to fit into a tradition.

Transposing the legend of the Sabine women to the Oregon timberland circa 1850 and blending in some elements from *Snow White and the Seven Dwarfs* was an intriguing conceit but could easily have led to excessive cuteness. While the early scenes make one fear that the pitfall won't be avoided, the film soon comes alive with the sprightly rendition, picked up in turn by various cast members, of a bouncy melody celebrating the return of spring and from then on proceeds with sustained, good-natured (although undoubtedly quite sexist) humor to its stunning climax, a barn-raising dance that turns into a gigantic choreographed fist fight between the abductors and the abductees' brothers. Michael Kidd's choreography and Donen's direction merge in perfect harmony for this hyperactive, endlessly inventive sequence, honing it into a set piece without any equivalent in the history of the musical. It is no surprise that Donen, who went to work on *It's Always Fair Weather* soon after *Seven Brides* was completed but didn't care much for teaming up with Kelly again, was enthusiastic over the prospect of directing Kidd as an actor and dancer in the last of the Kelly-Donen musicals. The semichoreographed free-for-all in the television studio at the end of the film was obviously inspired by the epochal fight in the earlier picture.

It was, ironically, not at MGM but at Paramount that Donen directed his best musical, *Funny Face,* a late masterpiece of the genre. The tie with his alma mater was far from completely severed, however, since *Funny Face* had originally been an MGM project and turned into a sort of home-away-from-home venture. The key link to the Freed unit, aside from the director himself, was producer Roger Edens, who had always been a vital element there both as composer and associate producer. Arrangers Conrad Salinger, Alexander Courage, and Skip Martin, all standbys of the Freed unit (Salinger had orchestrated both *On the Town* and *Singin' in the Rain*) were also brought in from MGM.

Funny Face demonstrates how a fresh, thoroughly original musical could be developed by drawing heavily upon past experience. The film may seem very unlike *Singin' in the Rain,* and understandably so; not only the studio but the screenwriters, composers, lyricists, choreographers, and stars were different; yet even a superficial comparison reveals numerous, surprisingly close similarities between the two pictures. Both used standard songs composed by one songwriting team some twenty years earlier, with a few originals added. (Roger Edens, who had written "Moses" to Comden's and Green's lyrics for *Singin' in the Rain,* wrote three numbers with scenarist Leonard Gershe to supplement the Gershwins' songs for *Funny Face.*) Both films are gentle yet incisive satires of a professional milieu: Hollywood in the late twenties; the contemporary fashion magazine. Both scripts focus on three principals (two females and one male in *Funny Face* instead of the reverse in *Singin' in the Rain*), who perform all the musical numbers either in solos, duos, or trios. Like Kelly in *Rain,* Astaire in *Funny Face* is involved in the professional milieu (as a fashion photographer), while the girl with whom he falls in love is an outsider reluctantly being dragged into the profession. The Audrey Hepburn character looks down upon the fashion world at the beginning of *Funny Face* with the same contempt the Debbie Reynolds character looked down upon the movie world at the beginning of *Rain;* Hepburn's dream of going to Paris to study with a famous philosopher being the counterpart of Reynolds's dream of being an actress on the legitimate stage. The Kay Thompson character in *Funny Face* performs the same function as Donald O'Connor's in *Rain,* that of a wisecracking, morale-boosting sidekick and accomplice to the protagonist (although she is nominally Astaire's boss, whereas O'Connor played a comparatively lowly studio employee). Most of the song-and-dance numbers deal with the same kind of feelings and/or perform the same plot-moving functions as the numbers in *Rain.* Thompson's "Think Pink" expresses a "philosophy" of fashion just as O'Connor's "Make 'em Laugh" expressed a philosophy of show biz. Astaire first conveys his attraction to Hepburn when he sings to her ("Funny Face") in his professional habitat (a dark room), like Kelly expressed his to Reynolds on a sound stage. "Bonjour Paris," performed by the three principals, projects the same optimistic joie de vivre as "Good morning" sung by the trio in *Rain.* "Clap Yo Hands," by Astaire and Thompson, is a comedy duo reminiscent of "Moses" (the lyrics for both numbers involve some semantic/phonetic byplay, and the orchestration—probably Conrad Salinger's—is quite similar for both songs). Astaire bursts out with joyful feeling in the street (although not in the rain) after leaving his girl at night, just as Kelly did in the title number of *Rain.*

Throughout the first half or so of *Funny Face,* one is thrilled by the exhilarating certainty that the miracle of *Singin' in the Rain* has been repeated and that this is going to be a "perfect" musical. From the very opening, after the stylish credit titles have unreeled, Donen shifts into a lightning-swift yet unstrained pace, smoothly blending fine satirical comedy and a series of brilliant numbers. The first sequence—Kay Thompson's high-powered "Think Pink"—wittily encapsulates the ethos of fashion and its silly arbitrariness, while delighting the eye with Richard Avedon's split-screen spreads. The world of fashion clashes with the intellectual world—the film's central theme—when Astaire and his Philistine magazine crew invade a murky Greenwich Village bookstore and confront a tweedy, indignant Audrey Hepburn. Then, after their departure and Astaire's casual kiss to her, comes a magical moment, Hepburn's rendition of "How Long Has This Been Going On?" as she stands on a ladder (another near-quotation from *Singin' in the Rain*), her untrained singing voice lending an unexpected poignancy to the song.

Fashion's voracious consumption of fresh faces, its bold annexation of alien areas in its endless search for novelty are comically illustrated when Thompson, inspired with a new "angle" by Hepburn's very reluctance ("Clothes for the woman who is not interested in clothes!''), lures the unsuspecting girl into her den of frivolous iniquity with a plan to turn her into the season's new modeling sensation. Hepburn's run for cover leads her into Astaire's darkroom, where, unflustered, he proceeds to develop, print, and enlarge a close-up of her face as he sings and casually dances around her in a model of purposefully functional choreography. The film's first half climaxes with the "Bonjour Paris" number, in which Hepburn, Astaire, and Thompson confess, first separately (Donen makes good use of the split screen here), then in unison that, despite their display of jaded indifference, they are "strictly tourists" yielding to the charm of the capital.

After that point, unfortunately, the film loses steam. For one thing, the satire shifts to a realm—the bohemian life of Paris's pseudointellectual underground—with which neither Donen nor, presumably, anyone connected with the film had any familiarity, with the result that the kidding becomes heavy-handed and pointless, a "satire" of something that didn't really exist. The character of the philosopher who turns out to be a slick womanizer—typical Hollywood anti-intellectualism—is uninteresting, and the scenes with him a mere pretext to generate lovers' quarrels. In the second half of the picture, too, a weakness for overprettified cinematography sneaks in, and the spectator is overcome by a surfeit of mistily filtered meadows, swan lakes, and fluttering doves. And then there is the big fashion show, which, unlike the one in *Singin' in the Rain,* is taken very seriously, and in the course of which ugly duckling Hepburn is supposed to be transformed into a striking beauty through the magic of divine dresses and sophisticated makeup and hairdos. The exact opposite occurs, of course, as most of her personality and charm are smothered in what—twenty years later at least—looks like typical haute couture schlock. Thus the film ultimately reneges on its satirical stand to endorse the pretensions and artificiality it had so convincingly debunked in the first part. The real phoniness, it seems to say, is intellectual phoniness, and now that Hepburn has been exposed to it, she will presumably give up her highfalutin notions and become a fashion model for good. Paris does strange things indeed.

It may seem slightly ridiculous to take a "mere" musical comedy to task on ideological grounds, but the film's first half is so good, and promises so much, that it justifies one's dealing with it as a serious work of art, which implies stylistic, thematic, *and* ideological consistency. It goes without saying that, even with all its flaws, the second half still provides above-average musical comedy fare to the aficionado. There is Astaire's "bullfighting" solo; the miniballet—a showcase for Hepburn's dancing— reprising "How Long Has This Been Going On?" and "Funny Face" with mock avant-garde orchestration and choreography; the hectic "Clap Yo Hands"; and a brief but charming Hepburn-Thompson duo ("On How to Be Lovely"). But they are only bright moments, and Donen cannot recapture the magically even, effortless flow of the first part.

It was a sign of the times that Donen's last two musicals were adaptations of Broadway shows and that he found himself back in a codirecting capacity but this time sharing the credit with the coauthor and producer of the two shows. Not that the sixty-eight-year-old George Abbott, by then a show business legend, was a total newcomer to movies; he had written and directed half a dozen pictures between 1929 and 1931—plus, as in an afterthought, the 1940 film version of his *Too Many Girls*— and produced a few others in the late thirties. Still, with his credits as a film director consisting of one picture in twenty-eight years, it is doubtful that his contribution to the direction was a great help to Donen on either *The Pajama Game* or *Damn Yankees.* Clearly, Abbott, who also produced, was there primarily, in both cases, to see to it that the stage property was faithfully consigned to film.

Damn Yankees, although it had many admirers both on stage and on film, is a negligible musical, almost marginal to the genre, and quite an anticlimactic close to Donen's brilliant career as a director of film musicals. A graceless, humorless fantasy, it is shrill and vulgar in a typical Broadway fashion, and Donen failed or was not allowed to tone it down and reshape it into something more amenable to screen treatment. A musical that boasts as its highlight Gwen Verdon's belting out of "Whatever Lola Wants Lola Gets" is strictly for Broadway Belting enthusiasts (whose name, of course, is legion), not something anyone else would care to dwell upon at any great length. *The Pajama Game,* however, although the effort to cinematize the vehicle was not much more elaborate, is quite another matter; by no means a major masterpiece of the movie musical, it is nonetheless a delightful experience, a rare instance of genuine empathy between two art forms separated—if one may transpose the phrase—by a common language.

The major reason for the success of *The Pajama Game* as a movie is almost ridiculously obvious. The original show was so good, and, unlike most Broadway musicals, so comparatively easy to transfer to the screen, that one feels it would have required gross incompetence to botch the adaptation. In a way, *The Pajama Game* did for the Broadway musical what *Singin' in the Rain* had done for the movie musical, achieving near-perfect evenness and unity in a medium whose very nature seems to breed unevenness. Each song in the amazingly fresh and original score by Richard Adler and Jerry Ross is both memorable and thoroughly integrated into the plot, a feat achieved by only a small handful of Broadway musicals before (*Kiss Me Kate* and *Guys and Dolls* come to mind as most likely candidates) and probably none since. *The Pajama Game* was undoubtedly the last musical the audience could walk away from humming the entire score. The songs, indeed, are the film's main attraction, as the production itself lacks the stylishness of *Funny Face* and the MGM musicals. It was made on an obviously modest budget and is often visually drab. In an extreme case, like the "Hey There" number, in which John Raitt just sits at his desk and sings the song into a tape recorder, then replays the tape and complements the lyrics with spoken remarks, Donen's direction nearly becomes a tongue-in-cheek comment on its own slumbering minimalism. At the other end of the spectrum, though, Donen and Fosse have a field day with the elaborate company picnic sequence, featuring the song "This Is My Once a Year Day," with joyous dancing by practically the entire cast spilling all over the screen, recorded in elegant, sweeping boom shots. On the whole, however, one doesn't really mind the fact that most of the film is set in such uninspiring locales as factory shops, small offices, union meeting halls, drab living rooms, and front porches by the railroad track. What matters is the irrepressible humor, the tunefulness and bounce of the songs. "There Once Was a Man," to take only one example, is one of the most infectiously energetic outbursts of ebullient amorousness ever penned by a songwriter, and its spirit is perfectly captured both by the choreography and Doris Day's and John Raitt's high-powered, enthusiastic performance of the number.

Donen's transitional period from musicals to straight comedies was not an easy one, and it would be pointless to try and salvage everything it yielded. In between the two Abbott shows, he had directed *Kiss Them for Me,* his first nonmusical variation on the motif of the trio out for a good time (three Navy men, as in *On the Town*), which had turned out to be an unexpectedly bittersweet romantic comedy, full of melancholy touches and delicate camera moves. *Indiscreet,* based on Norman Krasna's play, *Kind Sir,* although flimsy, revealed Donen's flair (still largely unexploited) for sophisticated comedy and was tasteful and brilliant enough to remind one of George Cukor at his best. *Once More With Feeling* and *Surprise Package,* on the other hand, two Yul Brynner vehicles, were undistinguished, their comedy as heavy-handed as *Indiscreet*'s had been delicate. One of Donen's major assets in the late fifties and early sixties was Cary Grant, who starred in four of the eight films he directed between 1958 and 1963. Indeed, all four films were casting coups of one kind or another. The Cary Grant–Ingrid Bergman combination worked beautifully in *Indiscreet*, one of Grant's best late pictures, and unquestionably Bergman's finest American film since Hitchcock's *Under Capricorn*. Donen brought together a potentially stunning quartet of stars for *The Grass Is Greener*; even Grant, Deborah Kerr, Robert Mitchum, and Jean Simmons, however, could not bring the endless conversations of this lusterless drawing-room comedy to life, and all, especially the forlorn-looking Mitchum, seemed bored by the proceedings. Clearly, Donen's crucial problem had become the dearth of suitable material.

After striking out three times in a row with the two Brynner pictures and *The Grass Is Greener*, Donen was not heard from for a couple of years. With his comeback picture, *Charade*, he seemed to be veering away from comedy proper into the realm of light adventure and suspense. His casting of Cary Grant and Audrey Hepburn was another coup, and this time a most felicitous one. He had an excellent rapport with both stars, whose relaxed elegance and distinction, common British background, and shared sense of humor made them an ideal combination. It may have been Grant's long-standing association with Hitchcock that prompted Donen to essay a Hitch-flavored suspenser, with Grant cast as an ambiguous character not unlike the ones he had played in *Suspicion* and, more recently, *To Catch a Thief*. Donen had already paid a kind of homage to Hitchcock by reuniting the stars of *Notorious* in *Indiscreet*, but the homage went far beyond mere casting in *Charade*, perhaps the most deliberately derivative picture ever made in the master's spirit until Brian DePalma's *Obsession* (Donen naturally leans toward the Hitchcock of *North by Northwest*, DePalma toward that of *Vertigo*) yet the respectful work of a talented admirer.

The distance that separates *Charade* from *Arabesque* might be said to be that between their respective stars, although the judgment would be somewhat unfair to Gregory Peck and Sophia Loren. *Arabesque* is certainly the latter's best English-language picture, with (and after) Cukor's *Heller in Pink Tights*, and Peck is quite enjoyable as a university professor caught up in international intrigue (the scene in which he drops a secret message in his soup and attempts to retrieve it without attracting attention reveals an unexpected flair for slow-burning comedy). Again, Donen borrowed heavily from Hitchcock (most conspicuously from *Notorious* and *North by Northwest*), but the film's formal extravagance—a new approach for Donen—went far beyond anything Hitchcock himself would have ever cared to consider. Done in a slick, showy style, replete with bizarre camera angles, extreme close-ups, superimpositions, aerial shots and incessant camera moves, *Arabesque* (a most apposite title) was, like Joseph Losey's contemporary *Modesty Blaise*, a product of the mid/late sixties pop craze. Where Losey used the spy-sex-violence format as a showcase for a display of neurotic obsessions, Donen worked in a spirit of light parody and fun, aiming to entertain rather than confuse or shock. Both films are overdone, but Donen's retains an unstrained elegance that is quite missing from Losey's. *Arabesque* is more tinsel than gold, no doubt, but its glitter is never obnoxious.

Donen dealt with more substantial material in *Two for the Road*, perhaps his most ambitious picture. An unusually perceptive anatomy of a couple's coming apart, it barely conceals, underneath the gloss of sophisticated comedy, a disillusioned quality that may be traced back in Donen's work to portions of *Kiss Them for Me* and *Indiscreet*, to say nothing of *It's Always Fair Weather.* For his third film with Audrey Hepburn, he again showed his casting flair by costarring Albert Finney as the husband; the two were equally convincing as enthusiastic young lovers and as squabbling spouses over the twelve-year period spanned by the story. Donen masterfully handled the script's numerous jumps in time, although the film's effectiveness is ultimately weakened by the juxtaposition of straight, or almost straight, dramatic scenes and moments of rather thin, superficial comedy. *Two for the Road* may nonetheless be considered Donen's best nonmusical effort, although at one time he cited his next film, *Bedazzled,* as his favorite. Brilliantly written (and performed) by the iconoclastic British comedy team of Peter Cook and Dudley Moore, *Bedazzled* is an occasionally hilarious and consistently offbeat variation on the Faust legend that combines the comically counterproductive granting of seven wishes with an exploration of the seven deadly sins (one of the film's more daring conceits is to expose God as the conniving old codger almost everybody at one time or another has suspected him to be). Despite all the talent involved, however, *Bedazzled* cannot quite escape the unevenness inherent in its episodic format, and one is left with a feeling that the medium of the feature-length comedy film has been used for material that doesn't quite belong there.

In a 1968 *Los Angeles Times* interview, Donen had this to say about *Singin' in the Rain:* "Why, it's very creaky. Friends asked me to show it not long ago. I was absolutely astounded. There are about four good things in it . . . but there are no characters except Jean Hagen. And that machine-gun tempo! In its time it was good, it may seem great in another twenty years, but not enough time has passed yet." Of course, a director has a right to criticize his own work, even if his severity is shared by practically no one else; still, the judgment seems very peculiar. It becomes more understandable, however, and even illuminating, if placed in the context of Donen's career in the sixties. A foremost concern of his had been to turn out fashionable products—as *Arabesque* most eloquently indicated—and it is not inconsistent that he should have felt embarrassed at what he considered *Singin' in the Rain*'s old-fashioned quality, even though it actually is one of the very few films that, over the years, has not aged at all, except in the most superficial and unessential manner.

It is ironic that the same man who failed to recognize the greatness of an earlier work because of his preoccupation with what was "in" at the moment was to produce and direct, in the following years, pictures that completely lacked the qualities formerly associated with his name and which, at the same time, failed to strike a responsive chord in the contemporary public, indeed, were severe commercial failures. Aside from the enjoyment he may have derived from directing Rex Harrison and Richard Burton as two middle-aged homosexuals, it is difficult to understand what impelled Donen to film the stage play *Staircase.* Anyone who has read Antoine de Saint Exupery's *The Little Prince* could have told Donen that it was the kind of book best left alone by the movies, that it would be almost impossible not to overproduce it, and that its fragile, whimsical charm was sure to be damaged, if not destroyed, by the literalness of film; but then, Donen must have been aware of the hazard himself. This unexpected and disappointing return to the musical was, at least, a noble failure. There was nothing noble, however, about *Lucky Lady* (the first of Donen's pictures since the fifties that he did not produce himself), a hapless hodgepodge of erratic comedy and overly graphic violent adventure, with too many ingredients in it and no chemistry between them or between its wasted stars.

A further and greater irony is that the man who, in 1968, repudiated *Singin' in the Rain* on account of its then unfashionable style, was to direct, ten years later, a homage to 1930s Hollywood musicals as part of a nostalgia-drenched re-creation of a prewar double bill. It would be somewhat misleading to speak of Donen's coming full circle, however, for whereas *Singin' in the Rain* was an early fifties movie looking back on early thirties musicals in an early fifties movie style, *Movie, Movie* (an unfortunate retitling of *Double Feature*) is a late seventies movie trying to duplicate thirties movie styles, a conceit that is both intriguing (if only because it had never been attempted before) and ultimately futile (if only because it can't really be done).

Precisely because the endeavor was self-defeating, however, Donen was forced to move beyond mere archeological reconstruction, and the result was, paradoxically, one of his more personal efforts—at least as far as the second item on the "bill," *Baxter Beauties of 1933,* is concerned. Despite the fact that Donen used the same cast in both films and, in sly acknowledgement of movie-making mores in the era of assembly-line mise-en-scène, opens both with the same stock shot (the camera panning down from a Manhattan street sign to establish the locale of a story otherwise entirely filmed on the sound stage), *Dynamite Hands* and *Baxter Beauties* are very dissimilar in concept and execution and cannot really be discussed as one movie. The former, literally the bottom half of the double bill, may be dismissed as a clever but overlong and intrinsically useless exercise. Donen is dabbling in the ambiguous art of the impressionist, to which there are two possible approaches: carbon-copy mimicry, or caricature, and *Dynamite Hands* keeps wavering between the two, drawing upon straight situations, characters, dialogue, and visuals from thirties movies (especially the Warners social melodrama) yet interspersing them with gag lines that spoof the models, so that homage and parody cancel each other out. The mimicry is so competent that one resents the intrusion of the derisive laughter that makes it impossible to enjoy the film as a piece of nostalgic reconstruction, while a spectator in the mood to laugh at a takeoff on corny old movies will probably find the parodistic element sparse and too light-handed. As for the hypothetical viewer with no familiarity whatsoever with thirties movies, he could only be thoroughly confused and nonplussed by this weirdly anachronistic artifact.

Donen's approach in *Baxter Beauties,* on the other hand, is neither mimicry nor caricature, or rather, both are subsumed in a less literal, more open and fluid method that deals freely with the corpus and uses it more as a springboard than as a model. Whereas *Dynamite Hands* could almost pass for a thirties movie, *Baxter Beauties,* despite its countless references to and quotations from thirties musicals, does not look, sound, or feel like one at all. The very fact that Donen decided to shoot the film in color when practically all thirties musicals were in black-and-white is indicative of a determination *not* to be slavishly imitative and makes it impossible to view the movie as typical— or archetypical. *Dynamite Hands* is a reflection of old movie styles, *Baxter Beauties* more of a meditation on them. Since Donen was himself a director of musicals, it is not surprising that he should have something to say about the genre and his relationship to it, and the fact that he was active in the genre in the late forties and in the fifties, rather than the thirties, suffices to account for his failure to focus on the ostensible referent.

A project like *Movie, Movie* could be conceived at all only because the kind of movies it evokes were a thing of the past. More specifically, *Baxter Beauties of 1933* could be made only because the movie musical, at least in the sense that term was understood from the beginning of sound until the late fifties or early sixties, had become a dead genre. Thus, in effect, the film's implicit theme is the passing of a genre that

Donen had illustrated decades earlier and to whose evolution he had contributed as much as anybody in Hollywood. And indeed, the death of Spats Baxter, the story's hero, may easily be read as a metaphor for the death of the Hollywood musical. By making sickness and death—taboo subjects in comedies until recent years—the mainspring of his plot, Donen placed himself at a huge distance from his so-called models and firmly rooted his film in a modern context that no amount of Busby Berkeleyisms could disguise. The hovering presence of death makes *Baxter Beauties* seem like a forerunner to the seemingly much more daring *All That Jazz,* which Bob Fosse (who had danced in and choreographed some of Donen's pictures in the fifties) was working on at the time of *Movie, Movie*'s release. Like *All That Jazz, Baxter Beauties* is concerned not only with death but with attitudes toward ailing and dying, as well as with the ambiguous mystique of show business, the glory and demands of showmanship, and the ultimate loneliness of the creative artist, all of which themes Donen managed to touch upon with seriousness, even pathos, while still keeping the surface of the film within the confines of the quaint homage to the old Warner musical it purports to be. A minor achievement, perhaps, but not a banal one. Donen's next picture after this ambiguously nostalgic hiatus, the empty-headed space thriller *Saturn 3,* was one more reminder of the predicament of the genre director in search of substitute genres.

16. *Gordon Douglas* (1909)

1936—*General Spanky;* 1939—*Zenobia;* 1940—*Saps at Sea;* 1941—*Road Show* (codirectors: Hal Roach, Hal Roach, Jr.); *Broadway Limited; Niagara Falls;* 1942—*The Devil With Hitler; The Great Gildersleeve;* 1943—*Gildersleeve's Bad Day; Gildersleeve on Broadway;* 1944—*A Night of Adventure; Gildersleeve's Ghost; Girl Rush; The Falcon in Hollywood;* 1945—*Zombies on Broadway; First Yank Into Tokyo;* 1946—*Dick Tracy vs. Cueball; San Quentin;* 1948—*If You Knew Susie; The Black Arrow; Walk a Crooked Mile;* 1949—*The Doolins of Oklahoma; Mr. Soft Touch* (codirector: Henry Levin); 1950—*The Nevadan; Fortunes of Captain Blood; Rogues of Sherwood Forest; Kiss Tomorrow Goodbye; Between Midnight and Dawn;* 1951—*The Great Missouri Raid; Only the Valiant; I Was a Communist for the FBI; Come Fill the Cup;* 1952—*Mara Maru;* 1953—*She's Back on Broadway; The Charge at Feather River; So This Is Love; The Iron Mistress;* 1954—*Them!;* 1955—*The McConnell Story; Young at Heart; Sincerely Yours;* 1956—*Santiago;* 1957—*The Big Land; Bombers B-52;* 1958—*Fort Dobbs; The Fiend Who Walked the West;* 1959—*Up Periscope; Yellowstone Kelly;* 1961—*Gold of the Seven Saints; The Sins of Rachel Cade; Claudelle Inglish;* 1962—*Follow That Dream;* 1963—*Call Me Bwana;* 1964—*Robin and the 7 Hoods; Rio Conchos;* 1965—*Sylvia; Harlow;* 1966—*Stagecoach; Way . . . Way Out;* 1967—*In Like Flint; Chuka; Tony Rome;* 1968—*The Detective; Lady in Cement;* 1970—*Skullduggery; Barquero; They Call Me MISTER Tibbs;* 1973—*Slaughter's Big Rip-Off;* 1977—*Viva Knievel!*

Television Movie
1975—*Nevada Smith*

"Don't try to see all the films I directed, that would turn you off movies completely," Gordon Douglas modestly advised once. "I have a large family to support, and I work on an interesting project only occasionally." One can only agree. Yet his career is far from negligible, especially the later part of it, during which his talent seems to have bloomed rather than faded.

His early efforts, if not his name, are familiar to several generations of youngsters who enjoyed the Hal Roach *Our Gang* comedies of the thirties in theaters then on television. Douglas directed about thirty of these before graduating to features in 1939 with *Zenobia* (Roach had allowed him one fling at features before, the 1936 *General Spanky.*) *Zenobia,* a quaint, nonslapstick comedy starring Oliver Hardy minus Stan Laurel and costarring faded comedy star Harry Langdon, was based on the daffy premise of a triangle involving a lady elephant and the two comedians vying for her affection (a very Langdonian premise, although Langdon was not credited for the story). A costumer set in the South in the 1890s, the film was closer to the tradition of thirties screwball comedies than to the usual style of either of its stars. No attempt was made to turn the Hardy-Langdon combination into a new comedy team, since Laurel and Hardy had had no intention of splitting up and had come to the end of their Roach contract anyway. (Stan explained to his biographer, John McCabe, that *his* contract had expired at the time, while Ollie still had one more film to go, hence the special arrangement for *Zenobia.*) The next year, Laurel and Hardy were reunited in *Saps at Sea,* their last really good feature, which Douglas also directed. Before he himself left Roach, Douglas helped him put together a curious semimusical called *Road Show,* which Roach was attempting to direct with his own son.

A contract director at RKO from 1942 to 1947, Douglas made over a dozen programmers there, most of them in the mystery category. He was assigned most of the entries in the *Gildersleeve* series, one in the *Falcon* series, and one *Dick Tracy,* as well as the fairly good prison film *San Quentin* (no connection with the Warners Bogart vehicle of 1937, except for the presence of Barton MacLane in both films). His last RKO assignment, *If You Knew Susie,* was also Eddie Cantor's last starring role. Douglas then worked three years for Columbia, directing, among other things, a number of swashbucklers that attempted to recapture the Warner Brothers–Michael Curtiz touch but with little success (*The Black Arrow,* however, is quite enjoyable). In 1950, Douglas was signed by Warners, the company for which he was to make most of his films until 1965. (He worked for other studios or producers only occasionally and then on a one- or two-picture basis.) His best Warner pictures of the early and mid-fifties were his two Cagney vehicles, *Kiss Tomorrow Goodbye,* a taut and faithful adaptation of Horace McCoy's novel, and *Come Fill the Cup,* about a newspaperman's fight against alcoholism· *The Iron Mistress,* a good biography of Jim Bowie; and *Them,* by now a minor classic and one of the few really outstanding science fiction films of the fifties. On the whole, however, Douglas's most interesting work is to be found in his Westerns of the late fifties and early sixties: *Fort Dobbs,* with its impressive opening reel; the powerful, antiracist *Yellowstone Kelly;* the relaxed and humorous *Gold of the Seven Saints* (all three starring Clint Walker); and particularly *Rio Conchos,* Douglas's favorite film, certainly his most inventive, in which, for once, he rose above his usual businesslike style of direction and introduced imaginative camera moves, boom shots à la Anthony Mann. Clair Huffaker's excellent script built to a splendid climax on a delirious set (a megalomaniac Southern officer's unfinished mansion, reduced to its facade) and provided Douglas with picaresque and violent material to illustrate various types of social injustice. In *Chuka,* a lyrical, nostalgic Western that contains some of the best scenes he ever directed, Douglas not only served the script competently but imposed a personal manner reminiscent of Raoul Walsh's Warners pictures.

One of the few movies Douglas made outside WB over that period was Fox's interesting Western remake of *Kiss of Death* as *The Fiend Who Walked the West.* Another later Fox remake Douglas directed was *Stagecoach,* no doubt one of those assignments he took on with his large family in mind. Yet, while one cannot think of any really good reason to remake *Stagecoach,* there certainly was nothing sacrilegious about it. Douglas handled the exterior scenes quite honorably (*his* version at least does not resort to the sloppy back-projections that mar the visual quality of Ford's classic), and the film, if anything, helped to expose the basic banality of the story. At any rate, Fox must have been happy with the result, for Douglas made a series of Fox films in the following years.

The Sinatra thrillers are quite interesting as part of a trend to revive the crime melodrama of the forties with the added attractions of color, semiexplicit sex, and foul language. While *Tony Rome* and *Lady in Cement* worked more or less within the tradition, *The Detective* went one step further but in a rather perverse way. Douglas and screenwriter Abby Mann transformed Roderick Thorp's splendid book, a brooding, actionless psychological novel of Jamesian subtlety, into a slam-bang, action-packed thriller with strictly one-dimensional characters. The "hero" was turned from a quite nonheroic small-town private investigator into a dashing New York detective, and the sensational element (the investigation of a gruesome sex murder), which the novel underplayed throughout, was dragged out into full view and splattered all over the screen. Still, if one is willing to disregard such boorish mishandling, the movie can be enjoyed for its pace and bounce alone. Indeed, it includes some of the most impressive scenes Douglas ever filmed (e.g., Tony Musante's capture and subsequent questioning by Sinatra) and, at least as far as camera work and use of locations are concerned, does stand out as one of his finest directorial jobs.

---

17. *Clint Eastwood* (1930)

by RICHARD THOMPSON and TIM HUNTER

1971—*Play Misty for Me;* 1973—*High Plains Drifter; Breezy;* 1975—*The Eiger Sanction;* 1976— *The Outlaw Josey Wales;* 1977—*The Gauntlet;* 1980—*Bronco Billy;* 1982—*Firefox; Honkytonk Man*

In an era of independent stars, and even stars turning director, Clint Eastwood and Malpaso, his production company, have an extraordinary critical and financial track record, and one with consistent integrity to it. Eastwood claims it was *Where Eagles Dare* and, particularly, *Paint Your Wagon* that prompted him to form Malpaso; he felt that he could provide a no-nonsense alternative to the wastefulness of such productions. And since forming Malpaso, Eastwood has not taken what must have been many opportunities to do three days' work in *Midway* or two weeks' work in *A Bridge Too Far* to make an easy large salary; he has focused his time and energy on projects he is interested in. One may question the projects but not the commitment.

Like Jerry Lewis, Eastwood developed expertise in, and took responsibility for, most technical and production specialities. (Also, Eastwood's transformation, like Lewis's, occurred under the influence of a mentor: Don Siegel for Eastwood, Frank Tashlin for Lewis.) Malpaso has remained small, efficient, and canny. Its emphasis has been on manipulating the current production opportunities in Hollywood to put the most apparent money on the screen for the least outlay. Rather like Roger Corman, Eastwood makes a practice of giving young professionals chances to step up. Bruce Surtees, Robert Surtees's son, got his first director-of-photography credits on Eastwood films; writer Michael Cimino and executive producer-production director Jim Fargo got their first director credits on *Thunderbolt and Lightfoot* and *The Enforcer,* respectively; second-unit cinematographer Rex Metz moved up to director of photography on *Gauntlet;* John Milius's rewrite job on *Dirty Harry* was a big boost to his career.

As a director, Eastwood has a much greater faith in human nature than Don Siegel, with whom he is often compared. Some try to group him with Robert Aldrich or Sam Fuller, but Eastwood has none of their hyperkinetic qualities; instead, he brings the male-action film tradition into contact with the perspectives of Douglas Sirk and George Cukor. And three absolutely necessary elements: deeply developed humor, a mise-en-scène visual style, and an intimate knowledge of the American marrow: its juices, its toxins, its contradictions.

Play Misty for Me, Eastwood's first film as director, shows a remarkable sense of place, an eye for interesting interior design—especially modern—and an ability to fix characters through visual description of an environment. His talent for tailoring landscape to fit a film's mood and theme is unsurpassed among recent American directors. His films are also superbly paced: unhurried, cool, and giving a strong sense of real time, regardless of the speed of the narrative.

Eastwood's pictures come from the male point of view, but this very one-sidedness gives them a certain truth and conviction beyond politics. Of all his films, *Play Misty for Me* best reveals Eastwood's need to test and compromise his own image, pushing it toward the limit of personal honor.

The movement of the plot is simple: As Eastwood tries to win back fair lady Donna Mills (a woman with whom he can be satisfied without putting out a lot of emotion), spurned dark lady Jessica Walter goes crazier and crazier, finally plotting to kill him. Eastwood sees the story as being about "misinterpretation of commitment," and his character as essentially victimized—but *Play Misty for Me* works on darker levels.

Walter is the exact opposite of Eastwood: impulsive where he is controlled, passionate where he is complacent. Consequently, we admire her a little, sensing some justice in her attack on the base of his self-satisfied life. She is nearly his alter ego, a projection of his suppressed furies and fear of love—a pull toward death and self-destruction that he must battle and exorcise within himself. In this sense, *Play Misty* is a companion piece to Siegel's *The Beguiled* (in which the antihero surrenders to dark passion and does die). They are two sexual mediations; both films show women archetypically as Innocent or as Corruptor. In *Play Misty for Me,* violence is equated with sex, and women with life (pulling man out of his isolation) or death. The film plugs into the mainstream of the male American romantic tradition and exerts a fascination well beyond the limits of the plot. If *Play Misty* benefits from these subconscious implications, it is finally satisfying because Walter is such a wonderful villain: a personal devil for Eastwood to fight, equaled only by Andy Robinson's prime psycho in Siegel's *Dirty Harry.* Regarding alter egos, one remembers how that film and its ad campaign stressed the similarities between hero and villain; in *Play Misty for Me,* as in all Eastwood's films, good triumphs in the fight with evil—but rarely has the devil lived so close to home.

The real inspiration of *High Plains Drifter* is its conception of the town, a sparkling clean main street that looks as much like a new condominium in northern California as it does the movie western towns of the past. This town, built on an oasislike lake in the middle of a scorched desert, ably serves the allegory of the film. Both it and Eastwood's man-with-no-name hero appear completely cut off from the world.

This is Eastwood's best revenge picture, and the most skillful thing about it is that, even after the picture is over, we never really know why he's taking revenge. The people in the town are so corrupt, though—worthy of Brecht and Weill's *Mahagonny*—that one can take special pleasure watching Eastwood get most of them killed. The overtones of Sodom and Gomorrah are deliberate, as is the devil quality of Eastwood's antihero—not to mention the film's homage to Japanese ghost-revenge melodramas.

The contrast of dark brown interiors and blinding white-light exteriors, added to the strikingly different look of the town, gives *High Plains Drifter* a stylized visual originality that goes beyond the expressionistic CinemaScope shots influenced by Sergio Leone and Don Siegel. The pacing casually makes the most of the action. Of all the films Eastwood has directed, *High Plains* has the best stylization of violence, with a laconic shooting from a bathtub being especially memorable.

Breezy is the only film Eastwood has directed in which he didn't star; its commercial failure minimizes the possibility for another directing-only project. Following *High Plains Drifter, Breezy* is again an allegory, with Eastwood still concerned with the hypocrisies and failed values of middle-class society—in this case, Los Angeles's idle nouveau riche. Directly, effortlessly, Eastwood conveys (and satirizes) the impotence of this dolce vita cocktail set, and this lack of equivocation gives his simple, tender love story a special grace quite different from the cold new crop of romances released since *Breezy.*

Breezy has the biting, moralistic wit of this period in Eastwood's work; one feels that here, in *High Plains* and in *Play Misty,* Eastwood enjoys stripping the mystique from the leisure class. *Breezy* evokes the spirit of his homeground, Carmel, more than it does the Laurel Canyon-Hollywood-West L.A. setting of the story. The use of the setting is rich. William Holden's elegant but lonely house—natural woods, rough boulder walls, indoor/outdoor jungle—is the perfect mirror of his soul in the balance. The mise-en-scène is so transparently simple, closest in style to *Play Misty for Me,* that *Breezy* overtly becomes an actors' showcase. Probably because he wasn't starring in the film, Eastwood gives freer rein to his sentimental streak; one of the many pleasures of the film is the degree of self-pity allowed the Holden character, as well as the unabashed hippy corniness of Kay Lenz's Breezy.

Part of Eastwood's strong appeal is that he seems too large for society. He embodies a dream: that a man can rise above the treadmill of bureaucracy and act on his own law. But the price of this independence is isolation. Eastwood's films often focus on this theme, as if to say that good can triumph in the world only when set apart from it.

Leone and Siegel nurtured Eastwood's image as a cutthroat antihero who could play dirtier than anyone as long as his motives justified his means. Treading the line between hero and devil in the characters he plays, Eastwood selects stories about bounty hunters, policemen, and revengers—all subjects where character motivation turns murky and paradoxical. With all moral values so compromised, Eastwood has only to maintain a tiny edge of purity so that the audience can identify with the self-righteousness that allows him to set himself above the rest of the world and act on his own predatory impulses. Regardless of director, the movement in all his best films is toward a dichotomy between the Eastwood character and, at the opposing pole, everybody else.

His recent films have moved toward softening this polarity, testing it through wider interaction with other characters and a continued belief in the potential of romance. From all indications, Phil Kaufman would have made a more sincerely communal *Josey Wales* than the one Eastwood finally made, one which would have incorporated Eastwood more completely into the whole. The crisis undoubtedly arose because Eastwood, conscious of "shorting" himself when he directs, felt he wasn't being covered well. The final version points up the standard dichotomy of his films even more than those that play off it more overtly. Close-ups of Eastwood as Josey Wales are less well blended into the style of the overall film than usual. An increasingly abstracted stylization of violence doesn't quite mesh with the theme of the film and its desire to be a tapestry or Breughel scene of the West. Despite a certain lack of tension, *Josey Wales* is an admirable attempt by Eastwood at broadening his scope and—no puns intended—the best things about this visually sumptuous movie are the remarkable Panavision master shots and an ease with the medium that gains in assurance as he looks for new challenges and directions in choice of subjects.

RECENT EASTWOOD

Since the above was written (in 1975) Eastwood has consolidated his position. Eastwood's later films sharply foreground themes that have their origin in the remarkable triad of films made at the end of the sixties—*Dirty Harry, The Beguiled,* and *Play Misty for Me.* Eastwood has progressively moved his hero down Northrop Frye's table of heroic modes; major components of this persona have moved from the superior (mythic) hero all the way down to the inferior (ironic) hero. Areas involved are: emotional completeness, intelligence, practical understanding of and ability to perceive and deal with the world, and relations with women. The terms of the hero's virtuosity are rethought, moving them from physical skill, wit, being the best, and compulsive, antisocial individualism to a new area marked out by stubbornness, fidelity to private ideals and style, and the survival value/necessity of friendship as an antidote to selfishness. It's as if Eastwood is trying to isolate the bare minimum of his persona—through an acting style that has always been on the minimal side, compared with the busy shifting of a Burt Reynolds.

The Gauntlet, Every Which Way But Loose (James Fargo, 1978), *Escape From Alcatraz* (Don Siegel, 1979), *Bronco Billy,* and *Any Which Way You Can* (Buddy Van Horn, 1981) show the powerful unifying effect exerted by Eastwood's producer-actor-sometime director role. Whether he directed them or not, these films expand Eastwood's central concerns more directly than the earlier films had. Eastwood continues to employ relative newcomers as directors, writers, and so forth, mixed into his regular production team. The effect of this apprenticeship system may involve a more complete domination of the films by Eastwood's vision—given the absence of any other strong, experienced personalities. (The exception, and apparently a difficult one for everyone involved, is *Escape From Alcatraz*, which has a Bressonian quality foreign to Eastwood's other films and which has been described by Jack Shafer as "what would happen if Dirty Harry were sent to prison.") At any rate, these recent films place Eastwood among those film makers most explicitly interested in dramatizing contemporary America and its social myths.

From *Josey Wales* through all the recent films, Eastwood pursues the ideal of a small, familial, self-sufficient social group that must plow through the obstacles of the dominant society to claim a place outside society—a farm, a house in the mountains, an insular and idealist traveling tent show (see George Romero's *Knightriders* for another recent articulation of this theme), even a bungalow in Burbank—where Eastwood and the group of losers he has taken responsibility for can be left alone.

The Gauntlet is the fourth and perhaps last of the police series. *Dirty Harry* was a rogue cop, against the police establishment, settling matters on the basis of justice rather than legalism. The next film, *Magnum Force,* seemed to be an apology for *Harry:* Harry extirpated a squad of vigilante cops. *The Enforcer* was an exercise in racial and sexual trimming. *The Gauntlet* comes full circle: an alcoholic, expendable loser of a cop is sent on a kamikaze mission by a police bureaucracy indistinguishable from the post-Mafia politics it responds to. The conclusion of the film is realized in the strongest possible terms: Ben Shockley (Eastwood) must drive a bus he has armored through a gauntlet of his fellow officers up to City Hall. All the cops have POLICE prominently stenciled on their riot helmets. One trooper asks the man next to him why they're going to shoot down one of their own. "Orders" is the answer. "Oh. OK."

The Gauntlet goes back to *High Plains Drifter* for an Oriental twist, but this time it has found as an action strategy, one that establishes Eastwood's difference from Siegel. Siegel's action mise-en-scène exemplifies the main American cinema tradition: progressive, kinetic sequences, structured rather like silent comedy: the initial proposition quickly moves from variations to the addition of other elements and propositions, mixing surprise and logic. *The Gauntlet*'s big action set pieces, notably the destruction of the bungalow and the bus/gauntlet climax, are structured without surprise and without graded, progressive kineticism. All elements of the action are posed before the action starts. The initial theme is one of excess: hundreds, then thousands of police gunners shooting at two reasonably innocent people. The action begins and continues without variation for a long time. The structural principle is repetition rather than building; the effect is contemplative, reflective. The viewer is not involved in keeping up with a forward-moving sequence but instead is invited to consider, over and over, the same, simple, outrageous image.

The film belongs to the recent cycle of American paranoid films. It is certainly Eastwood's most paranoid work, with the unusual twist that the hero is not bright and has not deduced/perceived the conspiracies around him. It is his prisoner, the college-educated prostitute, who must force him to understand the forces threatening them both.

Bronco Billy gathers into its Wild West show a microcosm of American losers, mostly members of the Eastwood stock company: Sondra Locke, Bill McKinney, Geoffrey Lewis, Sam Bottoms. Under the guise of nineteenth-century benevolent entrepreneurism, a would-be Buffalo Bill Cody struggles not to turn into a hard-luck Barnum. The group finds a new life through the catharsis of performance and through a commitment to an idealized version of the Western myth, which they use to keep the twentieth century at a reasonable distance. In *Bronco Billy,* Eastwood foregrounds notions about stardom, performance, and myth tested against American society. Its form (as is often the case with Eastwood) is the picaresque journey, and it fulfills the picaresque expectation to construct and operate unusual characters successfully. *Bronco Billy* is quietly ambitious in its theater/film/life transpositions.

Skill with characters reaches a strange high in the Clint 'n' Clyde films. (In discussing these, I am particularly indebted to Rolando Caputo's research.) The two films are a major narrative step for Eastwood. He had already worked with a series persona (the Dirty Harry films, the man-with-no-name films) and with a generic persona moved through several films. With *Every Which Way But Loose* and *Any Which Way You Can,* he tries a new form. In the first film (which did not conclude with a promise of a sequel), Eastwood poses Philo Beddoe, a *lumpen* car mechanic and star bare-knuckle fighter who lives with his mother (Eastwood has a mother—onscreen?) and Clyde, a sentient orangoutang who is both his animal alter ego and his bosom buddy. Philo is smitten by a sophisticated and hence untrustworthy country singer (Sondra Locke) whom he pursues across the country, bankrolling his trip by prize fighting. He wins the fights, mostly, and loses the girl, painfully. (Eastwood loses the girl?) Clyde comforts him.

Three years later, the same characters and situation are taken up again where they were left off. This time Philo gets the girl in the end. The two films are a single narrative, but each can stand alone. Though made by two different directors, they mesh together almost seamlessly.

Prior to *Every Which Way,* it had been said that Eastwood had a large redneck audience but had made no redneck films. *Every Which Way* can be seen as both a sympathetic subcultural salute to those of his supporters who don't read *The New Yorker* and as a smart move, in terms of the soft box office of his recent films, to compete with his major rival, Burt Reynolds, who is rightly touted as a new Cary Grant but who never forgets to make a redneck film every year or so, very profitably.

The films use Clyde and the sexual activities Philo sponsors for Clyde as analog and metaphor for human sexuality, connecting with an American tradition most clearly seen in the work of Hawks (*Bringing Up Baby, Monkey Business, Hatari!*). Animals are an example to humans (Aesop, Hollywood cartoons) and perform the service of liberating human sexuality (see the motel sequence, intercutting the motel rooms of a very old couple, a middle-aged couple, and a young couple, all of whom are imitating the sexual play of an orangoutang couple in a fourth motel room; if we have doubts about claims for the self-knowledge demonstrated by this scene, see its perfectly placed reference to Blake Edwards's *"10"*). Animal and human sex are not only compared, they are mixed—in some remarkable confessional scenes between Eastwood and the ape, which make it clear that this double film is the comic inversion of the *Butch Cassidy and The Sundance Kid*-style male bonding films of the past fifteen years.

Finally, through all these recent films, we should note a drift away from the structural and moral opposition of hero and villain. The villain drops out of the pattern as Eastwood becomes more interested in his social visions.

—Richard Thompson

18. Blake Edwards (1922)

by MYRON MEISEL

1955—*Bring Your Smile Along;* 1956—*He Laughed Last;* 1957—*Mister Cory;* 1958—*This Happy Feeling;* 1959—*The Perfect Furlough; Operation Petticoat;* 1960—*High Time;* 1961—*Breakfast at Tiffany's;* 1962—*Experiment in Terror;* 1963—*Days of Wine and Roses;* 1964—*The Pink Panther; A Shot in the Dark;* 1965—*The Great Race;* 1966—*What Did You Do in the War, Daddy?;* 1967—*Gunn;* 1968—*The Party;* 1970—*Darling Lili;* 1971—*Wild Rovers;* 1972—*The Carey Treatment;* 1974—*The Tamarind Seed;* 1975—*The Return of the Pink Panther;* 1976—*The Pink Panther Strikes Again;* 1978—*Revenge of the Pink Panther;* 1979—"10"; 1981—*S.O.B.;* 1982—*Victor/Victoria; Trail of the Pink Panther*

For the appearances are glimpses of the unrevealed.
—Anaxagoras

Blake Edwards, the most important comic stylist (along with Richard Lester) of the 1960s, and without peer today, parlayed deadpan farce and intricate gag construction into a profound comic metaphysic devoted to whatever possibilities remain for wit and romance in the postwar age. For Edwards, visual and verbal slapstick provide elaborate ways to meditate on his central issue: what civilized human behavior is still tenable? His masterpieces—*Darling Lili*, *"10,"* and *Gunn*—along with his other major works—*Breakfast at Tiffany's, Days of Wine and Roses, A Shot in the Dark, What Did You Do in the War, Daddy?,* and *The Tamarind Seed*—all embody a civilized, conservative attitude toward the absurdities of existence. (The same would apply to his other substantial, if lesser, works: *Mister Cory, This Happy Feeling, The Perfect Furlough, The Party,* and the butchered *Wild Rovers,* which in its original, now lost, cut was considered by Edwards to be among his finest achievements.)

Starting out in radio and later in television, Edwards worked in feature films as a writer, producer, and actor before directing his first features, two Frankie Laine vehicles (*Bring Your Smile Along,* a startling piece of self-portraiture in a Columbia "B" musical, and the trifling anecdote, *He Laughed Last*). As a screenwriter, he wrote many films for Richard Quine, including the best—*Operation Mad Ball* and *Drive a Crooked Road.* He originated the *Johnny Dollar* radio series and the *Peter Gunn* television series, as well as a pilot for *Kraft Suspense Theater* involving Robert Vaughn as a young Boston Brahmin sleuth called "The Terrier."

The most immediately recognizable quality in a Blake Edwards film is a wise-guy verbal facility keyed to visual fluidity across a lateral field. Edwards charges his surfaces with significance by using the appearance of objects to suggest their essence. The same principle applies to the behavior of his characters. The jokes and one-liners rarely express any deep commitment on the part of the characters delivering them; indeed, they serve as a means to keep them from communicating their needs and feelings, and so tacitly suggest them.

It wouldn't be mistaken to call Edwards's wit a well-conditioned reflex. The overall quality of humor tends to be clever, quirky, and mechanical. Audiences are encouraged to adapt completely to this style, so that the comic lines or events take on a familiar quality of convention, rather than becoming abstraction of movements or of heightened speech. The attitude expressed toward the environment, whether naturalistic terrain (*Wild Rovers*) or a stylized concoction (*The Great Race*), is invariably to take the world presented for granted. Though frequently morally charged, the films are singularly unconcerned with issues of good and evil, except as manifestations of a larger and more consuming chaotic universe. Edwards shares this strategy with Howard Hawks, though Hawks then fleshes out his artificial environment with extremely naturalistic behavioral detail, where Edwards prefers to follow through on the implications of his abstract situations: he is resolutely a man of his time, showing us how we all are out of joint.

The conflict central to all of Edwards's films is the opposition of a highly ordered and controlled existence to an existence characterized by anarchy and chaos. The former may carry with it elements of dignity, restraint (or repression), gallantry or calculation; the latter, a sense of spontaneity, emotional freedom, sensuality, immaturity or nervous confusion. Each mode of behavior has both advantages and drawbacks, and Edwards is capable of either condemning or endorsing, almost always indulgently, aspects of each as he seeks to forge a healthy synthesis of both.

This opposition forms the central action of his early comedy-dramas for Universal, each of which shows the basic Edwardian themes in gestation. The dramatic situations in these films are remarkably similar: in each, a character with a strongly developed sense of how he ought to lead his life finds this confidence/complacency challenged by an opposing life-style. Sometimes the protagonist is loosened up and made more responsive to life by the graded acceptance of degrees of chaos; conversely, a "wild" character realizes the private, internal value of social conventions, manners, morals, or values.

This modification of attitude, with its accompanying realignment of self-image, forms the dramatic center of Edwards's work, and because any notion of the self implies a role that that self will play, Edwards concentrates on changes in role as reflections of changes in personality. It is hardly surprising that he finds the theater, or more generally, any sort of pretense (such as Bing Crosby's drag episode in *High Time* or the numerous disguises donned by Inspector Clouseau) an effective metaphor for how people adjust themselves, and their views of themselves, to the exigencies that confront them. In some ways, the dramatic trajectory of an Edwards movie flamboyantly tracks the transference process in analytic treatment.

Curt Jurgens in *This Happy Feeling* retires to a country estate to breed horses because he feels uncomfortable with the newer "Method" style of acting. He resists all efforts to persuade him to return him to the stage in a meaty character role, which would require a tacit admission of his aging. But a prolonged tender acquaintance with Debbie Reynolds (a relationship paralleled by increasing pain and discomfort in Jurgens's back) enables Jurgens to surrender his courtly isolation and to triumph in the new kind of part, a metaphor for his acceptance of a modified image of himself, less afraid of growing old and richer for his fuller involvement in what he loves best— theater. In many ways, *This Happy Feeling* anticipates the more extensive and expressive treatment of a kindred story line far more sublimely subtle, in *Darling Lili*.

On the one hand, Jurgens and old undergrad Bing Crosby in *High Time* learn by their involvement with "young people" to manage their own lives with greater freedom and emotional fulfillment. Conversely, Tony Curtis acquires a rudimentary new moral awareness at the end of *Mister Cory* when he can overcome both class prejudice and the personal hurt he suffers as a result of his affair with a socially prominent but hypocritical Martha Hyer.

Edwards's special genius is for expressing these themes subtly by using gags as metaphors. Thus, in *The Perfect Furlough,* Tony Curtis tries to persuade a disbelieving Janet Leigh that a starlet could actually have fallen into a wine vat by directing her through the actions we have earlier witnessed. Of course, the pratfall, too, is reenacted. In *"10",* Dudley Moore's frantic efforts to answer the telephone (and make contact with his soulmate) only plunge him further away from a stable connection. In *What Did You Do in the War, Daddy?,* James Coburn takes on the job of directing extras in a sham battle in a real war.

In a related vein, Edwards also attaches significance to a mentor, who takes an interest in the protagonist to help him advance, succeed, and mature. In the earlier films, the relationships between Tony Curtis and Charles Bickford in *Mister Cory,* between Curtis and Cary Grant in *Operation Petticoat,* and between Jack Lemmon and Jack Klugman in *Days of Wine and Roses* reflect a positive need for solid guidance, though this theme is most poignantly expressed in Edwards's screenplay for *Soldier in the Rain,* far and away the best film Ralph Nelson ever signed as a director. The relationship grows more ambiguous in *Darling Lili,* where Lili must liberate herself from the influence of von Ruger to enjoy a safe and stable love relationship; and by the time of *"10,"* Dudley Moore can actually strike out on his dream date because he assumes the role of moral guide. By *S.O.B.,* everyone is on their own to twist in the wind, except to the extent succor is possible through friendship and loyalty.

Operation Petticoat summarizes the themes of the Universal comedies and perhaps is the most fully realized expression of them. Cary Grant's upright officer represents the voice of responsibility in a quandary, and Tony Curtis's playboy adjutant is the resourceful egoist, capable of novel solutions on the borderline of convention. Edwards's CinemaScope work is particularly acute here, and for the first time, his distinctive blending of dramatic weight with absurdist comedy becomes apparent. Edwards's propensity for violent nostalgia and the gay deployment of madness for sane ends culminates in the rescue of the pink submarine from destruction by the depth charges of its own destroyer by sending an inimitably American signal: women's underwear shot to the surface in the torpedo tubes.

The fundamental conflicts established in Edwards's Universal comedies were projected for the first time into the world at large in *Breakfast at Tiffany's.* Where the dramatic scale of *Mister Cory, This Happy Feeling,* and *The Perfect Furlough* was limited to the personal, in *Breakfast at Tiffany's* Edwards exercised his comic imagination on a larger social canvas. The opposition of Holly, the "free" character with no constructive outlets for her imaginative impulses, and Paul, the "repressed" character who is unable to express himself through his writing, sets up a distinctively Edwardian synthesis of personalities into a positive, romantic whole. The problem with each of them is that they cling with all the tenacity born of desperation to a false self-image in which ego and vanity predominate over recognition of harsh truths.

Superficially a frothy romantic comedy, the film intimates a lonely urban existence hovering just outside the movie's context, which in the later films will assume the characteristics of an implacable void. Here, however, the nervous hipness reflects Holly's own viewpoint. In Edwards's seminal party scene in Holly's apartment (which, characteristically, was improvised), the improbable, yet meticulously rendered, sight gags abstract these implications using comic terms. Formally, Edwards's camera follows Holly's name-less cat through the raucous goings-on, lightly suggesting the viewpoint of an isolated, anonymous outsider. In a paradigmatic gag, Holly's long cigarette lighter sets afire the bouffant hairdo of a woman guest; seconds later, she tilts the wrist of a man to look at his watch, spilling his drink onto the burning hair, extinguishing the blaze. The mechanical precision is only part of what makes the sight gag funny—it's also that no one there, least of all the perpetrator of unconscious disasters, Holly, takes the least notice of anything that is happening, so the comedy takes place on a separate dramatic plane from their own experience. Edwards's slapstick is laid like a grid over the social satire, deepening not the drama so much as the expression of his own viewpoint of the world in which he and the characters operate. It might also be worth comparing in passing the benighted fumblings of Clouseau with the amoral unawareness of Holly, who (as in the gag cited above) creates chaotic situations from which, through some divine (or directorial) intervention, she emerges blithely unscathed.

Holly's lack of self-irony crucially reflects the ambivalence of Edwards's own involvement with the hip, moneyed milieu. Holly accepts the conventions and appear-ances of swinging New York but as a matter of substance rather than merely as style. Consequently, she finds herself both capable of enjoying the party and yet unable to fend off the attacks of the "mean reds" that depress her. She is pertinently labeled "a phony, but a *real* phony," in that she actually believes the tinsel is real, but this legitimate superficiality cannot equip her to cope with the successive losses of husband, lovers, and brother.

On the other hand, Paul is cynical, disengaged, and hopelessly blocked on his novel. His typewriter has no ribbon in it. When he reveals this to Holly, Edwards cuts to a composition that distills the dramatic situation by using a divided frame, with Holly behind the shadows of a venetian blind's slats and Paul sprawled on a bed at the other side of the frame. The scene is punctuated by Holly's walk over to a mirror. Such mirror shots are deployed at critical narrative points to elaborate the film's theme of self-images in need of realignment. At the party scene, a middle-aged woman who is drowning her repressed unhappiness with drink laughs at her reflection. Later on, Paul will come out of Tiffany's with the engraved Cracker Jack's ring, only to mistake a stranger for Holly. Instead, he will happen upon her in the public library. Earlier, in the key romantic scene of growing to like one another, she had visited his haunt (the library) and he hers (Tiffany's). The discovery that each had been to the other's turf heightens the poignancy of their impending separation. Meanwhile, Edwards had emphasized not only the need for play in a relationship with their day's outing together but, by causing them to steal and don masks and then end the afternoon with her finally having the downstairs door key, he invests dramatic invention with metaphoric suggestion.

Holly's succession of relationships—with old Doc Golightly, with agent O. J. Berman, with two rich fiancées, and with jailed gangster Sally Tomato—all suggest a need for a mentor figure to free her from the need to confront her own feelings and channel her imaginative liberty into a sense of self-created personal worth. She helps Paul shake off his role as gigolo, which was destroying his creative abilities, and he then shows her that love can be the principle that transforms anarchy into order without losing its precious energy. The rain that engulfs their reconciliation, like all rain, is both wet and cleansing.

More important, though, is the undertone of neurotic panic in Holly's recurrent depressions—dubbed the "mean reds"—which would dominate Edwards's next two black-and-white dramas, *Experiment in Terror,* a technical exercise that nonetheless displayed a characteristic flair, and *Days of Wine and Roses.* Both are dark, unpleasant, full of threatening urban forms. The view of the modern world implied in previous films through dialogue and indirection are here expressed directly through a harsh visual style of strong contrasts and aggressive camera movements. The rapid fall from the reasonably secure office comedy of the opening section of *Roses* to the complete disintegration represented by Jack Lemmon drunkenly flinging away the flowerpot in the decimated greenhouse measures the instability of modern existence. Although visually atypical, these two films represent an alternate way of posing the Edwardian problem of attempting to create a balanced existence with some degree of dignity and emotional fulfillment in the face of overwhelming meaningless and omnipresent danger. The delicate balance between dignity and flexibility, between the controlled and the free, is bound up with the fundamental challenge of survival itself. In watching any of the comedies, and not merely through the grisly slapstick, it's useful to remember that the same man made *Days of Wine and Roses.*

At this point, the most important postulate of Edwards's universe becomes decisively evident: the sense of continual threat and undermined security. All characters live in a persistent shadow; annihilation (or its advance man, chaos) may descend at any time, in any fashion—and the characters know it. Edwards could be fairly called a director who is fundamentally "postnuclear," in a sense not unlike Stanley Kubrick, though Kubrick's alienation leads him to his own eccentric amalgam of absurdist escape and Calvinist opprobrium. Edwards rejects the releases of either total despair or spiritual flight, accepting instead the condition of the world as a given and attempting to deal in a forthright manner with the problem of how to live with it. The characters who are successful in their confrontation with chaos and the prospect of annihilation attack the problem head on: In *Days of Wine and Roses,* Lee Remick is unable to deal with her alcoholism, but Lemmon, through the new self-image he has constructed with the aid of Alcoholics Anonymous, is able to try to make the best life he can. Defenses may be vital, but artificial defenses are worth little in the long run; you can run, but you can't hide. Conditions must be confronted in order to be overcome. They need not even be faced clear-eyed: Clouseau's strategy of confrontation, however addled, leads him to his anarchic victories.

Edwards can accept the lack of intellectual guidelines to modern behavior, the extent to which we are condemned by our awareness to failures of understanding. He accepts unblinkingly the very banality from which a Kubrick so carefully alienates himself. The characters always remain wholly accepting of their world and totally of it, even if the world exists only in their imaginations. (The important exception is *The Tamarind Seed,* where the lovers create their haven more out of imaginative power than plot contrivance.) The deck is never stacked with characters who are superior to their surroundings, not even the dapper Peter Gunn; the problem in an Edwards film is to function in opposition to an environment, while remaining both a part and product of it.

If the situation is posed in intensely physical terms, the solutions are invariably internal. For Edwards, it is one's self-image, the style and manner in which a person lives, a self poised between elegant control of emotion and an ability to respond spontaneously, that can allow relationships of love (*Darling Lili, Tamarind Seed*), friendship (*Wild Rovers, The Party*), and decency (*What Did You Do in the War, Daddy?*). The Edwardian strategy is to keep one's head together as the only means to keep it from going under. We must make do with available materials, as Dudley Moore exultantly does at the conclusion of *"10"* when he appropriates the "Bolero" to consummate his love for Julie Andrews.

The conditions of just being alive are parlous in all Edwards's pictures, even the slapstick comedies. Clouseau may simply open a car door, but the possibilities for serious injury are innumerable. In *Experiment in Terror,* Lee Remick enters her garage, and a hand with a knife grabs her throat. Jack Lemmon introduces his wife to the pleasures of drinking, and a nightmare is unleashed. Curt Jurgens (in *This Happy Feeling*) runs after a train bearing away a friend, only to fall in a ditch and injure his back. Herbert Lom stabs himself with a letter opener, for a belly laugh. *Darling Lili* opens with the archetypal image of panic, as zeppelin bombs stampede an audience for the exits. *Wild Rovers* and *S.O.B.* open with deaths, *Tamarind Seed* with the recollection of one, and in *"10",* George mistakes his surprise birthday party for a wake. In *Gunn,* Peter can swear to a disbelieving girlfriend: "God strike me dead if it isn't the gospel truth!" cueing an offscreen explosion. Perhaps the most brilliant and compressed expression of the fragile state of human security comes in the opening sequence of *The Pink Panther Strikes Again,* in which Lom demonstrates his hard-won success with his psychiatrist, only to have the delicate construction of his new-found mental stability utterly unnerved by the insistent, intricately destructive sympathy of old adversary Clouseau.

Clouseau is perhaps the key invention of the Edwards canon, not only for his embodiment of certain aspects of Edwards's comedy method but also because he provided the means back to commercial viability for Edwards in the seventies. Sellers's Clouseau is in largest measure funny because of his sustained faith in himself, even in the face of the most outrageous challenges to his inner placidity. Attempting to sit on a modernistic couch, there is an incredible peace in his unyielding confidence throughout a 180-degree pratfall. Clouseau belongs to the tradition of the charmed fool, and his considerable virtues and minor flaws as a comic creation essentially derive from that benighted tradition. Yet in the context of Edwards's works, he represents considerably more, although it is not *The Pink Panther* but rather the subsequent *A Shot in the Dark* that is the richest of Edwards's Clouseau films.

The Pink Panther divides its spotlight between Clouseau and the dapper jewel thief Sir Charles (David Niven, still able to do *Raffles* after twenty-five years), with detours to include Sir Charles's nephew, George. The plot complications are elaborate, even though the film is largely given over to extended sequences that are irrelevant to the plot, notably a lengthy party scene and the comic cadenzas in which Clouseau tries to make love to his wife, who is intent instead on rendezvousing with Sir Charles, her lover and confederate. At first, it seems that Edwards might be juxtaposing Sir Charles and Clouseau as contrasts between "free" and "rigid" personalities, but Edwards keeps introducing material that makes the schematism more complex. Sir Charles is rather effectively upbraided over dinner for his Don Juan reputation, which he takes deftly but without attempting refutation, while Clouseau is really only a fool to the extent of his misplaced romantic passion for his wife. It makes a certain comedic sense that they should ultimately switch roles, with Clouseau mistaken for the notorious thief, although the glibness of that resolution dilutes any edge that the comic situations might have had. Still, *The Pink Panther* was Edwards's most convincing demonstration to date that slapstick and sophistication were not incompatible.

Though the outlines of the characterization are established in *The Pink Panther,* the character would change significantly through the course of the series. Clouseau's professed distrust of everyone is paralleled by his inexhaustible faith in the innocence of his women, in the face of all logic to the contrary. He can be open-minded to the point of irrationality. ("I believe everything. I believe nothing," he asserts in *A Shot in the Dark*.) His processes of deduction are completely chaotic, and yet the unyielding obsession of his superior and nemesis Herbert Lom is "What if Clouseau is right?" Ultimately, Clouseau's White Knight insistence on the innocence of Maria Gambrelli (Elke Sommer) proves his feelings and instincts more right, and more ordered, than all the social conventions upheld by the other corrupt characters in *A Shot in the Dark*, not to mention the more rational impulses of the audience. Clouseau maintains his dignity despite innumerable challenges to his aplomb, because his self-image, however deluded, is so secure as to render him unflappable. In a comic distortion of the central Edwards theme, Clouseau remains true to a sense of interior order that, however absurd, can prevail over the order of society, which turns out often to be corrupt, unsatisfying and ultimately just as chaotic. Since chaos is inevitable, we must find our own sense of order, rather than accept the inevitable disintegration operating behind imposed systems of social discipline. Edwards characteristically sees the ridiculous side of personal anarchy, while endorsing its liberating effects. The action of fate may be unpredictable, but the Clouseaus somehow survive with their sense of self-assurance crazily intact.

Clouseau's brand of anachronistic gallantry determines his elaborately disastrous manners and conduct. His solicitude proceeds from his sense of his own character and how it should function, regardless of what situation presents itself. In a world in which the kind of comic catastrophes concocted by Edwards can occur, who's to say that Clouseau's is not the proper response? The world created by Edwards in which Clouseau operates is patently not a real one but a bizarre abstraction that illuminates Edwards's own eccentric perceptions of behavior and the potential for disaster.

Clouseau represents the man of gallantry unaware of the havoc wrought by his singular devotion to a fixed idea. Critics such as Stuart Byron have focused on the gallantry of Edwards's males as a central motif, but what is important is not the gallantry itself but how it proceeds from their personal conceptions of what their character is and how it should function (*vide* Captain Larrabee in *Lili*, Cary Grant in *Petticoat*, or Culley in *S.O.B.*). Manners constitute the surface which the self presents to the world, and they can function as a defense or mask or response or challenge to society. Significantly, manners can neither dominate nor control a situation, but they do provide a means of maintaining a self-image in any confusion. Aplomb is akin to survival. Within the kind of world that Edwards postulates—heartless, cruel, dangerous, unpredictable, capricious, arbitrary—manners represent the means by which characters have resolved to manage their ways through this world. In this sense, he projects the philosophy of Lubitsch forward in time, rather than backward, and his distinctively different visual style represents an appropriately modern response to the very different world to which he applies his wiles.

As a result of his long skein of successes, Edwards moved into more and more expensive projects, and his plots became more and more elaborately constructed. *The Great Race* suffers from serious inflation, particularly over-elaborated in the distended climactic pie-throwing sequence, a slapstick concept far more successfully revived in *The Party*, which manages to make a virtue of showing all of its gag mechanics by elaborating intricate slapstick structures counterpointed to a very subdued Peter Sellers performance.

Between these two exercises in style, Edwards achieved two of his most complex and profound works. *What Did You Do in the War, Daddy?* and *Gunn*. For some unaccountable reason, critics likened the complex farce of the former to the adolescent antics of *Hogan's Heroes,* and the film became Edwards's first major commercial failure. Yet it was also his finest, most resonant achievement to date, a near masterpiece in which every comic conception contributed to a profound elucidation of Edwards's fundamental concerns.

The film opens with a distinctive blend of the parodistic and the ominous. The Sicilian campaign was bloody, and the credits are backed by convincing combat footage. We then see General Bolt taunt his adjutant, Captain Cash, in a deadpan takeoff on *The Naked and the Dead.* Cash is assigned to a decimated unit with orders to take the town of Valermo. Cash, a by-the-book fanatic, is shocked to find the lax discipline of the unit under Lt. Christian. Finding the town deserted, the soldiers fan out through the village square in their choreographed movements designed for effective lateral pans in widescreen format. Everyone is at the soccer field, as the GIs find when a ball is impaled on a bayonet. From that moment on, the colors of the film gradually brighten as the reality of war is forsaken for the lessons of farce.

The Italian commander, Captain Oppo (named perhaps after the assistant director on *The Pink Panther*), would rather surrender, provided of course that the evening's annual festival proceeds unspoiled. When Cash insists that the Italians march off as prisoners forthwith, Oppo redeclares hostilities. Cash's uptight officer is thrown up against the uninhibited hedonism of Oppo and the village, and the result is animosity and conflict (Edwards's extended single-take handling of the scene is more effective than conventional cross-cutting, since by keeping both officers in the same frame, he emphasizes them as contending forces in a situation, not as viable, individual alternatives). It remains for the resourceful Christian to conciliate these opposing forces.

The elaborate party, replete with sight gags, serves a decidedly different purpose from those in, say, *Breakfast at Tiffany's* or *The Pink Panther.* Here the frolicsome chaos is meant to serve as a positive counterweight to the demands of war and the rigidity of command discipline. The performance of Dick Shawn progressively metamorphosizes into an imitation of Daffy Duck, spitting out "I'm in command here!" while he gets a clutch of confetti in the mouth. Muttering about how it's all a trap, he is coerced into drinking a toast to the mayor's daughter Gina (Oppo's girl), when Christian proposes, "Not to drink is to call her ugly!" As often with Edwards, drinking becomes a device for dramatic revelation. With everyone safely soused, the mayor takes a photo of Gina and Cash. The motion picture camera assumes the point of view of the still camera, with an upside-down image. The world has turned topsy-turvy, as Cash surrenders to the revelers.

The morning after, Christian wakes up to the distressing news of an imminent inspection by intelligence officer Pott, only to have his own efforts to whip the company into shape stymied when Oppo, indignant over Cash's bedding of his girl, refuses to cooperate. Meanwhile, the Americans have lost their uniforms in a card game with the Italians, so all identities have been switched. The farcical mechanism is in place, as the implications of Cash's conversion are developed into a convoluted situation, until survival actually depends on the flexibility of the personality to accommodate impersonations of its opposites. Thus, Cash must sport both female drag and Nazi regalia, and in the manic exchanging of uniforms, their symbolic significance becomes thoroughly purged, merely the available materials in the scramble for self-preservation in a world ruled by comically sinister forces.

Edwards's development of the situations in William Peter Blatty's inspired script covers the gamut of possibilities, from Major Pott's mad foray through chaos into madness, as he wanders lost through the catacombs, to the frustrated criminal activity of two tunneling robbers whose miscalculations intervene in the plot (providing the equivalent of a portable trap door), to the terrorist activities of the local motley Communist cell (who perform the only ostensible killing in the film). In a sense, world politics have been reduced to farcical gestures and stratagems that serve to underscore Edwards's fundamental conviction that only individual balance creates stable meanings, while ideology, for all its apparent order, only invites functional anarchy.

The centerpiece of the film is the elaborate false battle engaged in by the two sides when the American command must be hoodwinked until an orderly surrender can be agreed to. Christian assumes the role of director, staging mock combat with zealous attention to detail. James Coburn slyly mimics Edwards's own physical gestures and movements, which accentuate his slight resemblance to the film maker. The sequence is perhaps the most concentrated expression of the Edwards philosophy that the maintenance of order can only succeed as a form of personal expression and that art is the means to survival.

The *Peter Gunn* television series had been the most successful of Edwards's various series (including Dick Powell as *Richard Diamond, Detective; Mr. Lucky;* and on radio, Edmund O' Brien as *Yours Truly, Johnny Dollar*), running three seasons, from 1958 to 1961. *Gunn* was intended to launch a series of films, like the Bonds, which never materialized.

The dialogue in *Gunn,* more than in any other Edwards film, assumes a ritual quality. Peter's putdowns never vary in their deadpan delivery, his interlocutors respond in kind, and Peter's topper signs off the scene. Clever, quirky, and mechanical, the conversations quickly lose their sense of heightened speech.

The world in which Gunn functions is equally eccentric and unparticularized. Although the setting is specified as San Francisco, we see no landmarks but move instead through a progression of netherworld locations without any ostensible directorial comment. Both Gunn and Edwards take this hermetic and exotically corrupt world for granted. They are not concerned with issues of evil or of crime, except as manifestations of a larger and more consuming chaos. The stylized world of *Gunn* is the most extreme abstraction of the Edwardian universe on film, a distillation of the world presented in the earlier films. Those attributes that typify Edwards's vision of existence—incipient threat, individual struggle in opposition to natural chaos, the "sick joke" response to an all-consuming, debilitating knowingness—are here combined to form a laboratory situation for the expression of Edwards's view of survival.

That's why the dialogue direction is handled as a form of artificial behavior, of manners. The characters share a trait in the way they talk—a device that propels the action much as, say, the foibles of Clouseau or the duplicity of the lovers in *Darling Lili.* The surfaces presented by the diverse characters are functionally identical as they exchange brother acts and put-downs with Pete. This stylized behavior creates a backdrop against which the progress of Peter's personality development can be contrasted, as Edwards flattens out the psychological and social details so his protagonist's smallest alterations are discernible.

The need to function as a distinct being in a world where it's hard to differentiate between cop, crook, and private eye requires an ability to find values one is capable of clinging to when value itself is no longer a meaningful concept. Peter maintains his dignity and aplomb no matter what forces attack, and he finds that there is more to love with Edie than a wisecrack. He finds reasons for doing things, when the world respects none. *Gunn* is primarily about the balance between self and society. The most stripped down of his works, it concentrates on the process that the other films only describe.

Unlike the parody of *The Great Race, The Party* represents Blake Edwards's genuine tribute to the silent slapstick comedies. In contrast to a vulgar exercise in condescending burlesque like Mel Brooks's ineffable *Silent Movie, The Party* recognizes that slapstick, in its meticulous requirements, requires great elegance of intellect, even as it appeals to the nether sources of laughter. He does greater honor to the techniques of silent comedy by refusing to compromise his own thematic concerns to fit the outlines of an exercise, instead appropriating the structure and style to fashion yet another meditation on the difficult preservations of personal values in a comically capricious society.

The $2.8 million film was quite unusual in that its script ran only about 65 pages (half an average-length screenplay) and that about one-quarter of it has no dialogue whatever. (The film isn't silent, but then neither were "silent" pictures.) Perhaps more than in any other film, Edwards relied extensively on the improvisational skills of himself and star Peter Sellers. Because of the spirit of experimentation, Edwards first employed during shooting a simultaneous videotape recording of the camera's view of a shot (the video camera mounted on the Mitchell), thereby permitting not only Edwards but also cast and crew the opportunity to analyze and evaluate each take.

Sellers plays Indian actor Hrundi K. Bakshi, imported to Hollywood for the role of a Gunga Din-like character. In his innocently overzealous way, Bakshi destroys the production to the consternation of the unsympathetically drawn director. Roger Greenspun has called the precredit sequence "the funniest slapstick scene since *Steamboat Bill, Jr.,*" and the insertion of the comic figure into massive settings, with so much undone by so little, is one of Edwards's most inspired inventions.

Sellers's Bakshi is one of his intently observant, grave, interior creations of this period, one of those few roles in which his gift for mimicry was submerged in the creation of a rounded, richly detailed character. In the Keaton tradition, Bakshi is imperturbable, though in his eagerness to please there are suggestions of the foreigner-as-Harold Lloyd. Bakshi evinces certain values of politeness, solicitude, gallantry and grace throughout the picture, and he is set against the stereotypes of the party guests as a man of integrity and character. It's not a coincidence that such a man wreaks havoc wherever he goes. A man so at peace with himself can only highlight how the world is out of joint. The scene in which Sellers plays the sitar in intense concentration at first seems like a startling choice in which to display a comic character, but in terms of establishing the solidity of the man's personality, it quickly confers an underlying sobriety that validates the later comedy.

Edwards's effort to invent continuous sight gags was probably foredoomed to unevenness, and there are extended passages that plainly do not work. But *The Party* is above all a concept film, and the arc of accelerating comic amplitude builds smoothly. As Bakshi himself observes, "Wisdom is the province of the aged, but the heart of the child is pure." Eventually, Bakshi becomes aligned with the children of his unwitting hosts in a flood of flower-child energy, as the party becomes awash with soap suds and the sunshine of what seemed in 1968 to be the coming of a new order. Edwards's expression of sympathetic faith in the power of uninhibited innocence to purge the excesses and hypocrisies of the older generation never seems disingenuous, largely because the conviction in his efforts to construct gags is translated into enthusiasm when those gags take on metaphoric significance. *The Party,* like many Edwards films, has an aspect of a fairy tale, but it also serves as Edwards's reminder to himself that there are values that are too precious to be lost. Experience has never seemed to equip anyone in Edwards's world to face the challenges of living in it; if anything, knowingness has brought characters to a pass where it eliminates possibilities of faith without generating acceptable alternatives.

In this sense, Sellers's Bakshi represents both an extension of and an advance on the Clouseau character. He, too, is a harbinger of chaos, as well as a man with a sublime sense of self, however misplaced. But Bakshi also maintains a dignity quite apart from his comic purpose, and in his shy, affecting encounter with his counterpart in innocence (Claudine Longet), he exemplifies the positive implications in those same traits that spell comic disaster for the corrupt world around him. (Edwards attempted to do something comparable in the last Clouseau picture, *The Revenge of the Pink Panther,* but by then the Sellers characterization had eroded to the point where there was no conviction that the development came from anything organic in the character.)

Darling Lili is probably Edwards's paramount masterpiece, a richly textured meditation on the role of art in love and love in art, a mixture of formalism, romance, slapstick, suspense, and musical numbers that explores the vagaries of loyalty, gallantry, love, and art with their necessary ambiguity intact. Edwards's camera has never been more precise in creating meanings out of situations nor more exquisite in his straight-faced way with passion and laughter, which for him are simply two aspects of the same indispensible impulse.

It's amazing how much sexual duplicity Edwards has worked into an ostensibly wholesome family entertainment. Julie Andrews, in the performance of her lifetime, plays the idolized theatrical entertainer Lili Smith, the inspiration to both soldiers abroad and the folks at home. A patriotic symbol, she is also a German spy, in league with her mentor (and possible lover), von Ruger. In perilous times, she is a model of surface control. When zeppelins bomb London during her performance, turning a panicked, crowded theater into an archetypal metaphor for insecurity (see also *Torn Curtain*), Lili is capable of calming the crowd and restoring not merely order but confidence and cheer. She is a masterly manipulator of sublime self-possession. Yet as she sings to an assembly of convalescent veterans, she is also "The Girl in No Man's Land."

Her assignment to pump playboy-flier William Larrabee for information confronts her with her match. Larrabee designs his own mise-en-scène for seduction, and Lili, while passing on his secrets, falls in love, which makes her angry, jealous, and less in control of her situation. Lili's objectives become mixed, leading to some of Edwards's most successful slapstick gags. In a jealous pique, she frames Larrabee and his former mistress, a remarkably chaste stripper, and in a fit of conscience (after receiving the Legion of Honor), she clears him by turning herself in, at which point she and von Ruger are both marked for assassination by German agents.

The characters, both brilliant and insipid, are the apotheosis of those in other Edwards films. Lili, a model of composure, is undone by her encounter with the dashingly irresponsible Larrabee. Each is trying to respond to the rigors of war in the way their personalities are best suited for survival, yet both are compromised in their professed loyalties. Whether comedy, romance, or melodrama, Edwards's movies are notably lacking in a quality of mercy, except for the occasional eccentric love scene. Here what the French have called "the special malice" of Blake Edwards extends to the games his lovers play. They are prone to strange confessions and gentle nostalgias as well as to outlandish mishaps, and that is all part of their valiant attempt to preserve some particle of self-awareness through the absurd, dangerous fray. In the end they overcome their rituals to unite as fantasy lovers in a forgiving postwar world.

Lili's relationship with von Ruger is the most complex and ambiguous of all the mentor relationships in Edwards's work. He is part father figure, part charismatic dominator, unassailably supportive. They remain linked even though she must also free herself of his influence. He makes an effective foil in comparison to Larrabee, because he is equally attractive in his opposing way. Lili's conflicts are probably insurmountable, which is why the film affords her recourse and refuge only in her art.

The opening musical number, "Whistling in the Dark," is shot in a startling 360-degree take that encloses Lili in a void in which the only source of light is upon her. This movement, and the song, is repeated at the end where she is reunited with Larrabee. Visually and musically, the number defines the metaphysical situation in which Lili and the rest are placed. She can only make meaning out of the nothingness through the power of her art, which at first draws only upon her own resources but which at the end is animated crucially by love. The freedom Lili attains is a debatable one—she is still circumscribed by the darkness—but Edwards suggests that since the world does not change because we do, all we can influence is our own sense of purpose and value. In that existential sense, the world is paradoxically both entirely of our own creation and entirely beyond our powers. Such subjectivity is acknowledged as unrealistic, but it marks the difference between egoistic absorption and satisfying human relationships. *Darling Lili* doesn't describe that relationship—*"10"* would do that, again with Andrews—but it unifies the need for love and the necessity of art as essential allies in the struggle against enveloping nullity. In its manipulation of planes of focus, the film suggests that while nothing is as it seems, we must decide for ourselves in what we shall have faith.

There followed two successive butcherings at the hands of MGM and James Aubrey, *Wild Rovers* and *The Carey Treatment.* The former was designed as a two-and-a-half-hour roadshow but was cut against Edwards's wishes by over forty minutes, gutting the narrative. Edwards believes it may have been his finest work, and Arthur Knight, who screened Edwards's cut for his USC class, agrees, but apparently MGM has not preserved the original cut. The latter film was shooting when Edwards realized that it would receive a similar fate, and he contends his heart went out of the project at that point. Edwards retreated from film production for two years and apparently considered giving up directing entirely. He returned to make *The Tamarind Seed* for his wife's company, a work of startling complexity of story and feeling, the most emotionally intricate of all Edwards's films and the best work he would do between the masterpieces of *Darling Lili* and *"10."*

In her first role since *Darling Lili,* Andrews played a vacationing Foreign Service employee who is recovering her emotions after a disastrous love affair she wandered into after the death of her husband in a fiery car accident. Determined to let her injured vulnerabilities heal, she rejects the suave advances of Omar Sharif's Russian agent. Because their contact could represent a breach of security, the respective forces of international intelligence are unleashed on the unsuspecting couple, whose romance blossoms despite Andrews's unwillingness to bed Sharif promptly.

The mechanics of the espionage establishment are plausibly exploited, as the endemic distrust that is the hallmark of the profession is counterpointed to the suspicion between potential lovers. As their guardedness melts, the alarm of governments intensifies. Finally, the world makes it impossible for the lovers to be together safely in it. In a controversial conclusion, the lovers are united in a somewhat implausible happy ending that asserts the transcendence of their romantic attachment over the political world that cannot countenance it. It's an ending with an ambiguous charge of fantasy, more disconcerting than the comparable conclusion to *Darling Lili,* because the earlier scene had the force of a formal device, whereas the shooting of this scene is apparently straight.

Although comparisons could be made to Hitchcock's *Topaz* (which, despite greater individual brilliances, is not nearly as thematically forceful or profound as *The Tamarind Seed*), the most pervasive cross-reference would seem to be Frank Borzage, not only in its romantic, somewhat delirious subject matter but also in the spiritual values Edwards discerns in the nature of his lovers' relationship against the backdrop of political intrigue. The forces set in motion by their encounter reflect the enormous energy released by their bond, and some of the international cross-cutting achieves the visual transcendence that was a hallmark of Borzage's cinema. Edwards is too modern and knowing to accept Borzage's strategies divorced from an astringent character context, yet this is his only film that suggests that love conquers all. In *Darling Lili,* he seemed content to assert only that it survived all. If *The Tamarind Seed* is ultimately less moving, it may be because Edwards cannot escape an element of wishful thinking for all his knowing avoidance of sentimentality.

Edwards's career was finally resuscitated by a return to the *Pink Panther* series, although none of the seventies outings rank with his better work, despite such flashes of inspired invention as the brilliant opening sequence of *The Pink Panther Strikes Again.* Since these three films grossed over $250 million worldwide, Edwards was at last afforded an opportunity to essay a personal project written during his exile, which became his biggest hit, *"10."*

In *"10,"* Edwards examines perfection, our ideas about it and how those ideas strike back, and he virtually achieves it. Dudley Moore plays George Webber, a super-successful songwriter in the throes of midlife crisis complicated by incipient infantilism. (In a deft touch, his lover's son is also named George.) Now literally some twelve years older than he was in *30 is a Dangerous Age, Cynthia,* Moore again essays an antic Everyman at a psychological turning point, flailing against impinging maturity mostly because he can't abide the terrible decisiveness of it. A rebel Wendy, he wants to go back to Never-Never Land.

That Edwards can credibly advance such a man as a surrogate for universal experience is part of his genius. Like all wise men and comic talents, he takes his wisdom where he finds it, and the emotions of the Beautiful Rich are for him no less genuine than those of Pietro Olmi's peasants. In fact, because the details of economic survival can be safely ignored, Edwards's characters are more trenchant examples, since their struggle to survive is more intently interior, though no less desperate. Edwards seeks the truth through his camera, and he knows, as his characters will discover through their peeping at their neighbors through telescopes, that it isn't where you look but how you see. For all its hysteria, *"10"* is a relentlessly sane movie; Edwards at fifty-seven was sufficiently distant from the age of George Webber that he could view the antics with compassionate objectivity.

Edwards has always taken the absurdity of modern life for granted, so he begins where many film makers have strained to end up. He takes George from a sense of his lost possibilities to the point where he learns from his misadventures that possibilities are never lost, only the sense of them. *"10"* takes us on a comic odyssey through mania to maturity, and it shows us how it can all be done.

Comedy in *"10"* is a source of wisdom. It demonstrates that in the cinema, too, the unexamined life is not worth living or at least can make the day one hell to get through. Scrutiny, tempered with compassion, might just bring one to the brink of reality, and the sense of vertigo is wild. Edwards is after bigger game than a rating system for women, weighing the burdens that our expectations of perfection place on our lives. Throughout the film, characters observe with relief that "no one's perfect!" (George himself rates Bo Derek not a "10" but an "11.") Robert Webber's homosexual lyricist calls perfection "a drag." The film works equally well as a study of the transition from romantic fantasy to romantic reality or as an examination of the reconciliation of the soul to the limitless glories of its just confines.

In this sense, *"10"* marks a culmination of the themes Edwards has been exploring in various contexts throughout his career. George undergoes grotesque transformations as his changes in role reflect his changes in personality. The comedy is always an extension of the dramatic argument. George's own fears of aging are hilariously mirrored in the flatulent Mrs. Kissel. His initial pursuit of Jennifer ends in a smashup with a cop car. The electronic-age farce of his missed telephone connections with Julie Andrews catapults him into a literal descent into hysteria.

Invariably, the Edwards characters who are successful in their confrontations with chaos and the prospect of annihilation are those who meet the problem directly, and no one rushes more headlong into disaster than George. Edwards knows that defenses are vital, but he also knows that artificial defenses are worth little over the long haul—you can run, but you can't hide. The confrontation needn't be clear-eyed (viz. Clouseau), but it must be complete. It is the very artificiality of George's fantasies of salvation that lead not only to his undoing but to his enlightenment. It is no coincidence that Edwards met Moore in group therapy.

Of course, Jennifer is not what she seems. Edwards doesn't judge her (as he does George when he permits a woman to blame his impotence on herself); any fault is in the eye of the beholder. Significantly, from the first delirious sight of her, we see her refracted through the long lens of George's subjective view of her, unnaturally magnified and distanced. When he starts to make love to her, the real person is finally revealed, and the romantic dream founders on the hard truth that, yes, no one is perfect.

Edwards has always been scrupulously honest, even courageous, about his own involvement in his themes. This goes beyond the obvious, though important, fact that he is married to Andrews. He is constantly seeking metaphors to link his own viewpoint with that of the audience, such as in the crowded theater threatened by a zeppelin bombing in *Darling Lili*. The cinema is an art where both artist and public are voyeurs, which Edwards highlights through the use of the telescope with which George watches his hedonistic neighbors and they him. When George returns to Sam, they give up, and the camera pans along the telescope, and, with a cut, assumes the viewpoint of the telescope's long lens, the same device through which he had expressed the deluded idealism of George. The iris shot carries associations with Griffith. Through this setup, Edwards achieves a great epiphany, as George starts to make love to Sam to the strains of "Bolero." I know of no more moving demonstration of how salvation is perforce a matter of found materials; the trick is to find whatever tools we can use. The elements of his experience have become the basis for a newly meaningful life. Not only funny, the moment, being seen as through the eyes of the cinema itself, manifests truths about Edwards's art as well. Meditation has settled into contemplation, and voyeurism has been transformed into enlightenment. No act of sex occurs in *"10"* until the frame after the last frame, and the film can justly end when the sex can truly begin.

Perfection, George's shrink notes, is something we no longer are. We all must live with the prospect of death. *"10"* shows that even if we start out knowing everything, we can still learn something and that at the start of every day of reckoning, we can look in the mirror, repeat that no one's perfect, and echo, as *"10"* does, thank God.

S.O.B. may well be the most personal project yet realized by Edwards, and it's obvious that the outlandish events in the film derive from his own decades of experience in the industry. It's a sour, bleak, occasionally bitter view of Hollywood, yet it's also an outrageous farce festooned with elaborate sight gags and smart-alecky one-liners. Its vision is dark, yet its final effect is surprisingly positive. *S.O.B.* is an intricately constructed argument, a stylistically forged abstract, absurd world in which the style gradually ekes out some particle of personal meaning from a hip, enveloping chaos.

S.O.B. boasts no heroes. It doesn't even have a protagonist, or even an individual through whose consciousness our observations can be filtered. We identify with no one. The characters are all types, representing a panoply of relationships between themselves and the business. Not one can be called an artist. They are all articulate spokesmen for their viewpoints, but the only soliloquy on art is given to the rantings of a madman. These are pawns in the malicious scheme of Blake Edwards, who surprisingly seeks not revenge but insight.

Edwards's screenplay exaggerates only a little, mostly by collapsing a lifetime of horror stories into a single spate of incidents and by pitching the performances just an edge over into caricature.

What differentiates these decidedly flawed characters from one another is a quality of decency, of maintaining some semblance of personal value despite a life of moral compromise. Gradually we learn that not all these selfish people are vicious, that some of them have learned to reserve some particle of integrity if only to preserve some sense of themselves as decent human beings. Edwards doesn't sentimentalize this redeeming decency; these men have all made their conscious decisions to sell out. But because it is so hard to sustain even a vestigial humanity in a corrupt and venal world, Edwards appreciates the real value of such small victories.

These characters—William Holden's director, Richard Mulligan's producer, Robert Preston's doctor, and Robert Webber's press agent—carry the burden of Edwards's search for something positive in the treachery of Hollywood. Preston sums up the theme in a drunken scene at a bar: "There isn't a man among us with half a conscience who doesn't keep a hair shirt as part of his permanent wardrobe." It's possible to view *S.O.B.* as a reverse angle on Edwards's *"10."* Where *"10"* examined the concept of perfection and found it pernicious, discerning positive value in the measure by which every man (and dream) must fall short of expectation, *S.O.B.* treats with the full measure of man's venality and corruption, and finds that in this context, even the smallest virtue can be redeeming. Edwards's comedies are ultimately so moving because they have a cathartic effect: The foibles and quirks of being human are what gives us what little nobility we have. In the pratfall is the seed of human value.

As usual, Edwards uses the appearances of objects to suggest their essence. His comedies are not drawn from character, but situation; these are metaphysical farces. People rarely express their feelings except when drunk. While his work is morally charged, Edwards is singularly unconcerned with issues of good and evil. Edwards doesn't play God, as comedy directors are wont to do (after all, they do call down plagues of slapstick upon their hapless buffoons). Rather, he implicates himself in the comic quandaries of his characters. He doesn't exempt himself from the madness of *S.O.B.* Tellingly, the one great speech about the rush of creative juices comes from the mad producer, whose notion of artistic fervor is to insert perverted sex and nudity into the family musical he's just flopped with. Similarly, the director played by Holden has no interest in artistry or self-expression. He's an amiable, decent, hedonistic man who long ago decided that he would not expect any personal satisfaction from his work, so he does his job and takes pleasure from his activities outside it, with the young girls and fancy cars and a few good friends. *S.O.B.* is no jeremiad on the misunderstood and maligned artist. Edwards doesn't proclaim his commitment to art; instead, he fights the Philistines with the only weapon in his arsenal, his ability to make a work of art.

Behavior represents the only means by which a person can distinguish himself from the maelstrom of meaninglessness. Small things, such as Holden's gallantry in picking up teenaged hitchhikers, define the sense of self. In the final analysis, *S.O.B.* suggests there aren't any grand hopes for human virtue. All one can hope to do is keep the compromises acceptable to one's core of value, to maintain half a conscience anyway, and hope that along the way one can find a few good, loyal friends who understand. While it's a bleak conclusion, Edwards so contrasts these small, pyrrhic victories of half-consciences with the childish rampages of characters whose superegos never grew up that we grow to appreciate the weight these blows for decency carry. Just as we must make the best of a harshly indifferent world, so we must strive to find that which is best within ourselves and cherish and protect it. *S.O.B.* lights a candle against the darkness and brings up the wind to a howling pitch.

Throughout his films, Edwards looks at lovers, and how they cannot quite get together, and at life, and at how hard it is simply to survive. The two problems are inseparable, yet only by the creation of mutual trust and, with it, the recognition that the nature of events is often the caprice of nature can they in some small way be resolved. The world is a hostile place, never more so than when inhabited by an impulse to slapstick, and we must find such particles of personal value and make them stick as we can. We forage and, sometimes, we find. The exhaustion at the end of *"10"* is not defeat. The struggle is less to hold onto our fantasies than to let go of them, to see the world truly and crazily, and master ourselves by surmounting it. Out of this struggle, Edwards has fashioned some of the funniest and truest work to emerge from the declining years of Hollywood artistry.

---

19. *Richard Fleischer* (1916)

1946—*Child of Divorce;* 1947—*Banjo;* 1948—*So This Is New York; Design for Death* (documentary); *Bodyguard;* 1949—*The Clay Pigeon; Follow Me Quietly* (uncredited codirector: Anthony Mann); *Make Mine Laughs; Trapped;* 1950—*Armored Car Robbery;* 1952—*The Narrow Margin; The Happy Time;* 1953—*Arena;* 1954—*20,000 Leagues Under the Sea;* 1955—*Violent Saturday; The Girl in the Red Velvet Swing;* 1956—*Bandido; Between Heaven and Hell;* 1958—*The Vikings;* 1959—*These Thousand Hills; Compulsion;* 1960—*Crack in the Mirror;* 1961—*The Big Gamble;* 1962—*Barabbas;* 1966—*Fantastic Voyage;* 1967—*Doctor Dolittle;* 1968—*The Boston Strangler;* 1969—*Che!;* 1970—*Tora! Tora! Tora!* (codirectors: Toshio Masuda, Kinji Fukusaku); 1971—*10 Rillington Place* (Great Britain;

U.S., 1971) *The Last Run* (uncredited codirector: John Huston); *See No Evil;* 1972—*The New Centurions;* 1973—*Soylent Green; The Don Is Dead;* 1974—*The Spikes Gang; Mr. Majestyk;* 1975—*Mandingo;* 1976—*The Incredible Sarah;* 1978—*Crossed Swords;* 1979—*Ashanti;* 1980—*The Jazz Singer*

Uncredited
1951—*His Kind of Woman* (John Farrow)

Among the talented craftsmen who graduated to direction in the forties, Richard Fleischer is one of the few still working steadily today. Following a four-year gap after the commercially unsuccessful *Barabbas,* one or two Fleischer pictures were released every year between 1966 and 1976, many of them expensive productions and quite a few esthetically ambitious. Back in the fifties, some critics, at least in Europe, felt that Fleischer had the makings of a major director, and such films as *Bandido, Violent Saturday,* or *The Vikings* seemed to bear them out. Later, at the time of *Compulsion* and *Crack in the Mirror,* there was a general feeling that he had traded his sense of pace and visual inventiveness for misplaced psychological ambitions. In the sixties, his work was erratic, with costly disasters like *The Big Gamble* and *Doctor Dolittle,* to say nothing of the abysmal *Che!;* yet, far from sinking to the status of a hopeless hack, Fleischer actually directed two of his best pictures, *Barabbas* and *The Boston Strangler,* during the decade. Indeed, his career has been so uneven that its ups and downs have become almost predictable: one interesting film is bound to materialize after a couple of duds. Thus, *10 Rillington Place,* sandwiched in between *Che!* and *Blind Terror.* His more recent thrillers, although they may be dismissed as mindless escapism, are remarkably well made and so is *Mandingo,* a production that was reviled by practically every single critic here and abroad, but for rather questionable reasons, and that should be rehabilitated as one of the director's major achievements. Now in his sixties, Fleischer has survived changes and failures and retained his ability to turn out entertaining and provocative pictures, reason enough not to consign him to benign neglect.

After his apprenticeship as editor, writer, producer, and occasional director in the shorts department at RKO, the son of cartoonist Max Fleischer graduated to feature direction with two tearjerkers starring child actress Sharyn Moffet, who was the title character in *Child of Divorce* and played an Orphan Annie type in *Banjo.* Fleischer was then assigned to a number of small-budget thrillers, including *Follow Me Quietly,* which dealt with a psychopathic killer, a theme that was to recur several times in subsequent films. There were two early, pleasant, non-RKO comedies, *So This Is New York* and *The Happy Time,* but it was with a couple of thrillers, *Trapped* and *The Narrow Margin* (his last film for RKO) that Fleischer really made his mark. Whether coincidentally or not, the films were reminiscent of two Anthony Mann thrillers, *T-Men* and *The Tall Target,* which had recently contributed to raise Mann out of the rank and file of "B" directors. *Trapped,* like *T-Men,* is a semidocumentary account of Treasury Department agents trying to crack a gang of counterfeiters (both films were produced by Eagle-Lion, and *Trapped* may have been launched in an effort to cash in on the box-office success of Mann's film). *The Narrow Margin,* like *The Tall Target,* takes place almost entirely aboard a train. Although not quite in a class with Mann's minor masterpiece, it is a consistently inventive demonstration of what a good director can do with a train despite a small budget and a routine script. Whereas in *Murder on the Orient Express*—to take a much later instance of rail-borne mystery—Sidney Lumet makes *his* train look as roomy as a luxury hotel on wheels and leaves it conveniently stranded by a snowdrift for most of the footage, thus eliminating the problem of noise, Fleischer systematically exploits the claustrophobic feeling generated by narrow corridors or cramped compartments and uses the whole range of train sounds to the best atmospheric and dramatic effect.

In the year of the 3-D craze, Fleischer was put in charge of one of the two MGM entries in the field, *Arena*, a rodeo story starring Gig Young. More importantly, he got a chance to direct his first big-budget (and first CinemaScope) film, the magnificently produced *20,000 Leagues Under the Sea,* quite possibly the finest live-action feature ever to come out of the Disney studios, as well as one of the very best screen adaptations of Jules Verne. In such moments as the awe-inspiring first apparition of the *Nautilus* as it emerges from the slowly dissipating fog, Fleischer recaptured the magic everyone remembers experiencing when first reading the novel. A sensitive performance by James Mason as Nemo and an infectiously ebullient one by Kirk Douglas as Ned Land, evocative art direction, effective special effects, and fine photography all contributed to a first-rate spectacle.

His next film, *Violent Saturday,* was an ambitious thriller that closely scrutinized the effects of a bank holdup on a sampling of a small town's population. In *The Girl in the Red Velvet Swing,* an intriguing recreation of the murder of architect Stanford White by millionaire Harry Thaw, the murderer's homosexual attraction to his victim was suggested with both subtlety and daring. *The Vikings,* although it could not avoid some degree of silliness in the intimate and "psychological" scenes, was a highly stimulating adventure yarn with superior location shooting and a climactic sword fight filmed with breathtaking bravura. As Fleischer's best film of the fifties, however, one might single out *Bandido,* a complex, tongue-in-cheek Western reminiscent of Robert Aldrich's *Vera Cruz,* in which Robert Mitchum, most unheroic as a quiet weapons and ammunition salesman in 1910 Mexico, unwittingly changes the course of the revolution by destroying the government troops' machine-guns out of sheer annoyance at being disturbed by the noise. Ernest Laszlo's fine deep-focus CinemaScope photography added visual excitement to the film's felicitous blend of humor and adventure. *Bandido* suggested that Fleischer had a flair for the Western genre, which he had not tackled before; however, he was to make only one more Western, *These Thousand Hills,* which was rather blandly directed despite strong characterization and a fairly realistic atmosphere.

Fleischer's subsequent Zanuck period started not unpromisingly with his adaptation of the Meyer Levin novel and play *Compulsion,* suggested by the Leopold-Loeb murder case (it gave Orson Welles a chance to impersonate Clarence Darrow), but floundered with *Crack in the Mirror,* a story doomed from the start by its preposterously artificial premise (the brainchild of Zanuck himself, who wrote the script under a pseudonym), and *The Big Gamble,* a confused African adventure in which Stephen Boyd kept getting into trouble while trying to truck-haul some beer on the Ivory Coast. *The Big Gamble* did not pay off and put an end to the Fleischer-Zanuck collaboration, as well as to Zanuck's African forays and to his protégée Juliette Greco's career as an aspiring international star.

The Zanuck fiasco was followed by what might be called the Dino De Laurentiis misunderstanding. A producer whose partiality to mindless spectacle was becoming more and more pronounced at the time, De Laurentiis may not have suspected that *Barabbas,* as adapted by Christopher Fry from the Pär Lagerkvist novel and directed by Fleischer, would turn out, despite its spectacular aspects, as a character study and the anatomy of a myth, rather than a traditional biblical epic. The film is a grimly powerful drama, focusing on the Caliban-like figure of Barabbas (a natural for Anthony Quinn, who did the part justice), a brute solely intent upon survival, puzzled and enraged by his own legend, unable to comprehend the moral upheaval the world around him is going through, yet slowly growing aware of the impact, if not the meaning, of Christianity, and eventually driven to an absurd act of solidarity with the Christians. Fleischer's work has moments of greatness, especially in the nightmarish sulphur-mine sequences, which depict the hopelessness and physical horror of slave labor with a harrowing, Dantean vividness rarely equaled on the screen.

Barabbas was too relentlessly somber to appeal to the audience for which it superficially seemed to be intended, and its failure caused Fleischer to remain inactive for several years. As if he had learned his lesson, he returned to directing in 1966 with a production that seemed to negate his previously demonstrated ability to create intelligent spectacle. Touted at the time as the most expensive science-fiction film ever made, *Fantastic Voyage* was a triumph of technology over creativity and of matter over mind. Its director's task must have been a largely logistical one, supervising and coordinating the fantastically elaborate work from the art and special-effects departments. It certainly did not extend to directing the cast in any imaginative way, for the performances were wooden and stolid in the science-fiction film tradition and in harmony with a script that effectively nipped in the bud the poetic, surrealistic potentialities of the premise. Neither did Fleischer do much to enliven *Doctor Dolittle,* a project that seems to have put him to sleep, although a few moments (e.g., the circus sequence) were inventively handled.

After these routine, if large-scale, assignments, *The Boston Strangler* provided Fleischer with material more suited to his talent, as it enabled him to combine suspense, psychology, and social comment in a way reminiscent of some of his best earlier films. The result is quite probably his finest work. One would be hard pressed to cite a contemporary film exhibiting more restraint in the handling of an admittedly sensational topic. Indeed, to eschew sensationalism seems to have been one of Fleischer's major concerns. The murders are suggested, rather than shown, and there is no lingering over the victims' bodies. Not a mere display of "good taste," this restraint is an essential feature of the film's style. The repeated cutting from "before" (women unsuspectingly opening their doors) to "after" (the discovery of the bodies by friends, neighbors, police) underscores the fact that the strangler himself, although occasionally heard, is not seen for the first forty minutes or so and helps to create a heightened sense of threat and inevitability and to build up suspense more effectively than any amount of terror and violence could. Fleischer's use of the split screen, which in some scenes seems a superfluous substitute for traditional cutting, is at other times highly efficient (e.g., the rounding-up of the suspects); on the whole, it functions as a logical stylistic outgrowth of the diversity of angles and wealth of detail (on police, politics, the media, and mass psychology) that Edward Anhalt incorporated to his tight, sturdy script. Equally well handled is the film's shifting of gears in midcourse and its focusing on a one-on-one confrontation that substitutes psychological suspense for the kaleidoscopic, action-oriented approach of the first part. Working in tension-filled long takes, Fleischer elicited an extraordinary performance from Tony Curtis as the schizophrenic DeSalvo painfully reconstructing his murderous activities—and discovering himself in the process—under the compassionate but relentless prodding of Assistant District Attorney Bottomly (one of Henry Fonda's best performances in the sixties).

Fleischer's directorial chores on *Tora! Tora! Tora!,* the American–Japanese coproduction about Pearl Harbor, concluded his association with Fox, which had produced all his films since 1966. The two pictures he then went on to make in England were, at least apparently, derivative, since one, *See No Evil,* was, like the successful *Wait Until Dark* a few years earlier, a thriller about a blind young woman and the other, *10 Rillington Place,* was, like *The Boston Strangler,* a study of a real-life sex killer. *10 Rillington Place,* however, is a major work in its own right and as underrated a picture as *Barabbas.* A meticulous recreation of the John Christie case (filmed in London and using the transcript of the Christie trial for added authenticity), it is so painstaking in its detailing of the sordid, the bizarre, and the pathological that its documentary realism, rather than an end in itself, becomes a means for Fleischer to explore the boundless and inimitable weirdness of reality. One of the puzzling points Fleischer had emphasized in *The Boston Strangler* was the ease with which the murderer gained access to his victims' apartments. Gullibility, and what almost appears to be a sheer willingness to be deceived, are a major theme in *10 Rillington Place,* too. No lie is blatant enough to alert Christie's naive victims, who blindly throw themselves into the most conspicuous traps. When he selects a married woman as his next prey her husband turns out to be an illiterate, moronic mythomaniac who lives in a fantasy world and makes things easier rather than more difficult for the killer. Were it not so doggedly factual, the film might join the ranks of such fantasies of organized extermination as *Kind Hearts and Coronets* or *Monsieur Verdoux,* whose corrosive humor it occasionally brings to mind.

Since Fleischer's parting with Fox, most of his films have been comparatively routine thrillers that came and went swiftly and without much fanfare, despite the presence of such stars as George C. Scott, Anthony Quinn, or Lee Marvin. The two outstanding exceptions were the expensively produced and commercially very successful *Soylent Green* and *Mandingo.* The former, faithful to a long tradition of pessimism in science fiction, took the direct predictions of ecologists and neo-Malthusians to the letter, combining the themes of food shortage and demographic expansion gone wild into an apocalyptic vision of overcrowding and starvation in New York City circa 2022. While the film's credibility is sometimes rather shaky, Fleischer derives his most spectacular effects from its questionable premise. The bleakly fantastic vision of helpless, starving thousands jamming New York streets, office buildings, churches and subways, being herded by police or shoveled away by riot control trucks is reminiscent of one of the most powerful achievements in his work, the sulphur-mines sequence in *Barabbas.* The plot proper, however, is disappointing, despite its coy toying with the taboo of cannibalism (excess population are turned into the title food substance—a fate that nearly befalls Charlton Heston). Ultimately, the best thing about *Soylent Green* is proba- bly the Edward G. Robinson character, an anachronistic relic from the past, and his relationship with Heston, and the film may be remembered as much for Robinson's moving performance in his last screen appearance as for its futuristic spectacle.

The case of *Mandingo* is a curious one and calls for some detailed comment. It was received with loud disapproval by the critics, who were too outraged to mention, or presumably to even notice, its formal qualities. The film, however, can and should be vindicated on the very ground upon which it was assailed. "Cheap sensationalism" in the treatment of slavery was the critical consensus. Granted, the source novel *is* sensational, and the screen adaptation in no way attempts to tone down its lurid aspects. It would be naive to suppose that producer De Laurentiis had other, nobler intentions in making the film than those the critics damned it for or even that Fleischer himself was not basically in agreement with them. Yet the end result provides a valid dramatic insight into the structure and meaning of slavery, and one might contend that it does so not despite its "sensationalism" but because of it.

The most common criticism against *Mandingo* was its obsession with sex and sadistic violence; the concentration on sexuality and, more specifically, miscegenation supposedly obscured the "real" issues, as if sexual behavior and attitudes were isolated phenomena bearing no relation to ideology and politics. What the film clearly verifies, on the contrary, is that the nature of sexual practice in a given culture is inextricably linked to its ethics, economics, and social structures. No matter how melodramatic, the events depicted in *Mandingo* are credible and, in a way, inevitable, for in a social system based upon slavery, interracial sex is bound to proliferate, and sexual behavior is bound to take a violent, sadistic turn.

Sexual availability is one aspect among others of the slave's total availability to the master, and it is therefore natural that the master should take advantage of it. Using slaves sexually is only one of the master's many ways of asserting his dominance over them. However, the master is likely to feel degraded by the act, since the slave is inferior, hardly human, and his shame and rage at his degradation naturally turn against the slave. This mental process is best exemplified by the Susan George character who orders a slave to have sex with her, warning him at the same time that she will tell her husband that he has raped her, whether or not he complies with her request. She thus simultaneously uses the slave for sexual gratification and takes her revenge upon him for allowing herself to give in to her lust. The film also shows, one might add, how the existence of the master-slave relationship tends to corrupt other kinds of relationships: white master humiliates his wife by sleeping with a slave and having a child with her; wife retaliates by sleeping with a slave and giving birth to a black baby. Thus the existence of slavery triggers an endless cycle of mutual degradation.

The film's emphasis on sadistic violence and torture, then, whatever its intended effect on the audience, derives from the very nature of the subject matter, not only because the ruthless, often overtly sadistic treatment of slaves by their masters is an historically documented fact (indeed, any objective, documentary attempt at depicting what actually went on would have to be considerably more shocking than any fiction film on slavery ever made, including *Mandingo*), but also because the perversion of human relationships entailed by the institutionalization of slavery has brutality built into it and naturally tends toward sadistic behavior.

As an example of "objectionable" but ultimately meaningful violence, one may single out the scene in which two wealthy gentlemen have their strongest slaves fight each other with no holds barred before a thrilled audience composed of the best local society. The fight is interminable, appallingly brutal and bloody, and quite unbearable. Yet, nothing could better illustrate the slave's subhuman condition (they fight "like animals," and clearly, to their audience, they are no more than that) or the utter hopelessness of a situation in which his survival depends on the maiming, and possibly killing, of his black brother for the amusement of the white oppressor.

Fleischer's direction makes almost palpable the atmosphere of sickness, corruption, and decay that permeates the film. It beautifully captures the oppressing gloom of the huge, rambling mansion with its barren rooms plunged in a perpetual semidarkness, orange sunlight seeping through heavy shades during the day, murky dinners lit only by candles held by a couple of black boys. This flair for atmosphere, combined with Fleischer's brilliantly dynamic handling of several exterior sequences (e.g., a manhunt and lynching), somewhat make up for the dramatic weaknesses and the trashiness of the characterization (which flaws, however, are, like the "sensationalism," a conse-quence of the very nature of the subject matter as much as of poor writing).

Fleischer's lush, elaborate camera work in *Mandingo* is typical of a style that has always favored the decorative over the functional, while, thematically, the film's bleak pessimism is in keeping with the dominant mood of a long, although not uninter-rupted, series of works dealing with neurotic loners and losers, pitiful psychopaths locked inside their sick private worlds, the helpless and the downtrodden. There is a curious discrepancy between this downbeat trend in Fleischer's films and his healthy professionalism, his cheerful willingness to tackle almost any kind of assignment. This is the only noticeable puzzle in the personality and career of an otherwise uncomplicated film craftsman.

20. John Frankenheimer (1930)

1957—*The Young Stranger;* 1961—*The Young Savages;* 1962—*All Fall Down; Birdman of Alcatraz; The Manchurian Candidate;* 1964—*Seven Days in May;* 1965—*The Train;* 1966—*Seconds; Grand Prix;* 1968—*The Fixer;* 1969—*The Extraordinary Seaman; The Gypsy Moths;* 1970—*I Walk the Line;* 1971—*The Horsemen;* 1973—*The Impossible Object* (France; unreleased in U.S.); *The Iceman Cometh;* 1974—*Ninety-nine and 44/100% Dead!;* 1975—*French Connection II;* 1976—*Black Sunday;* 1979—*Prophecy;* 1982—*The Equals*

Frankenheimer may not have directed more than a few completely satisfactory pictures, but he has rarely made an indifferent one, which is perhaps more important. His command of the medium, his taste for challenging topics, and the enthusiasm he brings to them bear witness to the soundness of his personality; so does his steadfast refusal to let himself be pigeonholed by producers, critics, or audiences. In some of his later pictures (e.g., *The Gypsy Moths* or *I Walk the Line*), he has evidenced a maturity, a deepening sensitivity that place him among the foremost directors of his generation.

"Serious" critics, however, have been fairly consistent in their dismissal of Frank-enheimer. At the beginning, he was saddled with his television background, as it was then taken for granted that a small-screen director could not make the grade in movies. Later, because of his association with Burt Lancaster, he was branded as a big star's yes-man, and his taking over the direction of *The Train* from Arthur Penn was grist to the mill of his detractors, who immediately cast Penn as the martyr and Frankenheimer as the ruthless opportunist. *Seconds* was vilified by a unanimously hostile press (and reactions at Cannes were so negative that the director refused to show up for his press conference). *Grand Prix* was sneered at for its commercialism. *The Gypsy Moths* and *I Walk the Line* were either ignored or dismissed as pretentious trash (they are much admired in France by the *Positif* critics, however). *The Horsemen* remains one of the most obscure and rarely shown films of the sixties. The succes d'estime of *The Iceman Cometh* did not quite extend to its director, whose name was not even mentioned in *The New York Times*'s lengthy review. *The Impossible Object,* a French production that has not been released in the United States and which Frankenheimer considers his most personal film, got scathing reviews from all the French critics. *French Connection II,* in some ways a much better picture than William Friedkin's multi-Academy Award winner, did not get a tenth of the earlier film's critical acclaim and went almost unnoticed. So it goes.

Frankenheimer's films are primarily distinguished by their visual impact. Although he rarely indulges in flashy techniques (what he calls "shooting through the wagon wheels"), his setups tend to be eye-catchers. They enhance reality, impart people and objects with a disquieting presence. He has a flair for slam-bang openings that grab the spectator's attention and keep him riveted: the blind boy's murder in *The Young Savages,* the demonstration outside the White House in *Seven Days in May,* the bewildering cross-cutting of the introduction to *The Manchurian Candidate,* the wide-angle traveling shot through Grand Central Station in *Seconds,* the Cossacks' raid in *The Fixer.* His endings, too, often take us by surprise, whether he wraps up a superspectacle in a minor key (*The Train*) or unsettles his audience with one of the most offbeat, and downbeat, conclusions on record (*Seconds*). Another Frankenheimer trademark, at least in his earlier films, is a taste for bizarre plot twists and dramatic shock effects. If one refuses to see beyond such characteristics, Frankenheimer may appear as a director more intent on sensation than suspense. However, he has proved with *The Gypsy Moths* and, to a lesser extent, *The Fixer* or *I Walk the Line* that he could eschew formal effect and successfully concentrate on relationships, feelings, and atmosphere.

Most of Frankenheimer's films deal with the individual's alienation in modern society, not an original theme to be sure but one he handles with honesty and an unusual disregard for easy solutions. The misunderstood adolescent of *The Young Stranger;* the drifter-rebel of *All Fall Down;* the ghetto youths of *The Young Savages;* the brainwashed soldiers of *The Manchurian Candidate;* the politicians, isolated and rendered helpless by their own power, of *Seven Days in May;* the executive of *Seconds* who seeks an alternative to his aimless existence and finds even worse aimlessness in his "second" life; the disenchanted sky diver and the bored, loveless housewife of *The Gypsy Moths;* the fatally infatuated sheriff of *I Walk the Line* are all examples of traumatic inadaptation and of an ensuing loss of intellectual and moral integrity. Although the emphasis has shifted from the predominantly social or political concerns of such early films as *The Young Savages* or *Seven Days in May* to a deepening insight into the characters' emotions in *The Gypsy Moths* and *I Walk the Line,* the typical Frankenheimer hero has always been a man alone and under stress. The height of physical and emotional isolation is reached with the incarcerated protagonists of *Birdman of Alcatraz* and *The Fixer* who, in their struggle to preserve their sanity and human dignity against crushing odds, turn out to be Frankenheimer's most positive heroes.

The theme of solitude as an inevitable fact of life is emphasized by the lack of "meaningful" relationships between men and women and by the inadequacies and ultimate failure of what few relationships are portrayed. Practically all the couples in Frankenheimer's films are mismatched, painfully and ludicrously so in *I Walk the Line.* There are unhappy married people in *Seconds, Grand Prix, The Gypsy Moths, I Walk the Line, The Impossible Object.* The only married hero who doesn't seem to have major marital trouble is Burt Lancaster in *The Young Savages;* still, the wife's characterization is not really sympathetic. A wealthy, liberal socialite, she almost gives the impression of having married her husband, an assistant district attorney who struggled his way out of the slums, as a form of field work. Relationships often end up in tragedy (Eva Marie Saint's suicidal car ride at the end of *All Fall Down,* Lancaster's deliberate jump to his death in *Gypsy Moths,* Montand's death in a car crash in *Grand Prix*). The hero of *The Fixer* is betrayed twice by women, first by his wife who leaves him for another man, then by a rich girl whose advances he scorns and who incriminates him when he is wrongly suspected of murder. In *I Walk the Line,* the sheriff is deceived and made a fool of by the teenage girl he has fallen in love with. In the latter case, as in *All Fall Down,* the failure is a result of one of the partner's immaturity and irresponsibility. A more pervasive sense of inadequacy prevails in *The Gypsy Moths,* where both Deborah Kerr and Burt Lancaster are dissatisfied with their lives but, despite their strong attraction to each other, find it impossible to overcome the differences in background and life-style that keep them apart. *The Impossible Object,* from what we know of it, also deals with the problems of middle age, marital dissatisfaction, and fear of commitment.

Frankenheimer's major professional problem lies in the fact that he has become an increasingly introspective artist in an industry that has him labeled as an action director. His handling of his own career bears witness to his dissatisfaction with the label, and his versatility is more an expression of his resistance to it than a proof of opportunism. A prolific director (he made twelve films between 1961 and 1970), he consistently worked against type during the sixties. His first three pictures seemed to establish him as a specialist of adolescent problems, yet most of his subsequent films were about adult, often middle-aged heroes. After the confined, claustrophobic *Birdman of Alcatraz,* a painstaking biography with an obsession for realistic detail, the broad political fantasy of *The Manchurian Candidate* was a complete change of gear. *Candidate* and *Seven Days in May,* both slightly paranoid fantasies about international relations, politics, and the power of the military, were highly successful yet did not turn Frankenheimer into a purveyor of speculative political thrillers. As a matter of fact, except for *Black Sunday,* none of his later pictures could be described as a thriller, political or otherwise, and only *Seconds* contains a fantasy element.

With *The Train,* Frankenheimer did not merely demonstrate his ability to handle a big-budget spectacle, he turned it into a work of epic beauty. It is doubtful that Arthur Penn could have done any better given the material. The material, incidentally, was nothing to be sneered at. Film seems to have a natural affinity for trains and railroads, and their power, their sheer poetry have rarely been as vividly captured as in Frankenheimer's picture. As for Lancaster, one understands, watching *The Train,* why he valued Frankenheimer so much as a director. He had given fine dramatic performances in *The Young Stranger* and *Birdman of Alcatraz,* but in *The Train* he is seen from beginning to end doing what he always was best at: purely physical action requiring speed, skill, accuracy, coordination, and total concentration. His boundless energy is at times curiously reminiscent of Keaton's in *The General,* probably the greatest railroad picture ever made and one *The Train* follows not too far down the list. After *The Train,* Frankenheimer recalls that he was "offered every action picture that was going to be made," but he again steered clear of the easy road and picked up an earlier project, *Seconds,* which he knew was going to be a gamble. Indeed, the film was a complete critical and box-office failure.

The most disconcerting of Frankenheimer's pictures, *Seconds,* like so many stories based upon an initial mystery, fails to sustain the excitement generated by its intriguing premise once the mystery has been cleared up. The opening sequences are fascinating in their conjuring of an eerie atmosphere out of the fabric of everyday decor and action, but the film bogs down after the hero, a New York banker tired with his life, has acquired a new identity through facial surgery and been relocated in California.

The attempt at depicting a West Coast artists' colony is unconvincing in a typical Hollywood way, and a drawn out grape-harvesting sequence, intended to convey a sense of communion with nature and healthy sexual abandon, only succeeds in being ludicrous. The true reason for the film's failure, however, may be its utter pessimism: unable to find any contentment in his new life, the hero returns to his home and family but can't readjust to them, and when he seeks help from the company that arranged the original change for him, they promptly murder him. We are stuck with our lives, the moral seems to be, and if we don't like them, the only way out is death.

From *Seconds,* his least commercial picture up to that time, Frankenheimer went on to make his most commercial one, *Grand Prix.* Although the themes most prominent in *Seconds* (dissatisfaction, loneliness) did recur in *Grand Prix,* they were submerged in an endless round of spectacularly engineered car crashes, and there is little about the film that could be called personal. Physically his biggest assignment (Cinerama, ten-million-dollar budget, three-hour running time, and, in his own words, "an immense undertaking"), *Grand Prix* could have been Frankenheimer's passport to the world of superspectacles. Instead, his next picture was a modest, satirical World War II comedy, *The Extraordinary Seaman* (which he has called "dreadful"), and the one after that, *The Fixer,* was the complete antithesis of a big-budget spectacular. A somber, brooding drama, deliberately drab-looking and oppressively claustrophobic (the entire second half of the film takes place in a prison cell), *The Fixer* is a shattering, almost physically painful but ultimately uplifting experience for the viewer. Frankenheimer gives tremendous impact to the depiction of his hero's ordeal through months of physical and mental torture, of his slow awakening to political consciousness (the film aptly illustrates the hero's remark at the end of Bernard Malamud's novel: "One thing I've learned, there is no such thing as an unpolitical man"), and to the notion that such values as dignity and basic human rights must take precedence over mere survival.

The Gypsy Moths was, again, a complete surprise, for a Frankenheimer picture dealing with professional parachute jumpers naturally suggested an airborne variation on the *Grand Prix* formula, whereas the film is actually a low-key, intimate study of complex mental states and relationships. Frankenheimer was aware of the problem when he stated before the film's release: "There will be no similarity whatsoever here between men in racing cars and the men who jump with parachutes. If anybody tells me this is a film about parachute jumping I'll feel like hitting them over the head." Metro, which couldn't have cared less, played up the parachute jumping and tried for the family market by opening *The Gypsy Moths* at New York's Radio City Music Hall (with some lovemaking between Burt Lancaster and Deborah Kerr removed to avoid an R rating). In an additional confirmation of the director's fears, the film was shown in France under the title *Les Parachutistes arrivent,* which must have suggested some kind of war movie to unsuspecting French audiences, since *parachutiste* usually means *paratrooper.* (*Cahiers du Cinéma* listed the film among current releases as *Les Parachutistes attaquent!*)

To say that *The Gypsy Moths* is not about parachute jumping is of course an exaggeration and actually does an injustice to the film's cohesion, for the aerial scenes (which were beautifully filmed and edited) are perfectly integrated to the thematic and dramatic texture of the narrative. Parachute jumping provides an apt metaphor for the deceptive sense of freedom the three sky divers derive from their drifting existence. The excitement of the jumps and free falls only leads to the despondency that accompanies the return to the ground; and the freedom of choice that the hero,

Rettig, insists upon as the one positive element in his life turns out to be nothing but a freedom to choose death over a meaningless life. After Rettig's suicidal jump, Malcom, his younger partner, realizes that the exhilaration of the stunt is dangerously conducive to the acting out of the death wish, as he experiences the temptation not to open his parachute during his own jump. The sky divers are attracted to death like gypsy moths to a flame. More generally, the film deals with the necessity for everybody to take jumps, i.e., to make choices; the woman with whom Rettig falls in love will choose not to leave her husband for him, although her own life is meaningless.

Thus, *The Gypsy Moths* confronts conflicting life-styles and values only to bring out the common disenchantment and suppressed anguish that lie underneath the masks of everyday attitudes. The five main characters all lead lives of quiet desperation, whether it is the wandering, aimless existence of the stuntmen or the loveless, stunted life of a middle-aged, middle-class couple. Frankenheimer depicts with equal delicacy the genuine, though at times strained, friendship among the three flyers and the subtle tensions that arise from their contacts with the townspeople. The uneasiness and diffidence that pervades their meeting with the Brandons—Malcom's aunt and her husband—is conveyed with acute, although understated, sensitivity, while a later scene brings gentle humor to the somewhat incongruous situation of Burt Lancaster's lecturing a group of local matrons on his craft and demonstrating parachute folding to them. Most remarkable, perhaps, is Frankenheimer's handling of the love affair between Rettig and Elizabeth Brandon, a rare instance of such a relationship being dealt with in a movie. The approach is tasteful, compassionate, and frank: the sexual attraction of the two for each other is not glossed over.

In many ways a companion piece to *The Gypsy Moths, I Walk the Line,* Frankenheimer's next film, proved even more pessimistic. It is another study of existential malaise set in small-town America (this time Tennessee), with the protagonist again a confused, disillusioned middle-aged man who seeks an escape from despair in a hopeless love affair. But whereas Rettig retained self-control and dignity even in the midst of his self-destructiveness, Tawes, the small-town sheriff of *I Walk the Line,* falls to pieces and gets into serious trouble as a result of his infatuation with a teenage girl, the daughter of a local moonshiner. Many of the structural patterns of *The Gypsy Moths* are reversed in *I Walk the Line.* In the earlier film, the protagonist, as part of a group of outsiders, brought a disruptive element to the town's ordered life; in *I Walk the Line,* that element is represented by the girl, her father and brothers, while the protagonist is the symbol (albeit inadequate) of law and order, a pillar of the community. *The Gypsy Moths* opens with the arrival of the disruptive group in town; *I Walk the Line* closes with their departure. Where Rettig was level-headed enough to realize that his relationship with Elizabeth could lead nowhere, Tawes realizes nothing until the last minute, when his girlfriend, who now has no more use for him, makes her rejection of him perfectly clear by slashing his arm with a bailing hook. The general mood of the film, however, is similar to that of *The Gypsy Moths* and so is Frankenheimer's attitude toward his characters. Despite Tawes's total loss of control of himself and the situation, the spectator is not encouraged to feel either contempt or pity for him; the girl and her relatives are not portrayed as degenerate or even, in her case, particularly bad people but rather as puzzling specimens of humanity, almost innocent in their amorality. (Pauline Kael's complaint that the film "oozes sanctimoniousness" is a clear case of the critic's confusing the film maker's material and his treatment of it.) In the end, the film leaves us, more than anything else, with a sense of bewilderment at the unpredictable vagaries of human nature and passes no judgment on them.

After *The Gypsy Moths* and *I Walk the Line,* Frankenheimer's career was, commercially, at a low ebb, and *The Horsemen,* which he shot in Afghanistan and Spain in early 1971, didn't do much to help, as the film only had the briefest of careers in the United States (as with the two preceding pictures, the distributors made little discernible effort to promote it). Then, in yet another shift to a totally different type of picture, he accepted the awesome assignment of putting on film a complete, four-hour version of *The Iceman Cometh,* to be the key entry in the first season of Ely Landau's American Film Theatre series. It has become a sort of tradition for ex-television directors to take on screen adaptations of O'Neill, and after the abysmal *Desire Under the Elms* (Delbert Mann) and Sidney Lumet's erratic *Long Day's Journey Into Night,* the smoothness and care Frankenheimer brought to the project (his first filmed play) may seem a huge step forward. Yet one wonders whether such endeavors are not ultimately doomed to remain exercises in futility. Indisputably the most thoughtful screen version of an O'Neill play, the film is also stupefyingly boring. While one may take exception to some aspects of Frankenheimer's direction, he can hardly be blamed for what is more probably the consequence of an irremediable rift between the material and the medium.

It is not on account of mere bad luck or lack of expertise that most of the dozen or so motion pictures made from O'Neill plays during the sound era were disastrous failures (the least dreary of them, Rouben Mamoulian's *Summer Holiday,* a semimusical version of *Ah! Wilderness,* was the one that tampered most with the original play; even John Ford's much-admired *Long Voyage Home* is weighted down by turgid writing and melodramatic plot contrivances). It can be reasonably argued that O'Neill cannot and should not be done on the screen. He was a "pure" playwright (how good or limited is another question) inasmuch as his characters and the speeches he put in their mouths need the actual presence of actors upon a stage in order to come alive. His writing is so fraught with dramatic convention that no other medium can do it justice. On the written page or on film, all that comes through is the bombast and hollowness of his stilted prose. It doesn't make much difference, then, what amount of talent and intelligence goes into the filming of an O'Neill play. There is undeniable elegance in Frankenheimer's deep-focus long takes, his careful, deliberately stagelike groupings, his sparse but effective use of camera movements, and many of his transitions from long shots to close-ups, from ensemble to individual playing. The photography, shadowy but sharp, has a Toland-like quality, especially in the latter portion of the film when the action moves out of the backroom into the bar proper. Fredric March in his last screen role and Robert Ryan in his penultimate one are frighteningly well cast: they look exactly like the dying men they are playing and which they actually were at the time. These are fine performances, but they never come to life in filmic terms and neither does the movie itself, which in this case, is little more than the sum of its performances.

Freed from the straitjacket of faithfulness to the Word, Frankenheimer went on to make one of his most interesting films, *French Connection II,* which he deliberately fashioned into an almost exact opposite of Friedkin's slam-bang hit. Largely shot in Marseilles, the film is a grim yet often funny essay on culture shock and alienation, a character study rather than an adventure yarn. The obligatory chases and shootouts are all bunched in the last half hour, while the bulk of the film is actionless and unsuspenseful. Popeye Doyle (again played by Gene Hackman, who had given one of his finest performances in a character part in *The Gypsy Moths* and who had requested Frankenheimer as director) is stripped of the seedy glamour that had made the personage popular and comes across throughout most of the film as an arrogant slob and chauvinist, blundering, erratic, irresponsible, and eventually driven to psychotic murderousness (in a frighteningly literal cleansing ritual, he spreads gasoline throughout the hotel in which drug dealers have kept him prisoner and doped and gleefully sets the building ablaze). What makes Frankenheimer's Popeye affecting despite this "ugly American on the beat" image is his utter loneliness, his helpless frustration at finding himself in a country whose language he can neither speak nor understand and whose ways are thoroughly alien and disturbing to him ("I'd rather be a lamp post in New York City than the President of France," he remarks bitterly). Whether buying drinks for a hopelessly monolingual waiter in a café called, with apposite irony, "Le Florida" or, half-drunk, tearfully blabbering about baseball to a French colleague who has never heard of Mickey Mantle or screaming for a Hershey Bar "with the nut in it" or desperately attempting to convey to a native the concept of "mayonnaise," Popeye in Marseilles is the epitome of alienation, an alienation with which Frankenheimer, as an American who has lived in France for years, can empathize without romanticizing it. Thus the character, while retaining basic psychological and behavioral features established in Friedkin's film, is enriched and deepened as he becomes truly a Frankenheimer character. Despite the initial handicap of being a sequel, Frankenheimer's film turns out to be a very personal effort. A somewhat unpromising property provided him with an opportunity to restate once more what his films had been stating for years: the fundamental inadequacy of the individual in his or any other environment.

21. Hugo Fregonese (1908)

1945—*Pampa bárbara* (Argentina; codirector: Lucas Demare); 1946—*Donde mueren las palabras* (Argentina; U.S., *Where Words Fail*, 1948); 1949—*Apenas un delincuente*, Argentina; *De hombre a hombre*, Argentina; 1950—*One Way Street; Saddle Tramp;* 1951—*Apache Drums; Mark of the Renegade;* 1952—*My Six Convicts; Untamed Frontier;* 1953—*Man in the Attic; Blowing Wild; Decameron Nights;* 1954—*The Raid;* 1955—*Black Tuesday;* 1956—*I girovaghi*, Italy; 1957—*Seven Thunders* (Great Britain; U.S., *The Beasts of Marseilles*, 1959), 1958—*Harry Black* (Great Britain; U.S., *Harry Black and the Tiger*, 1958); 1962—*Marco Polo* (Italy; U.S., 1962; credited codirector in Italy: Piero Pierotti); 1964—*Shatterhand* (European coproduction; U.S., 1967); 1966—*Pampa salvaje* (Spain; U.S., *Savage Pampas*, 1967)

It seems probable that Hugo Fregonese's reputation as a major director in his native Argentina was due more to a dearth of competition than to his own talent, for his subsequent Hollywood career was really quite modest. Before coming to the United States for the first time in 1936, he had briefly studied economics, gone into the cattle business, and worked as a sports reporter. An ardent filmgoer in his youth, he headed for Hollywood where he did some work as an extra (he was a prisoner in *The Hurricane*, a Spaniard in *The Firefly*, a pirate in *The Buccaneer*), was a technical advisor on a couple of productions with South American locales, studied cutting, and attended Jean Hersholt's drama school. In 1939 he returned to Argentina, where he worked in the local film industry first as a cutter, then as an assistant director to Enrique de Rosas, then to Lucas Demare on several major films such as *La guerra gaucha,* and finally as Demare's codirector on *Pampa bárbara,* whose subject bears a marked resemblance to Wellman's later *Westward the Women* (during the Indian wars in Argentina, a shipment of women is dispatched to a small outpost to reduce desertions by soldiers deprived of sex and families). Argentine film historian Domingo di Nubila, who called *Pampa bárbara* "one of the most cinematographic works in the history of the Argentine film" praised Fregonese's first solo effort, *Donde mueren las palabras* ("Where Words Fail") as "the highest quality musical film at that time in our country." In this melodrama about a night watchman who turns out to have been a famous conductor wracked by guilt at having caused his ballerina daughter's death, the main attraction is an audaciously long ten-minute ballet sequence choreographed by Margarita Wallman to Beethoven's Seventh Symphony. MGM bought the American releasing rights and signed Fregonese to a contract, but nothing came of it (except a marriage to Faith Domergue), and he soon returned to Argentina with the intention of making a semidocumentary in the *House on 92nd Street/Naked City* mold. That was *Apenas un delincuente* (*Hardly a Criminal*), after which Fregonese made one last unsuccessful Argentine film before being signed by Universal and returning to Hollywood, this time for good (or at least until the early sixties when he moved to Europe).

His first American movies are not without original qualities, the most interesting among them being *The Raid, Untamed Frontier,* and *Apache Drums.* The latter is a fine Western enhanced by an imaginative use of color, such as in a striking scene in which villagers are besieged all night in a church by gaudily war-painted Indians who from time to time appear, ghostlike, out of the darkness. This was Val Lewton's only Western (and last film; he died before its release) and it effectively transposed the master horror producer's exploration of the unseen as a source of terror. While most of Fregonese's pictures for Universal were Westerns or adventure yarns, his one film for Stanley Kramer, *My Six Convicts,* was in a different vein. An overly sentimental but quite affecting story of a prison psychiatrist fighting routine and regulations in order to help a group of inmates cope with their condition, it might have led one to think of Fregonese as an offbeat and personal artist, with qualities quite untypical of the traditional Hollywood director. Unfortunately he then set out to prove himself the "great" director his Argentine reputation suggests he had always wanted to be and piled effect upon arty effect in such pictures as *Black Tuesday* and *Man in the Attic* (in which Jack Palance played Jack the Ripper). *Decameron Nights,* primarily a cinematographer's picture, was pleasant but static and excessively tame. *Blowing Wild,* whatever its merits, did not seem to owe much to its director, while *Harry Black and the Tiger*'s interesting script and funny dialogue were marred by poor direction. Fregonese's career continued to deteriorate through a series of styleless thrillers in Germany and Italy (which he himself hated thoroughly). His remake of his own *Pampa bárbara* as *Savage Pampas* is a rather bombastic movie that does not recapture the alleged cinematic power of the original in spite of fine location shooting and some good scenes of violence. His only European film of more than routine interest is the unusual *I girovaghi,* about a puppeteer (played by Peter Ustinov) driven out of business at the turn of the century by the advent of motion pictures.

22. Samuel Fuller (1912)

1949—*I Shot Jesse James;* 1950—*The Baron of Arizona;* 1951—*The Steel Helmet; Fixed Bayonets;* 1952—*Park Row;* 1953—*Pickup on South Street;* 1954—*Hell and High Water;* 1955—*House of Bamboo;* 1957—*China Gate; Run of the Arrow; Forty Guns;* 1959—*Verboten!; The Crimson Kimono;* 1961— *Underworld, U.S.A.;* 1962—*Merrill's Marauders;* 1963—*Shock Corridor;* 1964—*The Naked Kiss;* 1969—*Shark* aka *Man-Eater;* 1973—*Tote Taube in der Beethovenstrasse* (Fed. Rep. of Germany; U.S., *Dead Pigeon on Beethoven Street,* 1973); 1980—*The Big Red One;* 1982—*White Dog*

Sam Fuller is, in the most radical sense of the phrase, "something else," and attempts to pigeonhole this most eccentric and anarchistic of American directors are doomed to fail. To begin with, nothing one can write about him seems to account for the physical impact of his cinema. The soundest piece of advice on how to approach Fuller was given by Andrew Sarris when he noted that the director's works "have to be seen to be understood. Seen, not heard or synopsized." Fuller's ideas and their fictional expression are either aggressively offbeat or banal with a vengeance—when not both simultaneously, for he has an uncanny flair for dressing up the commonplace in bizarre garb. His scripts are surrealistic junkyards littered with the by-products of a brilliant but aberrant imagination seemingly fostered on trash. Taste, moderation, selectivity are values foreign to him. His dialogue writing, while often clever, can be atrocious and is frequently at its most atrocious when at its most clever. Characters deadpan, or grimace, their ways through reels of contrived platitudes and slogans or blurt out flabbergasting statements ranging in length from pseudophilosophical one-liners to protracted lyrical speeches. Motivations tend to be inscrutable, when not incoherent, and sudden plot twists and mind-boggling behavioral turnabouts are sprung upon the audience without notice. In a Fuller movie, what will happen next is anybody's guess.

Fuller's admirers refuse to be embarrassed by the trashiness of his material. They either ignore it completely or attempt to rationalize it into a virtue. Phil Hardy's vindication (in his book *Samuel Fuller,* 1970) of the much abused *The Naked Kiss* is an example of the latter approach. The film, Hardy writes, "demands that we take Fuller seriously." But the trouble is, we can't take such a film "seriously" unless we deliberately turn it into something it is not, something interesting, no doubt, but bearing little relation to what is actually seen and heard on the screen. Hardy's dead-serious thematic analysis explains away the absurdities and makes perfect sense out of the chaos, thereby failing to account for the shock value of a fundamentally incongruous, cockeyed concoction.

For Fuller's appeal lies in his very outrageousness. Even when he makes sense, it is a "sense" that derives its worth from the nonsensical manner through which it is arrived at. It is for such reasons that Fuller cannot easily be evaluated in the usual terms applicable to other American directors of his generation. It is clear why his films exerted such an influence on Godard: In them we witness the breakdown of most of the rules, concepts, and values that governed traditional film making (realism, verisimilitude, consistency of tone and point of view).

Which explains why Fuller found it increasingly hard to make his kind of films within the still fairly rigid production system of early and mid-sixties Hollywood. Each of the three pictures he did manage to direct between 1963 and 1973 (*Shark*, he refuses to acknowledge as his own) has been more quirky in form and content than the one before, and they have met with mostly negative response from audiences and critics. Not that these films, however daring, are exceptionally provocative when compared with some commercially and critically more successful contemporary products. Audiences have become accustomed to the bizarre handling of bizarre material even in a cinema that makes no claims to being "avant garde." They do not, however, associate the modern mannerisms they now take for granted in fashionable films with the all but defunct type of low-budget genre movies Fuller's pictures outwardly belong to. When people laugh—as they usually do—at *The Naked Kiss*, their laughter is a reaction not so much to a jarring disharmony between style and content, as to a discrepancy between their experience of the genre and the film maker's approach to it. Fuller has never shown much interest in or respect for the genres as such, on the contrary, he has repeatedly used them to explode the categories and conventions upon which their very existence is founded. Whereas Aldrich in *Kiss Me Deadly* enhanced the virtues of the thriller through a process of intensification, Fuller in *The Naked Kiss* undermines them through a process of corruption. Fuller's film is as much an antithriller as Aldrich's is a super—or archetypal—thriller, both transcending the genre but in opposite ways. In *The Naked Kiss*, the genre seems to be spoofing itself, yet Fuller's obvious seriousness precludes the possibility of conscious parody, so that the audience ends up finding the film "ridiculous." By the time he made *Dead Pigeon on Beethoven Street*, after a seven-year hiatus of aborted projects, Fuller had become aware of the implications of parody in his approach. *Dead Pigeon*, while in many ways more bewildering than any other Fuller film, including *Naked Kiss*, is not as "ridiculous" as the latter—and is therefore easier to accept—because of the director's frank kidding of his material and of himself. Although there is much in the film that Fuller seems to take quite seriously, we are encouraged to view the whole thing as a travesty by the opening shots of the members of the cast, and Fuller himself, posing in carnival costumes under the credit titles. This introductory gimmick, reprised at the end with the introduction of the technical crew (among whom is an editor shown disgustedly dumping strips of film in a trash basket), testifies to Fuller's increasing self-consciousness, the result of personal evolution but also of influences. Between *Naked Kiss* and *Dead Pigeon* stretch seven years of self-conscious world cinema, seven years, most particularly, of Godard, starting with Fuller himself giving his definition of cinema in *Pierrot le fou*. We shouldn't be surprised to find a note of schizophrenia creeping into the director's late works.

Fuller, however, was a wildly individualistic talent from the very first picture he directed. He deserves the distinction of auteur not only because he has written most of his own original scripts, but also because of the consistency in his work, a consistency of attitudes, themes and forms, virtues and faults. No matter how bad a Fuller scene (or line, or sequence) may seem, it is bad in a manner that could not be anybody else's, which may sound like a backhanded compliment but is not. Whereas badness, as a rule, tends to be anonymous, Fuller's personality redeems his trashiness.

I Shot Jesse James, although not as brilliant or idiosyncratic as some of his later films, was already a microcosm of Fullerian cinema. It shows an amazing disregard for the "rules" of the Western genre. Built around the theme of defection and betrayal that runs throughout Fuller's work, it is full of typical absurdities (e.g., some dreadfully contrived business about a stolen ring; the two Frank James scenes; the hero's last words) and psychological inconsistencies which, whether "weaknesses" or bold ellipses, were by no means accidental, since such inconsistencies were to become a distinctive feature of Fuller's style of characterization. Superimposed on the motif of Bob Ford's guilt over shooting his best friend in exchange for amnesty is a triangle relationship the nature of which never becomes clear until the last reel, when Bob's girlfriend is revealed to be in love with a prospector she has seen only a couple of times and for whom she never evinced the least attraction in earlier scenes. The man's feelings are none too clear either. We are under the impression that he first sees the girl as an easy pickup (he all but propositions her within seconds of their first meeting), then forgets about her when he realizes she is stuck on Ford. Moreover, *her* feelings toward the latter are confused and contradictory throughout the film, while Bob's attitude toward the prospector shifts with amazing ease from murderous jealousy to friendliness, to suspicion (of theft), to renewed jealousy. It all adds up to a very murky set of relationships. (To top it all, Ford, shot to death by his rival, dies in the girl's arms, confessing that he really "loved" Jesse James.) Fuller might of course be praised for tackling complex psychology and the vagaries of human passions, but he never analyzes or even demonstrates the complexities. He takes them for granted and merely shows their consequences, so that undocumented ambivalence deteriorates into arbitrary incoherence. (*The Baron of Arizona,* Fuller's second picture, also hinges upon a startlingly unexpected and unmotivated character reversal.)

Psychological inconsistencies are only one consequence of the Fullerian method of juxtaposition and discontinuity, a method that eschews most traditional concepts of dramatic construction and development, as well as of stylistic coherence. Until *Dead Pigeon,* the most extreme example of this approach was probably *Forty Guns,* a Western which, considered from a traditional point of view, would suffice to rank Fuller among the worst "constructionists" in Hollywood history. Although the plot, when reconstructed in retrospect, appears quite simple, it is extremely hard, while watching the film, to grasp a story line that keeps breaking into wildly jagged patterns or branching out into idle doodlings. Individual scenes almost never seem to result from what precedes or to lead into what follows. Each one is a set piece with its own particular structure and mechanism. The general effect is one of shapelessness, of a film without a backbone or center of gravity, disconcertingly elusive but extraordinarily free and open in its construction.

Fuller's war pictures form a tight, independent group that deserves some special consideration. In view of his own definition of the cinema ("It is like a battleground. Love, hate, action, violence, death. In a word, emotion.") and of his personal experience in World War II, the genre would seem to be ideally suited to him. Yet, all of his war films are disappointing in some way, and none reaches the level of achievement of *Park Row, Pickup on South Street, Forty Guns, Shock Corridor,* or even *Underworld, U.S.A.* or *The Naked Kiss.* While the genre provides the perfect outlet for Fuller's obsession with physical conflict ("Life is a battle," one of his characters says. "Somebody has to get a bloody nose.") and violent death, it offers little opportunity to deal with his other major themes: education, deception, the innocence of children, woman as a moral influence (his attempts to integrate them into *China Gate* or *Verboten!* are most unconvincing). The Fuller war movie is disconcerting in that it does not fall into either of the two usual categories (militarist or pacifist) of the genre. Fuller is no war propagandist, yet it would not occur to him to turn his films into antiwar tracts. The horror of war is too obvious to him to necessitate formal indictment. The subject of his war films is survival, and it is a concern that leaves little or no place for ethical or political considerations. Fuller's war is very grim, but unspectacularly so. Men freeze to death, starve, collapse from exhaustion, get shot by snipers. Violence is never glossed over, but neither is it glorified or poeticized. There are few heroics, few big battle scenes (the generally modest budgets would have precluded them anyway). A brilliant action scene like the shooting in the maze of the tank trap in *Merrill's Marauders* is exceptional. Neither is Fuller much interested in providing a sampling of psychological types and pitting them against each other, a natural tendency of the genre with its heterogeneous groups of men thrown together by chance and forced to stick together through the most harrowing circumstances. Here too, the business of war and the will to survive supersede any other preoccupation. Fuller's war films are honest, uncompromising, and rather dull. At times, his concern with authenticity and a sense of history seriously backfires. Thus, in *Verboten!* the intercutting between newsreel shots of starving German civilians and Fuller's studio reconstruction of a similar scene makes the latter look hopelessly phony, and the use of footage from the Nuremberg trials, for the same reason, weakens the impact of the film instead of bolstering it.

To a certain extent, war is to Fuller what bullfighting is to his friend Budd Boetticher, a subject that fascinates him more than any other but has failed to bring out the best of his talent. Fuller's *Arruza* is *The Big Red One,* the autobiographical World War II saga that was his most cherished project since the fifties and that finally became a film in 1980. It is far from being the major disappointment *Arruza* turned out to be, to be sure; it can even be described as one of Fuller's better war pictures. However, much of his war experience had gone into his earlier films—especially *The Steel Helmet, Fixed Bayonets,* and *Merrill's Marauders*—and *The Big Red One* strikes one more as a recapitulation of themes and scenes than as an entirely original work, although some familiar statements do come across more successfully than before. Thus, Fuller manages to convey the horror of the concentration camps through a method that is the exact opposite of the one used in *Verboten!* (i.e., showing as little as possible and relying on suggestion). The theme of childhood, too, is more convincingly integrated, as it becomes one of the film's leitmotifs (there is a child in almost every sequence). In *The Big Red One,* as in his other war films, Fuller is more interested in what takes place in between battles than in combat itself, yet some fighting scenes stand out—not as spectacle (Fuller eschews the spectacular, lyrical violence that most war films exploit and that culminated, a couple of years before his film, in Peckinpah's *Cross of Iron*) but because they emphasize the plight of the individual soldier. Perhaps no other scene in the history of the genre conveys the terrifying vulnerability of the foot soldier in an attack with as much power and immediacy as the Normandy landing sequence. On the whole, however, the film does not add much to Fuller's body of war pictures; most of what he had to say in the genre he had said before.

As a contrast to the war films, a picture like *Park Row,* which deals with another kind of war, gathers all of Fuller's major themes in a burst of dramatic and visual excitement. To an ex-journalist who has stated that what he would like to do most of all would be to own and edit his own newspaper, the making of *Park Row,* a wildly romanticized paean to the birth of modern journalism, must have been not only a labor of love but an act of vicarious wish fulfillment. Perhaps Fuller's most personal film, it is one of his most controlled in spite of its ebullience. Even the small budget ($200,000 of Fuller's own money) seems to have contributed to the film's tightness. Practically all the action takes place in only three sets: a barroom, a printer's shop converted into a newspaper's offices, and two studio-built blocks of New York City's Park Row with a painted backdrop of the Brooklyn Bridge thrown in. This distribution of available space largely determines the film's pace. Fuller alternates crowded scenes in confined quarters with street scenes, using a predominance of tightly framed, static medium shots and close-ups for the former and long, fast dolly and boom shots tracking up and down the street for the latter. The spatial circumscribing is echoed, at the level of the plot, by the amazing compression of a multiplicity of momentous events—some of them nonfictional, others invented—within the shortest possible timespan. In less than a week's time, Fuller crams Steve Brodie's jump from the Brooklyn Bridge, the invention of the linotype, the founding of a newspaper, the launching of a subscription for the erection of the Statue of Liberty, a circulation war, and the development of a love-hate relationship between the owners of two rival newspapers. When such a degree of poetic lunacy is reached, verisimilitude becomes quite irrelevant. In *Park Row,* Fuller takes the structural conventions of the film biography and pushes them to their limits, achieving a kind of functional abstraction reminiscent of that resulting from the obsession with the "unities" in seventeenth-century French drama.

Fuller's addiction to technical "virtuosity" sets him apart from most other American directors of his generation and constitutes a permanent challenge to the Hollywood tradition of "invisible" technique. His trademarks include dizzying crane shots and lingering dissolves, ten-minute takes and near subliminal flash shots, scenes filmed with the camera strapped to an actor, and very slow zooms over huge distances. His taste for unexpected, insistent close-ups is notorious. Manny Farber felt that Fuller "would like to do a movie all in close-ups," and Sarris claims that *I Shot Jesse James is* such a movie (actually, the film does not contain more close-ups than most average productions, but Fuller's *do* startle). Even more characteristic are Fuller's elaborate compositions—especially in the old aspect ratio—using the range of camera setups in between the medium shot and the close-up, especially in shots gathering several characters within a a tightly framed space. Such shots are repeatedly used in *Park Row,* where they emphasize the closeness of the team of newspapermen assembled by the hero.

As for Fuller's seemingly fetishistic fascination for long takes, it has produced some of the most exciting sequences in modern cinema. Never of the single-set–fixed-camera variety, they often involve characters moving from one set to another and engaging in complex, often violent action. Fuller seems to be interested above all in the challenge presented by the difficulty of shooting such scenes in one take. In an interview filmed for French television and later published in *Cahiers du Cinéma,* he discussed a ten-minute take from *Pickup on South Street,* gleefully detailing the physical problems of going through the scene's thirty-two camera moves without a cut (that particular take was unfortunately recut in the final editing, against Fuller's wish). In another interview, for *Movie,* Fuller described his two favorite shots, which happen to be highly complicated long takes. One is a famous scene from *Forty Guns:* "It opens in a bedroom with one of the brothers talking. He comes out of the bedroom, walks down the stairs and meets the other brother. They start to walk. They meet the sheriff. They walk four blocks. They go to the telegraph office, send a telegram. Barbara

Stanwyck passes them with the forty horsemen, and then they walk past the camera. That is the longest dolly shot in Hollywood."

Fuller's description of his other favorite, a stunning shot from *Park Row,* is quite inaccurate, and understandably so, for the scene's speed, complexity, and violence are truly bewildering. It opens when Phineas Mitchell (Gene Evans) is told that one of his employees has been deliberately run over by the driver of a truck belonging to the rival newspaper. Here again the dolly shot is the backbone of the scene. Following Evans, the camera moves out of a bar, up the street, into the newspaper's office, then out again as Evans beats up the driver, dragging him across the street and symbolically banging his head against the pedestal of Benjamin Franklin's statue. The three sets (bar, street, office) are crowded with people milling about, and there is quite a lot of angry dialogue in addition to the physical violence. Although most spectators probably do not realize that the whole thing was filmed without a break, the continuous take applied to a sequence of actions, which, more traditionally approached, would have been broken down into anywhere between ten to forty different setups, generates a tension and intensity that could not have been achieved otherwise.

Quite as impressive, although not as spectacular, is one long single-take shot in the hotel suite shared by the two detectives of *The Crimson Kimono.* Again, the camera moves a lot, but the scene this time involves no violent action and concentrates on quiet dialogue. It opens with Glen Corbett waking up and calling room service for coffee. The camera follows him as he gets up, shuffles out of his room into the living room, opens the door to let in the waiter bringing coffee, talks with him for a while, walks into James Shigeta's room, wakes him up and talks to him. He keeps on talking as Shigeta goes into the bathroom and gargles. The camera then pulls back as the two men walk into the living room, follows Shigeta to a desk, and remains focused on him as he makes several phone calls, keeping up the conversation with Corbett in between calls. Such a scene—by no means a memorable one in terms of "content"—is impressive, of course, as a technical feat but even more for its functional quality. It makes us acutely aware, by contrast, of the arbitrariness of conventional editing. The most universally accepted manner of filming movies and putting them together (shifting again and again from one camera placement to another) is divested of its deceptive "naturalness" as we are reminded of its basic strangeness and mystifying power. With such experiments, Fuller was unwittingly paving the way for the young European directors who, during the next decade, were to become disenchanted with editing and made the long take their favorite means of expression. (Miklos Jancso, who at one time claimed he was "incapable of shooting a reverse angle" and has become an addict of the ten-minute take, is the most extreme example.)

Fuller's approach to technique, of course, is neither theoretical nor ethical, at least not explicitly. The reasons he mentions for using long takes, whether esthetic (e.g., the heightened realism of actors' voices when recorded in continuity) or economic (a carefully rehearsed long take saves time at the shooting stage), are purely pragmatic. His primary motivation, moreover, seems to be the excitement he derives from the technical challenge—the gamble of shooting for several minutes with the ever-present risk of something going wrong just before the takes reaches completion—and from the successful breaking away from what he considers a lazy, unimaginative way of making films. This motivation gives us a key, if not *the* key, to Fuller's personality and to his cinema. He enjoys filming dangerously, thrives on challenges and difficulty. Because he knows that cutting is a practical necessity at least as often as it is an esthetic choice, shooting a scene without a cut becomes, to him, a personal victory in the endless contest that pits the form-conscious director against the ponderousness of the film-making apparatus. Most of the great stylists of the screen love doing long takes. Alfred Hitchcock once went so far as to shoot an entire picture (*Rope*) in eight ten-minute takes made to look like one continuous eighty minutes through the use of screen-filling close-ups to bridge each reel change. Years later, it was, quite logically, Sam Fuller who came up with an idea to out-Hitchcock Hitchcock by doing away with the time limitation imposed by the 1000-foot reel.

Talking about one of his projects, *The Rifle,* Fuller told an interviewer: "I shall have a track which I want to shoot with a minimum of four cameras. The four cameras are on a dolly, but only one camera's in action. That's forty minutes, ten minutes a camera. It has to be continuous. I don't want a cut in the film. . . . I want to shoot just like you project, with a changeover. . . . I don't want the actors to stop. . . ." Of course, there is hardly any chance that *The Rifle* will ever be produced, and it is a sad loss, for far from a purely technical tour de force, the projected forty-minute track promised to be one of those rare, precious instances of total coincidence between form and content, intention and realization—not only the perfect stylistic expression of the relentless drive ahead that is at the core of Fuller's war films but also a portrait of the man who conceived it; a metaphor, really, for his energy, his love of movement, action, and danger, his "excessive" nature. There is something slightly insane, but also visionary, about Fuller's enthusiasm over the project ("Everything you can put into a movie has to be in those forty minutes. . . . This track never stops. Never."); and anyone who can think of his endless track as nothing more than some arcane entry for the *Guinness Book of Records* has little feeling for the cinema and little understanding of what Sam Fuller is all about.

23. Curtis Harrington (1928)

by PIERRE SAUVAGE

1963—(1960) *Night Tide;* 1966—*Queen of Blood* (includes reedited footage from one or more Russian films); 1967—*Games;* 1971—*What's the Matter With Helen?; Who Slew Auntie Roo?;* 1973— *The Killing Kind;* 1977—*Ruby* (uncredited codirector: undetermined)

Television Movies
1970—*How Awful About Allan;* 1973—*The Cat Creature;* 1974—*Killer Bees;* 1975—*The Dead Don't Die;* 1978—*Devil Dog: The Hound of Hell*

Miscellaneous
1966—(possibly unreleased) *Voyage to a Far Planet* aka *Voyage to a Prehistoric Planet* (pseudonym: John Sebastian), reedited, English-language version, *Planeta Burg* (Pavel Klushantsev, U.S.S.R.) with additional footage shot by Harrington.

"Inspired by admiration for those who have, even if only momentarily, crossed the commercial chasm, I am attempting to tread gingerly that hovering, swaying tight-rope as well," Curtis Harrington wrote in a statement to *Film Culture* in 1956. He remains today the most striking example of a once avant-garde film maker now making a living in Hollywood and was probably until the eruption of Peter Bogdanovich onto the scene the Directors Guild's most bona fide film buff—the author of a number of film-magazine articles and of an annotated filmography of Josef von Sternberg, the director he most admires and with whom he shares a preoccupation with visual dynamics.

Harrington embarked on his movie career at the age of fourteen with a five-minute 8-mm version of *The Fall of the House of Usher.* While a film student at the University of Southern California he moved up to 16-mm with his first real short, *Fragment of Seeking* (photographed by fellow student Gregory Markopoulos), a humorless, adolescently narcissistic essay in which he played the forlorn lead and revealed a predilection for skeletons that was to crop up later in his work (e.g., the pinball machine in *Games,* directly over his name in the credits to the film). *Seeking* in some ways resembles Kenneth Anger's more famous, homosexually narcissistic *Fireworks,* which it antedates, and Harrington was later to play Cesare in Anger's *Inauguration of the Pleasure Dome.*

But Harrington's most interesting shorts are the heavily symbolic *On the Edge* and *Wormwood Star,* his tribute to painter Cameron Parsons (the film became a true document when she destroyed most of her works shortly after it was shot). Harrington spent two years studying acting under Robert Gist, then went to Paris, where he was able to wallow in film at the Cinémathèque Française before returning to the United States armed with a letter of recommendation to producer-director Albert Lewin. He ultimately wound up as an assistant to the dynamic producer Jerry Wald (sometimes given as the prototype for Budd Schulberg's running Sammy Glick), symbolically starting his new commercial career working on *Peyton Place.* (He was later to serve as associate producer of Don Siegel's *Hound Dog Man,* Jose Ferrer's *Return to Peyton Place,* and Franklin Schaffner's *The Stripper,* of which he supervised a final cut different from the director's own.)

While still with Wald, Harrington managed to scrape together enough money to shoot his first feature, *Night Tide,* which he defined to Jonas Mekas as "an attempt to combine my efforts to create a poetic cinema with an effort to make a film that is commercially acceptable." The picture is an uneven, moody piece about a young sailor—played by a very square-looking Dennis Hopper with an openness, a disarming availability, that brings to mind Jacques Demy's young leading men—who falls in love with a young carnival worker who may or may not be a murderous mermaid. Though it never really works (belief is regularly suspended by acting that ranges downward from adequate, and there is a ponderousness to the whole enterprise), the film bathes in a low-keyed occult ambiance that is seldom attempted on screen, and occasionally it misses in ways that appeal and intrigue. Commercial acceptability became a moot point when the picture disappeared at the bottom of a bad double bill. Harrington's directorial career was resumed only several years later when Roger Corman hired him (and Bogdanovich) to make American movies around Russian space footage for which Corman had bought the American rights. For *Queen of Blood* Harrington concocted a bearably preposterous linking story involving a trip through outer space and a mysterious extraterrestrial woman who turns out to be a green-blooded vampire. (Far worse and better forgotten were the two segments he directed for Don Siegel's television series *Jesse James.*)

Harrington really came into his own with *Games,* an art nouveau suspense thriller with momentary supernatural overtones. The story is related to *Gaslight* and especially *Les Diaboliques*—Clouzot's star, Simone Signoret, was even brought in when Universal vetoed Marlene Dietrich for the part as just not being box-office—but if the plot's twists and turns are not all that unpredictable (except perhaps for the elegant crane-shot–crime-does-pay ending), the atmosphere of Upper East Side bourgeois idleness and aspiring funkiness is compelling. (The couple played by James Caan and Katharine Ross is said to have been loosely patterned after Dennis Hopper and his then wife.) Even more striking are the lush town house interiors resplendent with Tiffany glass, Van de Velde candelabra, Mackmurdo screens. . . .

If Harrington's ABC television movie, *How Awful About Allan,* adapted by Henry Farrell from his own novel (about a partially blind young man with guilt complexes who may or may not be the victim of a plot) was fairly lackluster despite a few good effects and good performances from Anthony Perkins and Julie Harris, and if *Who Slew Auntie Roo?* is a minor but well sustained fable that manages to survive being swallowed alive by Shelley Winters, *What's the Matter With Helen?* is probably Harrington's best film to date. A sardonic thirties period piece, it is another of screenwriter Farrell's two-women shows, here pairing a cool, platinum-blonde Debbie Reynolds and a broad, disturbed Shelley Winters in a well-charted story culminating in increasingly macabre touches and the inevitable psychologically, as well as physically, grisly murder. Superb musical throwbacks to the zeitgeist of the decade (a parody of the tango in *Wonder Bar,* some astonishing Animal Crackerish kiddie numbers, the catchy, honky-tonk "Goody Goody") are well integrated into David Raksin's superlative score, which along with the excellent sets and costumes gives the film an unusually tangy flavor. In *Helen,* Harrington came closest to merging his visual meticulousness into his favored chiller framework, and it is surprising that he went on to make only two other features in the seventies (the barely released psycho-suspenser *The Killing Kind,* in which Ann Sothern made a comeback, and the low-budget horror thriller *Ruby*), as well as a few television movies. His planned film version of Iris Murdoch's *The Unicorn* may be just the project that will allow him to fulfill some of the earlier promise.

---

24. *George Roy Hill* (1922)

by BARRY PUTTERMAN

1962—*Period of Adjustment;* 1963—*Toys in the Attic;* 1964—*The World of Henry Orient;* 1966—*Hawaii;* 1967—*Thoroughly Modern Millie;* 1969—*Butch Cassidy and the Sundance Kid;* 1972—*Slaughterhouse Five;* 1973—*The Sting;* 1975—*The Great Waldo Pepper;* 1977—*Slap Shot;* 1979—*A Little Romance;* 1982—*The World According to Garp*

George Roy Hill did not direct his first film until he was forty, an extremely advanced age in a profession that today is considered a young man's game. Yet this was probably fortunate timing for him since his career seemed to be waiting for the stylistic and temperamental changes the industry took in the late sixties in order to find its own attitude and direction.

He came to television in the mid-fifties from a varied background. A fighter pilot in World War II, Hill did graduate work in music under the G.I. Bill at the University of Dublin. His thesis on musical forms in the works of James Joyce was never completed since by that time he had become interested in acting and was working in various troupes including the Abbey Players. His career was interrupted when he was called up to active duty again during the Korean conflict, but while in the Marines he wrote a military-based script called "My Brother's Keeper," which he sold to *Kraft Theatre* and with which he became a staff writer for the show. Within a year he had become a director on the show and over the course of the next few years he directed for *Kraft* and *Playhouse 90* such well-remembered shows as "The Helen Morgan Story," "A Night to Remember," and "Judgement at Nuremberg" during what is now called the "Golden Age of Television."

With fellow television director Robert Mulligan, Hill was signed by Joseph L. Mankiewicz's Figaro Productions to direct films. A project called "The Harrigan Story," which also had a military background, went into development, but neither director actually made a film for Figaro, and Hill soon found himself directing on Broadway. His first play was the 1957 adaption of Thomas Wolfe's *Look Homeward Angel.* This was soon followed by *The Gang's All Here, Greenwillow, Moon Over Rainbow Street,* and Tennessee Williams's *Period of Adjustment.* This last play finally proved to be his ticket to film making when he was brought to Hollywood to do the movie adaption.

Both *Period of Adjustment* and his second film, an adaption of Lillian Hellman's *Toys in the Attic,* are the kind of films that are easily identifiable as having been made by a newly recruited theater/television director. Claustrophobic, one-dimensional, and inappropriately theatrical, neither film seemed to concern itself with the formal demands of the new medium or offer any promise that Hill would join the exceptions among his colleagues—Mulligan, Penn, Frankenheimer—who were trying to find their own truly cinematic ground in film directing. However, at this point Hill formed the Pan Arts production company with his former agent Jerome Hellman, and their first film, an adaption of the Nora Johnson novel *The World of Henry Orient,* became the first turning point in his career and offered a prophetic look at what his concerns would be once the climate for his kind of film had been reached.

The film deals with the friendship between two teenage girls (Tippy Walker as a disturbed, imaginative musical prodigy and Merrie Spaeth as her more down-to-earth companion). Disappointed at the conventionality of their lives at school and home, they improvise games of alternative personalities for themselves based mostly on pop-culture images. They are, randomly, World War II nurses trapped by the enemy in Central Park or soap-opera heroines building melodramatic scenarios for emotional fainting spells on an East Side street until they focus their attentions on an egotistical, not too talented concert pianist named Henry Orient (Peter Sellers). Orient's own attempts at secluded seduction with a wildly paranoid housewife (Paula Prentiss) had continually collided comically with the girls' fantasy plays in the park and on the street, so when they wind up seeing him in his own public expression, a bitterly comic parody of an atonal concert by former music student Hill, it seems almost inevitable that they would use him as the icon toward which they would channel their romantic energies.

From here it is the comic complications and disillusioning realization of life's stubborn refusal to live up to the girls' imaginations that give the film its tensions. Their blood-oath of devotion to Henry Orient is pure idealization based on a manufactured image of Orient derived from public appearances, album photos and notes, and puff-piece magazine articles. Indeed, it is the girls' dramatically public displays of adoration frustrating Orient's clandestine attempts at seduction that give the title its ironic bite. Further, the giddy liberation of the girls' alternative world seems dependant on asexuality, since it is also contrasted with the corrosive sexual tensions between Walker's parents (Angela Lansbury and Tom Bosley) and paralleled will the easy camaraderie between Spaeth's mother (Phyllis Thaxter) and female companion (Bibi Osterwald).

If ultimately the film gives too much rope to the comforting philosophies of the "good" middle-class adults Bosley and Thaxter and finally attempts to trivialize the girls' role playing as a stage on the road to maturity, it is best to keep in mind that at the time American film was not overpopulated with characters who made up their own images of themselves and played them out to the end. That the film, with Tippy Walker's marvelous embodiment of the joys of improvised emotion, succeeded for as long as it did paved the way for the more all encompassing expressions of the future.

Meanwhile, Pan Arts was not faring well. A project with Sidney Poitier fell through, and Hill wound up replacing Fred Zinnemann on *Hawaii.* It was not a happy project for Hill. He was fired once and quit twice before finally being ousted for good just before editing began. His name remains on the film, but he firmly disassociates himself from it. Neither was he happy with *Thoroughly Modern Millie,* on which producer Ross Hunter added twenty minutes to Hill's cut to inflate the film into a roadshow extravaganza. Hunter was patterning his ideas on such past Julie Andrews musical hits as *Mary Poppins* and *The Sound of Music,* while Hill's concept seemed to anticipate the attitudes filtering into the American cinema in 1967.

That was the year of *Bonnie and Clyde, Point Blank, The Graduate, You're a Big Boy Now,* and *Cool Hand Luke,* among others. A disparate list in terms of quality and effect, but a definite change in the direction of the medium. Stylistically there was a much looser approach to narrative, with elliptical devices borrowed from the French New Wave and television commercials used to call into question the continuity of experience. Simultaneously, our experience of the American movies was reevaluated with characters and attitudes placed into traditional genre films that embodied a contemporary commentary on how film history had affected our culture and consciousness. Clearly Hill's attitudes as expressed in *Henry Orient* would benefit from this approach, and indeed he would form the general structure to embody those attitudes in his next film, *Butch Cassidy and the Sundance Kid.*

In *Butch Cassidy* the girls from *Henry Orient* find a situation in which they can play out their pop-culture fantasies without being patronized or forced to grow up. Here they are placed in a Western movie and can act out their visions of themselves as western outlaws. Tippy Walker becomes Paul Newman, the instigator, the strategist, the imaginer of romantic characters and exciting adventures to be entered into by himself and his partner. The partner, Merrie Spaeth, becomes Robert Redford, the tag-along, the technician, the practical link between the naturalistic society and the theatrical visionary. Like the girls in *Henry Orient,* Butch and Sundance are aware of film genre conventions, but by being in a genre film themselves they can play off the society's expectations of the characters of western outlaws to become the characters without having most of the necessary skills.

The adventures of either one or both of these characters as they invent themselves as romantic legends built on film images would become the center of Hill's work, but, ironically, in the film where it all takes first form, it doesn't work. Perhaps most indicative of the film's failure is a scene not even in the finished work but which can be seen in the documentary made about the shooting of the film. Here Butch and Sundance are aghast and confused when they wander into a turn-of-the-century movie house that is showing a Western that presents images of themselves that totally contradict the images they have been building for public consumption. That Hill felt that the scene didn't work is related to why the film doesn't work as a whole. There is an uncertainty as to how the characters relate to the genre and thus as to how the process of film making relates to the creation of the characters. This uncertainty is also carried over into his next film, *Slaughterhouse Five,* an adaption of the Kurt Vonnegut, Jr. novel.

Hill would seem to be the natural director for Vonnegut's vision of shadow lives lived on the substance of our daily planet, which are exploded into the infinite possibilities of alternative life structures in alternative galaxies. Yet Hill chose not to concentrate on the dislocations of values through time and space but on Vonnegut's rather shallow political ideas. What emerges is a film perhaps not as bad as Mike Nichols's *Catch-22* or Arthur Penn's *Little Big Man* but one in the same tradition of humorless and one-dimensionally shrill social statements that deny the imaginative possibilities in the humorous language of the original.

However, in his next film, *The Sting,* Hill managed to pull it all together, finding the central metaphor from which all of the established attitudes can spring. Newman and Redford are back in their accustomed roles, this time as con men trying to exact revenge from syndicate king Robert Shaw by "taking" him in a big horse-betting swindle. In *Butch Cassidy* the characters were consciously trying to create the illusion of their images within the conventions of the "given" film; here the characters are creating their roles within the swindle plot that they are also creating. Thus they are creating the film as they create themselves. Toward this end, we see all of the components of the film coming into being as the characters need them. We see the signing on of the other major players (the recruitment of fellow con artists Harold Gould, Ray Walston, Eileen Brennan) and the casting auditions of bit parts, the construction of the set (the bookie joint), rehearsals, putting on of makeup, unforeseen problems causing changes in the script and impromptu improvisation—all of the components necessary to sting Shaw while leaving out enough to still sting the audience. The metaphor thus extends out; the Hill protagonists, bored with conventional life, are actors trying to con-vince the society that it is the audience for the movie that they are creating of their lives.

Since *The Sting* all of Hill's films have concerned the protagonists' inventing the movie that the audience is watching. Having established Newman and Redford as his contrasting con men/actors, he next examined their personalities individually; first with Redford in *The Great Waldo Pepper* and then with Newman in *Slap Shot.* The Redford character as far back as *Henry Orient* had always been slightly ambivalent about the world that his partner was creating for them. The more conventional of the two, he provided the practical influence and technical skill necessary to pull off the job, but *The Great Waldo Pepper* posits that left to his own devices he simply doesn't have the grandeur to make his own movie work. In *The Sting* Redford was continually wandering out of the character that the created movie was creating for him. Were it not for the support of his fellows, his lingering belief that satisfaction could be found in more naturalistic ways would have proved fatal to him. In *Waldo Pepper* he is an aerialist who is never quite able to convince people that he is the World War I flying ace that he is trying to play and never quite able to manipulate the conventions of the basic air-circus, barnstorming, or air-mail-carrier genre films that he is constantly drifting into rather than inventing. Ultimately he winds up in Hollywood literalizing his story by becoming the anonymous stunt double for a movie-manufactured, larger-than-life image of a hero of the skies. His one small measure of control comes in his decision to fatally play out the role he has chosen for himself, confronting his German opposite number (Bo Brundin) in a spectacular dog fight while the cameras capture the action for posterity. In the end, Waldo Pepper's greatness is as ironic as Henry Orient's world, and the bitter pessimism of the film stems from its admission that the worthy technician cannot sustain the film without the showman's hokum.

The showman's hokum is something that the Newman character in a Hill film never lacks, and in *Slap Shot* he stretches it almost to the breaking point. But the stretch is just barely enough to see him through for here Hill has also extended his metaphor to its logical conclusion. The space in which the protagonist can create his own movie in front of a passive audience society is gone; here the entire world is a movie and Newman merely one of many players struggling for survival. The film opens with a sportscaster and a hockey player facing directly into the camera in an on-air interview explaining how the game is actually played. It has almost nothing to do with what follows in the film: the building of the society of a minor league hockey-franchise-as-movie-company with Newman as the player-coach (star-director), Strother Martin as general manager (producer), an all-powerful and anonymous owner (studio), and on down through the ranks of lesser players, technicians, and audience-fans. The film builds a series of complex, interlocking performer-audience relationships that no-body controls and leaves everybody scrambling to find the proper character components that will attract attention to their conceptions of themselves. As the hockey players struggle to define themselves in front of their public, so they are ill defined by being paraded in public in Martin's publicity fashion show and then join the public, taking the place of the fans in the stands, searching for compatibly defined females in the ice show's pinwheeling chorus line. At the center of it all is Newman, using the advice that becomes the focal point of the film, "Use your imagination, that's what I'm doing," to wildly improvise faces to both hold together the various faces on the team and to create a team face that will convince the totally undefined absentee owner to salvage the club for the next season.

That advice came from Melinda Dillon who found that the unexpected solution to the problem of being a hockey player's wife was a lesbian relationship, and the fact that the advice comes not only from a woman but in a sexual context indicates just how far Hill has expanded the concept of life as an existential movie. Heretofore sex had always been considered an antagonistic element to the romantic world that Hill's characters were building. Angela Lansbury in *Henry Orient,* Dimitra Arliss in *The Sting,* and Susan Sarandon in *Waldo Pepper* were all corrosive characters who had to be destroyed in one way or another for the protagonists to succeed. Newman, fulfilling his traditional Hill role, has found that he cannot combine his life as hockey role-master with marriage, though even here, his scenes with estranged wife Jennifer Warren indicate that this is a failure that they both bitterly regret. It is with Michael Ontkean, who more or less takes the more conventional Redford role, that sexuality finds its place in Hill's world. Though philosophically opposed to Newman's "any tactic for the effect" approach to hockey, he finds that his own marriage to Lindsay Crouse suffers from the exact same contradiction of "performer" on ice and "real person" at home. It is only when he sees his wife as an audience member at the championship game that his own imagination expands to the realization that private feeling and public action are necessarily interdependent. Reversing sexual "role playing," Ontkean becomes his own pinwheeling chorus line doing a strip-tease mating dance for his wife before the crowd and copping the Academy Award (the championship cup) for his effort.

One could say that this freshly finalized formula was carried over into *A Little Romance,* but that film is so patently laid out as a summing up of Hill's career to date that there is no single antecedent. Here we get the romantic adolescents (Thelonious Bernard and Diane Lane) rebelling against the unimaginative adults (Sally Kellerman, Arthur Hill, and David Dukes as Angela Lansbury, Tom Bosley, and Peter Sellers) from *Henry Orient,* tying in with a con man (Laurence Olivier) in a horse racing scheme from *The Sting,* and becoming hunted outlaws from *Butch Cassidy* in their flight to Venice to enact their own romantic legend. As one would expect after *Slap Shot,* the antagonist world can no longer be seen as a naturalistic society but is literally a rival movie company presided over by Dukes in what is said to be a parody of director William Friedkin. The difference between the two movies is that the one Bernard, Lane, and Olivier are making of their lives is based on the conception of self-definition as myth-making while the literal movie company sees their work as an internal business. This Hill makes clear when film buff Bernard confronts movie company actor Broderick Crawford playing "Brod" with the image he projected in Ray Enright's *Sin Town,* and Crawford doesn't even remember the movie. Against this Hill posits—George Roy Hill films. In a film defining the career of George Roy Hill, the career of George Roy Hill is used as the fuel to fire George Roy Hill character/actor Bernard to become a George Roy Hill hero.

As such, *A Little Romance* could be seen as a rounding off of a phase in Hill's career. Certainly it is difficult to tell how his film version of John Irving's *The World According to Garp* is going to fit in with his previous work. But Hill remains committed to his basic vision of life. As he told Tom Toper at the time of making *Slap Shot:* "I *do* like the idea of the romantic ideal, of a character creating his own world. Waldo did it. Butch did it. And, of course, that's what making films is, creating your own world, seeing your own vision realized."

25. *Elia Kazan* (1909)

1945—*A Tree Grows in Brooklyn;* 1947—*Boomerang!; Sea of Grass;* 1948—*Gentleman's Agreement;* 1949—*Pinky* (uncredited codirector: John Ford); 1950—*Panic in the Streets;* 1952—*A Streetcar Named Desire; Viva Zapata!;* 1953—*Man on a Tightrope;* 1954—*On the Waterfront;* 1955—*East of Eden;* 1956—*Baby Doll;* 1957—*A Face in the Crowd;* 1960—*Wild River;* 1961—*Splendor in the Grass;* 1963—*America America;* 1969—*The Arrangement;* 1972—*The Visitors (16-mm);* 1976—*The Last Tycoon*

The films of Elia Kazan are the passionate work of a passionate man, and it is difficult—perhaps even unwise—to discuss them dispassionately. The osmosis between his life and work (whether films or books) makes them consubstantial to each other. That Kazan is thoroughly aware of the consequences in terms of audience acceptance or rejection is evidenced by the following statement from a *Cahiers du Cinéma* interview (a translation of a translation):

> What people get from my films, they get through me. It is myself they get, ultimately. They see life through my way of seeing it and expressing it. If I do it honestly, they can say: "That's him, that's the man . . . that is the way *he* sees things." But others may say: "I don't like that bastard. I don't want to see any more of his films!" Well then, that's fine with me! They go for it or they don't, that's natural.

Such awareness implies a reflexive attitude—which is only superficially inconsistent with Kazan's image as an essentially "instinctive" artist. One might say that his art is all the more analytical, perhaps, as it is instinctive, since its dialectical movement is based upon the relentless questioning of its own processes. In Kazan's cinema, passion and reflection are not mutually exclusive; to him, passion is the object of reflection, reflection the outgrowth of passion.

Kazan deals in visceral emotions: lust, rage, fear, shame, love and hate intermingled. His heroes are hypersensitive nonintellectuals (inarticulate "primitives," confused adolescents) struggling against themselves and the world in the darkness of an inchoate consciousness, groping for answers to dimly realized questions. They are engaged in an endless fight for physical or spiritual survival, usually both. The two are seldom distinguishable in Kazan's world, a world ruled by the "law of the jungle"; wild animal life is used as a metaphor for "civilized" life in *The Arrangement* and, most extensively, throughout the African section of Kazan's novel, *The Understudy*.

The fact that Kazan sees the world as a jungle helps to account for the importance of the theme of betrayal in his work. This obsession is usually interpreted as a result of his "informing" on his former Communist friends, but it might be as much a cause as a consequence. On the simplest level, one could say that betrayal, to Kazan, is a natural fact of life, an effect of the law of the jungle. Loyalty, and therefore the guilt that accompanies the breach of it, are unknown in the animal world, where "a survivor celebrates," and "each day's ease is bought by the life of a brother or sister" (*The Understudy*). Kazan's metaphor, however, is only that, and he stresses the difference as well as the similarity between man and beast. The fact is that man *is* capable of guilt feelings. Betrayal is never taken for granted in Kazan's works, it is a major source of conflict, and crisis.

Man betrays man not because—or not only because—he is an animal but because he is human. Individuals grow and change, and change entails betrayal. The Kazan hero is in a state of flux, ever changing and ever dissatisfied. In order to remain "true to himself," to survive as a human being, he may have to renounce everything: job, spouse, friends, peer group, status, beliefs, values. Total renunciation, of course, is an extreme case. The only such example in Kazan's work is Eddie Anderson in *The Arrangement,* not coincidentally Kazan's most personal effort, both as novel and movie. Anderson's evolution is so exemplary as to appear almost mythical. He reaches a point of no return, beyond conflicts and crises. Not so for the more ordinary hero, who is caught up in the essential ambiguity of betrayal, an act both good and evil, salubrious and deleterious. Only betrayal of oneself (e.g., Lonesome Rhodes in *A Face in the Crowd*) is presented as entirely evil in Kazan's films. Most Kazan heroes are under constant pressure, both from without (society) and from within (their own moral qualms) to betray themselves by betraying others *or* not betraying them, by rejecting values *or* not rejecting them.

The resulting tensions and frustrations are so harrowing that they *have* to be escaped, hence a recurring pattern of withdrawal in Kazan's works. Two paths into withdrawal present themselves to the hero, one instinctive, subconscious, the other deliberately chosen. On the one hand, there is the ever-present lure of madness. To those who live on edge, there is nothing more natural than going over the edge. This may take the form of "cathartic" acts of violence (from Cal's pathetically futile dumping of the ice down the chute in *East of Eden* to Archie Lee's murderous impulse at the end of *Baby Doll;* or Sergeant Flores's actual murder of his daughter's lover in *The Assassins*) or of an actual retreating into some form of "insanity" (Blanche's engulfing paranoia in *Streetcar,* Deanie's nervous breakdown and its long aftermath in *Splendor in the Grass,* Eddie's catatonia after his car accident in *The Arrangement*). The deliberate course consists in "dropping out," walking away, and starting from scratch. The move may be tentative and the experience short-lived, as in the case of Zapata or Lonesome Rhodes, who both attempt to "withdraw" at a point when they feel dissatisfied with the nature of their "success" and who both are drawn back into the situation they had withdrawn from—which ultimately leads to their tragic end. The withdrawal can also be a permanent change, a move into a new life, as is the case for young Bud Stamper in *Splendor in the Grass* and for Eddie Anderson. (Sonny, the narrator-hero of *The Understudy,* also falls into the pattern at the end of the book, duplicating Anderson's experience.) Whether suicidal or regenerative, however, whether a cataclysmic impulse or a reasoned choice, withdrawal is always the result of intense psychic stress. Kazan's films have often been described (by critics who dislike them) as "hysterical"; were the term to be used in an objective rather than pejorative sense, it would not be inaccurate, for the Kazan hero has hysteria built into his mental world, and Kazan's emotional involvement naturally determines a stylistic approach that is more mimetic than clinical. Where the hostile critics reveal their blind spot is in their downgrading of Kazan's approach as a matter of principle, as well as in their failure to perceive Kazan's dialectical ability to go beyond the hysterical realm into the analytical.

Kazan's film career neatly falls into three chronological segments characterized by an increasingly "personal" type of expression. Roger Tailleur, in his book, *Elia Kazan,* labeled the periods, respectively, the "HE" (up to *Pinky*), "YOU" (from *Panic in the Streets* to *On the Waterfront*), and "I" (the subsequent films). While slicing up a career in such a way often serves the critic's convenience more than it reflects the artist's evolution, it is not only appropriate but inescapable in the case of a cyclical creator like Kazan, whose chronic dissatisfaction with his work and himself keeps driving him, like most of his heroes, to turn his back on the past and forge ahead into new directions.

To say that Kazan's expression became increasingly personal from one period to the next does not necessarily mean that all the films of the last period are more personal in content than earlier films; it means, rather, that each new stage of development was marked by the conquest of a larger slice of the autonomy he needed to express himself more fully. After *Pinky,* he broke away from the confinement of studio work and the crippling adherence to prewritten scripts; after the triumph of *On the*

Waterfront, he was able to become his own producer, to select his material and collaborate on the scripts; finally, with the two semiautobiographical pictures based on his own novels, he reached the status of *auteur complet.* The fact that the commercial failure of both films silenced him for several years, and the curious turn taken by his career thereafter, are not to be regarded as a setback in his evolution; books simply took over from films when film making became too frustrating, and the one picture (*The Visitors*) he made in the six years between *The Arrangement* and his Hollywood comeback with *The Last Tycoon,* although a modest production, was a thoroughly personal statement.

Taken as a whole, the first period was somewhat timid and tentative, thematically conventional and stylistically unexciting. With *A Tree Grows in Brooklyn,* an unspectacular although often affecting piece of sentiment, Kazan did little more than feel his way around a movie studio and pick up the tricks of the trade ("I just staged the scene as I would a theatre scene, and then he [Leon Shamroy, the cinematographer] determined where to put the camera and so on."). *The Sea of Grass* was the lowest point in a career that has very few low points. *Gentleman's Agreement,* despite its good intentions, is perhaps Kazan's dullest picture. *Pinky's* premise was impossible, and the film lived up—or down—to it. All these early films, with the exception of *Boomerang!,* are weakened by their unreal, artificial, rather anemic studio look. Kazan, unlike many other Hollywood directors, was unable to transcend this artificiality. From the start, his uneasiness with a sound stage, backlot work, and the whole paraphernalia of Hollywood movie making was evident. He felt that *A Tree Grows in Brooklyn* should have been shot on location in New York, *The Sea of Grass* out West "in the country where there is grass and cattle," *Pinky* down South (although one may wonder whether the realism of actual locales might not have exposed, through contrast, the conventions of the dramaturgy).

On the evidence of Kazan's first five pictures, it would have taken real clairvoyance to predict his evolution in the fifties and sixties. He seemed to be shaping up as a specialist of the safely courageous social-minded picture, tackling some new social evil in each film: political corruption in *Boomerang!,* anti-Semitism in *Gentleman's Agreement,* racism in *Pinky.* The prefabricated, mechanical approach was emphasized by the fact that the last two of these pictures, both Zanuck productions, used parallel and equally questionable gimmicks (Gentile passing for Jew; black passing for white) to put their "message" across.

Yet, none of the five films is a totally anonymous product. Kazan managed to introduce some personal feelings and touches in all of them. Of *A Tree Grows in Brooklyn,* he has said: "I put into the film many of the feelings I had for my children, whom I had lost at the time," and this is certainly felt in the beautiful performance he obtained from Peggy Ann Garner. Moreover, the time period was approximately that of two of his later masterpieces (*East of Eden; America America*), and the theme of an immigrant family in New York was close to his personal experience. In *Boomerang!,* he did get a chance to experiment with what would later become his favorite working method: on-location shooting with some nonHollywoodian and/or nonprofessional performers. Kazan's ambivalent feeling toward the South—a mixture of fascination and repulsion— was first manifested in *Pinky,* a film that also featured for the first time the director's attraction for scenes combining sex, violence, and automobiles. Even though he disliked the script of *Gentleman's Agreement* and was dissatisfied with the overall look of the production, Kazan, as a Jew and a liberal, could not fail to be interested in the theme of the film. Even *The Sea of Grass,* was not, as one might think, a reluctantly accepted assignment but a project that had initially attracted Kazan as "the classic American story" and one whose theme bears some similarity to both *Viva Zapata!* and *Wild River*. Only working conditions (shooting a Western MGM-style, entirely in the studio) and a lack of rapport with the stars (Tracy and Hepburn on unfamiliar ground, and understandably nervous) caused his disenchantment and the film's ultimate failure.

Kazan's first really satisfactory picture was his sixth, *Panic in the Streets*, a bold assertion of stylistic independence. It is the most impressive of Kazan's "minor" films. Of course, *Panic* is a thriller, more ambitious than most in its critical implications, but a thriller all the same, with obvious limitations on personal expression (at least the kind we now associate with Kazan); yet, it was perhaps the most appropriate type of picture for Kazan to tackle at a time when his growth demanded that he free himself from his association with prestige producers' pictures, top-heavy with messages and social issues. In the forties and early fifties, the thriller—whether *noir* or not—seemed to stimulate the creative energies of most directors, and Kazan was no exception. Moreover, he had the opportunity of working on location in New Orleans with a flexible script and in more or less the same semidocumentary form as in *Boomerang!* but with the added asset of a talented and sympathetic cinematographer (Joseph Mac-Donald, who was also responsible for the superb black-and-white photography of Henry Hathaway's semidocumentary thriller, *Call Northside 777*). For the first time, a Kazan film is distinguished by its visual impact and its pace. Kazan uses the genre as a vehicle for baroque imagery; his flamboyant camera work distorts and transfigures places and faces into nightmarish poetry. *Panic in the Streets* is to New Orleans what Dassin's contemporary *Night and the City,* also starring Richard Widmark, is to nighttime London.

Reviewing *Panic in the Streets* in 1950, the young Jean-Luc Godard remarked that Kazan made no distinction between theater and cinema. The statement may seem excessive, even meaningless, but it provides an insight into Kazan's esthetic ambivalence at the time. *Panic* had brought theatricality to the street; *A Streetcar Named Desire* (also set in New Orleans) brought cinema to the stage. Theatre and cinema do not clash in the film version of *Streetcar,* and neither really "dominates" the other. Kazan makes little attempt to "open up" the play, to subdue the power of the Word or tone down the performers' bravura. Artifice is not denied, it is accepted, even welcomed. The picture shows no embarrassment at being a filmed play. Kazan's camera scrutinizes his own stage production (it was the first time in his career he endeavored to transfer his own work from another medium onto film), magnifying each detail and thereby, inevitably, each flaw; it is overdone, certainly, but one hardly sees how it could have been done otherwise.

Streetcar was Kazan's first and only filmed play, and it is easy with hindsight to see it as a negative experience through which Kazan realized the necessity of severing his ties with the stage. Indeed, his next picture was as far removed from the stage as can be. It did not, however, eschew theatricality, if theatricality may be defined, or redefined, as artful enhancement of one's material for greater dramatic and esthetic impact.

Viva Zapata! comes as close as any Hollywood film to being a successful revolutionary epic. Not close enough, however, in the view of many politically obsessed commentators whose indictments of the film do not so much deny as ignore its artistic merit. As a piece of liberal romanticism, *Viva Zapata!* predictably views with sympathy the uprising of the downtrodden against injustice and oppression but takes a dim view of the unglamourous and often dirty business of keeping a revolution alive and working. Kazan's and John Steinbeck's revolutionary hero is a man who, at least in the semihistorical fiction they have devised, remains a prisoner of an idealistic concept of revolution. Zapata's social consciousness does not develop into political awareness, let alone political practice. He is a rebel—and a somewhat reluctant one at that—rather than a revolutionary. His proud rejection of the presidency when he realizes that power is corrupting him is a noble but selfish gesture. Moreover, Zapata's retirement is not criticized, even implicitly, but shown as a wise, heroic act (although one may find the simplicity of the scene somewhat contrived, it is nonetheless one of the most effective in the film).

As a product of "liberal" ideology, *Viva Zapata!* was bound to be non-Communist, and therefore implicitly anti-Communist. But it is absurd to call it, as one critic did, "a sustained anti-Communist polemic." Communism is neither defined nor even mentioned in the film. The character played by Joseph Wiseman, who could easily have been made into a caricature of the Marxist-Leninist hardliner, is left politically undefined and actually stands for *any* kind of political opportunism. In order to be able to read the film as anti-Communist polemic, one must already be politicized (and politically biased) to a much higher degree than the average movie audience that Kazan was allegedly attempting to indoctrinate. Neither should we feel embarrassed by Kazan's own description of the film as "anti-Communist" (in a 1952 *Saturday Review* article and, shortly after, before HUAC). He had obvious reasons to do so at a time when his survival was at stake, but to take his claim at face value today is both unfair and obtuse. Indeed, the intense revolutionary spirit that runs through it might easily have been construed as "Communist" at a time when antired paranoia ran rampant.

The film makes many valid revolutionary points and makes them in so many words (e.g., Zapata's reminding the peasants of the vital power of the people and warning them against the cult of personality). It is not only through such statements, however, that the film makes its revolutionary point but also, and above all, through Kazan's formal approach to the subject. His feeling for the land and the people comes through in vibrant visual terms, with an absolute minimum of Hollywood glamourization and stereotyping. Perhaps the film's highest achievement is that, while concentrating on a revolutionary hero, it manages to keep the *people* as collective hero in focus all the time. Kazan's lyrical enthusiasm is akin to Eisenstein's and so is his esthetic control over the means through which this enthusiasm is conveyed. Both directors share an ability to subsume didacticism and transmute concepts into filmic imagery and rhythm. When Zapata's bullet-ridden body is thrown on the fountain in the center of the square at Morelos, the juxtaposition within the frame of dead hero and water running, in its unobtrusive simplicity, doesn't so much "express" the message as it constitutes it, and we know with utter immediacy that, although revolutions are doomed to be betrayed, the revolutionary spirit never dies.

Kazan's most famous, most commercially successful, most honored picture (eight Academy Awards), *On the Waterfront,* was also the most bitterly attacked. The hostility it first generated has hardly subsided. Nearly thirty years after its release, film journals still run sprawling indictments of its ethics and politics. To many people, it remains Kazan's unforgivable attempt to justify his own informing before HUAC.

Much of the criticism leveled at the film actually springs from a misunderstanding as to its true nature and purpose (a misunderstanding no doubt encouraged by Kazan's own statements). Superficial guarantees of "authenticity" (the actual facts on which the script is based, the on-location filming "where it all happened") lead one to expect a documentary-style exposé of crime in the trade unions, which *On the Waterfront* of course is not. Aside from the fact that such an exposé would have been impossible, it should be clear that Kazan was not primarily concerned with political, economic, or even social issues but with the moral dilemma set by a given situation and the mental anguish through which it puts the protagonist. His concept was strictly dramatic and as such, alien to a "documentary" approach. The same applies to the film's cinematic style, which is the heightened style of the "black" thriller, based on aural-visual violence and shock, to which Kazan brings his own brand of high-strung intensity. Seen as traditional crime melodrama, *On the Waterfront* is, as a matter of fact, highly successful, although its excesses (blares of nerve-racking music anticipating or duplicating action, jarring cuts to overemphatic close-ups or very low-angle shots, self-conscious groupings, assorted histrionics from the supporting players) tend to make us feel uncomfortable, if not guilty, about our engrossed involvement in most of the proceedings.

From the very opening (tension-building drum pounding on the soundtrack as Johnny Friendly and his henchmen file out of the waterfront shack housing their local and stride up the gangplank, photographed in a series of alternating high- and low-angle shots, until they gather beside the menacing bulk of a huge black Cadillac), one realizes that the style of the film will be theatrical, not to say operatic. Indeed, a lot of effort, either unconscious or deliberate, seems to have gone into the erasing of the "real location" environment and the careful reconstructing of a safely artificial atmosphere, so that, although we know that the film takes place and was largely made on the New Jersey shore, we get a mild shock every time Kazan throws in a shot of the Manhattan skyline across the river. (An instance of such a shift to "reality" striking a wrong chord occurs in the early scene of Terry and the girl's first getting to know each other. The first part of the scene is smoothly, tactfully filmed in one long take, with the camera tracking alongside the two as they walk through a playground, then pausing with them as they stop by a swing. When they start walking again and reach the waterfront railing, however, Kazan cuts to one of his long shots of Manhattan, and the magic of the scene suddenly evaporates as the growing intimacy previously suggested by the fluid long take disintegrates into a series of conventionally cross-cut shots.)

The film's artificiality derives largely from its subject matter, which is not crooked unionism but the awakening of a conscience. In order to dramatize this awakening, Kazan and writer Budd Schulberg rather arbitrarily place their hero, Terry Malloy, in a state of almost total intellectual and moral "innocence," as well as of social and psychological isolation. Despite frequent references to Terry's past as a promising prize fighter, he seems to have had no real existence before the film opens. He has no parents, no family except for his gangster brother, no girlfriend until he meets Edie. He is never seen at home, or even going home, indeed we don't know where he lives and with whom, if anybody. Throughout the film, people who have been looking for him conveniently stumble across him in a bar, on a street, on the waterfront. This device is a stage convention, but it is not used merely for convenience. Terry Malloy is not unlike the abstract heroes of traditional problem plays, and it is therefore logical that he should be handled in a somewhat stage-bound manner. The fact that the presence of such conventions does not seem to affect audiences' belief in the film's "realism" proves that they are coherent with its overall stylistic approach.

Most evaluations of *On the Waterfront* stumble upon the question of the film as a "justification" of informing and, thereby, of Kazan's testimony before HUAC. Critics usually take this intention for granted, then proceed to discuss the film in terms of what Kazan is allegedly implying about himself, rather than in terms of what actually appears on the screen. The story is seen as a sustained, coherent metaphor for Kazan's political ordeal, with the waterfront mob standing for the Communist party, the crime commission for HUAC, and Terry Malloy, of course, for Kazan himself. Kazan is then, understandably, taken to task for loading the dice: the two situations are different, Terry's informing is, to a certain extent, justifiable; Kazan's is not. At the same time, however, Terry's action is criticized not so much in reference to the story's context as in reference to Kazan's case. Since Terry "stands" for Kazan, his behavior deserves the same disapproval. Commentators seem unable to take the film at face value.

But even such an "innocent" approach would pose problems because of the overpowering moral prohibition against informing, that last of the unchallenged taboos. The automatic, programmed response to informing is that it is *bad* whatever the circumstances, an assumption that has colored most criticism of the film. That such a stringent prohibition can become as mystifying and oppressive as the glorification of informing for the good of the state in totalitarian regimes should be obvious, yet one always encounters extreme reluctance to even discuss the matter. The film's point—that one owes no loyalty to racketeers and killers, that loyalty, in other words, has to be deserved by those who expect it and *is* indeed a relative matter—is not deemed worthy of consideration. Of course, *On the Waterfront* does not analyze the taboo it deals with. Kazan was too emotionally involved in the issue to approach it dispassionately. Yet the film challenges stock responses, which is reason enough not to meet it with those very responses, even though it anticipates them and incorporates them in its strategy.

Baby Doll and *A Face in the Crowd*, made in between *East of Eden* and *Wild River*, are an enclave in Kazan's third, post-*Waterfront* period and in many ways a farewell to his past as a film director. They were filmed—both in black-and-white—in 1956, before a three-year hiatus in his film activity, the first of several such interruptions that were to be forced upon him by the financial failures of *A Face in the Crowd*, *Wild River*, *America America*, and finally *The Arrangement*. *Baby Doll* was Kazan's second and last film collaboration with Tennessee Williams; *A Face in the Crowd* his second and last with Budd Schulberg. They were the only post-1954 Kazan films until *The Arrangement*, with a story set in the present, and while the satire of Madison Avenue and television commercials in *Face* foreshadows *The Arrangement*, the film's central theme and moral message are much closer to *Viva Zapata!*'s.

Baby Doll is unique among Kazan's films as the only one resembling a comedy, although calling it a comedy would not be doing justice to its complexity of moods. It is his only other film derived from stage material, but whereas *A Streetcar Named Desire* was a faithful rendition of the text of a famous Broadway production, *Baby Doll* is a complete reworking, mostly by Kazan himself, of two of Williams's rather obscure early one-acters. Despite Kazan's cinematic approach to the adaptation, however (opening up, on-location shooting), *Baby Doll* is closer to theater than any other Kazan film. The script of this three-character (almost two-character) play is a mere, although brilliant, pretext for a performing and directorial tour de force that inevitably brings to mind Kazan's experimental work at the Actor's Studio (a feeling reinforced by the fact that the three players were Studio members, two of them giving their first screen performance).

The middle section (or second act) of the film takes two performers and a riveted audience through the many shifting moods of one hour-long scene without any distraction or external help, and it comes as close to perfection as anything Kazan ever put on film. The rest of the film can be faulted in several ways. The opening is overdone, with Karl Malden's Archie Lee made too much of a fool too soon. The hectic agitation of actors and camera seems unnecessary and fails to conceal the clumsiness of the expository dialogue. Later, the meeting at the Syndicate and the burning of the cotton gin are straight dramatic scenes (also largely expository) whose visual treatment (low-key lighting, low-angle shots) clashes with the style of the film as a whole. In the last sequence, Malden's ranting, as he scours the grounds for Wallach, seems, again, over-done. But these flaws pale beside the superbly controlled achievement of the Baker-Wallach scenes, especially the one on the swing, with its dolly-in imperceptibly inching from medium shot to close-up as Baker becomes increasingly flustered.

The commercial failure of *Baby Doll* was largely the consequence, it seems, of a misunderstanding over its "eroticism." It is a measure of the film's originality that two contradictory statements—Truffaut's "Only sex matters in it" and Kazan's "We're not dealing with a love story and not even with a sex story"—are equally accurate. The film derives its paradoxical eroticism from the fact that sex remains implicit, sub-merged throughout the portions one would expect to be the most sexually charged. Baby Doll, in Kazan's own words, is a case of "arrested development" and only dimly aware of her own sexuality, of her attraction to Vaccaro or his to her. Vaccaro is more complex and ambivalent, but clearly, revenge, not sex, is foremost in his mind. The two hardly ever touch; he never makes, or even hints at, sexual advances. Yet their entire relationship is placed under the sign of sexual attraction and seduction. Their exchanges work on three superimposed levels: the pleasant small talk conceals the cat-and-mouse play that itself conceals the sexual attraction. To Vaccaro, obtaining Baby Doll's signed confession of her husband's guilt is tantamount to an act of seduction, making actual intercourse between the two unnecessary: after getting what he calls his "affidavit," Vaccaro falls asleep, just as one would after sex. The piece of wood with the confession nailed to it that he thrusts at a frightened Baby Doll across the crumbling attic floor may even be seen as a phallic symbol, and the entire scene as a metaphor for seduction or rape. Baby Doll's changed, more adult attitude from that point, by implicitly referring us to the cliché of instant maturing through sexual experi-ence, suggests that she too has shared in this metonymic form of fulfillment.

A Face in the Crowd is one of Kazan's most ambitious and most superficial pictures. It is genuinely "courageous" and "different," yet its method and message are thoroughly banal and predictable. What is most admirable about it is Kazan's and Schulberg's spunk in taking on television, advertising, and politics—all easy targets but rarely dealt with intelligently—and in straddling comedy, drama, satire, and social comment. Unfor-tunately, the film never really deals with what it is supposed to be about: "the danger of power in the television medium." Or rather, while it tentatively comes to grip with the topic, it soon relinquishes all claim to relevance or seriousness by resorting to an exceedingly unlikely situation as an example of the "danger" it purports to warn us about. That a popular entertainer could become a dangerous (read: fascistic) political power through his influence upon television audiences is a paranoid fear based on a highly simplistic view of both television and politics. It is doubtful that Kazan or Schulberg considered it an actual possibility; more probably, they saw the situation as a good dramatic device, one conducive to satire. However, *we* have to believe in the situation in order to accept the film's message, or simply to enjoy it as melodrama, and the burden of proof is on the film makers. Predictably, they prove unable to carry that burden. We can accept Lonesome Rhodes's early success on radio or even television, but his transformation from an easygoing country-western singer with a winning homespun patter into a power-drunk megalomaniac manipulating presidential candidates remains unbelievable, not so much because we know it could not happen as because we are not shown *how* it happens (Rhodes's rise to influence beyond the realm of show business is dealt with in a cursory montage). In their eagerness to make their point, Kazan and Schulberg shift from satire to fable, from drama to melodrama, jettisoning verisimilitude in the process. The very nature of their premise forces them to hit harder and harder, until they reach the fantastically contrived climax of Rhodes's exposure and "fall." No doubt, *A Face in the Crowd* was a noble failure. By all standards of its time, it was a director's picture, a labor of love. Yet it is one of Kazan's least personal efforts. In the future, private concerns and autobiography were to take precedence over the social issues of the forties and fifties films. With *Wild River,* a new Kazan was to emerge.

East of Eden had already been a new beginning. It was the first Elia Kazan Production, his first venture into color and wide screen, his first really lyrical film. Stylistically, *East of Eden* is Kazan's most exuberant picture. His lack of inhibition with CinemaScope is as impressive as Cukor's in *A Star Is Born.* But one shouldn't take its more facile technical flourishes as typical of the film as a whole. The artistic achievement of *East of Eden* is of a subtler, although almost palpable nature: a sense of space and place and atmosphere that is an expression of camera work rather than a recording of any intrinsic beauty in the locations or sets; a sensual awareness of textures, shapes, colors, and the moods they can generate; a bucolic feeling for nature; the blending of characters with their environment. The film combines energy and fluidity to a degree Kazan had never reached before. His direction is focused on James Dean's highly physical performance, whose dynamism is reflected in the film's general movement, and most obviously in the sweep and bounce of the camera moves.

Half a dozen years and four pictures later, Kazan returned to the theme of adolescent turmoils with *Splendor in the Grass.* Although a box-office hit, it was, critically, one of his most misunderstood films, which was not surprising, for in no other did he take so many chances, inviting charges of both excess and dullness.

The dramatic construction of *Splendor* is unusually bold in that all its tension, conflicts, and violent outbursts—climaxing with the girl's attempted suicide and nervous breakdown, and the boy's father's own suicide—are crammed in the first half of the film, while the second half is slow, quiet, uneventful, as though dramatic energy, like the protagonists' own energy, had exhausted itself and, like them, needed a period of recovery. The relentless intensity of the first part is almost unbearable, and consequently laughable to many spectators. The pervasive obsession with adolescent sexuality, the didactic insistence on the evil effects of frustrated desires may seem overdone. But, as Roger Tailleur pointed out, "excess is in the subject-matter, and the stylistic option for caricature is a guarantee of realism."

The Prohibition era was the perfect setting for an indictment of puritanistic repression. Prohibition created a psychological atmosphere in which all pleasure (drinking, dancing, sex, one inevitably leading to the other) was cheapened and made sordid not only by its being branded as morally and/or legally wrong but by its being *experienced* as such and turned into a source of guilt feelings and self-disgust (as in the case of the Barbara Loden character). The failure to enforce Prohibition and the casual and overwhelming disregard of a law by the nation that had pressed for it pointed to a kind of double standard that also pervades attitudes toward love and sex throughout the film (believe in love, but don't make it; have sex if you must, but not with the one you love). Those attitudes are as perverted as they are traditional, from the spinsterish high-school teacher babbling about courtly love to the father "buying" his son a chorus girl to the mothers entrenched in their frigidity and denial of sex to the hero's sister's neurotic promiscuousness. In contrast, the young lovers' frank physical attraction for each other appears as the only healthy, normal response.

Kazan's point is somewhat blurred, however, by the fact that, as Charles Silver put it, he had "to make an antipuritan film under the puritanical rules of 1961." On the other hand, describing oppression from within a repressive system has its advantages. By having to submit its dramatic strategy to the strictures it denounces, the film exposes them in its very structure. The fact that it does not (is not allowed to) in the words of Pauline Kael, "come out for the rights of adolescents to sexual experimentation," emphasizes rather than invalidates its indictment of repression. Moreover, in a culture without any sexual hang-up—if such a thing could be—a film like *Splendor in the Grass* would have no point at all, except perhaps as a pure period piece. The film's popular success alone proves that early sixties audiences did relate to the emotions and frustrations it depicts.

Still, a good case can be made for the superiority of the film's immensely affecting second half. It deals with the "afterward" of the crisis, the uneventful postclimactic stretches of time that are usually excluded from dramatic action or at most are barely hinted at. It is no longer concerned with revolt, conflict, and violence, which is familiar ground, especially for Kazan, but with acceptance, an acceptance that is no mere resignation but involves a higher degree of awareness and understanding. In such moments as the girl's reconciliation with her parents or her last meeting with her ex-boyfriend and his wife, the film beautifully justifies its title's reference to Wordsworth. Those scenes, suffused with "the still, sad music of humanity," illuminate the text of "Intimations of Immortality," which was absurdly "discussed" by uncomprehending high-school students in an ironic early scene:

We will grieve not, rather find

Strength in what remains behind . . .

In the soothing thoughts that spring

Out of human suffering

All three pictures in the American trilogy formed by *East of Eden, Wild River,* and *Splendor in the Grass* deal with conflicts of generations, with past and present, with the changes time brings, and the price to be paid for change. However, whereas *Eden* and *Splendor* focus on the individual and on adolescent problems and parent-children relationships, *Wild River* broadens the scope to embrace the theme of progress versus tradition, and its protagonists are adults whose personal lives and private emotions are intimately welded to the social and human conflict at the core of the story. This sustained unity makes the film an exceptionally satisfying one. It is a completely mature and controlled work, lyrical without gushiness, compassionate without sentimentality, reflective without ponderousness, and, of all of Kazan's films, the one in which theatricality is most subdued, probably because, for once, he was more concerned with showing and understanding than with demonstrating and taking sides. Neither a belated homage to the achievements of the New Deal nor a sentimental paean to rural primitiveness, *Wild River* records, with a rare blend of humor and sensitiveness, the clash of abstract values against human realities, of grand designs against individual aspirations. It shows the inevitability and the throes of change and how there must be, inseparably, loss in the gain and gain in the loss. It could be Kazan's best film, and it is a shame that it is never revived theatrically (16-mm prints betray the atmospheric quality of the CinemaScope photography, an integral part of the film's achievement).

In the sixties, Kazan entered his period of "total authorship," turning away from the stage and devoting his time to writing. *America America* is the most personal of his first sixteen films, not only because it was the first he wrote himself, or because it is based on his own novel, or deals with the story of his own family, but also because it gathers all the major themes of his work. An extraordinarily powerful picture, it is a masterpiece inasmuch as the realization consistently rises to the high level of ambition of the project. Kazan's artistic control over the entire picture is all the more admirable as it was made abroad in unfamiliar, sometimes hostile surroundings, and the production was plagued with countless difficulties.

If one is willing to call "epic," rather than picaresque, a work whose hero is as unheroic (although, in his humble manner, admirable) as young Stavros, then *America America* is one of the great epics in film history. It never indulges in picturesqueness or spectacle for their own sake, never dwarfs characters or reduces them to symbols or types, and never strays from its central theme: the humiliations of oppression and poverty and a young man's indomitable determination to escape them, no matter what the physical or psychic costs. Stavros's struggle for survival in the pursuit of his American dream is an overwhelming tale of apprenticeship, told with seething passion and lucid compassion in a style that consistently transcends realism and sometimes (e.g., the admirable shipboard sequence) erupts into almost nightmarish baroque.

America America ended with young Stavros reaching the Promised Land, battered but alive, eager to achieve his dream of success in the New World. Half a century and three generations later, Stavros's nephew, Eddie Anderson, takes a disenchanted look at the dream, a dream that has come true but has also backfired. Anderson is that typical hero of contemporary American fiction, the upper-middle-class, middle-aged man obsessed with the emptiness of his material success; he is atypical, however, in his radical rejection of everything that had been his life until the symbolical accident that triggers his rebellion. *The Arrangement* is thus an echo of and an ironic commentary on the earlier film. It also turns the American trilogy into a tetralogy by adding its devastating view of the contemporary scene to the explorations of earlier decades in *Eden, River,* and *Splendor.*

Flawed and fascinating, the film is at once doomed and redeemed by Kazan's heroic struggle to sort out the unwieldy material of his novel and fit it into the mold of another medium. The book aimed at a sort of exhaustiveness ("It's everything I see and feel about America today," Kazan told an interviewer in 1966). The film is quite as ambitious. It is not only a confession, an assessment of Kazan's psychological, emotional, and moral evolution (through a fictional hero who is largely, although neither literally nor exclusively, autobiographical) but also a catalogue of all the conflicts and problems (familial, marital, extramarital, professional, economic, psychological, physical, or any combination thereof) that can beset the average "successful" American male, *and* simultaneously an indictment of an entire society and way of life. But films, of course, require more selectivity than novels do and are more likely to suffer from the shapelessness resulting from overabundance. Kazan was careful to give his adaptation a simpler structure than the novel's, yet, after eliminating huge sections of his narrative and sifting out a great deal of detail from the ones he did retain, he still ended up with too many episodes, too many themes and conflicts to do any of them full justice. While forced to spread himself too thin, however, he did not do so *evenly,* and his choice of emphasis is consistent with the general direction of his films since *East of Eden.* *The Arrangement* is closest, perhaps, to *Splendor in the Grass* in its two contrasting halves, the first one bitingly satirical and somewhat overdone (the satire of advertising is crude and, for sheer lack of time, even sketchier than in *A Face in the Crowd*), the second tender, nostalgic, and lyrical in its concentration on personal (and more specifically familial) relationships. The father-son relationship that gradually becomes the focus of the narrative (the film significantly ends, unlike the book, with the father's funeral) is the most developed and most affecting in Kazan's work. *Accepting* one's parents, coming to terms with one's conflicting feelings toward them, reconciling the love and the hate, is one of Kazan's major obsessions. *The Arrangement* is his definitive statement on the subject. Where the sons in *East of Eden, Splendor in the Grass,* and *America America* were adolescents, Eddie Anderson is a man who, thanks to the cleansing, rejuvenating effect of his crack-up, combines the uncompromising rebellion of youth with the experience of maturity. The film's bold merging of past and present within the frame as Eddie evokes painful childhood memories is Kazan's way of concretizing the veritable exorcism this reborn man has to perform in order to be rid of the old obsessions, the old images, the old self, and thereby be able at last to accept the loved and hated father.

The commercial failure of *The Arrangement* did not alter the direction of Kazan's preoccupations. *The Visitors,* a 16-mm independent venture written and produced by his son Chris, deals with the relationships between an aging writer, his daughter, her young lover, and two youths back from Vietnam in search of a father image. Indeed, it is amazing how many Kazan characteristics the script contains (it seems to have been elaborated in symbiosis with the writing of Kazan's novel *The Assassins*). Underneath its careful preservation of ambiguities and ambivalences, however, the film is rather schematic in its handling of motivations and conflicts, and one is reminded not so much of Kazan's late period as of earlier pictures, especially *Baby Doll,* which *The Visitors* resembles both thematically (sexual seduction as revenge) and stylistically (the action takes place entirely in or around one house, dialogue is of primary importance, the direction is focused on performances—by a small cast of unknowns—with the camera closely following the characters). Tension builds between the characters (as in *Baby Doll*) through subtle game playing—vague, unformulated threats and emotional teasing—until release finally comes in an almost orgiastic burst of savagery (rape and brutal fighting around cars at night, one of Kazan's obsessive motifs).

One is tempted to feel that Kazan put more of himself in this somewhat marginal project than into the eagerly awaited *The Last Tycoon,* a very good but, at least outwardly, not particularly personal picture. While the opportunity to direct it was, in view of Kazan's commercial status after *The Arrangement* and *The Visitors,* an unexpected break, such a return to big-time Hollywood production was not without its handicaps. Adapting a famous (and, furthermore, unfinished) novel and working from a script written by Harold Pinter, one of the most prestigious playwrights alive (not to mention the probable uneasiness of taking over the project from someone else) was a far cry from the ideal of total authorship Kazan had reached with *America America* and *The Arrangement.*

Curiously, there are many touches in the book that one would have expected Kazan to find congenial but which, for some reason, were either discarded or modified. Thus, to take one small example, although Kazan relishes scenes in the rain and has confessed that rain to him is an erotic turn-on, he neglected the opportunity—provided by Fitzgerald himself—to use it in the lovemaking scene between Stahr and Kathleen in Stahr's unfinished house. More importantly, while Kazan's heroines are usually earthy, rather aggressive women, the Kathleen of the film is stripped of the down-to-earth quality Fitzgerald had written into the character and idealized into an ethereal vision, the real-life counterpart of the "perfect" girl Stahr requests from a writer working on one of his productions. Kathleen's line "I *am* rather a trollop," for instance, is omitted, and Fitzgerald's reference to her speaking to Stahr "coarsely and provocatively" while they make love has been ignored; it is as though Pinter and Kazan, in the midst of unprecedented permissiveness, had paradoxically, almost perversely, gone out of their way to tidy up a novel already quite restrained even for its time.

The film is directed without any flourish, paced more quietly and smoothly than any other Kazan picture. Opportunities for satire or social comment are eschewed, there is none of Kazan's usual physical violence and exacerbated emotionalism, and the sex, excepting a few flashes of nudity, is hardly more explicit than something out of the thirties movies the hero produces. Still, all this may be due to Kazan's own evolution as much as to Pinter's influence. With the years, the anxiety, the manic intensity have finally mellowed into serenity, so that tenderness and subdued lyricism can prevail. Kazan's *Tycoon* is not concerned with Hollywood, its psychology, sociology, or mythology. It is not a study of power but rather an elegiac poem about a sad man who retreats from the burden of power into a world of private nostalgia, and attempts to act out a fantasy, to make a dream come true, with predictably disappointing results. Rex Reed, who, in the same article, praised *Network* (a kind of updated *A Face in the Crowd*) and panned *Tycoon* as a "dreary bore," nevertheless hit upon the terms that best account for its originality when he described it as "a film of pauses and silences" and referred to Kazan's "dreamlike direction." There is nothing flamboyant about the handling of the De Niro-Boulting scenes, but every glance, every hesitation, every tentative gesture suggest an overwhelming complexity of feelings, a world of yearning, wistfulness and regret, the ghost of happiness glimpsed and denied.

While it may seem at times little more than a painstakingly faithful illustration, *The Last Tycoon* achieves genuine greatness, and one that owes practically nothing to Fitzgerald, in its closing sequence, which is reminiscent of the telescoping of time and space in *The Arrangement.* Stahr's lonely reprise of his parable on "making pictures" (enacted, this time, for our sole benefit—a devastatingly distancing device suddenly disrupting the traditional narrative) is intercut with shots of Kathleen going through some of the gestures he is describing, an ultimate and ironically frustrating merging of fantasy and reality. After this brief, haunting moment, the final shot of Stahr walking away, engulfed by the darkness of a huge, empty sound stage, strikes a perfect minor-key note despite a hint of facile romaticism and leaves us with the same bittersweet sadness as the ending of *Splendor in the Grass.* Isn't *The Last Tycoon,* after all, everybody's (Fitzgerald's, Stahr's, Kazan's) attempt at recapturing a splendor that nothing can bring back?

26. Gene Kelly (1912)

1949—*On the Town* (codirector: Stanley Donen); 1952—*Singin' in the Rain* (codirector: Stanley Donen); 1955—*It's Always Fair Weather* (codirector: Stanley Donen); 1956—(1952) *Invitation to the Dance;* 1957—*The Happy Road;* 1958—*The Tunnel of Love;* 1962—*Gigot;* 1967—*A Guide for the Married Man;* 1969—*Hello, Dolly!;* 1970—*The Cheyenne Social Club;* 1976—*That's Entertainment Part Two* (documentary compilation), as director of new sequences

It is ironic—and, from a strictly auteurist standpoint, somewhat irritating—that one of the most universally admired American films ever made, the inexhaustibly exhilarating *Singin' in the Rain,* was the product of a collective effort rather than of one creator's vision and that Gene Kelly, its codirector, never directed one really good picture aside from the trio of musicals for which he shared screen credit with Stanley Donen—even though Kelly, not Donen, was clearly the major driving force behind these three, as well as many other important MGM musicals.

Any evaluation of Kelly's creative contribution to *On the Town, Singin' in the Rain,* and *It's Always Fair Weather* is bound to be arbitrary, as it must be arrived at through guesswork and little established evidence. Although the making of the films—especially *Singin' in the Rain*—has been abundantly documented in various articles and interviews and in Hugh Fordin's invaluably informative *The World of Entertainment!,* the exact nature of the two directors' collaboration has always remained hazy. Indeed, the professional relationship between Kelly and Donen (it was also, obviously, a close *personal* relationship) is one of the most curious situations in film history. Kelly had discovered Donen when the latter was a nineteen-year-old dancer in the chorus of *Pal Joey,* in which Kelly was starring on Broadway in 1940. Kelly soon made the young man his assistant, first for *Best Foot Forward* on Broadway, then in Hollywood for *Cover Girl* and *Anchors Aweigh.* In 1946 the two men jointly submitted to Arthur Freed a synopsis for a musical on baseball, which was to become *Take Me Out to the Ball Game.* Whatever Kelly's ultimate intentions in grooming his protégé for Hollywood work may have been, he was proved right in his confidence not only by Donen's contribution to their joint efforts, three of the finest musicals ever made, but also by his subsequent career as a director in his own right.

The three Kelly-Donen musicals—which should really be called the Kelly-Donen–Comden-Green musicals—are, in a sense, anomalies, flukes (if magic ones), the only successful instances of an actual directorial collaboration in Hollywood cinema. Both experience and logic said it could not work, yet it did and triumphantly so in at least two instances out of three. The team had come together for the first time in *Take Me Out to the Ball Game* (for which, unfortunately, Betty Comden and Adolph Green wrote only the songs, not the script). With Kelly and Donen staging and directing the musical sequences (although Busby Berkeley, who only took care of the dialogue scenes, received sole credit as director), and with four of the stars that were to reappear in *On the Town, Ball Game* may be considered a dry run (in more than one sense of the phrase) for the later classic.

The first Bernstein–Comden-Green collaboration, *On the Town,* was an innovative Broadway musical, and MGM approached it in typical Hollywood fashion, first securing the rights (in a preproduction deal, which at the time was *not* typical) then proceeding to strip the show of most of its original elements (including the majority of the songs) and injecting its own ingredients which, happily, turned out to be the right ones, so that the film eventually proved more revolutionary in terms of the movie musical tradition than the show had been in terms of the Broadway tradition. Comden and Green produced a thoroughly cinematic adaptation. The film innovated both in the area of stylization and in that of realism. On the one hand, the epoch-making "Miss Turnstiles Ballet," a showcase for Vera-Ellen's dancing using ultrasimplified sets and props and monochrome backgrounds, was the first musical sequence of its type on film. On the other hand, *On the Town* was also the first musical (and one of the very few) to move off the sound stage for important location shooting involving all the principals. Nearly thirty years later, when location productions have become commonplace and New York City has been displayed in countless films, the sight of Kelly, Sinatra, and Munshin romping all over the city is still a gloriously exciting sight, all the more so as the realism combines with an overall look (that of forties movies) one associates with a much more traditional, studio-bound approach. It would be a mistake to overemphasize the film's "revolutionary" aspect, however. Unlike *An American in Paris,* it made no attempt at dazzling the spectator by showing off its innovations. As Donen himself put it: "We never told ourselves, 'Now, we're going to do something no one has ever done before.' We simply thought that this was the way one should deal with, one should conceive a musical comedy. . . . We didn't realize we were making any innovations." If anything, the film is a little too anxious not to appear "highbrow," a little too broad in its handling of plebeian (although tongue-in-cheek) humor. Indeed, laughs and pace seem to have been foremost in the minds of all concerned. The comedy is at times of the "anything for a laugh" variety, and the pace is frantic, in the image of the heroes' cram course in the art of hitting the big city. After the opening shots, with the sleepy crane worker yawningly singing "I feel like I'm not out of bed yet," the sailors move in, and all thoughts of sleeping (although not of one's "lady's arms") is forgotten (the only ballad in the entire score is the affectionately ironic "Main Street," sung by Kelly to Vera-Ellen in a contrasting homage to small-town life). There is no such hectic straining for effect in *Singin' in the Rain,* although its pace is as fast as that of any musical on record, and probably more so. But then, *Singin' in the Rain* is a perfect musical, whereas *On the Town* is merely a nearly perfect one.

The notion of a "perfect" film would have little meaning if applied to any other category; movie musicals, however, unlike other genre films, always seemed to be striving toward the realization of an archetypal model, a perfection of the genre that the best among them approached from a distance but which one doubted any particular one would ever reach. Put in simple terms, the "perfect" movie musical would consist of a series of great song-and-dance and/or ballet numbers, all growing naturally out of the story, a film in which no dichotomy would be felt between the straight scenes and the musical ones, the former never seeming like expandable transitions between the latter; a film, most importantly, in which the peculiar euphoria generated by good musicals would not be felt in a few numbers but experienced as a continuous feeling throughout the picture. Before *Singin' in the Rain,* this may have seemed a purely theoretical proposition, an unattainable goal toward which the best one could do was strive. *Singin' in the Rain* made it look not only possible but deceptively simple.

What made *Singin' in the Rain* so radically different is not something that can be easily accounted for; there is a certain quality about the film that just seems to elude definition or description. Yet, one can't be content with filing it away as an ineffable experience. It has too many obvious outstanding qualities that beg to be mentioned. One of them is the film's extraordinary *evenness* in a genre that seems to have ups and downs built into its very formula. It is practically impossible to rate one of the musical numbers above the other, as all of them, from the almost thrown away "All I Do Is Dream of You" (Debbie Reynolds, fresh out of a giant cake, heading a wonderfully vulgar-sounding and looking chorus of pink-clad girls "from the Cocoanut Grove") to the elaborately produced "Broadway Ballet" are equally polished and stimulating; almost any one of them could provide the highlight of an above-average musical. Moreover, all the nonmusical scenes (with a couple of negligible—because very brief—exceptions) are first-rate comedy material that not only smoothly and logically leads into numbers but remains thoroughly enjoyable on its own even after many viewings of the film. They contribute, to almost as high a degree as the musical sequences, to the sustained euphoria that makes the experience of watching *Singin' in the Rain* so unique.

Less obvious than the film's evenness is the exact nature of its originality, which is quite peculiar. The appearance of novelty is often achieved by dressing up an old formula; in *Singin' in the Rain,* a genuinely original concept was cleverly camouflaged so as to appear as traditional and predictable as possible on the surface. The project came into existence at all because of Arthur Freed's remarkably *un*imaginative notion to use a bunch of his old songs in a new musical. No director (or cast) had been decided upon when Comden and Green started working on a script and came up with the idea of setting the film during the period most of the songs had been written and in the very place where they originated: a Hollywood movie studio. A brilliant inspiration, it had, however, its pitfalls. The film could have been a mere spoof of silent and early talking pictures, with all the built-in limitations of parody. Played more safely, it could have become an equivalent of the traditional backstage musical, a backlot musical, so to speak, with the background shifted from a Broadway stage to a Hollywood studio. But the team cunningly steered clear of both pitfalls. The "historical" element, although much more than a mere backdrop to the story line, with which it blends perfectly, was, nevertheless, never allowed to upstage it or to become the dominant ingredient in the film's musical and choreographic style. This delicate balance was achieved (whether deliberately or instinctively) by keeping the principals uninvolved in the nostalgic re-creations of early musicals. They do not take part in the anthology sequence—a montage spoofing those early efforts and leading into the equally "dated" rendition of "Beautiful Girl," which itself frames a fashion show, late twenties style. None of the song-and-dance numbers by Kelly, Donald O'Connor, and Reynolds are performed for the film they are supposed to be making but come about as spontaneous expressions of their feelings at the time, whether they be a lover's elation turning a rainstorm into a burst of joie de vivre (the title sequence), renewed optimism after a depression ("Good Morning"), or a philosophy of show biz ("Make 'em Laugh"). Even the "Broadway Melody" ballet, which is supposed to be the climax of the revamped *The Dueling Cavalier* (now *The Dancing Cavalier*), is introduced not as if it were the actual completed sequence but as Don Lockwood's description to his producer of what it will look like when produced. (A perfect example of the script's sly acknowledging of the absurdity of the conventions it toys with is the producer's remark after the whole sequence has unreeled: "I can't quite visualize it, I'll have to see it on the screen.") The only two song-and-dance numbers that are, in the story itself, performances by the principals (Kelly's and O'Connor's "Fit as a Fiddle" and Reynolds's "All I Do Is Dream of You" with the chorus) are placed early in the film to establish their professional background: third-rate vaudeville and burlesque for Don and Cosmo, tabshow-type chorus line for Kathie.

In these as in all the other musical numbers, the integration of plot, characterization, and song and dance is beautifully realized. Just before doing her number, Kathy has lied to Don about her achievements, claiming that she is "an actress on the legitimate stage." The incredulous film star has kidded her about her pretensions, but he had lied in exactly the same way in an earlier scene when asked to talk about his early career to the preview crowd. Later, in a charming nonmusical scene, Don and Kathy confess their respective shams to each other. As the story develops, they learn (for *Singin' in the Rain,* on top of everything, has a moral) not to despise their humble show-biz past but rather to utilize the skills and experience it gave them to reach a higher achievement, i.e., *The Dancing Cavalier,* and more particularly the "Broadway Melody" ballet (which is indeed such an achievement that it is literally twenty years ahead of its time, Monumental Pictures's 1928 premonitory dream of what could only take place at MGM around 1950—no wonder the producer "couldn't quite visualize it"!)

Singin' in the Rain even affords the highbrow luxury of a *construction en abyme;* the theme is reprised in the ballet itself, which has to do with the rise of a hoofer from burlesque to the Ziegfeld Follies and beyond to modern and classical—or semiclassical—ballet (the sequences with Cyd Charisse). In the "Broadway Melody" ballet, Kelly's most obviously personal contribution to the film, the director-dancer-choreographer identified with his hero (the sequence seems to spring fully armed from Don Lockwood's mind) in articulating his ambitions and at the same time realizing them. Whether he was aware of it or not, this was to be the peak, for him, of personal expression.

It's Always Fair Weather is a problem all its own. It was disappointing when it first came out, but while it cannot compare with the first two Kelly-Donen efforts, its disenchanted, even bitter, quality—quite unusual in a musical—has become more affecting than it was in 1955. As if in acknowledgment of the passing of an era, the satire in *It's Always Fair Weather* was directed at television rather than old movies, and the film itself was photographed in CinemaScope. The heroes are plagued with the deep-set tensions of city life and executive responsibilities, and, in a downbeat variation on the pattern set by *On the Town,* Comden and Green imagined a ten-years-later reunion of three army buddies who find out that they can no longer stand each other. Dan Dailey's destructive routine at a party, prompted by some Madison Avenue types' indiscriminate use of the suffix "-wise," is a neurotic display more in tune with the spirit of Jules Feiffer and the "sick" comedians (to use a term popular at the time) than with the good-natured optimism of the Arthur Freed tradition. The old feeling is recaptured only in a couple of scenes, one of them an exhilarating roller-skating promenade through New York streets by a supremely relaxed Kelly, recalling the unforgettable title sequence of *Singin' in the Rain.*

It's Always Fair Weather was a sunset production, the swan song of the MGM musical, and today it has become invaluable as such. No matter what its weaknesses may have been, it towers above most of the musicals that have been made since, simply because it represents a type of entertainment whose secret has been lost. The only successful Hollywood musicals (as opposed to filmizations of Broadway shows) to appear after *Fair Weather* were Richard Quine's *My Sister Eileen* (which was released six months after the Kelly-Donen film) and Donen's own *Funny Face*—neither, incidentally, an MGM production. (*Gigi* is a visually stunning spectacle at times, but it completely lacks the kind of charm that makes films like *Band Wagon, My Sister Eileen, Funny Face,* or the Kelly-Donen collaboration so unique; indeed, the script, score, and lyrics by Lerner and Loewe, although written for the film, were more reminiscent of a Broadway musical—particularly their own *My Fair Lady*—than of the Hollywood musical tradition.)

To deal with Kelly's solo efforts as a director after the Kelly-Donen musicals is almost unbearably anticlimactic. In 1951, with the two most ambitious film ballets ever made in Hollywood to his credit (he was, of course, the choreographer for Minnelli's *An American in Paris*), he was naturally—but, as he was to discover, unwisely—moving toward the concept of an all-dance picture. Curiously (and unfortunately for Kelly), there was no resistance from Freed to the project, on which Kelly started working soon after completing *Singin' in the Rain* and which, except for one sequence involving cartoons, was filmed in London but under the constant supervision of Lela Simone, who was referred to by Hugh Fordin as the Freed unit's "trouble-shooter." (The chapter on the making of *Invitation to the Dance* is one of the most detailed in Fordin's book and is more illuminating about the film's problems and weaknesses than any actual criticism of it ever published.)

Invitation to the Dance was an ordeal to make and a severe disappointment to its director. The film was in production for nearly six months, following months of preparation, and once completed remained on the shelf for four years before going into limited release. (It recouped only about $600,000 of its approximate $1.5 million cost.) An ambitious film in all the wrong ways Kelly had always avoided before, *Invitation to the Dance* is, cinematically and choreographically, a hybrid product, a plotless juxtaposition of three "modern-classical" ballets, drawing upon such prestigious European talents as composer Jacques Ibert, who wrote the score for the "Circus" sequence, and ballet dancers Igor Youskevitch, Claire Sombert, and Tamara Toumanova, with music also provided by the light classical standby Rimsky-Korsakov. "Circus" and "Ring Around the Rosy," both a little over thirty minutes in length, are overlong, uneven, and inevitably stage-bound. The clever, inventive "Sinbad the Sailor," in which Kelly dances with animated cartoon characters (a device he had first used in *Anchors Aweigh*), is more in the traditional Kelly spirit, but it, too, is overlong (twenty-seven minutes), as the gimmick loses its novelty after a while. The Quimby–Hanna-Barbera animation, moreover, is far from first-rate. Significantly, the one sequence that was filmed but not retained was one for which Kelly had used a medley of some twenty-five popular songs; it may have been the liveliest section of the film (one would certainly like to see it if it has survived), but it was not classically oriented and thus could not find its niche in a production that was doggedly dedicated to "culture on film." (The "Sinbad" sequence, although Hollywoodish, was "redeemed" by its music.) Probably for similar reasons, Ralph Burns's jazz suite "Summer Sequence," which had been written for the film, was not used at all.

Kelly's tribulations with *Invitation to the Dance* must have taken their toll, for the atmosphere during the filming of *It's Always Fair Weather* was notoriously tense and unfriendly. Fordin quotes Donen as recalling: "I didn't really want to codirect another picture with Kelly at that point. We didn't get on very well and, for that matter, Gene didn't get on well with anybody. It was the only picture during which the atmosphere was really horrendous." By the time *Invitation to the Dance* was finally released, Kelly had starred in Minnelli's *Brigadoon* and his own *The Happy Road,* which he directed and produced for MGM. A nonmusical comedy set in France, it was a very enjoyable satirical piece taking on—of all things—NATO and its field maneuvers.

From then on, it was all downhill for Kelly as a director. *Tunnel of Love,* an innocuous filmed play, may have attracted him on account of its topic—a couple's difficulties in adopting a child—as Kelly always liked children; one wonders, however, what drove him to tackle such a doomed project as the mawkish *Gigot. A Guide for the Married Man* is a smutty, mirthless comedy directed with a dirty old man's leer rather than Kelly's customary grin. He capitalized again on the new freedom with *The Cheyenne Social Club,* a GP-rated comedy Western about a brothel, in which James Stewart's and Henry Fonda's acting is as heavy-handed as the director's touch. Ironically, Kelly directed only one musical on his own, and it had to be the aggressively vulgar, overproduced, and uninspired *Hello, Dolly!* There were so many basic things wrong with the script and overall conception of the picture that Kelly can take only a limited amount of blame, a director's job in such a case becoming, more than anything else, an exercise in survival. *Hello, Dolly!* fails for some of the same reasons as did most of Hollywood's multi-million-dollar adaptations of Broadway musicals in the sixties and early seventies: a slavish respect for the vehicle, the tyranny of superstars, a deliberate policy of overproduction. The film and its makers were smothered by money, but Kelly's inability to cope with the problems inherent in that type of movie making does not spring from any particular ineptitude of his own at handling big budgets. After all, *Singin' in the Rain* had been quite an expensive production in its time; still, it could be controlled and was conceived as a basically controllable venture, whereas *Dolly* was bound to get out of hand and had esthetic failure built into its ponderous structure. A comparison of the two films, respectively the zenith and nadir of the modern movie musical, dramatically stresses the tragedy that befell the genre when, for economic reasons, the making of original Hollywood musicals gave way to the presold packaging of Broadway hits.

27. *Irvin Kershner* (1923)

by BARRY PUTTERMAN

1958—*Stakeout on Dope Street;* 1959—*The Young Captives;* 1961—*The Hoodlum Priest;* 1963—*A Face in the Rain;* 1964—*The Luck of Ginger Coffey;* 1966—*A Fine Madness;* 1967—*The Flim-Flam Man;* 1970—*Loving;* 1972—*Up the Sandbox;* 1974—*S*P*Y*S;* 1976—*The Return of the Man Called Horse;* 1978—*Eyes of Laura Mars;* 1980—*The Empire Strikes Back;* 1983—*Never Say Never Again*

Television movie
1977—*Raid on Entebbe*

Irvin Kershner had so firmly established himself in the margins of the American film industry, making harsh, bitter films about unsuccessful rebels, that his emergence as a hot commercial director in the 1980s is a bit disconcerting. While granting that whatever audience there was for stories of malcontents who have the vision but not the talent to break out of their confinements has probably vanished, it is still difficult to see how Kershner's own talent will survive the confinement of the larger, more commercially calculated projects.

As befits the teller of his tales, Kershner came to commercial film making from a varied background in the arts. A graduate of the Tyler School of Fine Arts in his native Philadelphia, Kershner studied design at the University of California, Los Angeles before joining the film making program at the University of Southern California. After a two-year stint in advertising, he went to work making documentaries for the United States Information Agency in the Middle East. These four films (*Malaria, Childbirth, Locust Plague,* and *Road of 100 Days*) are difficult to find now, but among those who have seen them, they have very good reputations. They led to further documentary work for the *Confidential File* television series in the mid-fifties and then into fiction television with the Nick Adams series *The Rebel.*

Kershner's feel for documentary has stayed with him all through his career. Initially it allowed him to break into feature film making without the necessity of going through the still-powerful studio system. *Stakeout on Dope Street* was shot independently for about $35,000 mainly because Kershner was able to use the available locations in a semidocumentary style with a cast of young unknowns, which included Jonathan Haze, of later *Little Shop of Horrors* fame, and Abby Dalton on this melodramatic story of a group of teenagers who find a stash of heroin and try to sell it. The film was then sold to Warner Brothers, thus insuring that it would get a wider distribution than usual for a film of its size.

In fact, after a brief foray into the more usual break-in territory of Roger Corman with *The Young Captives,* Kershner made his initial breakthrough as a recognized talent with *The Hoodlum Priest.* The film looked enough like a conventional liberal "do good" picture in the tradition of *Knock on Any Door* or *Crime in the Streets* to gather a good deal of favorable notice from the mainstream film press, but in retrospect the remarkable aspects of the film can be seen not as minor variations on an overly familiar theme but as indications of attitudes and strategies Kershner would later use with more congenially structured material. Kershner reinforced the documentary possibilities inherent in the story of St. Louis's Rev. Dismas Clark (Don Murray) by shooting the film in that city. The shifting of the focus from Clark to the rebellious youngster (Keir Dullea) and the sympathy for the rebellion of the youngster right up through his execution, plus the uncommonly fierce hostility toward the establishment antagonists all would become characteristic of Kershner's later work. Indeed, after the modest if characteristically gloomy thriller *A Face in the Rain,* Kershner entered his most productive period, most effectively fitting together his form of film making with his concept of society to produce in his next five films his four best works.

The Luck of Ginger Coffey and *A Fine Madness* can be considered together not only because they concern themselves with poetic, impractical central figures who cannot adjust to the demands of a middle-class society but because they also offer the opposite extremes of reactions by these characters to their situations. Kershner's strategy of location shooting, hinted at in the earlier works, becomes more evident in these films. The continuous tracking, panning, and hand-held following of Ginger Coffey (Robert Shaw) as he ambles through the dusty press room and dreary streets and buildings of Montreal and of Samson Shillitoe (Sean Connery) as he strides into and is chased out of the congested streets, gyms, and offices of New York eventually turns from a definition of the character through his environment into a definition of the limitations placed on the characters' aspirations by their environments. Kershner draws the location so tightly around the characters that no matter how restlessly they strive to physically dodge all of the responsibilities of middle-class society, they are continuously frustrated by having one or another of them pop up in the road just as they thought they had broken free. This can be seen perhaps most clearly in *A Fine Madness* in the sequence where, having just escaped from an imminent lobotomy at the "rest home," Shillitoe pauses on the bridge, strutting up and down the parapet, having finally risen above all of his pressures and pursuers only to have the police close in on him from both sides to arrest him for failing to pay his back alimony. Further, Ginger's passive resistance to and Samson's massive defiance of the responsibilities of family, work, social respectability, and whatever else interferes with the pursuit of their personal visions of self form the polar boundaries of Kershner's antiheroic outsiders, his Bartleby and Ahab as it were.

Kershner's next film, *The Flim-Flam Man,* is not without interest. It, too, ties the characters to the locations so tightly that it all but suffocates them, ultimately culminating in their capture by the authorities. Also, the relationship between the confused adolescent (Michael Sarrazin) and his mentor (George C. Scott) plays like an ironic commentary on *The Hoodlum Priest* with the mature character being the voice of bitter disillusionment. However, the film never quite captures the tone it wishes to present, suffers from a lack of definition in the Sarrazin and Sue Lyon characters and more acutely from a performance by Scott in the grand ham tradition of Paul Muni and, ultimately, from just too much middlebrow profundity and unfunny comedy.

It was with the next two films, *Loving* and *Up the Sandbox,* that Kershner created works that reestablished and in fact enriched and commented upon the ideas developed in *Ginger Coffey* and *A Fine Madness.* Ginger and Samson were professional outsiders, people who, by the definitions of their sensibilities, never would be able to fit into the mainstream of society. Kershner had always been sympathetic toward the qualities that made them unacceptable to a culture he sees as bland, smug, and deadening to the spirit, but in Jean Seberg's Mrs. West in *Madness* we see the beginnings of an expanding outlook. This character is a person who has adjusted to the demands of society but finds its rewards to be the same sort of trap that life as an outsider is for the earlier characters. Further, while Ginger and Samson would simply not be left in peace by a culture they wish to reject, Brooks Lawrence (George Segal) of *Loving* and Margaret Reynolds (Barbra Streisand) of *Up the Sandbox* are doubly cursed by the failure of their social success to fill their emotional needs and by their awareness that it is the failure of their personal aspirations that led to the compromises of social acceptance. The failed painter who settled for a career as a free-lance commercial artist and the educated housewife with fantasies of grandeur become the mirror reflections of blocked writer Samson and impractical dreamer Ginger, reflections imprisoned in the frame of defined jobs and sets of responsibilities.

Mrs. West had the sensitivity to be frustrated by the emptiness of her life and also the sensitivity to realize that she is not talented enough in the arts (her harp) or intellectual pursuits (her club meetings) to be able to escape her situation. The breakfast sequence between her, her husband (Patrick O'Neal), and their children seems to be the jumping-off point for these two later films. In fact, it is reproduced almost literally at the beginning of *Loving* to establish the tensions between Brooks's love for and irritation with his family and pride in and disgust at the definition of his life.

The character's attitude toward family becomes the central point around which *Up the Sandbox* revolves. In Kershner's usual manner, he uses the opening sequence of Margaret washing her children while waiting for daddy (David Selby) to come home to wed the home and children so tightly around her that they form the outer boundaries of her life. And as we see Margaret trudging through her routine chores, coping with the children and the boredom of housework and the terrors of New York City life, seemingly insignificant events trigger wild fantasies of the differing directions her life might have taken and seemingly might still take.

Yet while these fantasies are comic, they always end in humiliation and disaster for Margaret. She winds up not having either the nerve, toughness, or ability to cope with these situations. Her final fantasy concerning the abortion she is considering aptly visualizes her plight when she is dumped full-grown into her children's park sandbox. Similarly, Brooks winds up in his overcoat and undershorts being caught on closed-circuit television trying to seduce a woman in a child's playhouse. The final image of Brooks, while still in that outfit, being beaten by his wife (Eva Marie Saint) with her purse contrasts just as ironically with Samson's final swings at his wife (Joanne Woodward) as Margaret's fantasy failures do with Ginger's dreams. Whereas Brooks and Margaret are more aware of the implications of the childishness at the center of all of Kershner's protagonists, that extra awareness has directed them toward the kinds of childishness that keeps them dependent on the frustrating routines they have fallen into. For all of their faults, Ginger and Samson are failures who are living on their own terms; Brooks and Margaret are even failures at being failures.

These four films constitute the major body of Kershner's work, summing up his attitudes and approaches. Ironically, all are based on novels; by Brian Moore, Elliot Baker, J. P. Ryan, and Anne Richardson Roiphe respectively. Since *Up the Sandbox*, Kershner's own work has most often failed to succeed on its own terms and has been in steady decline. All of these films are from original scripts.

Still, on the plus side was a wacky spy spoof starring Elliott Gould and Donald Sutherland, which was retitled from *Wet Stuff* to *S*P*Y*S* in obvious imitation of that pair's previous hit *M*A*S*H*. No doubt fans expecting something along the order of that film were disappointed with this knockabout farce, though had they looked closer they would have found an underlying tone much more corrosive than the much admired Altman film had. Even on the surface level there were many good sequences of physical comedy, such as Gould's spritzing of nerve gas on Sutherland in a crowded restaurant to create a diversion and a long chase by the out-of-shape agents of some enemies through Paris back alleys.

Still on the interesting side was *Return of the Man Called Horse,* a nominal sequel to Elliott Silverstein's *A Man Called Horse.* Here English aristocrat Richard Harris voluntarily returns to his Sioux tribe to train and lead them in guerrilla war against the corrupt white settlers. The revisionist politics commenting on America's domestic and foreign policies was stronger than the usual Hollywood attempts in that direction, but the film seems to be blind to its own racial implications in having Harris being the thinking force behind the action, as if Pontecorvo's *BURN!* had never existed.

From there it is a quick slide to *Eyes of Laura Mars,* which was originally written by John Carpenter but which went through numerous hands before the finished product emerged. The film seemed at first to be raising interesting questions about the relationship between the artistic and criminal minds but turned out to be much less interested in answering them then in striking haughty, condescending attitudes toward the New York fashion scene.

And finally there is *The Empire Strikes Back*. George Lucas admired Kershner from the days when he was Kershner's student at USC, and his selection of his mentor to helm the second *Star Wars* film made Kershner a hot, bankable director despite the fact that he had never had a commercially successful film in his entire career. That *The Empire Strikes Back* is marginally superior to *Star Wars* is probably due to the fact that it plays like the middle third of a single feature and thus contains fewer of the agonizing scenes of exposition and more of the easy to take (or leave) special effects and action rather than anything Kershner might have contributed. That the film is just about the biggest moneymaker of all time certainly had nothing to do with anything Kershner contributed.

---

28. *Stanley Kubrick* (1926)

1953—*Fear and Desire;* 1955—*Killer's Kiss;* 1956—*The Killing;* 1958—*Paths of Glory;* 1960—*Sparta-cus* (uncredited codirector: Anthony Mann); 1962—*Lolita;* 1964—*Dr. Strangelove or How I Learned to Stop Worrying and Love the Bomb;* 1968—*2001: A Space Odyssey;* 1971—*A Clockwork Orange;* 1975—*Barry Lyndon;* 1980—*The Shining*

If an extraterrestrial, sent to gather data on the ways of mankind, decided after some observing to stay among us and take up movie making, his films, one suspects, might resemble Stanley Kubrick's. Kubrick's detachment is the most chillingly consistent in film history. Irony—coming in all shades from mild to bitter, sly to biting—seems to be not just his favorite but his only mode of response to the foibles of the human race. His visual style is as coolly formalized as his scripts are coldly engineered, the computerlike, geometrical necessity of his camera moves echoing the clockwork mechanism of the narratives. His vision of humanity is relentlessly pessimistic. The past, either distant (*Spartacus*) or recent (*Paths of Glory*), is the realm of injustice, cruelty, indifference to suffering, senseless massacres. The present (*Lolita*) is nightmarish, a world of ludicrous couplings and inexplicable, destructive sexual urges with a cultural wasteland for its backdrop. The near future is dominated by nauseating violence and pornography (*A Clockwork Orange*) or headed for nuclear holocaust (*Dr. Strangelove*), while in the distant future of *2001: A Space Odyssey,* man is so dehumanized as to become all but undistinguishable from his machinery. As for *The Shining,* it suggests that the present is condemned to endlessly repeat the evil of the past.

Kubrick's is a loveless world and essentially a womanless one. No women appear in *Paths of Glory* or *2001,* except in roles so incidental that they only emphasize the all-maleness of the whole. In other films, women are sex objects (Lolita, the Tracy Reed character in *Dr. Strangelove*—the only female part in the film—all the women in *A Clockwork Orange*), ruthless predators (Marie Windsor in *The Killing,* Nina Foch in *Spartacus*), or comical (Shelley Winter's giddy husband-hunting widow in *Lolita*). The female protagonists in *Barry Lyndon* and *The Shining* rise somewhat above the level of stereotypes or caricatures to which all of the above were confined, yet Kubrick's treatment of them remains perfunctory, almost contemptuous, and his very casting of the parts is revealing of his attitude to the characters. Susan Sarandon's cool beauty and ethereal aloofness in *Barry Lyndon,* emphasized by makeup, period hairstyle and clothes, as well as photography, help keep her at a distance from the spectator and turn the character into a cipher. Shelley Duvall's natural talent for projecting dazed vapidity (best utilized by Robert Altman in *3 Women*) is encouraged, rather than subdued, in *The Shining,* in which her character, although perhaps the only woman in Kubrick's work—alone with Jean Simmons's Varinia in *Spartacus*—toward whom the audience may feel empathy, has practically no personality of her own.

Of course, inasmuch as Kubrick sees *all* people as puppets, he tends to make caricatures out of men as well as women. Still, the action of his films—at least in the earlier, more traditional ones—revolves around three-dimensional heroes. They may be of less than heroic stature, but in the case of Humbert Humbert, for instance, compassion is evoked through understanding, whereas, in the same film, the characterization of Lolita's mother is so broad that her pathetic insecurity cannot possibly touch us. Not surprisingly, male-female relationships (a very minor theme in Kubrick's cinema at any rate) are usually warped, with men driven by sexual obsessions leading to their enslavement (Humbert's to Lolita, Elisha Cook Jr.'s to Marie Windsor in *The Killing*) or to sadistic outbursts (*A Clockwork Orange*). Barry Lyndon's marriage is doomed almost as soon as it is consummated, and there is not a single moment of intimacy or togetherness between Jack Torrance and his wife (*The Shining*), even before he starts breaking down. (Significantly, Kubrick filmed but cut out several "happy-family" scenes from the early part of the picture.) The only instance of tenderness—if one excepts the relationship between the prize fighter and the dancer in *Killer's Kiss*—is the doomed love that unites Spartacus and Varinia, and that occurs in Kubrick's least personal effort.

Failure is the common denominator to all endeavors depicted in Kubrick's films. The prize fighter and the would-be ballerina (*Killer's Kiss*) never rise above mediocrity; the holdup money is scattered to the winds (*The Killing*); innocent soldiers can't be saved from execution (*Paths of Glory*); the slaves' revolt is crushed (*Spartacus*); Humbert Humbert ends up in jail, a murderer (*Lolita*); nuclear annihilation can't be avoided despite frantic efforts on both sides (*Dr. Strangelove*); the space mission is sabotaged by the computer (*2001*); the therapy meant to "rehabilitate" Alex turns him into a spineless, passive victim (*A Clockwork Orange*); Barry Lyndon's schemes backfire on him, and his life is destroyed; Jack Torrance, the would-be writer, never gets beyond one single, meaningless sentence, becomes psychotic, and surrenders to the overwhelming powers of evil (*The Shining*).

A sense of inevitability—rather than of fate—pervades all the films. There is never any doubt as to the ultimate outcome of *The Killing, Spartacus,* or *Paths of Glory. Lolita* opens with Humbert's murder of Quilty, then flashes back to the story proper, a well-worn device, but still the most effective one to intimate that the chain of events in a narrative ineluctably lead to a specific ending. In Kubrick's more ambitious latter films, failure and self-destruction are viewed as built into the very makeup of the human race. The first weapon, which heralds the dawn of civilization (*2001*), is at the same time the first step toward the modern technology that will bring about the destruction of mankind (*Dr. Strangelove*). While man bears the responsibility for his own destructiveness, he can't be credited for his resourcefulness and creativity. According to the *2001* cosmography, major steps in the evolution of the human race have been monitored by some vastly superior, almost godlike intelligence. Because of the hopelessness of man's nature, this noble experiment backfires, and the "intelligence" has to plant danger signs (the ubiquitous monoliths) along man's path through space in an effort to offset the nefarious consequences of the initial impulse. Eventually, man can be "saved" from the combination of death wish and death dread that characterizes him only by being upgraded to superhuman status (this, at least, is one possible interpretation of *2001*'s ambiguous ending, and inasmuch as the ambiguity is deliberate, it is as valid an interpretation as any other).

Human beings, clearly, are not Kubrick's cup of tea, and even the compassion for the underdog, the indignation at injustice that seethed underneath the cold surface of *Paths of Glory* later disappeared to be replaced with a half-jaundiced, half-amused blanket rejection of the human race as a hopeless miscarriage. Hence, probably, Kubrick's fascination with everything that mocks or dwarfs the human shape: lifeless replicas of the body and face (the dummies in *Killer's Kiss,* the gangsters' masks in *The Killing,* the false noses and outlandish eye makeup in *A Clockwork Orange*); oversized sets emphasizing the individual's insignificance (the court-martial room in *Paths of Glory,* the war room in *Dr. Strangelove,* the spaceship in *2001,* the abandoned theater in *A Clockwork Orange,* the Overlook Hotel—reminiscent of the spaceship—in *The Shining*). Hence, too, his interest in the subhuman (the animal status of the slaves and gladiators in *Spartacus,* the soldiers as cannon fodder in *Paths of Glory*); in the crippled body (Strangelove, the writer in *2001,* both confined to wheelchairs, both turned into half machines with no control over their own bodies); and in the crippled mind (Humbert's, Strangelove's, Ripper's, Alex's, Torrance's, to name only a few). And then there is Hal the computer, the hero—or antihero—of *2001,* who belongs in all of the above categories. A giant replica of the human brain, it grows neurotic and destructive when it becomes human (or is it the other way round?), and its disconnection is a deliberate crippling, an incapacitating process that brings him to helpless disability.

A French critic once complained that all of Kubrick's films are vulgar. If vulgarity is less a matter of poor taste than of heavy-handedness, then Kubrick *is* vulgar. From the ponderously surrealistic artiness of *Killer's Kiss* to the snickering kinkiness of *A Clockwork Orange,* he never has had any use for understatement. Far from increasing in subtlety as they increase in complexity, his films seem to become ever more leadenly insistent. At his most facile, he is liable to turn out something on the level of *Mad Magazine* or the *National Lampoon. Dr. Strangelove* made it big by dint of its deliberate excesses. It seemed to derive its impact upon audiences solely from the shock power inherent in the clash between its subject matter and its treatment. Kubrick certainly couldn't miss with the subject matter, a problem one can safely assume every spectator had worried about at one time or another. Moreover, it was the first time it had really been dealt with in *any* movie—although Sidney Lumet's *Fail Safe* was released less than a year later. All previous "doomsday" pictures (*Five, On the Beach, The World, the Flesh and the Devil*) were harmless socio-psychological charades set *after* a nuclear war, using the war as a fait accompli and a dramatic convention and thus divesting it of any reality. No movie had ever dared picture the ultimate holocaust and the ineluctable chain of events leading up to it. The decision to turn the whole thing into a farce, although titillatingly outrageous, was, if not sound, at least logical, since the rationale behind the nuclear arms race (i.e., that neither side wants a nuclear war and that therefore the only way to avoid one is for both sides to build up ever deadlier atomic weaponry) *is* insane, a mind-boggling instance of topsy-turvy logic reminiscent of Lewis Carroll or *Catch-22.*

Kubrick, who had originally intended to make a straight dramatic adaptation of the source novel, found that "one had to keep leaving things out of it, which were either absurd or paradoxical, in order to keep it from being funny; and these things seemed to be close to the heart of the scenes in question." One sympathizes with the adaptor and his predicament, but shouldn't the whole point of the movie as planned have been to expose the "absurd" and the "paradoxical" in the political realities upon which the survival or extinction of the human race depend? The style of comedy Kubrick—abetted by Terry Southern—decided upon was so broad that it safely defused the explosive potential of the theme. They made the whole matter of nuclear policy seem too ludicrous to be taken seriously, thus managing to entertain and reassure the audience while treating it to nothing less than the end of the world. After all, there are no such people as General Jack D. Ripper, Dr. Strangelove, or Major T. J. "King" Kong in real life, are there? And doesn't it follow that what happens in the film couldn't possibly happen in real life? Underneath its satirical irony, the coy subtitle to *Dr. Strangelove* betrays its cynicism, for the film does indeed teach its audience how to stop worrying and love the bomb. And the audience, needless to say, was ready for that kind of teaching. *Dr. Strangelove* might not have worked ten years earlier, but it came at a time when the fear of the bomb that had overshadowed the late forties and the fifties was beginning to recede into the depths of people's subconscious minds. Kubrick's magnified crudeness—culminating with the shot of an insanely gleeful Slim Pickens riding the fatal bomb to its target—was intended, it seems, not to revive that fear but to make it appear as abstract and speculative as any "What if . . . ?" science-fiction proposition, thus encouraging the new prevailing mood. (Yet, to a certain extent, Kubrick attempted to have it both ways. Large portions of the film—the scenes aboard the bomber—are straight suspense, milked to the last drop, with Pickens's mounting patriotic hysteria the only touch of comic exaggeration.)

Kubrick's touch was at its most leaden in *A Clockwork Orange,* his most ponderously demonstrative film. Its coarseness is pervasive, one both of purpose and execution, and while it is the film's major flaw, it is also what brings it unity and distinctiveness. The effect is at the same time numbing and shocking. Every point is driven home with such insistence, the plot moves from one ironic twist to the next with such clockwork predictability that much of the film's second half seems almost unnecessary and induces mixed feelings of boredom and irritation. On the other hand, the spectator is repeatedly jolted out of his sense of familiarity by the grotesque distortions, the ghastly crudeness of Kubrick's touches: the graphic beatings and rapes cutely scored to Rossini or Nacio Herb Brown; the bashing of the art lover with her own phallic sculptures; Alex's groveling boot-licking in front of an applauding audience, and so on. Caricature is supposed to enhance the real by distorting it. Kubrick's caricature simply reduces life to an obscene Punch and Judy show.

To Kubrick, there doesn't seem to be any difference between the future and the past; they both serve indifferently as settings for his wry ruminations. In one case, of course, he has to create a world, in the other to recreate it, but the world ends up by being Kubrick's own in any case. After toying for years with the project of a film on Napoleon, Kubrick settled for a lesser (at least in terms of content) historical venture, selecting as a vehicle an obscure novel by one of the least appealing and most superficial of the famous Victorian novelists. An unpromising choice, but Thackeray's cynical ironies and cartoonlike satire were obviously congenial to him and served his purpose. In his rendition of *Barry Lyndon*, far from attempting to flesh out the one-dimensional characters or to inject excitement into the paper-thin plot, Kubrick seems determined to overwhelm the spectator with their insignificance, deliberately using the fantastically elaborate scale of the production to emphasize its lifelessness and ultimately, one surmises, the absurdity of all human endeavor. The film's stylistic leitmotif is the slow optical tracking out from a close shot to a huge panorama in which people are dwarfed by landscape. In interior scenes, Kubrick concentrates on decoration, props, lighting, groupings, and freezes setup after setup into a tableau vivant. The resulting visual distancing is aurally reinforced by the prevalence of "nondramatic" period music, the paucity of dialogue, and the impersonal dryness of the third-person narration (which has been substituted for Thackeray's use of the first person). The only response to the characters allowed us by Kubrick's approach is indifference, especially in the case of the hero, who, although almost as much of a scoundrel as the Alex of *A Clockwork Orange*, comes out looking almost as bland and remote as the astronauts of *2001*.

Reviewers raved about *Barry Lyndon*'s "breathtaking beauty," and indeed it is, pictorially, one of the most impressive films ever made, but the truth is that it is impossible to have one's breath taken away by pictorial splendor alone for three solid hours. Kubrick himself seems to have felt that some emotion had to be expressed and elicited at some point, since he devoted a large portion of the film's second part to the death of Barry's son and to the father's grief—practically the hero's only show of feeling in the film. But this shifting of gears occurs too late into the narrative to be effective. Our response has been so conditioned that we can't work up emotion; or rather, we *have* to work it up, if we want to be moved. Indeed, it is difficult to suppress a vague suspicion that Barry is somehow faking grief, an irrational impression that is solely the effect of Kubrick's handling of characters and situations up to that time. Since few if any of Kubrick's effects are accidental and unintentional, it is quite possible that he intended to prove (if only to himself) that form can be a leveler of content and can be used to program audience reaction regardless of narrative material.

The Shining, arguably Kubrick's finest artistic achievement since *2001*, propounds the same bleak world view as his earlier films, using genre conventions and traditions as a convenient channel to sneak in chilling metaphysical undertones. Previous Kubrick films had taken on a familiar film genre (the war picture in *Paths of Glory*, science fiction in *2001*) and broadened its scope to such an extent that a redefinition of the genre became almost necessary. The refurbishing is quite as drastic in *The Shining*, although at first glance it may not seem as spectacular and ground breaking as was the case for *2001*. Kubrick deals with the fantasy/horror genre—one that breaks down into many subdivisions—not by bringing in new themes (which would hardly be possible in such a codified field) but on the contrary by incorporating practically *all* the traditional themes from practically all the subgenres: ghosts, demonic creatures, pacts with the Devil, possession, reincarnation, ESP (telepathy, clairvoyance), déjà vu, as well as that staple of contemporary horror films, the murderous madman stalking his helpless victims (a woman and a child). In addition, the film borrows heavily from the related, but quite distinct, realm of the fairy tale, with Jack Nicholson cast as a combination ogre and big bad wolf and with fairy-tale imagery pervading the entire picture.

The more ritualized a genre (and few are more ritualized than the horror film and the fairy tale), the more predictable and immovable audience expectations are likely to be. Kubrick, however, has no interest in satisfying such expectations. The heterogeneous elements he brings together in *The Shining* are assembled in such a fashion as to cancel each other out, precluding logical explanation, frustrating interpretation, and generally upsetting the audience's accustomed way of reading a film narrative. The motif of the labyrinth, central to the film, is an apt symbol for both the film itself and the spectator's predicament. The narrative is labyrinthine; it keeps making abrupt turns that invariably lead us down the garden path into dead ends. All who enter this maze do so at their own risk and might as well abandon all hope.

The non-Aristotelian open-endedness of the script devised by Kubrick and Diane Johnson (with only limited "faithfulness" to Stephen King's novel) boldly rejects some of the implicit principles that underly most, if not all, fantasy fiction: the supernatural, being an intrusion upon the "normal," must be distinguishable from it; even the irrational must have its own internal logic. There is no such logic in *The Shining*. No distinction is made between the rational and the irrational, the normal and the supernatural; the latter must be taken at face value. What the film asks from the spectator is what he finds most difficult to manage: an unlimited suspension of disbelief, the willingness to accept everything that appears on screen as real, simply because it *is* on screen. The pivotal moment occurs when Torrance addresses an invisible bartender—whom we assume to be a figment of his imagination—in an empty ballroom of the Overlook Hotel (which we know is inhabited only by Torrance himself, his wife, and son). A reverse-angle shot suddenly reveals that there is indeed a bartender behind the bar, one who is more than happy to pour Torrance his first drink in a long time, thus celebrating his first contact with the forces of evil. From then on it becomes impossible to tell hallucination from reality—where demonic forces intrude upon the everyday world, hallucination *is* reality.

Throughout the rest of the film, however, our conscious or implicit assumptions keep being challenged and mocked. The irrational is denied any internal logic, and incoherence is turned into a narrative principle as the encroachment of satanic forces becomes pervasive, as though the breakdown of the categories set up by the civilized mind were a side effect of the triumph of evil. Soon after we have accepted the reality of ghosts and demons, for instance, we are required to accept what seems even more difficult—their ability to open locked doors. The parallel world, which we assumed was accessible only to Danny (who is gifted with the "shining") and his father (who has entered into a pact with demons), ultimately intrudes upon the one character who was our—and the narrative's—only link with normalcy, Danny's mother.

Kubrick keeps up this game playing to the very end. When, after the shot of Torrance frozen in the maze, the camera returns to the hotel to roam its deserted halls, we are led to expect some revelation that will somehow "make sense" of the bewildering sequence of events. The scene is reminiscent of the last sequence of *Citizen Kane*, with Kubrick's camera slowly tracking to a close-up of a photograph on a wall, like Welles's camera slowly tracked to a close-up of the burning sled. But whereas the close-up in *Citizen Kane* delivered a clue—the answer to the quest for "Rosebud" started at the beginning of the film—Jack Torrance's presence in a photograph taken on July 4, 1921 (long before his birth) at the Overlook Hotel not only explains nothing but perversely heightens our confusion.

Kubrick is playing with two familiar devices of fantasy stories, the last-minute switch, or revelation, and the coming-full-circle of the narrative that makes time a cyclical concept. He refuses, however, to use them for a neat wrap-up in the accustomed way. The last-minute switch, in its most common form, reintroduces the supernatural after a rational explanation has been provided (the end of Michael Powell's *A Matter of Life and Death* is a good example). But since no rational explanation of anything has been provided in *The Shining,* the device fails to fulfill its usual purpose—which is exactly, one suspects, what Kubrick wanted. The coming-full-circle is similarly deceptive, as it does not bring back the narrative to its beginning (the classic film reference here is *Dead of Night*) but suggests another beginning, and an incomprehensible one at that.

With *The Shining,* Kubrick devised quite a diabolical artifact. If the Overlook Hotel is a trap—with the labyrinth a trap-within-the trap—in which the Torrance family gets caught, the film itself is a trap for the spectator, a prime example of Kubrick's irony being exercised not only on content but on forms, on narrative and stylistic conventions we tend to take for granted and which his sly transgressions force us to reconsider. Part of the American audience apparently resented having its programmed responses disrupted—after outstanding box-office receipts in the first week or so, attendance quickly tapered off, probably as a result of adverse word-of-mouth from disappointed thrill-seekers. For the spectator who is willing to enter Kubrick's game, however, the rewards are rich. On one level, the film is a stimulating intellectual experience; on another, its dreamlike narrative flow, its wealth of primal imagery, its closeness to myth allow us to recapture a child's experience of the terrors and delights of popular tales, the spirit of which the film so successfully evokes.

Kubrick is, first and foremost, a creator of forms, and we cannot do justice to his cinema or, for that matter, to our response to it if we concentrate on analyzing his sterile, although multifaceted, pessimism. A film like *The Shining* reminds us that his *Weltanschauung* does not have to interfere with one's enjoyment of the forms he creates. Susan Sontag's remark that "interpretation takes the sensory experience of the work of art for granted and proceeds from there," applies only too well to the bulk of commentaries on Kubrick's work. A striking example is Pauline Kael's lengthy *New Yorker* piece on *A Clockwork Orange,* an indignant indictment of the director's indulgence in sex and violence, in the course of which the reviewer mentions in passing, almost parenthetically, Kubrick's "distinctive style," the fact that the film "doesn't look like other movies, or sound like them," yet immediately dismisses as "leering" and "portentous" a style that, by her own admission, impressed her as unique. One would expect such a rare experience to rate more than a couple of scornful adjectives, even from a disapproving critic. After all, we are constantly exposed to mildly, predictably pleasant *and* unpleasant esthetic experiences, but any work that manages to be disagreeable in an original way should deserve our undivided attention.

Kubrick's films—his *best* films, at any rate—are first and foremost sensory experiences, to be enjoyed and, if possible, discussed as such. Of all the living directors, he is perhaps the one who has the best understanding of the awesome technical possibilities of modern film making and of the ways to translate them into a totally controlled, thoroughly individual vision. *The Shining,* for example, shows the most successful artistic use of the Steadicam to date (although John Boozman's *The Exorcist II* comes a close second). Kubrick is at his weakest when he allows a thesis to take over and smother visual/aural excitement, as in *Strangelove* or the second half of *Clockwork Orange. 2001* is his greatest picture because its abstruse polysemy is entirely subsumed by its triumphant form, so that what it "means" ultimately becomes a moot point. Because *2001* has little dialogue and, unlike most other Kubrick films, no voice-over narration, our attention can focus on image, music, and sound effects and their interacting. There are countless interpretations of *2001,* and they, of course, have their value (although one might question, as a matter of principle, the validity of any attempt to explain away *deliberate* ambiguities), but what really counts, and should be accounted for, is the complexity of feeling—a mixture of euphoria, wonder, bewilderment, awe—evoked by the film, the hypnotic power of its cosmic choreography, the sense of timelessness its sights and sounds, pace and space impose upon us. Perhaps the film's highest achievement is indeed its thwarting of familiar intellectual responses and its inducement of a contemplative, uncritical, and nonanalytical absorption in sensual experience. Kubrick failed to recreate similar conditions in his next two pictures despite sporadic attempts in *A Clockwork Orange* and a systematic one in *Barry Lyndon.* He retained the outsized format and grandiose manner of his masterwork, but neither the extremes of caricature of *Orange* nor the extremes of pictorialism of *Lyndon* managed to do the trick—which would suffice to prove that there was more to *2001* than a mere "trick," no matter how elaborate.

The *Shining* did manage to do the trick again. Ostensibly "just" a fantasy tale, it carries no message or thesis beyond a bleak Calvinistic view of man and the prevalence of evil, which is not surprising from Kubrick but is too remote from us to be taken quite seriously. Like *2001, The Shining* creates its own self-contained world and generates a quality of pleasure that resolves the tension—which has always existed—between Kubrick the gloomy moralist and Kubrick the contemplative artist.

29. *Jerry Lewis* (1926)

1960—*The Bellboy;* 1961—*The Ladies' Man; The Errand Boy;* 1963—*The Nutty Professor;* 1964— *The Patsy;* 1965—*The Family Jewels;* 1966—*Three on a Couch;* 1967—*The Big Mouth;* 1970—*One More Time; Which Way to the Front?;* 1971—(unreleased) *The Day the Clown Cried;* 1981—*Hardly Working;* 1983—*Smorgasbord*

A French critic writing in English about Jerry Lewis for American readers is liable to become as schizoid as the object of his study. Whereas, in a country where Lewis's genius is practically taken for granted by the vast majority of critics, it is almost mandatory to apologize for expressing anything less than wild enthusiasm about his work, such enthusiasm is regarded here with the mixture of disbelief, amusement, and hostility reserved for highbrow aberrations of a particularly foreign nature. To complicate matters, this Frenchman's response to Lewis has itself changed over the years ranging from a 1960 putdown of the comedian (then not yet his own director) as "the lowest degree of physical, moral, and intellectual abasement" to this more sympathetic look ten years later:

An auteur is born. Underneath the clown's makeup there lay, well concealed, not a broken heart—although that is a possibility too—but a sturdy comic mind, a long-frustrated master of the film form. From his various—and variously talented—directors Lewis learned, to a degree, what to do, but more importantly, and even from Frank Tashlin, what *not* to do. Besides, it looks as if he forgot about it all when he switched to the other side of the camera, so original and aggressively personal did his directorial style turn out to be. As we watch his films we are not reminded of Chaplin or Keaton or any other director-comedian but rather of a Bresson (dedramatization, ellipses) or a Godard (filmic fiction redefined and reborn through its own destruction). Like today's most advanced film makers, Lewis questions the traditional relationship of audience to film. More than most, he trusts the spectator's intelligence to establish the required connections between images and supply the intermediary information he boldly skips over. Laughter must be deserved, he seems to tell us, let's meet halfway. His is a modern approach, which frustrates our expectations the better to satisfy them later on, emphasizes the obvious only to spring the unexpected out of it, dismantles or conjures away gags, tampers with traditional structures and slyly warps them. But while his hand may be trumped up, he plays it in all fairness, with his cards on the table: Don't you believe it, he insists, it's only a movie (which wards off identification and dubious sentimentality). In order to achieve an even higher degree of distancing, Lewis keeps switching disguises, multiplies himself by two, three, or seven, confronts his own self or his opposite, or even introduces Lewis the man himself, as he provocatively did in the first film he directed. This is inside joking, to be sure, but it all points to ethical, or at the very least thematic, content. Of course, the attractiveness of Lewis's themes and style tends to obscure a most vital question, that of comic content, for it is a fact that these fascinating films are not always very funny. But their originality lies precisely in the fact that, while nominally slapstick comedies, they so transcend categories that laughter in their case ceases to be the test of success or failure. There doesn't seem to be any reason, incidentally, why Lewis should be denied a kind of excuse that has been used—and not always too justifiably at that—in Chaplin's favor for the past fifty years."

Now that a few more years have elapsed, I suspect that this flare of enthusiasm, although quite sincere, was unduly influenced by the general excitement over Lewis among French critics at the time. Not that there is any ground for retracting the claims of originality and "modernism" made for his cinematic style. It cannot be denied today that Lewis is an auteur, and a completely personal one. Watching his films again— the ones he has directed—one more than ever notices how contrived and, at times, counterproductive their formal sophistication can be. Too, their frequent unfunniness shouldn't have been so breezily dismissed as irrelevant (comedy is probably the last genre left today in which a film maker can't get along on style alone, and Lewis is certainly no exception). Moreover, a certain degree of retroactive disenchantment has been made unavoidable by the brutal deterioration Lewis's inspiration has undergone since this eulogy was written. *The Big Mouth* and *Which Way to the Front?* are very personal *and* very unfunny efforts. The latter, which was Lewis's first box-office failure, was followed by ten years without a single screen credit (excepting the never released drama *The Day the Clown Cried*), and Lewis's 1981 comeback with *Hardly Working* was, to say the least, anticlimactic and could hardly be considered a new departure.

According to his own account, Lewis's directorial debut was quite accidental. *The Bellboy* was undertaken on short notice early in 1960 in order to provide Paramount with a Jerry Lewis picture for summer release, as the comedian felt that the just-completed *Cinderfella* should be held up until the Christmas season. Paramount agreed to leave him entirely free, provided he came up with some film for the summer. (As a matter of fact, *Visit to a Small Planet* was also completed at the time, so that three Lewis comedies rather than the customary two were released in 1960—which makes one wonder whether Lewis's version of the genesis of *The Bellboy* is quite accurate.) *The Bellboy* may not be Lewis's masterpiece (most of his admirers would rather single out *The Nutty Professor* or *The Patsy*), but it is quite possibly his funniest picture, an outpouring of highly idiosyncratic comedy ideas in an atmosphere of unpretentious— yet far from unambitious—relaxation. In joyful celebration of his newly acquired free- dom (not only was he, for the first time, his own director but also his own and sole writer), Lewis jettisoned a number of traditional encumbrances and turned out a plotless and virtually dialogue-less picture, a daring and healthy reaction to three decades of overplotted, overtalky comedies. Indeed his approach in *The Bellboy* harks back to the old silent-comedy principle of systematically exploiting the comic possibilities of a given locale (in this case a Miami hotel), so that gags are not subservient to a plot but are the direct outcome of those possibilities. The feeling of easygoing improvisation is deceptive, however (Lewis's shooting script, he has said, was 170 pages long). Loosely structured as the film is, there is nothing haphazard about its comic content. In fact, it turned out to be a complete catalogue of the raw material for Lewis's subsequent movies: "eluded" gags (the off-screen aerial stunt); game playing with time and space (an empty cafeteria suddenly becomes crowded with customers; hundreds of chairs are arranged in neat row by the diligent bellboy in less time than it took his boss to give him the order); camera work used as gag (the variation on the old silent-comedy routine with dozens of people coming out of a small car); and inspired flights of poetic nonsense (a flash bulb turns night into day). In 1960 *The Bellboy* looked like an interest- ing oddity, a one-shot unlikely to lead to anything else. It turned out to be the most logical of first steps, a film whose every gag, as Jean-Louis Leutrat and Paul Simonci put it in their book, *Jerry Lewis* (1965), was to become more significant with the release of each new Lewis film.

Although the comedy in *The Ladies' Man* is very much in the same spirit as *The Bellboy,* the two films are quite different, and the latter one more clearly points to some further developments. Whereas *The Bellboy* had a wonderful, slapdash, un- Hollywoodian quality about it, *The Ladies' Man* is a glossy, expensive, carefully engi- neered studio product that flaunts its production values with almost nouveau riche insistence. To be sure, these production values are not just that; Lewis uses them functionally and creatively. The huge open-faced interior set (four stories high and stretching "across two Paramount sound stages") and the elaborate crane shots (for which a special boom extension had to be constructed), which follow characters in and out of rooms up and down stairs and corridors in long fluid takes, have been sufficiently analyzed by admiring critics and require no further comment. The combina- tion of set design and camera movement for comedy purposes is perhaps most brilliantly effected in the opening sequence. The camera moves up from a close-up of a road sign ("Milltown, a very nervous city"), sweeps over a deserted town-square set, zeroes in on a lone elderly lady walking briskly down Main Street, tracks laterally to accompany her and record the catastrophic chain effects of a loud greeting as they pile up in quick succession.

Yet the lavishness of the production ultimately backfires on Lewis, and the film slowly disintegrates during the second half. The latter part may not be weaker, but it runs out of steam through sheer repetitiousness. One of the problems is that Lewis is doing too little with too much. The big set and the three-dozen girls who people it most of the time turn out to be a mere backdrop for spare routines involving Jerry's dealings with one character (e.g., the hat scene with Buddy Lester, the George Raft cameo) or with some objects (a collapsing bed whose resilient mattress engulfs him like quicksand, a butterfly case from which the butterflies escape when he opens it, a lady's portrait whose lipstick he smears when he attempts to dust it, priceless glassware and vases that he invariably shatters in record time). The most elaborate sequence (the television show) doesn't really come off and looks too elaborate in terms of the few laughs it yields. Another problem is the plotlessness, which worked so well for *The Bellboy* but which tends to become burdensome here. One longs for some kind of storyline—no matter how slender—onto which gags could be hung and that would lead the film somewhere. There is no build-up, no progression, no climax. Instead, there *is* a moral of sorts—something about feeling needed and being really needed— which a "nice" girl (inadequately characterized) somewhat solemnly enunciates in a little closing speech to her callous fellow boarders. This little bit of moralizing does weaken the film's ending. It is too perfunctorily handled, however, to become annoying, as will happen in latter films.

Although *The Errand Boy* develops and systematizes ideas already at work in the earlier films, it is arguably the slightest of Lewis's first six directorial efforts. It is structurally similar to *The Bellboy* and *The Ladies' Man*—that is, totally episodic—but it lacks both the spontaneity and inventiveness of the former and the visual impact of the latter. Sentimentality, moreover, rears its mawkish head here with considerably more insistence than in *The Ladies' Man*. Whereas the "fantasy sequence" in the previous film was weirdly surreal, not to say downright kinky (an unsuspecting Lewis walking into a white-on-white "forbidden" room inhabited by a black-clad, vampirelike female and the entire Harry James orchestra), it consists, in *The Errand Boy,* of a cute conversation between the hero and a puppet ostrich ("I love you and I believe in you," whimpers a dewy-eyed Lewis, stickily rephrasing a philosophy more forcibly stated earlier in the "If You Believe" number from *Artists and Models*). One tends to assume that the comic potentialities of a movie studio should be greater than those of a hotel or boarding house, especially given Lewis's flair for fooling around with audio-visual equipment, but, possibly as a result of his reluctance to do the obvious, little use is actually made of these possibilities.

Faithful to the oblique approach inaugurated in *The Bellboy,* Lewis gives gags a minimal build-up and concentrates on comic consequences rather than on comic action. Thus in the car-wash scene—in which both car *and* driver get sprayed—or in the film-within-the-film party sequence, ruined by a ubiquitous Morty (a gag already used in the TV sequence of *The Ladies' Man*), we are only shown the effects of Morty's blunders as the car leaves the garage and as dismayed studio executives watch a screening of the ruined sequence. This "before-after" gag structure does fit in with the looseness of the overall construction, but one gets the definite feeling—although this is admittedly hindsight—that the film exhausts the possibilities of the format and that Lewis would have to move on to more structured constructions in later films. Which of course he did with *The Nutty Professor.*

Lewis's fourth film is the first one to combine the "production values" of *The Ladies' Man* (color, expensive sets, sophisticated special effects) with the traditional story elements that had been absent from the earlier films. In contrast to the episodic structure that had become the Lewis trademark, each sequence in *The Nutty Professor* performs a specific narrative function. As the first in a series of variations on what was to emerge as Lewis's favorite—and obsessive—theme (split personality), the film utilizes the most traditional reference available—the Jekyll-and-Hyde motif—and manages to succeed on its own terms, i.e., as comedy rather than mere parody. Yet despite Lewis's virtuosity both as writer-director and performer, one can't help feeling that he has tried to handle more than he was capable of; more, perhaps, than could be handled by anyone in a comedy. The delineation of the two personae (Kelp, the timid, blundering professor and Buddy Love, the macho, self-centered pop singer); the paradox of Jerry Lewis playing the part of an idolized crooner and his necessarily ambivalent attitude toward the character (Buddy Love must be at the same time plausible and comical, the real thing and its caricature); the jarring overlapping of the two personalities and the rather confusing relationship between them; the gradual shifting of the girl's feelings and her continuingly ambiguous attitude toward both Kelp and Love—all these subtle complexities tend to get in the way of gag development and blunt the film's comic impact. The problem extends beyond the realm of the classic plot-versus-gags dilemma—one all creative film comedians have had to confront one way or the other—for in *The Nutty Professor* it becomes clear for the first time that Lewis is after something other than getting laughs, something that involves both the spinning out of thematic intricacies and the exhilarating exercise of mise-en-scène for its own sake.

Consciously or not, Lewis must have sensed the nature of his predicament, for he used the making and evolution of a comedian as the subject of his next film. In that respect *The Patsy* may be considered his most ambitious picture, as it tackles the crucial questions: What is funny? How do you make people laugh?

A popular comedian dies; his staff try to turn a daffy bellboy (called Stanley, as in *The Bellboy*) into a duplicate of their fallen star. The attempt fails miserably until Stanley finally breaks away from his mentors' stifling tutelage and becomes a hit by being true to himself. It is again a film about rebirth, about the struggle to cast off the slough of inadequacies and frustrations while remaining faithful to one's own self. As in *The Nutty Professor,* the split personality motif is central to the film and again involves an entertainer (all artists are schizoid, Lewis seems to be saying), with all sorts of attendant paradoxes and ironies (famous comedian plays failing comedian; being unfunny in a funny way). There is a total reversal in the treatment of the theme, however. Whereas Kelp was a failure at his job (at least the "performing" side of it, i.e., teaching) and became successful after his transformation, Stanley is "naturally" funny as himself but flops when required to use comic material unsuited to his personality (an obvious comment on the mediocre material Lewis was often forced to accept). Moreover, whereas Kelp was, like Jekyll, his own Pygmalion, Stanley is a puppet in the hands of his promoters until they give him up as hopeless, and he then comes into his own. The nature of the split is far more subtle—although less radical—in *The Patsy.* What took place in *The Nutty Professor* was a total psychological and physical upheaval. Stanley's personality, on the other hand, is not actually "split" at all; his two "sides" are only professional aspects of the same individual. Although *The Patsy,* like all the other Lewis films, deals with some of the seemingly endless avatars of the character's protean persona, it does so in a more specific, almost autobiographical way, as Stanley's ordeal can only be interpreted as a dramatized history of the growth of Jerry Lewis the comedian.

The comic quality of *The Patsy* unfortunately fails to match its thematic coherence. As a direct consequence of the film's premise, the comedy branches out into two distinct, almost opposite, directions. The grooming of Stanley provides an ideal showcase for traditional Jerry Lewis routines relying on the character's clumsiness and incompetence, and while there are some highlights (e.g., the sequence with Hans Conreid as Stanley's hapless voice coach), those routines are on the whole fairly predictable and simple-minded. The comedy in the "performing" scenes, on the other hand, is much less obvious and includes what may be the most sophisticated routines ever devised by Lewis, especially the climactic "Ed Sullivan" sequence.

In *The Family Jewels* Lewis discarded the linear construction of *The Nutty Professor* and *The Patsy* to revert to a looseness of structure more reminiscent of his earlier films. A brilliantly complex, often very funny picture, *The Family Jewels* is the ultimate in schizoid comedy, with Lewis playing seven different parts, a not unheard-of tour de force for a comedian (one more than Fernandel in *Le Mouton à cinq pattes* but two less than Alec Guinness in *Kind Hearts and Coronets*), but one that, in his case, has nothing gratuitous about it. The format has its drawbacks and its advantages. The film is a series of sketches strung together by a slim premise (a millionaire orphan girl must decide which of her six uncles will become her guardian), and a certain spottiness is consequently unavoidable. On the other hand, the variety of comic characters involved allows for such a wide range of activities, locales, and props that the supply of gags never runs dry. Moreover, Willard, the little girl's faithful chauffeur (also played by Lewis) gives the film cohesion by his presence throughout. The character is not merely functional; neither is it a "straight" part (like the hero of *Three on a Couch*). Although Willard, unlike the "uncles," is not a broad caricature, and therefore stands apart from them, he nevertheless has his share of the comedy and actually walks away with some of the best scenes in the film (e.g., the smoothly directed opening sequence in which Willard unwittingly foils a carefully planned robbery by simply retrieving a stray baseball or his superbly choreographed disruption of a military parade).

The Family Jewels contains some of the finest displays of physical clumsiness in Lewis's work, particularly a devastating pool game and a long scene recording the fumblings of a hopelessly unfocused fashion photographer. Clumsiness is not the unique source of comedy, however. One uncle, for instance—a tugboat captain seen in a flashback as a World War II navy enlistee successfully disconnects the fuses of a torpedo and removes it from the hulk of the ship into which it had lodged itself (of course the gap thus left open in the hulk immediately causes the ship to sink). Other uncles— a gloomy clown who hates his job and a would-be gangster who even fails to frighten children—are deliberately offbeat—even sinister—rather than funny characterizations and bring a not unwelcome touch of uneasiness in the midst of all the slapstick. Finally, Lewis concludes the film by bringing the six uncles together, and the effortless mastery with which he handles the task directorially makes up for the stickiness of the obligatory piece of sentiment. Even if one agrees with Andrew Sarris's judgment that Lewis "has never put one brilliant comedy together from fade-in to fade-out," one must admit that *The Family Jewels* comes reasonably close.

The Family Jewels was Lewis's thirty-fourth and last-but-one Paramount picture, and it turned out to be the last of his major comedies as well. From 1966 on he was to work either as star or director or both for Columbia, Fox, Warners, and United Artists, and whether because of the change in working conditions, the loss of some favorite collaborators, or the fact that, with one exception, he no longer wrote his own scripts, he never recaptured the inspired brilliance of his brief great period. He directed himself in a semistraight role in *Three on a Couch*, his first non-Paramount picture. Although the more traditional Lewis is allowed to manifest himself in a series of comic impersonations, the film is banal, with only an occasional flash of directorial invention. One of the impersonations (a girl-shy insect collector reminiscent of the two Juliuses-Kelp from *Nutty Professor* and the photographer from *Family Jewels*) is vintage Lewis, but the others are either tastelessly lowbrow (a protracted skit in drag) or confused and pointless (the cigar-smoking, tall-talking Texan). Lewis uses the plot— about an artist whose psychiatrist fiancée can't marry him because she is too busy with her patients—as a framing device for the impersonations, with the result that a sizeable portion of the footage is devoted to noncomedy scenes that do little beyond conveying information. Still, it is quite a personal film, and all sorts of profundities— real or imagined—can be read into its psychoanalytical premise. Auteurist critics certainly did not fail to praise its most glaring weaknesses. Thus Jean Louis Comolli in *Cahiers du Cinéma* argued that *Three on a Couch* was "the most constructed of Lewis's films, the one in which the comic system best coincides with the dramatic system," thus reasserting, in his own modish way, the traditional belief that the highest form of comedy is the one with the least comedy in it.

Outwardly, *The Big Mouth* might seem to be a return to Lewis's earlier brand of comedy, which makes its failure all the more disappointing. He was reunited with Bill Richmond, who had coscripted with him all the Lewis-directed Paramount pictures except *The Bellboy* (in which, however, Richmond does a symbolical walk-on as Stan Laurel, Lewis's comedy idol). This time around, Richmond provided the original story as well as help in the writing. Still, almost everything about the picture goes wrong. The trouble has a lot to do with the storyline, a mere pretext, but this time a decidedly cumbersome one. Lewis and Richmond use one of the most hackneyed comedy premises in the book—the hero is a dead ringer for a dangerous gangster—and fail, indeed don't even attempt, to do anything new with it. The other premise on which the entire film is supposedly based (the hero, a vacationer who has fished a murdered frogman out of the Pacific, can't get the police or anybody else to listen to his story) is one that can't possibly be sustained through more than a few initial scenes, yet Lewis keeps restating it again and again throughout the film, thus stressing the story's basic flaw. *The Big Mouth* is weakened by the kind of minimal motivations, slapdash transitions and shaky logic one expects from an average silent comedy short, but which just won't do in a 1960 sound feature. The Lewis touch has deteriorated into a pervasive looseness that sometimes verges on sheer amateurism. Scenes misfire because of poor writing, inadequate direction, or sloppy editing. At times the comedy becomes unbearably childish; thus when Jerry's pursuers (they don't recognize him thanks to his disguise) describe to him what they'll do to him if they catch him ("We'll beat him up, break his arm, hang him, shoot him," etc.), he cringes and grimaces in fearful anticipation.

Like *Three on a Couch*, though, *The Big Mouth* is fascinating in all sorts of marginal ways to anyone who is interested in how Lewis's mind works. As a metaphor about the struggle between the creator and his creatures, it certainly deserves attention. The importance of water throughout the film and its thematic relation to the motif of creation would also warrant a detailed analysis. The film begins and ends on the Pacific shore, several scenes take place in San Diego's Marine World, it is intriguing—albeit not very funny—to see Lewis pull his own double out of the ocean (an evolutionist's view of creation?), and the entire cast throw themselves into the same ocean at the end in mad pursuit of that same, indestructible double. Lewis has even equipped the film with his own version of a Greek chorus, a narrator who, in a precredit sequence, is discovered fully dressed, attaché case in hand standing ankle-deep in the ocean surf. (He, too, will return to the sea in the end, still carrying his attaché case, but this time wearing polka-dot underpants in acknowledgment of the basic nuttiness of a story he had insisted throughout the film was "completely true.") While the thematic paraphernalia do impart the film with a semblance of structural coherence, this does little to dispel the gloom engendered by the mirthlessness of the comedy. Beyond the irony of the title, the ultimate irony of the film is that this "tragic meditation on the theme of incommunicability" (as one French critic put it) is Lewis's first total failure to communicate with his audience in his chosen idiom, that of comedy and laughter.

One More Time should be of interest to students of Lewis as the only film he ever directed without acting in it. If one is to believe the all but unanimous reports, however, this sequel to *Salt and Pepper* merely proved that Lewis's work as a director is meaningful only in relation to his own comedy style. As for *Which Way to the Front?*, his latest and bleakest comedy, it comes very close to being a total disaster and may be viewed as an advanced step on the way to suicidal self-fulfillment. Like *The Big Mouth,* it is a study in frustration but with megalomaniac overtones added. The hero, Brendan Byers III (who happens to be the richest man in the world), can't stand rejection. The very word brings him to the verge of collapse. However, his immense wealth enables him to bypass rejection and rearrange the world to his liking. Since the Army won't have him, he sets up his own miniarmy to fight his own private war against Nazi Germany. Byers impersonates Kesselring, changes the course of history, and even subdues Hitler himself. It is an intriguing conceit and an ambitious one— reminiscent of Chaplin and Lubitsch—but the film is a dismal affair. Lewis seems to have had little confidence in his material. He surrounded himself with a bunch of other comedians, a generous but esthetically dubious decision. The action starts sluggishly and takes ages to get under way. A straight and unnecessarily protracted opening sequence is followed first by animated credits, then by *more* expository material, as Byers meets three other Army rejects and each of them explains in a flashback why he desperately wants to enlist. One, a small-time nightclub comic, is running away from a loan shark whose henchmen viciously beat him up when he failed to come up with the money he owed (the scene is played straight and very realistically). The other two flashbacks, while at least comical in intention, are hardly funnier than the first. The eventual comedy turns out to consist mostly of Lewis's broad burlesque of a German general, a routine that quickly becomes tiresome.

As in *The Big Mouth,* most of the comedy rests upon shaky foundations. The impersonation of Kesselring, for instance, inevitably raises the problem of language, and Byers does try to learn German from records at an early stage in his preparations, yet Lewis later adopts the more convenient convention of an English-speaking German army, so that he can rely on comic elocution—English rasped and squealed with a mock teutonic accent—for most of his effects. Now, we don't expect "realism," nor even verisimilitude, from a Jerry Lewis comedy; Byers's "private" war is an outrageous proposition to begin with, yet we have no trouble accepting it as a premise. (Incidentally, the use of a stereo console and LP records in the above-mentioned German learning scene is evidence of Lewis's lack of concern for material as well as for dramatic realism.) No matter how wild and nonsensical a comedy may get, however, there is one thing it can't get away with, and that's contradicting its own premises, which is exactly what Lewis does about his language problem. But then, this kind of contradiction is so pervasive in the film that it can hardly be accidental. It is probably naive to speak of "mistakes" in the face of such deliberate disregard not only for consistency but for the very concept of narrative. At the same time, the film remains at least superficially indebted to that concept—hence its vulnerability (one couldn't very well direct similar criticism against, say, *Blazing Saddles,* whose structural principle *is* the non sequitur).

What Lewis's evolution has led to with *Which Way to the Front?* is this most perverse of "modern" artifacts, a comedy that keeps destroying the very conditions of its functioning.

It may seem paradoxical to view Lewis's failure to make the pantheon of comedian-cinéastes as a consequence of his being too clever a film stylist, yet he does seem to have, so to speak, directed himself into a corner. In this as in almost any other respect, Lewis is the antithesis of a Buster Keaton. Whereas Keaton's mise-en-scène was a natural extension of his comedy—and, one may just as well say, vice versa—Lewis's formal concepts often tend to defeat the very purpose of all comedy. His roundabout approach to gags is a case in point. The next logical step to "suggesting" gags, after all, is to eliminate them entirely. It would be absurd to suggest that this technique led to his eventual discarding of comedy for drama, yet there must be *some* kind of connection. In Lewis's comedies, the "eluded" gag is evidently meant to produce laughter, but does it really? And if/when it does, how good a laugh does it yield?

In *The Errand Boy,* Lewis has a routine on a ladder with a huge glass jar which, against all expectations, he never drops. The scene is a variation on an old joke: In a candy store, one kid after another asks for a penny's worth of bubble gum; after each purchase, the storekeeper returns the jar to its top shelf, only to have to take it down again for the next kid in line. The audience knows exactly how the routine is supposed to unfold. The only surprise lies in the absence of a punch line, either verbal or visual. Nothing happens, and *that,* the Lewis fans argue, is the gag, as who needs to be told—or shown—what one already knows? They may have a point, yet what Lewis is doing is reminiscent of the story about the comedians' convention where they gave well-known jokes numbers and called out the numbers instead of telling the jokes. Very clever, but wouldn't you rather hear a *new* joke told?

The elimination principle may be applied to entire sequences, thus the airplane routine from *The Bellboy,* the whole point of which is that no use whatsoever is made of the hero's incompetence at flying a plane. All Lewis wanted from the scene, apart from the trick played upon our expectations, was a fine but minute sound effect of the DC-8 roaring over the hotel as the manager, who has just been told on the phone about what's going on, shouts a horrified "What?" into the receiver. ("We cut the sequence thirty times before finally deciding to drop two frames," Lewis comments in his book, *The Total Film-Maker.* "It was that critical.") Next thing we know, Stanley and the DC-8 are safely back upon the ground. We haven't seen them once in flight. Lewis's conceit does get a smile (it is certainly better than a hackneyed treatment of a hackneyed situation), but the effect is hardly commensurate with the effort. Underneath our pleasure at being tricked and our recognition of the director's cleverness, we experience real frustration at a letdown, which, although intentional, remains a letdown nonetheless.

As a method of comedy making, "playing tricks" upon the spectators is a hazardous practice, for it may turn out to merely confuse them. All film comedians seem to agree that, in order for a comedy scene or gag to work, the audience must be provided with all the relevant data: motivations, background to the situation, location, spatial layout, etc. The audience should be enabled to register all these readily and effortlessly, for otherwise they become puzzled, the underlying principle being that one can't ask oneself questions and laugh at the same time. One of Lewis's most famous comedy sequences—the silent routine at the end of *The Patsy*—boldly disregards this principle. In this scene, Lewis pulls a neat trick on the audience. The hero, Stanley Belt, has been groomed for months to become a comedy star but until now with dismal results. His press agent has managed to get him a booking on the Ed Sullivan Show, but his whole staff is so convinced he is going to flop that they walk out on him. Stanley gets their letter of resignation in his dressing room fifteen minutes before going on the air. He walks out of the building, looking disconsolate. A block away from the television studio guests are filing into a theater for a first-night gala performance. Stanley watches the crowd while, at the same time, Sullivan is going through his introductory speech for him on the air. A man and his wife walk out of the theater, having an argument. The wife throws her ticket on the pavement and walks away. Stanley picks up the ticket and walks to the entrance, but the ticket taker refuses to admit him because he is wearing jeans and sneakers. Stanley sneaks into a blind alley in back of the theater and, using some black paint, transforms his outfit into something quite convincingly resembling a tuxedo. He is thus able to enter the theatre without any trouble. Only at that point do we realize that Stanley had not given up going on the Ed Sullivan Show and that the whole routine we have just watched was actually his act for the show.

Deliberately, Lewis has made it almost impossible for us to grasp the true nature of the routine at a first viewing. The "clues" he has planted here and there, if and when we notice them at all, are too ambiguous to do more than perplex us. Cuts to Sullivan and his staff watching a TV screen (which *we* cannot see) are particularly confusing. They hint that Stanley's routine may be part of the show, but the logistics of the whole thing escape us. (One of several possible conjectures is that TV cameras started filming Stanley, unbeknown to him, after someone on Sullivan's staff noticed him doing funny things on his own back in that alley.) Another source of puzzlement—if we take the routine for what it is, i.e., a *performance*—is that Stanley's pantomime is so polished, so perfectly timed and executed, whereas he had proved a complete flop at each preceding rehearsal and performance. Of course, this is the very point Lewis wants to make: Stanley becomes successful once he gets a chance to "be himself." But there is an essential difference between the unintentional funniness of Stanley the bellboy—a typical Jerry Lewis "idiot" with his hopeless clumsiness—and the highly professional, graceful funniness of the television routine. If Stanley were really to be "himself," he would never be able to perform such an act. The sequence is a tangle of ambiguities, obscurities, and inconsistencies that work as jamming devices to distort Lewis's modest message, just as they deactivate his comedy.

At the time of *The Patsy* and *The Family Jewels,* the eschewing of traditional narrative and gag structure was leading Lewis toward an increasingly formal—and increasingly complex—type of comedy, with stylistics taking over from slapstick. Conflict between what he was doing as a comedian and what he was doing as a film maker was therefore inevitable. His more recent efforts, however, have indicated that there is no Jekyll-and-Hyde dichotomy between the two, as the director's tendency to deplete comedy content and spirit away gags is now echoed by the performer's reluctance to rely upon his traditional image as funny man. For quite some time he had been devising ways of dissociating himself from the "idiot," either by playing a straight part and relegating the clowning to impersonation skits (*Three on a Couch*) or by appearing *only* in impersonations (*The Family Jewels*), thus canceling out the Lewis character through the multiplicity of his own disguises.

A new approach to this phasing-out strategy was introduced in *The Big Mouth* and *Which Way to the Front?,* in which Lewis diverts our attention away from himself and onto various other performers. Something of the kind had already been suggested in *The Patsy,* which featured a quintet of well-known character actors, but theirs remained essentially straight parts, and Lewis was still in charge of all the comedy. In *The Big Mouth* and *Which Way to the Front?,* however, important comedy bits have been handed to a number of associate comics whose apparent function was to take the load off Jerry's shoulders and allow him to keep as low a comedy profile as possible.

This eagerness to delegate authority is at the same time emphasized and contradicted by the glaring similarity between these bits and Lewis's own performing style and the osmotic patterns that ensue. Thus, Charles Callas's gibberish and nervous tics in *The Big Mouth* are reminiscent of any number of previous Lewis routines and are more or less reprised in *Which Way to the Front?* by Lewis himself, whose outbursts are in turn faithfully mimicked by Jan Murray in a subsequent scene of the same film. Again in *Which Way,* Steve Franken, looking remarkably like Lewis as a henpecked husband and son, is put through a typically Lewisian scene of slavish submission to female tyranny (played with Kathleen Freeman, the perennial mother-image of Lewis's films). In interviews Lewis has claimed that he wants to "bring the audience relief from watching me all the time," but the purpose—if indeed this is his purpose—is obviously defeated as we are reminded of, rather than distracted from, him by what amounts to a series of impersonations of Jerry Lewis by assorted second- and third-string comics.

The yearning for self-obliteration transpires in the very anecdote of the late pictures. Jerry Clamson, the hero of *The Big Mouth,* lives in limbo throughout the film. To one group of characters—the gangsters—he can only be a ghost (they mistake him for his look-alike, whom they have painstakingly slaughtered). The rest of the world ignores Jerry so consistently that he is unable to convey to anybody the information he is burning to reveal. Only by renouncing his personality and assuming a false identity does he eventually succeed in establishing some degree of contact with the outside world. The millionaire hero of *Which Way to the Front?* is another limbo character forced into a vicarious mode of existence as a result of rejection. When his only desire— joining the Army—is denied him, he buys himself the means to act out an elaborate fantasy—involving, again, the adoption of a false identity—in which no less than the outcome of World War II is at stake. Byers is thus reduced (reduces himself) to his function as buyer (the name, like Clamson, is clearly symbolic). Characteristically, his first "purchase" is a trio of surrogates (he promises them $100,000 each to go along with his scheme), each of whom represents a facet of the Lewis persona. Rather than a "character" in the usual sense, Byers is a projection of Lewis the producer-director putting a show together—for that is what his contribution to the war really looks like, a supershow backed, cast, designed, staged and, performed by himself.

Lewis's evolution, then, is quite logical, no matter how paradoxical it may seem. The withdrawal syndrome has combined with directorial deviousness to create conditions in which laughter is seriously impaired or even becomes impossible. Under such circumstances, it was also logical that Lewis should lose much of his audience. He has attributed the commercial failure of *Which Way to the Front?* to Warners' lack of interest in it, and the film was indeed inadequately promoted and released, but it is unlikely that a more thoughtful handling would have turned it into a hit. After all, you can't work that hard at destroying your own image and still expect to retain your old following. The switch to straight drama in the film that followed (the still unreleased *The Day the Clown Cried*) is an equally logical, although startling, development. We already suspected that the clown of *The Family Jewels,* who hated "the makeup, the faces, the screaming kids" was expressing one side of Lewis's ambiguous feelings about his work. Ironically, the hero of *The Day the Clown Cried* is a clown who finds himself in such a situation that he can only hate his job, which consists in keeping the children in a concentration camp occupied as they wait to be taken to the gas chamber. While it is not surprising that Lewis should finally come round to disclose a fondness for pathos shared by so many comedians (there had been warning hints in earlier pictures), his selection of such a painfully bizarre theme does come as a bit of a shock. Clowns may all be closet sentimentalists, but this is strutting, not sneaking, out of the closet. Still, one should refrain from condemning the film on the face of its subject matter. Although the odds against it are staggering, it *might* turn out to be sublime. Indeed, it would have to be sublime not to be ridiculous or simply embarrassing beyond endurance. At the very least, one must admit that making the film at all took guts and that Lewis didn't opt for any easy way out of his creative problems.

Unlike Woody Allen or Mel Brooks, Lewis has always strived for the "universality" achieved by the great silent comedians. Unfortunately for him, the evolution of movie attendance in the past couple of decades may already have made his kind of universality obsolete. Once the archetypal lowbrow comic with enormous lowbrow appeal, he now seems to have lost touch with the masses and finds himself ironically cast in the role of misunderstood artist. He even kids himself—judging from his interviews—that European, and especially French, audiences are more intelligent and more receptive not only to his work but to comedy and film in general. Commiserating about the lack of recognition Lewis receives from his fellow Americans has become a traditional routine (*item:* on a *Mike Douglas Show* whose guests included Lewis and Marcel Marceau, the host at one point urged the latter—with somewhat excessive eagerness, as though Lewis were a has-been in dire need of any kind of plug—"Tell the audience how they love this man in your country"). But how could Lewis feel anything but resentment about the shabby treatment he has always received at the hands of American critics? Once all the necessary reservations have been duly entered (Sarris's eleven-count indictment in *The American Cinema* takes care of the most familiar ones), and once it has been recognized that Lewis's work, as a result of its inner contradictions, imposed some serious limitations upon itself, the inescapable fact remains that Lewis was the only Hollywood comedian to rise from mere performer to—in his own, quite accurate phrase—"total film maker" during the sound era. The uniqueness of the achievement alone deserved sympathetic attention rather than the hostility or indifference it met with. Yet it is easy to see why this very uniqueness worked against Lewis. Critics were not prepared to deal with a personal cinematic approach to physical comedy, because the patterns for that genre had been set thirty or forty years earlier by the great silent comedians. Lewis stood alone, and there wasn't any yardstick available by which to evaluate his contribution. The merit of the French critics, auteurist excesses notwithstanding, was their willingness to look at what Lewis was doing as a film maker for what it was, rather than with some preconception of what film comedy should be. This willingness is all the more commendable as, in many cases, it had to be conquered over an ingrained—and far from unfounded—prejudice against the Lewis of the Dean Martin period, a prejudice few people here seem to have overcome or even reconsidered.

30. Joshua Logan (1908)

by PIERRE SAUVAGE

1938—*I Met My Love Again,* codirector: Arthur Ripley; uncredited codirector: George Cukor; 1956—*Picnic; Bus Stop;* 1957—*Sayonara;* 1958—*South Pacific;* 1960—*Tall Story;* 1961—*Fanny;* 1964—*Ensign Pulver;* 1967—*Camelot;* 1969—*Paint Your Wagon*

Uncredited

1937—*History Is Made at Night* (Frank Borzage; uncredited codirector: Arthur Ripley); 1955— *Mister Roberts* (John Ford, Mervyn LeRoy)

It is bewildering now, but Joshua Logan was briefly taken very seriously as a film maker in 1956 when his new career began and was even interviewed respectfully by *Cahiers du Cinéma.* To be sure, *Picnic* and especially *Bus Stop* had affecting and effective moments, but today some viewers find it difficult to understand their initial excessive enthusiasm for the films, and whatever esteem the two films generated for Logan at the time has been irreparably battered by an uninterrupted succession of undistinguished pictures. In a letter to us, Logan himself volunteered: "I have hated most of my pictures."

Logan had actually worked in Hollywood prior to achieving his considerable Broadway fame as the director and occasional producer and coauthor of a dozen smash musical and comedy hits, including *I Married an Angel, Annie Get Your Gun, Mister Roberts,* and *South Pacific.* (In addition to coauthoring the latter two, Logan collaborated on the books of the musicals *Higher and Higher, Wish You Were Here,* and *Fanny* and had solo credit on *The Wisteria Trees,* a Chekhov adaptation whose "doctors" are rumored to have included Maxwell Anderson, Robert Penn Warren, S. N. Behrman, and Nunnally Johnson.) As a student, he had participated in the Princeton Triangle Club shows, then joined the University Players, an intercollegiate New England summer-stock company cofounded by fellow Princetonian Bretaigne Windust, participating first as an actor and later as a director. (Henry Fonda, Margaret Sullavan, and James Stewart were among the young players.) After spending eight months studying under Stanislavsky in Moscow, Logan shared a New York apartment with Fonda, Stewart, and Myron McCormick, making his Broadway directorial bow in 1935.

The following year he went to Hollywood where David O. Selznick imposed him on director Richard Boleslawski as dialogue director on the multiaccented *The Garden of Allah.* Logan was then paired with Arthur Ripley as (uncredited) second-unit director on Frank Borzage's 1937 *History Is Made at Night.* With the former comedy-short director blocking the camera moves and Logan directing the players, they turned out the much praised shipwreck sequence and later, after an unsatisfactory preview, created a new scene changing the plot to depict Colin Clive as the murderer. The film was a big success and a grateful Walter Wanger allowed the team to codirect *I Met My Love Again* (with George Cukor directing some retakes and a few additional scenes). By the time the enjoyable but indifferently received Henry Fonda–Joan Bennett romantic drama was released, Logan was back in New York, where he staged four hits in quick succession and remained very active for three decades (overactive at times: In order to publicize the benefits of a new drug, Logan publicly declared that— like Elliott Nugent who also had a notable career on Broadway and in Hollywood— he had suffered from manic-depression throughout most of his professional life, until he began taking lithium carbonate). Logan also appeared as himself in *Main Street to Broadway* (Tay Garnett, 1953) and has said he was extensively involved in blending the Ford and LeRoy footage for the film version of his *Mister Roberts* (he owned a quarter of the film), shooting retakes as well.

"I think we plan picnics just to give ourselves an excuse to let something thrilling happen in our lives," says a character in *Picnic;* Logan's film version of the William Inge play he had staged on Broadway (the published edition is dedicated to him) provides little comparable excitement. Daniel Taradash's screenplay retained much of the original dialogue, and the big helpings of Technicolored Midwestern flavor were perhaps not inappropriate, but *Picnic* now seems rather ponderous and unconvincing. A catchy wistfulness occasionally comes across, and Kim Novak is as lovely as she was ever to be (on the other hand, mature-looking William Holden never achieves plausibility as a wandering, unwashed stud); but Inge's lines, such as they are, required a more cutting psychological edge, and the dramatic scenes are fatally shallow in emotional undercurrents. Visually smooth, with some shots strikingly framed (James Wong Howe was cinematographer), the film had a particularly graceful closing helicopter sequence—which typically sacrificed the playwright's dubiously happy ending to a glossy, upbeat finale.

Picnic was a critical and box-office success, however, as was Logan's Inge follow-up, *Bus Stop* (whose play was opened up by George Axelrod). The film was much admired even by Jean-Luc Godard (who had it fourth on his ten-best list for 1956) and Roberto Rossellini. It was understandably easy then to overlook the picture's strident brassiness to respond only to the affecting and apparent ease with which Marilyn Monroe seemed to identify with her character's insecurity, implausible ambitions ("Hollywood and Vine!"), and demand for properly respectful love. Opposite Don Murray's boisterous rodeo rider (whose ingenuous gaffes and boyish persistence were played up with excessively indulgent gusto), Monroe also got a rare chance to convey comparative maturity; it was a refreshing switch to see her cringing at an enthusiastic gaucheness on his part, which her male partners had found gratifying to patronize in the many dumb blondes she had played.

After Inge, Michener. The saccharine benevolence of *Sayonara* was followed by the Todd-AO brashness of *South Pacific,* with both giving their blessings to East-West romances, although in the case of the former, it was reportedly only at Marlon Brando's insistence that his officer ultimately marries the Japanese heroine. The musical was right up Logan's alley: He had coauthored the book (drawing on his war service for the sailor dialogue) and had coproduced and staged the tremendous 1949 Rodgers and Hammerstein hit. Perhaps inevitably, the film was a smash, breaking all box-office records for a musical. It hardly seemed to matter that the blockbuster was a static, vulgar, witless affair that any Hollywood hack could have directed with just as little flair. Logan has written that the overlapping transitions between scenes he used on Broadway had been inspired by the movies' lap dissolves; his prime contribution to film technique in the fifties was the contrived, grossly overworked use of changing color filters, as in the gaudy "Bali Ha'i" number. Logan has since conceded it was a bad mistake, the seed of which can perhaps be traced all the way back to *Picnic*— William Holden and Kim Novak dancing prettily in and out of different color lights— and *Bus Stop*—Monroe kicking on the variously hued footlights while singing "That Old Black Magic."

Logan's two later contributions to the film musical—worse adaptations of lesser Lerner and Loewe efforts—complete a unique eight-and-a-half-hour trilogy of musical flaccidity. After *Camelot,* a festival of claustrophobic close-ups and graceless two-shots (the latter if not the former usually involving the obvious services of a stand-in whenever possible, each star presumably having better things to do than participate when avoidable in another's scene), it is incomprehensible why producer Alan Jay Lerner picked Logan to direct *Paint Your Wagon,* and the lumbering, tedious picture that resulted found few enthusiasts.

Logan's three early sixties nonmusicals were hardly better. *Tall Story* was a moronic collegiate comedy in which his goddaughter Jane Fonda made an insubstantial movie debut (that same year, Logan introduced her to Broadway audiences in a melodramatic bomb written by Daniel Taradash). *Fanny* was the uninspired film version of the Marcel Pagnol-derived stage musical, with which Logan had been closely associated, shorn of the Harold Rome songs and photographed in Marseilles. *Ensign Pulver* was a poorly received sequel to *Mister Roberts.*

The above is one possible rundown of Logan's film career. Another is the director's own, generously conveyed to us in 1974 in response to a request. It seems that the least we can do under the circumstances is to give him the last word, without any editorial tampering.

Your letter of January 12th was a truly unique experience for me. In a sense, it asks for a helping hand with fair warning that that hand might get bitten. Well, it can't be bitten any more than I've bitten it myself.

I have hated most of my pictures:

1. *Paint Your Wagon.* Too long. No script. I tried to resign, but wasn't allowed to leave unless I was fired, and no one would fire me; they just interfered with my work and made me stand around and watch. My chief regret is that it has made money.

2. *Ensign Pulver* was a bad idea, but Warner's had bought the rights to a sequel and, by God, they got it.

3. *Tall Story.* Not good enough, except that it introduced Jane Fonda.

4. I also loathed and despised the color changes in *South Pacific.* They were experiments which were left in because Magna needed money so bad they wouldn't hold back the release for the three months it would require to eliminate the color changes in the laboratory. As I had co-authored and directed the Broadway play, I was sick about the picture even though it's the most successful financially of anything I've done.

The films I loved:

1. *Bus Stop.* An almost perfect picture. Surely Monroe's greatest performance, and Don Murray was great, too.

2. *Sayonara.* Truly beautiful and moving. Brando was better than he got credit for being. He *made* the picture as well as Japan.

3. *Fanny.* A classic French story, beautifully cast and filmed in Marseilles.

4. *Picnic.* I love the picnic sequence, and particularly the dance to "Moonglow" with the "Picnic Theme." A great cast, and cameraman Jimmy Howe.

5. *Camelot.* It's *too long,* but it also is one of the most beautiful-to-look-at pictures that will ever be made, thanks to John Truscott's decor, Richard Kline (camera) and Vanessa Redgrave and Richard Harris."

In 1976, Logan published his autobiography, *Josh: My Up and Down, In and Out Life,* and he has since developed a nightclub routine mainly about his impressive Broadway career.

31. *Joseph Losey* (1909)

1948—*The Boy With Green Hair;* 1950—*The Lawless;* 1951—*M; The Prowler; The Big Night;* 1956— *The Intimate Stranger* (pseudonym: Joseph Walton, Great Britain; U.S., *Finger of Guilt,* 1956); 1957—*Time Without Pity* (Great Britain; U.S., 1957); 1958—*The Gypsy and the Gentleman* (Great Britain; U.S., 1958); 1959—*Blind Date* (Great Britain; U.S., *Chance Meeting,* 1960); 1960—*The Criminal* (Great Britain; U.S., *The Concrete Jungle,* 1962); 1962—*The Damned* (Great Britain; U.S., *These Are the Damned,* 1965); *Éva* (France; U.S., 1965); 1963—*The Servant* (Great Britain; U.S., 1964); 1964—*King and Country* (Great Britain; U.S., 1965); 1966—*Modesty Blaise* (Great Britain; U.S., 1966); 1967—*Accident* (Great Britain; U.S., 1967); 1968—*Boom!* (Great Britain; U.S., 1968); *Secret Ceremony* (Great Britain; U.S., 1968); 1970—*Figures in a Landscape* (Great Britain; U.S., 1971); 1971—*The Go-Between* (Great Britain; U.S., 1971); 1972—*The Assassination of Trotsky* (Great Britain; U.S., 1972); 1973—*A Doll's House* (Great Britain; U.S., 1973); 1975— *Galileo; The Romantic Englishwoman* (Great Britain; U.S., 1975); 1976—*M. Klein* (France; U.S., *Mr. Klein,* 1977); 1978—*Les routes du sud* (France); 1980—*Don Giovanni* (France; U.S., *Mozart's Don Giovanni,* 1980); 1982—*La Truite* (France; U.S., *The Trout,* 1982)

Uncredited
1951—*Imbarco a mezzanotte* (Andrea Forzano, Italy; U.S., *Stranger on the Prowl,* 1953) 1954— *The Sleeping Tiger* (Victor Hanbury, Great Britain; U.S., 1954)

The problem posed by Joseph Losey's evolution, although unavoidable, is one that should be easily disposed of, for the dichotomy between his American and his British films is more apparent than real. The look of films in general has changed a lot since the fifties, and Losey's are no exceptions, but in his case the evolution denotes a skillful adaptation to what could be called current film-making practice rather than any deep personal change. There is no actual break between the restrained, secretive style of his early efforts and the decorative, self-consciously mystifying style of most of the English films, for the former were as deceptively limpid as the latter are deceptively opaque. To divide his work into "periods" therefore only obscures the matter. Ultimately, Losey always faces himself, even in the very process of turning away from the early image he had established. What has endured beneath the stylistic novelties is an *attitude,* made up of pessimism, bitterness, contempt, a fascinated attraction to failure and degradation, a lack of emotion more enhanced than concealed by the hysterics and histrionics his players are occasionally allowed to indulge in. The latter trait should not be construed as a deliberate withdrawing from emotional involvement, for Losey, no matter what many critics and he himself may say, is no Brechtian director. Distancing to him is not an ethical concept of the artwork's relationship to its audience but rather, it seems, an almost pathological compulsion to keep the outside world at a distance. Hence the dialectics of Losey's cinema; as a result of his aloofness, he loses touch with reality, which he then gets busy reconstructing in a vacuum and in terms of his own obsessions and fantasies. The process was already at work, for instance, in *The Prowler,* whose abstract realism verges upon the eerie, and became glaringly evident in Losey's sixties films.

Since the outside world is there anyway and has to be dealt with in some manner, Losey choses to show it as a mere collection of things. There are only objects in Losey's world. Sets are stars, props proliferate, life becomes a reflection caught in mirrors, the camera pans away from actors to focus on statues or peeps through keyholes not at people but at buildings (*Eva*). People themselves are objects, for each other and for the director who monitors their relationships. It is no surprise, then, that those relationships should so often be of the master-slave variety, which accounts for the masochistic overtones in most of Losey's English films and in quite a few of the earlier ones.

A major theme in *Gypsy, Eva,* and *The Servant* and a more subdued but still traceable one in *Accident, Boom!,* and *The Go-Between,* masochism finds its way into all his plots under one guise or another (see, for instance, the beating and humiliation scenes at the beginning of *The Big Night* and *The Damned*). One may argue that the syndrome could just as well be characterized as sadism, since the distinction is essentially a matter of point of view. It is indeed impossible to decide whether Losey derives a masochistic or sadistic gratification from the situations he creates or whether he remains an unconcerned observer. No doubt, some degree of ambiguity is present at any time, and he cannot possibly be unaware of it. His point of view, however, always seems to settle on the receiving end of the SM relationship. His male protagonists (there is little if any female masochism in his films) are, more often than not, weak and easily dominated, especially by women, and Losey places them in situations that either reproduce echo or parallel masochist fantasies. The tendency reached the high-water mark in *Modesty Blaise,* which is one SM fantasy after the other, with Modesty herself every masochist's dream come true. The film, a minor achievement perhaps, but a telltale one ("It was a kind of purgative thing for me," Losey stated) goes beyond the SM ambiguity to bring into sharp focus the pervasiveness of the ambivalent vision in Losey's cinema. *Modesty Blaise* purports to be an indictment, through parody, of a movie genre (the James Bond-style thriller) that Losey finds, in his own word, "filthy" and of the corrupt type of audience response it implies; but while the film does make its critical point, it comes across at the same time as an exacerbated statement of Losey's own obsessions, which happen to coincide with some of the ugliest aspects of contemporary life and contemporary movies he is out to expose.

As for the "humanistic," "social-minded," "committed" side of Losey's work (quotes here seem to be de rigueur), while it cannot be entirely dismissed as a figment of the imagination of cultist critics, it should nevertheless be approached with the caution required by all cultist constructions. Because he is an admirer of Brecht, whom he knew and worked with, and because his American career was shattered by McCarthyism, some have been moved to cast him as the exemplary leftist thinker. He is actually as mediocre a thinker—leftist or otherwise—as he is a director. His interviews do disclose the intelligence and sensitivity of a creator who knows what he wants to achieve and is in complete command of the medium—which, after all, is all that counts—but they are also full of platitudes (e.g., "I wanted to do *King and Country* when I realized how many millions of people had died in that war") and of irritating pseudoprofundities that seem to echo the superficial complexities of his later films (e.g., his insistence upon the social significance of *The Servant* with statements to the effect that the characters stand for "the false values" of their society). As far as "great issues" are concerned, Losey may be genuinely concerned about racism, war, capital punishment, or the nuclear threat, but watching those of his pictures that deal with these issues, one gets the impression that he really couldn't care less. (It is characteristic that Losey's approach to a historical-political subject in *The Assassination of Trotsky* was to depoliticize it and play down the historical angle by shifting the emphasis from ideological conflicts to individual psychology.)

As used to be the case in traditional Hollywood movies, moreover, Losey's social statements are often subservient to dramatic conventions that tend to weaken them. Thus in *The Criminal,* the validity of his view of prison life as a microcosm of society suffers from contrivances more reminiscent of grade-"B" thrillers than of Brecht. One example is the character played by Gregoire Aslan, a bewilderingly efficient inmate who appears to rule the entire prison and to whom arranging a killing or a jail break is all in a day's work. He does arrange Stanley Baker's escape, but the odds against the plan working out are so overwhelming that its success all but destroys the film's credibility. With what can be described as either irony, cynicism, or plain irresponsibility, the writers even rehashed the old ploy (from one of the best known—and most improbable—Warner's prison melodramas, *Each Dawn I Die*) about the convict escaping then returning voluntarily to prison in order to take care of some unfinished business inside but with the intention of getting out again when that's settled.

It is possible that Losey, as an American living and working in England, tends to overestimate the meaningfulness of his own observations on the British class structure. One also wonders whether "social content" in his films is not used as a substitute for the traditional delineation of motivations and relationships he has shown himself increasingly anxious to eschew since his earliest pictures. The young aristocrat's behavior in *The Servant,* as he sinks first into a kind of pathological apathy and then to what both script and direction clearly designate as "degradation," remains psychologically unexplained except in the most abstract and general manner. (We know from the very beginning that he is "weak".) This reluctance to "explain" is of course typical of Harold Pinter who wrote the screenplay, but there is no doubt that Pinterism was highly attractive to Losey, whose art had been developing along somewhat similar lines for quite some time. (*Accident,* the second Losey-Pinter collaboration, is arguably Losey's English masterpiece.) Since the general tendency as regards Pinter's plays has been to overemphasize the importance of their "symbolism," it was unavoidable that the film would be approached in a similar way, especially with the director lending a helping hand in his interviews. To explain the character's degradation as a symbol of the corruption of his class and its values, however, is a rather complacent and not very meaningful justification for an opacity the authors shouldn't have to make excuses for. It cheapens rather than illuminates a film that, in spite of its basic theatrical artificiality, still sticks too closely to realism to be experienced by the viewer as a parable.

It is indeed one of Losey's weaknesses that he overloads his films with those visual crutches and signposts to "sense" usually referred to as "symbols." His commentators relish discussing how almost every action, reaction, event, and object "evokes," "stands for," "represents" something else. This plethora of signs and meanings, again, tends to be impoverishing rather than enriching, a fairly general phenomenon in the realm of motion pictures, as though pointing to a meaning through visual aids resulted in diminishing the amount of meaning involved and in cheapening its quality. But it would be absurd to reject symbolism per se. Losey occasionally achieves that rare coincidence of a directorial touch (a camera move, an actor's stance, the use of a set) with an idea, thus reaching the level of symbolic expression in which imagery acquires enough power and autonomy to stand for itself instead of for something else and becomes, so to speak, self-referential. Of course, the perception of the level at which a symbol operates largely depends upon individual response, and one spectator's symbolic meat can be another's poison. No matter how convinced one may be, it is difficult to prove, for instance, that the closing shot of *The Prowler* belongs to the higher level, while the closing shot of *The Criminal,* which was obviously patterned after it, is too contrived (although dramatically and visually effective) to achieve the unobstrusive concurrence of image and message that characterizes the former.

Dealing with "meaning" has always been a major concern of Losey's art, and this accounts for much of its self-consciousness. He has tried various approaches to the problem of the stylistic production of sense, from the false "simplicity" of *King and Country* to the aggressive kitsch of *Modesty Blaise.* His style is often made to suggest more significance than there actually is to be found, and the resulting sense of inadequateness gets in the way of the purely formal kind of enjoyment for which we were quite willing to settle down.

In a 1960 article entitled "The Individual Eye," Losey stated as one of his objectives the Brechtian "stripping of reality and its precise reconstruction through selection of reality symbols." Commenting upon this James Leahy wrote in his book, *The Cinemas of Joseph Losey* (1967): "Like Brecht, he rejects a naturalistic depiction of real life, preferring, rather, to show what life is really like, its bared, heightened conflicts. Losey does not set out to depict reality, rather he distills it—selecting the significant detail, the significant gesture, ignoring the rest." Perhaps, but the terminology used by both Losey and his commentator is so vague and confusing that any serious consideration of their statements immediately raises a multitude of questions, such as: What are "reality symbols"? Don't such symbols themselves belong to the realm of reality? Is there any valid reason to believe that Losey knows "what life is really like" (whatever that means)? Isn't real life just the opposite of a selection of "bared, heightened conflicts," and isn't this selection precisely what distinguishes drama from reality? While it is true that Losey selects "the significant detail, the significant gesture" (but isn't that what any good director—or writer—is constantly doing? Art, after all, is selective by definition), is he really free to "ignore the rest," as Leahy claims? Practically, how do you go about "ignoring the rest" in a movie? To what extent can you "strip" reality in a medium that, although it modifies reality in a number of ways, also functions as a means of recording it mechanically? The problem, as a matter of fact, is acknowledged, although unintentionally, by Leahy himself in the very paragraph under discussion. After the above passage, he goes on to write: "Despite a minutely observed naturalistic surface, Losey's films are essentially and clearly allegories or fables." How can the films of a man who "rejects a naturalistic depiction of real life" present at the same time "a minutely observed naturalistic surface"? If the contradiction does not seem to bother our critic it is, perhaps, because of the inescapable truth behind it: Losey, no matter how "modern" an artist he may be, still works within the traditional, mass-audience-oriented narrative format, one that allows the film maker only limited leeway in tampering with the raw material the camera feeds on. Losey's selection of "reality symbols" can only be accomplished against a wider, more comprehensive background, the basic stuff of filmic vision. Assuming that by "a naturalistic depiction of real life" Leahy means a depiction that takes that background into account, it seems difficult to conceive of a narrative film that is not, to some extent, naturalistic (and that would include even such highly stylized films as Bresson's or films that challenge the "reality" of their own material, in the Godard or Robbe-Grillet fashion). The tension between selective symbolism and the "naturalistic" approach is really never resolved. Because of the nature of the medium, the more "meaning" is injected into a film through symbolism, the less meaningful it often tends to appear. (The collapse of Losey's system is evident, for instance, in the pretentious vacuity of *Boom!*, a film whose stylistic principle is to suggest mountains where there aren't even any molehills. *The Go-Between,* although a far superior picture, is also marred—indeed in its very premise—by the director's tendency to tease and tantalize the mind while eventually failing to deliver.) But if Losey doesn't always get the upper hand in his struggle for—and with—meaning, it is a brave struggle, and it is his own, not anybody else's. The films that come out of this struggle clearly reflect it and are therefore more vulnerable to criticism, although they are also, and by the same token, quite seductive and likely to be overrated by those viewers who allow themselves to be impressed by intimations of profundity. The ideal Losey movie would be one eschewing the hints and thereby enhancing rather than obscuring the sense. The child hero of *The Go-Between* who carries messages but remains in a state of innocence may be seen as an unconscious symbol of what Losey's films strive for and never quite manage to be; for while Losey hasn't deeply changed since *The Boy with Green Hair,* he has nevertheless grown much too devious and self-conscious, or simply much too clever, to ever be able to recapture the bliss of esthetic innocence.

32. Sidney Lumet (1924)

1957—*Twelve Angry Men;* 1958—*Stage Struck;* 1959—*That Kind of Woman;* 1960—*The Fugitive Kind;* 1962—*A View From the Bridge; Long Day's Journey Into Night;* 1964—*Fail Safe;* 1965—*The Pawnbroker; The Hill;* 1966—*The Group;* 1967—*The Deadly Affair;* 1968—*Bye Bye Braverman; The Sea Gull;* 1969—(unreleased) *The Appointment; King: A Filmed Record . . . Montgomery to Memphis* (documentary—codirector: Joseph L. Mankiewicz); 1970—*The Last of the Mobile Hot-Shots;* 1971—*The Anderson Tapes;* 1972—*Child's Play;* 1973—*The Offence;* 1974—*Serpico; Lovin' Molly; Murder on the Orient Express;* 1975—*Dog Day Afternoon;* 1976—*Network;* 1977—*Equus;* 1978—*The Wiz;* 1980—*Just Tell Me What You Want;* 1981—*Prince of the City;* 1982—*Deathtrap; The Verdict;* 1983—*Daniel*

Lumet's nearly proverbial "unevenness" is the direct consequence of his versatility and pragmatism, of a concern with material output rather than personal input that has made him the most prolific director of his generation. A fast worker who earned an early reputation for professionalism and dependability by bringing in pictures on or ahead of schedule, he has directed more films since his 1958 debut than any of his contemporaries have over the same period of time. Many of those films were, in concept if not in execution, ambitious endeavors, and quite a few presented difficulties from which a less confident director might have shied away. Self-confidence, however, is one thing Lumet has never lacked, and after an initial "safe" period during which he concentrated on adapting stage plays, relying on his experience as a television director, he soon proved not only willing but eager to tackle challenging projects, even though he must have realized he was still ill-equipped to handle them. His uninhibited approach to the medium is reminiscent of those Hollywood veterans who worked their way up to prominence, learning the craft as they went along. Like many of them, it took Lumet quite some time to come into his own, but his erratic piling up of near hits and intriguing misses over nearly fifteen years has finally led, in the seventies and in the early eighties, to such films as *Serpico, Dog Day Afternoon, Network,* and *Prince of the City,* which exhibit not only far greater formal expertise but also a firmer personal point of view than any of his previous efforts.

One's opinion of a film maker is often filtered through one's response to his first few films, so that his growth, over the years remains unacknowledged. In 1966 Pauline Kael, in her essay, "The Making of *The Group,*" judged Lumet, after nine movies, to be "basically a TV director," directing "one-dimensionally." There was little ground then for challenging her prediction that he would go on using space in the same unimaginative, uncinematic manner, but her appraisal *has* been proved wrong, and it is no longer possible to file and forget Lumet as one of those television directors who made creditable, TV-derived first films in the late fifties and then bogged down into middlebrow ambitions and message-coated commercialism.

By no means a personal work, *Twelve Angry Men* nevertheless provided its director with an opportunity to display technical smoothness in handling a group of people in one small room for ninety minutes, and Lumet did rise to the occasion. Based on Reginald Rose's cleverly crafted television play and independently produced by Rose and star Henry Fonda, the film was praised as a courageous statement on racial prejudice and the frailties of human justice. Its message, however, had to be put across within the narrow limitations of the genre, i.e., the well-made suspense play, with its psychological and dramatic conventions. As a result, the very craftsmanship of the piece tends to defeat its generous intentions. In order to secure for the accused the benefit of doubt the law provides for, the Fonda character had to come on as a combination Sherlock Holmes and Perry Mason, as well as double as confessor, catalyst, and instant psychiatrist to a number of the jurors. (The play is based upon the dramatically convenient but otherwise simplistic assumption that people's prejudices can be traced to specific occurrences in their past and can thereby be accounted for and removed.) The film was, and still is, commendable for its fine ensemble acting by a cast of splendid character actors, which was probably instrumental in getting Lumet big stars to direct in his subsequent productions.

The occasional redeeming feature of Lumet's next five films (all but one adaptations from stage plays) was also good acting: from Raf Vallone, recreating his stage role in the rather ponderous version of Arthur Miller's *A View From the Bridge;* from a masterfully understated Brando and an unusually restrained Magnani in *The Fugitive Kind,* two performances emphasizing the best in Williams's play, its tenderness and compassion, while toning down its melodramatic overindulgence; and from all four stars, but especially Katharine Hepburn, in *Long Day's Journey Into Night,* provided one is willing to accept basically theatrical performances as satisfactory film acting.

The latter picture received enthusiastic praise from some critics, notably Pauline Kael, who called it "a great experience" and stated that she didn't see "how one can niggle over whether it's 'cinema' or *merely* 'filmed theatre.' " Still, there doesn't seem to be anything niggling about bringing up the matter in the case of a production that never allows us to forget that we are watching a stage play. Although it is possible to conceive of the film being a "great experience" to some spectators *as* filmed theatre (curiously, though, Kael's admiration for the film doesn't extend to the play itself, which, she feels, "has the worst American failings"), it is difficult to comprehend how it could be one for anybody *as a movie.* On the one hand, Lumet seems paralyzed by his awe of the spoken word (practically every line of the text is retained in the complete, 180-minute version, a token of producer Ely Landau's dedication to literal fidelity); on the other hand, most of his attempts at "cinematization" through camera movement and editing are inadequate. The camera roams and rambles aimlessly, the editing is jarring and arbitrary. Lumet will cut from a shot of a character making a small gesture at the close of a speech to a different angle of the same gesture being completed, the ultimate in unconscionable fussiness. Time and again, he cuts or pans or dollies away from a character delivering an important speech to concentrate on a largely predictable and superfluous reaction shot. Even one of the few felicitous directorial touches—the camera slowly pulling out during Hepburn's closing speech, leaving the four characters in darkness except for the bleak light from two naked bulbs overhead and the dim flashes from the lighthouse coming through the windows at the far end of the room—is ruined by the absurd insertion of a series of close-ups of the performers (as though the cast were taking a curtain call before the end of the play), after which the dolly out, to which Lumet awkwardly returns for his fadeout shot, just fails to conjure up the same mood as before. The film is at its best when the camera unobtrusively focuses on Hepburn's rambling soliloquies and the ever-shifting moods that race across her marvelously ravaged, anguished countenance. It *is* a fabulous performance, for the preservation of which one must be grateful, but Lumet's direction embalms rather than revives it.

Switching for the first time to adapting a novel, Lumet cast Henry Fonda, the star of his first two films, as the President of the United States in *Fail Safe,* a "serious" counterpart to *Dr. Strangelove.* (Columbia, the releasing company, copyrighted the two films on the same day, December 31, 1963, but Kubrick's film was released ten months earlier.) Sturdily scripted by Walter Bernstein and vigorously, if not very imaginatively directed, the film was even more grimly ironic, in a sense, than *Dr. Strangelove,* as it built to a climax in which the President had no choice but to order the destruction of New York City in order to convince the Russians that the atomic bombing of Moscow was indeed a mistake. Although now dated, alas, as a result of the evolution of technology (in an era when practically any target in either country can be reached by missiles within minutes, the days when a nuclear attack had to be delivered by bombers seem nostalgically primitive), *Fail Safe* remains a powerful and timely cautionary tale.

The Pawnbroker, however, was an unexpected and quite appalling fling at trendy film making, using Resnais-like stream-of-consciousness flashbacks, as well as on-location shooting with hand-held cameras and direct sound recording. Whether this was an opportunistic jump onto the New Wave bandwagon or an earnest attempt to adjust form to subject matter is open to question, but Lumet's clumsiness in handling such delicate stylistic devices is not. Unlike *Hiroshima mon amour,* the film's obvious inspiration, *The Pawnbroker* fails to achieve unity of form and content, and its indiscriminate use of modernistic tricks cannot conceal the fact that it is firmly rooted in melodramatic formula. *The Hill,* Lumet's next picture, although not so elaborately flashy, was an equally bad case of directorial heavy-handedness defusing a potentially valid subject.

Lumet's most hazardous project to date, *The Group* brought further evidence of his lack of inhibition in choice of material and rather curiously turned out to be more satisfying than practically any of his previous films. Not that it is really successful as a whole; indeed, it may be the most seriously flawed of Lumet's major pictures. Despite Sidney Buchman's tight, workmanlike adaptation of Mary McCarthy's unwieldy novel, the film is a glaring demonstration of the medium's inadequacies in certain fields that are the proper realm of literary fiction. Movies can do without action but not without interaction, and there is little of that in *The Group* despite the milling crowd of characters vying for our attention. There exists neither real friendship nor serious conflict or rivalry among any of the eight Vassar graduates who constitute the novel's collective protagonist. Away from the college, their banding together serves about the same purpose as an alumnae's association. Their function as members of the group largely consists in keeping tabs on each other and circulating news and gossip. Mary McCarthy's description of Norine's speech (she "talked continuously, emitting a jerky flow of information, like an outboard motor") may be applied to the film itself. It operates like a busy little computer processing and disseminating data (Lumet even resorts to "teletype" subtitles in order to cram in as much information as possible), and at times the flurries of names and facts flashed across both sound and image track, the frantic updating of ever-changing situations suggest a grotesquely speeded-up soap opera. It is all exposition and recap, 140 minutes of "the story so far" without any actual story.

Given the script's overwhelming emphasis on speech, one of Lumet's main concerns was, clearly, to avoid seeming static, which resulted in another of his flings into directorial overbusyness: swirling camera moves around girls breathlessly chatting away, erratic dolly shots shuttling listlessly between people in crowded rooms. But while Lumet's pedestrian style fails in its unifying ambitions, the film triumphantly comes to life whenever it focuses on one of the girls and her personal problems: Dottie's (Joan Hackett) rather sordid first affair; Polly's (Shirley Knight) relationships with her manic-depressive father and wavering married lover; Priss's (Elizabeth Hartman) breast-feeding agonies; Kay's (Joanna Pettet) clashes with her failed playwright husband. In 1966 the sensitiveness, compassion, and intensity of many of those scenes were almost unprecedented in American cinema; a decade later, they have lost none of their impact, and it is sad to realize that not one of the remarkably gifted young actresses that make them glow (Joan Hackett's performance is particularly memorable) went on to the great careers, which, from the evidence of the film, they thoroughly deserved. *The Group* is also notable for Lumet's atmospheric use of color in some of its scenes, although the director himself was dissatisfied with this first experience with color. (Boris Kaufman, who had photographed several of Lumet's early films, had himself comparatively few credits in color at the time—the only notable one being *Splendor in the Grass*—and, according to Lumet, never managed to adapt his style to color cinematography.)

After *The Group*, Lumet's activity continued to be intense and increasingly international. For his newly formed independent producing company, he went to England to make *The Deadly Affair*, a brooding, tedious adaptation of a John Le Carré spy thriller, only slightly redeemed by James Mason's affectingly forlorn presence. While shooting a scene of this film, a performance of Marlowe's *Edward II* by the Royal Shakespeare Company with David Warner in the title role, it suddenly occurred to Lumet that Warner and the two stars of *The Deadly Affair*—Mason and Simone Signoret—would be an ideal cast for Chekhov's *The Sea Gull*, respectively as Konstantin, Trigorin, and Arkadina. A Nina was promptly secured in the person of Vanessa Redgrave, who lived round the corner from the studio, and the very same day Lumet and the four actors agreed to make a film of the play together. *The Sea Gull* was filmed on location in Sweden. Some critics consider it one of Lumet's best pictures, and it is the director's own favorite among his filmed plays, along with *Long Day's Journey Into Night*.

The Sea Gull was followed by *The Appointment*, another European venture (it was filmed in Italy), which was poorly received at the 1969 Cannes Festival and was subsequently reedited and rescored for a belated 1970 release in the United States. Criticized for being "imitation Antonioni," the film was photographed by Carlo Di Palma, the cinematographer of *Red Desert* and *Blow-Up*, and Lumet has stated that he had taken on the project mainly for the opportunity to work with him, as he still felt uneasy with color at the time. Back in the United States, he directed the commercially unsuccessful and seldom seen *Last of the Mobile Hot-Shots*, a reworking, scripted by Gore Vidal, of Tennessee Williams's black comedy *The Seven Descents of Myrtle*.

Bye Bye Braverman and *The Anderson Tapes*, Lumet's most interesting pictures of the period, were thoroughly American efforts. Both are "group" movies (all-male groups in both cases), with stories focusing not on one here but on a bunch of characters brought together by circumstances, affinities, or occupation. In *Bye Bye Braverman*, they are four none too successful Jewish intellectuals driving from Manhattan to Brooklyn in a Volkswagen to attend a friend's funeral. The film is a crazy quilt of rambling conversations, alternately or simultaneously zany and pathetic, and of near-slapstick interludes projecting the characters' vague musings and fantasies. Based on Wallace Markfield's novel *To an Early Grave*, the film is literate, bright, and occasionally moving; it is marred, unfortunately, by a couple of arbitrary, overdone, and painfully unfunny cameos by comedians Godfrey Cambridge and Alan King, which were obviously dragged in in an attempt to inject some box-office value into the offbeat material (to no avail, as the movie did poor business anyway).

The group in *The Anderson Tapes* is as studiedly heterogeneous as was the one in *Twelve Angry Men*. The seven men planning and executing the large-scale caper masterminded by Sean Connery include a long-haired youth, an old convict who has just finished serving a thirty-five-year sentence, a swishy middle-aged antique dealer, two blacks (one active in a Black Power movement, the other apolitical), and a dumb, sadistic hood of the old school. However, there is very little of the psychological and racial tension such socio-ethnic cross sections might suggest and that is standard dramatic fare in "group" movies (and especially caper yarns since *The Asphalt Jungle* and *Odds Against Tomorrow*). The film's actual theme is the matter-of-fact invasion of privacy resulting from the use of modern technology—especially communication media—for "security" purposes. From the ubiquitous closed-circuit television of the opening scenes to the hasty "erasing" of all the gathered material in the end, the theme is so relentlessly and efficiently driven home that the people in the story become overshadowed by the gadgetry, and the film's actual protagonists seem to be TV and movie cameras, tape recorders, and bugging devices, rather than the individuals they are constantly monitoring. Lumet no doubt makes the point as much in faithfulness to the novel as out of personal conviction; yet the theme is by no means unexpected in a film whose director has repeatedly dealt with human failure and noncommunication. (It may be noted in passing that couples are absent from many of Lumet's movies; in most of the others, couples are of minor dramatic importance and/or the relationship is mediocre and unsatisfactory, sometimes ludicrous, or pathetically grotesque.) *The Anderson Tapes* reaches an extreme point where human endeavor recedes into the background, and relationships are revealed in all of their raw inhumanity. A prophetic pre-Watergate statement, the film points to such post-Watergate treatments of the theme as Coppola's *The Conversation* and, of course, Pakula's *All the President's Men,* as well as to Lumet's own *Dog Day Afternoon* and *Network,* two pictures that were to deal at length with the impact of the media on individual and collective psychology and behavior.

Lumet's eclecticism and unpredictability were again in evidence with his 1974 box-office hits, *Serpico* and *Murder on the Orient Express.* Two films can hardly be more dissimilar in either subject matter, style, or level of achievement. In *Serpico,* Lumet successfully undertook the arduous task of recreating actual events of the very recent past, while in *Murder,* he safely retreated to the nostalgic thirties as a setting for the most deliberately artificial of old-fashioned mysteries. *Murder* is all plot—plodding plot, at that; *Serpico* has no plot at all, but the energy of each of its sequences overcomes their repetitiousness. *Serpico* is, from beginning to end, a *sustained* movie; *Murder* builds up expectations with a cleverly handled opening montage sequence and richly atmospheric expository scenes, then settles down to offering nothing more distinguished than an expensive equivalent of the mystery quickies Hollywood once used to grind out for the bottom halves of double bills.

Serpico is built around one actor's stunning, beautifully diversified performance; in *Murder* the acting by the star-studded cast—each of whom was diplomatically alloted equal screen time—is uniformly nondescript and occasionally overdone. The New York location shooting in *Serpico* is consistently inventive in the choice of places, colors, textures. The action of *Murder* is confined aboard a train, and while this handicap may also work as a stimulant to a director's imagination (see Anthony Mann's *The Tall Target* or Richard Fleischer's *The Narrow Margin,* two small gems of virtuose direction), Lumet was clearly burdened with the handicap but failed to respond to the stimulation. The train is such a nuisance to him that he keeps it immobilized (with the help of a convenient snowdrift) for about two-thirds of the film's running time, perhaps so that the noise won't interfere with the nonstop, information-laden dialogue. (Even with this precaution taken, he is so unsure of his grip on the spectator's attention that he keeps flashing back to earlier scenes in an attempt to keep the proceedings clear.) Ironically, the calculated escapism of *Murder* fails to entertain, while *Serpico* manages to be as suspenseful and engrossing as the best of traditional thrillers.

While the contrast between *Dog Day Afternoon* and *Network,* Lumet's next two pictures, is not as striking—indeed, they have some major preoccupations in common—

their very thematic similarities emphasize basic dissimilarities of approach. Both films deal with the relationship between reality and its representation/transformation by television and with news reporting and the way it changes the people in the news *and* the viewers. Both films, too, stress the medium's tendency to dull audiences' reactions by making the outrageous seem commonplace and, to that extent, both are concerned with the dehumanization of contemporary societies and the part the media play in it. There are similarities (although one man makes the news and the other reports it) between the Al Pacino character in *Dog Day Afternoon*—the outlaw as instant electronic hero—and the Peter Finch character in *Network*—the anchorman turned mesmeric seer. Both are charismatic figures—albeit in a pathetic and, in the former's case, ephemeral way—who grab the public's attention through an act of defiance and indulge in confused, anarchistic but liberating indictments of the System, the Establishment, and the very medium that enables them to do so, thus bringing crowds a kind of cathartic exhilaration.

Yet the two films widely differ in both concept and method. *Dog Day Afternoon* derives its outrageousness from its very adherence to the facts of a real-life happening, whereas *Network* bases its on a satirical premise that has little if any credibility on a realistic level. *Dog Day Afternoon* is linear, driving, uncluttered; *Network* is convoluted and lumbering, with a script that keeps sprouting new threads, temporarily losing sight of them, then picking them up later. One film is as relentlessly phenomenological as the other is digressive and didactic. The direction of *Dog Day Afternoon* concentrates on raw action, behavior, gesture; even Pacino's rambling harangues to the crowd function more as physical flourishes than as verbal statements. *Network,* on the other hand, is dedicated to the written word and relies upon elaborate, florid language to make most of its points. Paddy Chayefsky utilizes the broadest range of moods and registers from straight drama to farce, and whatever unity the film achieves is through the sustained brilliance of its deliberately overwritten dialogue. *Network,* of course, is as much Chayefsky's film as Lumet's, and where *Dog Day Afternoon* coolly records the pervading madness without passing judgments, *Network* is fraught with the self-righteousness and moralizing typical of the writers of Chayefsky's generation.

As far as Lumet is concerned, both films brought conclusive evidence that he had at last reached beyond the one-dimensional style Pauline Kael once thought he would never outgrow. *Dog Day Afternoon* confirmed the feeling for the rhythms and moods, the pace and speech of New York City life that had been one of the major assets of *Serpico*. Both *Dog Day Afternoon* and *Network* have their weaknesses, but neither could be called one-dimensional. Perhaps the most obvious progress made by Lumet is in the area of camera work. The self-conscious, haphazard movements of earlier efforts have been replaced by a coherent, functional use of the mobile camera. The nervous, lightning-fast dolly shots inside the bank in *Dog Day Afternoon* do not just follow Pacino's hyperactive, bumbling moves, they are a perfectly apposite formal expression of his agitation. *Network,* in some ways, may seem a throwback to Lumet's earlier, stage-struck period, yet he rarely allows himself to become smothered by the flamboyance of Chayefsky's verbal overkill. For example, the scene in which Faye Dunaway and the network executives matter-of-factly plan the assassination of Peter Finch is as striking visually—with its studiedly scattered positioning of characters not looking at each other and its ominous underlighting—as for its writing.

After *Network,* Lumet was once again lured back to stage adaptations with *Equus,* which he says he should not have made (he disagreed with the "philosophy" of the play), and *The Wiz,* his only musical and by far his most elaborate and costliest production. Both were incursion into nonrealistic territory, another instance of Lumet's willingness to broaden his range. *The Wiz* has some impressive moments, but its total lack of charm—surprising if one considers the delightful Broadway show from which it is derived—and aggressive ugliness make it one of the most depressing movie musicals ever perpetrated. A born New Yorker who has made more films in his native city than any other director, Lumet may have seemed a logical choice of director for a black version of *The Wizard of Oz* set in Manhattan, but the relentlessly nightmarish vision and compulsive street-wiseness he brought to the project hopelessly distorted the simple virtues and wisdom of the original, which the stage show had skillfully preserved. The approach is just too bleak and bizarre for the vehicle and perhaps for *any* musical.

Fortunately, the indefatigable Lumet was soon back doing what has now become clear he does best—anatomizing the interaction of law and crime in the urban jungle. *Prince of the City,* faithfully based on Robert Daley's exhaustive account of Bob Leuci's covert investigation of corruption among his own colleagues on the New York Police special narcotics unit, is one of Lumet's most ambitious and most successful films, an overwhelmingly intense and at times almost unbearably gritty drama of conflicting loyalties in a nether world where the line between lawlessness and law enforcement has become hopelessly blurred. Written by Jay Presson Allen and Lumet, whose first screenwriting credit it is, the film is sprawling (167 minutes), convoluted—occasionally to the point of incoherence—overemphatic, and repetitious—a series of very powerful individual sequences that somehow do not quite add to the masterwork that they should, but these faults are due to the nature of the material, and the director's respect for it, rather than to any failure on his part. Indeed, by eschewing traditional dramatic progression and putting his hero through a succession of harrowing scenes that are largely repetitive both in style and content, he comes closer to the reality of the character's experience, a nightmarish and emotionally lethal ordeal that never seems to come to an end.

Prince of the City demonstrates Lumet's control of the logistics of film making, a control which, in the case of such a production, must be absolute. The fact that the film, with its 126 speaking parts (most of them played by nonprofessionals) and 131 locations, was shot in only fifty-nine days (eleven days ahead of the shooting schedule) would be remarkable in any case but in view of the end result is simply amazing. Lumet has indeed come a long way since his days as a "one-dimensional" director or even since the time, in the late sixties, when he could be somewhat patronizingly characterized as "a director to be followed, if only from a distance." He has shown more ability to grow as an artist than any other film maker of his generation, and although he will probably continue to get involved in dubious projects with dubious results—a consequence of his insatiable craving for making films and learning as he makes them—there is no doubt now that his every move should be closely watched in the future.

33. *Ida Lupino* (*1917*)

by RONNIE SCHEIB

1950—*Never Fear; Outrage;* 1951—*Hard, Fast and Beautiful;* 1953—*The Hitch-Hiker; The Bigamist;* 1966—*The Trouble With Angels*

Uncredited
1949—*Not Wanted* (Elmer Clifton; Lupino directed all or virtually all of this film.)

In 1949 Ida Lupino and her producer-husband Collier Young founded Emerald Films, later to become The Filmmakers, a small independent production company, and started to turn out some of the first low-budget, location-shot "problem movies." In contrast to the turgid, morally weighted, we-who-have-legs-salute-you-who-do-not Liberal Establishment treatments of the late forties and early fifties (*Gentleman's Agreement, Crossfire, The Men*), or their latter-day cousins, the made-for-TV-movies, with their carefully apportioned slices of social guilt, Lupino's movies, like many of Nicholas Ray's, are small-scale rite-of-passage films—passage into womanhood, into nightmare, into lack of control.

Cast out of familiar, protective environments, torn by conflicting desires or no desire at all, Lupino's characters do not know how to act. Their "problems"—rape, polio, illegitimate children, bigamy—have put them beyond the pale, beyond the patterned security of their forseeable futures. The problem is not how to reintegrate them into the mainstream; the problem is the shallowness of the mainstream and the void it projects around them—the essential passivity of ready-made lives.

The heroines of Lupino's films display none of the qualities—neither the vulnerable, tenderly probing love of one have-not for another (*High Sierra, Deep Valley*), nor the cool, vital self-assurance and on-line energy (*The Man I Love, Roadhouse*), nor the nervously alternating currents of neurotic drive (*Ladies in Retirement, The Hard Way*)—that illuminate her own stand-out performances as an actress. Instead, her characters are sleepwalkers—dazed, mutilated, displaced persons wandering aimlessly from half-way house to half-way house on the byways of small-city America. Passing through social diseases they can't quite make their own, unaware of their tentative search for identity, they live or flee from moment to moment. Yet their torn-out moments have an intensity, a naked unattached will-to-being that makes the shaped destinies of others seem an off-space dream.

They've worked for a living since high school, not as brisk, efficient secretaries or boss-struck little helpers but as waitresses, factory workers, bookkeepers, neither in glamour nor in drudgery, not for self-fulfillment nor independence nor upward mobility, but because their families needed the money. They've lived on girlish fantasies and half-formed expectations; they've dreamt of love in darkened bedrooms and brought fiancés home to dinner. Then suddenly, brutally, they become women—and can relate to nothing and no one around them.

Lupino as cowriter is an auteur in a very literal sense, and it is not difficult to schematize the overall pattern of her narratives: a brief opening positing a continuing "normal" life, a sudden traumatic interruption of that flow, an overwhelming sense of alienation and disorientation, a brief respite at some sheltered communal refuge, a reversal of trauma by the active assumption of what was initially passively experienced, and a tentative start of a new life. Yet within this narrative unity and even greater unity of style, there is constant exploration, experimentation. The topography and "feel" of the films change—from the mesmerized phasing in and out of *Not Wanted* to the claustrophobic, symbolically overcharged stasis of *Never Fear*, to the violent city-country contrast of *The Outrage*, to the tight orchestration of the three-way dance of death in *The Hitch-Hiker.*

Lupino's first film, *Not Wanted,** exploited as a daring exposé of the shocking plight of an unwed mother, resembles its publicity very little, remarkably free of both head-shaking compassion for the "poor unfortunates" and the tawdry sensationalism of the big-budget *Peyton Place* generation of teenage preggie pics. Its heroine Sally (Sally Forrest) is a pretty young girl waitressing in a café, frustrated by the narrow, unchanging colorlessness of small-town respectability. Her romantic dreams crystallize around the spotlit figure of a not-so-up-and-coming piano player Steve (Leo Penn), in town for a short gig.

Many of the story elements of *Not Wanted* recall *The Man I Love,* Raoul Walsh's Lupino-starring masterpiece of three years earlier: the driven piano player who can't settle down, the lovemaking and suffering-rhymed power of the piano—even a waitress named Sally. But where Lupino is the dynamic center of *The Man I Love,* holding the film and the family together, Sally Forrest leaves pieces of her life scattered across the map.

Sally's parents are no better equipped for life than is she. Her father's wistful indulgence and vague protectiveness, her mother's harried discontent and stock-in-trade hopes ("I want you to meet a respectable man who can do things for you") trace the limits of their quietly failed expectations, their uneasy apprehension of all that falls outside the perimeters of their own meagre lot. The house is a series of singly occupied rooms—the mother in the kitchen, moving from left to right in seemingly endless preparations, while her husband diffidently sneaks in the right corner of the frame and her daughter exits to her private dreaming space to the left.

For space is an emotional entity in a Lupino film, not that the space expressionistically reflects the character's emotional state but that his way of inhabiting it defines his relationship to the world. The two men in Sally's life present an opposition in spatial deployment. While Steve is perfectly willing to share his piano bench with Sally as he pounds the keyboard in half-committed, half-disillusioned virtuosity, he fends off with moody desperation all her attempts to penetrate the off-space of his anxieties, his uneasy transience (the Murphy bed closed before the door is opened, the crumpled, abortive musical arrangements carpeting the floor of his boarding house room).

---

* Ida Lupino took no directorial credit on *Not Wanted.* The film is entirely credited to Elmer Clifton who was to have directed and did in fact begin only to suffer a heart attack three days into shooting. Lupino, who had cowritten the screenplay, took over as director.

In contrast, Sally's subsequent boyfriend, Drew (Keefe Brasselle), is at home in any environment and puppy-eager to share it, even the seemingly barren scape of the "Gaseteria" where he and Sally work, yielding cozy oases in the form of an open-air back of a truck or a couple of chairs drawn around the Coke machine. Yet the miniature, enclosed world of model trains that the lame Drew enthusiastically brings to life for Sally (for him a fantasy of unhampered locomotion, of circled completion) and his offhand joking about losing his leg in the war ("Bad habit of mine. I never watch where I'm going") imply a loneliness as great as Steve's failure-dogged rootlessness.

Sally's discovery that she is pregnant by Steve, which comes immediately after her near acceptance of Drew's marriage proposal, casts her adrift. Her life takes on a nomadic purposelessness, marked by suitcases, bus stations, rooming houses, odd jobs. Sally is the first in a long line of Lupino wanderers, shell-shocked veterans who wonder if they can ever go home again.

There are temporary refuges; for Sally in *Not Wanted,* a home for unwed mothers constitutes a real community, with its domestic chores, its matter-of-fact sisterly solidarity. But it is a community, like the rehabilitation center in *Never Fear* or the rural enclave in *The Outrage,* defined by its insulation from the day-to-day world, overshadowed by its impermanence. Once outside the walls, each will again become other, alien, isolated. This is conveyed strikingly in the finale of *Never Fear* when its polio-stricken heroine finally ventures out of the center, limping on her cane, shrinking, bewildered and overcome by the street full of hurried purposefulness lying right outside the door—her tentative steps, hailed before as great milestones, here a snail's progress on the scale of functioning normality.

Even within the walls each is alone. Sally's baby happens to her in total passivity. She is lifted unyielding, almost inert, from the bed to the stretcher, her face beaded with moisture, the walls going by above her head as in sharp-edged hallucination, the white-clad nurses bending down before the lights go out. There are many such "spacey" moments in Lupino's films—moments of extreme emotional stress causing visual distortion, moments of total obliviousness.

But these spacey moments are never purely subjective nor purely indicative of stress. Rather, they bear witness to the radical dysfunction that forms the spoken or unspeakable subject of so many modern women writers (Jean Rhys foremost among them). The specific problems of Lupino's characters are neither exemplary nor causal, and the camera captures neither the judgmental nor the emotional content of their thought but rather the inwardness and intensity of a process of consciousness unrelated to ego, fixated on images of desire intuitively recognized as primordial and banal, vibrating with emotion that has renounced belief in itself and exhausted its own possibilities. Passivity in Lupino's films is no comfortable sinking into despair, no well-fed suffering spiced with revolt or self-abnegation but a stark, stock-still simultaneous inevitability and impossibility of consciousness.

In *Not Wanted,* when the economic impossibility of both caring for her child and earning their living forces Sally to give up her baby, it is neither a fifty-violin tragedy nor one woman's underlit descent into social iniquity but part of the exigencies of a real world that can no more be morally "resolved" than it can be ignored. A strong social sense, heritage of her Warners days, informs all Lupino's films. The options of her characters are inseparable from their precise social situation. Lupino can no more depict a character outside a vital social context than can Walsh; class is never a given but a lived.

Sally sits in a jail cell, having unconsciously kidnapped a baby to replace the one she has lost, surrounded by half-crazed women (it is not degredation but insanity that menaces Lupino's heroines, even the "degrading" aspects of her cellmates, from frowsiness to lesbianism, is overridden by their incipient or real madness) and asks "How did I get here?" For Lupino's characters are always on the verge of a breakdown, not of their ability to relate to others but to be congruent with the world. Their passivity is a force, an autistic integrity, hypnotically powerful in its absolute resistance to time and becoming.

Thus Sally's final instinctive headlong flight—Drew in painful pursuit along an improvised yet pitiless steeplechase, up endless flights of concrete steps, over railroad trestles, overpasses, bridges (the cruelest possible course for a one-legged man)—compresses, with extraordinary physical immediacy, the cumulative pain, desperation, and striving of the entire film into ten unrelenting minutes. When Drew finally falls forward, unable to go on, impotently pounding his fists against the slats of the wooden bridge, Sally stops running, her resistance powerless against his need, his aloneness.

The very specific topography traversed, not created, by the chase, the constant sense of a cityscape designed for quite other purposes (the gracious wide parklike steps, on the one hand, and the little-traversed footbridges and industrialized railroad yards, on the other), the exciting levels of dissonance and congruity a geographic sense of location-shooting creates with its preexistent labyrinth of possibilities (Sally's darting split-second seizing of every geographic opportunity, her whole-body plunge toward the railing, suicide less a desire than the only available route of escape) were explored by low-budget American films long before the New Wave "discovered" Paris. Lupino's almost "documentary" sense of locale, from city streets to the workings of a home for unwed mothers, and the intense emotional investment of the characters playing out their drama largely unaware of the world around them, creates a very special tension. It is the extent to which her character's consciousness fills the screen, but not the world, that allies her to Samuel Fuller, Nicholas Ray, Robert Aldrich and the modernist fifties films in general in their putting into question the subjective heroic consciousness structures of traditional Hollywood film.

Lupino's second film, *Never Fear,* is about an active, creative woman forced into a new, mutilated form of womanhood. The opening scenes spotlight a series of celebrations, as the personal and professional engagements of Carol (Sally Forrest again) and her partner/choreographer/fiancé, Guy (Keefe Brasselle again) are alike launched by the success of a sinuous provocative fencing number, enacting both within the mime narrative of the dance and in its flawless execution the vibrant responsiveness of Carol's body, her shaping of space, and symbolic mastery of danger, while the choreographed willing post-victory surrender of her emblematic heart, body and sword to her partner/rival, evokes the couple's remarkably well balanced personal and professional duality, their equalized interdependence.

Polio not only destroys Carol's career, it also destroys that equilibrium. The camera dollies in and holds on Guy, working on a new routine at the piano, offhandedly throwing enthusiastic remarks over his shoulder, only to unexpectedly cut to Carol behind him, literally hanging on the ropes of the stage in slowly dawning awareness of her illness, exploring the silent disaster, the invisible process of change within her. The inwardness of Carol's experience is intensified by a few out-of-focus, sound-distorted point-of-view shots of Guy at the piano, supremely unconscious of what is happening behind him.

Never Fear fully explores one of the most fascinating aspects of Lupino's films:

the interaction of a claustrophobic "woman's picture" emotionalism and a full-frame documentary realism (complete with extensively researched detail, nonprofessional actors and, in many instances, true stories), creating a kind of two-level space of alternating, shifting focus, neither pole of which subsumes the other. A wheelchair, square dance date, uneasy mirror of Carol's past partnership with Guy, is an excellent case in point.

Unlike the paraplegic basketball game in *The Men,* billboarding Bravery, Pathos, and the Indomitable Human Spirit, the square dance, with its authentic cowboy band and unstudied motley group of onlookers, rolls on with down-home, low-key matter-of-factness. In the coordination of the chrome-flashing wheelchairs and the shifting, patterned formations of the couples, the hero-centered inserts (the flustered tangle of Carol's machine with her partner's, her flushed, eager face) appear as colorful details in the long-shot fresco of the dance—until Carol looks up to see Guy standing against a giant-gardenia-papered wall holding a gardenia (signature throughout of his constancy), like some dream-doubled specter of her past life.

If most of the men in *Never Fear* are constantly supportive, "doctor" types whose positivistic therapeutic demands "cure" Carol, the women are linked by a mute, compassionate solidarity condemned to immanence, to incompleteness: a fellow patient's (Rita Lupino) silent concern over and concentration on Carol are confined to the frame-lines and borders of the main action for several scenes, to create a tension and resistance of what cannot come center-screen, promising more than her unwitting, example-setting, post-polio marriage. Women seem to help each other by accident or to their own detriment, not out of lack of generosity but because, not possessing their own lives, they have no funds to cover their largesse.

For in many ways, *Never Fear* is about "being a woman" or, more precisely, about the difficulty of accepting a dependent, truncated version of womanhood disturbingly close to its most traditional limited social definition. The film arouses very ambivalent feelings in a contemporary audience, feelings not unrepresented on screen (the opening caption proclaiming that this is a true story arouses heroic expectations—Carol will again become a dancer, found a school for legless acrobats, do *something*—that are never resolved or, in fact, denied). On the one hand, Carol's adjustment is treated much as a man's would be—"being a man" or "being a woman" is a question of guts through compromise with an unalterable situation. Yet, on the other hand, "being a man" and "being a woman" imply two quite dissimilar things, as strongly evinced by the fact that no future beyond Guy is sought or projected—Carol is able to salvage her personality but not her life.

Afraid and uncertain of her ability to "go it alone," distrustful now of her body and her will, her faltering rail-aided steps are voice-overed by a mixed track of pep talks by her coaxing by-her-side doctor and by memory-echoed reprises of first her father then Guy crying out their need for her, until she lifts her hands and lo she walks. The schizophrenia implicit in the sound/image split underscores the alienation latent in her recreated "autonomy." For Carol has realized through her dancing a synthesis of self-for-self and self-for-others, of potential and realization, quite unique in a Lupino film and quite unlike the constant need for male affirmation qua self-will that defines her "womanhood" by the end.

Never Fear is Lupino's most specifically autobiographical film (she had polio early in her career). But, like all Lupino's films, it is a road-not-taken autobiography, the story of a dancer who *couldn't* become a choreographer (read actress who couldn't become a director). Lupino has said that she wanted to make films about bewildered lost people—men and women—and she has perfectly understood the experience of passivity and the social forces that maintain and exploit it. Yet Lupino, as a woman who has gone very far beyond that stage in her own life (after years of undifferentiated parts as bleached-blond ingenues in countless Paramount flicks, Lupino moved heaven and earth to get her all-important role in *The Light That Failed* and never let go after that), is of necessity in a privileged position that makes her experience and destiny inapplicable to the situation of her characters.

Lupino's attitude toward her characters is not without a quietly understated, almost maternal, concern, not unrelated to her own complicity as director: to describe victims one must create their victimization and, ultimately, designate its source. In closing off to her characters the options she herself enjoys (and has fought for), Lupino finds herself in a very equivocal position; a liberal bind, it is both the strength and weakness of her films never to completely avoid or resolve. Lupino's third film, *The Outrage,* is an extremely curious one in the extent to which victimization by society in general and by men in particular is viewed alternately through a paranoia and a benevolence *both* of which are excessive, neither of which is quite real, the world vacillating between nightmare and dream.

A young girl, working overtime at a factory, locks up and starts for home. In the foreground, unseen by her, a man closes up a coffee stand. In the lonely silence of the empty city streets, both girl and man are caught up in the inexorable cross-cut logic of the chase. She is running now; darting into an alley, she pounds frantically on the metal sides of a barrack-shaped building. No one hears—except the man, drawn on by the sounds of her passage. For always, at each stopping place in her flight, the camera cuts back to an earlier stopping place, now occupied by the man, the twice-told topography, as through some dream-distorted memory-trace, laid out with the irrevocable clarity of a Walshian encounter with destiny. This destiny is neither of character nor of nightmare; no moral, psychological, or social determinism structures this experiential time and space. The rapist-to-be is no icky Behaviorist specimen of pathological violence loosed on an unsuspecting public, nor a lurking Expressionistic menace at one with the sexual darkness but just a background figure led by impulse and circumstance into a major role in an event he only half wills or understands.

In the closed-off maze of a truck yard, however, the event takes on a new configuration. The follow-the-leader chase, with its curious balance of active and passive (he precipitating the action she is impelled by, she carving out the time and space through which he must pass), resolves itself into a cat-and-mouse waiting game, the predator roaming free somewhere outside the fragile frame-lines, the prey huddled against the large, uncertain truck shapes until, breaking cover, she trips and falls onto a loading platform. As he advances out of the shadows toward her, the camera pulls up and away from the two figures soon lost to sight, pausing on the other side of an adjacent building where a man at an upstairs window peers out and, seeing nothing, closes the window on the rape scene of *The Outrage.*

Like *Never Fear, The Outrage* opens in celebration. Ann (Mala Powers) has a fiancé, the news of whose raise assures Ann's happy integration into the values and life-style of her community, her future cast in a familiar and familial mold: the announcement of the engagement at the office amidst effusive ring-admiring enthuiasm, the family dinner after which the fiancé must ask the unwilling father's consent, the mother's serene shepherding of the intended into the fold.

The rape perverts all this, radically and overnight. The slow ascending withdrawal of the camera from the actual rape not only places the event in the larger context of the unheeding city, it also locates it in the recesses of Ann's psyche. For Ann, the rape registers less as a specific shocking incident than as an irreversible sea-change, transmuting the familiar into the unknown, relegating her experience to a time and space that cannot connect up (even the rape's immediate sequel, Ann's stumbling walk home, is symptomatically dislocated, appearing out of sequence under the opening credits).

If the world has altered in Ann's eyes, she too has altered in the eyes of the world. When Ann finally ventures out of her parents' house, everything conspires to banish her to the other dimension of her trauma. In this very suburban backdrop, with its neat parceled squares of lawn, its flagged mailboxes, two gossiping neighbors break ranks and re-form as Ann advances warily, the streets a uniform patterned surface that parts to let her, the alien, pass. Reactions to Ann, from a busmate's fussy overprotectiveness to an office worker's heavy sympathizing hand on her shoulder, quiver with a funereal, almost squeamish unease, particularly on the part of the men, the women being more blankly curious or openly empathetic.

For the rape produces an instant male/female polarization—Ann's father and a detective pace downstairs, bent on action, while upstairs Ann's mother and a note-taking policewoman huddle around her bed. The men all feel vaguely implicated in the rape. The genteel solicitude of the small-scale professional classes (Ann's father is a teacher, Ann a bookkeeper) is at the price of a kind of bloodlessness, a cutting off from the more "brutal" facts of life, a nice ordered corner blitzed by this undomesticated intrusion of raw sexuality (as opposed quite specifically to the Sunday-best engagement rituals). Rape opens up the whole carefully wrapped sexual can of worms. In this threatened atmosphere, guilt veers from man (Ann's father: "They look at me as if *I* had done something") to woman (Ann as damaged goods). The foundations of both the nuclear family and the community are shaken by this maelstrom that has risen from its center—Ann's father and the police captain bound in a helpless, embarrassed intimacy, glancing insecurely at the bridallike confirmation photo of Ann, as they discover with simultaneous shock the sexual otherness of Ann and the sexual otherness of the rapist, their mitigated innocent/guilty relationship to both.

The police lineup procedure doubles the situation. Setting up a two-way paranoia (what others see in Ann; what Ann sees in others), it compels her to regard a whole series of men as potential rapists. The system works on one level to exonerate all other men by isolating the guilty one, though this is obvious only in the opposite effect it has—to implicate *all* masculine faces, including the policeman's and her fiancé's, in an insistent rhythmic montage of impossible demand.

The second half of *The Outrage* presents a violent contrast to the first, anticipating Nicholas Ray's *On Dangerous Ground* (in which Lupino starred and a few scenes of which she directed) in its radical city/country split. Ann boards a bus leaving the city, winding up in a pastoral farmland, where she is picked up unconscious on the wayside by the young local minister (Tod Andrews) and taken to a couple's home, accepting a job crating fruit in their factory. To the fragmented, highly compartmentalized collage of the city is opposed an organic panorama where nothing seems separate— all the locations in the rural valley into which Ann wanders seem extensions of each other—even the house where Ann lives and the factory where she works are joined. The menacing city glances, which at best polarize and alienate, at worst sexually violate, are here defused, defetishized.

The pipe-smoking minister, Doc, is the medium of this defusing. He begins to act as Ann's intercessor and shock absorber. As Ann increasingly gives herself over to him, becomes *his* problem, he functions, if not as hero, then as camera and action subject of the frame, with Ann its questioned object. The routine arrival of a sheriff causes a barely contained panic in Ann, but instead of cross-cutting between the ominous cop figure and the terrified Ann, all is encompassed in the back-and-forth of the minister's questioning, ruminative gaze.

The one time Ann does turn her gaze toward the community, during an outdoor picnic and dance, it sets off a complex and nearly murderous chain reaction. Ann, reluctantly moving away from Doc, goes toward the dance platform, the camera in a beautiful onward-flowing movement gliding among the slowly turning dancers while Ann, drawn to yet fearful of involvement, skirts the periphery. A country Romeo approaches her from an off-space, which has been identified with Doc as the other pole in a series of reaction shots, and playfully but insistently presses her for a kiss, until, confusing him with the rapist, Ann clobbers him with a wrench. Although it is the man's physical insistence that flashes Ann back to the rape, it is his naming of the desired, feared, and repressed sexual relationship between her and Doc ("No wonder Bruce Ferguson's been keeping you all to himself," Doc's full name deemphasizing his ministerial function) that triggers and further displaces an already multiply displaced sexuality.

For Doc's glance, witness to a mute struggle between "earthly" and "heavenly" love, effects a reversal, both of the lustful stare of the unseen rapist behind his coffee stand and of the queasy malaise-filled paternalism of the postrape reactions to Ann. By placing that malaise in a minister (in whom sexuality is itself problematic), Lupino shifts the center of sexual questioning from woman to man, through whom the drama of sublimation must be played. In many ways the second part of *The Outrage* seems flat and unsatisfying, particularly after the nonstop dramatic reversals and tremendous emotional energy of the first part. This is especially true of the formal hearings that anticlimax Ann's assault, where a juiceless, deadpan army of judges, prosecutors, doctors, and psychiatrists, nudged to justice by Doc's impassioned pleas, officially absolve Ann, and by that process, society itself of sexual guilt and bus her off to the further therapeutic ministrations of family, fiancé, and shrink.

The finally unresolved sexual and social tensions within *The Outrage* reflect perhaps equally Lupino's own uncertainties about male/female sexual identity and her variously empathetic, exploitative, and benevolent function as film maker. Through Ann's subjectivity is experienced the disconnection, alienation, and sexual victimization Lupino recreates, one must suppose, out of some past or present potential or realized self; through the self-repressed "objectivity" of Doc is represented the compassionate, half-impotent desire of a more distanced, mature self to respond to the terrible vulnerability and need of that other who Lupino both is and creates in the androgenous zone of the woman director.

The partial shift in center from Ann to Doc prefigures a gradual focus change in Lupino's films, a multiple, alternating point of view which, although structured around one character, nevertheless separates and localizes the social and familial forces that shape, develop, or limit his consciousness. In *Hard, Fast and Beautiful,* Florence (Sally Forrest), far from breaking with her family, embodies all its contradictions, fluctuating between the two conflicting role models of mother Claire Trevor and father Kenneth Patterson.

It is the mother who seems to hold the reins of Florence's life (e.g., the startling opening image of Trevor's scissors-wielding hands cutting the dummy-draped fabric of Florence's dress). Since her single-minded drive from poverty up the social ladder has fallen far short of acceptable goals, she has withdrawn all hopes from her nice-guy husband and centered them upon Florence. But in that transfer from husband to daughter, the vicarious (living through her daughter) and the exploitative (riding on her coattails) have become strangely mixed. Trevor's identity-confusion is at the heart of *Hard, Fast and Beautiful,* an alienation and near schizophrenia which, although manifested through ruthlessness, hypocrisy, and dedicated to the shallowest social aspirations, nevertheless renders her as much victim as victimizer.

Florence, however, is serenely unaware of her mother's ambition. Indeed Florence, thanks to her protective middle-class upbringing, is serenely unaware of just about everything around her—including the failure of her beloved parents' marriage. Her father, an understanding man with a healthy dose of ironic distance, still is wistfully in love with his ambitious, dissatisfied wife. Their bedroom is an encampment with lines firmly drawn, the single beds back-to-back forming a double barrier, insuring total isolation. Yet Florence moves through this polarized space understanding nothing—as unworldlywise as an eighteenth-century demoiselle fresh from the convent.

As it happens, social mobility comes to Florence not through "marrying rich" but through her tennis—elevating her to the country club, Forest Hills, and beyond. The family battle lines then extend to the living room, where the arrival of a fourth party, herald of a new stage in Florence's career, touches off a series of chess moves: Claire Trevor maneuvering herself into a commanding position on the soon-to-be-launched bandwagon, drawing the country club chairman into her corner, her husband brought in only for the polite wrap-up of negotiations in his patently titular role as head of the family.

Yet her father's passivity is ultimately more powerful than her mother's active manipulation. Although Florence is pushed along by her mother, it is continually stressed—through cross-cutting from the tennis finals to her father at home, stretched out on a couch or gravely ill in a hospital bed (his absence from the game exerting a magnetic pull through possible death)—that she plays tennis for her father, and all her will and energy are in her tennis. The quiet intimacy shared by father and daughter in brief early scenes constitutes by far the deepest emotional bond in the movie. Her father's undemanding support and back-off empathy are not entirely beneficial, however. His abdication of power within the family leaves Florence at her mother's tender mercy, and his overprotectiveness in shielding her from the reality of her situation leaves her unable to make conscious choices.

At the center of these conflicting loves, these spoken or unspoken demands, is Florence. Her concerted energy dominates the brilliantly edited tennis sequences, so that the cross-cut convergence of the hopes of others can but hang suspended on her forceful drives and hard-line serves. From the introductory scene of Florence determinedly thwacking practice balls at the numbered squares painted on the garage door to the grandstand finals, the film contrasts her coordinated meshing of will and action on the tennis court to her total inability to relate to the world outside, which she perceives as an unproblematic, supportive whole (all those around her concurring, through misguided love or calculation, to make it appear so).

In Fletcher Locke, her mother's somewhat sinister cohort in economic and perhaps sexual crime, Florence sees only her tennis coach. She accepts fifty dollars to make a rich kid look good and cannot understand her fiancé's disgust, any more than she can grasp his later refusal of a proferred token job which would allow him to trail along on Florence's tour-cum-honeymoon in nepotistic splendor. For she honestly has no conception of social or economic reality (being, significantly, the only Lupino heroine who does not work for a living). It takes her most of the tour to discover (via a pricetag on her dress) that Fletcher and her mother have exploited her amateur standing for large sums of money.

As the conflicting demands and contradictory meanings placed upon her tennis become more polarized (between her mother's waxing enthusiasm for greater and greater glory and her fiancé's waning indulgence for her last premarital fling), Florence begins to feel a pressure that visually overlays the built-in tensions of the tennis matches. For the tennis matches are not merely pretexts, semidocumentary recreations or loose fields of victory and defeat but rich, many-stranded, intensely dramatic events. The immediate consequences of each move, variously recorded by the linesman's call, the cheering or *ohb*ing spectators, the announcer's appreciative running commentary (carried via radio to her convalescent father), her mother's and Fletcher's lip-chewing reactions in the stands, both enlarge and constrict the field of play, converging in the high-angled shots of Florence energized and trapped by the narrow rectangular confines of the court, everything and nothing endlessly at stake.

Hard, Fast and Beautiful closes not on Florence but on mother Claire Trevor, abandoned by all on a wind-swept tennis court at night—for, in many ways, Sally Forrest and Claire Trevor portray two aspects of the same woman. Separated by profound generational and class differences, their complementary incompleteness both mirrors and analyzes the good/bad, rich/poor, blond/brunette oppositional pairs of traditional Hollywood film, the either/or absolutism of these pairings coming not from any inherent incompatability of "opposites" but from socially imposed feminine role models. For Florence to live happily-married-ever-after, she must renounce Claire Trevor and all she represents, including tennis.

Lupino affords a glimpse of what a synthesis of mother and daughter might be during the tour, the one and only time Florence takes control over her own life—when her eyes are finally opened to her exploitation. Despite the brittle cynicism of the mother-mocking role she then assumes, Florence is truly magnificent, playing her mother's game but for herself and by herself, with an assurance, decisiveness, and depth quite beyond the latter. She contemptuously flings a cheap tennis racket bearing her endorsement into the fire, denouncing the con with newborn social consciousness. She roundly tells Fletcher off, a long delayed consummation devoutly wished. She leaves Forest Hills the day before the finals to fly to her sick father in California and returns to battle fatigue and a hard-hitting younger opponent to win.

This Florence, a logical and inspired extension of the girl on the tennis court, by far the most vital and exciting woman in the movie, appears only to be repressed, to disappear into her hubby-happy-ending, as Ann in *The Outrage* disappeared into her problem—both fade into the unsketched greyness of social integration.

Hard, Fast and Beautiful is pivotal, midpoint between Lupino's more subjectively charged, single-focus early films and the colder, more detatched, multiple-viewpoint late films. Her films move away from subjectivity and also from women and adolescence—but never from passivity and its curious coloration, its dreamwalking, eternal present. But a young girl's passivity and a middle-aged man's are two very different states. In Edmond O'Brien, the perpetually pressured everyman of the fifties, Lupino found the embodiment of another kind of passivity—helpless entrapment between two irreconcilable modes of action.

The Hitch-Hiker, considered by many, including Lupino herself, to be her best film, is a classic, tension-packed tour-de-force thriller about two men (O'Brien and Frank Lovejoy) vacationing in Mexico on a long-awaited fishing trip, whose car and lives are suddenly and irreparably commandeered by a one-eyed psychopathic killer

(William Talman). The technical brilliance Lupino displays in all her films seems to have been more visible to critics when no longer in the service of her own very original, disorientingly "odd" perspective but placed within the familiar framework of a suspense actioner. Among the elements hard at work: the striking compositions (two blanketed figures, like shrouded corpses, separated by a narrow stream from a gun-cradling madman whose eye cannot close even in sleep); the on-pulse kinetic editing (the alternation of dramatically linear action with frozen, impossibly nervous waiting-time); the spatial integrity of a determined and determining sense of locale (the pitiless topography of a rock-bound, horizonless Mexico over which hovers an ever-present death); and the full utilization of contrasts between day and night, inside and outside (the night's saturation and day's terrible clarity, the friction felt among the three men in their fixed car positions and the even more fearful range of possibilities outside the car).

The precarious security of the petite bourgeoisie shattered by the dark sexual forces of the lower classes, hinted at in *The Outrage,* surfaces fully here—the focus less on a paranoid portrayal of tic-laden brutality than on the impact of that brutality. One of the fascinations of *The Hitch-Hiker* is its subtle, class-related differentiation of the two men's reaction to imposed passivity. Lovejoy, a skilled, precision white-collar worker (a draftsman), used to working to others' specifications, endures patiently Talman's sadistic needling and jumpy hair-trigger precautionary rituals barked out at each move, carefully awaiting his chance, following the laws of dependent social survival: "As long as he needs us we're safe. When he tries to get us we'll get him." O'Brien, a mechanic who owns his own garage and controls his own labor, goes almost mad under submission to another's absolute power. His need for direct, immediate action is continually thwarted by Lovejoy's phlegmatic practicality. O'Brien breaks down toward the end, crying hysterically, almost "womanish" under the strain of a passive role, caught between the compromising caution of the petite bourgeoisie and the petty vengeance of the dispossessed.

The Bigamist finds "middleman" O'Brien caught between two complementary spouses: Joan Fontaine, sterile wife of eight years, who compensates for her childlessness by managing her husband's business (selling freezers); and Ida Lupino, a lonely woman whom he meets, has a child by, and marries. As in *Hard, Fast and Beautiful,* the two-women dichotomy is firmly rooted in class. Fontaine, a "lady" from an upper-crust, patrician family, reverently attached to her dying pater and all he represents, obviously never worked before her marriage; Lupino, on the other hand, is a working woman from way back, waitressing in a joke Chinese restaurant and wryly enjoying the joke. Fontaine moves in multiroom, large, open, light-filled spaces; Lupino in much smaller, darkly intimate, somewhat shabby surroundings (Lupino reputedly used two different cameramen for the two different women).

If Lupino's films seem decidedly nonfeminist (*The Bigamist* provides a classic example, with Fontaine's career as alienating substitute for a more "natural" desire for children), they are far less endorsements of the status quo than thoroughgoing analyses of it. It's fine to applaud Dorothy Arzner for showing a daring young aviatrix in *Christopher Strong,* but it would help if Katharine Hepburn didn't waltz around palatial sitting rooms in a gold lamé art deco outfit complete with antennae. Arzner's feminism, with its run-of-De-Mille class-consciousness, strangely allies itself with the very forms, both filmic and societal, responsible for women's oppression. Lupino's Fontaine character may be an unfashionable version of the "career woman," but it's swell as a demystification of the whole class-based concept of careerism, distinguishing between independence and economic self-sufficiency—of the two women, the Lupino character is obviously better equipped to "go it alone."

But despite the definite interest in the two spouses, *The Bigamist* is no more "about" two women than *Daisy Kenyon* is "about" two men. It is O'Brien's indecision that dominates the film, the two women representing his former driving, future-oriented ambition versus the relaxed, unassuming, take-it-as-it-comes intimacy that tempts him in middle-age. What is extraordinary in *The Bigamist,* as in all Lupino's films, is the depiction of passivity as a process of consciousness. O'Brien's position is one of total clarity in terms of his feelings for the two women but of utter befuddlement as to how to reconcile the largely incompatible actions requisite in each case (except by complicated, disaster-risking juggling acts). He watches as from a distance his own dysfunctionality, dazzled by a kind of wonderment—it is the bigamist's deepening awareness of the complexities, values, ironies, and contradictions inherent in his situation, the literal coexistence of so many possible yet impossible alternatives, that the film traces.

Yet what one misses, less in the claustrophobic self-definition of *The Hitch-Hiker* than in the polarized see-saw of *The Bigamist,* is the unique excitement generated by the passage of a strong existential subjectivity, like some vacuum-powered negative force field of resistance, through a clearly delineated social structure that totters, shifts, and reforms in its wake. There are, of course, some brilliant scenes in *The Bigamist:* O'Brien's almost-failed pick-up of Lupino on a see-the-homes-of-the-stars tour bus; his clumsy attempts to use the driver's patter as conversation-starters thudding with consummate awkwardness in the silent irony of Lupino's self-contained gestures and precise comebacks until, won over by his very ineptness, she finally relents; Joan Fontaine's building fear and disorientation at O'Brien's hurried departure on his way to a self-inflicted arrest, as she runs from elevator to the wide-flung window, vertiginously unable to decipher the small figures below, the phone then ringing beside that window as if on cue to inform her of what happened, the diaphanous curtain flapping like a demented spirit behind her.

After a thirteen-year hiatus spent directing television shows, Lupino returned to features with *The Trouble With Angels* for Columbia. Beneath its somewhat unfetching-seeming subject matter—nuns—*Angels* is a study of sexual awakening. The film ends with convent-rebel Hayley Mills's "miraculous" conversion to the sisterhood. But the obsessional fascination that arch-rival Rosalind Russell exerts over Mills has little to do with the vocational calling to which it is officially ascribed. And the deep sense of betrayal that Mills's partner-in-rebellion feels at her capitulation has little to do with childhood friendship pacts. Few films have so unproblematically and unsensationally depicted love between women as a natural stage in a woman's life or confounded physical and metaphysical so completely. Hayley Mills watches in the chapel, sexual and religious curiosity comingled, as Rosalind Russell collapses on the coffin of a dead Sister, the slow arcing descent of the camera at once transcendent and painfully earthbound.

Unfortunately, few films have had so innocuous a frame (the two girls' pubescent prankishness versus Russell's Mother-Superior-knows-best profundity), Lupino having been granted far too little control over this assignment to escape its inflexible wah-wah setups. It is not the least of *Angels'* accomplishments that the all-but-moated isolation of the castle-cum-convent simultaneously reflects the cloistered recesses of Mills's self-absorption, the womb-space of woman's sequestration, and the anachronistic gargoyle-gated glories of the big Hollywood studio (the hothouse artificiality of an expensive, everything-in-its-place Hollywood location: 6 swans a-swimming, 5 pools reflecting, 4 nuns a-praying, and a sparrow atop Saint Francis).

The garishly colored odds and ends the two girls bring back, magpielike, from the outside summer-vacation world cannot compete with the cool blue and rich brown closed-off homogeneity of the convent, eons away from the black-and-white city streets of Lupino's Filmmakers work. And the brightly chatting schoolgirls who will go on to their rounds of bridge parties or live, perpetual virgins, in the confines of a cloister, seem but distant relations of the destitute sleepwalkers who wandered those streets.

---

34. Joseph L. Mankiewicz (1909)

by ERIC SHERMAN

1946—*Dragonwyck; Somewhere in the Night;* 1947—*The Late George Apley; The Ghost and Mrs. Muir;* 1948—*Escape;* 1949—*A Letter to Three Wives; House of Strangers;* 1950—*No Way Out; All About Eve;* 1951—*People Will Talk;* 1952—*Five Fingers;* 1953—*Julius Caesar;* 1954—*The Barefoot Contessa;* 1955—*Guys and Dolls;* 1958—*The Quiet American;* 1960—*Suddenly Last Summer;* 1963—*Cleopatra* (uncredited codirector: Rouben Mamoulian); 1967—*The Honey Pot;* 1970—*King: A Filmed Record . . . Montgomery to Memphis* (documentary), codirector: Sidney Lumet; *There Was a Crooked Man;* 1972—*Sleuth*

Television Movie
1964—*Carol for Another Christmas*

Joseph L. Mankiewicz has said that writing and directing are but different phases of the one process: film making. For him, a well-written script already has been directed. The screenwriter has not only created setting, event, character, and dialogue but has visualized how all these elements interrelate. Were a separate person to come along and direct a completed script, he would actually be "redirecting" it, thus setting up a possible tension (creative or destructive) between himself and the material. So, for Mankiewicz, it was necessary to become a director to insure that the process he had begun with his writing would be followed through, protected, and perhaps even enhanced during its actualization into a motion picture. Mankiewicz also has spoken of his awareness that editing, too, is a crucial step, and he has tried to stay on his productions through their completion.

Within this attempt to exert as much control as possible over his material, Mankiewicz also is something of a realist. Prior to being allowed to direct, he wrote extensively for others, and produced numerous projects in which he had no deep personal interest. During this time, he was introduced to all the rigors of Hollywood film making and certainly was made aware of all areas of potential compromise. Thus, when he did finally reach the exalted position, he chose, for his first few projects, scripts he hadn't written! Perhaps he sensed that if he had to worry about material that was too personal or deep-rooted, then he wouldn't be able to pay enough attention to the craft of daily film making. Once he was satisfied, however, with his ease at handling all the different on-set elements, he wanted only to create and realize his own material.

His need to be responsible for his work was not a function of ego or tyrannical personality. He quietly whispered stage directions to his actors, never yelling in front of a crew. He assiduously stayed out of sight during a take so as not to distract an actor or make one feel that he was playing "for the director." He consciously kept his camera work as unobtrusive as possible so as not to draw attention to any one aspect of the work at the expense of another. When awards and personal publicity came around, he remained as low-key as possible (with the grand irony being that he is the only one ever to win two consecutive sets of Academy Awards for writing and directing). When one thinks of Mankiewicz films, words like intelligence, sophistication, and wit come to mind. He applies these qualities to subjects that reverberate into all areas of storytelling. His dramas are not without comedy (*The Ghost and Mrs. Muir, A Letter to Three Wives*); his comedies are not without seriousness (*People Will Talk, Guys and Dolls, The Honey Pot*); his melodramas evoke tremendous darkness and violence (*Somewhere in the Night, House of Strangers, No Way Out*) as well as social concerns. This notwithstanding, he never is didactic. He has said, "Don't ask an audience to think or try to get them to think. Make them think."

The presence of real thought—which is to say, not only ideas but speculative processes—is one of the most notable elements of Mankiewicz scripts. It is important to stress, though, that the intellectual integrity and seriousness of his work is not pedantic and is not expressed simply through having erudite characters utter educated lines. Though Mankiewicz himself was trained in literature, he is well aware of the differences between novelization and visualization; between cerebral function and imaginative pictorialization. He strives for an intellectual depth, what he calls the "deep truth" in his material, but this is never at the expense of creative freedom.

These disclaimers notwithstanding, some have found Mankiewicz's films *too* literate or *too* talky. In general, before any criticism can be accepted as valid, one must locate the area a potential work of art sets up as its domain of concern. These parameters established, one then may determine to what extent a work succeeds or falls short in any of its modes. A film is "too talky" not as measured by the number of words spoken but only if something that could or should have a visual correlative is left open to the floundering support of dialogue. Likewise, a film might not be talky enough if a simple communication is translated into a massively obtrusive camera move or angle or if such a move or angle calls for an absent aural correlative.

Mankiewicz's work resides in the area known as *films théâtraux,* films whose effects depend on theatrical artifice. That is, given the kinds of characters and settings he creates, they *must* talk a certain way at a certain length in order to be true to themselves. If this mode of dialogue is more literate or extended than common street talk, what does it matter? Even when the characters are street denizens (*No Way Out*), the Mankiewicz world they occupy has an entirely different set of boundaries than the daily arena.

For Mankiewicz, *films théâtraux* are to be distinguished from a more obviously visual mode such as what's commonly called "avant-garde" or "experimental" cinema. For one thing, *films théâtraux* must rely on sound as an equally important determinant of their emotional and intellectual impact. Since sound is a sense available to most people, and since sound has all sorts of connotative as well as direct links to sight, it is the duty of the film maker working in such a mode to pay as much attention to the aural as the visual. Such attention would begin, in the traditional linear dramatic narrative form, at the script stage, and this is why, no doubt, Mankiewicz looks at script writing and film directing as inseparable creative moments. Thus, when his characters speak in a manner usually reserved for "legitimate" theater, Mankiewicz is not so much being uncinematic as he is pushing beyond certain accepted limitations regarding the literacy of screen leading personages. For this reason, Mankiewicz has expressed a preference for working with "intelligent" actors over and above the icons and mere presences so abundant in modern feature films.

If all we could say about Mankiewicz's work is that his scripts were polished and his actors spoke eloquently, then we would be commenting perhaps on his seriousness of purpose and his approach to role playing. What is most important in determining his ultimate value as a film maker is discovering precisely what, if any, are the correlations between these thematic regions and his visual style.

To begin with, an examination of the subject matter of his films indicates a preoccupation at one level with elements of the human social structure: class differences (*No Way Out, House of Strangers, Suddenly Last Summer, Sleuth*); surface appearances (*Dragonwyck, A Letter to Three Wives, Five Fingers, The Late George Apley*); obsession with wealth (*The Honey Pot*) and age (*All About Eve, Suddenly Last Summer*); commercialization (*A Letter to Three Wives, The Honey Pot*); elegance and style (*All About Eve, Guys and Dolls, Sleuth*). Such concerns can be treated in one of three ways—support of them as necessary evils or goods in a world made up of people; exposure of them as destructive, degrading, or false values; or neutral observation of them from a disinterested stance. Mankiewicz is closer to the latter two positions, with an emphasis most recently on the last. For all the havoc wreaked in people's lives (within the story) by Eve's aggressiveness (*All About Eve*), there is a love for and fascination with such machinations. For all the posturings and illusions described and perpetrated in *A Letter to Three Wives*, there is a generalized sympathy for everyone. Mankiewicz sees his characters not only as constituting those forces but as being constituted by them. To the extent that they attain awareness, they can neutralize the effects of the disruptive forces. However, most often the forces lead to an explosion that is not altogether cathartic but *is* necessary.

It has been suggested that Mankiewicz' films as a group may be seen as tales about the moral weaknesses that motivate conduct. If this is an accurate analysis, then *all* the forces listed above would have to be seen as derived from something inherent in human life itself. It has been suggested that a clue to the thrust of Mankiewicz's oeuvre is to concentrate not so much on the specifics of his characters' drives and hopes but on the idea that all such elements are on a footing when they are engulfed in the actual spaces (film frames) in which the people and their surrounding objects dwell.

Mankiewicz has said that illusions rule the world, and every point of view, thus, is false. Here we have the real power behind Mankiewicz's films—and the reason that they are not mere extensions of visualized theater but works of art in their own right. Mankiewicz sees all entities in a consistent and profound way as being constituted out of and contained within the physical geometry of their environment. This is the case in his films both theatrically and visually. Such a dynamic link, impossible in theater, vivifies all moments and allows Mankiewicz to use sophisticated dialogue and storytelling when it serves his purpose, and to eliminate it when it would cast attention on itself for nonspecific ends.

From his first film, *Dragonwyck,* we sense a concern as much with the creation of a mystical atmosphere as with obsessed and obsessive characters. Mankiewicz's mysticism is not derived from some vague or cloudy view of mansions and dark nights but from a precise and imposing gothic stature lent to all the objects he photographs. The correlations between people's surroundings and their actions are rendered strong and specific by their relative position and placement within the shots. The houses in *Dragonwyck, House of Strangers, The Honey Pot, Sleuth, The Late George Apley,* and *The Ghost and Mrs. Muir* sometimes mock and caricature their inhabitants, sometimes become active participants in the dramas, and sometimes sit back to observe and define the extent of movements within themselves.

The sewer in the *Guys and Dolls* "Luck Be a Lady" scene is not only where the men play their crap game, it is the exact counterpoint to Lindy's delicatessen, the mission, the Cuban café, and the theater dressing room. It simultaneously contains, characterizes, comments upon, and participates with its resident entities. Stubby Kaye's "Sit Down You're Rocking the Boat" number in the mission manifests the perfect self-awareness of how an individual is not only part of a group or movement but part of an altogether larger idea, which is a space, that allows him to be in the first place. Indeed, defining a space as an idea is one of the major consistencies within Mankiewicz's style. The houses in *Dragonwyck, Suddenly Last Summer,* and *Sleuth* make inevitable certain lines of action—and so, Mankiewicz is not really "theatrical" at all, since in the theater it would be impossible (and if it were possible, uninteresting) to show characters totally defined by and subservient to their dwellings. It is the cinematic mode that makes Mankiewicz's connections important and interesting. The "goodbyes, regrets, and disappointments" in which Mankiewicz evidently is interested are made poignant because of their settings within a superstructure.

The theater—the subject and location of much of *All About Eve*—is not a simple metaphor for life (though Mankiewicz's admiration for Shakespeare would at least make that theme predictable). Rather, it is an idea; it is *the way* for his characters. The most theatrical character in *All About Eve* is not Eve (Anne Baxter) or Margo Channing (Bette Davis) but Addison De Witt, the acerbic critic played by George Sanders. And the most theatrical scene is not in the building with that function or in Bette Davis's house or at her parties but in the plain hotel room at the Taft Hotel above the Shubert Theater in New Haven. When De Witt tells off Eve and informs her of the necessary pattern her life will follow, we transcend the world of conscious playacting and enter the realm of absolute equivalence between word, action, thought, and life. Eve tries to run away from De Witt's statements, leaves the frame, and enters . . . the bedroom. De Witt's words are not escapable, however, and he reenters the frame continuing his calling-to-the-fore of the deception Eve has perpetrated. His remarks on the inability to love and contempt for humanity are the climax of the film and render Margo (the true thespian), her life, and her career a world apart from the active viciousness of the Eves. This theater/life duality is cinematically conveyed in one of the most seemingly gratuitous shots in the film. After the Sarah Siddons Award ceremony and all its attendant drama and tension, all the guests leave, Sanders and Baxter being the last. We cut to a silent long shot of the awards room, empty except for tables in the foreground being cleared by waiters and Sanders and Baxter going out the door. The emptiness but strength of this space has contained and predicts for the future the kind of event that will occur there. Characters weave in and out of such areas, but when there, though they act according to their own needs and personalities, the parameters are predetermined.

This is how, effectively, Mankiewicz is so well able to speculate on another of his themes—the interplay and interference between past and present. By imbuing his sets (or locations or defining spaces) with an active role, they reverberate with all that has gone before and presage all that may come. Hence, the spaces containing and objects surrounding the role players themselves are vivified. In *Sleuth*, for example, the puppets and toys are more animated in expression and insightful in posture than are Laurence Olivier and Michael Caine. The former are seemingly in control of themselves (at least they know themselves), while the latter are prey to the forces that have put them there in the first place.

Mankiewicz's interest in the intermingling of past and present is reflected also in his use of flashbacks repeated from several points of view. In addition to observing the different narrative elements added and subtracted by the various characters' retellings, we see subjective lighting, camera placement, and camera moves. This renders all conceptions of an event as equally true—or equally false. Perhaps this is why in a Mankiewicz film when someone gets what he or she wants (*All About Eve, Sleuth, The Honey Pot, There Was a Crooked Man*) that goal is shown to be not only empty but destructive of the energy that had defined the quest for it.

Mankiewicz's films show a complete world—one in which the aural and visual, the thematic and stylistic, are unified in common pursuit: the description of a space where all entities reside on a footing. This footing is subservient to and acts because of a larger containing space. This region of engulfment is profoundly connected to the idea that the whole is greater than the sum of its parts but that we best can reach a sense of the whole by showing its interactions with its constituents.

35. *Vincente Minnelli* (1913)

1943—*Cabin in the Sky; I Dood It* (uncredited codirector: undetermined); 1944—*Meet Me in St. Louis;* 1945—*The Clock* (uncredited codirector: Fred Zinnemann); *Yolanda and the Thief;* 1946— *Ziegfeld Follies* as main director; other directors: George Sidney, Roy Del Ruth, Robert Lewis, Lemuel Ayers; uncredited other directors: Norman Taurog, Merrill Pye; *Undercurrent;* 1948— *The Pirate;* 1949—*Madame Bovary;* 1950—*Father of the Bride;* 1951—*Father's Little Dividend; An American in Paris;* 1953—*The Bad and the Beautiful; The Story of Three Loves,* "Mademoiselle" episode; other director: Gottfried Reinhardt; *The Band Wagon;* 1954—*The Long, Long Trailer; Brigadoon;* 1955—*The Cobweb; Kismet* (uncredited codirector: Stanley Donen); 1956—*Lust for Life; Tea and Sympathy;* 1957—*Designing Woman;* 1958—*Gigi* (uncredited codirector: Charles Walters); *The Reluctant Debutante;* 1959—*Some Came Running;* 1960—*Home From the Hill; Bells Are Ringing;* 1962—*The Four Horsemen of the Apocalypse; Two Weeks in Another Town;* 1963—*The Courtship of Eddie's Father;* 1964—*Goodbye Charlie;* 1965—*The Sandpiper;* 1970—*On a Clear Day You Can See Forever;* 1976—*A Matter of Time*

Uncredited
1942—*Panama Hattie* (Norman Z. McLeod; uncredited codirector: Roy Del Ruth); 1947—*Till the Clouds Roll By* (Richard Whorf; uncredited codirector: George Sidney); 1952—*Lovely to Look At* (Mervyn LeRoy); 1957—*The Seventh Sin* (Ronald Neame)

The quality of esthetic pleasure delivered by so many of Vincente Minnelli's films should secure him a choice position in the personal pantheon of any cinema lover, yet his reputation is currently at a low ebb. While some auteurists idolized him in the fifties and sixties, he has been increasingly taken to task for his "lack of substance," the perennial objection to Minnelli's "mannerism." In 1978 a *Cahiers* critic tersely dismissed him (along with Preminger) as a "typical false auteur." In his 1973 book, *Vincente Minnelli,* Marion Vidal, who obviously holds the director's work in high esteem, nevertheless bends over backward to give as full credit as possible to everybody who ever worked on a Minnelli picture—even at the risk of overemphasizing the collaborative aspect.* An apparently widely shared view was expressed most epigrammatically by Andrew Sarris in the last sentence of his Minnelli entry in *The American Cinema:* "Minnelli believes more in beauty than in art"—which smacks of the puritan disapproval of esthetic enjoyment for its own sake.

True, Minnelli has always been more interested in the look and feel of things than in their meaning, in textures than in substances, in atmospheres than in situations, in moods than in ideas. Although the tenor of his films is often surprisingly reflective for an allegedly "superficial" provider of elegant entertainment, they carry no profound message and lack the kind of strong thematic underpinning commentators can sink their teeth into. Minnelli's attitude is remarkably consistent, but it is an attitude to his material rather than to philosophical, moral, or social issues, a view of his art rather than a world view. Moreover, Minnelli is a notoriously inarticulate person, and his bland statements in interviews are grist for the mill of his detractors. Thus, in the introduction to *The Celluloid Muse,* Charles Higham and Joel Greenberg, after conceding him "a recognizable personal visual style" hasten to add, "but he has nothing to say, and the diffidence with which he discussed his films with us makes this fact entirely clear."

What we have here is a clear and familiar case of the old monster form-without-content rearing its ugly head, and the "serious" critic dutifully hacking at it. However, the claim that a director has "nothing to say" may actually be an admission that the *critic* can't think of much to say about the director's work. Obviously, it is easier to discuss ideas than visual style, no matter how recognizable. Minnelli's and George Cukor's "reluctance to discuss their films in intellectual terms" merely suggests that their films were not conceived in such terms. The point of all this is not to prove that Minnelli is one of the towering geniuses in film history, which he certainly is not; but, just as certainly, the reason for his comparatively minor stature is not his lack of a "deeply held outlook on life." As a matter of fact, it could be argued (and it has) that Minnelli does have his own recognizable world view. However, that world view is not the source of the pleasure we derive from his films; and, again, pleasure is the major, if not the sole justification for his cinema. Pleasure, unfortunately, has a

---

* The cog-in-the-machinery view of the Hollywood director, one that prevailed for decades and was first seriously challenged by auteurism, has been enjoying a new lease on life, as far as Minnelli is concerned, as a result of the publication of Hugh Fordin's *That's Entertainment!* and Donald Knox's *The Magic Factory,* whose implicit thesis, at least as far as the latter is concerned, is that the great MGM musicals were made by everybody and nobody in particular and that the director did little more than be around and vaguely coordinate the efforts of dozens of people. Minnelli himself sees it differently in his autobiography *I Remember It Well* (1974). Although he writes—less out of modesty, perhaps, than in typical old-Hollywood distrust of intellectualism— "I'd never presume, God knows, to use the word 'Minnellian' to describe anything I've done," he also strongly challenges the studio-as-auteur theory and insists that, in the making of *An American in Paris,* "Though I don't minimize anyone's contribution, one man was responsible for bringing it all together. That man was me."

perverse tendency to defy analysis, but that is no reason for critics to write as though there were no such thing.

What is unique about Minnelli's style is the acute sensitiveness that permeates all his films. His material has seldom been so adverse as to stifle self-expression, and the restless soul that hides behind the mask of elegance comes through in even the most unexpected contexts. While Minnelli was the last of the contract directors (he made all but three of his films for MGM), he was by no means a studio hack, and, unless one takes an unreasonably radical view of the American film business at the time, never behaved as the "slave" François Truffaut scornfully accused him of being. He may have worked on assignment throughout his career, yet his filmography indicates a high level of selectivity. Minnelli was, indeed, one of the most highly specialized among Hollywood's major-league directors. One simply can't imagine a Minnelli-directed Western, thriller, adventure film, or war epic (even though he did dabble in the latter genre—reluctantly and with dubious results—in *The Four Horsemen of the Apocalypse,* which is really a melodrama with a wartime backdrop). Minnelli's specialization, however, was not a genre, since he shuttled with the greatest of ease between comedy and drama, but rather a mood. His producers (not only the phenomenal Arthur Freed, who produced all of Minnelli's MGM musicals, but also John Houseman, Sol C. Siegel, and even the workmanlike Pandro Berman) all understood what his areas of expertise were and seldom attempted to force alien material upon him. When this did happen (less than half a dozen times in his entire career), the project would turn out to be a study in self-caricature, as Minnelli deliberately sought refuge in the gratuitous enhancement of his patented trademark, visual opulence, rather than anonymous craftsmanship. Perhaps the most striking example of this strategy is provided by *Kismet,* a vehicle Minnelli disliked and found himself directing under duress. Lavish and stupefyingly lifeless despite overgenerous helpings of comedy relief (the film's "humor" is uncharacteristically vulgar), *Kismet* has been singled out by some as the archetypical Minnelli musical but is really quite the opposite, an anomaly that displays the director's flair for decorative splendor at its most superficial level, that of a Radio City Music Hall pageant. In most of Minnelli's films, and certainly in all his best ones, the decorative element serves the story, characterization, and mood, it does not attempt to overshadow them; *Kismet,* on the other hand, is nothing but sets, props, and costumes. Minnelli's instinctive ploy when confronted with weak material (and the stage vehicle certainly *was* weak, as its disastrous late-seventies Broadway revival as *Timbuktu* confirmed) was to overload the screen with production values, feeling that, at least, the audience would have something to look at.

Another assignment Minnelli took on reluctantly was *Brigadoon,* both because, again, he didn't care for the Broadway show and because of his dislike for the new CinemaScope format (*Brigadoon* was to be his first Scope picture). Although he started developing a brilliant wide-screen style in the film (the hunt on the moor, done in one breathtaking long take, is one of his great set pieces, a forerunner to the boar hunt in *Home From the Hill* and the carnival sequence in *Some Came Running*) and although *Brigadoon* is far superior to *Kismet,* the director's uneasiness with the material can be sensed throughout most of the film. It may seem paradoxical that a director whose stock-in-trade was dreams and dreamlike atmospheres should not have been delighted to film what must have been the most explicitly oneiric show in Broadway history; but clearly, Minnelli was more interested in weaving his own personal web of dreams than in packaging the Broadway version for the screen. This may have been beyond even Freed's shrewd understanding of what made Minnelli tick—or else he may have felt that Minnelli, no matter what, was still the best man for the job. But Minnelli was at his best doing *Hollywood* musicals; it cannot be a coincidence that his four adaptations of Broadway musical shows are also his least successful contributions to the genre. (The other two are the sadly lackluster *Bells Are Ringing* and *On a Clear Day You Can See Forever,* a disappointing late effort despite the visually stunning "regression" sequences.)

Indeed, Minnelli brought new life to the Hollywood musical at MGM quite some time before Gene Kelly and Stanley Donen (or Charles Walters), and despite all the shared resources, they tapped thoroughly different lodes. The Kelly-Donen pictures, like all the Kelly-starring musicals before them, are down-to-earth, brash, plebeian, and indomitably mirthful. Minnelli's, on the other hand, are ethereal (Kelly's own term to describe Minnelli's work), dreamlike, nostalgic, and melancholy. It was inevitable that Kelly's and Minnelli's paths should cross at some point at the MGM studios (where both men coincidentally started their film careers in 1942). But although it would be excessive to claim that their personalities were incompatible (Minnelli has described their collaboration on *The Pirate* as "the most intense professional association I'd ever had with an actor," adding, "One idea would meld into another, and little difference who started the trend of thought"), it cannot be denied that their three films together, despite the great moments in each of them, do not rank among either man's best efforts. A markedly un-Minnellian straining for boisterousness runs through *The Pirate* (derived from a nonmusical Broadway show). It may be the best of the Kelly-Minnelli collaborations, yet it totally lacks the flowing effortlessness that characterizes the two men's best solo efforts.

An American in Paris is quite a special case, as it is really two different pictures in one. The epoch-making dream ballet is unquestionably the greatest set-piece not only in Minnelli's career but in the entire history of the film musical; otherwise, however, the picture is an uneven, pedestrian production saddled with a banal script, predictable humor, musical numbers that are, for the most part, merely average, and an overgenerous helping of "Gallic charm" and local color (one certainly could have done without French crooner Georges Guétary, an egregiously bad actor). Minnelli's most celebrated picture, *An American in Paris* is also one of his least personal—until, that is, it abruptly and mysteriously shifts gears and plunges into that climactic ballet, which could be said to be like nothing ever seen on the screen before if it did not so magically recapture the mood of two previous highlights of Minnelli's career: the "Limehouse Ballet" from *Ziegfeld Follies* and the "Will You Marry Me?" ballet from *Yolanda and the Thief.*

The two men had both been enthusiastic about their first two projects together. When it came to *Brigadoon,* however, Minnelli, had serious misgivings, and the rapport he had previously experienced with Kelly failed to repeat itself. Indeed, Kelly told Hugh Fordin, "Vincente and I were never in synch. . . . I think he only took this assignment because we all asked him to." Perhaps as a result, he himself seemed to grow disenchanted with the project, and the combined moods of the director and the star certainly took their toll on the finished product.

If the Minnelli-Kelly collaboration was comparatively disappointing, it would logically seem to follow that Minnelli's pairing with Fred Astaire, Kelly's antithesis, was destined to work wonders, and that indeed it did.* The two achieved greatness

---

* Astaire and Kelly's only screen encounter, directed by Minnelli for *Ziegfeld Follies,* turned out to be an anticlimactic throwaway number, with the two walking rather than dancing around each other.

from the very start, in *Ziegfeld Follies*, despite being saddled with the decidedly uncharismatic Lucille Bremer as a partner for Astaire in both "This Heart of Mine" and "Limehouse Blues," the revue's highlights. Almost simultaneously, Minnelli was directing Astaire in *Yolanda and the Thief*, one of the most original musicals ever made. Although poorly received at the time, both critically and commercially, it now appears (with *The Band Wagon*) as Minnelli's musical masterpiece.

Coming after Astaire's wartime string of thoroughly traditional and generally minor musicals, the Minnelli collaboration revitalized his career—although not at the box office—by opening up new choreographic vistas for a star who, in some seventeen films, seemed to have developed all the possible variations on his unique formula. Astaire's aristocratic elegance was more attuned to Minnelli's temperament than Kelly's plebeian buoyancy; but Minnelli also knew how to push Astaire beyond himself into an area of style and mood neither he nor anyone else had ever explored before on screen. Without the combination of their two talents, it is highly unlikely that such achievements as the "Limehouse Blues" ballet or "Yolanda's Dream Ballet" would ever have taken place.

Yolanda and the Thief is both thematically and stylistically one of Minnelli's most personal films. For the first time the dominant themes of his work—the ordeal of coming of age, the lure of the dream world, the tension between fantasy and reality and the effort to reconcile them—took shape and coalesced into a coherent whole. Yolanda, the innocent (and wealthy) orphan just out of a convent, whom a fortune hunter convinces that he is her guardian angel, is the first of several Minnelli heroines (Judy Garland's Manuela in *The Pirate*, Emma Bovary, the Lana Turner character in *The Bad and the Beautiful*, Shirley MacLaine's Ginny in *Some Came Running*) who are deceived, ostensibly by men, but actually by their own romantic imaginations, while Astaire as the thief acts, like many later Minnelli protagonists, as the catalyst between fantasy and reality, himself getting caught up in the middle.

The film elicits opposed, even contradictory, responses, which must be acknowledged simultaneously if one is to enjoy the show at all, its unique blend of gaiety and brooding, childishness and wisdom, innocence and cynicism. All the doubts, fears, and ambiguities upon which the story feeds find their perfect visual expression in the "Dream Ballet," the most complex and innovative ever filmed to that date. Not only does it recast all the elements of the plot in choreographic terms, it strips them of their superficial silliness to bare the underlying anxieties. Chronologically, *Yolanda and the Thief* can be considered the first of the modern film musicals.

The Band Wagon, Minnelli's third and, regrettably, last collaboration with Astaire, is in many ways unique among the director's musical pictures. All of the others, with the exception of the leaden, charmless *Bells Are Ringing*, rely on exoticism in space and/or time: turn-of-the-century Americana (*Meet Me in St Louis*); South American Ruritania (*Yolanda and the Thief*); the West Indies in the 1830s (*The Pirate*); Paris (contemporary—but with a salute to the past in the ballet—in *An American in Paris;* turn-of-the-century in *Gigi*); a dream village on the Scottish moors (*Brigadoon*); the Arabia of the *Thousand and One Nights* (*Kismet*); Regency England in the "regression" sequences of *On a Clear Day You Can See Forever*—to which one must add the Heaven and Hell of *Cabin in the Sky*, Minnelli's first film.

The Band Wagon, on the other hand, is set in the "here and now" of nineteen fifties American show business—one sequence even takes place on Times Square and Forty-second Street (albeit a Times Square of the mind, as detached from reality as any dream location in the other films). Moreover, whereas the other Minnelli musicals deliberately eschewed the conventions of the traditional (i.e., thirties) Hollywood musical, the premise and plot of *The Band Wagon* hark back to the hoariest of traditions, the backstage musical (even to the obligatory montage of train wheels, names of cities, and theater program pages turning, that timeworn Hollywood shorthand for a show going on the road.) It is as though Minnelli, after the "intellectualism" and Europeanism of *An American in Paris,* had purposefully set out to do an all-American musical, the backstage musical to end all backstage musicals.

With Betty Comden and Adolph Green, earlier associated with Kelly and Donen's own all-American musicals, in charge of the screenwriting, one might have expected *The Band Wagon* to emulate the ebullient good cheer of *Singin' in the Rain,* rather than the wistfulness of *Yolanda and the Thief.* There are indeed many external similarities between *The Band Wagon* and *Singin' in the Rain,* evidence of the writers' falling into a comfortably familiar pattern. Both films deal with producing a musical—one on screen, one on stage. In both cases, the protagonist is a performer who has reached a critical stage in his career (Don Lockwood, a silent-screen star, must adapt to sound pictures; Tony Hunter, a forgotten song-and-dance man is trying to make a Broadway comeback) and has to develop new skills. The disastrous opening night of the modern *Faust* in *The Band Wagon* parallels the equally disastrous Hollywood premiere of *The Dueling Cavalier* in *Singin' in the Rain.* Both shows are eventually salvaged through recycling into a different genre. The climactic ballet—which is supposed to be part of the show in both films—has the hero's quest for a dangerous, elusive woman (Cyd Charisse in both instances) as its central theme. Even the song "That's Entertainment" expresses much the same philosophy of show business (although more inclusive) as "Make 'em Laugh" in *Singin' in the Rain.*

With so many common points, then, it is remarkable that the mood of the film should be so unlike that of *Singin' in the Rain* and so much closer to other Minnelli films. *The Band Wagon* is indeed a very *moody* musical, replete with self-doubt, anxieties, tensions, conflicts, the fear—and the actuality—of failure. Of course, some of these elements are the very stuff of the traditional musical (shows must get into trouble before they are made to "go on," girl must spurn boy and/or vice versa before they "get" each other), but they are seldom if ever more than conventional plot-moving devices. It would be excessive to claim that *The Band Wagon* breaks away from the tradition in that respect; it is, after all, a traditional musical. Yet in no other musical comedy, perhaps, are the characters' emotions and the difficulties they encounter made to seem more convincingly real.

The film opens on a downbeat note, as an auctioneer fails to raise even a few dollars for Tony Hunter's once celebrated cane and top hat. Tony's status as a has-been is confirmed by a passenger's attitude toward him on the train to New York, then by the newspapermen who ignore him at Grand Central Station (they have come to meet Ava Gardner). Astaire's rendition of "By Myself," one of the most broodingly introspective ballads ever written, as he strolls down the deserted platform is a statement of stoic determination in the face of rejection. In contrast, his greeting by his friends Lester and Lilly Marton disguised as a delegation from an imaginary Tony Hunter Fan Club is ebullient, but their strained exuberance, and the irony implicit in the joke, only underscore Tony's plight.

The "Shine on My Shoes" dance solo in the next sequence is an exhilarating number in the grand Astaire tradition, but the mood becomes uneasy, even somber, again when he is introduced to his future costar (they keep involuntarily offending each other and end up convinced that they couldn't possibly work together) and to the producer, Jeffrey Cordova, whose idea of turning a musical-comedy script into a modern version of *Faust* makes Tony—and everybody else—uncomfortable. "That's Entertainment," although it briefly breaks the tension and seems to bring the star, producer, and writers together, is sung in such a context that its meaning becomes rather ambiguous and ironic. Written as a paean to the cathartic and exhilarating virtues of the theater ("A show that is really a show/ Sends you out with a wonderful glow . . ."), "That's Entertainment," in the film, is introduced by Cordova as his way to make the point that there is no hierarchy between the different forms of theater— musical comedy or Shakespearean drama, they are all entertainment. (Just before going into the song, he has an unforgettable line equating "the rhythm of Bill Robinson's feet and the rhythm of Bill Shakespeare's verse.")

The irony, of course, is that this seductive theory is invalidated by subsequent developments, as Cordova's musical *Faust* proves a miserable failure. The additional irony is that Cordova, in his aspirations if not his achievement, is very close to Minnelli, a director who, more than anyone else, strove for the fusion of so-called highbrow art and the lowly Hollywood musical. In that sense, the film's "philosophy" challenges the implicit premise of Minnelli's entire work within the genre. In order to salvage the show, Tony Hunter, with the help of a humbled and compliant Cordova, turns the modern *Faust* back into a safely routine Broadway revue. Thus Minnelli found himself directing the most traditional—not to say conventional—musical numbers in all his film career ("I Guess I'll Have to Change My Plans," "Triplets," "I Love Louisa," "Louisiana Hayride") within a context in which they are meant to represent the triumph of tradition over innovation. It is unfair to write, as Richard Corliss does in *Talking Pictures,* that "when the show-within-the-film is supposed to fall together, the film itself simply falls apart." The numbers are delightful within their limitations, especially the hilarious "Triplets" and the elegantly minimal "I Guess . . . ," and they lead up to the girl-hunt ballet, hardly an anticlimax. Yet, it is a remarkable paradox that *The Band Wagon,* one of the great classics in a genre dedicated to joie de vivre, is at its least creative when depicting success and at its most successful when dealing with failure and despondency.

Minnelli's melancholy streak is perhaps even more discernible in his "straight" comedies than in the musicals. They often seem to be comedies only by accident and tangentially, with laughter played down and sadness, even grimness, never far round the corner. The allegedly "charming" *Father of the Bride* takes a bitter look at middle-class mores, and its dream sequence, a typical Minnelli set piece, is an actual nightmare that spells out the real fear underlying the jocularity. *The Long, Long Trailer,* Minnelli's only incursion into broad, near-slapstick comedy, is done so realistically that the viewer is more likely to cringe than to chuckle at the spectacle of Desi Arnaz and Lucille Ball's all-too-plausible automobile mishaps. There is as much pathos as laughter in *The Courtship of Eddie's Father,* where cracks keep appearing in the surface cuteness to reveal depths of anguish. This is a world in which the death of a goldfish can take on traumatic proportions. Minnelli is too fascinated with the workings of the human psyche to play the rules of comedy straight, as comedy tends to schematize and dehumanize emotions, using them in a coded form merely to feed a specific mechanism. Unlike Howard Hawks, whose comic protagonists are the reverse of his dramatic ones, Minnelli is interested in the same kind of people in all of his films. The intensity of feeling has to be toned down in comedies, but Minnelli can't totally suppress it.

The sensitiveness Minnelli projects into his characters accounts for the uneasiness that pervades so many of his films. The Minnellian protagonist is typically maladjusted and misunderstood, a nonconformist and a loner, but one who suffers from the isolation and never quite reaches the point of becoming an actual rebel—which would free him (her) from painful ambivalences. Social pressure is a major source of discomfort. The individual's reluctance to accept middle-class values, traditional roles (sex roles, in particular), and conventional life-styles is a central theme in such films as *Home from the Hill, Some Came Running, Tea and Sympathy, The Sandpiper,* and *Madame Bovary*—which Minnelli characteristically turned into a vindication of the romantic outlook on life, whereas Flaubert's biting satire of Emma's bourgeois environment was played against a criticism of her own naive and ultimately destructive romanticism. The pressure to conform is everywhere, whether it is the pressure on males to live by the stereotypes of virility (*Home from the Hill, Tea and Sympathy, Designing Woman*), on women to fit into a prescribed social mold (*Madame Bovary, Gigi, The Reluctant Debutante*), on the artist to be more like everybody else (*Some Came Running, Lust for Life*), or on most everybody to dutifully go through the performance of social rituals.

Minnelli, however, is no social critic, and the conflicts in his films are more likely to be of a personal nature. He often depicts groups of individuals arbitrarily thrown together by one shared condition, or occupation (e.g., mental illness in *The Cobweb;* a common job—show business—in *The Bad and the Beautiful, Two Weeks in Another Town,* and *The Band Wagon;* unconventional life-styles in *Some Came Running*). In such circumstances, tensions become inevitable and escalate into serious clashes at the slightest provocation. Thus, the microcosm of the mental clinic in *The Cobweb* is shaken to its very foundations by a dispute over new drapes. Couples like the young adolescents (John Kerr and Susan Strasberg) in *The Cobweb* or MacLaine and Sinatra in *Some Came Running,* whose attraction to each other is frustrated by the very circumstances that brought them together, best exemplify the kind of strain under which relationships operate in Minnelli's world. Both uneasy romances end tragically, as though death were the only conceivable solution to the characters' emotional predicaments. In *Some Came Running,* it does not really matter which of the two—Dave or Ginny—dies. (In James Jones's novel, Dave gets shot; in the movie, Ginny does—trying to protect him.) Death is poetic justice, retribution for a union (Dave's spite marriage to Ginny after the Martha Hyer character eventually rejects him) that is a mockery of true love, with one partner doing all—or most of—the loving. There are indeed very few happy couples in Minnelli's films, but rather mismatched pairs that drift apart or people who fail to ever get together.

A critic wrote that "Minnellian heroes are all hyper-sensitive people, therefore artists," which makes the problem of the artist the dominant theme of his work. There is a definite correlation between this "artistlike" sensitiveness and the difficulties the characters encounter in their emotional relationships. As a matter of fact, an underlying theme to Minnelli's work is the choice to be made between "art" and "love"—a choice that indeed often imposes itself. *Lust for Life* would be the most obvious example (love is denied the artist because of the very intensity of his sensitiveness), but the theme is perhaps most clearly spelled out in *The Bad and the Beautiful,* in which producer Jonathan Shields (Kirk Douglas) insists that he must not allow himself to become emotionally involved with any woman because of the demands of his work. He uses an actress's love for him and pretends he responds to it only to make her happy and get the best out of her while her first starring picture is in production, then he rejects her pitilessly. Later in the film, the writer played by Dick Powell is told bluntly that his wife's accidental death was a good thing for him, as she kept interfering with his work. The point is made, not surprisingly, by Shields himself, but there is little if any indication that Minnelli disassociates himself from this view. Shields is tough, but he is usually right. The writer subsequently becomes highly productive and successful, and we are made to feel that his wife's death may indeed have been for the best—at least we are not made to feel the opposite. (The startling callousness of the attitude is underscored by the fact that the wife [Gloria Grahame] is depicted as a charming, well-meaning, although rather empty-headed young woman—quite the traditional lively, loving wife according to the Hollywood canons.) Emma Bovary, another "artist" in her desperate effort to bring beauty and style into her drab existence, makes the mistake of believing in love, and her disastrous affairs cause her downfall. On the lighter side of Minnelli's work, *Brigadoon* suggests that the ideal woman and the perfect romance may exist only in the dream world.

In an earlier essay on Minnelli, I ventured the claim that "this dreamer is also a realist," citing, in particular, the accuracy of his art direction and the use of authentic-looking locale in such films as *The Clock*—which, although entirely shot on an MGM sound stage, so convincingly captures some of the bleaker aspects of New York City life (e.g., the scene at the Automat)—or *Some Came Running,* of which I wrote, "The moment the bus pulls up at the station in the opening sequence, the town imposes itself upon us as thoroughly real" (I was not aware at the time that the film's exteriors were shot in Madison, Indiana, the very same town which the War Department had selected as "the typical American small town" for a 1941 documentary—*The Town*—directed, ironically, by the least "realist" of American film makers, Josef von Sternberg.)

Whether the "impression of reality" experienced watching *Some Came Running* was due to Madison's archetypal "ordinariness" or to Minnelli's flair for authenticity, or both, is really a moot point, and the paradox of the dreamer as realist seems a facile one that sheds little light on the central problem of the tension between dream and reality in Minnelli's work. But then, this is a problem upon which little light is likely to be shed anyway. All the critics who have dealt with Minnelli seriously, or even half-seriously, have dutifully tackled the issue, but it is one that seems remarkably conducive to arbitrary speculation. The fact that film is at the same time the most realistic *and* the most dreamlike art form (dreamlike, in a sense, because of its very realism) does not make an investigation of the dream-reality dialectics in Minnelli's work any easier.

A tension between reality and the imaginary exists, to varying degrees, in all films, and films involve and affect us because we acknowledge that tension and respond to it. Minnelli's pictures differ from others only in the superficial sense that they often explicitly deal with the tension rather than merely embody it. At the core of this confrontation as experienced by the viewer is our eagerness for an impression of reality, an expectation that may vary in intensity and application depending upon the individual, and the film, but is perhaps the most universal of viewers' expectations. If Minnelli's films are representative of the Hollywood tradition, it is in their ability to move and convince us, even when little about them bears any resemblance to our everyday experience of reality; in other words, when the impression of reality is achieved through (as much as in spite of) high artificiality. "Realism" being a highly relative and constantly redefined concept,* artificiality (especially of the coherent—if only semiconscious—

---

* The Italian "neorealists" are a case in point. What is most striking about their films today is not their much-vaunted realism but, on the contrary, and depending upon the case, their almost baroque stylistic exuberance (*Open City*), their epic, larger-than-life quality (Lattuada's *Il Bandito* and *Senza pietà*), or their old-fashioned melodramatic contrivances (*Bicycle Thief*).

Hollywood variety) stands a better chance of convincing, and aging well. French films of the thirties and forties, which were supposedly more "realistic" than their American counterparts, now more often than not seem appallingly false. Even a Renoir was apt to confuse the conventions of French stage acting of the time with "naturalness"— which is one of the problems with his own failed *Madame Bovary*, a film that was ruined as much by the drastic cuts imposed by the distributors as by the pseudorealistic histrionics of most of the cast, especially Valentine Tessier in the title role. (Renoir, however, found her "adorable," and the otherwise unenthusiastic French reviewers highly praised her performance.) The Minnelli version, despite the potential handicap of its "un-Frenchness" (the language and actors, the Hollywood studio look and style, not to mention the strictures of the Production Code) is by far the more *convincing* effort.

Working in a medium whose relationship to "the real" is inevitably ambiguous and within a system—the Hollywood film—that had evolved what must be the most arbitrary code of representation in Western cinema, Minnelli—the dreamer under contract to the dream factory, sheltered in the cocoon of the MGM studio—could filter reality through his personal emotions and reconstruct it as a projection of the inner world. This rearrangement is not only "dreamlike," it also involves a magnifying of the real into a larger-than-life vision. In the best films of Minnelli's middle period (*Lust for Life, The Cobweb, Home from the Hill,* and, in a more subdued register, *Tea and Sympathy*), both physical reality and the characters' feelings, personalities, and relationships are put through a process of intensification—which, as a matter of fact, does not always avoid the pitfall of caricature. Wade Hunnicut, the macho patriarch played by Robert Mitchum in *Home from the Hill,* is archetypal to a fault, and every artifact in his den—all red leather, guns, and hunting trophies—"reflects" his personality with an almost embarrassing obviousness. In *Some Came Running,* Shirley MacLaine and Martha Hyer play female archetypes at opposite ends of the spectrum (the prostitute with a heart of gold and the prim academic), whose characterizations are practically completed, before they even open their mouths, through the fastidiously selected details of their physical appearance—clothes, hairstyle, makeup, stance. Minnelli's films are not above the kind of streamlining and repackaging of human emotions and conflicts one associates with soap opera rather than with great drama.

But whereas *real* soap opera (i.e., the television product) matches the predictability of its ever-renewed crises with the blandness of its look (so that the emotional ordeals the characters go through seem as unfelt as the living rooms in which they tend to take place look un-lived in and the emoting as mechanical as the camera work that records it), the stylistic flamboyance that Minnelli brings to his material transfigures (rather than redeems) it by changing our perception of and response to it, in the same way music transfigures the trashiness of an opera's plot. A Minnelli drama is soap opera without the soap—an operatic experience (some of his dramas are more "musical" than his musical comedies). At the risk of quoting Dostoyevsky out of context, one is tempted to apply to Minnelli's heightened moments the words of Lyov Nikolayevitch Myshkin in *The Idiot:* "What does it matter if it is abnormal intensity, if the result . . . turns out to be the height of harmony and beauty?"

36. Robert Mulligan (1923)

by JOHN BELTON

1957—*Fear Strikes Out;* 1960—*The Rat Race;* 1961—*The Great Impostor; Come September;* 1962—
The Spiral Road; To Kill a Mockingbird; 1964—*Love With the Proper Stranger;* 1965—*Baby, the
Rain Must Fall; Inside Daisy Clover;* 1967—*Up the Down Staircase;* 1969—*The Stalking Moon;* 1971—
The Pursuit of Happiness; Summer of '42; 1972—*The Other;* 1975—*The Nickel Ride;* 1978—*Bloodbroth-
ers;* 1979—*Same Time, Next Year;* 1983—*Kiss Me Goodbye*

Over the past fifteen years, Robert Mulligan has, with little or no critical acclaim,
directed a series of films as astonishing for their stylistic subtlety as for their emotional
power. The sixties, due in large part to Andrew Sarris's auteur polemics, marked the
emergence of the director as superstar, each director with his name, like Capra's,
displayed prominently above the title of his film. Mulligan, however, sees himself
more as a collaborator than as a superstar; his name, more often than not, lays buried
in the credits. In spite of his popular success with films like *To Kill a Mockingbird*
and *Summer of '42,* Mulligan has kept a low public profile, rarely giving interviews
or publicizing his films. Even though the British Film Institute singled him out for a
retrospective in 1971, Mulligan has remained a director without recognition in his
own country.

Mulligan's self-effacing denial of directorial authorship and his relative anonymity
in the industry are part and parcel of the esthetic vision that makes him an auteur.
His films do not spring fully armed—like Athena—from his brain but rather are slowly
shaped into form through his sensibility. Mulligan is clearly not the author of his
films in the same way that Ingmar Bergman is; he does not create his own characters
or stories or write the dialogue. But Mulligan is a storyteller, *interpreting* the stories
of others. As Mulligan describes his role, "Things have to sift through me. That's
me up there on the screen. The shooting, the editing, the use of music—all that represents my attitude toward the material." In his role as storyteller, Mulligan interposes
his personality and sensitivity between the tale and the audience; he makes the story
his own by supplying *attitude.* It is this attitude or tone that becomes the true subject
of a Mulligan film, not character or plot. Thus in a Mulligan film, no single individual—
director, screenwriter, producer, or actor—stamps the film with his personality; the
feelings generated by Mulligan's view of specific characters in specific situations and
settings are what count most.

Mulligan, as interpreter, chooses preexisting plots and characters for the stories
of his films. His best films have been based on best-selling novels that have in common
strong subjective narrations and settings that are inseparable from character and plot.
To Kill a Mockingbird was based on the Pulitzer-Prize-winning novel by Harper Lee;
Baby, the Rain Must Fall had as its source screenwriter Horton Foote's play, *The Traveling
Lady; Inside Daisy Clover* was based on Gavin Lambert's novel about Hollywood studios

and stars; *Up the Down Staircase* on schoolteacher Bel Kaufman's popular book on her experiences in a New York City high school; *The Stalking Moon* on Theodore V. Olson's novel; *Summer of '42* on Herman Raucher's nostalgic best-seller; and *The Other* on former actor Tom Tryon's immensely successful, thirties gothic novel. Mulligan's flops during this period, on the other hand, were based either on original screenplays (*Love With the Proper Stranger,* though not a disaster, does not equal *Baby, the Rain Must Fall*) or on unremarkable novels (*The Pursuit of Happiness* and *The Nickel Ride*). Even in his period as contract director at Paramount and Universal, Mulligan relied heavily on best-sellers (Jimmy Piersall's *Fear Strikes Out* and Garson Kanin's *The Rat Race*), autobiographies (Fernando Waldo Demera's life was the basis for *The Great Impostor*) and novels (Jan de Hartog's *The Spiral Road,* a story of an agnostic doctor's discovery of God in the Lloyd C. Douglas mold).

The number of Mulligan films based on presold properties tells us less about Mulligan, however, than about industry practices in the sixties and seventies (though Mulligan's television work in the fifties also consisted largely of adaptations (e.g., *David Copperfield, The Bridge of San Luis Rey, The Moon and Sixpence, The Member of the Wedding,* and *The Catered Affair*). Original screenplays became less and less marketable; best-sellers whose popularity had been proven guaranteed film financiers a return on their money. Mulligan's films with producer Alan J. Pakula, though the director's best, do reflect the packaging psychology predominant in the industry during the sixties; a presold novel or play and a presold star (Gregory Peck, Steve McQueen, Natalie Wood, Christopher Plummer, Sandy Dennis, Eva Marie Saint) insured a profit at the box office. The Pakula-Mulligan team produced a string of distinctive films: *Fear Strikes Out, To Kill a Mockingbird, Love With the Proper Stranger, Baby, the Rain Must Fall, Inside Daisy Clover, Up the Down Staircase,* and *The Stalking Moon.*

After *The Stalking Moon,* Pakula and Mulligan dissolved their partnership, Pakula choosing to produce *and* direct his own productions. His first film, *The Sterile Cuckoo,* was an adolescent love story reminiscent of the films he and Mulligan had made, but with *Klute* Pakula established his own identity as a film maker, and his subsequent films all deal, as no Mulligan film does, with the struggle between the individual and the invisible machinery of a corrupt corporate power, striking a decidedly more moral attitude and a more political note than any Mulligan film, even the seemingly committed and political *The Pursuit of Happiness.*

Mulligan, on the other hand, has turned inward, toward a more personal, intimate drama (Mulligan himself delivers the first-person narration of *Summer of '42,* with whose adolescent experiences the director, seventeen years old in 1942, perhaps identifies). His recent films are clearly extensions of the sensitive Pakula-Mulligan best-seller projects of the sixties but without the star packaging on which Pakula seems to rely. Mulligan's films, retreating from the real world to which Pakula anchors his suspense melodramas, have become more and more subjective, beginning with *Summer of '42,* which concerns the real but nostalgically magnified memories of one character, culminating in *The Other,* which explores one child's fanciful recreation of his dead twin, and continuing into *The Nickel Ride,* which contains a quite disturbing fantasy sequence in which the hero imagines a bloody battle with the men sent to kill him.

Mulligan's choice of subject matter lacks the topicality of Pakula's. His choice of period setting—the thirties in *The Other* and the forties in *Summer of '42*—fortunately coincided with a revival of popular interest in these periods, and *Summer of '42* became the biggest box-office success of his career.

Mulligan's interest in the reality of feelings, imagination, and memory is apparent even in his very first film, *Fear Strikes Out,* which deals with the nervous breakdown of centerfielder Jimmy Piersall, played by a pre-*Psycho* Tony Perkins whose youthfulness and latent emotional instability Mulligan exploits to advantage. *Fear Strikes Out* also reveals Mulligan's interest in the dramatic potential of the parent-child relationship. Piersall's father (Karl Malden) is a frustrated sandlot ballplayer who pressures his son to become a major leaguer. Mulligan suggests the paralytic nature of this pressure early in the film with a high-angle shot of father and son playing ball together in a small, enclosed backyard. Later, when Jimmy starts to play pro ball, Mulligan repeatedly separates the two on either side of wire fences, hinting at the repressed and potentially explosive nature of the feelings within each.

The *Rat Race* is the first of Mulligan's New York films. Of all the graduates of the New York television industry in the fifties—Arthur Penn, John Frankenheimer, Sidney Lumet, Sidney Pollack, Martin Ritt—Mulligan is (with Lumet) the only member of the American New York wave who continued to project a New York sensibility and a concern for the cynicism and callousness of big-city life in his films. In addition to *The Rat Race, Love With the Proper Stranger, Up the Down Staircase, The Pursuit of Happiness,* and *Bloodbrothers* are all situated in New York.

The environment of Mulligan's films plays a major role in establishing tone. The impersonal setting of New York provides an atmosphere of isolation and loneliness against which his characters' attempts to reach out and make contact with one another are played out. Musician Tony Curtis and dancer Debbie Reynolds in *The Rat Race* platonically share an apartment, each so intent on making it in the big city that they ignore one another and their feelings for each other for two-thirds of the film. *Love With the Proper Stranger,* shot almost entirely on location in New York, deals, as its title suggests, with the anonymous nature of life in a city of crowds. Mulligan repeatedly stages intimate conversations between Rocky (Steve McQueen), a musician, and Angie (Natalie Wood), a Macy's salesgirl whom Rocky has gotten into trouble, in extremely public settings. The title sequence establishes the mood of the film: an empty musicians' union hall slowly fills with musicians looking for work. The chaotic movements and activities of the surrounding people, all heading in different directions and concerned with their own affairs, make meaningful communication between Rocky and Angie impossible. Rocky does not even remember his one-night stand with Angie, who angrily walks out. The union hall and the fifth floor of Macy's (where their second encounter is set) become settings that frustrate contact, preventing any growth of romantic feeling between the two. Indeed, romance seems impossible in an urban setting. Rocky, in love with himself as much as his showgirl mistress, Barbie, is in love with herself, is unwilling to take on the responsibility of a deep commitment to another; he is even estranged from his own parents, whom he seldom sees (as we see in a remarkable playground reunion with them as he attempts to raise more money for Angie's abortion), and he views married men as "prisoners of Zenda." But Rocky's cynicism yields to Angie's romanticism. Angie, dreaming of a lover as a knight on a white horse, says she will know that she is in love when she hears "bells and banjos." At the end of the film, Rocky, playing bells and banjos and carrying a sign that reads "Better Wed Than Dead," chases Angie through the crowded city streets outside Macy's. The high-angle long shot of these two "lovers" lost in a crowd recalls the opening sequence in the union hall, but here Rocky has rejected the deadness of his previous life-style, having taken a first step when he prevented Angie from going through with an abortion in a cold, desolate-looking abandoned apartment building. Rocky's actions here and at the end of the film reflect a triumph of feeling over environment, which is also the subject of Mulligan's subsequent New York films, *Up the Down Staircase* and *The Pursuit of Happiness.*

Actually, New York City is, like the Indian Salvaje in *The Stalking Moon,* rarely seen in *Up the Down Staircase,* but its off-screen presence is felt throughout the film. Mulligan's camera remains focused on Calvin Coolidge High School and the streets surrounding the school and refuses to explore the lives of characters outside of this setting. The school, with its banging lockers, grim halls and stairways, and bustling crowds of students and teachers, is the subject of the film, revealing quite clearly the primary role places play in the director's films. The immediacy of Mulligan's environment in this film excludes the existence of all others—there is no world outside of the school. When characters leave this setting, they leave the film (as do Ed Williams and Ellen O'Mara's romantically suicidal Alice Blake). Sandy Dennis's novice schoolteacher, Sylvia Barrett, is less in conflict with this environment than in awe of it, initially unable to understand it or to discover what it takes to survive in it.

The bustle and apparent confusion in the school's halls during class changes captures the directionless vitality of the place; an energy is there which teachers, in the semiorder of the classroom, attempt to channel. Miss Barrett's after-school encounter with Joe Ferrone marks an attempt to "recall him to life." But the sense of place has changed here: when Joe turns off the lights and approaches Miss Barrett, and Mulligan shoots the encounter in dramatic close-ups, the "schoolness" of the room vanishes; the order and stability of the setting has been transformed. Even within a single environment, a variety of moods can coexist, reflecting the complex interrelationship between specific people and specific settings.

The Pursuit of Happiness is less a New York film than an "estrangement of youth" film, though the city and the central character's experiences in it (e.g., the automobile manslaughter, the car's breakdown in traffic) contribute to his judgment that, "There's a nervous breakdown going on out there, and I don't want to be part of it." Environment—the city—becomes the focus of William's (Michael Sarrazin's) rejection of the values of his parents and of the society around him. Unable to understand it or come to terms with it, as Miss Barrett does at the end of *Staircase* when she makes contact with Jose Rodriguez, William can only dissociate himself from his environment. As Tom Ryan writes in *Movie* 21, "the film's final sequence provides an exhilarating if precarious feeling of liberation, as the tiny plane carrying William and Jane soars away from the urban landscape filled with skyscrapers, endless rows of cars, and a veil of smog. The only possibility for escape in the film has seemed to rest with individuals' ability to move away from the places with which their roles are linked. . . . and to move towards the discovery of an independent identity."

Mulligan's central characters frequently view the world around them as a hostile body which, after they establish brief contact with it, they ultimately flee, either literally as in *Pursuit* or figuratively, by withdrawing into themselves or into a world of memory or imagination. The "real" world in *To Kill a Mockingbird* is incomprehensible to Scout, who narrates the film. It is an adult world, represented by the courtroom sequence, which deals with adult problems: race and sex. The presence of Scout, Jem, and Dill in the courtroom as Atticus (Gregory Peck) defends a black accused of rape marks a confrontation between innocence and worldliness, much as Scout's taking of Boo Radley's hand at the end of the film represents her confrontation with and victory over the childish fears that Boo earlier represented. Yet the narration of the film, told from the point of view of a child, views the adult world with distance and incomprehensibility. The world of grown-ups has an alienating otherness.

Mulligan had suggested the separateness of parent and child earlier in his career by isolating them in the frame or by separating them with fences (*Fear Strikes Out*) or with screen doors (*Baby, the Rain Must Fall*). In *Summer of '42,* Hermie spies on adult experience, Dorothy and her husband, from a distance, a distance that Mulligan underscores by filming Dorothy from Hermie's point of view and in an idealized slow motion. Although Dorothy later initiates Hermie into this world, it remains a mystery to him: he returns to her house to find it locked and a note for him left on the closed door. The distance between parent and child, between the world of adults and of childhood experience is realized structurally in *Mockingbird* and in *Summer* via the narration that accompanies childhood memories. In both, narrators look back upon experiences of their youth and attempt to understand them, both as they really were then and as they seem now. We sense simultaneously the immediacy of these memories as they appear on the screen and the narrator's distance from them.

The "otherness" of one's own experiences, seen in the esthetic distance of *Mockingbird* and of *Summer,* becomes the literal subject of *The Other,* a film about a boy who, through imagination, restores to life his dead twin. Niles (Chris Udvarnoky) has a close relationship with his grandmother, Ada, who has encouraged his imaginative powers. (His mother has withdrawn into her own private world after the death of her other son.) As Mulligan explained Ada's character, "She was the heart of the house. She has a primitive sense of imagination and drama, which is the greatest thing an adult can give a child. . . . Her only failing is that she has a maternal love so strong that it blinds her to what is happening. Though she enriches and turns on the child's imagination, her gift is used in a destructive way by the child." Indeed, Niles becomes responsible for at least three deaths (four, if we count the Niles-induced heart attack of a neighbor).

The film's first shot, a slow, descending crane and zoom shot, like that which opens *Mockingbird,* initiates the audience into a very private world of imagination inhabited only by Niles, his recreated brother, Holland (Martin Udvarnoky), and their grandmother, Ada (Uta Hagen). The privateness of this world is so total that, as Mulligan pointed out, "If Niles could have life just the way he wanted it, his world would contain only Ada, Holland, and himself—preferably only Holland and himself"— which is the way the film ends. It is a child's world of imagination, drama and, magic (which Niles performs and which facilitates his escape from the burning barn at the end). It remains emotionally distanced and separate in tone from the world of those characters around him.

The descending crane shot introduces us to a world of subjective experience. As Mulligan has said, "I want to put the audience into the body of the boy with this shot and to make the experience of the film, from beginning to end, a totally subjective one." In putting the audience into the body of the boy, Mulligan, in effect, does exactly what Niles does when he puts himself into the body of a bird in flight: he celebrates the magical power of imagination.

Though Mulligan never cheats in the film—Niles and Holland are never in the same frame at the same time but are always separated by a cut or a pan across space—the audience believes in the existence of Holland, so totally are we immersed in the subjectivity of Niles's point of view, until Ada shatters that subjectivity for us. Late one night, Niles sneaks downstairs and talks to Holland in the living room. Mulligan pans from one twin to the other—always from Niles *to* Holland as he has done previously, affirming Niles's point of view. But when Ada comes downstairs, the camera suddenly shifts to her point of view, and we see that Holland is not there. The next day, Ada shows Niles Holland's grave but fails to undo the harm her imaginative powers have caused.

One of the major subjects of the film is the power of imagination both to liberate, as seen when Niles becomes the bird in flight, and to imprison, as seen when Holland must hide in the film's second half. This subjective reality—as Ada tells Niles, "your world is very real . . . for you"—lies at the core of all of Mulligan's work. Similarly, *The Great Imposter* features a childlike character whose fantasies give him moments of escape yet ultimately imprison him: he never comes to terms with himself or with those around him who care for him.

The Other ends as subjectively as it began. Mulligan tracks from the burning barn in which Ada, as an "angel of death," has killed herself and, supposedly, the evil Niles to the second-story window of the adjoining farmhouse from behind which Niles looks out at the burning barn. As in the film's first shot, Mulligan again zooms in—this time to a close-up of Niles's face. Niles blinks twice, the frame freezes, and the film ends. Again Mulligan's camera work leads us into the child, into the reality of his world. But this time, because of what has occurred during the course of the film, we draw back. The intervention of the window, which now separates us from the child, becomes a visual symbol of the distance that exists between his private world and the real world around him. Like the opening shot of *Baby, the Rain Must Fall* in which we see Georgette (Lee Remick) framed behind a bus window, this last shot of *The Other* affirms the impenetrability of a private world of feelings.

Mulligan's treatment of the Niles-Holland world makes it vividly real for us and, through visual stylization—internally framed compositions, zooms, freeze frames— makes it unreal as well. Yet Mulligan is not a mere stylist. Less interested in plot mechanics than in mood, he creates a mood that produces its own sense of reality. For example, the director carefully tries to reconstruct a thirties atmosphere through period detail. Yet as Mulligan points out, "Objects don't have specific meanings in my films; they are only part of mood I'm trying to create." Similarly, his controlled suspense techniques heighten the spectator's involvement in action by pulling back from violent or climactic events. Like Fritz Lang, Mulligan lets his audience imagine rather than see the violence and, as a result, magnifies it in their minds.

Mulligan's editing creates a rhythm that entrances his audience. "I cut a lot in *The Other* from long, open shots to tight, constricting close-ups," he explains, referring in particular to the bird-in-flight sequence. At the same time, Mulligan alternates long, fluid camera movements with short, static shots. Toward the end of the film, he breaks even spatial continuity (in the barn burning) to intercut shots of Ada's face with the face of the Angel of a Brighter Day (a stained-glass-window angel in a nearby church) and suggests Ada's transformation as it appears in Niles's mind. Mulligan's rhythmic editing reflects the film's narrative dialectic between imagined and real experience.

The alternation between subjective and objective reality in *The Other*'s narrative and the incorporation of the alternation into the film's visual style make it one of Mulligan's most complex works. At the same time, *The Other* appears to be Mulligan's most controlled work, every camera movement, every cut contributing to the film's suspense and plunging the audience in the labyrinthine subjectivity of a very private world.

37. Ralph Nelson   (1916)

by PIERRE SAUVAGE

1962—*Requiem for a Heavyweight;* 1963—*Lilies of the Field; Soldier in the Rain;* 1964—*Fate Is the Hunter;* 1965—*Father Goose; Once a Thief;* 1966—*Duel at Diablo;* 1968—*Counterpoint; Charly;* 1970—*Soldier Blue; . . .tick. . .tick. . .tick. . . ;* 1971—*Flight of the Doves;* 1972—*The Wrath of God;* 1975—*The Wilby Conspiracy;* 1976—*Embryo;* 1977—*A Hero Ain't Nothin' But a Sandwich*

Television Movies
1978—*Lady of the House,* (codirector: Vincent Sherman); 1979—*You Can't Go Home Again; Christmas Lilies of the Field*

It is perhaps not all that astonishing that the same director is responsible for *Lilies of the Field* and *Soldier Blue.* Both films, after all, reveal a capacity to pull out the stops, whether the purpose be to warm hearts or to curdle blood. Ralph Nelson's mildly ambitious undertakings are undermined by dramatic flaws, contrivances, and compromises, while his more conventional efforts are never more than mildly successful. Nelson feels that his best work is in character studies and character relationships, and, indeed, if he has yet to turn out a wholly satisfactory picture, there are interesting portraits (Cliff Robertson's mentally retarded *Charly,* Van Heflin's dogged police detective in *Once a Thief*) and deft and affecting two-shots (Jackie Gleason and Tuesday Weld's date in *Soldier in the Rain*) scattered here and there throughout his films.

Born of Swedish immigrant parents, Nelson started out as an actor at the Wharf Theatre in Provincetown, Massachusetts, became an actor and a stage manager for Alfred Lunt and Lynn Fontanne in 1936, collaborating on such hits as *The Taming of the Shrew, Idiot's Delight,* and *Amphitryon 38* (such future film personalities as Sydney Greenstreet, Thomas Gomez, and Richard Whorf were often in the casts). While serving as a pilot in World War II, he wrote two plays that were produced on Broadway: *Mail Call,* a one-acter, and *The Wind Is Ninety,* a war fantasy about the efforts of a dead flyer's spirit to communicate with his family (Kirk Douglas appeared as "a soldier"). Nelson then worked as an actor and a writer, becoming a television director in 1948. At first associated with routine programs (in particular, the unlamented *Mama* family series), he was very active throughout the fifties, and toward the end of television's ambitious decade he directed such prestigious presentations as the Old Vic Company's *Hamlet,* Noel Coward starring in his own *This Happy Breed,* Rodgers and Hammerstein's original musical *Cinderella* (starring Julie Andrews), and other shows for the highly rated *General Electric Playhouse, DuPont Show of the Month,* and *Playhouse 90,* as well as for the *Climax!* and *Dick Powell Anthology* series.

Nelson's first theatrical film was a remake of his Emmy Award winning *Playhouse 90* production of *Requiem for a Heavyweight.* Rod Serling's story of a washed-out boxer clinging to his honor and his dignity despite betrayal and humiliation is rather ponderously meaningful, and Anthony Quinn does not pull his punches in his hoarse, hammy portrayal of Mountain Rivera. In a letter to *Life* magazine, Nelson pointedly praised Jack Palance's "hauntingly gentle performance" on television, adding that Quinn "chose to play Sonny Liston instead." A viewing of a kinescope of the original *Playhouse 90* confirms that this live performance was indeed better all round, with some affecting moments rendered all the more powerful by the directness and lack of glitziness of the production. The later film, from its opening fight sequence (in which the aging pug is pummeled by a young Cassius Clay) to its gut-busting conclusion, lacks well-placed feints, and its jabs to the heart can be ducked.

It is also possible to resist, if not really to dislike, Nelson's second picture, *Lilies of the Field,* his favorite of all his films, in which Sidney Poitier plays a cheerful, itinerant handyman who stops to get water for his car's radiator and winds up lingering long enough to help some East German refugee nuns build a chapel for a Mexican-American community (and teach them how to sing "Amen"). The film, ably put together, over-flows with good feelings, and the National Conference of Christians and Jews' Brother-hood Award was well earned, if not, perhaps, Poitier's Oscar.

If Poitier's relationship with head nun Lilia Skala was more interesting than Anthony Quinn's with social worker Julie Harris in *Requiem,* far better still was the close friendship between the two peacetime servicemen played by Jackie Gleason and Steve McQueen in *Soldier in the Rain.* Like *Of Mice and Men*'s George and Lenny, McQueen's devoted simpleton and Gleason's wheeler-dealer dream of life in an idyllic world, a Pacific Island where the women go topless and "all the breasts point upwards." Blake Edwards produced and coscripted this curious adaptation of a William Goldman novel, which despite uneven and forced comedic elements and such unnecessary touches as the standard service comedy's sadistic sergeant, was appealingly tactful and surpris-ingly effective.

Far more conventional was *Fate Is the Hunter,* the story of an investigation of a plane crash (the ultimate results give the lie to the film's title). It is superior, however, to *Counterpoint,* a World War II film that Vincent Canby deemed "incredibly unimpor-tant" and more original than Nelson's only out-and-out comedy, *Father Goose,* also set during the war, in which Cary Grant was cast as an unshaven, boozing, baggily dressed South Pacific beach bum who is intruded upon by prim Leslie Caron and a band of schoolgirls, a theme with vague Hustonian overtones (*The African Queen, Heaven Knows Mr. Allison*).

There were overtones of *Les Miserables* in *Once a Thief* (which was supposed to launch Alain Delon on an American career), though the implications of this cops-and-robbers story were muffled by a flow of coincidence and a wavering approach to Zekiel Marko's semiautobiographical screenplay (he gives the film a ring of authenticity in a vignette as a drug-addicted loser), perhaps typified by the director's bewildering comment in an article he wrote for the *Los Angeles Times:* "There is no message in *Once a Thief.* It states simply that society creates criminals."

In *Duel at Diablo,* a violent Western, Sidney Poitier was interestingly cast as a foppish, petulant, horse-dealing ex-Army sergeant. Unfortunately, the film was overly static in its depiction of the main characters and in its dramatic progression and was further hampered by extraordinarily awkward action sequences, which made it difficult to understand the strategic considerations and led some spectators to relax and concen-trate instead on Neal Hefti's excellent musical score.

Duel's villains were the Apaches and indeed Nelson himself, who likes to act in his films—he is the hard-nosed contractor who is won over to charity in *Lilies* and a speaker at the psychiatric convention in *Charly*—plays the colonel who leads the relief detachment. A few years later, Nelson struck a different chord in the bloody, gruesome *Soldier Blue,* which starts with a violent attack by the Indians but culminates in an extremely gory, merciless recreation of a massacre of the Cheyenne by the U.S. Cavalry. The butchery, based on the Sand Creek Massacre of November 29, 1864, with elements from the December 29, 1890 "Battle" of Wounded Knee, is probably realistic. But like most cinematographic cruelty it seems dubiously self-righteous and is particularly uncompelling coming on the heels of an extended romantic interlude between a young, overly contemporary sounding white woman who knows the Indian's point of view and a naive, innocent, "soldier blue." The verdict of *Akwesasne Notes,* the newsletter of the Mohawk nation, is worth quoting: "The only good part of the picture was the massacre of the Indians by the cavalry. That saved it because it showed the truth. The rest was junk." Indeed, whatever its limitations, the film certainly was forthright in its depiction of white America's scarred past and capacity for cruelty. (The film's success abroad, if not in the United States, was not hindered by the news, shortly before its release, of the My Lai massacre.)

. . .*tick.* . . .*tick.* . . .*tick.* . . . , however, indicated that Nelson was not beneath pandering to the hypocritically "balanced" racial views set forth in James Lee (*The Green Berets*) Barrett's screenplay, which deals with the first day in office of a black sheriff (Jim Brown) in a southern cracker county (the defeated sheriff is played by George Kennedy, and Brown intermittently serves him as straight man, à la *In the Heat of the Night*). White extremists are of course carefully denounced, but the local black radical happens to be a rapist, while the Ku Kluxers stand up for the sheriff in the last reel.

Nelson's only hit besides *Lilies* was *Charly,* based on Daniel Keyes's story "Flowers for Algernon," which had already served star Cliff Robertson as "The Two Worlds of Charlie Gordon" on television's *The United States Steel Hour* in 1961. The film, about a mentally retarded adult whose mental faculties startlingly but temporarily increase after an operation, provided moments of genuine warmth and emotion, despite the limitations of Sterling Silliphant's script (the transformed, brilliantly perceptive main character is provided only with trite generalizations on the ills of contemporary society), a superfluous and implausible love interest (therapist Claire Bloom), and some ill-conceived, distracting screen effects.

In the last few years Nelson has been flip-flopping back and forth between opposite poles. The savage *Soldier Blue* and . . .*tick.* . . .*tick.* . . .*tick.* . . . were followed by an Irish-made family picture, *Flight of the Doves,* which died at the box office and sent its director hurtling back to violence in *The Wrath of God,* which he wrote himself. Many admirers of *Lilies* would probably be hard put to appreciate the casual jocularity of its sacrilegious imagery, such as a sequence in which Robert Mitchum, as a bogus, probably defrocked, submachine-gun-toting priest involved in 1920s banana-republic strife, is tied with barbed wire to a crucifix by insanely anticlerical Frank Langella, who finds himself crushed beneath it when it plunges downward. In such weirdly humorous moments, it is hard to tell whether one is laughing with the film or at it; the seemingly serious sections are by contrast only grotesquely operatic (lacking Sergio Leone's contemporaneous *Duck You Sucker* lyricism) or crudely violent—the work of a tinhorn Peckinpah.

There were overtones of Charles Laughton's superb *The Night of the Hunter* in the Mitchum character, and *The Wilby Conspiracy,* which reunited Nelson with Sidney Poitier, irresistibly evoked memories of the star's earlier Stanley Kramer hit, *The Defiant Ones.* After the poorly received sci-fi horror film *Embryo,* Nelson went "wholesome" again with the unsuccessful *A Hero Ain't Nothin But a Sandwich*. Working in television again, Nelson remade his favorite film as *Christmas Lilies of the Field* (Billy Dee Williams and Maria Schell were the leads), hoping that the movie would then turn into a series. Surprisingly it didn't.

38. *Robert Parrish* (*1916*)

1951—*Cry Danger; The Mob;* 1952—*The San Francisco Story; Assignment—Paris,* (uncredited codirector: Phil Karlson); *My Pal Gus;* 1953—*Rough Shoot* (Great Britain; U.S., *Shoot First,* 1953); 1954—*The Purple Plain* (Great Britain; U.S., 1955); 1955—*Lucy Gallant;* 1957—*Fire Down Below;* 1958—*Saddle the Wind;* 1959—*The Wonderful Country;* 1963—*In the French Style;* 1965—*Up From the Beach;* 1967—*Casino Royale* (Great Britain; other directors: John Huston, Ken Hughes, Val Guest, Joe McGrath); *The Bobo* (Great Britain; U.S., 1967); 1968—*Duffy;* 1969—*Doppelgänger* (Great Britain; U.S., *Journey to the Far Side of the Sun,* 1969); 1971—*A Town Called Bastard* (Great Britain/Spain; uncredited codirector: Irving Lerner; U.S., *A Town Called Hell,* 1971); 1974—*The Destructors*

Uncredited
1951—*Ten Tall Men* (Willis Goldbeck); 1952—*The Lusty Men* (Nicholas Ray)

Robert Parrish would be totally unknown in this country were it not for his charming book of reminiscences, *Growing Up in Hollywood* (1976), which modestly focuses on his early years as a child actor and says practically nothing of his career as a film director. It may therefore come as a surprise, even to well-informed American film buffs, that the Cinémathèque Française, back in 1963, organized a Parrish retrospective with the director attending several of the screenings and introducing his films. At the time, Parrish had only directed a dozen pictures, several of which had not been released in France, but he had enthusiastic supporters among French critics (especially the staff of *Positif*), essentially on the basis of his war drama, *The Purple Plain,* and his Western, *The Far Country,* and, to a lesser extent, *Saddle the Wind* (another Western), and *Fire Down Below,* an uneven but underrated triangle story that should have attracted more attention, if only because of a cast bringing together Robert Mitchum, Jack Lemmon, and Rita Hayworth.

An actor in several John Ford films between the ages of twelve and nineteen, Parrish became Ford's assistant editor in the late thirties and later followed the director when he was appointed Chief of the Navy's Field Photographic Branch during the war. There, he edited Ford's documentaries *The Battle of Midway* and *December 7th.* After the war, still in the service, he worked with Budd Schulberg at gathering and editing the prosecution's filmic material for the Nuremberg trials. After his discharge, he became the editor of such important films as *Body and Soul, Caught,* and *All the King's Men.*

Parrish's early directorial assignments were mostly thrillers, which he handled with a mixture of businesslike efficiency and sometimes sardonic humor (e.g., *Cry Danger,* his first effort). In his more personal films, however, he tended more toward romantic wanderings than physical action. His favorite mode proved to be introspective and hesitant, his dominant mood disenchanted and melancholy. *The Purple Plain,* his first important picture, dealt with war and some of its psychological effects with unusual sensitivity. The story of a neurotic pilot bent upon self-destruction, yet clinging to life after a plane crash in Burma, it used few battle scenes and little dialogue, succeeding solely through the director's remarkable instinct for suggesting moods and feelings. The film unobstrusively made its points about the many aspects of the situation: the death wish masquerading as heroism, the helplessness of men fighting in a strange land, their relationships with the natives, and the cultural gap between them. The film was one of the first to challenge the Production Code on the matter of miscegenation, and Parrish had the additional courage to impose an unknown oriental actress as the native girl with whom the pilot falls in love. (Gregory Peck, whose performance as the pilot remains one of his best, had also insisted that his leading lady be a native; "It took me a year to find the girl," Parrish recalls.)

Saddle the Wind was an ambitious, offbeat Western scripted by Rod Serling, with John Cassavetes giving an outstanding performance as a violence-prone rebel who eventually commits suicide, an unheard-of occurrence in a Western. (John Sturges directed a number of scenes uncredited, including a studio-imposed ending.) *Fire Down Below,* a brooding, sultry drama of passion, studied the relationship between two friends, the owners of a tramp boat off the coast of Central America, and a woman with a past who pays them to take her from one country to another and with whom they both fall in love. While the Rita Hayworth character was a stereotype, the relationship between the two men was thoughtfully delineated, and the climax, with Lemmon trapped in the burning, sinking boat, very powerful.

The Wonderful Country, Parrish's favorite among his films (he had wanted to adapt Tom Lea's novel even before he had started directing) is a sadly neglected masterpiece, one of the great Westerns of the fifties. Described by the director as a "historical" work rather than a Western, it is as remarkable for the meandering yet thoroughly controlled complexity of its story as for the understated but pervading sadness of its mood or for the beauty of its locale, a Mexico largely stripped of folklore and captured in fine, muted Technicolor by Floyd Crosby's camera. The film develops Parrish's favorite theme, a rootless hero's quest for inner peace, and Robert Mitchum's quiet desperation as the gunrunner torn between two countries and rejected by both comes as close to a perfect rendition of it as the director could have wished for. As in *The Purple Plain,* the direction is deliberately slow-paced, almost contemplative, and Parrish seems to dwell with relish on the long stretches of inaction provided by the script. In the early portion of the film, the hero breaks a leg and spends a great deal of time lying in bed with little more to do than stare at the ceiling; rather than skipping over the episode or filling it up with conversations or little incidents, Parrish makes us a party to his slow recovery, suggesting the weight of empty hours with barely perceptible tracking shots on the pensively stoical, bedridden Mitchum. Later, the hero's tentative romance with a disillusioned Army wife—movingly portrayed by Julie London—confirms the melancholy streak that seems to be so characteristic of Parrish. Which is not to say that he couldn't handle a traditional action scene, as witnessed, in *The Wonderful Country,* by a stunning Indian attack. Violent scenes, however, are exceptional in this as in most other Parrish films, which makes the occasional shifts to quick and brutal statements all the more impressive. The most memorable instance in *The Wonderful Country* is the opening of the film's closing scene, with the camera swiftly pulling away from Mitchum—as though abandoning him to his fate—after he has fired the shot that will send him running away once more from "the wonderful country."

Both the theme and mood of *The Wonderful Country* were taken up in *In the French Style,* whose Fitzgerald-like disenchantment, especially in the Jean Seberg–Stanley Baker sequences, must be credited not only to Parrish but also to Irwin Shaw's brilliant script (Shaw also wrote *Fire Down Below*). Parrish's later efforts (all filmed in Europe) have unfortunately been marred by meddling producers and/or inadequate material. Parrish's considerable but rather specialized talent is equally unsuited for broad comedy (*The Bobo,* in which he clashed with Peter Sellers; his sequences in *Casino Royale*), assembly-line spaghetti Westerns (*A Town Called Bastard*), the war epic (*Up From the Beach,* which he simply refuses to discuss), or cheap science fiction (*Doppelgänger,* an intriguing premise ruined by poor writing and shoestring special effects). A few personal touches in *Duffy* (e.g., Susannah York's farewell to James Coburn at the top of a lighthouse or her final scenes with James Mason) make up for the modish superficiality of the script, and the theatricality of *A Town Called Bastard,* although quite atypical of its director, is occasionally stimulating, the basic vulgarity of the project notwithstanding. Such intermittent flashes, however, provide only flimsy hopes as to the problematic future of a career that has been floundering almost ever since Parrish left the United States. Although one of his major films, *The Purple Plain,* is a British production, it is clear that European "freedom," whatever the reasons that made him opt for it may have been, was not the right solution for Parrish, and his masterpiece remains a film (*The Wonderful Country*) that could not have been made anywhere else but in America.

39. Sam Peckinpah (1925)

1961—*The Deadly Companions;* 1962—*Ride the High Country;* 1965—*Major Dundee;* 1969—*The Wild Bunch;* 1970—*The Ballad of Cable Hogue;* 1971—*Straw Dogs;* 1972—*The Getaway; Junior Bonner;* 1973—*Pat Garrett and Billy the Kid;* 1974—*Bring Me the Head of Alfredo Garcia;* 1975—*The Killer Elite;* 1977—*Cross of Iron;* 1978—*Convoy;* 1983—*The Osterman Weekend*

Uncredited
1982—*Jinxed* (Don Siegel)

The controversial artist always runs the risk of losing his glamour when, his shock effects having become familiar, the controversy subsides and acceptance settles in. In the case of Sam Peckinpah—undoubtedly the most controversial American director since Orson Welles—people have not so much come to accept the man's idiosyncrasies as they have resigned themselves to them. The debate raged for a few years, centering mainly on *The Wild Bunch* and *Straw Dogs;* as the seventies progressed, however, and new Peckinpah films kept appearing with awesome regularity (with seven releases between 1970 and 1975, he qualifies, after Altman, as the most prolific American director of the period), he seemed to become more and more of an embarrassment to everybody, somewhat like a raucously amusing yet ultimately tiresome guest who has overstayed his welcome. The vehemence abated, and critics started to perfunctorily dismiss his films, perhaps in the hope that, if no one paid attention to him, he would become discouraged and just go away. But no matter how much despair, or even self-hatred, may consume him, Peckinpah is not the kind to go away. His faithfulness (or is it subjection?) to his *Weltanschauung* is absolute, and far from attempting to curb his most criticized "excesses"—the gory, glorified violence, the supermachismo, the celebration of rape, the necrophiliac fascination with death—he has immersed himself in them with neurotic single-mindedness, emptying his films of almost anything else. The death wish that seems to be one of the keys to his cinema received its most stylized (although bloated) expression in that exemplary and much maligned fable, *Bring Me the Head of Alfredo Garcia.* Peckinpah keeps "wallowing" in his obsessions (but would they be obsessions if he didn't?), apparently reveling in the irony of his contradictions and heedless of the accusations of "pandering" or "mindless escapism" brought against his work. Cynical he certainly is, yet the enjoyment he derives from film making is genuine and, repetitiousness notwithstanding, continues to be at least sporadically infectious.

The pattern of Peckinpah's career is curiously cyclical, with alternating periods of fame and disrepute over a comparatively brief time span. Prior to *The Wild Bunch,* he was admired by film buffs for one single film—*Ride the High Country*—but otherwise was practically unknown. After the *Major Dundee* fiasco, followed by his dismissal from *The Cincinnati Kid* and his relegation to television, his chances of ever making it again as a major film director looked extremely flimsy. *The Wild Bunch* suddenly made his name a household word, opening the floodgates to a torrent of Sunday-magazine literature on violence-in-the-movies, an issue that had hardly exhausted itself when *Straw Dogs* burst upon the screens and reactivated the dispute. It was the film with which Peckinpah managed to alienate not only a large portion of the outraged public but also many of his former admirers. His disagreements with the producers of *Pat Garrett and Billy the Kid* recalled his tribulations with *Major Dundee,* and while this time his career didn't go under, the general disappointment in the film was instrumental in bringing about the era of benign neglect (a neglect that has unfortunately been applied in a blanket fashion to such potboilers as *The Killer Elite* or *Convoy* and to the much more ambitious *Bring Me the Head of Alfredo Garcia* and *Cross of Iron*).

Things indeed have changed since the days when Peckinpah was an exciting but problematic one-shot director, although in retrospect, his entire career appears to have been foreshadowed in *Ride the High Country* and even in the flawed and very minor but also very personal *The Deadly Companions.* In order to eschew the facile rationalizations of hindsight, however, as well as for the sake of nostalgia, this writer's pre-*Wild Bunch* evaluation of Peckinpah in *Trente ans de cinéma américain* is translated below as a prelude to further reflections:

> To make a Western on the death of the West, its myths and heroes, thereby acknowledging that the genre has become impossible, yet revitalizing it by this very acknowledgment; such was Peckinpah's remarkably modern purpose in *Ride the High Country,* a film whose historical importance lies in the fact that, inasmuch as it is intelligible only in relation to the past of the Western, it is both a product

and a symbol of the latest stage in the evolution of the genre and, to a certain extent, of the American cinema as a whole. Peckinpah, who came to the cinema after an abundant and far from negligible career as a director of television Western series, has specialized in the depiction of those weary, disenchanted losers who of late have taken over the action film, ridding it of action to the point that it seems to have lost its reason for being. The elegiac tone and autumnal hues of *Ride the High Country* celebrate the death throes not only of an era and a genre but also of the Hollywood traditions.

They are traditions, incidentally, that we have become unable to enjoy, except when revisiting the classic movies; which is why we respond to Peckinpah's modernism, with its somewhat senile antiheroes and vaguely Faulknerian degenerates, its camel races and Chinese clutter, its gunfighters-turned-sideshow-performers, and early automobiles driving down the old Main Street set. It doesn't really matter that this baroque treatment happens to be documented realism; the world it recreates, even though based on historical fact, remains strange to us because the movies had not exploited it before, and our bewilderment is exactly what the film is striving for.

Underneath its exotic surface, however, *Ride the High Country* still contained many traditional elements: a two-way itinerary, the theme of friendship and that of a young man's conscience being awakened by an elder's example, the misguided friend's final redemption, and above all a positive moral—clearly stated by the Joel McCrea character—the very traditional tenor of which was one of the film's paradoxical charms. *Major Dundee* went much further by either eliminating or thoroughly perverting the classic ingredients of the cavalry Western, a subgenre with particularly rigid rules of its own. Ironically calling upon Charlton Heston, the superhero of a string of superspectacles, Peckinpah cast him as a clumsy, stubborn officer losing control of every situation, piling up mistake upon strategic mistake, and increasingly isolated in his bitterness and resentment of the whole universe. Partly because of the nature of the story, partly on account of the producer-imposed cuts and reediting, the film's meandering plot unfolds in a total confusion of shifting allegiances and obscure fluctuations, alternately banding together or pitting against each other a bewildering array of Yankee troops, paroled Confederate prisoners, elusive Apache Indians, Mexican and French regiments. Never was such a doubtful fight or such an ill-starred loser depicted in an American film.

Why should such an original endeavor result in an ultimately disappointing picture? It is easy to blame the producer, but isn't it possible that he merely made worse a situation already jeopardized by the director's outlook? Just like the depiction of boredom tends to produce boring films, doesn't the depiction of confusion and failure run the risk of producing confused and failed ones? Or it may be that we are unprepared for such an upsetting of conventions in an area where we have been accustomed to view even minor variations as breakthroughs. At any rate, it is difficult to evaluate the picture fairly or to draw any conclusion as to Peckinpah's future evolution, since he has returned to television directing after his quarrel with producer Martin Ransohoff, who replaced him with Norman Jewison after a few days' shooting of *The Cincinnati Kid*. We may imagine that Peckinpah would have made this character of a professional gambler one of his beloved losers. Losers, however, also lose at the box office, and Ransohoff knew it well. Peckinpah's dilemma today boils down to this:

either renounce his vision or give up film making. It is to be hoped that he will find a way out of it and that his career will take a happier turn than his heroes'.

It is clear now that the dilemma was a false or merely temporary one, since Peckinpah's triumphant comeback with *The Wild Bunch* involved no renunciation or compromise but on the contrary a heightened restatement of his favorite themes. The bitterness and despondency that permeated *Ride the High Country* and *Major Dundee,* while still at the core of *The Wild Bunch* and subsequent films, is somehow counterbalanced by the director's exhilaration in depicting violence, escalating it into orgiastic celebrations of death, given and received, as the ultimate experience. This exhilaration, however, was already felt throughout the final shoot-out of *Ride the High Country,* a grandiose suicidal outing that *The Wild Bunch* reprised and expanded into the bloodiest massacre in screen history.

The Wild Bunch really picks up the thread where *Major Dundee* left off: the same romantic despair, same brooding aimlessness, same sprawling, convoluted narrative, same confused, frustrated protagonists. Despite his tendency to ramble and meander, the director never allows his message to get out of focus. There is no uncertainty as to his heroes' obsolescence and inadequacy. The automobile, for instance, appears in the film, not fleetingly as it did in *Ride the High Country* but as the central symbol of a modern world in which the outlaws no longer have a place and as an instrument of their downfall (Mapache's car is used to torture and humiliate a member of the Bunch). Peckinpah's rejection of moral Manichaeism is clearly stated too. From the very opening, with its metaphor on the universality of cruelty and killing (red ants eating a scorpion alive as delighted children watch), he is out to drive home the by then familiar point that there is no such thing as Good and Evil, only different forms and degrees of evil and different levels of awareness of that evil. The three major groups of men whose interaction make up the plot of *The Wild Bunch* (the Bunch, the bounty hunters, Mapache's army) are all motivated by self-interest and greed, they all engage in theft and cold-blooded murder. The only glimpse of a normal, lawful social structure in the film is provided by the ludicrous Temperance Union, a living symbol of moral and social hypocrisy. Law enforcement is abandoned to outlaws and irresponsible killers. Women are venal and treacherous (all the female characters in the film seem to be whores). Even the myth of childhood innocence is repeatedly deflated (kids thoroughly enjoy the torturing of Angel; a little boy shoots Pike to death).

Peckinpah's vision, however, is not one of utter pessimism. His characters cling to the one value left to them, comradeship, the instinctive adhering to an unformulated, dimly grasped code of virile togetherness. This togetherness is conveyed, with somewhat self-conscious insistence, through the leitmotif of the shared laughter that rescues the Bunch from disintegration in moments of internal strife and eventually transcends death itself as it reunites the old partners in a ponderously lyrical finale. There lies one of the film's (and Peckinpah's) serious limitations. There is something disturbingly contrived and shallow in such sentiment and its deliberate magnifying into epiphany; it is too much of a sleight of hand, performed for the sake of esthetic composition and emotional efficiency, and it prompts a nagging feeling that Peckinpah is trying to have it both ways, making a cinema of the absurd that ultimately salvages hope and meaning and humanistic values.

For the truth is that *The Wild Bunch,* like other Peckinpah films, works hard—

although underhandedly—at sneaking back in the values and rebuilding the audience responses it had supposedly set out to challenge. There is little consistency, and more than a little deviousness, in Peckinpah's alleged criticism of his heroes. On the one hand, we are led to believe that this is the death knell of the Good Guys versus Bad Guys Western; on the other, Peckinpah spares no effort to secure our sympathy for the Bunch and our contempt for the bounty hunters and the Mexican mercenaries. The Bunch may be thieves and killers, but they nevertheless exhibit characteristics that place them above their pursuers and employers. Among them, Pike Bishop stands out not only by virtue of his leadership but also for obvious moral qualities. Although no "traditional" hero, he achieves heroic status through this constantly reasserted superiority over his men.

A detailed study of the other members of the Bunch would show that even the worst among them have their "redeeming" features. The only entirely repulsive one, a half-crazed, sadistic youth who forces his helpless victims to sing hymns before he shoots them, is conveniently disposed of at the end of the opening sequence. The rest of the Bunch do behave in a brutal, revolting manner too, but significantly their most objectionable actions (killing innocent bystanders; using women to protect themselves in escaping) all occur in that same opening sequence, before we have become acquainted with them as individuals. The attack on the ammunition train, for example, is conducted in the tradition of "professionalism"—careful planning, flawless execution—with a minimum of bloodshed. The few soldiers who do get killed are dispatched unobtrusively and with atypical cleanliness—no blood spurting all over the place in their case. As for the apocalyptic massacre triggered by the remainder of the Bunch at the end, Mapache and his soldiers have proved to be such treacherous, sadistic monsters in earlier scenes that the audience is more than ready to accept their slaughter as an act of sheer justice, made heroic by the death-defying recklessness of the four men confronting a whole regiment. (Again, unpleasantness is carefully avoided; all the peasants, women, and children are somehow safely out of the way, and only the mercenaries get hurt.) What the film actually gives us is an updated reading of the old cliché about the good bad guy redeeming himself in the end through an act of heroism that costs him his life, a banality easily obscured, of course, by the dazzling pyrotechnics of the mise-en-scène.

The form of Peckinpah's films echoes their thematic contradictions. His two most famous stylistic devices, slow motion and fast cutting, are diametrically opposed in form, intent, and effect. Slow motion, which turns the most appallingly violent scenes into surreal ballets of uncanny beauty, imposes harmony upon chaos, while the hectic editing—sometimes alternated with slow motion within one scene—stresses the chaos of a disjointed universe. When values disintegrate, when sanity, order, tradition collapse, when all hell breaks loose, Peckinpah is not content to stage and record the resulting shambles; he savagely hacks at his footage in stylistic emulation of the general coming apart. The scene, early in *Junior Bonner,* in which the title character watches his father's old shack being torn down, is a collage of quick glimpses of a bulldozer crashing through splintering walls intercut with equally brief shots of Bonner driving his beat-up convertible around and almost running into another bulldozer whose goggled, Martian-looking driver looks down upon him like a silent reminder of the Bonners's obsolescence. Fast cutting is also Peckinpah's instinctive manner of conveying the failure of relationships and communication. It cannot be a coincidence that *Straw Dogs,* one of the most "overedited" films in the annals of American cinema, is also one in which the characters are totally alienated from one another, more so than in any other Peckinpah film. The argument between Dustin Hoffman and Susan George in their living room before she exposes herself to the local yokels is broken down into an amazing number of shots for a scene of this nature and length. This fragmentation duplicates and emphasizes that of the direction proper, which turns the confrontation into a game of hide-and-seek between the protagonists and the camera.

There is a fairly consistent pattern to the structure of Peckinpah's films. They usually introduce their protagonists and state their themes with strong action and sharp imagery, then slow down almost to a stop in their middle section, apparently a consequence of the characters' aimlessness as well as of Peckinpah's reluctance to follow the traditional routes of plot development. His films have no "second act" but, rather, prolonged intermissions. In *The Wild Bunch,* an enormous amount of directorial care is lavished on such activities as wandering about, riding, whoring, relaxing, drinking, squabbling, all of them meant to be significant but failing to signify enough to justify the expenditure of time and energy. Even after several viewings, what takes place between the slam-bang opening and the attack on the ammunition train tends to blur in one's memory. The middle section of *Junior Bonner* is devoted to an interminable rodeo-day parade which turns out to be almost as tedious as if it had been clipped from an old FitzPatrick Traveltalk. The whole thing is, of course, fraught with symbolism, loaded with dismal caricatures of the hero's life-style and values (e.g., a cowboy riding a wooden rocking horse pulled by a car, glimpses of which Peckinpah intercuts with shots of Bonner Junior and Senior cavorting through deserted parts of the city on Junior's horse in celebration of their shared attachment to the past), but their very abundance, their obviousness and self-indulgent lack of selectivity blunts a point that had already been made more forcefully earlier in the film anyway.

The structural looseness of Peckinpah's films is too clearly a stylistic preference to be attributed to outside tampering (and it does have its charm, most particularly in *Ride the High Country*), yet the fact that he has often been denied final cut may have a bearing on the more negative aspects of that looseness. The whole matter of authorship, however, is a complicated one in Peckinpah's case, for no matter how personal his cinema may seem, he has always managed to deprecate his films while waiving much of the responsibility for them. Not only does he habitually complain that his films have been butchered by producers and distributors, but he claims having been forced to direct many projects he didn't approve of. Interestingly, his most controversial picture, *Straw Dogs,* the one Pauline Kael felt he had been moving toward all along and which with *The Wild Bunch* is considered his most typical by the vast majority of viewers is also the one he claims to have been most reluctant to undertake at the start ("What really turned me on was the amount of money I was given to do it," he stated with unusual candor in his 1972 *Playboy* interview. "David Goodman and I sat down and tried to make something of validity out of this rotten book.").

Taking him at his word, then, it would be logical to look for the "real" Peckinpah in a film like *The Ballad of Cable Hogue,* which, he said in the same *Playboy* interview, was "the only movie I ever picked to do" and which doesn't seem to have suffered any serious postproduction tampering. Superficially, the film is quite atypical in that it is devoid of violence. Not only is Cable Hogue a naturally nonviolent individual, but, unlike most Westerns with a nonviolent hero, the film doesn't make an issue out of his reluctance to kill, which is put to the test only twice. In an unexpected twist on the traditional pattern of vengeance yarns, Hogue ends up not only sparing one of the two men he had been yearning to get even with for years (the other one he shoots in self-defense) but even handing over to him the management of the prospering stage-coach station he had built from scratch around a water hole. Neither is the film *about* nonviolence—which would just be another way of being about violence; it simply ignores it as a theme.

Despite this deliberate eschewing of what passes for Peckinpah's foremost preoccupation, *The Ballad of Cable Hogue* is unmistakably a Peckinpah film, again about an aging loner caught up in the death throes of the Old West. It is, indeed, more specific in its statement of familiar Peckinpah themes than any of his other films. This time around, the obsolescent hero is not just being phased out by progress, he is actually run over by its mechanical symbol, the automobile, and dies the most absurdist of Western deaths.

The real trouble with *The Ballad of Cable Hogue* (for no matter how much one would like to love the film, it is ultimately a failure) is not that it rehashes well-known themes but that it doesn't come up with a satisfactory dramatic structure for them and lacks a coherent style. Peckinpah strings on one scene of tedious comedy after another—the rowdy, bawdy variety he is so fond of and handles with such a leaden touch—then shifts into sticky sentiment as love and tenderness are allowed to prevail upon chamber-pot throwing. The two moods clash and, to a large extent, destroy each other. After reels of crude jokes about Stella Stevens as archetypal sex object, it is difficult to believe in, let alone be touched by, the intimate relationship that is supposed to develop later between Hogue and Hildie (especially when it is conveyed through such dubious devices as their incongruous singing duet).

This is a prime example of an ineptitude at depicting love that is probably an emotional rather than esthetic failing, the direct consequence of Peckinpah's view of women and sex roles. In dealing with a relationship, Peckinpah invariably starts by establishing the female's status as sex object and/or whore. To him, prostitutes are the only truly honest women because they openly acknowledge woman's "natural" role, which is to service men sexually and be paid for their services. (Peckinpah subscribes to the old misogynous view that, in his own words, "most married women fuck for the money that's in it.") Thus, the fact that his female characters are, more often than not, prostitutes could be seen as his own peculiar homage to womanhood were it not for the transparent insincerity of his theory. Admiration for the whore as whore is a facile paradox that has often been put forth by antibourgeois intellectuals but proves rather too theoretical to be really tenable. Surely, Peckinpah's alleged respect for the honesty of the prostitute must be counterbalanced by a conviction that a person who defines herself solely in terms of her venality and sexual availability thereby proves her dependence and inferiority (and how honest can one be in a state of dependence and inferiority?). Even a Peckinpah can't help being ambivalent in his feelings towards whores. He praises them the better to scorn women in general, for the whore is emblematic of woman's subservient function. To be an honest whore is the best achievement to which a woman can aspire, since the only alternative is to be a dishonest one.

Peckinpah's sexism per se is not at issue here, only his artistic achievement. Clearly, one could approve of very few films and very few directors if they had to pass the test of current feminist standards. At any rate, men-women relationships are too marginal a concern in most of Peckinpah's films for his blind spot on the subject to make much of a difference. It becomes a serious deficiency, however, in a film that attempts, as *The Ballad of Cable Hogue* does, to be a love story. The same applies to *Bring Me the Head of Alfredo Garcia* (although it would be inaccurate to describe the film as a love story or even an attempt at one), in which Peckinpah's ambivalence toward the hero's prostitute-girlfriend is so radical that it renders him incapable of presenting their evolution from a purely erotic relationship to a loving one in a coherent manner. For the sake of the narrative and the hero's motivations and audience involvement, the girl has to be shown as a basically decent person, yet Peckinpah goes about the task in a halfhearted, ironic manner, balancing each positive touch with sly putdowns, overt or subliminal reminders that the girl is, after all, "just a whore." In their first scene in bed together, her boyfriend (Warren Oates) discovers that he has caught crab lice from her, Peckinpah's typical and quite successful move to ground the relationship firmly in sordid detail (as in the early scenes of *The Ballad of Cable Hogue,* the treatment is broad comedy); Oates curses at his sleeping friend and douses his genitals with tequila in a futile attempt at destroying the vermin. Later in the film, at a point where the couple are contemplating a permanent relationship, and Peckinpah has devoted a long—and typically ambiguous—scene to their discussion of their feelings for each other, they get involved with two bikers, one of whom rapes the girl while the other holds her boyfriend at gun point; she thoroughly enjoys the experience.

Such an account of the scene is, to be true, misleading, and the statement should be qualified, but the very qualification will indicate how devious Peckinpah can be with his sexual dialectics. What actually happens is as follows: The rapist (who is not, incidentally, your average Hell's Angel-type slob but Kris Kristofferson projecting his customary cool, sensitive, if scruffy charm) takes the girl into the woods and tells her to remove her clothes. She complies, resigned to the situation, but doesn't conceal her contempt for him. She slaps him hard, with determination, and gets slapped in return. At this point, Peckinpah unexpectedly scrambles the psychological programming of the scene. Instead of getting more violent and forcing himself upon the girl, the biker quietly walks away and sits down at a little distance; whereupon her own attitude instantly changes; she comes to him freely, and their coupling turns into a very tender and erotic moment of shared sexual pleasure.

The sequence is a complex one, both in its purpose and effect. It has a twofold function: one at the level of the narrative, the other, more general, as an illustration of Peckinpah's views not only on rape but on sexual relationships at large; the two, however, are naturally difficult to separate. As part of the narrative, the whole sequence may seem gratuitous, as it bears no relation to the rest of the story. It ends, in an additional ironic twist, with Oates interrupting the embrace and shooting down the "rapist," but the murder plays no subsequent part in the plot; neither does the other biker reappear. It is more significant as a comment on the personality of the protagonists, but here again, ambiguity prevails. What are we supposed to make of the girl's enjoyment of her sexual encounter? She has just been humiliated and brutalized and so has the man she claims she loves. For all she knows, they both might end up being murdered (not to mention her being raped for real) by Kristofferson's sidekick, who has been established as a sadistic nut. Under such circumstances, the amazing ease with which she shifts from the role of potential rape victim to that of passionate lover may be variously interpreted as the mind-boggling acting out of a masochistic fantasy (except that there is nothing masochistic about the way she handles the situation); a reminder that she is, after all, promiscuous by virtue (if that is the word) of her trade (except that there is nothing suggestive of the prostitute about her lovemaking in that scene); or simply a manifestation of the profound mysteries of sexual attraction and female sexuality, to be accepted without questioning. In terms of the film's general themes of jealousy and revenge (which the sequence echoes with its suggestion of a *construction en abyme*), Peckinpah's concern seems to be not so much the rape itself as Oates's reaction to it. The unexpected turn taken by the situation underscores the wrongness of his killing the rapist and the destructiveness of his love for the girl. The ambiguity here lies in the fact that, while we may disapprove of Oates's action, we understand and to a degree excuse it, all the more so as he doesn't know how the situation has developed. (He might, of course, be even more enraged and murderous if he did know, and although "what would happen if . . ." is, or should be, outside the realm of critical analysis, we do, as spectators, ask ourselves such questions, and our speculations contribute to the complexity of our reactions.) Peckinpah is playing a rather perverse game with the audience, enrolling our sympathy for Oates against Kristofferson, then turning the tables and confusing our response to lead to his moral, which is, apparently, "don't shoot the rapist, for there is more to rape than meets the eye."

As a general "statement" on rape and the nature of sex relationships, however, the sequence, far from using ambiguity to confusing ends, conveys Peckinpah's point with almost didactic clarity (the double rape in *Straw Dogs,* one of his great directorial tours de force, made a somewhat similar point but in much less explicit a fashion). By allowing his victim to believe she has a choice to have sex with him or not (whether she actually does is immaterial), the rapist makes the very concept of rape appear meaningless. If the border between sexual assault and consensual intercourse can be so easily crossed, then rape is an elusive, highly subjective notion, a mere form of seduction. Conversely, Peckinpah suggests, all seduction is a form of rape. This is why his fascination for the subject is more than just prurience; rape, to him, is a metonymy for all sexual intercourse between man and woman. The sequence dramatizes what Peckinpah spelled out in (again) the 1972 *Playboy* interview: "The basic male act, by its very nature, starts out as an act of physical aggression, no matter how much love it eventually expresses, and the woman's begins as one of passivity, of submission. It's a physical fact."

To deal with *Bring Me the Head of Alfredo Garcia* from the angle of this significant but rather marginal sequence is doing an injustice to the film, though; for it happens to be Peckinpah's most personal and uncompromising—if most bizarre—effort since *The Wild Bunch* and certainly the only one since *Straw Dogs* that can be considered an important picture. It is so single-mindedly consistent in its outrageousness, its contempt for "taste," its disregard of verisimilitude and logic (except perhaps that of the unconscious) that it manages to impose its excesses as a legitimate, indeed necessary, esthetic and ethical choice. Provided, that is, that the viewer is able to overcome his initial distaste and shock—which few critics did, judging from the film's reception. It is not an easy film to like. The premise is far-fetched to the point of lunacy; most characters are repulsive grotesques; unsavory, even nauseating episodes keep turning up; and the "look" of the film is one of unrelenting ugliness. It is an endless succession of sordid hotel rooms; squalid tenements; impoverished Mexican villages; bleak, blighted landscapes through which incredibly battered automobiles careen, raising engulfing clouds of dust (dust and grime are the visual keynotes of the film, and there are more and more of them as the story progresses); all of which makes the romantic opening shot— a young girl dreamily reclining beside a swan-inhabited pond at sunset— seem perversely sarcastic. Moreover, Peckinpah manages a steady escalation of unpleasantness from mere seediness to sheer revolting horror; thus the protagonist has to rise to more chilling situations than just battling crab lice when he gets buried alive with two corpses (one of them his girlfriend's) or tries to keep a dead man's head from decomposing as he drives for several days through the Mexican desert, the head wrapped in a grimy cloth and bouncing up and down on the car seat with swarms of flies buzzing about.

Although it is easy to dismiss the plot as Peckinpah's pretext for yet another series of choreographed, ritualistic massacres leading up to a grandiose finale, the dream-like (nightmarish) quality that pervades the entire film hints at more complex intentions. The form of which *Alfredo Garcia* is most suggestive is that of the fairy tale, with its coded situations and narrative patterns, its glorification of arbitrariness and adherence to an otherworldly, yet not inconsistent, internal logic. As in any number of fairy tales, the narrative is thrown into gear by an authority figure/father image (the enormously wealthy and powerful patriarch of the film is the closest modern equivalent to a fairy-tale king) who expresses a highly eccentric wish and promises a fabulous reward to whomever will satisfy it. As a result, a number of characters are sent on a difficult quest, with many trials and hazards along the way. An unprepossessing hero eventually outwits all his competitors and wins the reward.

The Quest and the Fabulous Reward, of course, provide the basis for countless stories that have little if anything in common with the fairy tale. Two famous film examples are Huston's *The Maltese Falcon* and *Treasure of the Sierra Madre*, and *Alfredo Garcia* also belongs to their tradition (which Peckinpah acknowledges by having a character give his name as Fred C. Dobbs, the protagonist's name in the latter film). *Alfredo Garcia* may be read as another morality play on the destructiveness of greed, but its originality lies in the fairy-tale method of eschewing realism in favor of symbolism dealt with at the most literal level. When the patriarch demands "the head" of the man who seduced his daughter, he does not speak metaphorically but actually wants the man's head brought to him. It is an unnecessary request and one that will come to pose serious practical problems (here, the naturalistic exigencies of the modern dramatic narrative comically clash with the fairy tale's disregard for natural laws). But, aside from its obvious symbolical significance (i.e., castration), it works as a sign of the patriarch's power. In fairy tales, the more powerful a character, the more excessive and arbitrary his/her demands are likely to be. The king in one of Grimm's fairy tales rules that his twelve sons will be put to death if his thirteenth child turns out to be a girl. Absolute power best asserts itself through absolute arbitrariness (although, of course, the decisions are far from arbitrary at the unconscious level; both the king and Peckinpah's patriarch clearly have a problem with repressed incestuous desire).

It goes without saying that Peckinpah's flirting with the fairy tale form can only result in a subversion of its principle, not just because innocence is no longer possible but also because the Peckinpah hero is a "modern" hero, that is, one who only exists to challenge the status quo (implicit acceptance of set hierarchies and a static social order; absolute submission to authority) upon which the form is predicated. The purpose of the Reward in fairy tales (usually a kingdom—or part of one—and/or a princess) is to raise the hero to the top of the social hierarchy in acknowledgment of his allegiance, so that, even when it seems to bring about an arbitrary upheaval of the existing order, the Reward actually reasserts it. The traditional tag end "they lived happily ever after" suggests that, as the tale comes to a close, order has been established or reestablished, and nothing will ever change again. But Peckinpah's cinema, precisely, is obsessed with the inevitability of change and deals with disturbances of such magnitude that nothing after them can ever be the same again.

The fairy-tale hero lacks the questioning faculty. He is concerned only with the "how?", not the "why?" of things. In *Alfredo Garcia,* the Warren Oates character gradually develops from this purely pragmatic "fairy-tale" stage (*how* to get the head and the reward) into a "modern" questioning hero who eventually reaches a point where he simply *has* to know the reason for his quest, or else his whole effort becomes meaningless. The reward is so huge that the recipient feels he is entitled to an explanation for it, failing which it will be worthless to him. In other words, the hero challenges the arbitrariness of the premise that makes the tale possible, a challenge that remains unthinkable in a fairy tale. Ironically, far from bringing some sanity to the proceedings, the challenge only results in the hero's actions becoming themselves more arbitrary. From a mere instrument in a crazed revenge ploy, he becomes the perpetrator of his own, equally crazed revenge, thus sharing in the sin of the Father whom he denounces and kills. The destruction of the evil order represented by the patriarch and his corrupt network of power does not usher in a new order but only leads to chaos and death, including the hero's. *Bring Me the Head of Alfredo Garcia* is so preposterous in realistic terms that it can easily be disregarded as an aberration, a meaninglessly morbid shocker; yet, in no other Peckinpah film is the rule of dark, destructive instincts over human behavior more cogently asserted. And while Peckinpah has projected his fascination with death in dramatically and graphically more appealing ways, none can match the elemental poetic horror of the image of the protagonist digging his way out of the grave in which he had been literally buried alive while unconscious. There can be honesty in cynicism, and *Alfredo Garcia* is an almost desperately honest film, and one, moreover, for which the director must have known he could expect neither critical recognition nor any but the most modest box-office success. Indeed, none of his films was made with so little apparent concern for public response. It is the kind of endeavor an artist launches into both to please himself and to deal with his obsession as uncompromisingly as he possibly can, and the world be damned. Only serious artists yield to, or even experience, this kind of hazardous compulsion.

40. *Arthur Penn* (*1922*)

1958—*The Left-Handed Gun;* 1962—*The Miracle Worker;* 1965—*Mickey One;* 1966—*The Chase;* 1967—*Bonnie and Clyde;* 1969—*Alice's Restaurant;* 1970—*Little Big Man;* 1973—*Visions of Eight* (documentary episode); 1975—*Night Moves;* 1976—*The Missouri Breaks;* 1981—*Four Friends*

Uncredited
1965—*The Train* (John Frankenheimer)

Arthur Penn's is the cinema of the elemental and the inchoate, of consciousness struggling to emerge from darkness. His films concretize with startling immediacy the ordeal and pains of defining oneself, the travails of the mind reaching for self-awareness and self-knowledge. Their chaotic presentation of the physical world is an extension of, and a metaphor for, the inner confusion of their protagonists. Penn's heroes are all children of darkness, peering at reality and themselves "through a glass darkly" and almost totally cut off from either. Although their plight may be filed under "quest for identity," it is perhaps more accurately described as a straining to ascertain a *place* for themselves in a scheme of things that seems to offer none. Only when reassured that they do have such a place can they reach a sense of self-identity; for, paradoxically, Penn's outsiders, outcasts, and outlaws experience at the most visceral level the need to belong in order to be. They look for, and look up to, surrogates of the parents, teachers, or guides they have missed and unconsciously attempt to recreate the familial and communal ties and rituals they never knew or have lost or rejected. But mostly, they seek their way out of the paradox through an intensification of it: they come to equate belonging, and therefore being, with being recognized, and, more often than not, what they achieve is only the recognition of the disruptive, "antisocial" nature that made outcasts out of them in the first place. As far as they are concerned, however, any kind of relationship to the world will do, as long as contact, no matter how self-defeatingly incoherent and destructive, is established.

Thus, the chaos that Penn's heroes bring to the world (or that the world imposes upon them, for the odds against a Helen Keller or a Jack Crabb [*Little Big Man*] are admittedly staggering) only renders them more opaque to themselves. They are wanderers, drifters, always on the move, always on the run, whether pursuers or pursued, running away from the self they confusedly yearn to discover. The "notorious" ones, Billy the Kid or Clyde Barrow, will identify with their own budding legend rather than look inward; they will choose to recognize themselves in an image pieced together by the outside world, because it is the product of the world's recognition of their existence.

Clyde symbolically "becomes a man" (i.e., overcomes his sexual impotence) after Bonnie has read to him the "Ballad of Bonnie and Clyde" from the newspaper. Other characters have various ways of turning their backs on themselves. Mickey One retreats into anonymity and ultimately becomes engulfed in his paranoia. Harry Moseby (*Night Moves*) goes through the motions of investigating his own life but refuses to interpret the clues and to find out the truth. Tom Logan (*The Missouri Breaks*) won't admit to himself that his vegetable garden is not a mere front for his outlaw activities but has become the expression of still unrecognized yearnings. The Penn hero exhibits a stubborn, almost passionate reluctance to learn, to see the light. The fight to break down this resistance and to force not so much learning as the *concept* of learning upon a restive mind is the very subject of *The Miracle Worker*. And a hopeless fight it seems to be, for how, one thinks, could such savagely instinctive refusal ever be conquered? We know that it *was* conquered, but that knowledge does not make the feat any the less miraculous. This is why the most intense moment in the whole of Penn's work is Helen Keller's climactic discovery of the relationship between signifier and referent, which finally opens her mind to the outside world. (The episode faithfully recreates what actually happened, as recounted by both Helen and Annie Sullivan, but it is one of those rare cases when the dramatic power and concentration of reality surpasses that of any fiction; its impact, both conscious and subconscious, on Penn was clearly enormous.)

Chronologically Penn's second picture, *The Miracle Worker* is nevertheless a seminal work, the film of his that, in a way, contains all the others, the matrix of his cinema. (As a matter of fact, he directed the television version of *The Miracle Worker* a year before making *The Left-Handed Gun,* so that his involvement with the material does predate his first film.) Helen Keller is *literally* what other Penn protagonists are only metaphorically—blind, groping, stumbling, inarticulate. She is the ultimate outsider, an outcast from life itself, with nothing but the most physical, animallike behavior at her disposal to make herself recognized. Annie Sullivan, on the other hand, is the supreme teacher and guide, a combination mother and father image. She gives Helen life (a new, real life) by bringing her the Word, and indeed, there is something almost godlike in the character. When, in the closing sequence, Helen's fingers decipher the word *water* spelled out in sign language by Annie's hand and her lips start forming the syllables of the word as she simultaneously feels the water trickling from the pump on her other hand, one can't help being reminded of the finger of God touching Adam's in Michelangelo's painting. But Penn's creation is steeped in the physical and derives its greatness from its very physicality. If the scene is one of the most overwhelming ever put on film, it is not only because what it deals with is nothing less than the birth, or rebirth, of intelligence but because it does so in so direct, concrete, and sensual a manner that all distinction between the concept and the physical experience of it is abolished. Woman, child, and water pump are a closed-circuit system through which meaning suddenly starts running, as though a switch had been thrown, and Helen's mouthing of the word, combining with the spurting of water and the convulsive, passionate clasp of hand upon clenched fist is truly an orgasmic moment, dimly linking the scene to ancient myths of the creation as the ejaculation of a god.

Penn's dissatisfaction with *The Miracle Worker* (he has said he would like to remake it) is understandable. The film suffers from the dichotomy between the conventional theatricality of the play's dialogue and the direct, brutal authenticity of the physical confrontations between Helen and Annie, a dichotomy that becomes particularly jarring when the two elements clash within the same scene or shot, as in the first dining-room scene in which Annie grapples with an exceptionally mischievous Helen, all the while exchanging improbably elaborate lines with the girl's parents. Still lacking confidence in himself and the medium, Penn did not realize that much of what may have been necessary on stage could be dispensed with on screen; and, after all, he was expected to bring a Broadway hit to the screen, not to spirit it away. Still, one may dream of what the film might have been had it focused entirely on the Keller-Sullivan relationship, discarding the largely superfluous cast of supporting characters.

Thus, *The Miracle Worker,* although in many respects an extraordinary and admirable picture, was not a "conclusive" one. But then, none of Penn's films ever was. Despite their strong thematic and stylistic resemblances, they are all, in a sense, "one-shots," as none sets a pattern for the subsequent ones. They can't be arranged into "periods," each picture is a period unto itself. Indeed, Penn's career looks almost as erratic as his heroes' lives. He made only nine films in the twenty years between *The Left-Handed Gun* and *The Missouri Breaks,* and there were prolonged periods in between pictures when there might have been good reasons to suspect he had given up film making for good. Throughout the early and mid-sixties, he kept returning to Broadway as to the safety of the womb, maintaining a cautious distance from Hollywood, and when he finally became disenchanted with the New York dramatic scene, it was to withdraw to the substitute womb of a repertory theater in his summer retreat of Stockbridge, Massachusetts. His early films were modest productions, family affairs, so to speak, for which he surrounded himself with old friends (e.g., Fred Coe, Leslie Stevens, William Gibson) from his television and even pretelevision days.

Penn was fired from his first big-time assignment (*The Train*) after a few days' shooting, and, by his own admission, was completely bewildered by the methods and working conditions imposed upon him for the second, *The Chase*, which he describes as his "first and only 'old Hollywood' venture." (With *The Chase*, Penn's parallel involvements with stage and screen finally came to a head, as his commitment to direct *Wait Until Dark* on Broadway prevented him from going to London where producer Sam Spiegel had the film edited, with allegedly disastrous results.) Neither did success substantially alter the pattern established in the early years. After *Bonnie and Clyde*, one of the most talked-about films in history, and a huge box-office hit, Penn turned down all offers in order to make a small-budget picture in Stockbridge, *Alice's Restaurant*, using a cast of unknowns and the slimmest pretext (Arlo Guthrie's hit recording) on which to hang a script. Even more surprising, although both *Alice's Restaurant* and *Little Big Man* were far from commercial failures, Penn went into a prolonged retreat after the latter, with his only film credit until *Night Moves*, made four years later, consisting of the pole-vaulting sequence in *Visions of Eight*, the documentary on the Munich Olympiad. During the period his stage activities were also negligible. (Penn is reluctant to discuss this period and insists that his professional eclipse was largely due to private, familial problems.) In 1975 he returned to films with the fascinating *Night Moves*, which quickly came and went amid general indifference (Penelope Gilliat's perceptive *New Yorker* review, a notable exception, failed to generate any sizeable following for the film). *Night Moves's* quiet flop was soon followed by a resounding one, when *The Missouri Breaks* was panned by most American critics with the kind of savagery they once held in reserve for late Kazan. Understandably discouraged by the failure of the two films (especially *Night Moves*, which he considers one of his best works), Penn threw himself into a new Broadway venture for the first time since 1966, and having secured a hit for himself with *Sly Fox*, started making statements to the press to the effect that, while the sixties had been the perfect period for film, the seventies were the right time for theater. Thus, twenty years after *The Left-Handed Gun*, Penn's film career seemed to once more have petered out.

Of Penn's ten features to date, at least four (i.e., *Mickey One*, *The Chase*, *Alice's Restaurant* and *The Missouri Breaks*) are seriously flawed, although *how* seriously is opened to debate for each of them; and *Little Big Man*, Penn's most ambitious picture, is also his most uneven. Even the most sympathetic student of Penn's work must give these flaws close attention, not only because the films make up almost half of his modest output but also because they are quite as "personal" as his more successful achievements and represent important steps in his evolution.

The Left-Handed Gun, although ignored by American critics, was hailed by many European buffs as a highly promising first film. *The Miracle Worker* brought Penn much wider fame (together with two Academy Awards for performances) without alienating his cult following. *Mickey One*, a film made in complete freedom from producers' interference, was therefore eagerly awaited. When it arrived, the general response was dismayed bewilderment.

Penn's first two films were derived from existing material: a teleplay and a Broadway play (itself based on a teleplay). With *Mickey One*, he was freed from the strictures of the theater—or so it seemed, though, curiously, the basis for the script was an unproduced play (whose author, Alan Surgal, wrote the adaptation). This origin is unacknowledged by the film's credits, probably because the changes wrought on the play in the adapting were considerable; still, the basic premise was retained, and its artificial conceit does strike one as better suited for the stage than the screen. Penn felt differently, however, and concentrated on opening up and visualizing what must have been a rather claustrophobic intellectual exercise (the entire action took place in one room), turning it into a kind of *Pilgrim's Progress* of modern angst.

Superficially, *Mickey One* bears a strong (and perhaps not accidental) resemblance to Ken Hughes's fine and much underrated British thriller, *The Small World of Sammy Lee* (1963), originally a teleplay broadcast both in England and on American network television in 1958. Each film deals with a night-club comic whose gambling debts to the mob cause him to run for his life. The resemblance, however, stops there. The only common point between Sammy and Mickey beyond their trade and initial predicament is that they both run a lot, and not just metaphorically. Hughes's film could be retitled *What Makes Sammy Run,* Penn's *What Makes Mickey Run?* The change from the declarative to the interrogative points to the two film makers' radically different approaches. While the purpose of Sammy's frantic activity is very clear (he must raise a certain sum of money within twenty-four hours or face a beating or worse), the menace Mickey is running away from is kept so abstract that it soon begins to look like a pretext for self-punishment, the rationalization of an inflated guilt complex ("I'm guilty of not being innocent!"). *Sammy Lee* is a straight thriller, *Mickey One* its absurdist, Kafkaesque version. Unfortunately, audiences confronted with night clubs, gangsters, gambling, and the like are conditioned to expect a straight thriller, not a study in paranoia with existential undertones and surrealistic overtones. It was Penn's fatal mistake to disregard these expectations or to think that he could get around them without some thorough restructuring.

The quasi-universal consensus on *Mickey One* is that it is a failure of a major magnitude (Robin Wood: "Any anxieties one has about Penn are centered on *Mickey One*"), and the feeling is quite understandable. Failures, however, do not have to be boring, and *Mickey One* happens to be quite enjoyable if taken in the right spirit (which, of course, may not be the spirit intended by the director). What made most viewers unable to enjoy the film in its time was their grim determination to comprehend what the story was all about. In 1964, movies, American movies at least, were supposed to "make sense" at the most literal level. *Mickey One* predated *Blow-Up* by almost two years, and the absurdist-nihilistic mood of late sixties movies was still quite a long way off. As a result, the film was dismissed as pretentious, arty, and hopelessly obscure. It *is* pretentious but not half as much as it could have been. It *is* murky, but the murkiness is not really annoying unless one insists upon probing it for some elusive "meaning." The best way to experience *Mickey One* is to forego interpretation and simply enjoy (if such "simplicity" is possible, and it should be) the bizarre imagery, the sprightly editing, the soaring improvisations of Stan Getz's tenor saxophone. More of a stylistic tour de force than anything else, *Mickey One* is obviously a film that Penn had a lot of fun making, and it should be viewed in a spirit of fun.

True, Penn himself makes it difficult for us to relax to such an extent. He perversely sticks to a minimal realism that prevents his film from actually being taken over by the kind of nightmarish fantasy it keeps courting. Penn's guideline for this project could have been Mack Sennett's motto, "Always the improbable, never the impossible." Thus when Mickey, in a state of intense paranoid agitation, runs into the bedroom of his second-floor apartment and is confronted with the weird sight of a man bobbing up and down just outside the window and staring into the room, as though in vertical levitation, one thinks for a brief moment that Penn has finally given up the pretense of realism and given in to a phantasmatic approach. A "rational" explanation, however, is promptly provided, as we discover that the man has been bouncing up from a trampoline placed in the building's backyard. The explanation satisfies our craving for logic, no doubt, but at the same time thumbs its nose at it; it is so far-fetched that the audience may find the bouncing man harder to accept as "real" than as an allegorical projection of Mickey's fears.

The trampoline is used as a springboard for a gag such as one might encounter in a silent comedy (it is reminiscent of some Keaton gags, especially the "captain's portrait behind the porthole" routine in *The Navigator*). Penn even tops it by having Mickey jump out the window, land on the trampoline below, and run away as the intruder stares in puzzlement, a neat reversal in the grand tradition of visual comedy. Clearly, no "straight" thriller would resort to such a bit of business, and the spectator, once reassured that the bouncing man was an explainable phenomenon, may very well resent the nature of the explanation, this unseemly intrusion of the comic mode, which seems to be the film maker's way not just to have some fun but perhaps, too, of having it at his—the spectator's—expense.

There is a great deal of such toying with the audience in the film but not with a mystifying intention. Penn was engaged in a difficult balancing act, trying to preserve the ambiguity of a narrative that has much affinity with the surrealist principle of fantasy and reality as indistinguishable extensions of each other. Penn's vision is not a surrealist vision, however (although the thought of surrealism must have been at the back, or even the front, of his mind). In order to produce a truly surrealist work, one has to be either completely committed to the surrealist method or completely naive and unaware of it. Penn was neither, and surrealism is not the key to *Mickey One,* despite the truly surrealist ring of some of its touches.

Mickey One may be an odd film, but it is by no means an oddity in terms of Penn's stylistic and thematic development. It is the first full-fledged instance of the director's fashioning of a kaleidoscopic style—fragmentation, syncopatic punctuations, abrupt transitions, visual and aural collisions—out of the systematic manipulation of the filmic material (which reminds us that Penn's fascination with the expressive resources of editing predated his collaboration with Dede Allen, the editor for all his films starting with *Bonnie and Clyde,* whom some critics see as the determining influence on Penn's editing style). Thematically, *Mickey One,* like Penn's first two pictures and like all the subsequent ones, deals with the individual's struggle to ascertain his own identity through his relationship to the world. The film's peculiarity lies in the fact that Mickey's "quest" for identity takes the paradoxical form of a craving for anonymity. The initial phase of Mickey's psychological itinerary is the inverted version of Helen Keller's final one: Helen's conquest of speech leads her to self-awareness and an awareness of reality; Mickey's forsaking of verbal expression (the comedian's glib articulateness gives way to a period of near muteness after he has decided to go into hiding) is his first step in a self-imposed process that cuts him from himself and from reality. Later, however, Mickey struggles back to articulateness, and self-recognition. The scene in which he visits a strip joint and, first tentatively, almost reluctantly, then with growing exhilaration, starts to cut in on the M.C., ending up by trading jokes with him, actually duplicates, whether consciously or not, the climactic moment of Helen's first words, that seminal scene of Penn's cinema. The nature of the breakthrough is the same in both cases. (The reading of the poem and subsequent sexual fulfillment of the protagonists in *Bonnie and Clyde* is the most clearly enunciated among other such "breakthrough" scenes in Penn's work.)

Thus, no matter how eccentric it may seem when viewed as an isolated item, *Mickey One* becomes reasonably intelligible when placed in the context of Penn's work. Mickey is a character in search, not of an author—or auteur—but of a *form*. Robin Wood identified what may be the film's basic weakness when he pointed out the "curious split between the immaturity of the overall conception and the extreme sureness of the execution." As it is, *Mickey One* very much resembles that cryptic conversation piece, the kinetic sculpture called *Yes,* which could have been meant as a metaphor for the film: a bold construction, it gives off fireworks when set into motion but self-destructs in the process.

With *The Chase,* as with *Mickey One,* the dominant impression is of something fundamentally wrong at the core of the project. The dichotomy between conception and execution that Wood noted about *Mickey One* does not exist here, however. On the contrary, the overstated theatricality of the direction quite matches the extravagance of the dramatic content, with the paradoxical result that a unity of sorts emerges from the baffling incoherence and disjointedness of the whole affair.

One of the few common points between the two films is their nightmarish quality; another, but related one, their disregard for verisimilitude. Unlike *Mickey One,* however, *The Chase* belongs to a naturalistic tradition predicated on the spectator's suspension of disbelief (which was neither required nor even desirable in the case of the dream world inhabited by Mickey) and which therefore demands that, within its own conventions, a degree of psychological and dramatic consistency be observed. The fact that motivations and behavior are consistently unbelievable throughout the film frustrates the spectator's legitimate expectations, as he realizes that a familiar genre (the melodrama of small-town mores, southern variety) is being used as a pretext for a crude morality play in which allegory is substituted for character, and the plot boils down to a series of contrivances pointing to the moral.

Although he is not as emotional today about *The Chase* as he once was (he disowned it in a number of interviews), Penn still considers its making the unhappiest experience of his career. His plight was that of a talented but still comparatively inexperienced director struggling with hopeless material and, simultaneously, with all the constraints, pressures, and frustrations of a big Hollywood production. (The two battles were fought on the same battlefield and at times became indistinguishable; no matter how inadequate Lillian Hellman's script may have been, it could only be made worse by the daily rewrites—the uncredited work of Ivan Moffat, Horton Foote, and perhaps others—which producer Spiegel imposed upon Penn.)

The umbilical cord that linked Penn to the theater was still strong when he undertook *The Chase,* and the fact may account for his initial misjudgment of the material and its cinematic potential. Like his preceding films, *The Chase* was derived from a play, and although the author, Horton Foote, had subsequently adapted it into a novel, the end result on the screen has an unmistakable stage quality about it. (One may assume that Hellman based *her* adaptation primarily upon the play; at any rate, whatever she borrowed from the novel, she translated into something closer to her favorite idiom.) Penn has mentioned his admiration for Hellman (whose *Toys in the Attic* he had directed on Broadway) as one of his major reasons for accepting the assignment, which is indicative of his allegiance to the values and hierarchies of the stage world at the time.

Penn's only opportunities to get away from his Main Street set and cardboard characters are the scenes of Bubber Reeves's escape from prison and all-day flight through marshes, woods, and swamps. These are energetically paced and visually beautiful, especially the opening sequence, with its camera work reminiscent of the swamp scenes in Minnelli's *Home from the Hill*. Those moments, however, have little relationship to the action proper and are even detrimental to it in at least two ways: they underscore, by contrast, the stagebound nature of the rest of the film; and they focus our attention on a character who is hardly a character at all but rather a dramatic device, that old standby of the playwright's craft: the "catalyst." One feels that Reeves should have been either considerably developed, and integrated to the action, or else entirely confined to his symbolical role as the Menace from Without, and kept off-screen throughout. Because he has no reality of his own, the climactic auto-graveyard sequence—in which Reeves at last encounters his wife, his old pal and now rival, as well as a lynching mob that seems to include the entire community—completely collapses dramatically despite its visual brilliance.

The Reeves character starts the creaky machinery of the play moving and to a certain extent conditions the level of credibility of the whole proceedings. The premise (a whole community going frantic at the news that a local boy, who may have reasons to dislike some people in town, has escaped from the penitentiary) is so preposterous that, even were the people involved portrayed with a great deal more subtlety, their reactions would remain basically unbelievable. The film boasts a multitude of characters, but most of them are stereotypes, which the script, instead of fleshing them out, turns into caricatures; the few that escape that fate are so sketchily drawn that they remain ciphers. Penn's heroes are always complex—if inarticulate—individuals whose complexities are revealed through their emotional and physical clashes with the surrounding world. There are no complexities to be revealed in *The Chase*, and although Penn's flair for physical expressionism reasserts itself in an occasional touch, the performances remain the most conventional and uninventive in any film of his.

A monster of a film, it both repels and fascinates, the way freaks do. It becomes truly impressive, however, when it comes to terms with its monstrosity and instead of making excuses for it, flaunts it. The last fourth of the film—where Penn seems to have had the most input—does exactly that, starting with the indescribably brutal scene in which a trio of irate citizens beats up sheriff Calder (Marlon Brando) in his office. (In some takes, according to Penn, the actors actually hit each other, but the footage was deemed "unbearable" and left out when the film was edited. Even so, it is quite possibly the most realistic scene of its kind in any fiction film.) The fact that the aggressors' behavior seems absurdly out of proportion to their motivation makes the scene all the more startling and upsetting. From then on, we feel, the most grotesque happenings can take place. And they do.

Calder's hideously deformed face after the beating can be seen—like the kinetic sculpture in *Mickey One*—as a metaphor for the film and its esthetics. The impact of his ghastly appearance reaches beyond the shock effect of a particularly successful makeup job; it is as though Brando, the star of the film, had been turned into a monster *in the image of the film itself*. At that point, the monstrosity is extended to the entire world of the film, as Calder's fellow citizens, seen in subjective shots through his impaired vision, become in turn mishapen images whose physical ugliness and deformity manifest the moral evil they are meant to represent. The image that Hellman's lumbering dramatics had been trying to conjure (the South as Pure Evil) is suddenly brought home in grandiloquent but superbly visual terms. In a collective celebration that brings together hitherto carefully segregated age and social groups, an auto graveyard is bombarded with fiery tires, flooded with gasoline, and set ablaze for the ritualistic burning at the stake of the returned native, the hated conscience of the town. This having failed, the Menace is moments later swiftly disposed of in a stunningly mounted reenactment of Jack Ruby's shooting of Lee Harvey Oswald. None of it makes much sense as social comment, but the visual and emotional impact comes in time to make it clear that, even in the most uncongenial circumstances, Penn could still come up with one of his visions of engulfing chaos.

Alice's Restaurant, the third of Penn's failures, is, like *Mickey One* and unlike *The Chase,* a small-scale independent effort, and a very personal one. Unlike both films, it presents a controversial issue, for whereas almost everybody agrees that *Mickey One* and *The Chase* are failures (Wood's opinion on the latter is the only notable dissent), many critics hold *Alice's Restaurant* in high regard. They have no trouble relating its thematic content to that of other Penn films; what they fail to account for, however, is the distressing physical experience of the film's deliberate disjointedness.

Sitting through this bleak, chaotic throwaway of a movie is somewhat like taking a bumpy ride across a debris-strewn city park at the end of a summer holiday—not an entirely gratuitous comparison considering that litter is such a prominently featured ingredient of the film. Indeed, there is something ironically symbolic about Penn's attention to garbage and garbage dumping (an attention that verges on fascination; the two dumping scenes are filmed and edited with quasi-Eisensteinean lyricism). What may have been intended as a metaphor for the discarding of bourgeois values, a flippant farewell to the consumer society, can thus also be seen as a metonymy for the overall style of the film.

Alice's Restaurant does look like a city dump; its cluttered setups tumble across the screen like so many pieces of refuse pouring from a sanitation truck. It is as though Penn's old fondness for the depiction of messiness had been raised to the status of an esthetic principle. Confused agitation prevails in nearly every scene, and whenever agitation is not required by the action of the scene, the cutting supplies it anyway. In *Alice's Restaurant,* Penn's editing is not just nervous but spastic. The simplest dialogue scene is broken down into a bewildering multitude of shots, with desultory switching of angles and constant cross-cutting between meaninglessly emphatic reaction shots. Such fragmentation further weakens performances that largely rely on the limited set of facial expressions (head tiltings, squints, ubiquitous nodding) favored by the dropout generation as a substitute for articulateness.

One might argue, of course, that the film's formal chaos reflects the very chaos it depicts. After all, *Alice's Restaurant* is supposed to deal with the malaise of a confused, rebellious generation searching for new values and new life-styles (although, in point of fact it hardly deals with it at all). But the film is not so much deconstructed as unconstructed, not so much dedramatized as undramatic, with Penn's familiar preoccupations scattered all over the place, rather than organized into any kind of coherent pattern. It is typical late-sixties sloppiness posturing as free-form narrative.

In Penn's successful films, social relevance is attained through the immediacy of his depiction of an individual experience. Characterization in *Alice's Restaurant* is too sketchy for any such thing to happen, so that this most topical of Penn's films fails to make any significant comment upon the society it purports to analyze. There is no central character, which, again, might be an appropriate approach for a movie dealing with communal, or semicommunal living. However, Penn's concern turns out to be not so much with communal life as with its impact on the personal problems of a few individuals who, although they have opted for that life-style, prove unable to cope with some of its consequences. In effect, the film quite traditionally concentrates on three or four characters (Arlo, Alice, and Ray and, to a lesser extent, Shelly, the drug addict), and if none of them may be called "central," it is only because Penn leaves them and their relationships largely undefined. Arlo is too passive and detached a character to fulfill any dramatic function. A bystander, rather than a protagonist, he is denied a chance to act, react, and reveal more about himself, as nothing of any consequence ever happens to him. The threat of the draft is conveniently disposed of as soon as raised (Penn treats the induction sequence as broad slapstick farce anyway, thus defusing the situation while appearing boldly satirical). Moreover, we are told nothing about Arlo's feelings, either about his father's death or his relationship to the girl with whom he almost literally rides away into the sunset in the end. (The relationship is no more than hinted at; the girl—the epitome of adoring docility—is seen only fleetingly and hardly speaks more than a couple of lines in the entire film.)

Thus, we have no choice but to accept Arlo as an uninvolved outsider passing through on his way to whatever awaits him in the problematic future of mildly talented dropouts. We are led to expect much more, however, from Alice and Ray, the film's actual focal characters. There, unfortunately, Penn failed to devise a valid alternative to the traditional characterization and dramatic construction he had resolved to eschew. Alice and Ray are hardly less sketchy than the dim hippy types who gravitate around them. He comes across as a blundering idiot, she as a would-be earth mother with an innate inadequacy for the role. The nature of their relationship is anybody's guess, so that their fights and reconciliations seem arbitrary and meaningless.

That Penn should have placed these rather pathetic parental figures at the center of a film on the dropout generation is symptomatic of his uneasiness toward the phenomenon as a whole. Alice and Ray are a basically straight couple who delude themselves that they have a vocation for "alternate" life-styles, and signally fail at them. *Alice's Restaurant* is such a bleak, depressing film not just because it is esthetically sloppy to the extreme but also because it deals almost exclusively with failure, not grand, noble failures but the dismal petering out of modest, well-meaning endeavors. Penn sees the dropout movement as a worthy but doomed attempt to revitalize some of the values and rituals that traditional society had degraded into meaninglessness. He is both sympathetic to and critical of the scene he observes, but the outcome is tentativeness rather than any productive ambiguity.

It can't be denied that there are moments in the film (e.g., the fight between Ray and Shelly while the racing film is running; Shelly's burial; the closing sequence) in which Penn's formal approach not only perfectly expresses the particular scene's intentions but functions as exemplar of the mood of the film as a whole. For example, the closing tracking shot, with its combination zoom-in-dolly-out that seems to simultaneously increase and diminish the distance between Alice and the camera—thereby keeping it constant—is a brilliantly conceived formalization of the ambivalence that permeates the entire film. But its very brilliance weakens its effectiveness; the self-consciousness of the conceptualization gets in the way of emotion. The same may be said of the studied arrangement of figures in space in the burial scene or of the intricate counterpoint between the action and the film-within-the-film in the fight scene. Thus the film keeps wavering between two stylistic approaches, as well as between two moods, and manages to escape sloppiness only at the price of contrivance.

Unlike *Alice's Restaurant,* which was a spur-of-the-moment endeavor, *Little Big Man* was a project Penn had nurtured since the mid-sixties, and while there is no telling how he would have handled it at the time of *Mickey One,* it bears a strong thematic resemblance to the earlier film. Jack Crabb is, with Mickey, the most allegorical of Penn's protagonists. Both characters are fabrications serving the purpose of a demonstration rather than actual individuals. Mickey is hopelessly alienated, Crabb hopelessly rootless, and both are unable to adjust to what appears to be a hopelessly insane social scheme. Whereas Mickey's alienation remained an essentially abstract proposition, however, Crabb's rootlessness is rooted in history. Where *Mickey One* bravely attempted to create its own myth, *Little Big Man* more safely goes about deflating familiar ones, in tune with the kind of late-sixties iconoclasm that had also inspired *Alice's Restaurant.*

A further step in Penn's move away from traditional narrative structures, *Little Big Man* paradoxically relies upon the conventions and structures of a traditional *literary* genre for its purpose. The film is one of the closest equivalents to a picaresque novel the American cinema has produced. To what extent it is a *successful* equivalent is open to debate. Although the picaresque form, with its emphasis on action and movement, physical detail, and surface picturesqueness, would seem to be naturally suited to the film medium, very few movies have actually managed to master it. Perhaps because pictures are meant to be consumed in one sitting while novels as a rule are not, film requires more tightness and structure than does fiction (in this respect, it is closer to the theater than to the novel). An answer to Penn's eagerness to break away from the "well-made" three-act script, still a prevalent concept in Hollywood at the time, the picaresque approach also offered the built-in pitfall of unevenness. In a picaresque novel, the looseness of the narrative content is counterbalanced by stylistic unity, the consistency of the author's tone and delivery. The style of a film, however, is a combination of so many heterogeneous elements that such unity is all but unattainable. No matter how personal, even idiosyncratic a director's point of view may be, what is shown on the screen always retains a high degree of independence, an objective presence. Penn was aware of this, of course (thus, the bloodlessness of the massacres was intended to prevent the film from capsizing into sheer horror), but seems to have been concerned with *structural* unity rather than consistency in point of view.

The film so skilfully utilizes the picaresque principle of the cyclical recurring of characters and situations that it never becomes rambling despite its length and the huge mass of material it encompasses. Penn's *approach* to this material, however, so much lacks unity that it verges on sheer arbitrariness. The film's many moods range from near slapstick to straight drama, but their distribution is far from being even within each sequence. At one extreme, Penn offers traditional comedy routines (e.g., Jack's first meeting with Wild Bill Hickok, which, in concept if not in all its details, could be out of a Bob Hope or Jerry Lewis film); at the other, epic tableaux of relentless intensity. Most sequences, however, are played on two or more levels, with constant shifts from straight to comic (and the constant readjustments in audience responses these entail).

The Indians' attack on the stagecoach is a characteristic, and quite complex, example of this method. At one level, it is an archetypal scene, and as such intended to generate thoroughly familiar responses. It is so *self-consciously* archetypal, however, that an element of parody inevitably sneaks in (Penn approaches the scene the way we approach a word when we place it between quotes to maintain an ironic distance; it is, so to speak, a scene between quotes). Much of the scene, moreover, is deliberately played for laughs, which is still another level, for the comic and the parodic elements, although overlapping, remain quite distinct. At the same time, the action is extremely violent, with graphically brutal incidents alternating with comic touches in such rapid succession that the notion of comic relief hardly pertains (one might as well speak of dramatic relief to the comedy). To top it all, the scene is set to a brisk, bouncy harmonica score—somewhat reminiscent of the banjo music in *Bonnie and Clyde*—which, although thoroughly *un*dramatic, also eschews "comic" effect, so that a distance is maintained, and the ambivalent mood of the picture is musically reasserted. The score doesn't "duplicate" the action, since it is neither "dramatic" nor "comic," whereas the action is both; rather, it suggests a mode of response to it, a noncommittal suspension between the two moods.

No matter how expertly all this is done—or, rather, precisely *because* it is done so expertly—there is something disturbing about the ambiguity of such scenes; they raise the question not just of the purpose but of the legitimacy of the comic approach. Why, for example, should the slaughter of white men by Indians be treated as fun, while the reverse, in other scenes, is treated as tragedy? It is not that Penn is guilty of reverse prejudice—although the Indians *are* idealized in his film. More simply, Indians attacking a stagecoach are enough of a film cliché to be played for laughs, while the extermination of an entire Indian village by the U.S. Cavalry clearly is not. Still, the problem remains. Intended to preserve the picaresque mood, the injection of funny business in basically noncomedy scenes cheapens rather than enriches their contents. Only infrequently does the film hit upon the right balance of irony and pathos that seems to be the answer to its esthetic and ethical dilemma. The Little Big Horn sequence, in which the swift wiping out of Custer's troops is staged as a background to his megalomaniac rantings about politics and power, goes beyond the mock-heroic mode to give us an inkling of what an *epic* demythifying (an apparent contradiction in terms) of historical legend might be.

In no other Penn film is editing as essential as in *Little Big Man;* not just the film's formal strategy, but through it, its entire dialectics rest upon it. Only through editing can Penn achieve the modal shifts, ruptures, and ironic juxtapositions that are the backbone of his discourse. But perhaps the most important function of editing in *Little Big Man* is one of concealment and excision, a consequence of Penn's determination to deal with extreme violence while eschewing too graphic a representation of it. No act of violence is ever shown in its entirety, brutal clashes are treated in a flurry of brief shots, with the point of impact, the gory detail always ablated, cut away from. Editing virtuosity thus becomes a form of conjuring, the cutter's scissors a magician's wand. In other words, Penn's editing in *Little Big Man* is basically a technique of deception. Just like the use of comic elements, it manifests the clash between the implications of the material and the requirements of the genre, and as such, its legitimacy is equally open to question. From the strict standpoint of efficacy, however, Penn's ideological program imparts his editing with a purposefulness that makes it the exact opposite of *Alice's Restaurant's* aimless cutting style. But in their diverging ways, both films are typical examples of what could be called, without too much exaggeration, the tyranny of editing over Penn's work. To him, editing *is* filmic specificity, and its mastery the sure indication of a film maker's maturity. It is no surprise, then, that the two pictures he made after *Bonnie and Clyde* (the film he considers his first mature, fully controlled work) are his most "cutting oriented." In a very true sense, *Alice's Restaurant* and *Little Big Man are* their editing styles; which is another way of saying that that style sets their limits. Film makers who are fascinated, as Penn obviously is, with the "possibilities" of editing often underestimate the power of the shot itself; cutting, after all, is always, by definition, cutting *away from* something. True, it is also, by the same token, cutting *to* something else; but then, what has been cut to is in turn cut away from, and the compulsive jumping from shot to shot almost becomes an end in itself, while the content of the shots remains subservient to their alternation. It makes little difference that the rationale for most cuts is unclear in one film and obvious in the other; they are both instances of a filmic discourse tending to become reduced to its articulations.

A believer in genre films with a difference, and a daring, if not always successful explorer of the territories the difference covers, Penn has given us highly idiosyncratic readings of the gangster saga (*Bonnie and Clyde*), the thriller (*Mickey One; Night Moves*), and the Western (*The Left-Handed Gun; The Missouri Breaks*). His approach is quite unpredictable; at his least convincing, he can be irritatingly coy and self-conscious in his dealing with a genre; at his best, he is so uninhibited that he gives the impression he is hardly aware of the existence of the genre and has just invented it all over again. In either case, he is likely to displease both those traditionalists who like their genres untampered with and those highbrows who insist upon equating film genres with trash.

The Western is the most highly specialized of American film genres. No other is more limited in geographical space and historical time or in the types of stories and characters with which it may deal. The genre is so identified with the set of conventions that define it that any significant departure from them is met with resistance, often from the very same people who dismiss the genre *because* of those conventions. *The Missouri Breaks* is unlike—or at least not quite like—any other Western one can think of, and this very originality (in the objective—neither laudatory nor derogatory— sense of the word) probably accounts for much of the negative response to the film, although few critics cared to acknowledge such a reason for their hostility. Where *Little Big Man* is picaresque, *The Missouri Breaks* is baroque, or perhaps "precious" or "euphuistic" would be more accurate terms, for there have been baroque Westerns before (e.g., *Duel in the Sun* or *Johnny Guitar*) and they have little in common with Penn's film, which is quaint rather than flamboyant, Brando's performance notwithstanding.

As many critics have noted, *The Missouri Breaks* is much influenced by Thomas McGuane's personality (McGuane was editing his own *Ninety-Two in the Shade* while *Missouri Breaks* was in production). The major problem in evaluating the film as an Arthur Penn film is the dichotomy between the writer's and the director's respective visions, a dichotomy that exists in no other picture Penn has made. For both his successes and failures, he had worked in close harmony with writers, whether they were modest collaborators helping give shape to his own ideas (as seems to have been the case with *Mickey One* or *Alice's Restaurant*) or a Thomas Berger adapting his own hit novel. The end result had always been, first and foremost (with the possible exception of *The Chase*), an Arthur Penn film. In *The Missouri Breaks,* however, two personalities coexist rather than blend. And the film's quaintness, its ostentatious cleverness are definitely McGuane's contribution, not Penn's.

Immediately recognizable as familiar Penn elements are the depiction of the gang as substitute family, the camaraderie and tensions within the group, the adolescent horseplay (all reminiscent of *The Left-Handed Gun* and *Bonnie and Clyde*). Recognition sometimes comes as a shock, however, as we are confronted not so much with Penn's themes as with their caricatures. Thus, his characters' tendency to view themselves as performers with the world as their audience—a tendency that is unmistakable, yet neither articulated nor even realized in the case of Billy the Kid or the Barrow gang—

is blown up into a big joke, an explicit running gag. As the owner of the general store/saloon/post office wearily complains after one of Logan's gang more or less playfully threatens to blow his brain all over the mail, "It's got so's nobody can get through the day around here without doin' these outlaw skits in my store!" Since the hero and his gang can't be turned into a regular vaudeville act (although one of them remarks that "every outfit's supposed to have a comedian"), marginal show-biz types are provided. Thus, when a pathetic young man, tried for an unspecified misdemeanor, is asked by the judge to make a "colorful" statement (the trial is only an excuse for giving the town's people a show), he spills out his fantasies of himself as a dangerous outlaw and requests to be called "the Lonesome Kid," whereupon he is laughed out of the courtroom. But the biggest joke of all is, of course, Clayton (Marlon Brando) the "regulator," the quick-change artist, sharpshooter, impressionist, and female impersonator, who has turned his life into a nonstop performance and makes his living out of it.

Clayton doesn't resemble any character in any other Penn film; but then, he is a rather unique character, a grotesque, wholly fantastic creation, almost something out of an animated cartoon; one thinks of Chuck Jones's wolf or coyote, tirelessly contriving ever more elaborate (and superfluous) disguises and contraptions in order to catch their prey. The outrageously anachronistic character of Jane Braxton, with her Women's Liberation rhetoric, further contributes to the general unreality, and so does old man Braxton, an overexplicit version of the evil father that underlies all of Penn's films but is usually much more subdued. (An all-powerful dictator neurotically obsessed with the fear of losing his kingdom, Braxton seems—although Penn denies it—a caricature of Richard Nixon, and Clayton his one-man team of plumbers.)

What is totally unlike Penn, above all, is the teasing narrative mode adopted by McGuane: withheld or delayed information, private jokes, hints, tricks and surprises, all intended to keep the spectator thinking that there is more to what's going on than meets the eye, or ear. In a number of scenes, McGuane kills two birds with one stone by setting up some characters (Logan and his gang) as the outsiders, while we too are the uncomprehending spectators to a lot of chuckling, giggling, and amused, knowing glances over cryptic remarks by insiders. It is clear, however, that, of the two birds to kill, the audience is the main target. Occasionally, McGuane's conceit pays off, because it serves an actual dramatic purpose, as in the opening scene, which lulls us into a relaxed, almost pastoral mood until the brutal revelation that one of the three riders whom the camera has been following in slow, elegant boom shots is being escorted to his own hanging by the other two. But most of the time, the only purpose served is the writer's self-gratification. To a large extent, the direction was preprogrammed into such writing, and Penn had little choice but go along with it.

It may seem perversely circuitous to come around to Penn's first film after discussing most of the subsequent ones, but there is much to say for the old method of accentuating the positive by dealing with it last. Three films (*The Left-Handed Gun, Bonnie and Clyde, Night Moves*) have been set aside for final consideration because—to this writer at least—they are (together with *The Miracle Worker,* whose special situation in Penn's work has already been discussed) the basis for an admiration that survives the disappointments.

In the opening shot of Penn's first film—an extreme long shot of the New Mexico desert—a man stumbles on, as though out of nowhere, carrying a saddle. The owner of a cattle drive and his cowboys rescue him and ask questions; he squints and shrugs, uncomprehending, and doesn't answer. The first words he eventually speaks are his name: "William Bonney." To us, he is Billy the Kid, a legend of the West; to the men he has just met, however, he is nothing but this as yet meaningless name. One of the two young cowpokes who befriend him and will become his "gang" starts calling him "Bill"; the other insists on addressing him as "William"; the indeterminacy of this double rechristening points to the embryonic status of the legend at that point.

Except for a brief (but significant) reference to nine-year-old Billy's stabbing of a man who had insulted his mother, the film deliberately ignores the boy's short but tumultuous past. He seems to be born then and there, as Tunstall, the cattleman, an instant father image, ignites the spark of life in him with an explication of I Cor. 13:11–12 and the gift of a Bible (i.e., the Word; the relationship with *The Miracle Worker* is clear). After Tunstall is murdered, Billy (to his friends' astonishment: "He hardly spoke ten words to you!") will literally devote his life to the avenging of the man who metaphorically gave it to him.

The film is obsessed with endings and new beginnings, fraught with the imagery of death and rebirth. Believed to have been burned to death in a fire, Billy recovers at the place of a friend (a gunsmith). His two pals bring him a newspaper clipping telling of his death and stage a mock ceremony over his bed. Some time later, completely recovered, Billy throws the clipping in the gunsmith's forge, fans the flame, and, phoenixlike, declares "I'm no longer dead; I am born again." (Again, one is reminded of the climactic scene in *The Miracle Worker;* in both films, the character's "rebirth" is associated with an element; the forge is to fire what the pump is to water; the two mechanisms even look alike.) Governor Wallace's general amnesty is another of those new starts that give the film its pace and structure. The amnesty eradicates the past, gives the outlaw a new lease on life. But Billy sees things differently; there is one more murderer to be tracked down and killed, and the amnesty must therefore be broken. To him, it is the completion of his avenging mission that will mean a "new lease" on life. The implication of his words after he has shot that last man ("Now it's done and I am clean") is not just that he has done what he had to do but that the deed has somehow given him a clean slate, freed him to turn a new page. Thus, new beginnings conflict and cancel each other out; but Billy never seems to lose his confidence in the possibility of rebirth, of a renewed state of innocence life somehow holds in store for him.

It has been said that Penn "demythologized" Billy the Kid and his legend, but if he did at all, it was only to substitute his own variation on the myth. Indeed, the mythical aura that surrounds the hero is intensified by the Oedipal overtones of the characterization. (In addition to Tunstall, Billy has ambivalent relationships with two other father substitutes, Pat Garrett and Saval, the gunsmith. Significantly, he disrupts the former's wedding and has sex with the latter's wife.) Neither is the character "demythologized" through stricter adherence to historical truth; Penn's Billy doesn't seem to be much closer to the real-life Billy (at least from what little is known about him) than, say, King Vidor's version. In *The Left-Handed Gun,* Billy is not seen as a thief and killer but as the avenger of his spiritual father's cold-blooded murder and as such takes on a heroic and tragic dimension the real William Bonney most certainly didn't have. Even Billy's death has been rewritten, turned into a virtual suicide for tragic impact: although unarmed, he reaches for his empty holster to force Garrett to draw and shoot him (moments before, Saval had realized the relationship between his wife and Billy, and the latter had handed him his gun, begging to be shot). The paradox of the film—a paradox inherent in any fictionalization of history—is that it confronts the growing of a legend with "facts" (inasmuch as the story in traditional fiction is always given as factual) that are themselves largely legend.

Also, and in a more important way, Penn's concept (fully developed in this first film) of the hero-as-showman inevitably results in aggrandizement and glamourization. His Billy is a consummate, flamboyant performer who keeps devising clever, often histrionic routines in order to con, convince, or compel. After Tunstall's death, feigning unconcern to conceal his plans of vengeance, he throws himself into an exuberant dance number, using a broom as his partner. To remind his drunken friends of their mission, he pushes them into a puddle and empties his gun at the moon's reflection in the water, shouting "Moon! Moon!" (which happens to be the name of the man they are after). He strikes up a conversation with a lawman, surreptitiously removes two bullets from his gun while admiring it, then subtly taunts the man until he draws on him and is publicly humiliated by a triumphant and self-righteous Billy. His shooting of Hill during Pat Garrett's wedding party is planned and staged with unerring showmanship, after Billy's photograph has just been taken and he is the focus of all the guests' attention. Even dying, he can't refrain from a theatrical flourish; slumped on the ground, he dramatically holds out his gunbelt, displaying the empty holster to Garrett, a pathetic but also taunting gesture that seems to be saying, "I tricked you once more!" Through all these inspired bits of business that immediately established Penn as a master of behavioral invention, the hero seems to be deliberately working at the building of his own legend.

The modernity of *The Left-Handed Gun* lies not in "demythologizing" but in the fact that it forgoes the innocence (genuine or feigned) of the traditional Western vis à vis its mythical material and concerns itself not so much with the reworking of an oft-told tale as with an examination of the genesis of myth itself. It may have been the first Western to acknowledge the existence of a myth-making apparatus (which, in the transitional society of William Bonney's lifetime, was a combination of oral tradition and—if one may venture the anachronism—media hype) and to look into the relationship between the raw material this apparatus feeds on and the finished product. The printed word, an essential tool in the myth-making process, is ubiquitously present in the film, from Tunstall's pointing out of the biblical phrase and his presenting Billy with the book to Billy's dumping of a bagful of Billy-the-Kid literature on Moultrie's back at the end. The kid, who, ironically (but quite appropriately for a legend in the making), cannot read, is constantly provided with various types of reading matter: the Bible ("I may use it to look up some words"); the amnesty poster (to him, the most enigmatic of messages); the reward posters (which he collects and decoratively hangs from the rafters of his hideout); the newspaper articles (which tell of his death when he is still alive); the dime novels (which spread his legend when he is about to die). The printed word, then, is a two-edged sword, a source of information and misinformation, of enlightenment and confusion. Billy's persona emerges with the discussion of the biblical text and becomes diluted in the journalistic and fictional text. The media are symbolized by Moultrie, the legend-peddler, who throughout the film acts as groupie and self-appointed press agent to Billy, following him everywhere, feeding the eastern newspapers with tales of his exploits (real, embellished, or imagined), and dutifully bringing him up to date on the progress of the legend. Eventually, however, Moultrie realizes that the real Billy and the image he has helped create have little in common: "You're not like him!" he cries in dismay, as though the image was the real thing and Billy himself a fake. Moultrie then turns against his hero for not conforming to the image and betrays him to the law. While it can be said that

Penn's Billy dies because of an unresolved Oedipal conflict, it is just as true that he dies because of an equally unresolved conflict between the hero's private persona and his public image. Some ten years later, Penn was to reexamine this conflict in his second major achievement, *Bonnie and Clyde.*

Thematically and narratively, *Bonnie and Clyde* is the Arthur Penn film that most closely resembles *The Left-Handed Gun* (it is an apposite coincidence that *Bonney* and *Bonnie* happen to be phonetically identical), although it is quite a unique film, with a mood and look all of its own. *Bonnie and Clyde* revived (and radically altered) an all but extinct subgenre, the gangster-on-the-run saga (as opposed to gangster movies dealing with organized, or semiorganized, crime figures). In this subgenre, the outlaw's status, his relation to the law and the outside world are much like what they are in Western films. The Western outlaw rides; the modern gangster drives. As Penn himself pointed out in 1967, "In American Western mythology, the automobile replaced the horse in terms of the renegade figure. This was the transformation of the Western into the gangster." Penn's Clyde Barrow is a Depression-years Billy the Kid. The two have so much in common that it is hardly necessary to belabor the point.

Like *The Left-Handed Gun*, *Bonnie and Clyde* deals with young people who can think of no alternative to lawlessness in order to express themselves; like the earlier film, it concerns itself with their growth into folk heroes and with their participation in the development of their own legend. *Bonnie and Clyde,* however, strives for far greater complexity in its approach to relationships. Whereas Billy stood alone and his gang remained embryonic, the subject of *Bonnie and Clyde* is as much the group (a gang of five sharply differentiated people) and the relationships between its members as the personality of Clyde Barrow or even the Clyde-Bonnie couple. The gang is a closed unit, a true substitute family perturbed by tensions not unlike those found in real families. (Indeed, actual family ties are the major source of disruption within the group: most of the trouble comes from Blanche, Clyde's brother's wife, who tags along by necessity but never becomes integrated to the gang.)

Penn's Bonnie Parker is an exceptional character in that she is the only female to be granted full protagonist status in any Penn film. (With the obvious exception of *The Miracle Worker,* all his other films focus on male heroes and tend to keep women in the background; very few of his females are more than schematic silhouettes or caricatures, and even the occasional complex characterization—e.g., the Jennifer Warren character in *Night Moves*—remains subservient in importance to the male protagonist.) Clyde Barrow does not exist without Bonnie Parker. They meet as the film opens, immediately team up, and stay together until they are both shot in the final ambush (a departure from historical fact that emphasizes their togetherness). Bonnie is a far cry from the traditional gun moll, that decorative and expendable appendage to the macho gangster. She is thoroughly involved in all the activities of the gang. More mature, less instinctive than Clyde, she is, in a sense, the "brains" of the outfit. Not only is she capable of perceiving Clyde and herself as mythical figures, but she produces a text that casts this perception in the perfect mold for public consumption.

Bonnie and Clyde was the first American film that esthetically *and* dialectically challenged the "transparence" of traditional Hollywood cinema, its effacing of the narrative voice behind evenness of discourse and consistency of tone. In a time of ideological strife and generalized contestation, it made irony, ambivalence, and distancing vital dimensions of the fiction film, bringing to a close the era of straight narrative. Penn did not jeopardize the entertainment value of the narrative film, however. *Bonnie and Clyde* was a triumph of neoglamourization (as opposed to the decorous, well-scrubbed glamour of classic Hollywood); the more scruffy the heroes, the more winning they seem to become. The strategy was so canny that Robin Wood, for example, was moved to marvel at the "unglamourous commonness" of Bonnie and Clyde, not realizing that the very uncommonness of their "commonness" made it glamourous. It would even be a gross exaggeration to claim that Penn eschewed traditional glamour altogether; thus Faye Dunaway, in the grand tradition of Hollywood period pictures, is the epitome of standard female beauty at the time the movie was made, with only the faintest suggestion of a period look. The film makes no claim to documentary accuracy; it is a seminostalgic fantasy, the thirties viewed through the filter of a sixties sensibility. With a visual style that alternates between hard-edged glossiness and soft-focus mistiness, it is, essentially, a *pretty* picture (although it doesn't "paint a pretty picture"). One would say that Penn was faced with the extreme difficulty of making things look drab in color, except for the fact that he clearly never had any intention of making them look so. Even the violence, the bloodiest and most graphic ever seen on a screen at the time, is canceled out, in the finale, by the balletic unreality of slow motion. It may be, as some have complained, that Penn's manipulative strategy in *Bonnie and Clyde* is both esthetically and ethically questionable. It is true that its enormous influence on the American film has been, to a large extent, nefarious. Formal freedom degenerated into license, irony into cynicism, ambivalence into contempt for the audience; but the meretriciousness of so many of the followers, precisely keeps reminding us of the magnitude of the originator's achievement. Like *Citizen Kane*, *Bonnie and Clyde* is one of those few landmarks in the history of film that has retained all of its power long after the novelty has worn off.

Night Moves is unlikely to have the slightest influence on the evolution of the American film. Although it approaches the crime thriller with at least as much originality as other Penn films did other genres, it does so in such an unobtrusive manner as to render the feat all but invisible. (Its aim, it seems, is not so much to "renew" the genre as to make us forget it ever existed.) Outwardly Penn's most modest and unprepossessing work—which caused most critics to dismiss it as a routine effort, "unworthy" of its director—*Night Moves* is the mature masterpiece of an artist who, until then, and even at his best, had dealt with the medium in an experimental, somewhat tentative fashion, seldom resisting the temptation to flaunt his discoveries. The brilliance of *Bonnie and Clyde* often verges on—and occasionally lapses into—showiness; it is one of those films that manages to impose the ostentatiousness of their virtuosity as an esthetic necessity. *Night Moves* belongs to an altogether different category of films, in which the work on forms, though quite as elaborate, effaces itself and is subsumed into a pervasive quality that seems to emanate from the narrative flow itself.

Which is not to say that *Night Moves* is more "traditional" than earlier Penn films; it does belong to a traditional, indeed obsolescent genre, but the distance it keeps from it (*not* an ironic or critical distance, just a distance) is such that genre-related expectations become irrelevant. Most of the time, the story line seems to meander aimlessly, taking in extraneous material, doubling back, going round in circles (the aimlessness is deceptive, a smoke screen obfuscating the complex, rigorous organization of an exceptionally well-structured script). The "mystery" aspect of the plot is dealt with in the most peculiar, topsy-turvy manner, withholding not the solution of the problem but the problem itself until the very end, when, in a dazzling visual tour de force, both are conjured up almost simultaneously. Yet, the old machinery of the thriller is dutifully cranked up: the detective works on a case, going through the usual motions of looking up people, asking questions, trying to sort out lies from half-truths; only, the machinery keeps running down, as though exhausted, producing ever-diminishing returns.

The vacuum created by this rift between an apparently operational apparatus and its deactivation on the level of the plot proves most conducive to what is perhaps the film's major virtue, the free, evocative play of poetic imagination. It runs throughout the film, elusive but unmistakable, transmuting matter into moods, weaving dreams out of the ordinary. An intensely introverted picture, *Night Moves* is at the same time vibrantly attuned to the realm of the physical, to shapes, textures, colors, motions, to the elements, all of which become dreamlike reflections of the inner world. No one sensed it or put it better than Penelope Gilliatt: "I don't remember any other film that so freely moves, like a sleeper's imagination, among the realms of air, land, and water."

The film's dominant themes and moods coalesce in its title, whose palimpsestic allusiveness reflects the multilayered construction of the narrative. Harry Moseby moves in the dark. The job for which he has been hired proves to be ridiculously simple, yet everything connected with the situation eludes him. He senses a real mystery underneath this open-and-shut case, but he misinterprets clues, suspects the wrong people, and has no idea of what has actually been going on until he stumbles upon the truth. He is haunted by wrong moves, moves not made at the right moment or not made at all. He keeps brooding—as though he himself had been involved—over the "three little knight moves" a chess champion back in 1922 could have made to win a game but did not.

Penn's heroes are all seekers for clues groping in darkness. Nothing would seem more natural than casting one as a detective. The detective's quest, however, is of a different, even opposed nature. The truth he is seeking is not the truth about himself; he can't function *unless* his individuality is kept subservient to his function. As a fiction character, the detective is doomed to always remain somewhat *less* than an actual character (an infirmity many mystery writers attempt to conceal, or make up for, by equipping their heroes with a set of colorful mannerisms and idiosyncrasies, which, however, only succeeds in rooting them more deeply into convention). He is a kind of surrogate of the omniscient narrator; he who "makes sense" out of an arbitrarily scrambled configuration of facts. This peculiar status is, in a sense, the subject of *Night Moves,* and Penn's treatment of Harry Moseby *as an individual first and foremost* constitutes its perfect reductio ad absurdum.

No matter how "humanized" and "demythologized" the investigator may have been in some films of the seventies, he was never denied the interpretive faculty that is the fiction detective's only reason for being. In *Night Moves,* the detective is demoted to the rank and file of ordinary characters, stripped of his seerlike status as supreme decipherer and interpreter of signs. His fallibility is the price to be paid for his humanization. Failure to solve a case has occasionally been used in crime fiction but as a mere gimmick that never jeopardized the detective's prestige or altered his status within the fiction. Penn, on the other hand, is interested in the relationship and conflict between the man's function and his personality. Harry Moseby fails not only to solve the mystery at hand but even to identify its true nature, and the failure is a consequence, not of the difficulty of the case itself but of Harry's emotional shortcomings. There is a murky relation between his inability to grasp what is going on in the outside world and his inability to grasp what is going on inside himself. He is blind to the truth, and the blindness is largely self-inflicted. In a symbolic gesture, he places his hands over his eyes when his wife questions him about his father; and when handing someone his professional card, he apologetically points out: "at least it doesn't have an eye on it." The missing eye suggests the failure of insight into the private "I." Moseby is the negative side of Oedipus, that granddaddy of the flatfoot. He goes around looking for the father he never knew, and when he has found him, takes one look at him and walks away. (In terms of the Oedipal conflict, Harry is a middle-aged version of Billy the Kid; not surprisingly, everything concerning Harry's relationship to his father was Penn's own contribution to the script.)

Night Moves is a somber picture. The thriller, since *film noir* and the Chandler legacy, has always been characterized by its cynical, pessimistic view of life, but the fact that *Night Moves* transcends the genre and deals with characters who strike us as real people rather than just cogs in the machinery of a mystery plot makes the quality of despair in Penn's film particularly intense and affecting. The dominant theme is failure—failure of insight, of communication. The many relationships the film deals with (husband-wife, father-son, mother-daughter, stepdaughter-stepfather, assorted pairs of lovers) remain opaque to their participants as well as to the audience. When questioned about their feelings toward another person, the characters invariably turn noncommittal, cryptic, or inarticulate. Most of the relationships actually are, or develop into, triangles of one kind or another (husband–wife–lover, mother–daughter–stepfather, stepdaughter–stepfather–mistress), which increases their basic ambiguity. Largely as a consequence of Harry's "moves" (in all senses of the word) the triangles keep overlapping, and crossovers ensue. (The motif of the triangle is stated in an early scene that deftly superimposes three triangular relationships—past, present, and fictional: while listening to a taped biographical profile of his client, who obtained a divorce on grounds of adultery, Harry drives up to a movie theater showing *My Night at Maud's* and watches his wife coming out with her lover.) The exact position of each individual on his/her triangle, or any other triangle, is never ascertained, and the ambiguities are never resolved. In such context, relationships and life itself become a losing battle, no matter which "side" one is on. As Harry remarks about a football game on television: "one side is just losing slower than the other." At least games have clear rules (which is perhaps why Harry, an ex-football player with a passion for chess, is attracted to them). There don't seem to be any intelligible rules to the games people play in *Night Moves.*

Yet the film does not leave one with a feeling of despondency. It is too full of creative energy, too swarming with sensory and sensual stimulation, too alive with a sense of anticipation and discovery. In the end, as Harry lies wounded, perhaps fatally, in the circling boat, peering through a glass bottom darkly at the "pieces of the puzzle" coming together out of murky depths, our sense of absurdity and despair becomes strangely mingled with an exhilaration not unlike that experienced in the matrix scene of Penn's cinema, Helen Keller's discovery of language. In a visual roundup reminiscent of Helen's ecstatic enumeration of things, all the operative items of the narrative—airplane, boat, statue, diver, water—are called upon simultaneously, dragged out of darkness into the light of sense. For Harry on the brink of death as for Helen on the brink of life, signs at last begin to signify, the indecipherable is illuminated. Perhaps because the elements—water, air, and their unifying power—are again summoned, this celebration of sense regained holds intimations of a cosmic order underlying epiphenomenal chaos. Much of Penn's work is concerned, even obsessed, with chaos, sometimes to the point of becoming engulfed in it, but it is most precious for those flashes of recognition in which a poet's voice sings the doxology of the sensible.

POSTSCRIPT

Four Friends, released after this essay was written, provides a particularly sharp illustration of its opening remarks. Young Danilo, the hero (despite its title, the film definitely has a central character), is the quintessential Penn loner-outsider, desperately looking for his place in a chaotic universe. The range of experience encompassed by his search is surpassed only by *Little Big Man*'s Jack Crabb, and indeed there is a picaresque quality about *Four Friends* that is reminiscent of the latter film. *Four Friends* revisits the sixties with considerably more distancing than the immediacy of *Alice's Restaurant* had allowed. The characters' relationship to their time is of less importance than individual relationships within the group—one of Penn's favorite themes from *The Left-Handed Gun* to *The Missouri Breaks.*

Danilo is too immersed in his personal quest—an obsession with roots, efforts to communicate with a perpetually resentful father, a tragically aborted attempt at social climbing, a frustrated and periodically reactivated love for the elusive Georgia—to be more than marginally involved in the political and social turmoil of his time. The civil-rights movement, the Vietnam war and antiwar protests, the psychedelic craze, and the drug subculture are all acknowledged but appear as the context rather than the text of the narrative, as Penn seems less concerned with the historical events and social climate than with their indirect, almost subliminal echo in the hero's and his friends' consciousness. Thus, when Danilo on his way to New York where his marriage to a society girl is being planned, is passed by a busload of young blacks, including one of his old high-school buddies, he starts following them, then at the last second, as roads part, veers off—a striking example of Penn's ability to translate inner conflict into strong yet unobtrusive symbolism—and continues east as the bus drives south. Similarly, much later when Danilo drives past a draft-card-burning demonstration in Greenwich Village, this iconic ceremony is placed there, to be sure, as a *sign* of the times, but the real focus of the scene is the unfurling by a protester of a burning American flag in front of Danilo's windshield, a gesture we know must be perceived with ambivalent feelings by this immigrant who passionately loves his adopted country. (Vietnam itself is never discussed, or even mentioned, by the characters, even though one of them is drafted and brings back a Vietnamese wife and her two kids; we will know nothing of his war experience and, unlike any other movie Vietnam veteran, he seems thoroughly happy and untraumatized.)

Penn's approach is consistently oblique and elliptical, and the film's dramatic structure is perhaps the most complex and unpredictable he ever essayed. About two-thirds into what looked like a minor-key, half-comic, half-nostalgic chronicle, he throws in a scene of demented violence—in the midst of the wedding party, the father of Danilo's bride shoots the newlyweds, killing his daughter and seriously wounding Danilo, then takes his own life (one is reminded of Billy's murderous disruption of Pat Garrett's wedding in *The Left-Handed Gun*). After this major trauma, the narrative becomes more and more erratic (if one may use the adjective descriptively rather than pejoratively), as though it patterned itself after the dazed aimlessness of the survivors. Yet the film ends on an unexpectedly upbeat note, with the happy, even idyllic reunion, ten years later, of the members of the original group—with the various spouses and children collected along the way. Although Danilo sets fire to the trunk he had been carrying everywhere with him since his arrival in the United States, this symbolic burning of his past is balanced by the permanence of the past that the reunion reaffirms, in the same manner as, in the preceding scene, his parents' departure on a pilgrimage to the old country provides the occasion for Danilo to make some kind of contact with his father at last (the old man relents and smiles at him for the first time).

In the end, Danilo seems almost ready to settle down. After a fling at a working-class experience (he takes a job in the East Chicago, Indiana steelworks where his father worked all his life since coming to the United States), he announces in the reunion sequence that he is going to teach school—"English; what else can a Yugoslav teach in America?" The quest for self and the pursuit of the American dream are inextricably interwoven in *Four Friends,* a remarkably harmonious encounter of Penn's world and that of screenwriter Steve Tesich—himself a Yugoslav immigrant—who brought much of his own experience to the script and worked with Penn not only on the writing but on every phase of production and postproduction. There is something gratifyingly ironic in the fact that one of the most personal works by the painter of generational conflicts and of the search for father images resulted from a close collaboration with a writer who could be Penn's son.

41. Sydney Pollack (1934)

1965—*The Slender Thread;* 1966—*This Property Is Condemned;* 1968—*The Scalphunters;* 1969—*Castle Keep; They Shoot Horses, Don't They?;* 1972—*Jeremiah Johnson;* 1973—*The Way We Were;* 1975— *The Yakuza; Three Days of the Condor;* 1977—*Bobby Deerfield;* 1979—*The Electric Horseman;* 1981— *Absence of Malice;* 1982—*Tootsie*

Uncredited
1968—*The Swimmer* (Frank Perry)

A stylist with a message, Sydney Pollack, in his first decade and a half as a director, has not quite managed to harmonize talents and ambitions which, although not necessarily exclusive of each other, tend to clash in all his films. His form and his content are sometimes strangely at odds, and one occasionally gets the impression that he is working hard at undercutting his own best qualities. Pollack is a sensitive artist whose taste for formal flourish gets in the way of his sensitiveness. His flair for realistic detail seems to suggest a talent for straightforward storytelling, yet he consistently eschews realism or, rather, uses it deceptively, as a pretext for allegorical explorations.

These conflicting tendencies account for Pollack's difficulty in achieving dramatic, structural, and atmospheric unity. His films frustrate expectations even as they foster them. They usually open on a fairly realistic plane, then gradually veer off into one form or another of fantasy in order to deliver their message, leaving the spectator confused as to what kind of response is expected from him. Thus, *The Scalphunters* starts as a straight, somewhat solemn Western dealing with easily recognizable types and motivations but shifts to picaresque jocularity and piled-up ironies after its "real" theme—the dialectics of the black man–white man, master-slave relationship—has been introduced. *Castle Keep* uses World War II as a pretext for character studies rather than heroics and action and grows increasingly allegorical as it moves toward its climax. In *They Shoot Horses, Don't They?*, the grim inhumanity of the dance marathon is magnified out of all plausible proportions, and what had begun as a naturalistic narrative is transformed (the painstakingly accurate period re-creation notwithstanding) into an abstract, absurdist-existentialist morality play, a kind of *Huis Clos* on the dancing floor. *Jeremiah Johnson,* in its first half a near-documentary study of survival in hostile natural environment, later turns into an account of the growth of a folk legend, with Pollack conjuring an almost fantastic atmosphere through various stylistic devices. *The Yakuza* opens as a fairly traditional (aside from its exotic location) thriller and works itself up to the operatic grandiloquence of choreographed massacres and exalted symbolic gestures. Such shifts usually result in a loss of audience involvement, and the greater commercial success of *The Way We Were* and *Three Days of the Condor* may be due to the fact that the latter films are more respectful of genre conventions and do not swerve much from the mood and mode they establish at the start.

The chaotic and competitive fashion in which most of Pollack's shooting scripts seem to be developed may be cited as either cause or consequence of the schismatic tendencies of the finished products. All but two of his first eight films were written by two different scenarists (three in the case of *This Property Is Condemned*), one of whom took over from the other at some point, pulling the film in a new direction. The replacement of James Poe, who had been originally hired to direct as well as script *They Shoot Horses, Don't They?*, by Robert Thompson after Pollack was called in is a cause célèbre, but there have been similar, if less publicized changes in connection with most of Pollack's films: David Rayfiel substituting for Dan Taradash on *Castle Keep*, John Milius for Edward Anhalt on *Jeremiah Johnson*, Robert Towne for Paul Shrader on *The Yakuza*. Additionally, Rayfiel, whether credited (*Castle Keep, Condor*) or not (*Jeremiah Johnson, The Way We Were*) has been involved, according to Pollack himself, in the writing of most of the eight films, and, in the case of *The Way We Were* and *Three Days of the Condor,* effected considerable changes on the adaptations of the source novels originally written by Arthur Laurents and Lorenzo Semple respectively. From all this one may infer that Pollack's method of evolving a script consists in playing, if not one writer, at least one concept against another and eventually falling back upon a trusted accomplice when tensions escalate. A strange procedure, which, whether deliberate or instinctive, betrays the director's ambivalence toward his material and uncertainty as to his esthetic purpose.

The ambivalence and the uncertainty are reflected in Pollack's own comments upon his films. For example, he told *Positif* that the Redford-Dunaway love scene in *Three Days of the Condor* (which keeps cutting from brief shots of the two in bed to shots of the girl's photographic work on the walls of her apartment) had become "romantic" and "lyrical" *in spite of* his efforts not to make it so, a bewildering statement since such a scene, treated in such a way, can have no other conceivable purpose or effect than being romantic and lyrical. The very concept of the scene is lyrical in essence, since it establishes a connection between a sexual encounter and the psyche of the woman, as represented by the style of her photographs: these are of cold, dark, empty places, suggesting (as the Redford character has pointed out earlier) the artist's loneliness and diffidence. The connection is, in theory, ambiguous; it may denote either an escape from, or a reaffirmation of, her loneliness; but precisely Pollack's handling of the scene all but eliminates the latter possibility: the misty texture of the filtered color—which contrasts with the stark black-and-white of the pictures on the wall—the tastefully selected and edited close-ups of lovemaking, the slow camera moves gliding over the bodies and the photographs, the balladlike piano score (quite romantic, although it is kept tuneless enough not to be mistaken for a theme song), all combine to impart the scene with positive connotations: we are made to feel that a loving, "meaningful" relationship is being started. Pollack's claim to *Positif* reveals a characteristic mental process, from his initial uneasiness at dealing with a stock situation (innocent fugitive forces girl—a complete stranger—to help and shelter him) to an attempt at eschewing the traditional, and therefore expected, outcome (i.e., the two falling in love after a period of distrust and hostility) to the eventual, reluctant yielding to the built-in demands of the situation.

Pollack is so defensive about some of the most obvious features of his style that he will occasionally deny their existence. In a 1972 interview with the French magazine *Ecran,* he paid lip service to the old dogma of the superiority of uncluttered, "functional" form and insisted that he had played down symbolism, allegory and "philosophizing" in such films as *They Shoot Horses, Don't They?* and *Jeremiah Johnson.* While Pollack did tone down, or eliminate, some of the more excessive flights of fancy in James Poe's script for *Horses* (as described by Poe himself in the "Hollywood Screenwriter" issue of *Film Comment,* Winter 1970–71), the formal and thematic portentousness of the picture can hardly be denied, and it is difficult to go along with the director's claim that *Jeremiah Johnson,* a film that strives for stylistic effect as steadfastly, although possibly not as blatantly, as any of his previous efforts, was deliberately made in a very "simple" style to fit the simplicity of the story itself. Clearly, we must "trust the tale," not the artist; yet the artist's comments should not be disregarded, for the discrepancy between alleged intentions and actual results *is* a constituent of his art.

The discrepancy may account for the remoteness of Pollack's heroes, a remoteness that is part of their attraction but also makes it difficult for the spectator to relate to them, even in more indirect ways than plain old "identification." They are monoliths, allegorical figures, rather than individuals. Their psychology is either oversimplified or murky. They are immovable objects (e.g., Streisand in *The Way We Were*) or else go through sudden, unexplained mutations (e.g., Fonda in *Horses*). The personality of Hubbell, the writer-hero of *The Way We Were,* is defined almost entirely in negative terms and never really comes into focus. Harry Kilmer in *The Yakuza,* played by Robert Mitchum with immense weariness and as if in a trance, exudes a quiet desperation that the film fails to account for satisfactorily, and his self-inflicted finger amputation, with its uneasy mixture of heroic flamboyance, pathos, and ludicrousness, and its inevitable psychiatric connotations, further confuses the audience's response.

Jeremiah Johnson is a particularly enigmatic character. We are hardly given any clue as to his emotions, his purpose, the psychological impact of Indian culture upon him, or the motivations for his ultimate transformation from a peaceful settler into a blood-thirsty Indian killer (for the avenging urge that drives him at the outset cannot alone explain the epic proportions his one-man crusade takes on in the end). In this case, Pollack's reluctance to be didactic blurs his point and results in an inarticulateness not unlike Johnson's, who communicates with his Indian bride and mute adopted child through pantomime and has difficulty speaking English after a long period of time away from civilization.

While Johnson constitutes an extreme case of a character's withdrawing from his own culture and background, most of Pollack's heroes *are* outsiders, running away or insulating themselves from the mainstream of social and historical events. In *Castle Keep,* a French aristocrat and an American officer escape the reality of war in the enjoyment of art. The protagonists of *They Shoot Horses, Don't They?* escape the economic reality of the Depression in fantasies of success and, when the dream collapses, seek oblivion in suicide. Hubbell doggedly rejects commitment in the midst of political strife. The hunted hero of *Three Days of the Condor* has civic consciousness foisted upon him but, before his nightmarish adventure at the hands of the CIA, lived in the ivory tower of his byzantine research work, apparently unconcerned by its connection with the sinister realities of international spying (as an immediately identifiable symbol of his bohemian disconnectedness, he is seen as the film opens riding a Solex motorbike, a remarkably timeless vehicle whose design has hardly changed since the first model appeared in the late forties).

Rejection of the present usually entails a fascination with the past. Thus Pollack's preference for stories set in earlier days (he considers *Condor* his first truly contemporary film), while it coincides with an ongoing fashion for period movies, seems to be a natural expression of his sensibility rather than just opportunism. His brand of nostalgia is not an archeological taste for the quaintness of other eras' decor, props, looks, and manners but a yearning for lost innocence. It is a feeling that Pollack shares with his protagonists, so that the films usually deal with two superimposed layers of past: the period in which they are set and the earlier times of the characters' memories and dreams. Johnson rejects civilization for a utopian return to the "state of nature"; Katie Morosky clings to the hopes of the New Deal through the disillusioned postwar years; Kilmer adheres to an alien and anachronistic code of honor. Even the thirteen-year-old Willie Starr (*This Property Is Condemned*) lives in (and on) a dream out of the past, the idealized memory of her dead sister. While the present and future are hopeless or threatening, however, the lure of the past only leads to dead ends. Hence the disenchantment, endemic to Pollack's cinema and particularly acute in a film like *The Way We Were,* whose very theme is the passage of time. One of the most melancholy moments of the film, and of Pollack's work, is the final sequence, in which Hubbell and Katie run into each other in New York outside the Plaza hotel years after their divorce. A wistful evocation of a lost, irretrievable happiness, the scene also confronts two individual itineraries, the failed dreams and ambitions of a talented writer who has deliberately sold out (he now works for television) and the incorrigibly naive idealism of the compulsive activist (Katie is collecting signatures for a ban-the-bomb petition). The implicit opposition between the two is negated, however, by the interminably held long shot of Grand Army Plaza, a purposefully drab, empty shot that stresses the permanence and indifference of the inanimate world and the victory of time over the futility of all human endeavor.

Like many other American directors, past and present, Pollack has received more sympathetic attention in Europe than in his own country. His continuing association with Robert Redford, while a commercial asset, has probably damaged his status in the eyes of the many American critics who are loath to take Redford seriously or, more generally, tend to view such teams as detrimental to a director's personality. There may be some danger involved to Pollack in the collaboration, a temptation to rely a little too much on the actor's good looks and charm. In *The Way We Were,* with the addition of Streisand playing opposite Redford, the acting tends to become a catalogue of coy reactions by two "beautiful people" to each other's mannerisms, as though the stars' very presence, quite independently of their undeniable talent, inevitably imposed a glamourous superficiality upon the director and his material. An inkling of the mundane yet not negligible problems the collaboration with a star like Redford may entail can be derived from Pollack's answer to an interviewer's question about the actor's modern hairstyle in *Jeremiah Johnson:* "I just got him to cut off as much hair as I could. . . . If you pay an actor a million dollars because he looks like what he looks like, it's a little silly to put an artificial nose on him, even if it's right for the character. . . . if I had gone any shorter with his hair—we experimented— he would have started to look like somebody else."

But such strictures seem insignificant when compared with the mutual benefits derived from the association. Redford handles his career very much like a responsible film maker does his, or tries to, as an expression of personal feelings, preferences, and convictions. The two men do not just get along well, there seems to exist a two-way creative osmosis between them. Some cross-references are instructive in this respect. Michael Ritchie's two underrated Redford pictures (*Downhill Racer,* 1969, and *The Candidate,* 1972) have some interesting common points with Pollack's, while the mood of Ritchie's subsequent efforts is completely different. In *The Way We Were,* Pollack used a variation on the curious scene from *Downhill Racer* in which Redford, after meeting Camilla Sparv for the first time, retires to the privacy of the men's room, apparently to mull the situation over. A comparable instance of the protagonist's seeking isolation to confront his emotions occurs in *Bobby Deerfield,* when Al Pacino, alone in his car, looks at the heretofore neglected family snapshots in the seclusion and near-total darkness of a tunnel.

After using Redford in three of the four pictures he made in the early and mid-seventies, Pollack proved that he could establish a most productive rapport with a very different type of actor when he selected Pacino to play Deerfield, perhaps Pollack's most cryptically remote hero to date. Pacino delivered what may be his most sensitive screen performance, and the film, although largely misunderstood by critics who dismissed it as a *Love Story* in travelogue form, stands out as one of Pollack's very best works. Underneath the picture-postcard prettiness of its locations, the conventional glamour of the milieu (beautiful rich girl, world-famous racing car driver) and the potentially cloying sentimentality of the theme of the dying heroine, *Bobby Deerfield* is an unusually subtle study of a self-centered, inarticulate introvert who has insulated himself from his own feelings as well as from the rest of humanity and who resists being dragged out of his quasi-autistic inner world with a kind of catatonic desperation. In contrast to, and as though in defiance of, his unflaggingly morose countenance, the Marthe Keller character affects a carefree life-style whose abandon and unpredictability are almost reminiscent of screwball comedy heroines. Attempts at communication between the two are frustrating, not so much because they are so totally different as for the lack of a common language that would enable them to acknowledge the differences and deal with them. Ironically, their only common ground (both insist on keeping a central personal problem—his denial of his roots, her terminal illness—out of the relationship) is also the ultimate obstacle to mutual understanding. Thus Pollack and his scenarist Alvin Sargent set up a situation that precludes any discussion of the film's major themes by the protagonists, simultaneously eschewing the pitfalls of shallow philosophizing and challenging themselves to devise alternate ways of dealing with those themes. Pollack focuses his attention almost exclusively on his characters' behavior, a behavior that is more often than not erratic or neurotic, or both, and always eccentric, both in relationship to a "norm" (what we, as spectators, consider it to be) and to the other characters' behavioral patterns. The eccentricity reaches a high with Pacino's pathetic impersonation of Mae West, which could have been just a coy contrivance but is genuinely moving because Deerfield's retrieving this unlikely item from his past in response to his girl's questions about what he did as a child is so curiously in character, so symptomatic both of his emotional inadequacies and of his effort to overcome them.

Bobby Deerfield is, to a large extent, free of the tensions, discrepancies and contradictions that were so central to most of Pollack's earlier films. The narrative is more straightforward, the symbolism more integrated to the storyline, the visual style more sober; thus, the film may prove to be a new departure for its director. Yet, it was not a success, and the misunderstanding between Pollack and American audiences—and critics—continues. His only real hits since *They Shoot Horses, Don't They?* were *The Way We Were* and *Three Days of the Condor,* comparatively superficial efforts, and more recently *The Electric Horseman,* not a major achievement either, although its protagonist shows obvious affinities with earlier Pollack heroes, and the film deals with several of his familiar themes—nature versus civilization, selling out, roots, and so on. Paradoxically, while such films have been branded for their "commercialism," Pollack's difficulties spring from his willingness to take chances that no truly commercial director ever would. His oblique approach to his material, his often confusing narrative strategies keep him in constant danger of losing touch with his public. More specifically, many important scenes or sequences in Pollack's films are built around elements whose likelihood to trigger the wrong audience response is very high indeed. The Mae West impersonation in *Bobby Deerfield* was certainly one of those. Pollack's decision to deal with blacklisting in such a basically "romantic" film as *The Way We Were* was also serious risk taking. In the latter case, the gamble payed off. Although most of the people who flocked to the movie presumably couldn't have cared less about the Hollywood Ten and HUAC, the film's political background did not hurt its commercial career. On the other hand, audiences visibly could not accept Robert Mitchum's self-amputation in *The Yakuza.* Once it was done, they lost whatever interest in and respect for the character (and the story) they had until then. Pollack took very much the same kind of chance in *Bobby Deerfield* with Marthe Keller's unexpected loss of a strand of hair in her sleep. Both scenes, unhappily, sent audiences into uncontrollable giggling for several minutes. In both cases, the dramatic impact is obscured by what is perceived as the incidents' physical ludicrousness. The similarity underscores Pollack's determination to ignore audiences' adverse reactions and to repeat his "mistakes" when he feels that he is doing the right thing. This is esthetic integrity of a kind that is far from common in commercial movie making.

42. Abraham Polonsky (1910)

by ERIC SHERMAN

1949—Force of Evil; 1970—Tell Them Willie Boy Is Here; 1971—Romance of a Horse Thief

Rarely are a director's politics discussed more frequently than his films. However, this often has been the case with Abraham Lincoln Polonsky. His stand during the McCarthy blacklisting era and his "underground" writing activities (many with Walter Bernstein, author of *The Front*) are a part of film history lore, but careful critical analyses of the three pictures he thus far has been able to direct are conspicuously lacking. While this is regrettable in one sense, it may provide an entrance into some of the deeper concerns and significances of Polonsky's work—both unto its own and as a part of Hollywood's veiled output.

Polonsky is one of the few trained and "accredited" intellectuals to make a career in feature-film work. A student and professor of law, philosophy, and literature in New York, he came west to apply some of his writing talents to narrative fiction. Teaming with other political liberals and radicals (including Robert Rossen, Robert Aldrich, and John Garfield), he participated in Enterprise, a young production company whose first project was *Body and Soul*. This Garfield-starring boxing picture (with an original script by Polonsky and direction by Rossen) was a huge financial success, and Enterprise next produced *Force of Evil*, Polonsky's adaptation of Ira Wolfert's novel, *Tucker's People*. Since Polonsky had exerted such on-the-set influence during *Body and Soul*, he was allowed to direct this new Garfield vehicle. *Force of Evil* evoked the sense of growing corruption, both possible and actual, in the capitalistic system. Perhaps for this reason, the picture was received coolly, and Polonsky's next assignment was to script *I Can Get It for You Wholesale* (directed by Michael Gordon, 1951), a vicious tale essentially about money-grubbing in the garment industry. Also known as *Only the Best*, this picture's release more or less coincided with the mounting anti-Communist hysteria in Hollywood and Washington. Polonsky's good friends included most of the "Hollywood Ten," who were called to testify as to whether they were now or had ever been Communists. The Ten all refused under First Amendment rights to testify, were promptly found in contempt, and were jailed. Polonsky was in the next wave of witnesses, most of whom refused to testify under Fifth Amendment rights. Though they were not found in contempt nor jailed, they clearly were "uncooperative" and were thus stigmatized for the rest of their careers. Finding no open-market work for a blacklisted radical Communist writer/director, Polonsky returned to New York and started turning out articles, book reviews, novels—some under his own name, others using "fronts" or altogether false names.

Talent such as Polonsky's was too rare for Hollywood to ignore completely. Many of the Ten and subsequent unfriendly witnesses returned to the movie business via complex and hidden routes. (With a typical dark sense of humor, they now proudly take credit for "every good Hollywood film of that era" as their only way to get revenge!) Of course, their salaries were only a fraction of what they were during the above-ground days and often double and triple sets of income taxes had to be paid through their fronting compatriots. One of the ironies of this period is that Polonsky and his partners scripted every episode of the Walter Cronkite television series *You Are There,* writing about such topics as moral and ethical freedom, freedom of the press, armed revolution, and all such human rights.

After more than fifteen years of such an existence, Universal Pictures, via Jennings Lang and Frank Rosenberg, called Polonsky back to work in 1968 to rewrite, under his own name, the Richard Widmark detective picture, *Madigan.* Though this was largely a Don Siegel–directed action picture, some of the moral ambiguities characterizing Polonsky's style were apparent in the script. Film buffs hailed *Madigan's* release as the return to open activity of the man whom Andrew Sarris and many others considered to be one of the key post-Wellesian film makers. The force and forward thrust of Polonsky's creative energy carried through to another writing/directing project— the dramatization of a true tale from the American West. Concerning an Indian who had killed another Indian, *Tell Them Willie Boy Is Here* did not become so much a revisionist Western as a period vehicle for Polonsky's mature speculations on the questions of determinism versus free will, key issues derived from his earlier interest in Marxist political and metaphysical thought. Though the picture starred Robert Redford, Robert Blake, and Katharine Ross—all popular from recent film successes—it was *Butch Cassidy and the Sundance Kid,* released at the same time with Redford and Ross in the cast, that attracted the greater part of the box-office attention. This was understandable not only for the usual reasons but because Vietnam War–era Americans were not particularly anxious to see films that intensified a sense of guilt and underscored such notions as individual responsibility and moral stagnation.

On the other hand, *Willie Boy* was obviously a fine enough picture with a remarkable script and performances so that Polonsky's career did seem to be mobilized again. His next project, *Romance of a Horse Thief,* derived from a script by David Opatoshu, was filmed entirely in Europe. Stuart Byron's perceptive critical writing made it clear that *Romance* marked a substantial departure from traditional dramatic structure. The film was not centered on an individual hero's or antihero's quest but rather on a large group of people and how all their destinies interrelated.

Polonsky's growing ease with the craft of directing was apparent in his probing for new cinematic forms to suit his ideas. *Romance* broke with several Hollywood traditions, and his next two scripts (yet unfilmed) further this trend. *Mario and the Magician,* based on Thomas Mann's short story, establishes a paradigm for the way fascistic or authoritarian mentality can invade an individual or collective unconscious and cause subservience to become a valued personality trait. *Childhood's End* is a science-fiction tale from Arthur C. Clarke, author of *2001.* Polonsky sees *Childhood's End,* one of the classics in the genre, as a means of expounding all his metaphysics, replete with contradictions, frustrations, hopes.

It should be clear that the interrelationships between Polonsky's work and life are extensive, and became the necessary repository for all his bottled-up creative drive, so frustrated by his years of subterranean work. It is not sufficient to examine his politics to the exclusion of the esthetics of his films; nor will it do to apply strictly formal considerations to the three films directed by a mature man whose personal life has been so overwhelmingly affected by his social views.

In all of Polonsky's films, the major character's basic ethics, morality, and drives are questioned. John Garfield, ambitiously pursuing a boxing career in *Body and Soul,* has to put up with his mother's admonitions against such a terrible profession. "Better," she says, "you should buy a gun and shoot yourself." Garfield's only possible response is, "You need money to buy a gun." Garfield, like all of Polonsky's protagonists, is not ruling out moral considerations, merely suggesting that they are presently irrelevant to certain other primal needs. He, like all the others, does pay the price, however. His black trainer (a former champ whom Garfield had pummeled into oblivion) dies as a direct result of Garfield's moral dilemma. But Polonsky's view of the black man is equally ambivalent—for he, too, had made certain compromises in his own rise to the top, and this tragically unattended death is only the necessary conclusion of a pathetically misled talent.

Money, and the vices to which it is heir—and cause—is, in a sense, the villain in *Force of Evil.* Garfield, now playing Joe Morse, a smart lawyer-mouthpiece for the Mob, has knowingly and willingly sacrificed all—including his own brother, Leo—to accumulate "more." Numerous others are exploited or fall by the wayside. However, it is a tribute to the maturity of Polonsky's vision that no one—and everyone—is seen as a victim. All the characters are participants in a crime, the crime of misplacing their energies in the direction of baseless values. When Garfield is made apprehensive about information he might have leaked over a tapped phone, he tries to cover his emotions by protesting, "I'm not a nickel, I don't spend my life in a telephone." But in a certain real sense, he might just as well have. His collection of gambling debts—most of them small change—is as close to a faceless crime as possible. The "victims" gladly give their dimes to a game that offers no real hope. When they lose their coins, it's never, "I've got to stop playing this," but rather, "If only I'd have bet another number." Everyone has sold out to a hopeless hope. When Thomas Gomez, Garfield's brother and the operator of a small local numbers' bank, protests that he's a "legitimate businessman," without his brother's Mob affiliation, Garfield rightfully counters that the crime according to the penal code is the same, only the stakes are different. In fact, Garfield may even be the more honest of the two, since he acknowledges that he's given up moral righteousness in order to pursue fully that which he's decided to live for. He tells his brother that "money has no moral opinions," and when his brother responds, "I find I have, Joe, I find I have," Garfield can only express sincere frustration that Leo has gone just so far but will not make the full plunge. There are not even situation ethics operating here, only levels of lawlessness and daring.

Similarly, Garfield's temptation of Beatrice Pearson in the famous taxi scene is not met by her with revulsion but rather the insight that if she falls in love with him, it's only to love something evil in herself. Fred Bauer, the bookkeeper, turns in his employers not because he realizes the wrongs of their work but because he himself doesn't want to be arrested. In fact, it really is Bauer, a small cog in the operation, who sets up Gomez's death over and above any moral dilemma that Gomez experiences regarding his brother. Again, with the flashes of insight peculiar to Polonsky people, Gomez points out to Bauer that his squealing will put the mark of Cain on his brother. "How could you do that, Freddy?" Earlier, Gomez had told Garfield that "All Cain did to Abel was kill him." In other words, *that* betrayal was an action of human weakness not fraught with such implications of moral decrepitude.

The events of *Force of Evil* occur in a homogeneous field where action is what it is, not what it seems. The cinematographer, George Barnes, was asked by Polonsky to recreate the shaded street lighting of Hopper paintings. The towers of Wall Street loom like gothic pillars over the antlike movements of pathetic people scurrying to get and keep a buck. Telephones, adding machines, coin sorters, wall safes, all become the objective correspondents of the ethical anomie in which *Force of Evil*'s characters live. A walk down a stairway becomes a descent into hell; a knock on a door becomes a demonic imperative; the presentation of flowers is a summoning to act against one's judgment of right and wrong. Everyone—Joe, his brother Leo, his girlfriend Doris, his boss Tucker, his bookkeeper Bauer—occupies a world where words and intentions are irrelevant in light of the results of actions.

Polonsky's aural equivalent to this condition is to have his characters speak in what amounts to blank verse. Key phrases are repeated, setting up rhythms that are more indicative of latent meanings than the words themselves. When Leo Morse first turns down Joe's invitation to join the combine, it's not a simple "no thanks" or "no, it's impossible." Rather, we hear him wail, "My answer is no, absolutely and finally no, finally and positively no, no, NO, no." He doth protest too much, for in nearly the next scene, he *has* joined. Of course, says he, it's just a way to pay off his debts, so he *then* can become honest. It has come to be a Polonsky trademark that his people act as though they must follow certain lines of action in order to free themselves of the necessities that made those lines their only potentials to begin with. Seldom do they realize that those potentials don't exist in a vacuum but are the logically determined results of all their previous actions.

The effects of Polonsky's years in exile only made this vision more permanent and, if possible, more austere. When asked in a recent interview how his politics have changed, he replied, "They're the same as ever, except more so." *Tell Them Willie Boy Is Here* was, in a way, twenty years in the making. Working with a tragic but typical turn-of-the-century incident involving a "renegade Indian" who had killed another Indian, Polonsky put his own particular vision on the events to yield for us a post-atom bomb, post-Korean War, mid-Vietnam War description of—again—how people set themselves up for their own undoing. In this case, a sheriff, played with great intensity by Robert Redford, tracks Willie Boy, played with a quiet strength by Robert Blake. Redford reluctantly follows through with his assignment, seemingly "hating to do it" all along the way. It is almost as if Willie Boy is leading him on rather than fleeing from him. When Redford stops for a drink at a creek and bends over to find that his own hands are in the same spot where Willie Boy's hands must just have been, a look of recognition comes over him, as in *Force of Evil* when Garfield begins to understand that he has, indeed, caused his brother's death. But, as with Garfield, it is essentially too late to stop the course of events. As Polonsky often says, at this point in life, all you can do is "remember and know" what happened, emphasizing the how and why.

Willie Boy, as the other films, is no simple morality play with right and wrong clearly defined. There is a metaphysics operating over and above all the socio-political references throughout the film. At one point during the chase, Redford encounters a farmer who comments that "This doesn't make any sense." Redford replies, "Maybe that's the sense it makes." It's this edge injected by Polonsky that gives all his films their richness and their impossibility at being read simply as extensions of any Marxist or revisionist historical tracts. Even the despicable professional Indian-hunter played by Barry Sullivan is rendered pathetic when he's shot down by Willie Boy. It's as though when one pays his price, even the lowest individual is seen simultaneously as a function of himself and of the other constituent entities surrounding him. Renoir's edict from *La Règle du Jeu* comes to mind: "tout le monde a ses raisons."

This idea is given its most complete fulfillment in *Romance of a Horse Thief*. Again, there is an essentially socio-economic tension—Russians oppressing Jews in 1902 at the Polish border. Some leave, some stay. Horses become of great value; song and drink are revered as necessary releases; people "flee" to America but don't really seem that anxious to get there. Everyone seems capable of love, and of cheating.

When criticized for taking too lighthearted an approach to such a serious situation (which recalls attacks on Lubitsch after *To Be or Not to Be*), Polonsky remarked, "I know about pogroms . . . this isn't a picture about pogroms." It's as if to say, "Why should I make a film about that. This is a side you don't always see; perhaps a more interesting side—because here we see what people can be." Is there a reason why any subject can't be treated as a romance or, as Polonsky sometimes says, a pavane?

Yul Brynner, playing the local commandant, the potential source of all evil, is himself a sympathetic figure, exiled in fact because of his own zest for life. ("Malava was to be my prison; I tried to make it my home.") Brynner is also the source of what is perhaps the major theme in the film: everything changes, whether we want it to or not. This universal principle is profoundly applied by Polonsky to occurrences in the film that would ordinarily be taken by liberals to be political givens. A "cell" meeting turns into a romantic picnic; an impossible impersonation leads to the escape of everyone who wants to escape; a horse being led through the halls of a whore house goes unnoticed by the "villain" Brynner; a young horse thief risks all just to ride a beautiful white horse. In fact, this last scene is one of the most lyrical in film memory, evoking the transient quality of "real" time and space. In the midst of a dire circumstance we are treated to a montage of dancer Oliver Tobias at loose in a field with this horse.

So, in *Romance,* thieves don't really steal; commandants don't really command; politicos don't really revolutionize; emigrants don't really emigrate. The last image of the picture—an ensemble of the leading characters blending in with the woods that have provided them camouflage—is perhaps the most succinct statement of Polonsky's overriding ethic: the determinism apparent in all dogmatizations of social behavior is but one aspect of the way humans interact with the universe. To get the complete story, one must look at how people become other than what they start out to be.

43. *Richard Quine* (1920)

1948—*Leather Gloves*, codirector: William Asher; 1951—*Sunny Side of the Street; Purple Heart Diary;* 1952—*Sound Off; Rainbow 'Round My Shoulder;* 1953—*All Ashore; Siren of Bagdad; Cruisin' Down the River;* 1954—*Drive a Crooked Road; Pushover;* 1955—*So This Is Paris; My Sister Eileen;* 1956—*The Solid Gold Cadillac;* 1957—*Full of Life; Operation Mad Ball;* 1959—*Bell, Book and Candle; It Happened to Jane;* 1960—*Strangers When We Meet; The World of Suzie Wong;* 1962—*The Notorious Landlady;* 1964—*Paris When It Sizzles;* 1965—*Sex and the Single Girl; How to Murder Your Wife; Synanon;* 1967—*Oh Dad, Poor Dad, Mama's Hung You in the Closet and I'm Feelin' So Sad,* uncredited codirector: Alexander Mackendrick; *Hotel;* 1968—(unreleased) *A Talent for Loving;* 1970—*The Moonshine War;* 1974—*W;* 1979—*The Prisoner of Zenda*

Television Movies
1973—*Columbo: Requiem for a Falling Star;* 1974—*Columbo: Double Exposure;* 1975—*The Specialists*

Like Stanley Donen, his contemporary, Richard Quine came to film directing from the musical stage (at nineteen he was the juvenile lead in Vincente Minnelli's Broadway production of Jerome Kern and Oscar Hammerstein's *Very Warm for May*), and, like Donen, he naturally specialized in film musicals, was hit by the demise of the genre in the mid-fifties, and rechanneled his talents into other types of endeavor, often with considerable success. Unlike Donen, however, Quine went through a fairly long period as a screen actor before taking up directing, his work in *Very Warm for May* having led to an MGM contract (indeed, he had been a child actor, on and off, both on stage and screen, since 1931). Hollywood musical fans will remember him as one (the other two being Mickey Rooney and Ray McDonald) of the Three Balls of Fire, singing and dancing to "Anything Can Happen in New York" in Busby Berkeley's *Babes on Broadway* and as Judy Garland's brother in Berkeley's next film, *For Me and My Gal.* He also had parts in nonmusicals, including one starring role in a 1943 Walter Wanger production, *We've Never Been Licked,* in which he played a young American raised in Japan and torn by conflicting loyalties when the war begins. He continued to appear in small screen parts until 1950, although his first directorial effort took place in 1948. *Leather Gloves,* which he coproduced and codirected with William Asher (later to become a specialist of "beach" movies), was an unprepossessing but engaging first film about a boxer in trouble. A supporting part was played by Blake Edwards, whom Quine had known in the Coast Guard during the war, and who was to become a close associate, scripting or coscripting seven of Quine's films, while the latter reciprocated by writing Edwards's first two pictures.

Quine's early musicals, shoestring Columbia productions swiftly put together, with Edwards usually aiding and abetting, are actually quite negligible, although occasionally amusing (Mickey Rooney's "When Knighthood Was in Flower" dream sequence in *All Ashore* comes to mind.) Somewhat more ambitious, at least budgetwise, was *So This Is Paris* (made at Universal), with its three sailors' ebullient cavorting through the French countryside in early sequences or, for whomever relishes this kind of humor, Gloria De Haven's rendition of an aggressively slangy French version of "I Can't Give You Anything But Love." Quine had time for only one major achievement in the genre, *My Sister Eileen,* which was to be his last musical.

This belated spinoff on a protean property (from short stories to stage play, to first screen version, to Broadway musical, to second movie version) turned out to be one of the finest, most enjoyable musicals of the postwar years, certainly the best of non-MGM origin. As an adaptation of the same material, it triumphantly rose to the challenge of being different from, and at least as good as, *Wonderful Town,* an undisputed masterpiece of the Broadway musical. The script—cowritten by Quine and Edwards— is actually tighter and stronger on characterization and motivation than Betty Comden and Adolph Green's book for *Wonderful Town.* The songs, by Jule Styne and Leo Robbin, are fresh and bouncy, with complex yet catchy melody lines (e.g., the delightful "There's Nothing Like Love" or Betty Garrett's comic dirge, "As Soon as They See

Eileen"). Not only are all the musical numbers first-rate, but none of them are gratuitous interruptions of the plot; they all make psychological points and keep the story moving. Two highlights are particularly intriguing in view of their performers' subsequent evolution. One is a semiacrobatic dance which pits Bob Fosse (in an early Hollywood part as a soda jerk in love with Janet Leigh) against rival Tommy Rall; the other is a scene in which Jack Lemmon *sings*—or pretends to—"It's Bigger Than You and Me" to a flustered Betty Garrett as he pursues her around his apartment.

One of the joys of Quine's direction in *My Sister Eileen* (a property he knew very well, since he had been in the cast of both the stage play and the 1943 movie version) is its effortless steering of dialogue into song through semirecitative (especially in the Janet Leigh–Betty Garrett number, "There's Nothing Like Love," with its brilliant shuttling back and forth); another is Quine's talent for keeping his performers credibly and gracefully busy while they sing, even when there is no choreography to fall back on. Such qualities are enough to suggest that hadn't the genre foundered, he might have become one of its foremost exponents.

Quine was not as successful with his rather derivative Judy Holliday comedies, *The Solid Gold Cadillac* and *Full of Life,* the former somewhat Capra-ish (the Capra of *You Can't Take It With You*—George S. Kaufman authored both source plays), the latter vaguely McCarey-ish. Quine, however, had proved more personal as early as 1954 with two crime melodramas, *Drive a Crooked Road* (another Edwards script) and *Pushover* (Kim Novak's first film), in which his understanding of female characters and his flair for conjuring gentle, tender atmospheres were already in evidence. Subdued melancholy was to be the dominant atmospheric quality of *Bell, Book and Candle,* a charming fantasy visually characterized by the choreographic elegance of its camera moves and the excellent direction of a cast including Kim Novak as a witch and James Stewart as the publisher she bewitches, Jack Lemmon (Quine's favorite star—they made six films together in less than ten years), and Ernie Kovacs, another Quine regular (he used him in four films in a row). The same formal elegance, the same taste for melancholy atmospheres, and the same felicitous way with performers again graced *Strangers When We Meet,* one of Quine's best films, in which his mature and compassionate treatment of relationships transcended the soap-opera material provided by Evan Hunter's source novel. The birth, growth, and death of a love affair between a suburban housewife (again played by Kim Novak, an actress of limited means whom Quine directed better than anyone else did, with the exception of Hitchcock in *Vertigo* and Billy Wilder in *Kiss Me Stupid*) and an architect (Kirk Douglas) who lives nearby are paralleled with the building of a house he has designed, which reaches completion when the lovers part. Such obvious symbolism, presumably derived from the novel, may seem obnoxious on paper, but Quine's direction makes it quite convincing and moving. (The house-building theme was later taken up and inverted in *How to Murder Your Wife,* in which a New York City neighborhood is being torn down all around Jack Lemmon's apartment.)

Paris When It Sizzles and *How to Murder Your Wife,* both written by George Axelrod, are underrated comedies, companion pieces tackling the themes of creation and of fiction intruding upon reality. The former, a wacky remake of Julien Duvivier's *La Fête à Henriette,* plays fantasy and real life against each other with a complexity not unworthy of a Borges story. Dealing with writer William Holden's frantic efforts to put a script together in two days for an irate producer, with only a title (*The Girl Who Stole the Eiffel Tower*) to work on, it ironically inventories the professional screenwriter's bag of tricks as Holden tries out one cliché situation—in a whole range of different genres—after another, using his secretary (Audrey Hepburn) as a sounding board and simultaneously giving her a crash course in the dos and don'ts of his craft. The two act out the situations he makes up and which become the action of the film, an action, however, that keeps breaking down due to Holden's inability to sustain it. Underneath the flippancy and Pirandelloish games, the tone of the film is quite bitter—a trait less attributable, perhaps, to Quine than to Axelrod, although Richard Corliss certainly overstates his case when he writes in *Talking Pictures* of the "uniquely strong sense of self-pity and self-loathing that pervades Axelrod's characters," taking the Holden character in *Paris When It Sizzles* as a prime example. Corliss defines the film as a "writer's movie" with a "fatal absence of any directorial style." There is no doubt that Quine's usually nimble style was somewhat cramped by the peculiar nature of the film's premise, its constant starts and breakdowns, the—by definition—clichéd nature of the situations and flimsiness of the characterization; to bring stylistic unity to such material was an impossible challenge. Yet, Quine is far from absent; indeed, in the context of his career, a scene like the one that wittily demonstrates that movie musicals can no longer be made has more relevance to him than it does to Axelrod, who never was involved with the genre.

Paris When It Sizzles was largely unappreciated and so was *How to Murder Your Wife,* which toyed tantalizingly with the intriguing notion of a comic-strip character and his creator infringing upon each other's private life. A somewhat farfetched (like all of Axelrod's scripts) but consistently funny comedy, it again features Quine's usual qualities: fluid camera work, a way of using sets both functionally and decoratively (the artist's apartment and the surrounding chaos), and a sympathetic treatment of female characters (the Virna Lisi character could easily have become unbearable; yet she shatters the stereotypes of dumb blonde and earth mother to come across as a person, in spite of the language barrier). This ability to humanize seemingly stock characters is in evidence even in such a broad farce as *Sex and the Single Girl,* whose characters are treated as human beings in spite of the nonsensical changes Joseph Heller's delirious script put them through.

These fine comedies marked the peak of a career that subsequently wavered uncertainly, eventually to come to an untimely stop. *Synanon,* a project Quine believed in but directed with a restraint verging on barrenness, made it clear that realistic drama and social issues were not his strength. (It may not be pure coincidence that this film on drug addiction was made less than two years after Blake Edwards's *Days of Wine and Roses,* a film about alcohol addiction.) On the other hand, his too literal, overrealistic treatment of *Oh Dad, Poor Dad, Mama's Hung You in the Closet and I'm Feelin' So Sad* (an unbearably coy title to begin with) turned Arthur Kopit's absurdist play—not a very funny one in the first place—into a sinister farce, whose only redeeming feature was a stylish and hilarious movie-within-the-movie done silent style. Mindless producers tried to salvage the film but actually dealt it the death blow by inserting some dismal additional footage (shot by Alexander Mackendrick) of Jonathan Winters commenting upon the proceedings from Heaven and indulging in one of the most vapid and vulgar series of wisecracks ever committed to a soundtrack.

Hotel, while far superior, was saddled with a conventional and gratuitous script, a mere showcase for an odd assortment of quasi stars, old-timers on tentative second careers (e.g., Melvyn Douglas, Michael Rennie, Merle Oberon), appearing in disconnected scenes. The most unkind cut came from Paramount executives who, for obscure reasons, decided against releasing *A Talent for Loving,* Quine's next film. *The Moonshine War,* which sneaked in and out of sight with excessive swiftness, is untypical of Quine, not only in subject matter—set in Prohibition times, it deals with a revenue agent's attempts to take over the production of a Kentucky moonshiner—but because of the viciousness and cynicism with which it treats most of its characters (the women, as usual, fare better than the men).

Quine directed only two more films in the seventies— *W,* starring British model Twiggy, which disappeared as quickly as *The Moonshine Wars,* and a comedy version of *The Prisoner of Zenda*—starring Peter Sellers, Blake Edwards's favorite male star— which came a very poor second to the definitive spoof of the old chestnut Quine's old accomplice had inserted in *The Great Race.* The petering out of Quine's theatrical career (he did direct a few television movies during his lean years) since the late sixties is one of the saddest occurrences in recent Hollywood history.

44. Bob Rafelson (1935)

by MARK LeFANU

1968—*Head;* 1970—*Five Easy Pieces;* 1972—*The King of Marvin Gardens;* 1976—*Stay Hungry;* 1981—*The Postman Always Rings Twice*

The history of Bob Rafelson's early life initially suggests the image of a sophisticated wanderer not unlike the Jack Nicholson figure in *Five Easy Pieces.* A Dartmouth dropout (philosophy), he wrangled in rodeos, served on an ocean liner, and played jazz in Mexico. But Rafelson in those early years also became adept at television production. After writing scripts for *Play of the Week,* he invented a rock-and-roll group, The Monkees, and exploited it through a successful series and a delightfully whimsical first feature, *Head.* By 1970, when he astonished the film world with *Five Easy Pieces,* Rafelson was thus a combination of classic, old-time Hollywood knockabout and successful media manipulator.

Already, when *Five Easy Pieces* begins, the family ties of its characters have long since been broken. This absence of a background is not uncommon in the cinema. Indeed, it is an advantage of the medium in terms of immediacy and spontaneity. The story is simply there; we plunge into it assuming that a life only becomes interesting the moment the hero has broken free of family confines. With Bob Rafelson, however, this attempt to break with everything that holds the individual back from attaining freedom, mastery, and creativity becomes the main subject, which is unusual—in this case somewhat autobiographical—for the American cinema.

In *Five Easy Pieces,* as in *The King of Marvin Gardens,* the final upshot of this break is defeat; but a more recent film of Rafelson's, *Stay Hungry,* is not content to end in this way. The happy ending is both optimistic and intelligent, it is the *right solution,* the complement to Rafelson's open style. In general Rafelson's ideological position is suggested by the nuance on the word *easy,* meaning relaxed, open, pleasantly ironic in front of the possibilities of life, and precisely, in the last resort, *not* paralyzed by distinctions of class. His is an extremely attractive aspect of American culture, and it imparts to the films in question a certain documentary freedom, part of their power and their interest, as if America, seen through the eyes of this director was still a country full of opportunity and occasion. Thus Rafelson's stories are both "about" his heroes and not about his heroes: at a certain stage they leave behind the manic egocentricity of the protagonist in order to contemplate, with a greater detachment, the world that surrounds and encompasses them. When we see films by directors like Rafelson (or Robert Altman, Hal Ashby, or Michael Ritchie), we have the unmistakable feeling that the society they depict is culturally and semiologically rich.

The gestures of the characters in Rafelson's films are intense, violent, full of repressed emotional force; but they are never theatrical in the pejorative sense of the term, and they are balanced in the overall rhythm of the film by a sort of tender and intelligent naturalism that is equally in its own way a language of gesture. More than any other form of art, the work of the film is concerned with the way people live and behave; the care that the scriptwriter and the director put into giving life to these gestures on the screen can never be too tender or passionate. What is at issue in *Five Easy Pieces* is the decisive presence of Jack Nicholson, one of those actors— perhaps *the* actor—whose 'gesture' has to be taken into account in any contemporary description of the American cinema, on the one hand by virtue of of a sort of serene suavity of allure (*Easy Rider, Chinatown,* the whole element of "easiness") and on the other hand, by virtue of a sort of furious and concentrated energy, at the same time both powerful and obsessive (*One Flew Over the Cuckoo's Nest, The Last Detail,* and *The Shining*).

Yet, *Pieces* is imbued with this richness of gesture in all its performances: Karen Black in the role of his working-class southern girlfriend; Ralph Waite as Nicholson's older brother, pompous and overweight, wrapped up in his music and living, it seems, in a nineteenth-century world of privilege and culture; Susan Anspach as the outsider for whom such a life-style proves fatally interesting and attractive; and finally Lois Smith as Nicholson's sister, large, gentle, lachrymose, gifted, unhappy. The characterization of these people is exact and well observed in all its details—alive and instantaneous, as if the camera had been able to foresee the genesis of a particular emotion and to place itself with unfailing rightness in the best place to exploit it. The naturalism of Rafelson's camera is such as to surprise the fleeting shafts of exaltation or disappointment on his actors' faces, as if their very moods were hatched from the scene itself and not from some preordained script (Karen Black, in bed with Nicholson after a quarrel because they have not made love, exclaiming with a mocking and ironic smile: "Is that a happy face I see in front of me?").

Indeed the actors themselves are so integrated into their roles that for long stretches one does not notice they are acting (which is why, as often in the cinema, we call the actors by their real names). The action seems completely *fluid,* as in Chekov's plays or the cinema of Orson Welles. Here one sees, perhaps, how Rafelson justifies the musical metaphor in the title of *Five Easy Pieces,* a metaphor that also evokes the film's contrast between old and new—between the "classical" music of the story's plot line and the contemporary music of the sound track—a contrast without irony or tendentiousness, it seems to me, that is generous to both types of endeavor.

The type of gesture Rafelson draws from his actors is in its essence the opposite of that demanded by Brecht, that is, the gesture that identifies his actors immediately as representing a certain social "type." Rafelson aims rather for the natural, as in the striking scene in which Jack Nicholson comes to see his sister in a recording studio. Lois Smith is bent over the piano, in an absorbed and fervent attitude, attempting to find the right notes to the growing anger of the studio's artistic director. Here, as everywhere in his films, what interests Rafelson is the way people really move, the way in which emotion is registered on a face, what people really do look like when they are working or relaxing. And what is interesting is that the extraordinary precision on the part of the actors still does not exclude the possibility that these gestures *may* possess, Brechtianly, the significance on a wider scale that makes them representative types.

As an example: For most of the film Nicholson's brother has his neck in plaster—he has had a fall from a horse—and because of this, in the dinner scene, he continually turns his head to judge the effect of his witticisms; in this jerky movement the actor expresses to perfection a kind of strange and limited superiority that is equally appropriate both on the personal *and* on the social level, so inseparably are they united. We see it also in a marvelous outdoor scene, where Waite is playing Ping-Pong and has to get down on his knees to look for a ball that has rolled under an adjacent car: the actor, we see, is big and imposing, and for a moment the look he gives to his brother expresses an indefinable and suffering pathos; there is defeat in his eyes but also the persistent conviction of a superiority, based on his birth and position. How subtly and economically the cinema establishes these unspoken relationships!

With Rafelson, gesture is above all *newly minted*—it is seen for the first time; it is freshly invented and yet at the same time it is illuminating, precise, and unambiguous. This emerges most clearly in Nicholson's role, all the more as the "Nicholson style" is by now so well known from other films. But the celebrated energy of Nicholson is never deployed in a facile or hackneyed way. Nothing is so admirable as the freshness of its invention. We recall the manner in which a love scene is shot at the beginning of the film, Nicholson carrying the girl from one room to another, the girl holding onto everything she can lay her hands on to balance and get a grip—a delirious, violent, excessive scene from start to finish and yet surely inconceivable in any other medium than the cinema for the emotion and truth it expresses. Or another example, showing admirably what good use the cinema makes of everyday objects by effortlessly endowing them with a sort of semisymbolism, rather as poetry searches for new and intriguing metaphors to mint. It is the scene where Nicholson, unable to leave Karen Black in Texas as he intended, vents his rage on the car's *steering wheel,* anticipating here the opening sequence in Antonioni's *The Passenger,* where Nicholson gives up the attempt to get the wheels of his Landrover out of the sand and instead smashes the vehicle with his shovel. The important point in both cases is that the scenes are short, lively, unworded, yet precise in the emotions they convey.

There is another aspect of "gesture" in this film as far as Nicholson is concerned, which ties up with a more general problem of cinema. We could call this the problem of finding an objective correlative for *ideas:* the difficulty, that is, of finding an equivalent in space and movement—in architecture—for what in literature is put forward discursively. How, specifically, does the film maker portray *Intelligence?*

In films like *Five Easy Pieces,* the dramatization of a break between two different cultures never assumes the form of an unbridgeable gap between intellectuals on the one hand and everybody else on the other. This seems to constitute, in a generally pessimistic film, a sign of optimism and hope—that, according to films like Rafelson's, there does not exist a specific intelligentsia that it ought to be someone's ambition to be part of. But we add straight away that the argument can obviously be reversed;

the *absence* of an intellectual class for someone like Nicholson to fit into, the failure on his part to institutionalize intelligence into paths that are appropriate and productive is precisely the reason why he is forced back again and again into the company of people who are unsuitable—like the girl played here so magnificently (and fecklessly) by the wonderful Karen Black. Thus the "heavily charged" gestures of actors like Nicholson in the contemporary American cinema come to symbolize not so much optimism and intelligence as their opposite, *frustration,* and instead of opportunity and openness we alight upon, as more "typically" American, the empty violence of the three comrades in Hal Ashby's *The Last Detail* or the way in which, in the same director's *Shampoo,* the Warren Beatty character is perpetually *under pursuit,* pressed, harried, and restless or finally the fruitlessly expensive energy—an energy canalized into cunning and madness—that is the dominant feature of Nicholson's performance in *One Few over the Cuckoo's Nest.*

A propos Karen Black, it will be recalled that in *Some Came Running* (Vincente Minnelli, 1959), the formal difficulty that is incurred in leaving the hero with a girl who is morally sympathetic but intellectually his inferior is "resolved" by having the young woman shot. As a sanction this is perhaps acceptable in a film as preoccupied as Minnelli's is with the actual problem of endings. But Rafelson's films are predicated on openness, which means that we must accept indeterminacy in the endings. Jack Nicholson abandons Karen Black in the filling station and climbs onto a truck headed for Alaska; perhaps it is not such a bad ending after all. It leaves a little room for irony, and I think we can take it or leave it. In short: pessimism and optimism seem to be subtly graded in this film. As an allegory about America it is difficult to categorize, and this is one of its merits.

Some Came Running is implacably arched; its plot follows the curve of a destiny, it finishes with a death, and its structure, appropriately, is tight, formal, and continuous. *Five Easy Pieces,* as the title suggests, has a musical structure that is more open and relaxed than Minnelli. Yet the title is finally puzzling. To an ordinary viewer, it seems at first sight that the film is divided into *two halves* rather than into five identifiable segments: it rests on the axis *North and South,* Texas and the Pacific North West, the coach journey joining the two. But distinctions like this are sometimes delicate. The unease we feel concerning the structure, if it is an unease, takes us back to the essential business of *content* and the fact that Rafelson has found himself a genuine subject. (The necessity of breaking with constraints of class, balanced by the "message" that Susan Anspach communicates to Jack Nicholson: that one cannot do without courtesy and intelligence, whether or not they appear to be tainted with those very same aspects of class that it is essential to try to fight free from.)

There is no need to worry that this subject is too autobiographical on Rafelson's part. Rafelson's life up to the making of *Five Easy Pieces* is after all sufficiently different from that of his hero. He has already, for example, made a delicious film called *Head,* with the Monkees; he has achieved a distinction in his profession. It is not Rafelson in the guise of Nicholson who moves off to the frozen North. The statement of a film maker is perhaps more anonymous here than the equivalent statement of a writer. And in any event, whatever the truth, *Five Easy Pieces* is a successful film by all accounts, in its conception, preparation, and in the full-blooded facing of its chances.

Rafelson's next film, *The King of Marvin Gardens,* employs a larger canvas: the old Atlantic City, New Jersey, whose turrets and cupolas rising from the vast seafront hotels recall the fantastic architecture of *Amarcord.* Even the light is almost the same: the azure sky conceals the fact that it is winter and the characters burn pieces of driftwood on the beach to keep warm. Grandeur and decadence are here where one least expects them.

The film is based on a wonderful paradox: its subject is failure, but its underlying emotion is happiness. The petit-bourgeois loan shark (played with astonishing fluency by Bruce Dern) fails to pull off the deals in real estate that would allow him to say that the city of his dreams belongs to him; he is ruler of an imaginary kingdom. But at the same time, Atlantic City is filmed with such severe beauty and apprehended with such imaginative power—we inhabit it so completely—that in the end defeat turns into victory, and Bruce Dern comes to possess the city without it actually belonging to him, like the hero of Henry James's *The Ambassadors* who discovers, seated in a Parisian café, that everything he looks upon is his. Film makers celebrate their love affairs with cities by the simple happiness of filming them well. One thinks of the Geneva of Godard in *Le Petit Soldat* or of Parma seen by Bertolucci in *Prima della Rivoluzione,* and we may observe how frequently a young film maker's first substantive act is to return to the city of his youth and affirm his dominion over it by taking it into the dream of his art.

This is what we see in the sequence where Bruce Dern takes Jack Nicholson to the top of a switchback, from which they enjoy a panoramic view of the coast—of the city they both possess and do not possess. The scene is shot in a simple and masterly fashion. In another episode, Bruce Dern shows an auctioneer how to bring in the customers; instead of just hoping they will come in, one must go out into the street to look for them. Rafelson films the scene in such a way that the sale, directed by Bruce Dern with a bunch of fanatical ladies pushing up the bids, seems to have moved out onto the sidewalk, while at the same time the sidewalk takes on the dimensions of the theatrical stage. Here, style confers a metaphysical beauty on Bruce Dern's insolence—and it says: one can realize one's desires provided one imagines them with sufficient intensity.

The King of Marvin Gardens is like Chekhov—the film is based on the same structural irony as *The Cherry Orchard*—but it also resembles the cinema of Robert Altman (who is Chekhovian in another way, through his admiration for everything that is contingent and fortuitous). The relationship of the girls Jessica (Julia Anne Robinson) and Sally (Ellen Burstyn) is like some of the numerous indeterminate relationships that are found in Altman, e.g., the scenes between Gwen Welles and her prostitute buddy in *California Split.* We find in these scenes precisely the same unselfconsciousness that seems to have for the director the function of suggesting a utopian image of sociability, like the happiness of the whores in the bath sequences of *McCabe and Mrs. Miller.* It's as if utopia were to find its most potent image in a structure of erotic tenderness. preferably the tenderness between women. In Altman and Rafelson, rather as in Japanese films, women always seem to find the time to brush each other's hair, imitating the indolence of Utamaro's courtesans. Ellen Burstyn combs Julia Anne Robinson's hair while sitting on the bed and talking about the future; here "gesture" isn't linked so much to action as to those *moments gratuits* outside the development of the story that suggest a sort of documentary fascination on the part of the film maker himself for the actors and actresses he admires. He seems to want to catch not only the precision of life but also the movements that memory recalls from dreams.

A dream is a fine subject for a work of art if the story itself carries a sufficiently strong counterpoint in the direction of reality. In this film the element of reality comes from the fact that the actions of the characters are simultaneously seen and criticized by the director as if they belong to a world of fantasy—the world, shall we say, of the Monopoly board. In which case *The King of Marvin Gardens* might be seen as an oblique version of films like *Lucky Luciano* (Francesco Rosi, 1973) and *The Godfather Part II* (Coppola, 1974): the real estate deals take place on the largest scale, but here they are always empty and unreal. The town has been sold long ago, behind the characters' backs, and to somebody else. The film is thus partly about how it is that the white petite bourgeoisie no longer has any say in the way America is run and is clearly a recapitulation of some of the anxieties of *Five Easy Pieces* (a nice twist being that Jack Nicholson plays the role played by the elder brother in the earlier film). Such symmetry confirms the importance Rafelson attaches to *subject* and prompts us to ask again what part autobiography plays in it all. There is always a father who refuses to die—there is always this dead weight of the past that ruins lives that would otherwise be sane and intelligent. We think of the scene at the beginning of the film, where Nicholson indulges in an amazing existentialist confession about his past and his childhood that the film later reveals to be a tissue of lies. (His grandfather is still living, whereas on the radio Nicholson says he has killed him or allowed him to die.)

This last scene establishes by a few sure and rapid strokes the reasons why Rafelson has chosen the art of *cinema* and not poetry or writing. His films are extremely well written and yet writing as the old-fashioned task of *converting lived experience into closed narrative form* is here made to seem false or suspicious. Experience, in the context of an excessively cultivated personality—like that of the Nicholson character—instead of being close to reality is actually cut off from it by barriers that are poignant and real. Modern writing is narcissistic, and the performance of Nicholson *as writer* is addressed merely to the self-ratifying microphone. Indeed Rafelson is so convinced of the truth of this observation that he is prepared to use irony to demonstrate it. For at first it seems as if Nicholson's tormented confession is addressed to *someone who is present with him in the room,* and only gradually does the camera draw away to show Nicholson in the recording studio alone above the microphone, separated by a pane of glass from the technician and producer, while weaving his fantastic yarn.

It is by virtue of its very complexity that the cinema seems to dispose of such cumbersome and too heavily autobiographical areas of false consciousness. The film maker's voice, we find, cannot so easily be pinned down to any exact existentialist "truth." Film belongs equally to the scriptwriter, to the director, and to his actors, and since the cinema is a popular art form, to the public as well. These considerations help to eliminate from cinema that peculiar anxiety that is found in modern writing, allowing the film to operate on a level that is autobiographical and nonautobiographical at one and the same moment. Although the mise-en-scène, like everything else, is clearly the subject of painstaking preparation *in writing,* there is always the possibility in the cinema that chance has a happy role to play in the final product. In the film at hand we think of the innumerable street signs and billboards characteristic of American cities, each sending out its own individual message: the cabarets, the bars, the neon signs—the whole way in which Rafelson in filming them manages to forge out of their winking brilliancy an ironic counterpart to the dialogue unfolding on another level in the foreground.

What an excellent film this is—serious, unpretentious, and of a precise and original texture.

Stay Hungry is a film that speaks about tolerance and courtesy but in a positive way by linking them to a certain sense of pride, rather than to their somewhat less attractive embodiment in apathy or mere politeness.

The film is extremely violent, but the violence is portrayed as healthy and cathartic, an indication of sincere emotions. The contradictions confronting the characters are not allowed to degenerate into despair but are, as it were, activated and resolved by a prolonged outburst of physical energy. The setting, Birmingham, Alabama, is contemporary America and once again Rafelson examines it with a kind of documentary respect—mildly intrigued and ironical but at the same time extraordinarily attracted by its energy: it is the same verve Altman brings to a similar exercise in *Nashville.* In both films exactness of observation is mixed up with a kind of craziness, and it is difficult to say at a given moment whether the humor is black and satirical or in the final count more optimistic and friendly. Rafelson's film, much more than Altman's, concerns itself with the movement of one class into another.

This would be a sensible moment to look at a maxim that could stand as a leitmotif in all Rafelson's films. "Stay Hungry!" is the advice Arnold Schwarzenegger gives Jeff Bridges in the course of a training session and it means—live at a high voltage, as dangerously as possible, see to it that you are always in charge of your decisions. Rafelson believes in personal authenticity and thinks it can be achieved by courage, determination, and intelligence. It is represented on the screen through the metaphor of physical courage as a sort of *bodily tautness;* more metaphysically, bareness of soul is given to us sculpturally in the concentrated image of the naked, or almost naked, body—firstly in the image of the body builders themselves; but also and one is tempted to say, just as importantly, by the girl, played here by Sally Field—an actress whose incredibly small, slender, lithe body somehow seems to be naked even when she is clothed. (And indeed we do see her naked in one or two scenes. One notices how Rafelson continually invents new ways of showing simple actions, as in the staircase scene where, after Jeff Bridges has examined her foot, Sally Field curls herself around him in a great embrace that seems to express—encompass—her entire body. She clasps him between her legs and folds herself into his arms.)

Nakedness, then, as "authenticity." But it is much more complicated than this. The culmination of the film has two alternating sequences. In one of them, the Mr. Universe contest is in progress and the body builders are going through their routines; the other sequence has the drunken owner of the gymnasium (played by the spectacular R. G. Armstrong) in the act of raping Sally Field (she has returned to the gym to collect her equipment). He grasps her in front of a mirror while he breaks and crushes a capsule of amyl nitrate, while in his rage he inadvertently tears off his wig, revealing a haggard and aging face. At this exact moment the camera switches to the scene in the auditorium where, the stage slowly rising, Arnold Schwarzenegger is making his bid for the title.

Two images of nudity, therefore. But they are essentially ambiguous; the shock of the one transfers itself to the other; Schwarzenegger's body (it's the first time we have seen his torso, since he has carried out his training in a Batman outfit!) appears in the contrast as gigantic and grotesque; his muscles form a sort of metallic and mechanical carapace—like the clanking suit of armor which, in a curious image, Scatman Crothers takes as a souvenir from Jeff Bridges's aristocratic mansion (where he has served as the family butler for fifty years).

It seems to me that what we have here is an excellent and complex artistic statement. Nakedness is presented as *metaphor* rather than truth, and it implies that even this monolithic image can be subliminally transformed and acquire new and contradictory meanings. Here it suggests that there is no privileged truth to be found in the pose—the "gesture"—of the body builder played by Schwarzenegger. The matter is open and ironic, as art ought to be. Thus, on the level of content, Rafelson approves of what Schwarzenegger represents (and Jeff Bridges is shown as accepting his advice); but on the level of the image and the subtle correspondence between the different images across the film, this approval is subtly withdrawn, and the whole subject matter remains neutral and enigmatic; we do not know what Rafelson really thinks of his body builders, any more than we know what Altman really thinks of his collection of singers in the earlier and more famous movie.

There seems to be an odd twist implied in all this; the energetic and very specific image of the body, which makes this film such a delicious paradigm of gesture in American cinema, becomes the focus of so many contradictions that it finishes paradoxically by losing its symbolic value altogether, and the naked bodies of the athletes respond by seeming as banal and deprived of significance—as essentially enigmatic and neutral—as the marvelous image of the American flag flapping in the wind (all things to all men) that immediately precedes the assassination attempt in Altman's disquieting masterpiece. In short: in both films, a neutral irony, in a minor key, strongly based on realism of image. (Michael Ritchie's *Smile* and the films of Frederick Wiseman might also be considered in this context.)

But *Stay Hungry* is essentially a happy film, and the relationships in it are imagined, as usual, with a fine and tender economy. It crystallizes curiosity and even affection between members of different classes, each of whom have their own way of life, in turn picturesque and exotic to the others. After their first meeting at the swimming pool, Sally Field runs her hand through Jeff Bridges's hair; it is cut differently from that of other men she knows (cut "like a squirrel's tail," she says: in other words, it's charming, bourgeois, a little childish). It is with pleasure and tenderness that she registers this difference. (Rafelson's camera shows all this with his usual speed and economy.) We might also consider the sequence where Schwarzenegger takes Bridges into the hills to listen to the fiddlers, and one sees how skilfully Rafelson succeeds in rendering the cultural identity of these people as being rich, various, and "courteous" in the sense in which I used the term at the beginning of this section. All without the slightest condescension on Rafelson's part toward their passionate and relaxed enthusiasm.

Rafelson's attitude toward his "picturesque" subjects is far removed from that of the tourist or anthropologist. On the contrary, the essence of the film consists in showing the amazing interlocking of the destinies of these groups and the vehement questioning of fundamental moral values that this interlocking gives rise to. Rafelson here partakes of a fine tradition of American cinema and the fierce moral emotion that accompanies it. The intense emotion set off by an episode like the one where Sally Field walks out of the reception given by Jeff Bridges's friends recalls in this context the best of Douglas Sirk and the best of Minnelli. Everywhere there is the same exemplary precision, the same skill in portraying detailed aspects of the different social classes through confrontations that are powerfully imagined and crisply delivered.

Yet in spite of everything *Stay Hungry* is a comedy or, in the terminology of the classical theater, a "romance." Enemies are reconciled, lovers forget their quarrels and prepare for marriage—all's well that ends well. The film overflows into dream, as in the final sequence where the body builders, leaving the Mr. Universe contest, spill out into the streets of Birmingham. After a reconciliation, Jeff Bridges's chief enemy, Jabo (Joe Spinelli), is strangely seen to climb into the sauna establishment through a window that hasn't been repaired, rather than going in through the door, thus transforming the real location used by the film into the décor used by a stage set. The intensity of the various groups' engagement in one another's machinations and power struggles has the curious result of leaving them all good friends; it is as if they have been through too much together not to end up as allies. And to cement their friendship, Rafelson even gives his actors a final bow (the credits come up at the end, thirties fashion, shown over cameos of the smiling actors; it is a pleasure to see them out of costume).

Stay Hungry is a remarkably serious film. But one notices how the breakup of Jeff Bridges's aristocratic world is in the end less *tragic* than it would have been in a film by Losey or Visconti; this is the magnificent openness of American culture. As for the aristocratic mansion itself, Jeff Bridges has already moved out long before it falls into decay. Scatman Crothers is left in peace; the old uncle returns to his scientific and naturalistic observations. Society continues on its unpredictable way but with an overall humor and a tolerance.

45. Nicholas Ray (1911–1979)

1947—*They Live by Night;* 1949—*A Woman's Secret; Knock on Any Door;* 1950—*Born to Be Bad; In a Lonely Place;* 1951—*Flying Leathernecks;* 1952—*On Dangerous Ground; The Lusty Men,* uncredited codirector: Robert Parrish; 1954—*Johnny Guitar;* 1955—*Run for Cover; Rebel Without a Cause;* 1956—*Hot Blood; Bigger Than Life;* 1957—*The True Story of Jesse James; Bitter Victory* (U.S., 1958); 1958—*Wind Across the Everglades; Party Girl;* 1961—*The Savage Innocents; King of Kings;* 1963— *55 Days at Peking;* 1981—(1979) *Lightning Over Water* (codirector: Wim Wenders)

Uncredited
1951—*The Racket* (John Cromwell); 1952—*Macao* (Josef von Sternberg); 1953—*Androcles and the Lion* (Chester Erskine)

Miscellaneous
Ray's unreleased and possibly unfinished 16-mm film work in the sixties and seventies included *Gun Under My Pillow* aka *We Can't Go Home Again.*

More than any other American director, Nicholas Ray *belongs* to the fifties, not only because his career practically began and ended with the decade but also because the Ray cult was the extreme and archetypal manifestation of a mode of response to film that developed and was most forcefully verbalized during the period. Seeing Ray's films *again* today is sometimes a disappointing experience, but while one is certaintly entitled to jump to the conclusion that they have not aged well, it might be more accurate to say that a certain critical—or rather uncritical—attitude toward them has not aged well. A typical example is Jean-Luc Godard's famous nonreview of *Bitter Victory,* in which he not only refused to discuss the film but insisted that it could not and should not be discussed. The piece was full of the kind of meaninglessly sweeping statements so fashionable among young French critics at the time ("Now there is the cinema and the cinema is Nicholas Ray. . . . It is not cinema, it is better than cinema"). Such outbursts unquestionably served a purpose, since they helped awaken an entirely fresh perception of cinematic values. Their enthusiasm did preclude serious analysis, but serious analysis was not what early auteurists were primarily concerned with. Given the atmosphere of stifling conformity that pervaded French life at the time, overreacting to the movies of revered American directors provided a rare and far from minor emotional outlet.

Ray's brooding pessimism, his high-strung, rebellious individualism struck a responsive chord then, as they still do now (to a lesser extent) among younger film buffs. This is not to imply that Ray chiefly appeals to adolescent sentimentality. What can hardly be denied, however, is that his films are steeped in the somewhat facile romanticism of failure, self-pity, and despair, a "weakness" that may also be their strength and with which, at any rate, one has to come to terms in order to understand his cinema. Ray's heroes never belong, they drift in search of a meaning, a reason for being, their own identity. They could all say, quoting the title of one of Ray's unrealized projects, "I'm a stranger wherever I go." They are lonely, weary, and scared, confused both about the nature of their problems and the ways to deal with them. In their fumbling for an answer, they turn to violence and the deceptive sense of freedom and "living" it provides (*In a Lonely Place, Johnny Guitar*), to the pursuit of money and success (*The Lusty Men, Party Girl*), to drug-induced fantasies of power (*Bigger than Life*), to a total rejection of society (*Hot Blood, Jesse James*), or to a stubborn fight to preserve endangered values (*Wind Across the Everglades, The Savage Innocents*). Their failure is as much the result of their self-destructive tendencies as of outside circumstances. Love does offer an escape from violence and confusion (in Ray's world woman stands for stability, reassurance, hope for an ordered life), but although Ray's heroes desperately need love, breaking away from their isolation and adjusting to the demands of a relationship requires agonizing effort from most of them. Coming together is a groping, painful process hindered by instinctive distrust and antagonism. Ray's lovers have little in common but seem to be irresistibly attracted by the very chasm that separates them and into which they throw themselves as one jumps off a cliff. Not surprisingly, there are few happy endings in Ray's work, and the few there are seem arbitrary or ambiguous, at odds with the mood of the films they are tagged upon.

Ray has been quoted as saying that he considered *They Live by Night* a near-perfect film and that, were he given the opportunity, he would change very little in it. One can hardly quarrel with this view. With the obvious exception of *Citizen Kane,* one would have to go back to Rowland Brown's stunning *Quick Millions* (1932) to find such a personal and stylistically controlled first film in the history of the Hollywood sound film prior to 1950. Any reservations we may have about *They Live by Night* are not concerned with the film's esthetic achievement. There is hardly a shot in it that doesn't evidence intelligent care in setting up the camera, placing the actors within the frame, selecting gestures and attitudes, controlling the pacing of action and delivery. Ray proved especially good at directing his actors in confined spaces—cars, small rooms—rarely resorting to traditional cross-cutting, over-the-shoulder shots, or close-ups but relying instead upon imaginatively composed two-shots or three-shots, alternating high and low angles, to emphasize the sometimes uncomfortable physical and emotional closeness of the characters. Like all his subsequent films, *They Live by Night* is essentially a study of moods and relationships, and it keeps suspense and action—

especially violent action—to a minimum, in almost total disregard of the traditions of the genre—the gangster film—to which it at least superficially belongs. The only bank robbery scene unfolds quietly in a couple of minutes, with the camera staying inside the getaway car. A less successful bank job, in the course of which one of the gangsters is killed, is not shown at all but only heard of on the car radio as the two survivors drive away. Of the two killings in the film, one, the shooting of a cop, takes place off-screen. The other, the gunning down of the hero by police, is the briefest, most understated climax of its kind. Ray exercised almost as much restraint in his treatment of the young couple's developing relationship, and, ironically, it is perhaps this obvious concern to avoid the pitfalls of sentimentality that undermines the film's emotional impact, for the understatement is so sustained as to become ostentatious, thus bringing out the mawkishness it was meant to eliminate. Moreover, beneath the careful stylistic checking of maudlin excesses runs a strong undercurrent of strident despair. A sense of doom and tragic inevitability is conveyed through repeated hints that the two fugitives have no way out, no future, no hope, a point stressed by the piling up of mishaps and fateful accidents as the story unfolds. The very presence of Farley Granger, whose facial expression, even in repose, rarely suggests anything less than anguished helplessness, is a permanent reminder of Ray's gloomy outlook.

Six years and ten films later the proportion of restraint to overt sentimentality was practically reversed in *Rebel Without a Cause,* as if the widening of the screen (*Rebel* was Ray's first CinemaScope film) had triggered a broadening of the director's touch. Ray's expansive mood was no doubt encouraged by the personality of James Dean, whose provocative—and now somewhat dated—display of adolescent angst amounts to an exploded version of Granger's pent-up intensity. But the two films do not differ in emotional emphasis only. Whereas *They Live by Night* focused on individuals and blurred the social background, *Rebel,* in its eager commitment to sociological relevance, dramatizes the period's fashionable commonplaces on the causes and cures of juvenile restlessness. Ray enthusiastically espouses the view that adults are to blame for every teenage problem, and loads the dice against his young heroes' parents accordingly. *Rebel* features not one but three disturbed adolescents in desperate need of love and guidance from parents who fail them in one way or the other. In the opening sequence at the police station, as well as in all the subsequent scenes in which they appear, Jim's parents come across as coarse caricatures, saying all the wrong things and forgetting the kid's plight as they bicker endlessly over who's responsible (there is even a stock mother-in-law tagging along). The father—as myopic and fumbling a character psychologically as Jim Backus's cartoon alter ego, Mr. Magoo, is physically—strikes us as more hopeless than necessary even for Ray's biased purpose (to his son's desperate appeal for advice he responds by nervously suggesting: "I'll get a pencil and paper and we'll make a list"). Ray conveys Backus's inability to stand up to his wife by confining him to sitting or even kneeling positions at crucial moments and has him wear a frilly apron throughout a key scene. Too, there is more than a shade of dishonesty in the final cop-out with its convenient disposing of a surrogate victim and its suggestion (admittedly studio-imposed) that everything is going to be all right from now on. But to point out such weaknesses—which certainly were quite as glaring in 1955 as they are now—is not to deny the film's stylistic effectiveness. With *Rebel,* Ray opted for theatricality as an ideal outlet for his neurotic sensitivity, and if the film is still affecting it is not because of its sociological window-dressing or simplistic psychologizing but for the flavor of its poetic paraphernalia, momentous cosmic symbols, and hysterical outbursts. Its real greatness lies in the operatic quality that accounts for moments of contrived but irresistible beauty, such as the low-angle shot of James

Dean holding out his hand to Natalie Wood without looking at her as they peer down the cliff that has engulfed Jim's rival in the "chicken" run. Ray's high level of formal awareness is attested to by the fact that almost every shot in the film is composed with the CinemaScope screen in mind, and although he used the new aspect ratio more self-consciously than a Cukor in *A Star is Born* and borrowed a couple of dubious devices from Kazan's *East of Eden* (e.g., tilted camera setups), he did convey, through purely visual means, a sense of oddness and unbalance directly related to the use of the Scope format.

Rebel was not, of course, Ray's first venture into baroque territory. This side of his personality had first clearly emerged in *Johnny Guitar,* made the previous year for Republic as, it almost seems, a gesture of rejection of the more subdued style of his RKO period. In an article on Ray, Mike Wilmington remarked that "Audiences will either laugh at his films or be deeply moved by them." *Johnny Guitar* is a case in point. Indeed, no other Ray film better illustrates the observation than this weirdly poetic soap opera in western garb. While Ray's admirers may be put off by the boorishness of semisophisticated audiences snickering at the film's wild flourishes, one shouldn't refuse to acknowledge the very real element of ludicrousness that causes such reactions, for that would be missing the nature of the film's originality. Allowing for varieties of movie watching experience, *Johnny Guitar* may be regarded as camp, and although camp followers, because of the circumscribed and superficial area upon which their attention is focused, are ill-equipped to appreciate such a film's beauty, there must be something of the camp follower's perverted innocence in anyone who is to appreciate it properly. Ray steers an uneasy course between the sublime and the ridiculous— and does it, incidentally, in complete awareness of his predicament—but steering clear of the ridiculous is by no means what Ray is trying to do in the film. *Johnny Guitar* is not sublime "at the risk" of becoming ridiculous, it is sublime because, and only inasmuch as, it is ridiculous. The distinction between the two opposite notions is really not in the film at all but rather in the eye of the beholder. One could no doubt use some less pejorative term than "ridiculous" ("delirious" always comes in handy in such situations), but the silliness at the core of Ray's pathos shouldn't be ignored any more than the pathos at the core of his silliness, for they are essentially one and the same thing. We are not talking here, of course, of the superficial silliness inherent in a leather-clad, gun-toting Joan Crawford; nor of the female-impersonator aplomb with which she sports her white gown in the famous piano-playing scene; nor even of such absurd moments as the improbably lengthy autobiographical speech she delivers while holding a threatening mob at bay but of the deeper silliness permeating the painfully intense emotions that are the stuff of the film's lyricism. In their half-reluctant, half-passionate attempt at reviving a relationship that floundered years before, Crawford and Sterling Hayden (another of Ray's typical adult couples, threatened, wavering, antagonistic, scarred, and scared) look and sound more than a little absurd; there is something hopelessly awry, sadly laughable about their combination, but that is how it should be, for therein lies their pathetic appeal. Ray doesn't "redeem" his material through distancing, his style is proof that he is completely in tune with his characters and their emotions. Thus, when at the climax of an agonizing showdown with Crawford a haggard Hayden suddenly storms out of the kitchen and strides into the deserted saloon, he is accompanied by a dolly shot that seems literally to wrench him away from the confrontation. It is perhaps this very harmony of form and content that determines the ambivalence of our response, as though Ray's intimacy with his characters somehow made him as pathetic as they are.

Ray's theatrical lyricism and his steady drift toward a total rejection of contemporary society culminated in *Bigger Than Life,* another major CinemaScope explosion, this time equipped with built-in thematic and stylistic hysteria. Ray's direction of the film is the faithful mirror image of his hero's mounting imbalance and increasingly distorted perception as his delusions of grandeur escalate into fits of egomaniac insanity, and the menacingly heightened visual style generates tremendous tension. *Bigger Than Life* thus represents the most satisfying convergence of theme and style in Ray's work. The film's statement is ambiguous, however, for while it condemns drug-taking as an escape from the mediocrity of everyday life, it makes no attempt at either suggesting other means of escape or at evaluating the individual's own responsibility for this mediocrity. The film criticizes not the hero's original boredom and disenchantment but only his addiction and demented excesses. To paraphrase Eric Rohmer, there is wisdom in Ed Avery's madness, even though we eventually realize the wisdom itself is madness. At the time, Ray was still seeking an alternative to the frustrations of modern life. The film's implicit conclusion seems to be that there is no such alternative. This is perhaps why *Bigger Than Life* was to be Ray's last look (except for his 1973 and 1979 postscripts to his filmography) at contemporary America. He turned to the country's past (*Jesse James, Party Girl*) and to a Rousseauist study of "uncorrupted" communities, the gypsies of *Hot Blood,* the Eskimo of *Savage Innocents,* and, marginally, the Seminole Indians of *Wind Across the Everglades,* a film which, ten years ahead of its time, dealt with the disastrous impact of civilization upon the environment.

Everglades actually makes it clear that there is no ultimate difference between harming nature and harming man. The hero, a young ecologist fighting the destruction of wildlife in the Florida swamps at the turn of the century, befriends a Seminole Indian who joined an outlaw gang of egret killers after his tribe banished him for lying. Through their conversations the Indian comes to grasp the similitude between the destroyed birds and his own people's plight: they are both species endangered by the white man's civilization and greed.

Although the hero is, for once, a rebel *with* a cause, he is no less confused and helpless than Ray's earlier, more "negative" heroes. The character, remarkably played by Christopher Plummer in a completely nonheroic vein, is yet another "stranger" who doesn't seem to fit anywhere in the social scheme. The band of outlaws he fights are greedy, ruthless destroyers of beauty and life. On the other hand, their way of life—free, close-to-nature primitiveness—sets them apart from the civilization that has created a market for their destructive activities and therefore bears the ultimate responsibility for them. Plummer's constant shuttling between Miami (civilization) and the Everglades (nature, primitive life) symbolizes his isolation. Eventually he succumbs—if only temporarily—to the attraction of the outlaws' life-style, not just because it is close to nature but because they, too, like the birds they kill, are an endangered species threatened by the civilization that tolerates them. When captured by the outlaws, Plummer engages in an all-night drinking bout with their leader (a formidable, red-bearded Burl Ives), and each comes to a certain understanding and appreciation of the other's values. The range of feelings and moods conveyed in this extraordinary sequence is amazing; few moments in Ray's work so subtly yet forcefully express his own ambivalence. Where the audience expects a battle of wits ultimately won by the hero, what we actually see is an increasingly befuddled Plummer, and the emergence of a feeling akin, if not to friendship, at least to mutual respect. Ray provides no pat answer, refuses to take sides, and leaves us with a bewildered sense of the relativity of all values.

Ray's career foundered after the brief flirtation with Bronstonian gigantism that produced the flawed but often inventive *King of Kings* (but for the fear of damning it with faint praise, one would be tempted to call it the best biblical epic ever made) and the hopelessly rambling *55 Days at Peking,* which Ray was forced to abandon before shooting was completed. There followed over fifteen years of unproductive wanderings—unproductive, that is, if one chooses to disregard the huge amount of unreleased material he did shoot during the period, much of which went into the never-completed *We Can't Go Home Again,* a multiple-screen, semiimprovised collective effort on which Ray worked off and on from 1971 to 1973 with his students at Harpur College in Binghamton, New York. It is sadly ironic that Ray's only directorial credit on a released film after 1963 (except for the posthumous *Lightning Over Water*) was for a segment of *Wet Dreams,* a pornographic omnibus film made in Amsterdam in 1973.

One must resist the temptation to gloat over Ray's collapse (if that is indeed what it was). It would be too easy, and only superficially meaningful, to draw parallels between his heroes' self-destructive bent and his own failure to get any "real" (i.e., commercially viable) project off the ground until his death in 1979. His withdrawal from conventional film making, whether involuntary or self-imposed (or both), was in some ways similar to that of Godard and, even more, that of Welles, a director with whom Ray otherwise shared so little. Both Ray and Welles were associated with "works in progress" that never reached completion; both were increasingly involved with experimentation; and each seemed too immersed in a reflection upon himself, his artistry, and his past to ever be willing to work again in a traditional fictional mold. Unlike Ray, however, Welles was always a marginal artist in the Hollywood—indeed in the American—context. Ray, on the other hand, seems to have been one of those Hollywood directors whose talent, although at odds with the system, was nurtured by the antagonism and could not survive without it. When the system changed, he found that he, literally, could not go home again.

Although forgotten by Hollywood and the general public, Ray became something of a cult figure in the seventies for the new generation of film buffs, not so much, perhaps, because of his fifties films as for his aura as a prestigious dropout, an ex-luminary of the movie establishment (the protégé of Howard Hughes, the director of Bogart and James Dean, the onetime husband of Gloria Grahame) turned radical and underground artist. Conflicting rumors about his ongoing campus project kept his followers intrigued. David Halpern, Jr.'s (and Myron Meisel's) feature-length documentary, *I'm a Stranger Here Myself,* created a moving and tantalizing "Portrait of Nicholas Ray" out of a mosaic of interviews with the director, clips of his old films, and footage of him and his students working on *We Can't Go Home Again.* The German director, Wim Wenders, met Ray while shooting the New York scenes of *The American Friend,* his highly personal homage to *film noir* and gave him a small part, which they concocted together, as a painter of fakes involved with gangsters.* This was to lead

---

* Ray's interest in the theme of fakery—which, incidentally, parallels Welles's—is also manifested in a project of his about a very ill painter who sells copies of his old, high-priced paintings in order to pay for a costly medical treatment. The subject—which Ray and Wenders discuss in *Lightning Over Water* as a possible storyline for their film but decide not to use—is too transparently autobiographical and allegorical to require much comment; yet it says a lot about Ray's own ambivalence. It alludes to the artist's dream of regaining, not health (Ray was past hope at the time) but some of his former status by leaving behind a last work and testament; yet at the same time it seems to suggest that such a last work would be a fake (a duplication of Ray's earlier films?).

to a close friendship and to a unique collaboration on an extraordinary document, *Lightning Over Water.*

Written (although no writing credit is given) and directed by Ray and Wenders, who "play" themselves, and mostly based, according to Wenders, on Ray's ideas, the film—which was known for a while as *Nick's Movie*—was shot over a period of three months in the Spring of 1979, with several interruptions due to Ray's poor health, and was actually completed after Ray's death in June of that year. Whatever Ray and Wenders intended it to be (never quite clear), the fact that Ray was visibly a dying man at the time and that he did die before production was completed inevitably turns *Lightning Over Water* into a document of and a reflection on his last days and death. That in itself makes for a unique experience and an almost unbearable one for the viewer, as it must have been for Wenders and his crew. Our passive voyeurism as spectators generates mixed feelings of embarrassment, shame, shock, and anger, which the artists must have been able, to a large degree, to exorcise through their active involvement in making the film. The fact that the dying man is himself staging, directing, and "performing" his own death for the camera—what more romantic gesture could there be?—does not make it easier for us but rather adds to our uneasiness.

The term "document" used above is actually misleading. *Lightning Over Water* might be described indifferently as a documentary drifting toward fiction or as fiction drifting toward the documentary. It can only disappoint and irritate if approached as either, for it is neither one nor the other. Its own dialectics lie in the constant shuttling between fictionalization and raw fact, in the tug-of-war between the straining for distancing and the irrepressible pull of reality. It is perverse dialectics, with no reconciliation of the opposites. Wenders's dissatisfaction with the first version (the one shown at the Cannes Festival in 1980 and in the editing of which he was only marginally involved) led to his entirely reediting the film. He felt that his editor had treated the material like a documentary, thus eliminating the fictional aspect of the project. Although Wenders feels that his new version is "as close as I could ever get to the film Nick and I had shot," critics who have seen the two versions have suggested that Wenders's editing weakens the film's impact.

From whatever angle one looks at it, *Lightning Over Water* is too thoroughly self-centered (this is intended as an objective observation, not pejoratively) to allow for the kind of distance Wenders sought through fictionalization. Not only is it a film by Nicholas Ray about himself, and, simultaneously, one by Wim Wenders about himself as well as about Ray, but the very making of the film is its central preoccupation. Throughout the film, the method's purpose is to keep reminding us that this is no cinema-vérité-type document we are watching but a reconstruction, a "dramatization" that allows itself flights of fancy away from reality. Most of the time it doesn't really matter whether the "dramatization" is faithful or fanciful. The widest conceivable margin between whatever actually took place and what we are shown still seems negligible when compared with Ray's irrecusable *presence,* which keeps reinstating reality in the midst of distancing games.

Even if, as Wenders insists, "most of the ideas" are Ray's, death steals away the film from him, shifting its authorship and responsibility to Wenders. It then becomes possible to see *Lightning* as Wender's symbolic acting out—no matter how reluctant—of the ritualistic murder of the Father, a thought that may have a lot to do with his continuing ambivalence toward the film. (Wenders indirectly reveals his awareness on the matter in at least two scenes. In one, he maintains that Ray is *not* a father image to him; in the other, he tells Ray, "If I felt that I was being attracted to your weakness and suffering, I would stop the film.")

Whatever Wenders's conscious and/or subconscious feelings toward Ray may have been, however, there is little doubt that Ray saw himself as a father image (this is made clear in a long clip from *We Can't Go Home Again*), although his attitude is never "fatherly" in any traditional manner during the film (as a matter of fact, the sad privilege that his situation as a sick, dying man gave Ray allows him to regress, at times, to an almost infantile state). In *We Can't Go Home Again* Ray had already staged his own death, by suicide—a suicide agreed to by his students. In a way, fathers have to die for their spiritual children to be able to develop. At any rate, Ray's romantic fascination with death is nowhere more apparent than in this posthumous work. Underneath the understandable desire to leave one last film behind after fifteen years of aborted projects, there lies, in "Nick's movie" a more obscure one: the desire to experience death (identified in Ray's diary—which Wenders quotes in the film—as a most natural one) and perhaps, who knows—such is the folly and wisdom of romanticism—triumph over it by turning it into an artistic statement.

46. Michael Ritchie (1938)

by MARK LeFANU

1969—*Downhill Racer;* 1972—*Prime Cut; The Candidate;* 1975—*Smile;* 1976—*The Bad News Bears;* 1978—*Semi-Tough;* 1980—*The Island; Divine Madness*

Unreleased
1979—*An Almost Perfect Affair*

Uncredited
Ritchie reportedly directed all or part of *Student Bodies* (1981), credited to the pseudonymous Allen Smithee

Television Movie
1968—*The Sound of Anger*

In comparison with the films of Robert Altman or Martin Scorsese or perhaps of Francis Ford Coppola, most people where they know them would think of Michael Ritchie's as small-scale, minor, particular, intimist work. Ritchie does not appear to have come into the prestige of his more celebrated contemporaries. Ritchie's films are unpretentious, closely observed, finely textured works, about which critics have not made much of a fuss. And yet there comes a point when, looking back, one sees that their consistency itself—their consistent excellence—is telling us something: something about the way that cinema itself is able to move out and *look around.* Why it is that cinema has taken over from all other art forms as the milieu in which strong, inquisitive, and ironic talent would wish to situate itself? Why is the cinema more attractive than the theater? Ritchie who started at Harvard in the theater and has since expressed the wish (I don't know how seriously) if the chance came round to take up theater directing again, gives us in each of his movies many decisive instances of an answer to this question. His films have a kind of richness and freedom (and here I would make him rejoin people like Altman and Scorsese, as well as other artists like Rafelson and Frederick Wiseman)—a freedom that makes the theater by comparison in everything that it executes clumsy and didactic. The cinema gives a kind of passionate and ferocious attention to its subject by paradoxically effacing itself. Whereas the division of the stage play into the traditional *acts* and *scenes* (different in this from the lightning switches of perspective made possible at each instant by the editor's art, the skill of the *final cut*) is condemned to lumber behind its clumsy symbolic baggage.

In *Downhill Racer* the female lead, foxily played by Camilla Sparv, is abandoned three-quarters of the way through the film. Reconciliation impossible: she plays her cards and loses. The film strikes me as being overall extraordinarily unromantic, austere, serious—even humorless, as if right from the start one senses the need in Ritchie to establish a kind of total distance from anything that could be accused of being romantically "theatrical." Instead: the ice, the snow, the tension and tedium of the ski events, everything that is *outdoors* given to us with an effort of documentary seriousness and objectivity. However it was initially conceived of by Robert Redford (who owned the property), the film arrives before *us* with a bleak, wintry intransigence. Its drama, where it exists, comes not so much from anything distinctive in the plot, as from something you sense about the circumstances themselves in which the film was made— the very sense of adventure, and fear, that is involved in being alone, in a foreign country, aged twenty-eight and shooting a first feature. The whole fragility and precariousness of the enterprise communicates itself in a kind of existential authenticity to the final product as it comes out in the movie theaters. One feels in this sense that Robert Redford's loneliness, perched on the top of an icy mountain at the beginning of a *downhill run,* doubles, beautifully, for that of the director himself—and that of every new director. Everything is about *risk,* and the film communicates this in its precise, elegant, swiftly cut formulations. The technical difficulty must have been: how to organize the tempo of the film so that the different skiing competitions can be seen to lead up to an overall climax, the Winter Olympics. (A problem, then, about time-keeping and thus about the technical nature of all movies in so far as they have to subscribe to a habit of precision: Ritchie's *television training* here, as a lesson in the *economy* of all good drama.)

Is it a film about ambitiousness? about "winning"? (the point most usually made about Ritchie's movies). So far as the plot is concerned, it is. The hero Chappellet drives himself furiously and unthinkingly to success in his chosen enterprise, and then in the midst of triumph finds himself confronted by a moment of lucidity. (He looks around. He sees the person who has *nearly* beaten him. What is it all about? What has the cost been?) So it is in *The Candidate;* so it is, more obliquely and spread over a larger number of protagonists, in a movie like *Smile.*

Yet there comes a moment when such a formula is no longer genuinely exploratory about the concept of success—it moves over into being something else: a plot device, perhaps, something to provide the minimal dramatic structure demanded by a work in its exposition but which, of itself, is not the focus of the film maker's keenest inquiry. And thus we find Ritchie himself, in some of the various interviews he has given, dissociating himself from, or at least being vaguely ironical about, a "theme" that his critics are everywhere united in having found at the center of his films.

But even if competition were not the specific *theme* of all his movies (and Ritchie draws attention to a number of unrealized projects where this seems to be the case), there is nonetheless a kind of *energy* observable in each film, for which "competition" and "winning" could be seen as simply a convenient metaphor. One sees in miniature in films like Ritchie's how forcefully it should be argued that the drive and energy that motivated the novel in its classical period—the novels, say, of Balzac and Stendhal— have now migrated entirely to an artform like cinema. There is a point to be made here about different art forms in different periods: cinema would now seem to offer the opportunities—in terms of expressiveness, opportunities for audacity and richness of observation, and moreover for the *subject matter itself*—that were once the province of the written word. Cinema is *the* modern medium of narrative. All this seems to me unpretentiously present in the simplicity, the linearity, and the un-self-consciousness of a movie like *Downhill Racer.* Its inquiry is turned outward, onto the world of people, rather than inward, into the mechanism of its own productivity. Its pace is both calm and fast-moving, as if holding fast onto an absolute confidence about its own transparent legibility.

On the specific question of winning, there is in fact, I think, an excellent ambiguity surrounding the figure played by Robert Redford. He is presented, after all, as being just a tiny bit stupid. "I wanted to make a satire on the jock ethic," Ritchie is reported as saying about a movie that most people have found, on the contrary, somewhat chilling, austere, and unfunny. "Satire" in Ritchie's cinema is a complex and essentially serious business, even in films as close to the heart of comedy as *Smile* and *The Bad News Bears.* What one *can* say is that this slight stupidity in the character of Chappellet prevents the ending (in which, as we have said, he "looks around" and confronts his victory with the possibility of defeat) from falling into an available and sentimental pathos. Chappellet through Redford is situated *ambiguously,* seen from the inside and yet seen from the outside, seen warmly and seen coldly, seen seriously and seen satirically, seen in real life and seen "on television"; this gives the movie a certain unasked for complexity of tone, and invites comparison with a film like Sidney Pollack's *Bobby Deerfield,* another movie about the ambiguity of male ambition and achievement.

In the meantime, we content ourselves with noticing in general how sharply Ritchie manages to draw the minor characters in this small, unpretentious movie: the coach (Gene Hackman), Redford's teammates on the American ski team; along with all the various hustlers, entrepreneurs, media men, "sportsmen" who materialize out of nowhere to surround and accompany a champion on his long and somewhat forlorn journey to success. Is it *downhill* or uphill? Hard work or plainsailing? Glamour or grind? The film puzzles about these things while remaining essentially true to its milieu— very few concessions to the public at large—with just enough of the allegorical about it to hint at a more generally conceived vision of affairs.

Prime Cut is a thriller set in the meat and harvest lands of Kansas. It is extremely well written (by Robert Dillon) to produce just that effortless continuity between the actors, the action, and the milieu that makes one think of American naturalism as somehow the great, and perhaps the only, true dramatic language of our time. The wit of a movie like *Prime Cut* is paradoxically much denser and much *sharper,* much harder to get hold of than that in such more literary collaborations as those of Alain Resnais and David Mercer or R. W. Fassbinder and Tom Stoppard. It is inseparably linked to the gesture of the actors who deliver the lines and the authentic locales in which the action is situated.

Prime Cut was a project Ritchie accepted at the last moment, and it provides

an interesting opportunity to test some notions of authorship—always a more complicated and more interesting problem than people think. Robert Dillon wrote the script,
but the film is still in many ways, even thematically, an authentic work of Ritchie's.
What is mysterious is that just the parts belonging to Ritchie are the parts that one
would suppose must have come *first.* Thus, in the confrontation between the gangster
from Chicago (Lee Marvin) and the Kansas meat boss "Mary-Ann" (Gene Hackman)
there is an underlying inquiry integral to the film and parallel to inquiries in Ritchie's
other movies, about who wields political power in the nation: who "owns" different
parts of America. (Chicago has gone soft and "Italian"; "You speak spic? Si?" Hackman
taunts Lee Marvin's Nick Devlin. Only the West—the Kansan wheat plains—holds
onto its pristine and somewhat sinister WASPishness). Similarly, underneath the conventional *gangster morality* there seems to be a real moral question being plied round the
figure portrayed by Lee Marvin—a question central to the position of all Ritchie's
protagonists in the context of that energy I spoke about as constitutive of the American
cinema: namely, whether success in an enterprise necessarily carries with it the moral
compromise of the person who succeeds. Is energy *itself* corrupting? Marvin's route
to success in this particular enterprise involves leaving behind him the traditional trail
of corpses endemic to gangster movies—a histrionic and overdetermined symbol that
can be interpreted on one level quite seriously as the *moral havoc* left behind by any
human enterprise of force and decision. One has to repeat how *extrovert* American
culture continually shows itself to be, as opposed to the interiority and psychological
circumspection of European culture. (There is a difference to be gleaned here that
Brecht would have liked—between the possibilities for epic art and for tragic art in
general.)

 Prime Cut is however a black comedy first and foremost. The Kansas wheat
plains of *The Wizard of Oz* are photographed under glowering skies and in the middle
of thunderstorms. The nodding fields of sunflowers at dusk that make up the landscape
of Ritchie's film impart a new meaning tinged with vice to the poppy-strewn meadows
over which, in the famous children's classic, Judy Garland skips whistling her famous
melody. As for little girls themselves, they end up in this movie being sold to meat
farms. (Sissy Spacek is rescued by Lee Marvin from the meat pens of Gene Hackman's
packaging plant: *Prime Cut,* like *The Wizard of Oz,* is also a fairy tale!) The fact that
the film comes from an already well defined and traditional fictional mode (the "gangster
film") allows Ritchie a tremendously vivid and metaphorical freedom in his imagery.
The film is shaped like a nightmare: the objects from the gangster film's traditional
iconography find themselves squeezed together and metamorphosed into astonishing
new combinations and conjunctions—squeezed together, like the bales of straw mixed
with motor parts that, in an amazing sequence, tumble out of the back of a combine
harvester that has just demolished a limousine. *Prime Cut* is like Polanski's *Chinatown*
in that *after dark* everything becomes brighter, more mysterious, more allegorical,
more tinged with poetic meanings. The opening sequence of the movie, shot in a
slaughterhouse, is a condensation into five short minutes of something like the entire
trajectory of Frederick Wiseman's marvelously poetic, Buñuelian reverie *Meat* (1976):
"From hoof to hamburger in five easy stages." Flesh, women, cars, wheat, opium—
the individual counters are all mixed up in nightmarish confusion, but as with dreams,
the confusion is somehow lucid and, as it were, striving to establish some normality
point of daytime ordinariness. In sum: a poetic movie, based on realism, like the best
of Hitchcock (and like Hitchcock, full of a kind of mysterious and *farouche* humor).

 The Candidate is very different—less wild, less metaphorical, though by no means prosaic. The title itself possesses a kind of suggestive anonymity, like the anonymity hidden in the title of Francesco Rosi's *Illustrious Corpses* or indeed much more famously in that of *The Godfather*—an anonymity sinister, ambiguous if you like, that seems already to bear a profound affinity with the practices of *films noirs*. The opening sequence of the movie, in which we see a professional campaign manager (Peter Boyle) and his advertising buddy (Alan Garfield) giving the slip to an unsuccessful "candidate" after his failed campaign, sliding into their limousines, and heading off to the West Coast in search of new material, has something of an indefinable aura of crime about it, which sets the film in motion on a *fictional* path that differentiates it altogether from mere examples of "reportage."

This metaphorical freedom makes the film difficult to interpret: it is "about" the corruption of American politics, but it is actually much more complicated, much *better*. The film has a corresponding idealism, a sense of vigor, that cancels out its pessimistic conclusions on the level of narrative. Far from wanting to satirize the mechanics of power, you feel that Ritchie wants above all to know how power operates: there is a kind of *forensic* interest over and above, *prior to,* any question of moral condemnation that succeeds in keeping the film cool in the heat of its bustling activity and manages to impart to the proceedings a particularly fine and subtle brand of moral irony.

The narrative itself shows how a successful radical lawyer (Robert Redford) is persuaded to leave his grass-roots constituency and run for the Senate, but this movement is never presented exclusively in terms of a *sell-out*. On the contrary, Ritchie is very subtle and ambivalent about this. The pact Robert Redford makes with his Mephistopheles, like all such pacts, is a serious one—or has serious possibilities—in that behind it lie authentic desires. And thus one has to be careful of saying that it is a film about Robert Redford's vanity. As "candidate," of course, he is (within reason) vain, ruthless, ambitious, but Ritchie seems to be just as interested in showing aspects of his activity that are not marked by any easily moralizable cynicism. How does one actually go about meeting one's potential constituents, building up a following, standing at factory gates, milling about beach resorts, visiting the poorer parts of the city, addressing complacent and pampered interest groups? The speeches that are actually made, the words that come across on these occasions are full of opportunism and shallowness, but what saves them and what makes them interesting for our purposes, and even poignant, is that the parties to the whole bizarre ritual *see* their inadequacy, and the atmosphere is full of a kind of fazed dramatic embarrassment—which can be accommodated by brashness and stupidity but also by genuine courage. "Learning to be a public figure" is in one sense learning how to act—an education in the art of insincerity— but on the other hand (and perhaps this is where one shouldn't renege on a certain optimistic spirit in the film despite everything), there is also the puzzle of genuine eloquence, genuine ability to get things done—even when *that* means speeches as conservatively homespun, action as egregiously calculating, as the cynical wisdom of Redford's opponent, the Republican Crocker Jarman (played with a wonderful assurance and a kind of weary insolence by Don Parker).

I return to a comparison with Rosi. There is the same inquisitive interest about social institutions between the two artists; the same desire to show the mechanisms of power at work in our society in strong, bold, essentially realistic strokes; along with the same fastidious and minute attention to detail, as if in the observation of detail lay the guarantee of one's seriousness as an investigator in the first place; (that detail itself is *serious* and governs the *complexity of elements* surrounding a given situation).

But one also immediately notices that what makes Ritchie different from Rosi is the relative lack of paranoia in the American artist, all things considered: the sense that politics in Ritchie's movies won't be translated into some elegant theory of conspiracy. No one is better than Ritchie at showing the ways in which the phenomenology of popular democratic politics is dominated by the day-to-day innovations of technology— the omnipresence of the television screen, the televised "political debate"—but Ritchie's forensic dramatizations of these institutions go hand in hand with a curious off-handedness. Unlike Rosi, Ritchie doesn't really think technology is sinister. His film is left-wing in its analysis, but curiously ironical, neutral, and aesthetic in his attitude toward that analysis. *The Candidate* is humorous, sharp, and tender in tone—tender at any event to the democratic American crowd that is *being* manipulated—rather than bitter and disillusioned as one might have expected. Forgive and forget: the film is different from real life—as films have to be. The reflections that art offers have a momentum of their own that is different from the reflections arising out of life, no matter how much, as in the case of both Ritchie and Rosi, art itself is found to be scrupulously grounded in reality.

Here for instance (to take a small example), one has the sense that there is a kind of *technical challenge* involved in rendering the entire spectacle with accuracy, and that this itself—a problem as it were of *logistics*—becomes a major part of the subject of the film. There are parallels between setting up a movie and setting up a political campaign, as Altman shows in a film like *Nashville,* and the pleasure of the one is almost bound to reflect on, and even turn into, the pleasure of the other (to the detriment, perhaps, of some harsh vision of politics that the film maker had previously contemplated).

The Candidate, while it bears certain thematic similarities to *Downhill Racer,* is a much richer and more psychologically nuanced work. The character played by Redford himself is more intriguing; it remains harder to tell in this movie in what way he is a mere cipher and in what sense, on the contrary, he impels his own destiny. In keeping with this greater richness and density of composition—this altogether greater freedom and wit—the characters who surround the central figure are also portrayed with a greater life of their own; we signal out Robert Redford's scheming and ambitious wife, beautifully, tenderly played by Karen Carlson; the tough, selfish and somewhat formidable father—onetime governor of the state (a crisp, resonant cameo role for the aging Melvyn Douglas); in short the *private background* against which ambition can become plausible and even authentically tragic is all here in this movie, economically suggested. The film beautifully and calmly winds together these public and private destinies, yet remains essentially generous, without making expensive allowances in the area of its rigor and of its formal precision.

Smile on the other hand is an amazing masterpiece, the prime justification for treating Ritchie as preeminent among younger American directors. The film demonstrates the ways in which naturalism—the documentary technique in general—is capable of drawing not merely sociological but metaphysical truth from the subject that engages it.

The subject of *Smile* is a beauty contest, and I suppose it could be said that in the subjection of women to art one has already one of the great iconographies through which metaphysical truth is potentially available. But a "subject" as such means nothing, or nearly nothing. Everything depends on a kind of initial conviction on the part of the artist that there is something there beyond the merely factual to bring out and illuminate—and then subsequently on the delicacy and poetic force with which he can coax such convictions into reality. Such insights are simultaneously momentous and incredibly simple and spring originally from an ethical rather than from an intellectual starting point. That is the artist's great strength. It's as if one has got to *believe* seriously enough in one's objective for it to be able to reward you with the privilege of its truth. (One comes back for comparison to an artist in genuine documentary like Frederick Wiseman.)

I think of a scene deep into this movie where one of the girls (Miss Anaheim, Annette O'Toole) gives a solo performance of her "speciality act." The girl in question is vain and silly (but nice) and her act is *predictably embarrassing.* Yet embarrassment is already one of the great vectors by which art communicates its propositions. (Most art, especially on film, is too polished, too finished to be embarrassing, and therefore one misses the existential knife edge—a kind of openness to chance—in which alone the emotions catch fire and are converted into truth.)

The act itself couldn't be more suitable or schematic; it is a strip tease. The girl begins dressed in boas and furs—imitation of a grand lady of fashion—which she then discards item by item, meanwhile treating us (the audience, the judges) to an excruciating homily (in verse) on the virtues of simplicity. "If you want to be real cutey / You'll rely on *inner* beauty" she concludes, discarding the last of her wrappings to reveal—a rather pretty figure in a bathing suit.

And yet: the whole thing is excessively complicated. The girl is surely sincere in her mistake that the best symbol for her soul is her body. In a way she is right: the two things can not and will not be separated. Virtue is all very well; but the girl's *destiny,* the things that really matter to her, are bound up in her looks. That is what beauty contests are all about. Not to be able to say this out loud is the gauge not of hypocrisy but of a kind of incredible poignancy. Everything in this movie is inadequate to its real truth, and yet the real truth is there in front of us the whole time, mediated into these weird, bizarre forms that make up the anthropology of the American beauty contest. (One says this about the woman characters in the film, but it is equally true about the males, busy organizing the event or in some way commenting on it.)

The film starts with a shot of the van taking the girls to the contest overtaking a *mobile home* on the back of a trailer. The character played by Bruce Dern subsequently and by coincidence turns out to be a *caravan salesman* (when he is not helping, as he is here, to organize the pageant). The contest itself is firmly set in Santa Rosa, California, but on another level the film speaks of a kind of spiritual homelessness in the American psyche—a longing within its customs for a genuine culture—which it seems to me has rarely been better dramatized. In *Smile* the girls in the contest have the name of their home town printed on a sash across their breast for us to identify them—and yet they are homeless. When Bruce Dern wants to promise his wife a holiday after the pageant is over, the first place he thinks of is—Disneyland. (His own house is like Disneyland: simultaneously cheap and expensive, profoundly anonymous, and yet to European eyes strangely exotic.) One repeats: there is no satire in this—the level of seriousness and the complexity of example remove these statements from the gaze of mockery.

The paradox of popular American culture as incarnated by beauty pageants such as those in *Smile,* then, could be summed up by saying that they are at once so ebullient and yet simultaneously so forlorn. Is it a coincidence that figures like Sissy Spacek—the figure of the ingenuous, innocent teenage girl in general—have come to dominate the storyline of so many of the most serious American films of the last few years, whether in a documentary sense, as here in *Smile,* with its bevy of Sissy Spaceks, or alternatively, mediated through an opposite genre like the horror film (*Carrie, The Fury, Exorcist II: The Heretic*)?

Is Ritchie's a horror film? Well, *Smile* has two meanings. One can smile because one is happy or smile because one has to. It is usually taken that Ritchie's film belongs decisively to the first of these categories, and yet it seems to me that the film is even ferocious. As in *Prime Cut* (perhaps the two films are interchangeable), there is the rather sinister sense in which the subject of meat slides into the possible fictions that the film could be about (as it does for that matter in a movie like Rafelson's *Stay Hungry.*) I don't mean here any obvious and crude reference to sexuality—on the contrary, the reference is to the original culinary metaphor itself. The freshness of the girls in the beauty contest finds a bleak, ferocious contrast in the antics among the town's males in the "Exhausted Rooster" ceremony and in their drunken gourmandising. There are everywhere strange references to food and to eating in *Smile* that are excessive to the narrative and function as a kind of permanent syntagmatic disturbance—a confusion on the metaphorical level, which, as in *Prime Cut,* seems always to be threatening to carry the film into nightmare. Like the best of documentary, *Smile* is edged by surrealism. The neatness with which the references in the syntagmatic chain tie up is always there to offer an alternative, darker logic, that tracks down and casts into a permanently somber focus the spontaneous gaiety and somewhat touching naiveté of the beauty pageant.

Perhaps this is putting the matter too explicitly (the film is after all on the surface, like all Ritchie's efforts, lighthearted and witty). And yet one thinks of an important scene like the moment when the drunken husband (Nicholas Pryor) comes back to his wife's spotless house, with its shampooed carpets, and elegant, tasteless nicknacks. The furious quarrel that ensues—it is dark, ferocious comedy—suggests that the only true comparison for the forlorn greatness of such scenes (in which for a moment a whole civilization is summed up by the decor of a single room) is with an artist as pitiless as Ibsen. Nothing else will do. *Smile* is Ritchie's *Doll's House* and even his *Hedda Gabler.*

The Bad News Bears is a comedy. Apparently every child in America has seen it twice: it has provided Ritchie and the companies that back him with their only substantial financial success. And as a matter of fact, it is a very good film. The attitude that Ritchie shows toward adolescents in his films seems to me in general to be interesting and worthy of note (we have already touched upon it in *Smile*). He obviously likes children and is able to put them into his movies in witty, unaffected roles; but at the same time there seems to be something more serious and more interesting—perhaps even something symbolic—in the fairly prominent positions that children have tended to occupy in so many of his movies. For instance, the weird, awkward alliance that Sissy Spacek strikes up with Lee Marvin in *Prime Cut* finds itself echoed here and opened up in the relationship Ritchie draws between Walter Matthau and Tatum O'Neal. What kind of relationship is it exactly? As in all the best "movies about children" (for example, *Moonfleet* [Fritz Lang], *Les 400 Coups* [François Truffaut], *High Wind in Jamaica* [Alexander Mackendrick]), the seriousness comes from an implied adult world that is somehow present in the very *texture of realism* with which the films are originally conceived. Criticism shows its inarticulacy by trying to specify in greater detail how it is that this should actually come about, *where* it is that we identify it. Is it in the script or in the handling that this mysterious rightness finds its way in, like some liquid infiltration? The generally poor quality of the sequels to Ritchie's movie

(*The Bad News Bears in Breaking Training* [1977], *The Bad News Bears Go to Japan* [1978], neither of them directed by Ritchie in person) seems to answer this question in one way, but in another way it is not really answered at all. Certainly there is nothing "heavy" about this film, nothing pretentious; it is brisk, lighthearted, and if one were looking for a way to sum it up one would say, full of character. It is another example of the truth that observation itself, when it is so totally without prejudice as it is in Ritchie's movies, has already in it all the moral element that art could desire. By "moral element" one simply means a kind of essential truth about the real relationship people occupy toward each other in society—something different from the romanesque, different from "verisimilitude," since these relationships stand at the same time (especially in children's films) as a utopian ideal and as the true, accurate embodiment of how we have actually come to be constituted.

The title of Ritchie's next film, *Semi-Tough,* has an obvious etymological resemblance to that of Bob Rafelson's *Stay Hungry.* There is the same rather humorous (*semi*-humorous) attitude toward keeping oneself in good shape, the same resort on Ritchie's part to black comedy and exaggeration to mask what strikes me as an essentially serious investigation of individualism (individualism in its up-to-date varieties, which in America today still implies a paradoxical conformism); the same resort, finally, to the *body* to make observations that really belong to the soul. One should not at the start separate the serious from the humorous parts of either movie: the investigation is serious *because* it is humorous; the humor is a shorthand for the swiftness and audacity with which either film is able to make its connections.

Semi-Tough, like *Stay Hungry,* is a film that could have been designed for Europeans to show how crazy and exotic America remains. As with *Stay Hungry,* the location is all-important. *Semi-Tough* was shot in Florida—the Florida of *The Heartbreak Kid* (Elaine May, 1972) with its rich golden light bathing Jill Clayburgh's face in a perpetual glow and a kind of general promise in the air of a prosperous al fresco existence. Clayburgh, by coincidence, is the star of both *Semi-Tough* and Paul Mazursky's *An Unmarried Woman,* two films that portray a "modern" woman and her relationship with men. But whereas, in the latter film, the men she is portrayed as getting mixed up with exist only as a *past* and a *future* (and in other words, for the purposes of the film hardly exist at all), what is excellent about *Semi-Tough* is that it is about a choice (between Kris Kristofferson and Burt Reynolds) that exists perpetually in the present tense—a choice therefore that can be serious and truthful, since, dramatically speaking, the only choices that are of interest to us are the ones that are given in front of our eyes.

Clayburgh's beauty is a beauty of voice. The film is full of glorious cadences, difficult for criticism to reconstitute in words. Her head thrown back, her eyes at a certain angle, the words that issue from her lips have a tender, deprecating irony that guard her privacy in the midst of the rather boisterous friendships that the film is engaged in portraying. It is a fine, serious performance, full of shades of womanliness, if it is still permissible to say such things. You feel that the part has been beautifully written for the actress so that, as in all the best cinematic writing, there is a constant and almost miraculous dialectical passage between the actor's own personality in real life and the personality assumed for the demands of the story. Its triumph is that it leads to a kind of annulment of acting altogether, so that the film in its description becomes something else entirely (perhaps a documentary).

Semi-Tough, which never once mentions movies, is permeated by what must properly be called a love for the cinema. One doesn't need Ritchie to tell us explicitly that behind this movie is a reworking of *Jules et Jim*—that its boisterousness refers us back to *The Philadelphia Story,* its comedy to a film like *Design for Living,* and its gallantry to the beauty of Margaret Sullavan in Frank Borzage's *Three Comrades.* The point of course is not the multiplicity of references that the critic adds up but rather a more general consideration about the use of history itself in conjunction with contemporary cinema. A film isn't better because it refers back to previous films; and yet to be open to such influences is to be open to the possibilities of one's art.

Semi-Tough, makes one want to look back again for a moment to *Downhill Racer*—back to the very beginning. There is the same drive and energy, but by the time Ritchie arrives at *Semi-Tough* it is all much more good-humored and colorful (as if the monochrome of the ski slopes has been exchanged for a kind of permanent chromaticism endemic in the American sunshine). There is a kind of erotic freedom in this last film that was either repressed or simply failed to surface in the earlier movies that mark Ritchie's collaboration with Redford. The scenes in *Semi-Tough* set in the various encounter groups also have an ideological freedom reminiscent of a film maker like Dusan Makavejev. For Makavejev and Ritchie the spectacle is always more wonderful than any comment that could possibly be made about it. There are these extraordinary customs in which ordinary people lay themselves open in their total vulnerability—this frantic search for some truth that will provide them with sense and identity: all these antics the film maker watches with no sense of condescension, but on the contrary a feeling of the utmost friendliness—a feeling very strongly that after all this is his culture too.

---

47. *Robert Rossen* (1908–1966)

by JEAN-LOUP BOURGET

1947—*Johnny O'Clock; Body and Soul;* 1950—*All the King's Men;* 1951—*The Brave Bulls;* 1954—*Mambo* (Italy; U.S., 1955); 1956—*Alexander the Great;* 1957—*Island in the Sun;* 1959—*They Came to Cordura;* 1961—*The Hustler;* 1964—*Lilith*

For most of his career, Robert Rossen was regarded with suspicion by formalist critics. The evident seriousness of his ambitions and his near ponderous approach gave him the appearance of a producer miscast as a director. Then he made *The Hustler* and *Lilith,* and his reputation underwent a sea-change. In particular, *Cahiers du Cinéma* hailed both works as highly original examples of psychological film. Unfortunately, Rossen, already very ill during the shooting of *Lilith,* died in 1966, and *Lilith* remained his last completed project. His earlier films, however, were searched for possible pointers to his mature style. This led to a reappraisal of *Body and Soul, All the King's Men,* and *They Came to Cordura* (1959).

In retrospect it is easy to see what *The Hustler* has in common with films of the forties. As Alan Casty has said in his excellent monograph *The Films of Robert Rossen* (Museum of Modern Art, 1969), "Rossen worked almost entirely within the conventions of socially oriented realism, established by the social-problem and gangster films and plays of the thirties." In fact, Rossen himself had helped establish these conventions as a playwright and a script writer for Warner Brothers. He had been responsible for the screenplays of Lloyd Bacon's *Marked Woman,* Mervyn Le Roy's *They Won't Forget,* Raoul Walsh's *Roaring Twenties,* Anatole Litvak's *Out of the Fog* and *Blues in the Night,* among others. These conventions could be described as mildly Marxist (at this time Rossen was a member of the Communist Party). They argued that gangsters were primarily the product of their social environment and therefore that the responsibility for their crimes was collective rather than individual. The opposite view, which could be termed psychoanalytical, saw gangsters primarily as psychopaths suffering from hubris: cf. Raoul Walsh's *White Heat* or Gordon Douglas's *Kiss Tomorrow Goodbye.* It should be noted, however, that when Rossen turned to directing he made only one gangster film, his first (*Johnny O'Clock* with Dick Powell, a minor achievement by all accounts). Rather, he specialized in describing male environments or "rackets" functioning on the borderland between gangsterism and legality: boxing in *Body and Soul,* regional politics in *All the King's Men,* bullfighting in *The Brave Bulls,* and finally, pool games in *The Hustler.*

Three men were together largely responsible for *Body and Soul.* John Garfield's company, Roberts Productions, started the project, and he starred in the film as Charley Davis. Robert Rossen directed it and apparently collaborated with Abraham Polonsky on the script. Rossen and Polonsky drew heavily not only on the conventions of the social-problem film but also on their own experience of the New York Jewish ghetto; Davis's friend in *Body and Soul* (Joseph Pevney) is called "Shorty Polansky." Davis himself and his mother (Anne Revere, an actress with left-wing leanings) are also Jewish. Both Rossen and Polonsky were committed to their Jewish heritage, and the biblical references of Polonsky's *Force of Evil* (also with John Garfield) have often been pointed out. According to Jean Seberg's testimony, Rossen kept up the practice of his religion until his death. Rossen and Polonsky also made full use of Garfield's screen persona as it had been developed by Michael Curtiz in his *Four Daughters* series and in his adaptation of Jack London's *The Sea Wolf,* scripted by Rossen himself. (Rossen had written the screenplays of two more Warners films starring Garfield: Lewis Seiler's *Dust Be My Destiny* and Litvak's *Out of the Fog.*)

Charley Davis becomes a boxer in order to escape from the ghetto. However, his economic and social ascent is achieved at the expense of his inner freedom. To rise above his condition, he must sell his soul. When he eventually makes up his mind to break with the racket, he knows that he will not be able to fight again. *Body and Soul* set the pattern for subsequent films about boxing. Thus Mark Robson's *Champion,* made two years later, reproduces the same success story, with Kirk Douglas rising "from the depths of poverty" (this time the slums are Irish rather than Jewish), losing his own soul, and retrieving it at the eleventh hour, only to die. Douglas even has an affair with an amateur sculptress, as Garfield in *Body and Soul* had been befriended by the artist Peg (Lilli Palmer); but the sculptress in *Champion* is otherwise more of a reincarnation of the vapid Hazel Brooks character in *Body and Soul.* Robert Wise's *The Set-Up* again espouses a similar pattern of material rise and fall contrasted with moral loss and rebirth.

This pattern is typical of much Hollywood drama, as Pauline Kael has shown in her discussion of *Citizen Kane.* It is a frequent assumption of popular literature that the rich and the mighty are fundamentally unhappy, that their quest for the "Rosebud" of inner satisfaction is always in vain. Rossen's dramatization of this traditional concept expresses his belief in the need both for material betterment and spiritual growth. Rossen was at the same time a Communist intellectual who favored radical social change and a Jewish pessimist who felt that power and wealth inevitably corrupt man. This tension between social and personal commitment, between thirties optimism and forties disillusionment, gave his films their special character.

All the King's Men is Rossen's adaptation of Robert Penn Warren's novel. A beautiful and complex film, it uses techniques borrowed from the *film noir* (the menacing portrait) and from the private-eye movie: John Ireland plays a journalist whose voice-over narration conducts an inquiry into Willie Stark (Broderick Crawford), a populist politician who is himself a twisted mixture of idealism and greed. Rossen has often been accused of unsubtlety. Yet All the King's Men is far more complex and ambiguous than All the President's Men, directed twenty-five years later by Alan J. Pakula. Treating a subject whose similarity is underlined by his film's title, Pakula is almost Manichaean, turning his journalist heroes into St. George figures slaying Nixon's dragon. Rossen shows the ambivalence in Willie Stark, a character reminiscent of Citizen Kane, and the tone of the film—a study of political and moral imposture—is akin to that in Richard Brooks's Elmer Gantry and Elia Kazan's A Face in the Crowd. Rossen also shows the confusion of the journalist's motivations, underlines the fact that Burden (John Ireland) too is moved by personal ambition, describes the fascination which Stark exerts over Burden. By the end of the film, Burden has been led to question his own credentials, and he turns against the photographers who harass the fallen Stark.

The conventions of the bullfighting film are similar to those of the boxing film: women, wealth, glory, and other external rewards tend to be gained at the expense of personal integrity. Rossen's The Brave Bulls is an honorable achievement in this difficult subgenre. But it remains markedly inferior to Mamoulian's admirable Blood and Sand. Among Rossen's next films, which include Mambo and Island in the Sun, the most interesting was probably his epic Alexander the Great, which, like All the King's Men, suffered from extensive cuts made at the producer's insistence. Rossen also had to compromise on certain aspects of They Came to Cordura, notably the fact that Gary Cooper is not allowed to die at the end. Nevertheless Cordura is a powerful allegory. The theme is the definition of courage and the realization of the gap between manifest (military) heroism and inner courage. Once again, Rossen, who had considered directing The Treasure of the Sierra Madre, is close to John Huston, who treated a similar subject in The Red Badge of Courage (later, Huston's Fat City revived the drab realistic tradition of Body and Soul). Ironically, Gary Cooper, supposedly a coward, is assigned to select a number of American soldiers, distinguished for bravery in combat, and to take them to safety in Cordura. Gradually, through the symbolic journey, the crossing of the desert, which is characteristic of so many Westerns and American films in general, roles are reversed. The true motivations of the pseudoheroes are laid bare, and it is the coward who becomes a Christ figure, displaying superhuman power and abnegation. The cavalry charge singling out the "heroes," at the beginning of the film, was shot by second-unit director James C. Havens, and Patrick Brion has criticized this sequence for being out of tone with the rest of the film (in Cahiers du Cinéma, April 1966). In fact, it is entirely appropriate that flamboyant heroism and true courage should be painted in different styles and even by different hands.

Rossen's last two films, The Hustler and Lilith, are among his best. He had complete control over them since he wrote, directed, and produced them. The Hustler owes a great deal to the atmospheric *films noirs* of the forties. The main characters are variations on those of *Body and Soul:* Paul Newman's pool shark for Garfield's boxer; George C. Scott for Lloyd Goff's gambler-promoter (cf. also Anthony Quinn in *The Brave Bulls*); and Piper Laurie for Lilli Palmer, whom she resembles physically. Peg (Lilli Palmer) was an artist, Sarah (Piper Laurie) is a writer. *The Hustler* is entirely satisfying on the realistic level as a depiction of the world of pool and billiards. The two long games between Fast Eddie (Newman) and Minnesota Fats (Jackie Gleason) are riveting. But the work also contains metaphysical connotations. The CinemaScope format and Eugen Shuftan's splendid photography (black-and-white having become unusual by 1961) lend the film a solemn poetic form. Rossen turns Scott into a satanic character, a tempter, and the billiards room in Louisville into a "sophisticated hell" (Alan Casty). The fact that Sarah is lame (a traditional melodramatic device) reflects the other characters' moral infirmities. Eddie commits the sin of pride in refusing to acknowledge failure. Sarah is more complex than earlier Rossen heroines. She is seen as a victim, but she bears a measure of responsibility for her tragic plight. In *The Hustler* Rossen achieved the most subtle balance between outside and inner pressure, between man's responsibility to others and to himself.

The delicacy and despair with which Rossen draws Sarah's character looks forward to Lilith (Jean Seberg) in the film of the same title. Specifically, the scene that has Sarah write "TWISTED, CRIPPLED, PERVERTED" on the mirror before she yields to Bert and kills herself announces the enigmatic words in Lilith's room, "HIARA PIRLU RESH KAVAWN." *Lilith* can also be seen as the antithesis of *Cordura*. In Spanish *cordura* means prudence, wisdom. While Major Thorn's journey took him from cowardice to courage, Vincent Bruce (Warren Beatty) goes from sanity to madness. Besides, from *Cordura* and *The Hustler* to *Lilith,* the shift of emphasis to the heroine is significant. For Lilith herself undergoes no change. She remains Lilith, a female devil according to ancient Jewish mythology, an embodiment of madness and beauty simultaneously, akin to the "mad spider" that spins the "most beautiful" cobweb. All the more fatal as she looks like a healthy country girl, Lilith is a prisoner of her own self. She traps men and drives them literally mad ("You know what is wrong with Lilith? She wants to possess all the men in the world"). She humiliates Vincent and uses him as an accomplice in her lesbian affair. Above all, she is in love with herself and with her own Harpy's reflection she narcissistically contemplates in the water of a fairy lake. In a mock tournament at the village carnival, Vincent becomes her servant knight and crowns Lilith "Queen of Love and Beauty," but the insidious aquatic element takes over, and the fun-fair doll is soon found drowned in Vincent's aquarium. *Lilith* is a chilling look at a chilling subject. Rossen rightly felt that the gentle, reassuring depiction of madness in Frank Perry's *David and Lisa* was "a big lie" and that his own, almost fantastic approach was in fact more realistic. Thus *Lilith* is not foreign to the Rossen corpus. It retains links with earlier films—*Island in the Sun* and *The Hustler* in particular—at the same time as it breaks new ground. The only reason why it appears relatively isolated is because of Rossen's premature death.

48. Martin Scorsese (1942)

by ALAIN MASSON

1968—*Who's That Knocking at My Door?*; 1972—*Boxcar Bertha*; 1973—*Mean Streets*; 1975—*Alice Doesn't Live Here Anymore*; 1976—*Taxi Driver*; 1977—*New York, New York*; 1978—*The Last Waltz* (documentary); *American Boy: A Profile of Steven Prince* (documentary); 1980—*Raging Bull*; 1983—*King of Comedy*

Miscellaneous
1970—*Street Scenes* (Scorsese is credited as postproduction director as well as production supervisor on this 16-mm film); 1974—*Italianamerican* (16-mm short included in compilation *A Storm of Strangers*)

How many people is Martin Scorsese? At least two: the intellectual, experimental film maker of *The Big Shave* (1967) and the Hollywood director (and apparent right-wing ideologue) of *Taxi Driver*. Or perhaps three—if a single added category could encompass the "B"-movie-fan who made *Boxcar Bertha* under the protection of Roger Corman; the thoughtful romantic who loaded the meditative *Alice Doesn't Live Here Anymore* with passion; and the documentarist of *Italianamerican*. Some might even identify a fourth Scorsese in the careful architect who built *New York, New York* on a calculated contrast of art and experience, showmanship and egotism—an artist whose taste for traditional narrative devices seems inconsistent with a passion for modern characters and rough formal innovations. Indeed, on second thought, each Scorsese film seems impossibly complex, even to the point of contradiction, but each scene, almost each shot, can be identified at first sight as Martin Scorsese's.

Except for two student sketches (*What's a Nice Girl Like You Doing in a Place Like This?* [1963] and *It's Not Just You Murray* [1964]), it all began with *The Big Shave*, in a perfectly illuminative way: in a television-commercial bathroom, a man seen meticulously shaving, and nothing exceptional is going to happen, until, having shaved, he begins to soap his face again; then the result is precisely what the audience was afraid it would be, and his face steadily turns into a wound, the logical completion being achieved when the character cuts his own throat. Almost everything in that short film seems to work as a mark of Scorsese's art, and a thorough analysis of its formal requirements should sum up his esthetic purpose.

The most obvious point, however, might not be the most important. The theme of facial destruction, as a result of the character's violent relationship to his mirror image will be used many times again. In *Taxi Driver*, Travis Bickle changes himself into somebody else, and into somebody who is not anybody, not even himself: just a selfless, symbolic figure drawn from the American stock of emblems—which paradoxically makes him stand out from the general selfishness. The conceit of the hero making-

326

up to kill finds its antithesis in two other behaviors: the taxi driver nosing around town with insatiable curiosity and the Peeping Tom watching blue movies: thus the cab, that is to say the selective authority of the script (once you get in that car you are a character in the film), and the cinematographic medium in itself come to demonstrate how decisive and universal is that search for images. And again in *Raging Bull,* Jake La Motta is evidently obsessed with his like, whether he reacts to likeness with brotherly love and rivalry or with homosexual hatred and jealousy. The recurring motif of glass breaking (*New York, New York, Alice Doesn't Live Here Anymore;* Scorsese once complained he could not have one character go through a windshield and another through a shop window in *Mean Streets*) must have some link with all that, since it affords the intruder an emphatic way of asserting his transcendence in relation to plane projections by seemingly cracking the surface of the screen.

This motif is important not only because it points to a stable thematic organization but mainly because it shelters Scorsese's themes from useless psychoanalytic musings: narcissism and castration may very well be of great consequence to Scorsese as a person, but they need not be preponderant as far as movie making and film viewing are concerned. On the other hand, the determination of vehemence by likeness and the qualification of image as self-estrangement must be taken into consideration, since they make up an iconographic figure explicitly related to narrative structure and film communication. This is what one has to learn from *The Big Shave,* instead of looking for intricate feelings or wild impulses.

As a matter of fact, the events in Scorsese's films cannot be comprehended and much less understood from the sole evidence of the characters' feelings. Jimmy Doyle in *New York, New York,* La Motta, or the touchy lover played by Harvey Keitel in *Alice Doesn't Live Here Anymore,* and even Alice herself at times, are all as unpredictable as the suicidal shaver. The logic of their behavior does not belong to their person, nor to some deus ex machina. The fate is the machine itself. The shaver has to cut his throat because this is what we expect as a film audience: not out of any deep thirst for blood, but because of the nature of time and of events. Since the narrative possibilities are explicitly closed by repetition, nothing can happen, nothing but that little accident, a slight razor cut, and since nothing else can happen, the paroxysm of the story has to be a monstrous hyperbole of that little nothing. Form is defined as expectation, and this would be true as well in many other sequences. Violence has to come up from the insistent regularity of form and at the same time to break with it.

Seen strictly in terms of characterization, Scorsese's heroes come out of a novel by Dostoyevsky: they are prone to anything crazy; their sudden and complete changes do not come out of hidden developments but have their only justification in an inveterate passion for excess and an unquenchable thirst for things absolute. It would therefore be preposterous to study them by analyzing their capricious moods. Many modern works of art have failed because of the contradiction implied by this sort of characterization: audiences do not want characters to obey rational motivations any more, but neither do they accept as a character someone who can always become anybody and decide anything. Most great works have escaped this dilemma through formal ideas. Dostoyevsky's heroes, for instance, must not be taken as individuals but seized in their interplay, as a network. Thus they cannot be seen as illustrations of an introspective inquiry, which would certainly weaken them. Scorsese's characters can much less be interpreted within a psychological frame, since they do not even speak out their minds. But they do have a formal justification.

To begin with, rationalization in *The Big Shave* could depend on a pun: the meaning of a *cut* varying from scratch to murder. Or again there might be some grim humor about how *clean* a shave can be. These explanations sound far-fetched, but anyone can notice that in *New York, New York* an "extraneous" factor dominates the story, as the harmony or discord between lovers serves mainly to express the relationship between jazz and pop music. Much in the same way, the necessities of boxing, rather than the historical figure of Jake La Motta, define the character in *Raging Bull*. This explanation of course is not sufficient, but before disproving it as idle, one has to remember that formal ingenuity, in spite of a romantic myth, is no enemy to sincerity and seriousness. Many times in his interviews Scorsese has stated that his films derive from established patterns and that he has always been surprised, in the end, by the way traditional forms could reflect his most vital interests.

There is a second point, however. Verisimilitude has been so extended these days that we tend to accept in a fictitious context the most unlikely people: people whom we would not care to consider as real if we had any choice. Seen as people from yesterday's paper, Alice is foolish, Johnny Boy is whimsical, Jimmy Doyle is insane, La Motta is crazy, and Travis Bickle is mad. But from what we know of them as fictitious characters in a movie, not only do we comprehend them but we sympathize with them as well. Now what does this mean?

First, it suggests that we might have to change the standards by which we understand, not exactly everyday life but the current representation of life: magazines, photographs, stories, gossip, legend. The epilogue of *Taxi Driver,* with Travis Bickle's violent quietness, after a paroxysm of violence, seems to call for such a criticism. It appears as a supplement to what was expected from the form of the plot; and the famous traveling shot looking downward into the site of the murder works as hiatus disentangling us from our suspect interest in Bickle's passions. The flashback construction of *Raging Bull* achieves the same result.

It must be added that the behavior of those people has much to do with connotation: the childhood prologue of *Alice Doesn't Live Here Anymore* does not tell us much about Alice but a lot about what the picture will be like: it will be like some other pictures. Glamour, ambition, art, and magic, in the Hollywood acceptation of those terms, appear as concepts indispensable to the understanding of the film. *Alice Doesn't Live Here Anymore* is in some ways a traditional "women's" picture. *New York, New York* clearly belongs to the genre of the musical biopic, and *Raging Bull* makes one think of other boxing films, while *Mean Streets* and *Boxcar Bertha* refer to the tradition of the realistic thriller. Therefore it must be said, however trivial it may seem, that Scorsese's characters act as movie characters because they are movie characters.

Why then should they sometimes act so crudely? Why should they be so inconsequential? Simply because it is their vocation not to accept being reduced to an image. Hence the interplay of established form and intense breaks in Scorsese's films. *Unlikeliness* is the perfect word here. As connotation builds up an expectation and defines the character in a way extraneous to the action of the plot, that character has no worse enemy than the types he or she is likened to. Everything happens as though the characters had felt this pressure of type and acted accordingly, to save their freedom. The ultimate means is a kind of retreat from their own image, illustrated first by Alice, then by Travis Bickle and Jake La Motta. Of course this does not result from a miracle: form and content have simply been conceived as a whole.

The advantages of such formal organization are evident: the seriousness with which an esthetic affirmation is displayed (the camera movement when Alice sings) cannot become a perfunctory exhibition of academic virtuosity, since it is bound to contrast efficiently with the characters' mishaps; on the other hand, the pathetic expression of the heroes never seems exaggerated, since it is going to be seen as an awkward and precious breach within a formal constraint. But this does not imply that Scorsese's films are easy variations on a simple formula. Simple as the formula may be, it does not amount to a recipe, for all the material must be invented and shaped.

The ultimate meaning of the device is transfiguration as a criticism of vision in as much as it consists merely in referring an object to its like. The simple alternation of close shots of moving feet and large framing of a happy crowd at the beginning of *New York, New York* points out that every image takes its strength not only from its own design but also from its individuality. Although it simply records a concert, *The Last Waltz* is a wonderful movie because no image is reduced to its informative value: frame, light, distance, and movement are contrived to give each and every shot its meaning. Movies are not made for recognizing things: they must bring out those differences through which beings manifest themselves. Such is Martin Scorsese's artistic lesson; it might also be a lesson of morals, the flight from one's likeness being a definition of liberty.

49. George Sidney (1916)

by ALAIN MASON

1941—*Free and Easy;* 1942—*Pacific Rendezvous;* 1943—*Pilot No. 5;* 1944—*Thousands Cheer; Bathing Beauty;* 1945—*Anchors Aweigh;* 1946—*The Harvey Girls; Ziegfeld Follies,* episode director (main director: Vincente Minnelli); *Holiday in Mexico;* 1948—*Cass Timberlane; The Three Musketeers;* 1949—*The Red Danube;* 1950—*Key to the City; Annie Get Your Gun;* 1951—*Show Boat;* 1952—*Scaramouche;* 1953—*Young Bess; Kiss Me Kate;* 1955—*Jupiter's Darling;* 1956—*The Eddy Duchin Story;* 1957—*Jeanne Eagels; Pal Joey;* 1960—*Who Was That Lady?; Pepe;* 1963—*Bye Bye Birdie; A Ticklish Affair;* 1964—*Viva Las Vegas;* 1966—*The Swinger;* 1967—*Half a Sixpence* (Great Britain; U.S., 1968)

Uncredited
1942—*Babes on Broadway* (Busby Berkeley): prologue; 1947—*Till the Clouds Roll By* (Richard Whorf)

Television Movie
1965—*Who Has Seen the Wind?*

George Sidney must have been in love with the musical, but what he seems to have liked best is genre universally. No absurdity was too much for him as long as it had some tradition or some conventional excuse. Under the assumption that faithfulness to the rules of the genre would ensure verisimilitude, or that verisimilitude was none of his business, he made musicals, comedies, and dramas without wondering whether they were going to look foolish or not and seemingly enraptured by scripts as bad as Dorothy Kingsley could ever write them. Chance may not be the only reason Gene Kelly and Stanley Donen used footage from Sidney's *The Three Musketeers* when they wanted to make fun of the swashbucklers in *Singin' in the Rain*. Indeed the plot of *Scaramouche* is very much like the script of *The Dancing Cavalier*, the fictitious film in their musical. Yet *Scaramouche* is one of Sidney's best films; and once it has been accepted, through sheer good will, its script can be esteemed as clearly built and highly efficient.

Sidney's achievements, however, must not hide the truth: he was theoretically wrong and historically isolated when he took genre for granted. *Singin' in the Rain* significantly includes a lot of jokes about genre, and every major musical of the Arthur Freed era is an attempt to reestablish a rich and complex motivation, in order to prevent the genre from degenerating into bizarre customs; at the same time people like Anthony Mann, Delmer Daves, and Nicholas Ray were doing the same thing for the Western. While Donen and Kelly, Vincente Minnelli, Charles Walters, and even Busby Berkeley used scripts by Betty Comden and Adolph Green, thus joining, with various degrees of enthusiasm, in the playful meditation about the musical, Sidney stuck to serious stuff, "serious" bearing here an embarrassing synonymy with guileless, gullible, pompous, and even square.

Though critics have been proclaiming for years that the American cinema is great, first because it is popular art, deeply rooted in the people's preoccupations and easily understood by ordinary folks and second because the films surpass their subject matter, no critic as yet has praised Sidney as the paragon of American movies. And no one should, for, even though his films meet both qualifications, it must be observed that there is no merit in surpassing poor material, and popular art need not be clownish. Besides, the separation of form and content is quite out of tune here, and there is no reason to assume complexity of form to be more palatable than complexity of thought nor to consider the one possible without the other. Pronouncements about the triumph of form over content therefore sound like a wrong way to rescue Sidney.

Sidney at his best considers not art but nature to be simple and easy to grasp; he does not want to transcend his material because he feels it is boorish; indeed, he does not consider it to be such (although it often is). Rather, he thinks adornment is the proper office of art. Hence the artistic musing that inevitably transforms the content of the films.

His use of color has constantly illustrated those principles. While other directors tried to tame Technicolor, he insisted on raw and brassy colors: *Annie Get Your Gun* and *Show Boat* immediately come to mind, but this stylistic feature is still more striking in *Bye Bye Birdie* or *Half a Sixpence*, since no technical explanation can account for their tremendous garishness. Sidney must have thought Technicolor at its beginnings was an artistic grace, as well as a natural effect; to some extent he was right: Donen and Minnelli demonstrated how the artificial quality of the medium could be put to good creative use. On the contrary, Sidney never tried to conceal the limitations of color photography by organizing a seemingly purposeful palette: he made no attempt at neutralizing the contingencies of chemistry through a careful and exclusive selection of costumes and scenery. Technical bindings must not be allowed to determine style, but neither are they to be thought of as a restraint ruling out extravagant vividness. Indeed the artistic device and the technical process are necessarily joined in the creative process. That is the reason why Sidney's colors always seem so convincing, even though they sometimes clash.

The brilliancy of Sidney's colors sometimes results in a glow, producing a transitional constituent between two types of scenes in which Sidney most completely gives way to his colorist disposition: the bright multicoloured tableau and the crepuscular romance piece. For instance, the lighthearted and glittering arrival of the show boat directly contrasts with its departure in a misty twilight halo. The opposition is enhanced, not only by common features in the general construction of both scenes but also by the diffuse energy of color dimming the shapes; this is all the more clear because the in-between scenes are handled in a more controlled chromatic manner. Although the finale of *Bathing Beauty* seems to be dominated by two complementary colors, green and red, each of them materialized by a substance, water and fire, and both of them meeting on the bathing costumes of the chorus girls, the scene cannot be accounted for in terms of general stylization. The colors are neither stable nor simple, and the blending of reflections, which is the purpose of the whole riot, definitely rules out any consistency of form and color. Here again the same dimming of shape is produced by opposite causes: the lack of light underwater and the excess of light outside.

Color seems typical of Sidney's implicit conceptions. An analogy with the history of art might be helpful here. Such a use of color is certainly not classical, but its lack of restraint does not make it baroque, for it does not achieve unity through dynamism. At his best, Sidney seems nearer a mannerist image, with its dazzling variety. Whether his *maniera* is on the side of the stylish *manieroso* or the affected *manierato* is a questionable matter but not merely a matter of taste, since approval clearly requests nothing more than an open understanding of art, broad enough to allow form to be a complex combination of styles and meanings, though critics have generally insisted on immediate unity or continuity.

What is really transcended by such a boisterous virtuosity is the narrative, which is not completely unexpected in a musical (though it might overstretch the definition of the genre as romance interrupted by musical numbers), but it is quite out of place in a drama and *a fortiori* in a swashbuckler. Yet *The Eddy Duchin Story* and *Jeanne Eagels* or even *Scaramouche* and *The Three Musketeers* share the same treatment. The duels and the theatrical interludes in the swashbucklers always seem to hesitate between advancing and delaying the unfolding of the plot. In *The Eddy Duchin Story,* the first big scene shows Eddy (Tyrone Power) and Marjorie Wadsworth (Kim Novak) taking a walk in Central Park. The length and rhythm of that eventless episode vividly contrast with the beginning of the film; since it is the first exterior sequence, it calls up the impression of nature as opposed to social hypocrisy; walking around and quietness contrast with progress and sudden changes (he is an ambitious young musician come to New York in order to achieve success and fame; he thought he was answering an invitation to the Wadsworth's party, when in fact he had been hired to play the piano!) and the lyrical tone of the scene impedes the narrative. The motif is thus transformed into an excuse for a thematic variation. The atmosphere gets darker and darker, and at the end the lovers' reflection in a puddle is blurred by a pigeon.

Several conformations of meanings and forms are at work in such a scene, and it would be unfair to dismiss it for bad taste before specifying them. First the interruption of the biopic by a lyrical stanza makes it clear that marriage is in the air; but *she* is going to propose to him, which breaks with tradition in a customary way but results in an interesting antagonism between lyricism and irony. Second, the content of the interruption sets apart the image of taking a walk and gives it an iconographical status:

from then on walks will be of great import in the film (Eddy feels bored during a walk with his son, remembers him on leave when walking through a bombed town, takes him for a walk to tell him that he is going to die; even Chiquita's relationship with Eddy has to be measured by that yardstick, for she follows him out to answer his timid proposal). Third, the progressive darkening of the scene foretells the misfortune that is to put an end to their love affair; it has to be connected with the symbolic function of meteorology throughout the film: wind (air) is, figuratively speaking, going to kill Marjorie and reconcile father and son, thus hinting that there is some kind of link between their mutual love and the mother's death. Such a meaning need not be clear or logical, neither must it be unintended or unconscious to be of human importance. Water will be associated with separation and reunion: Eddy spends the war in the Navy, wonders after his wife's death how it feels to be under the snow, and discovers by dipping his hand in the water that he is not suffering from a momentary cramp but is seriously (and in fact mortally) ill; Chiquita will catch up with him by the river; the contradictory meaning is neither surprising nor distressing, for the function of the form is to suggest an affective context and not to spell out a definite commentary.

This looks like a rather naive use of symbolism, but the symbolic function is only one of at least three formal layers in the scene. In bad or good taste, the whole must be considered as a rich exercise in variation. It must not be reduced to useless ornament since each arrangement associates form and function. Furthermore, these conformations can be used to describe the general form and meaning of the whole film. Interruption is a dominant narrative device; disclosure of feeling through space and movement has all the more importance because it is related with music as an expression of the deep self; the working out of symbols, some of them explicit, is a constant feature of the film and a frequent preoccupation of the characters.

The coherence of the sequence must not be sought within its own bounds, and to many it may look like a glittering waste. The same can be said about everything Sidney ever directed. But some harmony can be found; the different constituents do build up a style. Formal prowess manifests a deliberate intention and a set purpose. Thus *The Eddy Duchin Story* and *Jeanne Eagels* interweave sentimentality and spectacular effects; *Bye Bye Birdie* alternates rhythms, moods, etc.; *Show Boat* crumbles after an enchanting beginning, not because the story is worthless for the movies but because Sidney forgets his general pattern. *Pepe* is the best example, because Sidney never establishes a general structure: it is Sidney's worst film. It must be observed finally that artistic unity in Sidney's films is never an immediate experience, it implies the realization of a specific pattern framing the various stylistic constituents.

At least one of the three formal tendencies in *The Eddy Duchin Story* is characteristic of Sidney's style and can be considered as a major cinematographic virtue: the use of space as a means of lyrical expression. This stylistic feature is also found in films directed by Nicholas Ray, Richard Fleischer, and Samuel Fuller, so that it might pass as a mark of the fifties, part of an artistic reaction against the flat tints and clear shapes of the previous era. The way the camera finds Janet Leigh when she tells Stewart Granger of her love (*Scaramouche*) is touching without being obtrusive, and one could find many instances of the same quality as that moment, which has been discussed by Gérard Legrand, Sidney's most perceptive critic, in his review of the film (*Positif*, no. 114). But it seems easier to call up memories of emphatic camera work. *Thousands Cheer* has a very elaborate crane movement from Kathryn Grayson singing "Three Letters in the Mailbox" to Gene Kelly listening. Sidney's way of organizing space was already sketched in his mind by 1944, even if it was not yet definitely settled. This organization can be outlined in a rather abstract manner. Temporally it consists of four moments, the first couple being rather slow, while the last is accelerated. The first and third of these "movements" insist on dispersion, whereas the second and fourth stress reunion. The first moment builds up an expectation, a suspense, the object of which is space itself. A minor example of such an enigmatic space is the stage, surrounded with mirrors, wherein Lena Horne enters from the back to sing "Honeysuckle Rose" (*Thousands Cheer*). In more developed numbers, a kind of enumeration of the parts of this space takes place. The second movement then establishes clear relations between them. The third is an explosion: it freely carries out all the virtualities. With it must be associated Sidney's complicated and unusual angles, his frequent use of trick photography, and his dizzy cutting. The fourth movement shows everything has found its place in a new order. It makes an extensive use of long shots and pyramidal figures.

Of course this abstract description needs some qualification. It applies to musical numbers and with unequal adequacy. It is meant to be an abstract pattern rather than an exact description, but big crowd numbers in *Half a Sixpence*, as well as orchestra pieces in *Bathing Beauty* or "A Lot of Living To Do" in *Bye Bye Birdie*, illustrate it with some precision. As a general scheme of cinematic invention, it could even explain the use of space and rhythm in the finale of *Pal Joey* and other intimate numbers. As a symptom of Sidney's artistic sensibility, it may help to understand the structure of a scene or a movie. That such a patterning is possible is in itself of great interest. Walters and Minnelli would not yield such a possibility and neither would Kelly and Donen. The tendency to conceive the musical number as a fixed form seems to belong to Busby Berkeley's manner, though Berkeley works according to quite a different canon. Fred Astaire, who significantly never worked with Sidney except for a brief number in *Ziegfeld Follies*, never complied with any rigid conception of the musicals numbers and probably never felt the urge to fit them with a self-asserting form, and though Walters, Minnelli, and Donen have used either typical schemes or topical figures, they cannot be summed up and systematized that easily. As to the tendency to conceive the shooting of musical numbers as an epitome of a style, it certainly belongs to Sidney's "mannerist" views.

This pattern outlines Sidney's intuitive conception of space which he generally exerts through an active cutting and a free choice of shooting angles. Some visual motifs are, of course, particularly suitable for such purposes; rapid movement, like dance, provides an opportunity to constantly transform space perception through multiplication of points of view. Both *Half a Sixpence* and *The Swinger* involve some parallelism between musical numbers and bravura speed sequences, the former in its boat race and the latter with motor racing, but a similar use of space can be found in the duels of Sidney's swashbucklers. Theater, curiously enough, seems to produce the same effects: *Jeanne Eagels, Scaramouche*, and *Kiss Me Kate* all introduce the same image of the theater seen from backstage, with the audience clearly visible in the upper half of the frame: emblematic of broken space and of lost unity, this image could be Sidney's trademark. *Bye Bye Birdie* and *Pal Joey* show traces of similar preoccupations.

There may be more than childish pleasure in the way Sidney breaks up space. Or perhaps that "childish" pleasure means more than is generally assumed. His films do not tell a story: he clearly despises any idea of attending to an inner transformation. Trial, memory, experience are not to be conveyed by any obvious process, and since hinting and understatement are foreign to him, Sidney uses an external signification. In *Pal Joey* and *Bye Bye Birdie*, stripping is an equivalent of acting. No director of Sidney's generation was further than he from the Actor's Studio. Esther Williams,

Kathryn Grayson, Kim Novak, Ann-Margret, and even Elvis Presley (smooth features and sparkling eyes, round flesh and dazzling smiles) must have felt at home under his direction. The way he had so flexible an actor as James Whitmore play a caricature of himself in *Who Was That Lady?* is also significant. Sidney's films look like fantastic struggles of gestures and songs, colors and looks, outbursts and rushes, and that is precisely what has been considered as bad taste but follows from his basic views. Characters and plot lines are not considered as continuous and substantial beings but as mere pretenses; space therefore has to take such an appearance as is appropriate for each particular episode or motive.

Since there is no deep expression of self, characters must be thought of as figures. Better still: they must think of themselves as figures. As a matter of fact, Sidney's characters always act and play, that is to say live, in an unashamedly theatrical way. They know they are being watched, and since acting implies a deeper involvement and some use of affective experience, they must be considered as modeling. Of course that attitude implies no intended philosophical meaning but a strong sense of the body as a broadcasting machine. The opposite pole is speeding and appropriating as much space as possible. The finale of *Bathing Beauty* is a case in point: while the swimming pool is exactly measured by camera movements, the audience is made to think that underwater space is bigger than expected. "A Lot of Living to Do" (*Bye Bye Birdie*) shows characters struggling for space; and the much-misunderstood *Half a Sixpence* consists largely of an open and dynamic organization of spatial themes (the triangular relation of the racing boats versus the one-to-one relation of beginning love, the cheerful awakening versus the delirious wedding, the stage opening to a dream versus dream expressed by theater). These themes have uncommon strength. It is likewise fitting and moving that when Eddy Duchin's son (who once asked his father why he did not build a toboggan course from his room to the casino where he works, thus stressing the importance of materializing space relations) is confronted with his father, several swings embody their separation. A father telling his son he is going to die is a simple and naive idea of tragedy, but this scene is a strong example of how Sidney's passion for adornment and sense of space, improper as they may seem, completely renew awkward material: not by deepening the characters' psyches but by materializing the passional strength of the situation. This is an original allegory of grief.

In truly mannerist fashion, art imitating nature results in nature looking like art rather than in art looking like nature. The ladies (actresses?) in Sidney's films are theater figures, just as the individuals Bronzino painted: they do not express anything, they wear an expression. Only Frank Sinatra, not so much in *Anchors Aweigh* as in *Pal Joey*, ever looked like a person, and the contrast is interesting. As a rule, characterization in his films rather looks like an effort at self-assertion. A code of demeanor is at work, but it is not based upon *virtu:* its values are sexiness, fun, and glamour. In that respect Sidney does not belong to prewar Hollywood as much as he dreams of it.

Looking back at Sidney's career with these "mannerist" values in mind, one will find that he never made a flawless film. *Bye Bye Birdie* is marred by the sped up version of "Swan Lake," although the film had kept a beautiful balance up to that point: the trickery in "Put On a Happy Face" is justified by the contrast with the simple "One Boy," according to an alternation of the two pairs of lovers, which belongs in the structure of the film. *Pal Joey, Bye Bye Birdie, Half a Sixpence* clearly show he never made any exact distinction between directing films and manipulating special effects. There is nothing to blame in that conception; only the audience sometimes feels that special effects took the place of directing, since these two operations are sometimes irreconcilable. Such is the case in the much-overpraised sequence of Gene Kelly dancing with Jerry the cartoon mouse, because technical problems paralyzed the camera and because dancing can have no special grace when set beside the anything-is-possible world of animation. (Of course, this defect might also receive a mannerist interpretation: difficulty as a merit per se.)

If the above has seemed too indulgent, at least Sidney's originality should be clear. Although he was an MGM musical director from 1941 to 1955, when *Jupiter's Darling,* a good film, lost him his contract, his work bears little ressemblance to that of Minnelli, Donen or Walters; although he worked a lot with Joe Pasternak and Jack Cummings as producers, his films never look like standard Richard Thorpe, Roy Rowland, or Norman Taurog. Cheap ideas maybe, but he always had plenty, and he cannot be mistaken for anyone else. And going over to Columbia did not change him. Even his film with Presley is not only pleasant but bears his trademark. An artist of the fifties, with his enthusiasm for color and space, but with a prewar Hollywood conception of his art, Sidney is a curious case; but, if pleasure has not to be ceaselessly justified by humanist values, he can be recommended. He directed no masterpiece, but from an ingenuous idea of the world, he derives a rich image through constant artistic activity, and his films are fun.

---

50.   Don Siegel   (1912)

by JOHN BELTON

1946—*The Verdict;* 1949—*Night Unto Night; The Big Steal;* 1952—*Duel at Silver Creek;* 1953—*No Time for Flowers; Count the Hours; China Venture;* 1954—*Riot in Cell Block 11; Private Hell 36;* 1955—*An Annapolis Story;* 1956—*Invasion of the Body Snatchers; Crime in the Streets;* 1957—*Baby Face Nelson;* 1958—*The Lineup; Aventura para dos* (U.S., *Spanish Affair,* 1957; credited codirector in Spain: Luis Marquina Pichot); *The Gun Runners;* 1959—*Hound-Dog Man; Edge of Eternity;* 1960—*Flaming Star;* 1962—*Hell Is for Heroes;* 1964—*The Killers* (television movie released theatrically); 1968—*Madigan; Coogan's Bluff;* 1970—*Two Mules for Sister Sara;* 1971—*The Beguiled;* 1972—*Dirty Harry;* 1973—*Charley Varrick;* 1974—*The Black Windmill;* 1976—*The Shootist;* 1977—*Telefon;* 1979—*Escape From Alcatraz;* 1980—*Rough Cut* (uncredited codirector: Robert Ellis Miller); 1982—*Jinxed* (uncredited codirector: Sam Peckinpah)

Uncredited
1969—*Death of a Gunfighter* (Allen Smithee, pseudonym for Siegel and uncredited codirector: Robert Totten); N. B. Allen Smithee is also the credited director on *Fade In* (1967, unreleased but sold to television, reportedly directed by Jud Taylor), *The Challenge* (1970, television movie) and *Student Bodies* (1981, reportedly directed in part by Michael Ritchie).

Television Movies
1964—*The Hanged Man;* 1967—*Stranger on the Run*

A study of Don Siegel's career reveals a paradox: Siegel styles himself as a rebellious outsider, as "the last of the independents," but, in fact, he relies heavily on others. Although Siegel, since *The Killers* in 1964, has made films that bear the stamp of his personality, the quality of his films varies with the talents of his collaborators. Siegel's prominence as a director coincides with his association with Clint Eastwood and with writers Dean Reisner and Howard Rodman. *Madigan,* written by Rodman and Abraham Polonsky, marks a major turning point in the director's career. With it, his scripts become richer, giving greater attention to minor characters and employing them as foils for his major characters. Eastwood's presence in Siegel's next picture *Coogan's Bluff,* written by Herman Miller, Reisner, and Rodman, catapulted Siegel to the status of "major director," but Eastwood's performance would have been undefined, dimensionless, and perhaps even as allegorical as it is in the Sergio Leone Westerns without the presence of Lee J. Cobb, Susan Clark, Don Stroud, and Betty Field. The flat, Dickensian quality of these minor characters gives dimension to Eastwood, who, through his reactions to them, reveals qualities in himself that belie his silence and the implacable intransigence of his surface appearance. Leone's *Man With No Name* would never reveal his humanity as Coogan does in his last gesture, offering a cigarette to his prisoner. Siegel's success with Eastwood and Walter Matthau (*Charley Varrick*) and his failure with Michael Caine (*The Black Windmill*) and John Wayne (*The Shootist*) can be traced, in part, to the quality of his scripts. Albert Maltz, over the objections of Budd Boetticher, rewrote *Two Mules for Sister Sara* and *The Beguiled* (with John B. Sherry); H. J. and R. M. Fink and Reisner worked on *Dirty Harry,* and Reisner and Rodman collaborated on *Charley Varrick,* Siegel's best work to date. *The Black Windmill,* a disappointing film that fails in spite of Michael Caine, was scripted by Leigh Vance, and *The Shootist,* a flawed film rescued by John Wayne's performance, was written by Scott Hale, a friend of Siegel's.

Siegel's earlier work is similarly mercurial, rising and falling in direct relation to the abilities of those who worked with him. *Count the Hours,* though full of characteristically Siegelian treacheries and betrayals, is remarkable solely for John Alton's lighting and camera work. *Riot in Cell Block 11* and *Invasion of the Body Snatchers* were both produced by Walter Wanger, one of Hollywood's most independent and daring producers. Wanger's earlier work with Fritz Lang (*You Only Live Once, Scarlet Street, Secret Beyond the Door*) and his recent stretch in jail (he had shot his wife's agent, Jennings Lang) surely contributed first-hand experience to the realistically nightmarish quality of both films. By contrast, none of Siegel's earlier work is as intensely felt as are these two Wanger pictures. Siegel's screenwriter on *Body Snatchers* was Daniel Mainwaring, whose screenplays for Siegel and others reveal a concern for characters in similar situations, for the individual struggling against the impossible odds of a larger, impersonal organization. For Siegel, Mainwaring, a staff writer for RKO, also wrote *The Big Steal, An Annapolis Story, Baby Face Nelson,* and *The Gun Runners.* More characteristic of Mainwaring's concerns, however, are his screenplays for Jacques Tourneur (*Out of the Past*) and Phil Karlson (*Phoenix City Story*). Mainwaring's pessimistic, paranoid vision of postwar America provides Siegel with a psychological background for his largely physical foreground of chases and action sequences. The stakes involved in Siegel's chases are no longer material riches (the stolen loot in *The Big Steal*) but the preservation of his central character's emotional identity.

I do not suggest that Siegel's contribution to *Riot in Cell Block 11, Invasion of the Body Snatchers,* and *Baby Face Nelson* was any less than that of his collaborators, but a look at his other films of the period—*Duel at Silver Creek, China Venture, Private*

Hell 36, and *Crime in the Streets*—reveals a director of only minor talent. With the notable exception of *The Lineup*—and even here Siegel leans heavily on a strong screenplay by Sterling Silliphant and the format of a preexistent television series—Siegel failed to prove himself during the fifties.

The visual style of Siegel's best films of the fifties is lean and economical, eschewing the expressive interplay of light and shadow that characterizes the *films noirs* of the period. His decor, unlike that of Minnelli or Welles, is neutral and tends to depersonalize those within it. This neutrality becomes a major stylistic factor in a film like *Invasion:* the drab houses with blank walls seems to literally drain the protagonists' humanity out of them, much as the pod in the foreground on Jack's pool table slowly soaks up his distinctive features. Siegel's characters must struggle against the drabness of their settings in order to stay human. Siegel's lighting, Alton's *Count the Hours* to the contrary, tends to be flat. Similarly, his camera lacks expressive movement, panning only on motion or to connect one motion or character with another, and his camera angle, though rarely eye-level, avoids extremes. In effect, Siegel's camera does not interpret action, but rather records it in short, prosaic, simple statements, making him an ideal director, stylistically, of Hemingway material, as in *The Gun Runners* and *The Killers.*

Though Siegel's camera is unobtrusive, its placement in *Riot, Invasion,* and *Nelson* is hardly haphazard. Siegel positions his camera to emphasize the moments of encounter between characters and between a character and the world around him. By that I mean that there is a restive uneasiness to the lines of each frame's composition; there is no place for his characters to relax in his sets nor is there time for them to become human; nor can they domesticate their space, as characters in Hawks and Walsh films do. Siegel's sets and camera positions are designed to keep his characters on the move, and the camera, which is rarely static, is prepared to follow them to their next encounter with other characters or places. There is a deadness to Siegel's backgrounds that the positioning of his camera poses as a threat to his characters: the moving characters encounter this deadness, lose some of their energy to it, and are forced to continue moving to stay alive. This is in marked contrast to the relationship between character and setting in Hawks films in which a constant exchange of energies takes place. In a larger sense, Siegel's dynamic characters passionately fear stasis and fear entrapment either in claustrophobic settings or in relationships with other characters that involve serious commitment.

Siegel's interest in energy, vitality, and movement naturally draws him to the action genre and, though some of his films exist outside of this genre, his best work draws on the conventions of the male-oriented action picture. His police films, Westerns, and crime dramas focus on physical action, and character relationships are largely expressed in physical terms, i.e., violence. His characters display few, if any, domestic qualities: they have neither homes nor families. Charley Varrick, whose wife is killed in the opening sequence and who lives in a trailer, is the exception that proves the rule. Most Siegel heroes wander from hotel to hotel; the bare, nondescript decor of their rooms tells us nothing about them. Siegel defines his characters partially through the absence of certain relationships: his heroes lack parents, wives, and children. Even in *The Black Windmill,* British spy Tarrant (Michael Caine), though married and a father, is estranged from his wife and loses his child to a kidnapper. He rescues the boy only by functioning as a professional spy, not as a vengeful parent.

Siegel's women emerge as threats to his men in action because they seek to remove their men from the world of action. In *Dirty Harry,* Chico's wife persuades him to leave Harry and the police force after he is seriously wounded by the "Scorpio" killer. Both Tarrant's and Madigan's wives dislike their husbands' professions. Though Hawks's women initially disapprove of the dangerous professions of their men in films like *Only Angels Have Wings* and *Red Line 7000* and remain outside of the world of action, they come to admire and respect the professional identity of their men, finally participating in this world of action as spectators. Siegel's women—and his men—lack the flexibility of Hawks's characters; his films are unable to bridge the gap between the worlds of melodrama and action. The vulnerability of Siegel's action-figures in melodramatic situations is no better illustrated than in *The Beguiled.* A wounded Union soldier named McBurney (Clint Eastwood) hides from Confederate soldiers in a southern girls' school; intrigues with the school's headmistress, her assistant, the students, and the black cook; loses his leg and, finally, is poisoned. McBurney brings on his own death in daring to compete with women in the more feminine sphere of domestic interiors and love triangles. If the involvement of Siegel's heroes with women results in treachery and betrayal (Becky in *Invasion,* Sheila Farr in *The Killers*), then the only alternative for them is to go it alone.

All of Siegel's heroes involve themselves in the quest of certain goals that they can only attain on their own. The dramatic action in his films is the drama of conflicting goals. Clustered around the major conflict between the hero and his antagonist are an assortment of minor characters: they all struggle, independent of one another, to achieve disparate, often conflicting, goals. Each character in *Coogan's Bluff,* for example, becomes a foil for and an obstacle to Coogan in his pursuit of Ringerman (Don Stroud). The social worker, Julie (Susan Clark), wants to rehabilitate Ringerman's girl and prevents Coogan from seeing her. Mrs. Ringerman (Betty Field) shields her son from Coogan. And the bureaucratic New York police chief, McElroy (Lee J. Cobb), has too many other problems to worry about Coogan and his. Similarly, the goals and procedures of the mayor (John Vernon) and the police chief in *Dirty Harry* conflict with Harry's: their bureaucratic caution makes it more difficult for him to do his job. The bleakness of Siegel's later works is the result of his characters' inflexibility in pursuit of their goals. Though their tenacity—e.g., Lee Marvin's Charlie in *The Killers*— is seen as a strength, their refusal to compromise, to reconsider their goals, leads to their further alienation from society or to their deaths. As American policemen have pointed out, Harry need not have thrown his badge away after killing Scorpio at the end of *Dirty Harry;* he could have stuck it out until he was eligible for his pension (which *Magnum Force* and *The Enforcer* lead us to believe he did). But, for Siegel, Harry is incapable of adapting to the codes and goals of society. Harry, like many other Siegel heroes, is the victim of his own inflexibility. He himself refuses to change, and he cannot change the world around him. The result is less a stalemate than a defeat. He has attained his goal but become in the process as much an outlaw as Scorpio.

All of Siegel's best films focus on conflicts between the individual and the hostile society around him, ending, quite often, with that individual's defeat. Siegel often involves his characters in situations in which they must struggle to stay alive; his films are essays on survival. Films like *Invasion* and *The Beguiled* treat this issue quite directly, incorporating it into the plot, but the mood, spirit, and atmosphere surrounding actual life-and-death struggles pervade all of his films, even *Dirty Harry* in which Harry's own life is never in question.

Siegel clearly establishes but varies the terms of his characters' struggle for survival in his films. He often surrounds his central characters with hostile minor characters.

In *Invasion,* the entire town becomes an impersonal unit that seeks to transform the hero into an emotionless pod. (The film, though definitely antifascist, is ultimately ambiguous in terms of American political history. Are the pods Communists or are they McCarthyites?) Similarly, the western towns in *Stranger on the Run* and *Death of a Gunfighter* turn against Siegel's main characters; the police pursue his outlaws in *Baby Face Nelson* and *The Lineup* and both the police and the Mafia track Charley after he robs a bank that contains Mafia money in *Charley Varrick.* The environment of hostile characters that surrounds Siegel's heroes is paralleled in the architecture and setting of his films: the physical environment becomes hostile and alien. New York City in *Madigan* and *Coogan's Bluff* becomes his policemen's chief antagonist, and cities in other Siegel films—San Francisco in *The Line-Up* and *Dirty Harry,* London and Paris in *The Black Windmill*—range in character from deadeningly impersonal to cruelly threatening. Even his western landscape is full of dangers. The credit sequence of *Two Mules for Sister Sara* establishes the wildness of the setting through which Hogan (Eastwood) rides. Siegel pans from close-ups of wild animals in the foreground to long shots of Hogan in the background, setting up a rhythmic sequence that climaxes in a shot of a snake that is suddenly crushed by the hoof of Hogan's horse and setting up the terms of violence and physical pain that are to dominate the film.

The hostility of the world around them frequently produces paranoia in Siegel's characters. In *Invasion,* in which children fear their parents and Dr. Bennell ends up in a police station raving like a madman about "pods," the paranoia is justified. The pods are really out to get Siegel's characters. Less extreme forms of a similar paranoia emerge in all of Siegel's films. His heroes distrust the people around them; they can go to no one for help, because, as in *The Black Windmill,* their apparent allies are often, in fact, their enemies. Their actions are automatically self-protective. When Charley Varrick breaks into the dentist's office to remove his dead wife's x-rays (so that the police cannot trace or identify her remains), he switches his own x-rays with those of Harman (Andy Robinson), an action that later enables him to substitute Harman's body for his own and to escape both the police and the Mafia. Charley does not plan Harman's death, but he does not pass up an opportunity to safeguard his own life by using it.

Varrick is Siegel's cagiest character. He engages in a battle of wits with the police and with the Mafia's Molly (Joe Don Baker), surviving only by forcing them to make mistakes and by making none himself. Siegel's other heroes are less perfect; they are vulnerable and make mistakes. In Siegel's first feature, *The Verdict,* Scotland Yard inspector Grodman (Sidney Greenstreet) errs, and the wrong man is convicted of a crime and executed. Forced into retirement by the scandal, Grodman acts independently to bring the real murderer to a kind of justice: he kills the man himself, making it look like an unsolvable, perfect crime. He watches his successor at the Yard make the same sort of mistake he himself made when he convicted the wrong man on circumstantial evidence. Grodman is a prototype for Siegel's Madigan and Harry, cops who take the law into their own hands. In the first scene of *Madigan,* Dan Madigan (Richard Widmark) makes a mistake: he takes his eyes off his suspect for an instant, the suspect takes his gun and escapes. Madigan spends the remainder of the film in pursuit of the suspect, occasionally employing questionable tactics to track his man down. Harry violates the rights of the Scorpio killer when he arrests him, torturing him to discover the whereabouts of a kidnapped girl. Harry's lawlessness forces the D.A. to drop the case against the killer, and Harry embarks on a personal crusade to get the killer behind bars, watching and waiting for him to commit another crime. Harry takes his job personally, transforming his pursuit of Scorpio into a battle of wills. The challenges he presents to a bank robber in the first scene and to Scorpio in the last underscore this aspect of Harry's battle with his opponents. After a gun battle, Harry addresses his antagonist: "I know what you're thinking," he says. " 'Did he fire six shots or only five?' Well, to tell you the truth in all this excitement I've kinda lost track myself. But seein' this is a 44-Magnum, the most powerful handgun in the world, and would blow your head clean off, you've got to ask yourself one question—'Do I feel lucky?' Well, do ya, punk?" Scorpio, unlike the bank robber, accepts the challenge; his will is as strong as Harry's, but, in accepting the challenge, he makes a mistake and pays for it with his life.

The conflict between Siegel's heroes and his villains, as Jon Landau points out in a *Rolling Stone* review of *Charley Varrick*, is one of ego versus alter ego. If Scorpio is Harry's nemesis, he is also his alter ego: Scorpio is pure violence and lawlessness. In *Varrick*, Molly is Charley's opposite. A member of the organization, he wears business suits and smokes a pipe; Charley, who is "the last of the independents," wears work clothes and chews gum. Landau explains that, "In the end, every element of the film is directed toward defining the gulf between Charley's and Molly's worlds. Thus the former's antiquated plane and the latter's souped-up car become perfect extensions of their characters. And when, at one point, Charley tries to start an auto that won't ignite, he stares at it with his patented look of disgust for all things modern. . . . That moment lasts for all of five seconds, but seen in context, is a small piece of poetry, dwarfed only by the much larger moment when Charley and Molly face each other on the battlefield—an automobile graveyard—in a fight between the plane and the car." Charley wins his battle for survival but at the cost of his identity. Though he outwits the organization and, as an individual, triumphs over modern anonymity, he himself is forced to become nameless. He fakes his own death, and the film ends with the image of his crop-duster uniform, with his name on it, going up in flames.

Dirty Harry and *Charley Varrick* are unquestionably Siegel's best films; brilliantly structured in terms of character and action and stylistically unpretentious, they are disturbing portrayals of loss in gain, of defeat in triumph, a bleak reversal of John Ford's more positive vision of gain in loss and triumph in defeat. Siegel's less successful films present similar thematic concerns but are flawed by obtrusive stylistic excesses. In these films, Siegel's own ego comes between the action and the audience; he forces his signature upon the content of the film with his camera. *The Beguiled,* which Siegel considers his most personal work, plays with color and camera angle in ways that seem irrelevant to the action. The sepia opening evokes the atmosphere of gothic horror, but lasts only for the credit sequence, changing there to full Technicolor. What is the point? At the same time, Siegel exaggerates camera angle, especially in close-up and medium shots, calling attention to his own presence behind the camera. (The director has even named these camera setups "Siegelinis.") In a similar way, Siegel overstates his symbolism: the crow with the broken wing that is tethered outside McBurney's room symbolizes the wounded soldier's predicament. Siegel has rarely practiced restraint in such matters, even in his best films. *The Killers,* a film obsessed with sight and time, begins with a shot of Charlie (Lee Marvin) reflected in the sunglasses of his partner (Clu Gulager); they enter a school for the blind, where all the students wear dark glasses, and kill a man. Close-ups of a glass of carrot juice ("It's good for the eyes"), of Braille watches and of stop watches, coupled with Charlie's, "Lady, I haven't got the time," hammers home the blindness and haste which plague the film's characters, first Johnny North (John Cassavetes) and then Charlie. As Charlie and his partner approach the school for the blind in the first scene, they pass two blind children who are playing cops and robbers on the lawn; one child shoots the other, who feigns death. The film's last scene brings its hero (Marvin) full circle. Shot by Browning (Ronald Reagan), Charlie staggers down the walk outside Browning's house (in the first scene he goes up a walk). He falls. With tortured effort, he vainly tries to shoot at an approaching patrol car summoned by his earlier gunshots. But he does not realize that he has lost his gun and shoots, in a reflex action, with his fingers—his gesture recalling that of the blind children in the first scene. Siegel's narrative neatness and use of symbols is almost, but not quite, slick, rescued only by the intensity of Marvin's gut-physical performance.

Even *Dirty Harry* suffers from a heavy-handed use of symbolism, Siegel transforming Harry into half-gladiator (the Keezar Stadium sequence) and half-Christ figure (the cross in the park on which Scorpio crucifies him). Yet Siegel refuses to indulge these moments; the momentum of his action narrative pulls us from these overdirected scenes into other, less obtrusive ones. *The Shootist* sets up an obvious parallel between the passing of an era with the death of Queen Victoria, headlined in the newspaper J. B. Books (John Wayne) buys when he enters town, and that of Books himself, the last of the Old West's legendary gunfighters. But Books's repeated references to Victoria's death ("Queen Victoria went out in style") overstate the parallel.

The Shootist, as a collaborative effort, has too much Siegel and too little Wayne. Siegel makes his presence felt in elaborate crane shots, low-angle wagon-wheel shots, shots taken through glass doors, mirror shots, whisky-glass shots, sunbursts, and hand-held camera. The director's transitions are occasionally pointlessly slick: he slowly zooms in on the face of Mrs. Rogers (Lauren Bacall) watching Books going off to his last gunfight through her window, then cuts abruptly to a close-up of a pair of handcuffs being taken off one of the men who will shoot it out with Books, zooming out from close-up to medium shot in a reversal of the earlier movement. Only the most forced of interpretations, i.e., all of Siegel's characters are confined in one way or another, can justify the editing together of the two, quite different images.

Like *Buffalo Bill and the Indians,* which Dino de Laurentiis also produced, *The Shootist* reexamines the myths of the American West. Siegel surveys the Wayne persona with clips from Howard Hawks, John Ford, and John Farrow pictures, before the action of his own story begins. His emphasis on Wayne's potential for violence in the clips reflects a narrow approach to the actor's persona: most of Wayne's performances are built less around action than reaction. At the same time, Siegel ignores Wayne's gregarious sociability. Though Wayne is often simultaneously apart from and a part of the communities around him in his films, he always reveals in his performances a sense of the value of that community. Eastwood is an ideal actor for Siegel in that he is laconic, self-contained, and a loner; he is cynically independent, willing to take on the whole world but unwilling to ask anyone for help. Wayne, especially since *True Grit,* had become somewhat garrulous, his gestures more open and his characters more frequently seeking the company of others. Siegel's mistake is to frustrate this side of Wayne, shooting his conversations in one-shots rather than in two-shots, thereby aborting Wayne's scenes with James Stewart and Bacall.

Siegel reduces Wayne, at times, to cliché, playing upon the actor's own bout with cancer by afflicting him with it here and by setting up his final shootout with television cowboys (Richard Boone and Hugh O'Brien), confronting a figure of Western myth with his decidedly less mythic successors.

He surrounds Wayne's J. B. Books with unbelievably hostile characters, making, by contrast, even the pods of *Invasion* look friendly. Even before he gets to town, a highwayman tries to hold Books up. The local milkman insults him. Once his presence is known, Mrs. Rogers tries to evict him from her boarding house, calling in Marshal Thibido, who rejoices to learn that Books is dying and vows to dance on his grave. Siegel gathers vultures around him: a newspaper reporter wants to syndicate Books's life story, capitalizing on his death. A former girlfriend (Sheree North) turns up, willing to become Mrs. J. B. Books and hoping to cash in on his name by authorizing a biography of him after his death.

Books, one of Siegel's heroes forced to yield to the present, lives by an outmoded code, but one with which Siegel surely sympathizes. Books tells young Gillum Rogers (Ron Howard): "I won't be wronged. I won't be insulted. I won't be laid a hand on. I don't do these things to other people, and I expect the same from them." But Books, even if he did not have cancer, could not survive in the modern world: everyone wrongs, insults, and lays hands on him. Books decides to go out in style (like Queen Victoria). He stages a shoot-out in the Metropole café with three local gunmen. What is fascinating about this shootout is that even though it is suicidal for Books, he struggles to survive it. Even having made the decision to die, he fights to stay alive; killing the three gunmen, Books, in turn, is shot in the back by the Metropole barman. Siegel's world proves too treacherous for heroes of the Old West.

The impact of the film's final scene, the shootout, is dissipated by subsequent action. Gillum avenges Books, killing the barman, and he and Books exchange ambiguous glances before the former discards his bloody gun and the latter dies. The film ends with a series of highly angled shots and hand-held shots of Gillum returning home, Siegel making a final directorial intrusion upon the action only to obscure the significance of Gillum's gesture and of the final exchange of looks.

Siegel's career remains one of promise. He has elicited performances from Eastwood that no other director, save Eastwood himself, has been able to equal. Siegel's masterpieces, *Dirty Harry* and *Charley Varrick,* are clearly two of the very best American films made in the seventies. Like the characters in his films, he has struggled to survive in a hostile industry, but, unlike his heroes, he cannot make it alone. His directorial tag should read, "The Last of the Dependent Independents."

---

51. Steven Spielberg (1947)

1974—*The Sugarland Express;* 1975—*Jaws;* 1977—*Close Encounters of the Third Kind;* 1979—*1941;* 1981—*Raiders of the Lost Ark;* 1982—*E.T. The Extra-Terrestrial*

Television Movies
1969—*Night Gallery,* one episode (other directors: Boris Sagal, Barry Shear); 1971—*Duel;* 1972—*Something Evil;* 1973—*Savage*

When still barely in his mid-thirties, Steven Spielberg had had the unique distinction of directing, within half a dozen years, three of the top box-office hits in film history (as well as one unusually expensive flop). Thus he qualifies as the archetypal movie boy-wonder of the seventies. An uncharitable critic might describe him as the ideal provider of those commodities most appreciated by seventies audiences: cheap thrills (*Jaws*), cheap dreams (*Close Encounters of the Third Kind*), cheap laughs (*1941*), but that would be unfair. The amount of intelligence Spielberg was able to bring to *Jaw*'s idiotic premise, especially in terms of characterization, was remarkable. *Close Encounters,* despite its sticky religiosity, its general incoherence, and occasional disjoint-edness, is an exhilarating, sensuous experience and contains moments of almost magical cinematic grandeur. *1941,* while a dismal failure as *comedy,* is a highly original *directorial* experiment, in which the crudeness of the gags is constantly contrasted with the dream-like atmosphere generated by Spielberg's amazingly complex and inventive staging. As for *The Sugarland Express,* his first theatrical feature, although ostensibly a marathon car chase top-heavy with cheap laughs and cheap thrills, it was, underneath all the senseless agitation, a rather biting indictment of contemporary American society.

Perhaps Spielberg's most distinctive trait is the good-natured irony with which he views his fellow man, his audience not excluded. It *seems* good-natured, at least, because of Spielberg's laid-back "Californian" touch and total commitment to entertain-ment values, but a certain underlying nastiness is unmistakable. Spielberg has been called an unabashed optimist because of *Close Encounters of the Third Kind,* but it is difficult to detect much faith in humankind in a fable that, in effect, proposes communica-tion with extraterrestrials as an alternative to the lack of communication between men.

Aside from the benign, fetal-looking creatures glimpsed at the end of *Close Encoun-ters,* the life we find in Spielberg's movies is dominated by pettiness, greed, violence, prejudice, and utter stupidity. Selfishness and corruption eat at the social fabric, and relationships are habitually mired in misunderstanding. The failure to communicate is Spielberg's most regularly recurring theme and dramatic (or comic) device. The premise of *1941* is based on a prolonged misunderstanding, a failure to *interpret,* and in *Close Encounters*—a film whose central theme is interpretation—many scenes involve encounters between people who, either in the literal sense or figuratively, do not speak the same language. Scientists may be able to work out a means to communicate with visitors from another galaxy, but there seems little likelihood that anyone might devise a language through which the Richard Dreyfuss character and his wife could understand each other.

It has been said many times already that Spielberg's films (especially *Close Encoun-ters*) appeal to the child in all of us—which immediately raises the question of whether his cinema is childlike or childish; the line is not always easy to draw. Spielberg's evident relish for messiness, disruptive behavior, and wild confusion, for example, is even more suggestive of the infant than of the child. The hero's vision in *Close Encounters* is an excuse for him to regress to infantile behavior—messing around with mashed potatoes, building a tower of mud, etc. The character's kinship to children is repeatedly intimated; he gazes at the spaceships with the same wide-eyed wonderment as Melinda Dillon's son does (as Dillon remarks, "It's Halloween for grownups!"). His favorite movie is *Pinocchio,* the theme song of which "When You Wish Upon a Star," takes on a special meaning in this new context. It is first heard on a child's music box and comes over the soundtrack when Dreyfuss gazes at the inside of the mother ship at the end—his dream come true.

The true spirit of childhood, of course, has nothing to do with age. Dreyfuss's son, who may be seven or eight, responds contemptuously to the suggestion to go see *Pinocchio,* "a dumb cartoon," and tears of shame and dismay come to his eyes when his father abstractedly plays with his mashed potatoes at the dinner table. In a scene included only in the "Special (1980) Edition," the boy angrily denounces the distraught Dreyfuss as a "cry-baby." It is a shrill, almost hysterical scene, perhaps the only dramatic moment in the film that is not softened by a touch of whimsy or humor. The boy already belongs—along with his infuriatingly down-to-earth, no-nonsense mother—in the herd of smug sceptics who are so accustomed to, and comfortable with, the ordinary that they refuse to acknowledge the extraordinary, even when it stares them in the face.

Spielberg's eagerness to reach the child in us, and in himself, is nowhere more apparent than in *Raiders of the Lost Ark,* his celebration of old movie serials (made largely for the benefit of a generation of viewers who have never seen a serial—at least not in a movie theater). Although the inspiration for the film originally came to George Lucas (who ended up as producer) long before Spielberg became involved in the project, it was probably the ideal material—and the ideal collaboration—for the director who stated, referring to his producer and friend, "We both see movies through youngsters' eyes . . . I don't make intellectual movies." Spielberg is by no means childlike, however, in his determination to make it perfectly clear that his aim in making films is to provide audiences with the pure, undiluted escapism they now seem to crave almost exclusively. Certainly, no one can take *Raiders of the Lost Ark* to task for intellectualism (although its very clever, self-conscious toying with genre conventions might be viewed as a form of intellectualism).

What Spielberg is trying to recreate in *Raiders* is not, of course, old serials themselves, but rather the excitement of watching them as a kid, an excitement that is usually considerably dampened by later viewings in mature years. Only the most hard-core fans of the stuff would deny that the overwhelming majority of thirties and forties serials were decidedly mediocre, even by the undemanding standards of that particular type of cinema. The fact that we loved them as kids and will probably carry loving memories of them to our graves merely verifies that taste and discrimination are acquired traits—notoriously lacking in children. With few exceptions—William Witney's meteoric career, which produced the best of the genre from *Daredevils of the Red Circle* to *G-Men vs. the Black Dragon,* is a towering one—sound serials can only be enjoyed as camp, if at all.

Moreover, serials derive their distinctiveness, and much of whatever charm they retain for adults, from their very tackiness, the fact that they were made by hacks working on miniscule budgets and the briefest of shooting schedules.* A serial is a serial because it looks like one—cheap and trashy (barring, again, the odd exception). As a consequence, the better a film like *Raiders* gets, the more estranged it is from its models. For one thing, color, wide screen, stereophonic sound, and "production values" are thoroughly alien to the esthetics of the genre. In *Raiders,* moreover, the tongue-in-cheek humor of the script, Spielberg's directorial brilliance, the high-class cinematography, the elaborate special effects, the inventive production design (who ever heard of such things in the days of *Jungle Jim* and *Raiders of the Ghost City?*) all combine to make it impossible for us to respond to the film as serial.

There lies *Raiders*'s major problem, for there is, unfortunately, no other way to respond to it. When the craftsmanship of a production reaches such a level of excellence, one expects to find some substance in it, but the very nature of the project

---

* In that respect, Spielberg paid homage to the businesslike swiftness of serial directors by emulating it, shooting *Raiders* in a mere seventy-four days, which involved sometimes putting as many as forty setups in the can a day.

precludes any such substance. The emptiness and, ultimately, the futility of such an endeavor are numbing. Lucas has compared his films to amusement-park rides; if *Raiders* is not supposed to be anything else, then it must be praised for what it is—a good ride on which no effort has been spared to give the customer his money's worth. However, it is not unreasonable to expect something more (or at the very least different) from a movie—especially one made by highly talented people—than from a ride on a roller coaster. It is quite possible to be entertained by *Raiders of the Lost Ark,* to be amused, even, at times, thrilled by it, and yet to leave the theater vaguely dissatisfied, unfulfilled, and with no desire to repeat the experience.

Spielberg's movies are highly kinetic. They all revolve around chases, pursuits, quests (for the big shark, the magic mountain, the lost ark). Vehicles (cars and trucks, boats, airplanes, spaceships) are featured in every film and play as important a part as the people in them. Spielberg's camera, like his characters, seldom sits still. Movement is compulsive and often escalates to excited agitation, pandemonium, chaos—which is probably what Spielberg does best. He arranges for all hell to break loose and then delights in directing the traffic. Many of the best moments in his films are scenes of utter confusion: the panic on the beach in *Jaws,* the barroom brawl in *1941,* the evacuation sequence in *Close Encounters,* or the opening of the same film with all the excited scurrying and shouting when the "returned" World War II planes are found.

Spielberg's dedication to action and movement has steadily increased in the short time span between his first theatrical feature and *Raiders of the Lost Ark*—to the detriment of characterization. He started out by placing ordinary people in extraordinary situations and seemed at least as interested in their personalities and reactions as in the sensational happenings themselves. Indeed, what rescued *Jaws* from being a technically impressive but otherwise run-of-the-mill, slightly ridiculous horror movie was the delineation of the characters played by Richard Dreyfuss and Roy Scheider, their idiosyncrasies and weaknesses as well as their moments of triumph, the way they relate to each other and to other characters and to the situations they have to confront. In *Close Encounters,* however, although the Dreyfuss character is equipped with a lot of personality traits, he comes across mostly as a restless eccentric—the result of his "vision"—not very different from the assortment of crackpots who pursue the same grail he does, while the other "major" characters (his wife, the boy's mother) are mere sketches. With *1941* we enter cartoon territory, the crudely nihilistic realm of *Saturday Night Live* and the *National Lampoon,* with its endless orgy of parody and destruction and the caricaturelike characters it entails. In *Raiders of the Lost Ark,* characterization *must,* by virtue of the laws of the genre, be kept to an absolute minimum. Serial heroes have no psychology, they are entirely defined by their ever-renewed, indefatigable action. The reference, in *Raiders,* to an earlier affair between Indiana Jones and Marion, the heroine, is a startling departure from the tradition, not only because serial characters don't have affairs but also because they have no pasts; they only exist in and for the current adventure.*

* Of course, playing at observing the old-fashioned rules of a long-defunct genre is fun only to the extent one knows they can (and occasionally will) be broken. *Raiders* is scattered with such transgressions—as when Indiana Jones shoots a scimitar-wielding Arab, thus ignoring the unwritten but fundamental rule that the hero should never fight with a weapon more powerful than his adversary's. This transgression of romantic convention for the sake of expediency is greeted by the audience with the biggest laugh in the film, a laugh that, like the laughter triggered by profanities uttered in polite society, acknowledges the transgression of the rule rather than anything intrinsically funny.

Together with his emphasis on action and movement, Spielberg's tendency to pursue sensational effect has been, if that is possible, increasing. He will go to almost any conceivable effort and expense in order to make his audience gasp in shock, surprise, or delight, even if the effect is on screen only for a fleeting instant, even if it serves no particular dramatic purpose or involves throwing logic and verisimilitude to the wind. Again, *Raiders of the Lost Ark* provided the ideal format for this kind of indulgence, with its loose, episodic structure allowing for a storyline that is a mere string of cliffhanging situations (each sequence could be titled in the style of serial episodes: "The Revenge of the Idol," "The Deadly Snake Chamber," etc.). But Spielberg's most memorable effects are to be found in *Close Encounters,* a film dedicated to "mind-blowing" experiences from the very opening blast—a musical outburst that shakes the theater, almost, it seems, to its foundations even before the first image has appeared on the screen.

This physical impact on the spectator occurs only when the film is seen under the best possible screening conditions, such as the ones provided by the Ziegfeld Theatre in New York, where *Close Encounters* had its first run. Seen on a smallish screen with tinny sound and in less than pristine prints, it quite simply becomes another film— the magic is gone, and one becomes much more aware of the weaknesses. Of course, one's enjoyment of *any* film is diminished by inadequate projection, but rarely to such a degree. It is legitimate to wonder—although the question is such a tough one that I wouldn't presume to suggest even the beginning of an answer to it—what exactly is the relation to art of a film that so thoroughly depends for its effect upon the conditions under which it is exhibited.

A perfect example of Spielberg's huge investment of time and effort into the production of brief, spectacular effects is the oft-cited Indian scene in which thousands of upraised fingers point to the sky in perfect unison in response to Lacombe's question, "Where did the sounds come from?" The surprise is sprung upon us suddenly, and the scene is as suddenly over. Spielberg's surprises are not just sprung, however, they are led up to by flurries of excited activity that have become a virtual Spielberg trademark. This is part of a teasing technique (the spectator is kept wondering, "What's all the excitement about?") that works best in the opening sequence, or in the (Special Edition) scene leading to the wonderfully surrealistic discovery of a rusty ship in the middle of the desert. Before *we* discover it, others do, and we are puzzled witnesses to a hectic ballet of helicopters, crammed with media people, hovering above what to us looks just like sand dunes, until Spielberg at last cuts to the breathtaking marvel, only to spirit it away again seconds later.

Interestingly, most of the time there is little if any logical reason for the excitement. When the scientists inspect the returned airplanes in the opening sequence, they act as though they had just stumbled upon them, when in fact they knew exactly what they were coming to see. The excitement is put on strictly for our own benefit. Similarly, the Indian sequence's only reason for being is to treat the audience to one startling shot. The question asked of the natives is entirely superfluous, since Lacombe and the other scientists already know the answer. It is asked, then, only for our sake. It is pure mise-en-scène, proudly pointing to itself and its own gratuitousness.

But these raised fingers are not—as Ernest Lehman suggested in a brilliant, hilarious takeoff on *Close Encounters* in *American Film*—the film maker's contemptuous way of telling the audience, "Up yours." Spielberg's disregard for logic and verisimilitude is certainly not intended as an insult to the viewer's intelligence. To him, the end justifies the means, and the end is always to create an audio-visual experience that seeks to please the senses, not the logical mind. In his films, and especially *Close Encoun-*

ters, Spielberg is not so much telling a story as providing a series of privileged moments. How these moments are held together is not a major concern of his. With a famous response to the question: "Why didn't the Indians shoot the horses during the chase in *Stagecoach?*" (answer: "Because if they had, it would have been the end of the picture"), no less classical a director than John Ford reminded us that a storyteller's first duty is to make it possible for his narrative to continue, even if credibility has to be strained in the process. Spielberg is all for never shooting the horses. Most of the time, however, he doesn't even expect us to suspend our disbelief; he wants us not to bring it into the theater at all—to be like children. Playfulness is the keynote of his cinema. He just wants us to have a good time, and he knows how to show us one, provided we are willing not to play adult games with him. Spielberg is an immensely clever film maker, but he has no interest in being an adult one. Whether he will remain a perennial *enfant prodige* or will mature into a "serious" artist some day is open to debate; time will tell, and he still has a lot of time ahead of him.

52. *John Sturges* (*1910*)

1945—*Thunderbolt* (documentary), codirector: William Wyler; 1946—*The Man Who Dared; Shadowed; Alias Mr. Twilight;* 1947—*For the Love of Rusty; Keeper of the Bees;* 1948—*The Sign of the Ram; The Best Man Wins;* 1949—*The Walking Hills;* 1950—*The Capture; Mystery Street; Right Cross;* 1951—*The Magnificent Yankee; Kind Lady; The People Against O'Hara;* 1952—*It's a Big Country: An American Anthology* episode); *The Girl in White;* 1953—*Jeopardy; Fast Company; Escape From Fort Bravo;* 1955—*Bad Day at Black Rock; Underwater!; The Scarlet Coat;* 1956—*Backlash;* 1957—*Gunfight at the OK Corral;* 1958—*The Law and Jake Wade; The Old Man and the Sea* (uncredited codirectors: Fred Zinnemann, Henry King); 1959—*Last Train From Gun Hill; Never So Few;* 1960—*The Magnificent Seven;* 1961—*By Love Possessed;* 1962—*Sergeants 3; A Girl Named Tamiko;* 1963—*The Great Escape;* 1965—*The Satan Bug; The Hallelujah Trail;* 1967—*Hour of the Gun;* 1968—*Ice Station Zebra;* 1969—*Marooned;* 1972—*Joe Kidd;* 1974—*McQ;* 1976—*Chino; The Eagle Has Landed* (U.S., 1977), Great Britain

It is difficult today to understand what impelled some critics, back in the fifties, to hail John Sturges as a master of the contemporary Western, putting him in a class with such outstanding champions of the genre as Anthony Mann and Delmer Daves. The two pictures that seem to have been at the source of this reputation, *Escape From Fort Bravo* and *Backlash,* are actually quite undistinguished, sluggish and, at least in the latter's case, weighted down by too much "psychology." Promises in Sturges's early efforts were rather to be found in such thrillers as *The Capture* (written by Niven Busch, who considers it his finest script) or *Jeopardy,* a contrived but efficient suspenser (Barry Sullivan is trapped under his stalled car on a deserted beach; Barbara Stanwyck as his wife searches for help as the tide rises, meets and falls for an escaped convict

. . .) that exhibited one of Sturges's distinctive traits, a flair for the depiction of technological problems and the ways to solve them.

His first major assignment, which was to remain his best film, was *Bad Day at Black Rock,* on an outstanding script by Millard Kaufman and using a fine, almost all-male cast including Spencer Tracy, Robert Ryan, Ernest Borgnine (at his most despicably villainous), Walter Brennan, Lee Marvin, and Dean Jagger. Set in a tiny town by the railroad track right in the middle of the desert, its CinemaScope frame was brilliantly, if a bit self-consciously filled by Sturges's strategic positioning of his actors in relation to the huge, empty expanses around them. Andrew Sarris was certainly unfair to remark that it had been "naive . . . to deduce that Sturges had solved the problems of Cinema-Scope by his allegorical groupings." It is doubtful that anybody ever made such a deduction in the first place, since there wasn't one "solution" to the "problem" of CinemaScope but as many as there would be creative uses of the format; whatever one may think of Sturges's career as a whole, it should not be forgotten that his was one of the very first among such creative uses.

To say that Sturges's subsequent efforts never reached the level of *Bad Day at Black Rock* is an understatement. His non-Westerns since the mid-fifties make up a haphazard collection of almost invariably tedious forays into any number of genres, from war movies to soapers to comedies to science fiction, while the Westerns grew increasingly derivative and dishonest. A couple of fairly good entries were *The Law and Jake Wade* and the uneven and overrated *Gunfight at the OK Corral,* mostly memorable for its casting of Burt Lancaster as Wyatt Earp and Kirk Douglas as Doc Holliday and for the graphic, well-handled reconstruction of the historical showdown. Later, however, Sturges virtually appropriated the plot of Delmer Daves's *3:10 to Yuma* in *Last Train From Gun Hill,* a hodgepodge of all the then current Western clichés, in which he did not fail to pay lip service to fashionable antiracism through some unlikely dramatic contrivance. He went one step further when he remade Kurosawa's *Seven Samurai* as *The Magnificent Seven,* a film now interesting solely for its inspired casting of the then little-known Steve McQueen, James Coburn, and Charles Bronson, whose charismatic presence made the early scenes a most exciting experience before routine and confusion settled in. *Sergeants 3,* an *avowed* remake of *Gunga Din,* was Frank Sinatra's clan's idea of an in-joke (with Sammy Davis Jr.—who else?—as Gunga Din). The best thing about this picture may have been the trailer, devised by Stan Freberg, in which the stars are seen discussing the project: "I hear they're going to remake *Gunga Din* as a Western." "I can't accept that . . .", etc.

Anybody who thinks the Gunga Din joke fizzled should see *The Hallelujah Trail,* a ponderous comedy-Western that looked like a monstrously stretched-out version of an *F Troop* segment. A more interesting effort was *Hour of the Gun,* a sequel to *Gunfight at the OK Corral* that follows Earp and Holliday in their little-known later years. This rambling Western opens with a bang (a reprise of the *OK Corral* gunfight), then drags to a whimpering end as its heroes age none too gracefully. Still, despite its weaknesses, and on the strength of potentially fascinating subject matter, *Hour of the Gun* makes for better fare than most of Sturges's previous Westerns. In the seventies, Sturges contributed a Clint Eastwood Western (*Joe Kidd*), a John Wayne non-Western (*McQ,* a film made, apparently, for the sole purpose of casting Wayne as a cop), and *Chino,* a Clair Huffaker script, with Charles Bronson. Sturges seemed headed for the small-time when he was entrusted with a big-budget production, *The Eagle Has Landed.* Whether he lands other high-paying jobs on the strength of this effort is not really the critic's concern.

53. Frank Tashlin (1913–1972)

1952—*The First Time; Son of Paleface;* 1953—*Marry Me Again;* 1954—*Susan Slept Here;* 1955— *Artists and Models;* 1956—*The Lieutenant Wore Skirts; Hollywood or Bust; The Girl Can't Help It;* 1957—*Will Success Spoil Rock Hunter?;* 1958—*Rock-a-bye Baby; The Geisha Boy;* 1959—*Say One for Me;* 1960—*Cinderfella;* 1962—*Bachelor Flat; It's Only Money;* 1963—*The Man From the Diners Club; Who's Minding the Store?;* 1964—*The Disorderly Orderly;* 1965—*The Alphabet Murders* (Great Britain; U.S., 1966); 1966—*The Glass Bottom Boat;* 1967—*Caprice;* 1968—*The Private Navy of Sgt. O'Farrell*

Uncredited
1951—*The Lemon Drop Kid* (Sidney Lanfield)

In the staid fifties, movie comedy and satire hit such a low ebb (with Ernst Lubitsch dead, Preston Sturges silenced, and Frank Capra in semiretirement) that any film maker gifted with a modicum of madness and willing to be even mildly outrageous was bound to stand out and be recognized as some kind of master. Frank Tashlin was such a man, a giant among dwarfs who later turned out to be not all that towering and whose stature has dwindled ever since. Tashlin was almost absurdly overrated by French critics and film buffs who, upon seeing his Jayne Mansfield and Martin and Lewis movies, felt that the American Way of Life was at last getting what was coming to it. Since it was then customary, among Tashlin fans, to rate his films according to the number of allusions and private jokes one was able to identify in them, a reasonably well-informed viewer easily became convinced of Tashlin's genius. Some even stuck to his name the awesome label of "moralist," to which he himself seemed to aspire, as is clear from his three books of children's stories. In 1965 he informed an interviewer that if there is a sense of comedy in his films "it is all based on a bitter hatred of the foibles of society, the nonsense we live with, the nonsense we call civilization. I guess it comes out funny because everyone else feels it's funny. I see it as being bitter, and I'm ashamed of myself that I go that far."

Actually, Tashlin's comments upon the foibles of his time remained circumscribed and quite superficial, and predictably so. The man who bites the hand that feeds him can't afford to sink his teeth in very deep. In any case, one should not blame Tashlin for the limitations of his satire but rather for the obviousness of his targets. The rock-and-roll stars and dumb blonde sex symbols of the fifties were avowed self-caricatures and as such extraordinarily difficult to spoof. Such material required a degree of subtlety Tashlin was unable—perhaps unwilling—to achieve. As a matter of fact, his system was largely based upon a deliberate crudeness of approach. His admirers would patiently explain that the shot of Jayne Mansfield clutching two milk bottles to her bosom in *The Girl Can't Help It* was irresistible precisely because it was so crude and obvious.

Tashlin was also praised for the unusually high number of gags he was able to come up with in each new film. Gags were indeed plentiful, and sometimes excellent, in some of his comedies, especially the earlier ones (e.g., the hilarious *Marry Me Again*),

but in later efforts, they tended to become few and far between and not always worth the waiting for. Even at the height of what is generally considered his peak period, Tashlin could turn out such a feeble effort as *The Lieutenant Wore Skirts*, which can hardly boast more than a half-dozen sight gags, all of them forgettable (to make up for this dearth of visual invention, the dialogue is crammed with belabored double entendres). As for the influence of the animated cartoon on Tashlin (it used to be de rigueur to mention his early work for Paul Terry, Disney, and Looney Tunes and to describe his gags as "cartoonist's gags"), it may be credited for the streak of nonrealistic, nonsensical humor in his comedy. Still, "borrowing" would probably be a more accurate term than "influence" to describe it. Some of Tashlin's gags are easily identified as "cartoon gags" because they have been used in countless cartoons. They do not acquire originality just from being sneaked into live-action features.

Indeed, inasmuch as it is at all possible to compare achievements in the two respective fields, one is tempted to argue that Tashlin did his best work during his early days as an animation director. The frantic pace, inexhaustible inventiveness and weird sense of humor of some of his Warner cartoons are on a par with the best of Tex Avery. *Speaking of the Weather*, for instance, a 1937 "Merrie Melodie," is a stupendous minimasterpiece that takes a "cute" premise (magazine covers come to life) and turns it into a breathless, surrealistic romp jam-packed with delightfully clever conceits. Tashlin's cartoons definitely point to his later development as a full-fledged comedy director, but rather than merely "promising," they are more in the nature of succulent hors d'oeuvres leading up to a somewhat disappointing main course.

It took Tashlin quite some time to ease himself out of what one could call the Paramount style of comedy, best exemplified by the Martin and Lewis vehicles, the *Road* series and Bob Hope's movies in general. After all, Tashlin's first (uncredited) stab at direction was on a Bob Hope comedy. Prior to that, he had scripted Hope's *The Paleface*, and he later wrote and directed the sequel, *Son of Paleface*. (His *last* picture was also to be a Bob Hope vehicle, but this is a mere coincidence, although a symbolical one.) Tashlin's two Martin and Lewis pictures are closer to the *Road* pictures than to any specifically "Tashlinian" comedy style. The resemblance is not just a superficial consequence of the crooner-comedian combination (the Crosby-Hope relationship and the Martin and Lewis relationship are quite different despite some common features). Tashlin truly was at home with that brand of comedy. He was obviously not responsible for the similarities between Hope's and Lewis's comic personae (although mostly accidental and not particularly meaningful, the similarities are unmistakable, and it is not quite a coincidence if one of the Martin and Lewis comedies was a remake of a Bob Hope picture), but it is characteristic that he often devised the same type of situations and material for both comedians.

More generally, recurring features of Tashlin's comedy style—sly sex innuendos, facial and bodily contortions, foolish little skits (e.g., the kangaroo-patrol routine in *Artists and Models*), inside jokes and topical allusions—all seem to be derived from the *Road* pictures and are to be found in many of Hope's solo efforts as well. The top of Jerry Lewis's shoes popping up when he receives a kiss from Shirley MacLaine is nothing but a variation on a similar gag in *Road to Morocco* (in which the toes of Hope's curled-up slippers phallically straighten out when Dorothy Lamour kisses him). It is not a question of imitation, let alone plagiarism, in such a case, as we are dealing with gags from a huge reservoir of visual metaphors for sexual arousal, the original authorship for which can be credited to no one in particular. Such variations on a given theme are much like the countless jazz compositions and improvisations based

on the same standard chord sequence, and the cartoonists are the people who have most systematically run those changes.

Which brings us back to the subject of Tashlin as cartoonist: Tashlin is always closest to cartoon esthetics when he deals with sexual arousal, and his mode of approach is fairly consistent. His favorite metaphor is the rise in temperature: ice melts and milk boils out of milk bottles as Jayne Mansfield walks by; the water in a water cooler is brought to the boiling point as Jerry Lewis, standing with his back to the glass container, is receiving a passionate kiss (in *Artists and Models,* he literally gets hot pants at the sight of Eva Gabor—her cigarette sets the seat of his trousers on fire). Unfortunately, the live action film, by its very nature, is unable to compete with cartoons in this realm. Who could ever hope, for instance, to match or even approach the delirious display of erotic frenzy by Tex Avery's wolf in *Little Rural Riding Hood?*

Tashlin's career as a feature-film director falls into clear-cut periods. The first one is brief, consisting of two comedies starring Robert Cummings (*The First Time* and *Marry Me Again*) and *Son of Paleface* and *Susan Slept Here.* (The last seemed delightful back in the fifties but is today an ordeal to sit through, moronically coy in a typical fifties way and unusually ugly to look at, with the redeeming feature of one elegant dolly shot in a kitchen as a refrigerator door swings open—and little else.) Then came Tashlin's somewhat overrated but still enjoyable "great" period, with the two Martin and Lewis vehicles and the two starring Jayne Mansfield, a quartet upon which, rightly or wrongly, most discussions of Tashlin have always focused.

The Jerry Lewis period, which stretches from 1958 through 1964 and includes six pictures (interspersed with forgettable non-Lewis comedies) could be subdivided into two chronological categories: the films made before Lewis started directing his own (*Rock-a-Bye-Baby, The Geisha Boy, Cinderfella*) and those made after, which happen to be much better. The years between the break with Martin and the making of *The Bellboy* were an awkward transitional stretch for Lewis, and Tashlin was not particularly helpful in easing the growing pains: *Rock-a-Bye-Baby* and *The Geisha Boy* are uneven and not up to either man's best, and *Cinderfella* is a low point in both men's careers. *It's Only Money* and *Who's Minding the Store?,* on the other hand, are very funny, although uneven, and so is *The Disorderly Orderly* despite long stretches of un-Tashlinesque, but quite Lewislike, mawkish sentimentality. On the whole, though, the Tashlin-Lewis films are less remarkable for the blending of two comedy methods than for the tension between them. Rather than a collaboration, it seems more often a case of each man letting the other do his own thing. Some of the finest moments, for instance, are verbal routines in the Lewis tradition (his double-talk monologue as a television repairman at the beginning of *It's Only Money,* his impersonation of a Japanese television announcer in *Rock-a-Bye Baby*), which seem to owe little, if anything, to Tashlin. In *Who's Minding the Store?,* several scenes are variations on routines from Lewis-directed films (e.g., his dealing with a lady's wig in much the same way he treated Buddy Lester's hat in *The Ladies' Man* or the typewriter routine, an echo of the conference-room pantomime in *The Errand Boy*). Conversely, the Tashlin touch, when it does manifest itself, tends to shift the attention away from the comedian on to various props, for while objects are essential to all visual comedy, gags usually develop out of their relationship to people, whereas Tashlin finds objects themselves funny as long as he can pervert their functions and lead them into aberrant behavior. "Behavior" is used deliberately here, as Tashlin's pathetic fallacy turns inanimate objects, if not into human beings, at least into something akin to animals—nefarious ones invariably. Hence the rampaging lawn mowers of *It's Only Money* that ravage an estate with purposeful malignancy or, in *Who's Minding the Store?*, the monstrous vacuum cleaner that swallows up everything in sight—objects, people and their dogs, even the walls—a scene that almost reaches the cosmic proportions of Tex Avery's dizzying open endings in *King-Size Canary* or *Bad-Luck Blackie.*

A major problem Tashlin had to grapple with throughout his career, and which became particularly acute during his last period, was the paucity, if not the total lack, of performers with talents suited to his style of comedy. Jerry Lewis was, quite simply, the only one around. Tashlin had been able to work around the difficulty in the Jayne Mansfield films by focusing on topical satire rather than on a comic character. Over the years he had used Robert Cummings, Tom Ewell, Tony Randall, Terry-Thomas (the last in combination with Tuesday Weld in *Bachelor Flat,* a reworking of the basic situation of *Susan Slept Here* and one of Tashlin's most vapid pictures: its comedy chiefly consists of Terry-Thomas running around in his underwear, socks, and garters, pushing a variety of girls in and out of bedrooms, closets, windows, and back doors for no discernible reasons).

After his parting with Lewis, Tashlin tried to revitalize his old formula (effete comic plus bosomy blonde) by teaming Anita Ekberg with Tony Randall as Hercule Poirot in *The Alphabet Murders* but with little success. He ended up directing Doris Day and, finally, the infamous, and fortunately short-lived, comedy team of Bob Hope and Phyllis Diller. Curiously, it was Doris Day, of all people, who proved his wisest choice during those bleak late years. *The Glass Bottom Boat* and *Caprice* are no comic masterpieces, but they made good use of her gifts as a comedienne and injected some welcome slapstick into her usual, more tepid fare. Typical of Tashlin at his best is a scene in a fully automated kitchen whose circuitry goes haywire and Day's entanglement with a robot vacuum cleaner that pounces out of its lair at the drop of a crumb on the floor (when affected by the general breakdown, it keeps obscenely sucking at her toe). But the two films were really the tail-end of Day's screen career (she "retired" from films two years later), just like *The Man from the Diners Club* and *The Private Navy of Sgt. O'Farrell* were Danny Kaye's and Bob Hope's.

As a matter of fact, the decline of Tashlin's career is paralleled by the even sharper decline of most of his star performers: Mansfield's career foundered miserably throughout the sixties, and the last few films she made before her death are so obscure as to be almost untraceable; Ewell only got a couple of supporting parts after *The Girl Can't Help It;* Randall starred in three minor productions after *The Alphabet Murders* then disappeared from the screens in the seventies (except for a small part in Woody Allen's *"Sex"*); Ekberg, never much of a major star anyway, has only been seen in a few supporting roles and guest appearances since *The Alphabet Murders.* Was Tashlin a jinx? Actually, his performers' predicament was the same as his own in that they were all associated with a certain type of fifties movies and never managed to outgrow the image and adjust to new styles.

Tashlin's grim sense of humor, his jaded, jaundiced view of humanity, his relish for weird distortion and uncompassionate caricature, his attraction for objects and mechanisms running wild in a world itself gone mad, all were quite in tune with the times, yet he got stuck with unfashionable and uninspired material, quickly became anachronistic, and died in near obscurity. Tashlin may have been a cult figure among film buffs in the fifties and early sixties, but the Hollywood establishment never recognized him as a big-time comedy director, possibly because of his long association with Jerry Lewis, whose movies have always been considered lowbrow. During the years of their off-and-on partnership, the Tashlin-Lewis team was more often on than off, with Tashlin directing eight Lewis films (including the two with Dean Martin) and only six other comedies, half of them negligible. Tashlin may thus have become identified as "that Jerry Lewis director" and been accordingly treated with dwindling consideration by producers. While Lewis may thus be seen as one reason of Tashlin's downfall, it could also be argued that a major contribution of the director to film comedy was coaching Lewis through a period of growing self-awareness into the full-fledged comic auteur who emerged in the early sixties. Which is a somewhat vicarious kind of glory but by no means an insignificant one.

Tashlin was always criticized for his vulgarity, his reliance upon caricature rather than character, his anything-goes outrageousness. It is ironic, then, that the laugh-starved, undemanding seventies elected as their comic genius writer-director Mel Brooks, whose comedy style may be described in exactly the same terms. Brooks's facile, frenzied spoofs and satires are very much in the Tashlin tradition, and they seem to be more outrageous, more iconoclastic only because of the much-increased permissiveness that makes them possible. The contrived double entendre "What knock-ers!" (elicited by the juxtaposition of Madeline Kahn's bosom and the castle's huge gate) in *Young Frankenstein* is the verbal correlative of Tashlin's visual joke juxtaposing Mansfield's breasts and two milk bottles. If films like *Blazing Saddles* and *Young Franken-stein* are really, as some critics insist, "comic masterpieces," then Tashlin must have been doing something right back in the dark ages, and his work may be due for reappraisal.

54. Charles Walters (1911–1982)

by ALAIN MASSON

1947—*Good News;* 1948—*Easter Parade; The Barkleys of Broadway;* 1950—*Summer Stock; Three Guys Named Mike;* 1951—*Texas Carnival;* 1952—*The Belle of New York; Lili;* 1953—*Dangerous When Wet; Torch Song; Easy To Love;* 1955—*The Glass Slipper; The Tender Trap;* 1956—*High Society;* 1957—*Don't Go Near the Water;* 1959—*Ask Any Girl;* 1960—*Please Don't Eat the Daisies;* 1961—*Two Loves;* 1962—*Billy Rose's Jumbo;* 1964—*The Unsinkable Molly Brown;* 1966—*Walk, Don't Run*

Uncredited
1958—*Gigi* (Vincente Minnelli); 1960—*Cimarron* (Anthony Mann); 1961—*Go Naked in the World* (Ranald MacDougall)

Charles Walters's best films certainly have a charm of their own. This nobody denies, but it is quite another matter to understand how it works, so that many critics yielded to the temptation of assigning most of the merit to the studio and to the genre. Truly enough, Walters made only his last film outside MGM (*Walk, Don't Run*), and his masterpieces are musicals. So he will be considered as the typical MGM musical director and nothing more. His films do not convey a personal vision like Vincente Minnelli's; Gene Kelly and Stanley Donen have shown much more inventiveness than he did; George Sidney's visual style can be grasped and appreciated more easily. It may be argued, however, that the typical MGM director in those years was Richard Thorpe or Norman Taurog and that both the genre and the studio tradition look brilliant now because people like Walters polished them. His work is not an individual achievement and will not be of any support to the auteur theory, but his films have a special tone and a recognizable mood, fanciful and romantic, tense and genial, melancholy and lively.

Granted, for example, that Walters's musicals are just musicals, they certainly are not plain musicals. Some clarification seems to be needed here, for the word *musical* not only means, in an objective way, a set of rules and habits but also inescapably suggests the achievement of a certain esthetic quality within this frame. The musical tends to appear as an aggregate of merits and values, so that a lot of films with song-and-dance numbers but coming short of the sought-for atmosphere will hardly qualify as musicals. A bad Western is still a Western, but a musical needs to be good or at least festive. This is admittedly an equivocal definition, open to abuse, yet it is ably sustained by John Russel Taylor in his *Hollywood Musical* and by Jerome Delamater in his contribution to Stuart M. Kaminsky's *American Film Genres*. The double meaning certainly helps to understand Walters' work, insofar as making a musical was not for him a way of sheltering behind conventions but essentially an attempt to take advantage of the values implied in the genre.

In that respect Walters's musicals are not simply typical musicals nor can his work be accounted for in terms of musicals only. His comedies are pleasant and sometimes weak, but a drama like *Two Loves* is interesting and significant. Yet Walters's purpose is most openly disclosed by the way he tried to explore the borders of the musical, not only in the bittersweet *High Society* but also in *Lili* and *The Glass Slipper*. They may not be his best films, but they demonstrate that Walters did not consider the musical as a closed set of rules. In *The Tender Trap* he embedded the comedy in a musical frame. This means he was not fascinated by the musical in itself; on the contrary, he wondered how far the genre could reach.

Lili and *The Glass Slipper* tend to reduce the scope of dancing to a world of fantasy, and the link between the musical numbers and the story sometimes seems rather loose. In *The Glass Slipper* the audience would even gladly do without Roland Petit's strained choreography, but, bad as it is, the dancing hardly spoils the film inasmuch as restrained gestures and unaccomplished impulses make up the substance of the story: significantly enough the capital moment of the ball is when Cinderella slowly walks down the flight of steps. This restraint is connoted when she has to bring down the arm she had lifted in imitation of her dancing partner: as she obeys a code of propriety, she not only acknowledges the ritual ruling the relations between men and women, she also makes the difference between expressive dancing and ballroom dancing perfectly clear. But of course checking impulses is vital to the content of the film as well as to its form, Cinderella being the symbol of passion (fire) preserved by what is supposed to choke it (ashes). Scarce, restrained, and sometimes abruptly and beautifully terminated, the musical numbers find a new meaning: instead of expressing a feeling, they suggest the girl's surprise, bewilderment, and fear when discovering the depth of feeling.

Lili more precisely deals with a girl becoming conscious of her own sexuality through two dream numbers: in the first she becomes Rosalie's rival and must display her charms before Marc's eyes; in the second she discovers the man behind the puppets, Mel Ferrer as Berthalet, dressed in black. The simplified scenery in both numbers contrasts with the picturesque quality of the carnival. This contrast is underlined by the numerous camera movements that reveal "real" world in its diversity, whereas Walters films the dreams in a much more controlled manner. A second contrast opposes Marc the magician to Berthalet the puppeteer; even the type of entertainment they perform heightens their difference: the former is visible and works miracles, the latter stays out of view and operates in a perfectly ordinary way. The two images embody Lili's desires and suggest an interesting interplay of the pleasure principle and the principle of reality, while Berthalet's black and injured figure seems to assume the work of mourning, when Lili understands the other image cannot be grasped. A third contrast separates the clear and narrow character of the puppets and Lili's doubtful identity; the intelligible world of the puppet show forms a counterpoint to her own perplexities and sorrows. This wealth of meaning is based upon a clever use of a device belonging to the musical genre: the autonomy of meaning granted to the show-within-the-show.

Though the choreography in *Lili* is more efficient, it plays altogether the same part as in *The Glass Slipper*. Rather than advancing the action, it changes it into something unreal. The musical numbers do not result from the plot or atmosphere of the film; on the contrary they are an excuse for the general tone of the work. Thus in *Lili,* the last time Lili comes back to reality is seen through the eyes of the puppets, which casts a fundamental ambiguity upon the "happy ending." The musical has been used as a pretense to work out a new form. The reference to a well-known genre, compared to such a minor and ill-defined genre as fairy-tale movie, not only makes everybody more comfortable but helps to build new meanings. *Lili* and *The Glass Slipper* pretend to be musicals in order to find a clear formal definition but pursue their own purposes beyond that definition. For they are meant to arouse emotions (fear and pity) more easily associated with tragedy than with musical comedy.

The general device in Walters's films could be summed up in the following way: for some reason the artist is not confident he can bring about a deep perception of feeling unless he underlines the truthfulness of the sensibility by contrasting it with the unreality of the general atmosphere. In a similar way, the general simplicity of the film sets off the intricacy of the characters' emotions. The best example is certainly the "walking on air" of the loving couple in *The Belle of New York.* Unlike the similar walking on the ceiling in Donen's *Royal Wedding,* which brings on a lot of elaborate choreography when Astaire gets up there or uses three surfaces, the conceit here materializes in a very simple solo or pas de deux, and one cannot help seeing the trick photography just for what it is, since air is no extraordinary dancing floor, and however subtle Astaire's art, he cannot float but must walk. But the number need not be convincing, just as the ballets in *The Glass Slipper* need not be good. The unreality of the material world is supposed to prove the honesty of the feelings: the sudden lifting is the unquestionable manifestation of true love. This shows in the most ingenuous manner what kind of use Walters had in mind for the coordinate set of rules and values the musical seems to imply. For it is a rule to express the beginning of love through a musical number, and one of the values of the genre is traditionally described as a "momentary lift into another world of fantasy," in John Russel Taylor's phrase.

A romantic idea of the gap between the soul and the world may be implied in the formal process, but Walters never disclosed it clearly in his musicals. The blind pianist in *Torch Song* is cut off from the outer world in a more dramatic way than Lili. In *Two Loves* the old maid's inhibitions can be interpreted as an expression of the incompatibility between the self and reality. Interviewed by Pierre Sauvage (*Positif*, 144–145), Charles Walters explained he had filmed a dream that was to be used as a prologue but was eventually cut by the producer; it made clear that Anna (Shirley MacLaine) was deeply affected by sexual desire and frustration. But what is clear in a dream may be quite difficult to enact in real life, as another deleted scene was to show: she was going to sleep with her lover (Laurence Harvey), but he refused because she appeared to him as "a lamb before the sacrifice." As it stands, the film still retains something of that lost sense in the way it contrasts sensuousness with puritanism or sweetness and reserve with occasional outbursts of passion and disorder.

However unsuitable this dark mood may be in a musical, the controlled bitterness of a disappointed romantic can be felt in most of Walters's films. His characters do not live up to their archetypal figure. In *Easter Parade,* Astaire will significantly end up with a girl who can't dance except for comical numbers; in *The Barkleys of Broadway,* the famous dancers split, and this is all the more funny because the film reunited Fred Astaire and Ginger Rogers ten years after *The Story of Vernon and Irene Castle;* in *The Belle of New York* Astaire appears to be as much afraid of life as Vera-Ellen; he even gets drunk on the eve of his wedding. Such characters account for Lili's love for puppets who cannot disappoint her. Even in the early *Good News* one can trace some signs of blasé sophistication: June Allyson expresses her heartbreak by saying she is going to stay home and read *Les Misérables,* and if that kind of humor has been customary from the first days of the genre, the reference to a foreign culture seems more alarming. College girls are not what they used to be! Generally speaking, in Walters's films, oblique expression is to be associated with full passion and obstinate reluctance to yield to its solicitations. Dinah Barkley's passionate temper bursts out when she plays Sarah Bernhardt reciting *La Marseillaise;* religious sayings written under the pulpit find a new meaning during a lovers' quarrel (*The Belle of New York*); the French lesson in *Good News* changes into flirtation; the crescendo on "Gesundheit!", expressive of the characters' growing embarrassment at somebody's allergic sneezing, becomes the perfect example when the sneezer himself infuriatedly repeats "Gesundheit!" (*Summer Stock*). Thus Astaire expresses himself best when he dances on stage without Judy Garland, with a kind of vacant passion and lively expectation of happiness (*Easter Parade*). Again, this oblique expression is enhanced by a general law of the musical, and the number "You, Wonderful You" in *Summer Stock* shows the manifold implications of confusion (or distinction) between stage and off stage, thus going very deep into the basic metaphors of the genre. Compared with the famous "Dancing in the Dark" number in Minnelli's *The Band Wagon,* which was filmed three years later, the functionally similar number in *Summer Stock* is much more ambiguous. In Minnelli's film, the overt meaning (we dance well together) veils the expression of desire without leaving anybody any doubt about the covert meaning (we love each other), whereas Walters's characters do not know for sure where they stand. Everything *may* have been inspired by the stage and the lights, and indeed a clear example of inspiration by the scenery is to be found in Kelly's extraordinary "newspaper dance." Minnelli's characters' only problem is to speak their love; Walters's must feel the deficiencies of speech. One is then induced to a kind of amorous casuistry that reflects the uncertainty of both characters: he was on stage, but this was not part of a show; she surrendered to his kiss but only as long as she thought it was part of the falsehood, since acting is his natural language; but since he is an actor, can he be capable of any genuine feeling? And this can go on ad infinitum.

This subtle treatment of the rules of the genre is also illustrated by the inverted relation between solos and pas de deux in *The Belle of New York:* "Oops," the number in the tramway, plays with space in much the same manner as "Baby Doll" plays with words; in both cases there is some misunderstanding; even though point zero is not determined, they always have to come back to it, whether it is an ethical point of view or a moving vehicle, so that movement and expression lack freedom and authenticity. On the contrary, the solo numbers genuinely convey an impression of eagerness to live and love at the same time they express consciousness of one's limitations. "They Can't Take That Away From Me" in *The Barkleys of Broadway* is interesting in a similar way: the duet works smoothly but the marriage is on the brink of breaking up; the automatism of the dance is felt as such at the same time it is used as a pretense for remembrance, and of course the lyrics manifest the same contradiction between perennial love and parting.

Of course these subtleties express Walters's will to consider the genre as a means rather than an end. He is a modern film maker insofar as his films, instead of working out a compromise between an established form and a new picture of life or conveying a personal meditation through an intended classicism (as Donen and Minnelli may be said to have done), involve a play with the genre itself. The musical offers a motif generally set forth in a musical number: a girl is waiting and preparing for love or for her lover. In postwar musicals this convention can be interpreted as a reduction of the bring-on-the-girls type extravaganza. Both Minnelli and Donen have used it in a straight manner and with wonderful results. Walters always carried it a little too far. The general assumption is that the ability to dance displays the ability to love, called up with some male chauvinism by the ability to be loved, which is made perfectly evident by the dancing girls. The chorus numbers stress the sensuous side of love, whereas the solo numbers insist on its romantic aspects. But when Ann Miller "shakes the blues away" in *Easter Parade,* when Judy Garland "feels like singing" under her shower (*Summer Stock*), when Esther Williams swims through Howard Keel's daydream in *Texas Carnival,* or when Vera-Ellen, of all people, decides to get "naughty but nice" (*The Belle of New York*), Walters challenges the separation of sex and feelings and offers a picture of women's sexual desire. Cinderella getting ready for the ball belongs to the same structure and so does Grace Kelly's emotion when she hears Sinatra telling her she is "sensational" or overhears Bing Crosby singing "I Love You, Samantha" (*High Society*). Yet Walters has never blatantly broken the rules: he just dressed Ann Miller or Vera-Ellen in yellow and black and watched them display the richness of their movements; he decently filmed Judy Garland behind a screen; he had Grace Kelly lightly caress her glass. But what he did is expose the implications of the traditional motif: there is something pathetic in a woman's desire since it has to awaken men's desire in order to find its own expression: to desire is to be desired. There is nothing shocking in a sensuous parade or a romantic expression, but the rules do not permit the mixing. Hence the intricate blending of shame and showing off, risqué lingerie and psychological reluctance in these scenes.

Their moral ambiguity is all the stronger because they can be interpreted as a sympathetic comment upon women's burden or as a way of making the girls more appealing since they are subject to the necessity of changing into sexual objects. But of course this ambiguity makes these scenes more moving. These portrayals of repressed but passionate girls, unabashed and shy, resolute and awkward is a leitmotif in Walters's films, especially in his comedies. Even though his direction of actors is unequal, actresses are often interesting in his films. One remembers Judy Garland's tense sensibility in *Easter Parade;* he also worked well with Shirley MacLaine and Doris Day. One example will be enough to illustrate his sense of feminine vulnerability. The main difference between Katharine Hepburn in George Cukor's *The Philadelphia Story* (1940) and Grace Kelly in *High Society* lies in the fact that whereas Hepburn, though she may lose her composed image, always seems to master the game at least intellectually, Kelly sometimes is really at a loss.

This complex characterization is based upon Walters's open direction. His main quality seems to be an uncommon sense of continuity without monotony, which was already distinctive of his style as a choreographer. The merging of gesture and dancing, that special grace with which the stylized movements elate but never sublimate the body, each new emotion being a fresh one instead of following from the previous ones, but without any uncomfortable break in the expression, already was the forte of the musical numbers in Minnelli's *Meet Me in Saint Louis* and Rouben Mamoulian's *Summer Holiday,* which Walters staged. An analogous merging of the calculated gestures of a singer and the spontaneous movements of a talker can be observed when watching Sinatra in *High Society,* a film that is certainly not flawless but can be borne in mind as a singular exercise in overlapping (talking and singing, jazz and Cole Porter, character and commentator, reluctance and compliance, bitterness and sweetness).

This sense of the progressive fading of a movement into new movement or of an emotion into another emotion is another way of dealing with the contrasted image that is the dominant feature of his art. As the musical numbers show, Walters has always tried to visualize situations as totalities and to film them synthetically. He does not divide them into small bits as Sidney often did, he does not try to gain through them a new dimension of space like Donen, nor does he plan the camera movements according to a subtle and changing relation with the dancers and their own evolution, as Minnelli sometimes did, but he achieves a clearly constructed complete vision. Every camera movement can be easily foreseen, but he manages to avoid lazy long shots as well as ponderous close-ups. The "Swing Trot" in *The Barkleys of Broadway* and "Baby Doll" in *The Belle of New York* illustrate Walters's sense of measure. The camera regularly follows to and fro the evolution of the dances without anything trite or inflated in its movement. "Oops" in *The Belle of New York* or "Get Happy" in *Summer Stock* have a more complex and deeper comprehension of space, and the camera work is still quite openly planned. Both the choreography and the mise-en-scène have a form of their own, in order to make the interplay of these two forms the special interest of the numbers. Were the camera work granted complete autonomy, the choreography as a form would disappear, as it did more or less constantly in Busby Berkeley's numbers. On the contrary, when the connection is narrowly determined, it gives the impression of a forced phrasing, which Minnelli used in his dream numbers to connote the compulsive working of the imagination (Walters's fantasies, "Shoes With Wings On" in *The Barkleys of Broadway* or Esther Williams meeting Tom and Jerry in *Dangerous When Wet* show no interest in the surreal). Each director had to find a just proportion between these two excesses. Walters succeeded in leaving the dancers enough space in the frame, so that the camera and the choreography are related in an even but not frozen way, which is suitable for the characters' expression. The tracking shot of Judy Garland driving her tractor in *Summer Stock* or the memorable crane shot of

Sinatra in *The Tender Trap* illustrate well that interplay of free movement and clearly built shooting.

The same synthetic planning may be observed in the way Walters deals with colors. Whereas Minnelli always works on a chromatic pattern inspired by memories of paintings or based upon oppositions of simple colors, Walters tries to keep everything under control without any evident limitation. He always keeps a free hand and never feels dependent on a model: the calendar number in *Easter Parade* and the prints number in *The Belle of New York* develop freely, if not convincingly. Walters's genius as a colorist is in fact dynamically oriented. He is confident movement will not result in chaos but in liveliness. In that respect his attitude toward color and his consideration of his characters are much alike and have indeed deteriorated at the same pace, *The Unsinkable Molly Brown* balancing caricatures with chromatic monotony. The "Varsity Drag" (*Good News*), "Stepping Out With My Baby" (*Easter Parade*), or the "Bachelor Dinner Song" (*The Belle of New York*) achieve a colorful harmony through common planning of the colors and the choreography, the dance defining changing chromatic keys and areas.

An outline of Walters's work would have to distinguish his four classical musicals as the core of his output: *Easter Parade, The Barkleys of Broadway, Summer Stock,* and *The Belle of New York.* But it would be wrong to isolate them either from his other musicals, which bear the same qualities to a lesser degree, or from a group of works situated on the borders of the genre, from *Lili* to *High Society,* since they have a great illuminative power and a good deal of charm, while *Two Loves* discloses something of Walters's romanticism. Such an outline suggests that Walters's achievements are based upon a conflicting relation between the established motifs and the characters' strengths. This would explain why most of his attempts at comedy have been unfortunate: *Ask Any Girl,* for instance, gets interesting only in its sentimental moments.

Walters finally appears as an original artist, subtle and sensitive, whose delicacy and charm are not evanescent qualities but are deeply rooted in an unobtrusive yet thoughtful meditation on the musical form itself.

55. *Don Weis* (1922)

1951—*Bannerline;* 1952—*It's a Big Country: An American Anthology* (episode); *Just This Once; You for Me;* 1953—*I Love Melvin; Remains to Be Seen; A Slight Case of Larceny; The Affairs of Dobie Gillis; Half a Hero;* 1954—*The Adventures of Hajji Baba;* 1957—*Ride the High Iron;* 1958—(unreleased) *Catch Me If You Can;* 1959—*The Gene Krupa Story;* 1963—*Critic's Choice;* 1964—*Looking for Love; Pajama Party;* 1965—*Billie;* 1966—*The Ghost in the Invisible Bikini;* 1967—*The King's Pirate;* 1968—*Did You Hear the One About the Traveling Saleslady?;* 1979—*Repo*

Television Movies
1967—*The Longest Hundred Miles;* 1968—*Now You See It, Now You Don't*

Don Weis's *The Adventures of Hajji Baba,* mostly dismissed in the United States as an inept programmer with some pretty girls, created quite a stir among Parisian film buffs and soon became one of the causes célèbres of the fifties, arousing violent controversy for several years. To its ardent supporters, the movie was the archetype of pure mise-en-scène; to its detractors—usually admirers of Fellini or Bresson—it was just childish nonsense. It must be added that the latter often refused to see the film at all, while many of the former were known to have sat through it as many as ten times. Now that passions have died down, *Hajji* may be reconsidered more soberly. While no deathless masterpiece, it is still a delightful experience. Its unusual status among oriental adventure-fantasy movies comes from the fact that the pleasure it generates is somewhat different from—and more subtle than—both that induced by straight examples of the genre and by tongue-in-cheek parodies like, say, Ted Tetzlaff's *Son of Sinbad. Hajji*'s joy is closer to the physical thrill one derives from good musical comedy.

As a matter of fact, Weis's first notable movie before *Hajji was* a musical, the equally exhilarating *I Love Melvin. Melvin* is blessed with the kind of deliberately silly plot that keeps you chuckling along with it rather than at it and, provided you find yourself in the proper frame of mind, makes you feel so good that you sit watching even the duller parts with a foolish grin on your face. Among other goodies the movie boasts an intricately choreographed football game (a pert Debbie Reynolds is the football), a charming roller-skating routine by Donald O'Connor, a couple of infectious song and dance numbers by the latter and Reynolds, and some airy location scenes actually shot in Central Park. But *Melvin*'s highlight is O'Connor's mad romp through *Look* magazine's photographic studios—a worthy follow-up to his "Make'em Laugh" routine in *Singin' in the Rain*—a sequence that grows more and more surreal as O'Connor pops in and out of strange disguises and sets an increasingly rapid pace.

Weis's third and last memorable effort was *The Affairs of Dobie Gillis,* a musical graced by the nimble presence of both Bobby Van and Bob Fosse in addition to Debbie Reynolds. *Hajji, Melvin,* and *Dobie* were all released in between 1953 and 1954, a period during which MGM kept Weis hard at work, also assigning him to direct studio comedians (Mickey Rooney and Eddie Bracken in *A Slight Case of Larceny* and Red Skelton in *Half a Hero*) and a stage success, the mildly entertaining *Remains to Be Seen.* Weis, a graduate of the University of Southern California's School of Cinematography and a former script supervisor (first, during the war, on Army and Air Force films, then in Hollywood on features including *Body and Soul, Home of the Brave, The Men,* and Joseph Losey's *M*), had become a director at MGM in 1951 and made all his films for them until the mid-fifties. When the studio more or less collapsed at the time, so did Weis's film career, and he became increasingly active in television, where he has directed over 200 segments of various series. In 1958, he shot what was probably the last American film made in Cuba (*Catch Me if You Can,* a jewel-theft story starring Gilbert Roland, Dina Merrill, and Cesare Danova). It was never released, which was unfortunately not the case with his more recent pictures. After *The Gene Krupa Story,* a clichéd biography of a jazz figure more notable for misfortune and showmanship than actual percussive greatness, and *Critic's Choice,* a dreadful Bob Hope vehicle and a waste of the Ira Levin play Otto Preminger had produced on Broadway with Henry Fonda, Weis slipped to the bottom of the ladder with his two teen-and-beach AIP productions (*Pajama Party* at least served up Buster Keaton masquerading as an Indian chief and cavorting with a Martian), a cheapie swashbuckler, and a Phyllis Diller rehash. He seems to be trying to obliterate all our fond memories of a more cheerful period.

56. Orson Welles (1915)

1941—*Citizen Kane;* 1942—*The Magnificent Ambersons;* 1946—*The Stranger;* 1948—*The Lady From Shanghai; Macbeth;* 1952—*Othello* (U.S., 1955); 1955—*Confidential Report* (U.S., *Mr. Arkadin,* 1962); 1958—*Touch of Evil* (uncredited codirector: Harry Keller); 1962—*Le Procès* (U.S., *The Trial,* 1963); 1966—*Chimes at Midnight* (U.S., *Falstaff,* 1966); 1968—*Histoire immortelle* (France; U.S., *The Immortal Story,* 1968); 1975—*F for Fake* (U.S., 1977, contributing director: François Reichenbach); 1978—*Filming Othello*

Uncredited
1943—*Journey Into Fear* (Norman Foster)

Miscellaneous
Unfinished films include: 1942—*It's All True;* 1955—*Don Quixote;* 1967—*The Deep;* 1970—*The Other Side of the Wind*

As the first American film maker to question the then universally accepted tenet that style must remain an unseen servant to the "story," Orson Welles, who made form the very content of his films, did deserve to be called the father of modern cinema. His approach, however, although in many ways revolutionary, was also largely a throwback to a creative attitude that, no matter how exceptional, had dominated the silent era, and one without which, incidentally, the movies would never have outgrown their Nickelodeon stage. Welles, like Griffith, battled not only for complete artistic freedom but for a use of that freedom that would change the look and the very shape of movies. An even more obvious silent-day counterpart to Welles was von Stroheim, another genius silenced by an industry for which he was too big. Both were men of vision who simply refused to acknowledge the economic and logistic limitations of the medium in their time and place and blithely embarked upon the road to predictable—although not necessarily unavoidable—frustration and failure. (Welles, of course, managed to make one film *and* have it released exactly the way he wanted, a privilege Stroheim never enjoyed.) As a contrast, all the great American directors of the sound era, whether newcomers or holdovers from the silent days, worked within the system, both economically and esthetically. Even von Sternberg, the supreme stylist, went through the motions of making commercial pictures. Welles, with his unusual background (unusual from any standpoint but positively outlandish for Hollywood), his boy-wonder reputation, and the unheard-of freedom his RKO contract granted him, stood alone and apart in Hollywood's eye even before he walked onto a sound stage. A maverick from the start, he consolidated this image with every move and somewhat uncomfortably settled down to perpetuate it throughout decades of European exile.

Welles's films reflect this isolation. One might call them "classic" or transitional just as well as modern. They are at the same time daring and old-fashioned, dated and timeless. Above all, they exist in a kind of vacuum and seem almost completely unrelated not only to the films made at the same time but also to the ones made later. Welles's influence is allegedly immense, yet only his first two pictures can be said to have been in any way influential. *The Lady From Shanghai* was a by-product of, rather than a model for, the *film noir* esthetics. *Touch of Evil* and *Chimes at Midnight*, two major masterpieces, seem to have had little if any influence on anybody. Even the impact of *Citizen Kane* and *The Magnificent Ambersons* was diffuse and indirect, largely limited to an increased reliance upon long takes and upon a deep-focus, highly contrasted photographic style that they systematized but by no means introduced. The people who paid Welles the highest tribute—i.e., the young French critics who were to constitute the so-called New Wave—were the ones whose films turned out to owe him the slightest debt. What influenced them was not Welles's style but his spirit, his insistence upon making "personal" films in an era of "assembly-line" movie production.

"Self-destructive genius"—the phrase has been used countless times, acknowledging the madness in Welles's method. Like the scorpion in Arkadin's parable, Welles is a victim of his "character," whose dominant feature is an uncontrollable energy. Even before he started making films, his pattern of behavior was to plunge into scores of simultaneous projects no single individual could ever handle successfully. There is something vaguely miraculous about the way he so often managed to disentangle himself from seemingly inextricable predicaments. The odds against him were too high, unfortunately, for the miracles to happen often enough. Because of his insistent disregard for the time factor and the limitations of even his formidable energy, this most autocratic of creators found himself forced to delegate much authority or, when unwilling or unable to do so, to have it delegated for him. After every one of his pictures, *Citizen Kane* excepted, he complained that producers had betrayed his intentions and ruined his work by either deleting, adding, or reediting; but much, although obviously not all, of the sometimes irreparable (*Ambersons*), sometimes minor (*Touch of Evil*) damage resulted from the fact that Welles had made himself unavailable when his presence was needed or from his endless hesitations when it came to editing a picture.

Indeed, one salient aspect of Welles's "self-destructiveness" is his apparent reluctance to complete whatever he undertakes. Anxiety about what the finished product will be like and the compulsion to keep tinkering, with ultimate perfection in mind, are not uncommon traits among artists ("a poem is never completed," Valéry used to say. "One merely abandons it"), but they are the bane of the film maker, whom economic necessity usually compels to "abandon" his work at a much earlier stage than he would have wished. To an artist thriving on constant change and accustomed to the malleability and impermanence of the theater (a stage production can be modified at each performance, and it returns to nothingness when the show closes), the prospect of *releasing* a film—the very word suggests severance—may become a source of despair, a terminal stage to be postponed as long as possible. Hence the countless takes, for which Welles soon became notorious, and the agonizing in the cutting room. Noting Welles's "fear of completion," Charles Higham relates it to the obsession with death that overshadows all of his films: "For Welles, his own films are dead, which is one reason he cannot bear to look at them again." Clearly, they are "dead" because they can no longer be altered. A completed film is not a mere memory, unlike a play after the last performance, it keeps confronting its maker, naggingly reminding him of what it might and should have been. Of course, the immutability of the finished film is not an attribute of the medium but only an economic and practical requirement that may occasionally be by-passed. Welles was able to make important changes on a film (*Journey Into Fear,* which, ironically, he didn't officially direct) after the release prints had been prepared and the picture trade-shown and previewed. One suspects that he would have availed himself of this exceptional expedient for most of his other films had he been allowed to. As late as 1972, he was entertaining the extraordinary project—"fantasy" would be a more appropriate term—to rerelease *The Magnificent Ambersons* with a new ending, set ten years later, which he would film with members of the original cast. As for his most "recent" pictures, most seem doomed to remain perennial "works in progress." The ostensible reason for the unending delays—i.e., lack of money—is not one to be lightly dismissed; yet *The Deep* and even the legendary *Don Quixote,* over fifteen years in the making, are reportedly completed (or "nearly" completed, one never knows for sure) but still unreleased. *The Other Side of the Wind*—fragments of which were shown on television as part of the American Film Institute's 1975 homage to Welles—appeared to be still far from completion at the time, although Welles started working on it in the late sixties. Even if all these films are eventually shown, one wonders what level of esthetic unity can be attained by works made in such a desultory manner and over such extended periods of time.

Welles's is a cinema of organized chaos reflecting the disorganized chaos of his own life. The most immediate visual expression of this chaos is clutter, the piling up of props within the frame. Welles again and again returns to such images: Kane's furniture being moved into the already crowded *Inquirer* offices; the staggering jumble of accumulated possessions surveyed by the long tracking shot at the end of the film; the huge crates in the freight yard in the opening sequence of *Mr. Arkadin;* the rows upon rows of shelves crammed with bulging files and tied-up bundles of documents in *The Trial;* the paraphernalia of battle preparation in *Chimes at Midnight.* A related effect is sometimes achieved through a weird, Warhol-like use of duplication: Kane's endlessly repeated image as he walks past two facing mirrors; the multiplication of the three characters' reflections in the Hall of Mirrors in *The Lady From Shanghai;* the hundreds of stenographers' desks in the oversize typing pool of *The Trial.* In order to fill up the screen, Welles uses people and movement as effectively as he does inert masses. He loves crowded scenes, the noisier and more agitated the better: the welcoming party for Kane, the frenzy on stage before the curtain rises on Susan Alexander's "Salammbô," the sequence in the suspect's apartment in *Touch of Evil.* Even with only a few characters on hand, Welles gets his crowding effects by using cramped locations and tight framing. Although one tends to remember most vividly such huge sets as Xanadu or the Ambersons' mansion, what is truly striking about Welles's choice of interiors is the recurrence of small rooms, made to look even smaller by art direction (low ceilings, cumbersome furniture) and photography. Most of the interiors in *Touch of Evil* belong to that type. In *The Trial,* the painter's windowless studio induces claustrophobia, and the unexplained beating-up of the two detectives by their colleague takes place in what looks hardly more spacious than a broom closet. (In *The Stranger,* a comedian heard faintly over a radio quips about a hotel room so small that "every time I closed the door the knob got into bed with me." Welles's selection of that particular one-liner proves not only that he was quite conscious of his own predilection for cramped quarters but also quite willing to sneak in a private joke about it.) Occasionally, Welles uses his own body as a space-filling prop. In *Touch of Evil,* for instance, Quinlan's enormous bulk seems to occupy most of the tiny room in which he murders Grandi. While this kind of effect is, for obvious reasons, more frequent in later films (e.g., *Mr. Arkadin, Chimes at Midnight*), it goes back to Welles's very first film (Kane's lumbering shape looming disproportionately in Susan's bedroom as he smashes her furniture).

The symphonic complexity of Welles's sound tracks tends toward overloading as deliberately as do his picture tracks. He plays upon saturation effects, the punctuating overamplification of a single sound (from one typewriter key hitting the page to the sudden roar of an entire crowd), as well as upon the intricate polyphony of overlapping lines of dialogue, shouted or thrown away in frenzied, wonderfully confused exchanges. Most consummately crafted among many such scenes is the trial in *The Lady From Shanghai,* with its Alice-in-Wonderland pandemonium of constant interruptions and wisecracks from Everett Sloane against the background of a restless, coughing audience. Another memorable moment of vocal ebullience is the moving-in scene at the *Inquirer,* with Kane and Leland drowning a bewildered editor, then Bernstein, in a nonstop flow of bragging, teasing chatter, a perfect fusion of visual and aural clutter.

Charles Higham's criticism of this delightful scene raises an interesting point: "People interrupt each other pointlessly," he writes, "and the showing off of the ceilinged set seems very much like 'Look, no hands.' During the conversation in which the editor refuses to indulge in a circulation-building stunt, the handling is so fussy and confused that the whole point is lost and understood only on a re-examination of the sound track: here Welles is indulging technique to such an extent that an important aspect of Kane's character—his brutal use of people for dramatic effect—is lost."

To begin with, it seems strange that a Welles admirer should feel so negatively about such characteristically Wellesian treatment of a scene. But even granting that the response to the elaborate confusion devised by Welles is a matter of individual taste, Higham's central objection (i.e., that Welles's indulgence in technique blurs the psychological point of the scene) is certainly not a valid one. Welles's interest in his characters' psychology has always been minimal. His reluctance to spell out their motivations and probe their inner world is indeed an essential feature of his approach to drama. Both *Citizen Kane* and *Touch of Evil* end with the observation that a man must ultimately remain a mystery to the rest of the world. Characterization in Welles's films—and in *Kane* more than in any other—is always fragmented, oblique. Higham's criticism, pursued to its logical extent, would lead to a rejection, on the same grounds, of most of what Welles has ever done. The scene under discussion *is* intended, among other things, to provide information on Kane's character, but its "point," if any, is the very confusion it pictures, the feeling that momentous decisions are being made playfully amidst pervasive chaos—a chaos reflected in any number of scenes throughout the picture. Lucid, logical characterization could never jibe with such a vision of things. It is clear that Welles's esthetics of clutter is not a purely formal option but part of a strategy to submerge the presentation of character in the universal chaos and thereby, ultimately, to foil the search for identity with which most of his films are ostensibly concerned.

Citizen Kane, a triumph of disjointed, nonlinear narrative, achieves total adequacy of structure to vision, of style to subject matter. Its form is its theme and vice versa, for both deal with chaos. It may not be Welles's greatest film (one may prefer *The Magnificent Ambersons, Touch of Evil,* or even *Chimes at Midnight*), but it is, in that respect, his most perfect. Welles knew it and tried to repeat his feat a dozen years later when he made *Mr. Arkadin,* a bloated but formidably inventive caricature of his first film (and, with *Kane,* the only "original" script among Welles's released films).

Kane's most symbolic prop is not little Charles's sled, or the snowstorm paperweight, but Susan's huge jigsaw puzzle, for it represents both the form and content of the film. Charles Foster Kane is a puzzle, so is his life, and so is the construction of the picture Welles devotes to them. *Kane* opens with a collage of disconnected, as-yet meaningless images (the close-up of the dying man's lips, the whispered "rosebud," the paperweight falling) followed by a kaleidoscopic newsreel reconstruction of Kane's life—again, pieces of a puzzle thrown at us. The structure of the rest of the film is an expansion of the newsreel's, a juxtaposition of sometimes overlapping, often conflicting, points of view. But the pieces of this particular puzzle never "fall into place." Just before the final missing piece turns up, we have been warned that, even if found, it would not make the picture complete.

"Rosebud" is a false key that opens no door. It is, on the other hand, a serviceable structural device, an Ariadne's thread to guide us through the maze of Welles's narrative. We know from the start that it will not "explain" the mystery of Kane's personality, except—as it eventually does—in the most rudimentary fashion (Kane spent his life buying things and people to "compensate" for the loss of his sled and parents?). It is quite possible, in the last analysis, that there is nothing "more" to Kane than this simplistic explanation, but it does not make Welles's achievement any less remarkable, for his greatness is all on the surface, in what is seen and heard and not in what is "meant" (which is what Pauline Kael seems to be saying when she calls *Kane* a "shallow masterpiece").

No two Welles films look alike, but the same obsessive themes recur throughout his work: hunger for power and the loneliness it entails, nostalgia for the irretrievable past, the inevitability of aging, decay, and death. Indeed, dying, whether physical or metaphorical, whether it affects individuals, moods, or—as in *Ambersons*—an entire era, appears as Welles's most pervasive preoccupation. (It is fascinating to find that Welles played Death in *The Hearts of Age,* his 1934 amateur short discovered by Joseph McBride, and that, in the planned introduction to the never-produced *Heart of Darkness,* he used the example of a convict being led to the electric chair and executed "to instruct and acquaint the audience as amusingly as possible with the special technique used" in the film, i.e., the "subjective" camera.) Most of Welles's films end in death— usually the death of the character he plays—but such men as Kane or Quinlan have been spiritually dead long before the end, and Falstaff has lost something more vital to him than life itself. O'Hara (*The Lady From Shanghai*), a rare Welles hero who is allowed to live at the end, has had his dream shattered and muses, as he walks out of the devastated Hall of Mirrors, "Maybe I'll live so long that I'll forget her. Maybe I'll die trying." A quarter of a century after *Citizen Kane* and its opening death scene, Welles repeated the situation in *The Immortal Story* with the death of an immensely wealthy, immensely powerful lonely old man obsessed with the past. Both men die immersed in thoughts of unfulfilled potentialities, holding an object—Kane's paperweight, Clay's shell—that symbolizes their yearning. In both films, the object drops from the old man's hand at the moment of death. Welles's handling of the scene is as quiet and understated in *The Immortal Story* as it was flamboyant and hyperbolic in *Citizen Kane*—we do not see Clay dying, or dead, neither do we see the shell falling, whereas both Kane and the crashing paperweight were photographed in extreme close-up. One might say that the latter film is evidence of Welles's achieving both supreme esthetic simplicity and philosophical acceptance of death. McBride argues that the two scenes have quite different, indeed opposed, meanings. His reading is suggestive, yet the shock of recognition we experience when we see Clay's shell still gently rocking on the floor of the porch establishes this minor-key reprise of one of Welles's earliest evocations of death as the most effective reaffirmation of the permanence of the theme in his work.

All of Welles's films, as he himself has often pointed out, are about some kind of search, but it is a search that always ends in failure. Interestingly, the theme of the search is related, in Welles's mind, to the image of the labyrinth: "If we are looking for something, the labyrinth is the most favorable location for a search." A paradoxical remark, and a revealing one. It would seem logical to see the labyrinth as the *least* favorable location for a search, unless, like Welles, one is interested only in the search, not in the finding. What Welles did not point out in the interview from which the remark is quoted is that the labyrinth is also a trap, with the Minotaur—that is, death—waiting at its end. Welles's heroes are all caught up in a maze, whether it be a physical place, a dramatic situation, or both. They are prisoners of themselves and of their pasts, a confinement symbolized by Kane's Xanadu, the Ambersons' mansion, Macbeth's or Henry IV's castles. Only one of the heroes, the atypical O'Hara, breaks away from the maze as he leaves the dying Bannisters behind in the Hall of Mirrors.

Plot-wise, Welles's favorite version of the trap is the frame-up: Gettys frames Kane; Elsa Bannister frames O'Hara; Quinlan frames the Mexican boy—as he has framed many a suspect in the past—and later tries to frame Vargas's wife; Iago frames Desdemona; Macbeth frames the grooms for the murder of Duncan, then is himself caught in an elaborate plot arranged by fate through the witches' tragically misleading prophecies; and K in *The Trial* is the victim of what could be called the essential frame-up (in the sense Camus used the word "essential" in reference to Kafka's novel).

Most of the victims, however, are really guilty, although not necessarily of the crimes they are being framed for (O'Hara, while not a murderer, accepts being a party to fraud and embezzlement). The exceptions are two comparatively minor female characters (there are only two *major* female characters in Welles's work, and they, Elsa Bannister and Lady Macbeth, are thoroughly evil), whose very innocence condemns them to remain minor in Welles's scheme of things. Of K, who may seem to be the one totally innocent hero in his work, Welles has said: "I consider him guilty," a judgment made all the more significant by the fact that, when asked to elaborate, Welles failed to support it coherently ("Who knows? He belongs to something that represents evil and that, at the same time, is part of him. He is not guilty as accused, but he is guilty all the same. He belongs to a guilty society, he collaborates with it. In any case, I am not a Kafka analyst"). If the statement is to be taken as more than a glib paradox meant to tease the interviewer (who had just described K as "a sort of Prometheus"), then it applies to any ordinary human being, and the film becomes an indictment of the common man. While Welles's other heroes are guilty of setting themselves above and apart from society, its codes and its laws, K is guilty of doing just the opposite. In other words, there is no escaping guilt, and evil is universal. Innocence, in Welles's films, is at best a lost state, recollected and yearned for, never a reality.

In the last analysis, the secret of the fascination exerted by Welles's cinema lies in the extraordinary tension between its stylistic dynamism and its thematic despondency. The photographic pyrotechnics, the jolting transitions, the breathtaking camera moves, the audiovisual clutter, the frantic activity provide a constant sensory—and sensual—stimulation that irradiates the pervasive gloom. *Touch of Evil,* for instance, may be Welles's bleakest film in terms both of the moral universe it depicts and the physical location in which it is set, is also his most exhilarating to watch. The physical excitement it generates is not unlike that derived from the great moments in Hollywood musicals. Indeed, characters in the film often behave as though they were about to break into some kind of futuristic dance routine: Menzies's hop as he gleefully extols Quinlan's investigative acumen ("He did it! He did it again!"), Grandi and his boys' clownish gesticulating as they fuss with a hairpiece in the middle of an empty moonlit square, the motel clerk's bizarrely jerky movements of panic that make him look like an automaton going haywire. *Touch of Evil* is replete with electrifying kinetic shocks: the brutal, lightning-quick thrust of the camera following Vargas as he wildly careens through a bar, knocking over people and furniture; a car suddenly wrenching itself away from the foreground and the fixed camera to plunge into the deep-focus, wide-angled perspective of an empty street; the hectic editing of the final sequence, with its constant aural-visual jump-cutting from Quinlan and Menzies to Vargas's lumbering progress as he follows them through Welles's most cluttered location set ever. This style is meant to deprive the spectator of his bearings and immerse him in nightmare and chaos. The paradox is that, while it brilliantly succeeds in doing so, our actual response is not uneasiness or despondency but joy.

Welles's claim that he is an optimist is supported by the experience of watching his films more than by what they are about. He betrayed his ambivalence when he once remarked: "I don't think that an artist may take total despair as a subject; we are too close to it in daily life." It comes as no surprise that, to Welles, "daily life" is not the domain of the work of art and that artists should not acknowledge the existence of despair among us. "A film is never a report on life," he also said. "A film is a dream." Like the painter of fakes in *F for Fake,* the only reality Welles is ultimately concerned with is the reality of art, and despair cannot prevail in an artist's vision that sifts the raw material of life to turn it into poetry in motion, that weaves a "ribbon of dreams" out of the ever-present fear of decay and death.

57. *Robert Wise* (1914)

1944—*The Curse of the Cat People* (codirector: Gunther V. Fritsch); *Mademoiselle Fifi;* 1945—*The Body Snatcher;* 1946—*A Game of Death; Criminal Court;* 1947—*Born to Kill;* 1948—*Mystery in Mexico; Blood on the Moon;* 1949—*The Set-Up;* 1950—*Three Secrets; Two Flags West;* 1951—*The House on Telegraph Hill; The Day the Earth Stood Still;* 1952—*The Captive City; Something for the Birds;* 1953—*Destination Gobi; The Desert Rats; So Big;* 1954—*Executive Suite;* 1956—*Helen of Troy; Tribute to a Bad Man; Somebody Up There Likes Me;* 1957—*This Could Be the Night; Until They Sail;* 1958—*Run Silent, Run Deep; I Want to Live;* 1959—*Odds Against Tomorrow;* 1961—*West Side Story* (codirector: Jerome Robbins); 1962—*Two for the Seesaw;* 1963—*The Haunting;* 1965—*The Sound of Music;* 1966—*The Sand Pebbles;* 1968—*Star!* 1971—*The Andromeda Strain;* 1973—*Two People;* 1975—*The Hindenburg;* 1977—*Audrey Rose;* 1979—*Star Trek—The Motion Picture*

Robert Wise belongs to the last generation of directors trained within the studio system, and who, unlike the "star" directors of the sixties and seventies, slowly rose to prominence from lowly positions (in his case, odd jobs around the cutting room).

Indeed, Wise never became a star and, in true "Hollywood professional" fashion, always kept a fairly low profile, even at the height of box-office and/or critical success. He is a highly competent film maker whose prime commitment, however, has always been to his commercial career rather than to personal expression. His progress from the small-budget pictures of his beginnings to the multi-million-dollar musicals of the sixties testify to his concentration on upward mobility. While equating this concentration with a lack of artistic integrity would be unfair and naive, it is a fact that Wise's more creative efforts predate his blockbusting period and that his films tended to grow more impersonal and vapid as they grew bigger.

Wise's versatility is impressive (he has made films in practically every known genre), but it is *mere* versatility; no unifying vision underlies it. One would be hard pressed to find a link between *The Set-Up* and *The Sound of Music* beyond the fact that the same man directed both. A thematic analysis of Wise's work could dredge up little more than an occasional and not particularly significant similarity (the theme of racism in both *Odds Against Tomorrow* and *West Side Story;* the use of the science-fiction film as cautionary tale in *The Day the Earth Stood Still* and *The Andromeda Strain*). Neither is there a distinctive Wise style, although a number of his early films did exhibit enough stylishness to justify expectations that his later work failed to satisfy. He seems to have a preference for medium-close shots and low-angle camera placements and for cutting rather than dissolving from one scene to the next. More generally, he relies upon editing a great deal (*The Set-Up* is the most striking example). He has always been interested in the creative use of sound (which plays an essential dramatic role in *The Haunting*) and says he always tries to have his set designers and cinematographers work together, which makes sense, is rather unusual, and may or may not have a visible impact upon the finished product. In interviews, Wise likes to emphasize his preoccupation with realism and authenticity—whether in filming a fist fight (in *Blood on the Moon*, his first Western) from which the hero emerges, although victorious, almost as battered as his opponent; or doing extensive research (e.g., on small-time prize fighting for *The Set-Up;* on the Barbara Graham case for *I Want to Live*); or insisting that the submarine set for *Run Silent, Run Deep* be built the exact size of a real sub. All of which, ultimately, doesn't add up to very much, although it does confirm that Wise is a conscientious craftsman.

Wise was twenty-six and had been a full-fledged editor for only two years when Welles asked the studio to assign him to *Citizen Kane* (the reason, Wise speculates, was that Welles wanted someone his own age). Although Wise's later work as a director can hardly be described as Wellesian, his use of cutting and sound in some of his own films may have been influenced by their momentous collaboration. In 1942 Wise was faced with the nightmarish responsibility of editing *The Magnificent Ambersons* after Welles had left for South America and then of making drastic cuts and shooting some additional footage after the film's disastrous previews. As Charles Higham wrote in his book on Welles: "No one in the Mercury group recalls exactly who directed what in the picture." (As evidence of the continuing confusion, Higham attributes the closing scene to Wise, while Wise denies shooting it and attributes it to Freddie Fleck.) No matter who directed what, the non-Wellesian footage is easily identifiable, as no one involved attempted to duplicate Welles's style; the visual flatness of the additions is the obvious clue to their spuriousness. Whatever portion of the film Wise directed— and he must have hated doing it—it was as inauspicious a directorial debut as one could imagine.

Wise's two horror pictures for Val Lewton, *The Curse of the Cat People* and *The*

Body Snatcher are generally held in high esteem today, especially the latter, which some critics consider his best picture (it is Wise's own favorite among his early films). There is no denying that *The Body Snatcher* is an unusually literate and carefully made picture. Its superbly photographed and edited climax (a hearse rushing through a stormy night, its half-crazed driver hearing the mocking voice of the dead man he is transporting) reaches heights of genuine gothic horror seldom equaled in a Hollywood film. Most of the film, however, is lifeless and strangely lacking in suspense. James Agee found it "a little dull and bookish," and the observation is still valid today. Was that, one wonders, the price to be paid for bringing intelligence and literacy to the horror genre? Or is it simply that British period pieces cramped Lewton's style (the same tasteful lifelessness mars Mark Robson's *Bedlam*, which was also set in late eighteenth-century England, while Jacques Tourneur's Lewton films were completely free from it.)

The Curse of the Cat People, although uneven, is a much more interesting film and an altogether exceptional item in Wise's filmography. This first directorial assignment was by no means entirely "his" film; indeed, if DeWitt Bodeen's statement that about 40 percent of it was directed by Gunther Fritsch (whom Wise replaced after twenty days' shooting) is accurate, then the two men should share the praise as well as the criticism. It may be tempting to assume that the weaker portions (e.g., early scenes with the children or with the schoolteacher) were Fritsch's, yet he was dismissed for his slowness, *not* incompetence, and the weak scenes certainly do not amount to 40 percent of this remarkable film. The truth is that it is impossible to distinguish between the two, which should not be too upsetting; for this is a case in which the producer's personality takes precedence over the director's. As Tom Milne wrote in a reappraisal of the film: "It is undoubtedly Lewton's most personal production, drawing into one tight knot all the dreams, fears and obsessions that turn this disparate series of eleven films into an *oeuvre.*"

The story of *The Curse of the Cat People* is the kind of fragile, ambiguous fantasy whose built-in resistance to the literalness of the filmic image presents an awesome challenge to the film maker. Bodeen's script (the end of which was filmed but then discarded and rewritten by Lewton himself) is made up of two distinct and almost completely independent plot lines, which it was the director's difficult task to balance and harmonize as best he could. One is a sequel to *Cat People* (using the same actors—Simone Simon, Kent Smith, Jane Randolph—in the leading grown-up roles) with Irena—the "cat woman" who died tragically at the end of the earlier film—returning as a ghost to befriend her husband's daughter Amy. The other plot involves an eccentric old woman, a former actress, who lives in a rambling Victorian mansion nearby with her evil-looking, enigmatic daughter (whom she claims is not her daughter but an impostor). The "horror element" is totally absent from the ghost story, since Irena is a thoroughly friendly ghost—a startling reversal, incidentally, from the live Irena of *Cat People*—and the menace has been shifted to the "old dark house" part of the story. The two plots, however, are closely related thematically. Both are based upon ambiguity and uncertainty: is the ghost "real"? are the old lady's stories true? Moreover, the old woman befriends Amy just as the ghost does and obviously for similar reasons: to the old actress, Amy is the substitute for a daughter she lost when the child was Amy's age; to Irena, she represents the child she might have had had she not died (since Amy's father was her husband once). Amy keeps shuttling between the two fantasy worlds of her own house and the old lady's, thus providing the necessary link between the two story lines. These intersect twice, in interesting ways. When

Amy first meets the old woman, the latter gives her a ring; Amy later wishes upon the ring, and her wish (that she get a friend) comes true: Irena materializes. Thus, story B turns out to be the condition for story A to take place. The second point of intersection is a kind of reversal of the first one. At the end, when the daughter wants to kill Amy, the little girl calls out to her friend, and Irena appears superimposed on the other woman, who then gives up her murderous project.

Although Irena's appearances are supposed to be a figment of Amy's imagination (based upon a photograph of her she saw), the treatment of all their scenes together contradicts this premise; most of the things Irena does and says in those scenes could not possibly be "imagined" by a child. The "actuality" of her presence is awkwardly acknowledged by the direction in the two scenes in which a third person (Kent Smith) is present. In the first one, he asks his daughter if she can see Irena in the garden. She can (so can we), and she says yes. He is outraged at her "lie" *but never looks in the ghost's direction,* so that, even if he could see Irena, he would not. In the second scene, the last one of the film, which is intended to suggest that the father's affection for his daughter has at last taken over from the ghost's, he claims that he now can see Irena, thus recognizing Amy's right to her own fantasy world. (His acknowledgment of Irena's presence, however, is really a way of getting rid of her; in order to go away, she has to be there in the first place!) For the close of the picture, Wise cuts from a shot of the father and daughter walking back into the house to one of the ghost slowly disappearing. For the first time in the film, a shot of Irena cannot be interpreted as Amy's perception of her, since Amy has (physically and symbolically) turned her back on her, and Irena is now alone in the garden. No one in the film "sees" the content of this shot, only the spectator does. Since it cannot be a "point-of-view" shot, it has to be an "objective" one. Thus the direction in effect tells us that the ghost did exist after all. The directorial inconsistencies are the inevitable corollary of the medium's inability to equivocate. But the film's contradictions are part of its charm; like Amy, we want to believe in Irena, and we are grateful for any encouragement to do so against our "best" (i.e., rational) judgment.

The balance of Wise's RKO period includes such rarely seen films as *Mademoiselle Fifi,* a period piece (also produced by Lewton) whose script combined de Maupassant's eponymous short story with his famous *Boule de suif; A Game of Death* (the first remake of *The Most Dangerous Game*); the controversial *Born to Kill,* which most critics dismiss as inconsequential but some consider one of the forties' best *films noirs;* and *Blood on the Moon,* Wise's first "A"-budget picture, which William Everson describes as having some of the starkness and austerity of the silent William S. Hart films." *The Set-Up,* Wise's last RKO film and his first major critical success, was made at the time of Howard Hughes's takeover of the studio, and Wise credits Dore Schary—then still in charge of production—for convincing Hughes to let him direct this pet project of his. The earlier success of Robert Rossen's *Body and Soul* probably influenced the decision to make a boxing film, despite the comparative unconventionality of Wise's project.

The film eschews the melodramatics and moralizing of *Body and Soul* and Mark Robson's *Champion* (which was released within a month of *The Set-Up*). Both are rags-to-riches, rise-and-fall morality plays about unscrupulous—but charismatic—heroes driven and ultimately destroyed (or almost destroyed) by ambition and greed. The only thing that drives the hero of *The Set-Up* is a grim determination to survive. Wise's film focuses exclusively on the seamy side of boxing, the dark underside that was barely glimpsed amid the glamour of the other two films. It is a simpler but in many ways a more honest film than either. When John Garfield defies the mob at the end of *Body and Soul,* it doesn't cost him anything for the simple reason that the film ends on his gallant flourish. When Robert Ryan refuses to take a dive in *The Set-Up,* he knows what the consequences are, and his ordeal at the hands of the mob (they crush his hand so that he won't be able to fight again) has the inevitability of tragedy. As a consequence, critics—unlike audiences—tended to prefer *The Set-Up* to the other two films and praised its uncompromising realism. Wise's work, however, is a little too self-consciously down-beat to be completely convincing. Moreover, its strict adherence to the unities, its stylized dialogue, its virtuoso use of editing in the fight sequences, and emphasis on quasi-expressionistic reaction shots of the crowd all add up to a somewhat mannered and artificial style. These are the very qualities for which *The Set-Up* is usually praised, and there is no denying their strength, but the total effect is closer to the enhanced, dreamlike realism of *film noir* than to documentary accuracy.

Wise was kept very active by the studios throughout the fifties, and his output testifies to his versatility. The eighteen films he directed during that busy period include three war pictures, two Westerns, two soap operas, two comedies, two biographical dramas, one science-fiction film, and one costume spectacle. Several among the earlier of these films were curiously derivative. *Three Secrets* was obviously intended to exploit in a dramatic vein the gimmick that had worked so well in Joseph L. Mankiewicz's comedy, *A Letter to Three Wives,* the year before. Both films are about three married women kept in suspense by delayed information. In the earlier film, the suspense revolves around the question: which of the three husbands has eloped with another woman? In Wise's film it becomes: whose child has been killed in a plane crash? *Two Flags West,* based on a story by Frank Nugent, bears similarities to John Ford's *Fort Apache* (which was written by Nugent). *The Desert Rats* was Fox's companion piece—with James Mason cast again as Rommel—to their own highly successful *The Desert Fox* (directed by Henry Hathaway).

There were a few mildly interesting items in the grab bag of Wise's minor efforts of the fifties: *Destination Gobi,* a tongue-in-cheek war adventure; the third version of *So Big,* a tale of mother love and sacrifice in the grand tearjerking tradition, providing unique instance of Americana in Wise's work; and *Something for the Birds,* a quaint comedy (one of I. A. L. Diamond's pre-Billy Wilder scripts) dealing with, among other things, ornithology and party crashing in Washington.

A cut or two above these was *Odds Against Tomorrow,* Wise's last film of the decade and the first one he produced himself. Basically a traditional caper story, and in some ways reminiscent of *The Asphalt Jungle,* the film cleverly exploited a number of then new trends: extensive location shooting (New York City and upstate New York); a semi-improvised jazz score (by John Lewis and the Modern Jazz Quartet); and the theme of racial prejudice, which had become fashionable with such films as *A Man Is Ten Feet Tall* and *The Defiant Ones.* (Indeed, Wise recalls that the script's first draft so much resembled the latter that he decided upon major alterations, turning the optimistic moral of Kramer's film upside down in order to show that "hatred destroys.") The caper eventually fails, not because of external circumstances but as a result of psychological tensions among the participants; a white man's racist distrust of his black partner leads to their bungling the job and even killing each other. It may be ethically dubious to make a plea for racial tolerance by showing a criminal act being defeated by racism; it is a fact, however, that audiences invariably wish to see bank robbers get away with it; so that, by rooting for the robbers, they ipso facto espouse the film's antiracism, a simple but shrewd maneuver on Wise's part.

The highlights of Wise's career in the fifties are arguably the science-fiction classic *The Day the Earth Stood Still* and *Executive Suite,* although his prestige hits, *Somebody Up There Likes Me* and *I Want to Live!,* probably were the most highly praised. The latter two were portentously somber screen biographies in which Wise managed to avoid only some of the pitfalls of the genre. They both relied—unlike any other Wise film—on a virtuoso performance, in each case by a star exhibiting more energy than restraint. Any evaluation of *I Want to Live!* depends to a large extent upon the viewer's response to Susan Hayward, the all-stops-pulled, anything-for-a-cry specialist of heart-tugging biographical roles whose florid emoting had won her no fewer than four Academy Award nominations before she finally received the Oscar for this film for her portrayal of Barbara Graham. A painstakingly researched—although not necessarily accurate or impartial—dramatization of a famous criminal case, *I Want to Live!* is a passionate and often impressive indictment of the death penalty, which, however, tends to confuse the two distinct issues of the legitimacy of capital punishment and of Graham's disputed but probable guilt (Wise arbitrarily holds that she was framed), so that the film's stand becomes somewhat muddled. (The impact of Wise's stark, uncompromising re-creation of the gas chamber execution is undeniable, however.)

In *Somebody Up There Likes Me,* the life story of Rocky Graziano, Wise's stylistic strategy was, apparently, to combine the frantic pace and ebullient grittiness of old Warners plebeian actioners with the histrionics peculiar to many fifties movies. As a result, the numerous clichés—derived from a number of subgenres the film draws upon in chronicling Graziano's stormy adolescence and rise to fame—are magnified rather than rejuvenated. The veneer of realism and accuracy is belied by the slam-bang, imitation-Kazan direction. A street-gang fight on a rooftop is so choreographically stylized that, in retrospect, Wise seems to be warming up for *West Side Story.* Paul Newman's performance (his second screen appearance and first starring role), although enormously lively and highly personal, is broad to the point of caricature, the kind that once caused eyebrows to be raised at the mere mention of the Method. (Newman's Billy the Kid in Arthur Penn's *The Left-Handed Gun* two years later exhibits an obvious kinship to his Graziano, but the similarities in both character and performance emphasize the gap between Penn's creative refining of a still-wild talent and Wise's mere showcasing of the actor's raw material.) Adding to the general impression of sketchy realism is the almost total absence of a period look; although the action takes place in the late thirties and the forties, the entire film has a uniformly mid/late fifties look about it (the most notable attempt at a period flavor is Newman's wearing a pork pie hat with its brim upturned during the war years). This perfunctory approach to the near past was, of course, standard movie procedure until the nostalgia craze of the sixties, when production designers and art directors were encouraged to develop a nearly archeological attention to period detail. It was not perceived as a weakness by critics at the time, and it may be unfair to bring it up against Wise from the vantage point of the eighties. Still, certain conventions are not as readily accepted in a film like *Somebody Up There Likes Me* as they might have been in earlier productions. It was made at a transitional point in the evolution both of the American cinema and of Wise's own career. Films were becoming less simple and direct but not necessarily more subtle. Wise was beginning to overextend his talent, turning his back on the very real but modest ambitions of his early films and reaching for broader horizons. *Somebody Up There Likes Me* is symptomatic of these growing pains in its failure both to recapture the flavor of the classic Hollywood boxing films (including Wise's own *The Set-Up*) and to come up with a genuinely new, personal approach.

The Day the Earth Stood Still, conversely, resembles—in spirit if not in content—Wise's early work. A small picture done with skill and honesty, it courageously set out to make a serious statement within a genre without any tradition or respectability. It is, in effect, an antiracist parable and as such can claim a thematic relationship to West Side Story and Odds Against Tomorrow.

Chronologically one of the first entries in the science-fiction cycle that was to become so popular in the fifties, The Day the Earth Stood Still seemed to promise more exciting developments than the genre would actually yield. It has often been noted that an era dominated by McCarthyism and the Cold War was ripe for a type of movie obsessed with "alien" menaces, be they in the guise of extraterrestrials or giant insects. The originality of Wise's film lies in the fact that the aliens it depicts are benevolent, not hostile, and that it reminds us that the real menace is man's own destructive instinct. The aliens' benevolence, however, is far from unmitigated, and the film is actually closer to the mainstream of fifties science fiction than has generally been acknowledged.

Klaatu, the visitor from outer space who assumes a human appearance in an attempt to communicate with men, is a vaguely Christ-like figure (he calls himself Carpenter), but the message he brings is more in the nature of a warning, and even a threat, than one of love and peace. His mission is to convince men to stop fooling around with nuclear weapons, not that his people care about the future of life on earth but because they are afraid of the future consequences to themselves. In the closing sequence, before returning to whatever galaxy he came from, Klaatu explains that they have created a highly sophisticated breed of robots that patrol the universe in search of planets whose war technology is a potential threat to other worlds. Such planets, if they fail to heed the warning, are destroyed in the interest of the rest of the universe. In other words, Klaatu speaks softly, but he carries a very big stick. The fact that his people believe they have a right to annihilate entire worlds on the ground that they might become hostile some day suggests that their advanced stage of evolution, although it has eliminated war, still leaves something to be desired as far as ethics are concerned. The policing of the universe Klaatu describes is imperialistic in nature, even if it is conducted in a defensive rather than expansionist spirit. Moreover, the unlikelihood (in 1951) of men being able to bring nuclear warfare to other inhabited worlds makes those extraterrestrials appear suspiciously overzealous—not to mention a little foolish—in their alarmist vigilantism. It is strange that no leftist critic has ever thought of drawing the obvious parallel between their attitude and the United States' habit of waging war (Korea, Vietnam) in the name of world peace. Nowhere in the film does Wise suggest that the aliens' intentions are anything but noble and admirable. The villains are the authorities (they can think of nothing but capturing Klaatu dead or alive), and the extraterrestrial—whom soldiers eventually shoot quite unnecessarily—is cast as the heroic victim of men's hopeless stupidity. This grim view is typical of the period (the film has been cited as a forerunner to Close Encounters of the Third Kind, yet its mood is totally alien to Spielberg's irrepressible optimism). Like most fifties science-fiction films, The Day the Earth Stood Still is based on the concept of the Menace, a menace from the outside that is a projection of a menace from within. The film strongly suggests that the human race will disregard the warning, thus bringing destruction upon itself. In the symbolic closing shot, when the receding spaceship is about to vanish in the night sky, the tiny white dot it has become suddenly zooms back toward us to form the words "the End."

Although it never achieved the critical status of some other films by Wise, Executive

Suite may be, in terms of pure craftsmanship, his masterpiece. His tight, authoritative direction of Ernest Lehman's sturdily constructed screenplay made a remarkably functional and efficient use of a once-in-a-lifetime cast of major stars (William Holden, Fredric March, Barbara Stanwyck, Walter Pidgeon) and first-rate supporting players. John Houseman, who produced the film, commented in a 1975 interview: "Different directors had different strengths. If you wanted a very accomplished technician, one with great skill in cutting and shooting, you'd choose Bobby Wise for *Executive Suite,* which required a great deal of skillful and accurate shooting and editing to hold the thing together." *Executive Suite* was the third in a series of highly successful pictures Houseman produced for MGM in the fifties. Like the earlier *The Bad and the Beautiful* and the later *The Cobweb,* it deals with the interpersonal conflicts within a group of people thrown together by their work, and its central theme is ambition, the fight for power (which was also the case, of course, of the Houseman-produced *Julius Caesar*). *Executive Suite* may paint a somewhat naive, schematized, or romanticized picture of power struggles in the world of big business; still it is one of the more complex and dramatically satisfying ever presented by the movies. Subtle characterization (even June Allyson in her perennial role as the perfect wife and mother escapes stereotyping) more than makes up for some dramatic contrivance, and the overall balance of the performances (with eight or nine characters of about equal importance) is quite exceptional. Characters and performances are indeed what one remembers best about the film, especially, perhaps, the supporting roles (Paul Douglas, Dean Jagger, Nina Foch, and, above all, Louis Calhern as a suave, ever-conniving scoundrel whose ploys eventually backfire on him). In one of the best moments in his entire career, William Holden, addressing the board of directors of the furniture company whose top designer he is, makes an impassioned plea for corporate pride against profit-minded, assembly-line shoddiness that climaxes with his dramatic shattering of a piece of furniture ("One of our products!"). The scene is emblematic: the ideal of good craftsmanship it expresses is best represented in the motion picture industry by products like *Executive Suite.* Unlike the chair Holden breaks to make his point, the film has been crafted never to fall to pieces.

The musical was just about the only genre Wise had never tackled when he was approached by Mirisch Pictures and Seven Arts to produce and direct the film version of *West Side Story.* The choice is indicative of the status Wise had by then achieved in the industry but may otherwise seem rather baffling; not only did Wise lack any previous experience with musicals, but he was noted for his reliance upon editing, whereas the best approach to filming musical numbers has always proved to be based upon long takes and fluid camera movements, with cuts kept as few and unobstrusive as possible. Such stylistic considerations, however, must have carried little weight beside Wise's reputation not only as a highly competent technician but also as the director of films dealing with racism (*Odds Against Tomorrow*) or juvenile delinquency in New York City (*Somebody Up There Likes Me*).

West Side Story was packaged as the first "socially conscious" musical, a work of art with "relevance." It was destined to become—as Pauline Kael called it in her refreshing, although overstated, debunking of its pretentions—"a great musical for people who don't like musicals," just as *An American in Paris* was ten years earlier (or as *High Noon* and *Shane* are great Westerns for people who don't like Westerns). In *An American in Paris,* the appeal to middlebrow snobbism was purely esthetic (i.e., musical and pictorial); in *West Side Story,* it is both esthetic (ballet; an intermittently operatic score) and sociological (the slums; street gangs; racial tensions). Both films received the same kind of accolades: a host of Academy Awards, rave reviews from "serious" critics. Both films are indeed exceptional but frustratingly uneven (the former achieves greatness only in its final ballet, the latter in three or four sequences at most) and as such decidedly inferior to a score of more traditional musicals.

West Side Story may be one of the better films derived from a Broadway musical, but its kind of achievement pales beside such masterpieces of the *movie* musical as *Singin' in the Rain* or *The Band Wagon. Singin' in the Rain* is one of the most original musicals to come out of Hollywood, but its makers went to a great deal of trouble to camouflage its originality, dressing it up with so many clichés and conventions that it seemed a distillation of all the musicals ever made. In *West Side Story,* on the other hand, we are constantly reminded of the daring of the project; the originality is so strained and self-conscious that the production is ultimately defeated by its very ambition. The stage show, moreover, had its deficiencies—a serious dichotomy between the vitality and wit of the satirical numbers and the stilted pretentiousness of the Romeo and Juliet romance with its bland dialogue and uninspired love songs—which the filmization only succeeded in magnifying, thus coming dangerously close to ludicrousness when it is supposed to be at its most pathetic.

The integration of choreography to the urban landscape, which is the film's major esthetic ambition, is successful as far as it goes, but it just doesn't go far enough. Wise and Robbins always seem on the verge of achieving a miraculous fusion between the convention of balletic expression and the concrete realism of street life, but whenever the miracle materializes, it is promptly snatched away, as though too fragile to be sustained. Thus the opening sequence, with the Jets strolling down the block, alternately breaking into tentative dance steps, then falling back upon walking, symbolically spells out the show's entire program of teases and frustrations.

Before becoming engulfed in the anonymity of blockbuster manufacturing, Wise had the time to direct two "small" black-and-white pictures, *Two for the Seesaw* and *The Haunting.* The former was mere canned theater, but the latter is arguably the most interesting of his post-*West Side Story* efforts. Wise's first "horror" film since his Lewton days, *The Haunting* returned to the "old dark house" motif that had provided the suspense in *The Curse of the Cat People* and, like the earlier film, emphasized the psychological element, preserving a basic ambiguity as to how much of the supernatural happenings are real and how much created in the heroine's imagination. Considered purely as a haunted-house yarn, the film is among the best of its genre. The house itself, the obligatory New England mansion, is appropriately rambling and ominous, without some of the more obvious gothic trappings, and David Boulton's heavily shaded cinematography is not unworthy of the great Nicholas Musuraca. But it is Wise's use of the sound track that makes the film truly exceptional. The supernatural presence is manifested only by means of a variety of noises—poundings, moans, screeches— and violent gusts of wind, which prove more effective than any ghostly apparition. What prevents *The Haunting* from being the masterpiece it might have been is its clumsy characterization, a clumsiness made all the worse by naive attempts at psychological subtlety. The two central female characters, played by Julie Harris and Claire Bloom, are complex in a conventional, unconvincing way, and the suggestion of a lesbian attraction (that may or may not develop into a relationship) between them seems irrelevant, a gratuitous attempt at sneaking an "adult" theme into the script (Bloom's lesbian tendencies are more or less lumped together with a talent for ESP to connote weirdness, which is an indication of how adult the approach really is). There is something irritating about a film that tries to be smarter than its own genre and fails. The failure in *The Haunting* underscores the genre conventions the film was intended to transcend.

A complete commercial flop, *The Haunting* is followed, in Wise's filmography, by the film that was to become the top grossing motion picture of all time, a record it held until the phenomenal superhits of the seventies came along. This unprecedented financial career is the only exceptional thing about *The Sound of Music*. It is not even an exceptionally bad film, and although the commercial triumph of mediocrity is always distressing, one must resist the temptation to adjust the criticism to the success, as though the film had to be as awful as it was profitable. Wise was no less the professional when doing *The Sound of Music* than he was with other films, but some material seems to impose its own schlock treatment, and the Trapp family saga (already the topic of a couple of German films before being turned into a Broadway musical) decidedly belongs in that category. Wise's responsibility lies more in his decision to take on the project (originally scheduled for William Wyler) than in his handling of the direction.

It is ironic that Wise's next—and last—supermusical, *Star!* proved as disastrous at the box office as *The Sound of Music* had been successful, especially in view of the fact that, despite serious and ultimately fatal flaws, it was on the whole a much more enjoyable effort. One of the very few sixties musicals to be written directly for the screen, thus eschewing the safety of a presold property, it aroused the naive hope of a return to *original* film musicals; although Wise had hedged his bet (or thought he had) by patterning the show after *Funny Girl* in an attempt to do for Gertrude Lawrence what the Broadway hit had done for Fanny Brice. Musical biographies, however, are a hybrid, notoriously hazardous genre, and *Star!* did not avoid any of its pitfalls. The film opens promisingly enough, à la *Citizen Kane*, with a newsreel account of Lawrence's career, and the reconstruction of English music-hall shows and reviews of her early career is done with extraordinary care and evocative power. As the film drags through its 175 minutes, however, and Lawrence's not especially engrossing sentimental problems take over, the lack of a strong dramatic backbone becomes increasingly evident. Most of the last hour or so seems pointless and feels interminable. Excessive length also plagued *The Sand Pebbles,* eventually edited down to 155 minutes, which made the sprawling narrative even more confused.

The consequences of *Star!'*s failure at the box office went beyond Wise's (or Andrews's) career. Fox had hoped for a hit of the magnitude of *West Side Story* or even *Sound of Music,* and the film was promoted accordingly (one may recall that advance booking for the roadshow presentation started some sixteen months before the scheduled release date). When the expected crowds failed to materialize, the film was withdrawn and then rereleased a year later, again unsuccessfully, in a two-hour version and under a different title. *Star!* was instrumental in bringing the cycle of supermusicals (and, more generally, of multi-million-dollar productions) to a close, at least for quite some years. By the mid-seventies, of course, inflated budgets were back in fashion, and, interestingly, history was to repeat itself for Wise when *The Hindenburg* ("Two years in the making at a cost of $15,000,000" as its posters proclaimed) failed to break even at the box office.

Like the earlier film, *The Hindenburg* failed because of an initial misjudgment of the dramatic potential of its subject matter. As a disaster film, *The Hindenburg* had the initial handicap of dealing with a disaster that was over in a few minutes. To fill up the two hours leading to the Lakehurst crash, Wise opted for the mystery angle. But just as the excitement in *Star!* was not Lawrence's love life but the re-creation of legendary stage shows, the airship itself is the attraction of *The Hindenburg,* and one finds it difficult to work up an interest in the question of who (if anybody) destroyed it. Both films are caught up in the fascination exerted by artifacts of the past but are unable to sustain our curiosity for them.

Wise's finest films all have a contemporary setting, while the ones set in the past (with the very early exception of *The Body Snatcher*) are all more or less seriously flawed. Not surprisingly, therefore, his best post-1965 effort is *The Andromeda Strain,* a science-fiction story.

Like *The Day the Earth Stood Still,* although in a different way (and with a vastly greater budget), *The Andromeda Strain* deliberately sets itself apart from run-of-the-mill science-fiction movie fare. "Seriousness" here is manifested not only by the eschewing of some of the more obvious genre clichés but also by a rather pontificating insistence on scientific and technological accuracy. No other film, perhaps, contains so many shots of data flashing on computer screens or so much dialogue whose sole purpose is to translate said data into layman's language. Characterization is minimal, since the function of the main characters (a team of scientists) is almost entirely a decoding one. What makes *The Andromeda Strain* stand out among Wise's late films is the electrifying sense of tension and suspense it initially conjures and manages to sustain for the better part of its running time, although unfortunately not quite to the end. In fact, the excitement generated by the opening sequences—the hush-hush rounding up of scientists snatched away from work or home by ominously noncommittal secret agents; the search through a village (with very effective use of the split screen) whose inhabitants have all been killed by a mysterious disease—is too intense for the film's own good, for they promise much more than will eventually be delivered. It is only in the last third or so that Wise discards the pretense of seriousness and builds up to a typical space-opera climax in which one man, Flash Gordon-style, races against the clock to save the world from annihilation and succeeds, quite literally, at the last second. This ludicrously artificial suspense, although well handled, is quite different from the suspense of the early scenes, which shows Wise at his very best. What he achieves in those fine moments is reminiscent of what he did in *Executive Suite.* It may seem a strange parallel, as the two films, at first glance, have absolutely nothing in common; yet, the pleasure experienced viewing them is quite similar in nature and quality, and the similarity, to the extent that the same causes produce the same effects, suggests the existence of others.

Underneath their totally different plots, characters, and conflicts, the two films share a common substructure. At the start, sudden, unexpected death (the chairman of the board's/the villagers') strikes, creating a menace for the immediate future (of the company/of the world). A flurry of activity ensues, as concerned individuals (the board members/the scientists) are contacted and brought together to deal with the situation. The objective is to restore a disrupted balance by getting rid of an undesirable element (the villainlike candidate for the chairmanship/the disease from outer space). At this point, of course, the details of the structure vary considerably; in *Executive Suite,* balance is upset by the disappearance of one element (the chairman) and the vacuum thus created, whereas, in *The Andromeda Strain,* it is upset by the addition of an element (the death-dealing organism from space). In one case, the undesirable element is a member of the group striving to restore order, while in the other, it lies outside the group and is of a completely different nature. But such inevitable (and superficial) variations do not invalidate the basic similitude of the two films' structures. It is reasonable to assume that Wise's directorial expertise in both cases derives from a natural affinity for the common pattern he was dealing with. Perhaps his training as a film editor made him a natural for this type of complex, fast-moving action involving many characters and a wide variety of points of view (indeed, the sharpness and bounce of the editing is a major quality in both films).

All this simply verifies that "mere craftsmen," like auteurs (along with practically everybody else), are better at doing certain things than they are at others. However, they usually lack the auteur's instinctive ability to identify his forte and exploit it artistically. Wise seems to stumble across germane material rather than to deliberately seek and mold it, which accounts for the hit-and-miss quality of his work. Unlike most auteurs, he doesn't repeat himself, but that is because he has little to repeat and doesn't quite realize what it is anyway. His eclecticism is a reflection of this fatal lack of awareness.

58. Fred Zinnemann (1907)

by JOHN FITZPATRICK

1934—*Redes* (Mexico; U.S., *The Wave*, 1937, codirector: Emilio Gómez Muriel); 1942—*Kid Glove Killer; Eyes in the Night;* 1944—*The Seventh Cross;* 1947—*My Brother Talks to Horses; Little Mr. Jim;* 1948—*The Search;* 1949—*Act of Violence;* 1950—*The Men;* 1951—*Teresa;* 1952—*High Noon;* 1953—*The Member of the Wedding; From Here to Eternity;* 1956—*Oklahoma!;* 1957—*A Hatful of Rain;* 1959—*The Nun's Story;* 1960—*The Sundowners;* 1964—*Behold a Pale Horse;* 1966—*A Man for All Seasons;* 1973—*The Day of the Jackal;* 1977—*Julia;* 1982—*Five Days One Summer*

Uncredited
1945—*The Clock* (Vincente Minnelli); 1958—*The Old Man and the Sea* (John Sturges; uncredited codirector: Henry King)

By conventional standards Fred Zinnemann must rank as the most honored American director of his period. His seven Oscar nominations (two awards) and his four citations from the New York Film Critics Circle are unexcelled in the postwar era, and he holds the D. W. Griffith Award of the Screen Directors Guild for lifetime achievement. Yet the absence of retrospective critical interest in Zinnemann's films has been noticeable, and the reaction to early honors correspondingly severe. Auteurists have dismissed him for pursuing precisely those Important Subjects that earned such esteem in the fifties and—more pertinently—for treating them in a flat, impersonal, "objective" style.

Zinnemann's decline in critical favor has roughly paralleled that of the other significant "establishment" directors, William Wyler and David Lean, and it is significant that all three experienced career difficulties in the seventies. With Wyler retired and Lean effectively sidelined by his own uncompromising perfectionism, Zinnemann, though he has completed three films since 1970, has had to bear the brunt of the attack on the "impersonals." Lacking both Wyler's intensity with actors and Lean's visual mastery, Zinnemann has been an easy target.

Nevertheless, the attack is in some ways surprising, for *thematically* Fred Zinnemann has always been one of the most personal and consistent of Hollywood directors. In this he stands at the opposite end of the spectrum from Wyler, who quite consciously subordinated his own concerns to the narrative demands of each particular property. For Zinnemann the individual conscience has always been his theme of choice. *The Seventh Cross* and *Julia* both concern individual resistance to Nazism, and every significant film between these two revolves around a crisis of personal conscience or identity— in painful growth (*The Men, The Member of the Wedding*), in conflict with society (*High Noon, A Man for All Seasons*), or in discord with threatening institutions (*From Here to Eternity, The Nun's Story*). Few directors have been so consistent. The problem is that Zinnemann's neutral style, with the stationary camera seemingly always at a safe middle distance, has not always been adequate to such interior subjects.

Zinnemann was born in Vienna on 29 April 1907. He studied music and law before pursuing film studies in Paris in 1928, making him one of the earliest "film school" directors. There followed a long apprenticeship in Berlin, where he worked with Billy Wilder and Robert Siodmak as assistant cameraman on *Menschen am Sonntag;* in Hollywood, where he served as an extra in *All Quiet on the Western Front;* and in other quarters of the film world. The most important influence was that of Robert Flaherty on a film that was never made, for in 1929 Zinnemann spent some months with the father of American documentary planning an essay on a Central Asian tribe. Soviet intransigence killed the project, but from this encounter Zinnemann took his lifelong aspiration for the Flaherty brand of humanistic documentary realism. Indeed *The Wave,* Zinnemann's first completed full-length film, is a Flaherty-like documentary, the product of a year spent with the fishermen of Vera Cruz.

From this effort Zinnemann moved to two-reelers, most notably in MGM's *Crime Does Not Pay* series, which also nurtured the talents of Jules Dassin, George Sidney, and Jacques Tourneur. Two "B" pictures followed before Zinnemann made his first significant feature, *The Seventh Cross,* in which the prevailing themes and problems of his entire career are immediately apparent. *The Seventh Cross* is a film of some courage, daring (in 1944) to treat of "good Germans" (albeit in a prewar setting). It concerns the escape of an anti-Nazi (Spencer Tracy) from a concentration camp and thus proposes a series of confrontations of conscience. Tracy—himself a sort of German conscience— seeks aid from strangers and former friends, thus presenting each one with a crisis of courage, a test that is passed most strikingly by the decent, timid, and (presumably) Jewish soul played by Hume Cronyn. Unfortunately the very daring of the project serves to inject it with a double dose of the sanctimoniousness that afflicted most Hollywood war propaganda. Zinnemann's aloofness was scarcely suited to overcome such an effect and resulted in an oddly muted film, wherein Spencer Tracy seems paralyzed and even a series of crucifixions (for the recaptured prisoners) fails to stand out from the murky gray background.

Still lacking a great commercial success, Zinnemann established his reputation in the emerging mode that came to be known in the late forties as semidocumentary, or even American neorealism. In practical terms this meant a turn toward down-beat subjects filmed on authentic locations with some use of nonprofessional players—in other words, the prevailing trend of the postwar era, in which Zinnemann was simply one of the early participants. These tactics have become so commonplace today and two of the fresh, new faces—Montgomery Clift and Marlon Brando—so familiar, that the early Zinnemann films no longer possess any special immediacy. Nevertheless, they made his reputation.

The Search is an odd amalgam of styles. Its best parts take their impact directly from the authentic locales—the bombed-out rubble of postwar Germany—in which orphaned children flee even their United Nations benefactors in silent fear. The scenes in which they escape from ambulances that (they believe) are returning to the gas chambers have a cold terror not easily replicable in any other setting. Yet the studio-made concentration camp flashbacks look every bit as synthetic as—and far less appropriate than—the sound-stage Germany of *The Seventh Cross*. Such failings, plus the sentimental narration and score, vitiate the power of the outdoor images and mark *The Search* as a film for its time only, rather than the enduring classic it was initially hailed to be.

More impressive is *The Men*, in which the carefully limited settings are under firmer directorial control. As the embittered paraplegic veteran, Marlon Brando in his first screen role makes an effective contrast with the other painfully adjusting patients in the real Veterans Administration hospital where the story was filmed. His physical rehabilitation is detailed in crisp documentary fashion, while his love scenes with Teresa Wright naturally emerge in a more heightened, theatrical style. The hospital wedding, full of ominous new shadows, naturally brings these two strands together and sets the stage for the inevitable climax of the failed wedding night. This last scene, complete with symbolic spilling of champagne and expressive music, is a deliberate contrast with the hospital scenes and puts an indelible mark on Brando's—and the viewer's—consciousness. The ensuing return to the hospital is thus inevitably unendurable, leading to Brando's famous tantrums, his punishment, and his final discharge back to the problems of the real world in an only mildly hopeful ending.

Brando's tortured adjustment of self to society of course expresses Zinnemann's central theme of moral growth through suffering—a theme that he explored more fully in the famous successes of the early fifties *High Noon* and *From Here to Eternity*. Both are films of unrelenting visual drabness, yet both became tremendous popular and critical successes. It is as if the mode of humane realism—for Zinnemann had by this time largely dropped the documentary approach—was suddenly adopted as the official style of the times for serious drama.

For *High Noon* the realistic approach meant violating the conventions of the Western, thus transcending—or traducing—the genre. It has always been a controversial film. Despite, or perhaps because of, its archetypal simplicity, interpretations have multiplied: a modern *Everyman*, a parable of McCarthyism, or of international politics, an anti-Western. Genre directors like Anthony Mann and Delmer Daves disliked it intensely. John Wayne hated its "weakness" (the hero breaks down and weeps at one point). Yet the film early established itself in the popular mind as *the* classic Western. It has been imitated incessantly, transcending even the Western genre itself to emerge in outer space as *Outland* (Peter Hyams, 1981).

More germane to the present discussion than problems of interpretation is the additional problem of credit, for this, too, has been in dispute from the start. The film is known to have previewed badly, at which point producer Stanley Kramer had certain changes made: Dimitri Tiomkin was asked to add the unifying ballad, "Do Not Forsake Me Oh My Darlin'," to his score, and Elmo Williams was asked to fine tune the editing, this last to brilliant effect as the greatest climaxes of this talky film are creations of pure montage. One thinks of the build-up of clocks and cuts leading to the smashing of a bottle by an impatient outlaw and above all the retrospective views, just before the noon train arrives, of virtually every character in the film—the rhythm suddenly breaking with the whistle of the approaching train. Even Gary Cooper's famous performance has been credited to circumstances out of the director's control, for the actor's convincingly anguished expression throughout the film is at least partly the result of a stomach ulcer: the most pain-filled shots were actually reinserted after Zinnemann had left them out of his first cut.

What is clearly Zinnemann's is the *look* of the film. He engaged Floyd Crosby, the photographer of *Tabu* and *The River,* to give the picture a harsh, unfiltered aspect. There are no scenic cloud formations in *High Noon*—only a burning white sky against which Will Kane, in somber black, faces alone the fears that society would prefer to avoid. It is an image that shows no sign of fading.

From Here to Eternity examines the theme of conscience on a vastly larger scale. It is Zinnemann's most ambitious film. Most of his dramas of integrity, no matter how large the canvas, focus on a single character; here he attempts a complexly interacting quintet. Montgomery Clift as Robert E. Lee Prewitt, the "hardhead" soldier who refuses to box, is of course the catalyst. It is he who articulates the film's—and Zinnemann's—key theme: "A man don't go his own way, he's nothin'." Prewitt's way is to do his duty better than anyone else and to suffer for it. He is as much of a martyr as Julia or Sir Thomas More, only he is a victim of his own institution. The corrupt pre-World War II Army, even in the film's muted portrayal, is seen as an implacably brutalizing organization pushing the gentle Prewitt toward murder, court martial, and death. A "smarter" man, like Burt Lancaster's top sergeant, makes his accommodation to the system and emerges a conventional hero when war brings the army to life. A lesser figure, like Frank Sinatra's Maggio, is simply crushed trying to escape. But Prewitt's way is to return to his unit precisely when danger, both personal (a murder charge) and corporate (the Japanese invasion) threatens most. "What has the Army ever done for you?" complains his anguished girl, and Prewitt's reply, moments before he is shot by nervous American troops, has the simple dignity of tragedy: "I'm a soldier."

Prewitt's humanity is necessarily offset by the unrelenting drabness of army life and of the film's visual texture, which makes even Hawaii look dreary. The performances are perfectly cued to the prevailing bleak mood, especially that of Deborah Kerr, whose harsh, flat American tones are such a contrast to her previous work that attention is momentarily called to Zinnemann's unobtrusive contribution. Even her famous scene on the beach with Lancaster is cast in an ugly day-for-night glare, as if to mock any hope of romantic escape. Yet the film does offer one moment of undeniable and indelible beauty. Just as Prewitt's deepest feelings only emerge through his bugling, so Zinnemann allows the film only one true moment of release: Clift playing "Taps" at dusk for his murdered buddy while the music and the shadowplay of quiet barracks and soldiers preparing for bed render this scene on the eve of Pearl Harbor an elegy not only for a friend but for an era.

The tremendous success of *High Noon* and *From Here to Eternity* made Zinnemann a potent force in Hollywood cinema for the remainder of the fifties, so it is distressing to ponder how his freedom and opportunity were largely wasted on unsuitable material. Stage adaptations predominate in this period, a surprising choice for a director so attuned to semidocumentary realism. *The Member of the Wedding* and *A Hatful of Rain* show Zinnemann's typical concern for "sensitive" subjects—adolescence and drug addiction respectively—but neither film achieved much success, and the former is a classic instance of a common Hollywood mistake: adapting a stage version instead of the less restrictive original novel. The most surprising choice of all—Zinnemann himself calls it a "mistake"—was the gigantic *Oklahoma!*, the first film ever made in 70-mm and Zinnemann's first in color. It was an ambitious and commercially highly successful effort to recreate a stylized theater piece in screen terms, with Agnes De Mille herself adapting her celebrated choreography. The dream ballet is retained; offbeat casting choices (Gloria Grahame as Ado Annie, Rod Steiger as Jud) are used to liberate the picture from familiarity; and there is the occasional startling attempt at something "cinematic," such as a shot from underneath a moving buckboard, its wheels enclosing the screen with motion. Yet for all its energy and all its popular success, the film never really takes off. Unlike Wyler, who actively sought out different genres for the creative challenges they posed, Zinnemann has always seemed at sea when confronted by material outside his limited range. He was literally at sea with his aborted effort to adapt Hemingway's *The Old Man and the Sea*, a story whose interior symbolic drama would seem as foreign to Zinnemann's realistic sensibilities as the black-and-white CinemaScope look of *A Hatful of Rain* was to his visual skills.

Nonetheless, it is an interior drama that marks Zinnemann's greatest achievement, for *The Nun's Story* concerns an individual struggling to maintain her integrity in an institution devoted precisely to the annihilation of self and thus probes the innermost recesses of the soul. The film, which resembles no other Hollywood drama, concerns a woman's seventeen-year quest for perfection in the religious life, from her initiation into a strict Belgian order in 1927 to her leaving the convent amid the stresses of war and conscience in 1944. For Gabrielle Van der Mal (Sister Luke), the root of her inner struggle is accurately diagnosed by her surgeon father when he tells her at the beginning: "Gaby, I can see you poor, I can see you chaste, but I cannot see you, a strong-willed girl, obedient to those bells." Like Prewitt, Sister Luke is a "hard-head," an unbending soul whose quest can know no compromise. Yet here the central figure's struggle takes place in an institution that is at once more strange and foreign than the army and more universal. For the demands of the convent are absolute over mind as well as body, as announced in the opening narration: "He that loses his life shall find it. . . . Each sister shall understand that on entering the convent she has made the sacrifice of her life to God." (This speech is heard after the opening credits, during which we first see the figure of Audrey Hepburn thrusting skyward as she approaches the side of a bridge, then looking down to regard her inverted image in the water below, in the first of the film's many images of inner conflict.)

The Nun's Story is a profoundly ambiguous film. The sense of desolation when Sister Luke finally leaves the convent encourages a tragic reading: the inevitable failure of human aspirations toward perfection. On the other hand, the film can also be viewed as the triumph, however painful, of the individual spirit (or even—in a feminist reading—of the "new woman") over a restrictive environment. The Jewish Zinnemann, who deliberately engaged a non-Catholic cast and crew, took considerable pains to preserve this compassionate distance that permits the film such a variety of interpretations. For Zinnemann, the struggle itself is the subject. Gabrielle falls short, like the Quaker wife who kills to save her husband in *High Noon*, because her values are absolutes and human beings cannot live up to absolutes. But as Zinnemann said of the Grace Kelly character in the earlier film, "I don't think one should be blamed for that; *it's in the trying.*"

To say that the subject of *The Nun's Story* imposes a certain austerity is a considerable understatement. It is a long picture (149 minutes) covering seventeen years on two continents, yet the entire drama is internal to Sister Luke; none of the secondary characters in the large and distinguished cast have any importance except as they affect the heroine. For the first hour, the camera never ventures outside the convent, where, to compound the cinematic challenge, the nuns observe long periods of the Grand Silence. Zinnemann's success in surmounting these challenges belies his reputation as an "impersonal" film maker. Thus, the first hour, which has been rightly praised for its documentary-style exposition of the making of a nun, is subtly individualized in numerous ways. To capture the gliding movements of the postulants, Zinnemann engaged a ballet troupe as extras (hardly a documentary touch), making Audrey Hepburn's contrasting Sister Luke stand out at every turn. The long periods of silence force the camera to examine faces more closely than in any previous film and ensure that Sister Luke's involuntary lapses into speech, when they do come, are all the more devastating.

The rigor of visual design is likewise impressive, the first hour being composed almost entirely in the blacks and whites of the nuns' habits. As Sister Luke's career ventures into the outside world, the screen takes on more varied hues, finally exploding in the Congo sequences with the reds, greens, browns, and golds of Africa. The turning point is Sister Luke's intense relationship with a skeptical Congo surgeon who keeps puncturing whatever serenity she may have achieved with his perceptively barbed comments. Thus when, after the emotional, flower-strewn farewell to the Congo, Zinnemann cuts in a single dramatic stroke back to the rainswept motherhouse, the change of color itself signals the onrush of the inevitable denouement.

Fine as it is, Franz Planer's camera work could not have so structured the film into a three-part color symphony. Robert Anderson's screenplay and Audrey Hepburn's performance are likewise crucial to the dramatic realization of the internal subject, the former converting thought and narrative to dialogue and action with astonishing fluidity, the latter bringing a complex character into being before our eyes, largely without benefit of makeup, hairstyle, or change of costume. Yet there can be no doubt that Zinnemann, who initiated the project after seeing galleys of Kathryn Hulme's novel, is chiefly responsible for its excellence.

Three scenes, each almost wordless, encapsulate the drama entirely in terms of mise-en-scène and would by themselves mark Zinnemann as a major director if he had done nothing else. The first is the formal profession of vows, staged as a wedding procession in the glowing blue chapel light and climaxed by the unforgettable image of the haircutting, viewed from above, as with two rough snips of the scissors, counterpointed by delicate string harmonies, Gabrielle sees her own image in a silver platter obliterated by the falling tresses.

There is the climax, as she reads in her cell of her father's murder by the Nazis, the final blow that shatters her ability to forgive and forces her out of the convent. The setting is spartan: Sister Luke in black against bare white walls with a darkened window at the center. She paces back and forth in agony, her three cries of "Father!" each punctuated by a musical outburst, until, turning to the window on the third cry, black on black, she disappears from view entirely, and we know that her struggle is lost.

Above all, there is the conclusion, with the woman left alone in an anteroom to depart the convent forever. She begins to undress, and as the music fades away, the camera drifts to the austere image of a window cross against a plain blue field. When our view returns, it is no longer Sister Luke but Gabrielle Van der Mal, dressed in the same clothes she wore at the start of the film. With impersonal coldness the door springs open, revealing a long Belgian street. Slowly at first, then with resolve, she walks into the distance, hesitates, turns, and is lost from view—returned to a world of war and hate.

Such an ending, with its trapped stationary camera and absence of musical comment or release, can of course be seen as "impersonal" and "noncommittal," exactly the sort of thing that has made Zinnemann anathema to auteurists. Yet the director fought hard to preserve its balance. Ever the documentarist, he had originally wanted no music in the film except such Gregorian chants as might emerge from within the context of the action. Warner Brothers, the studio of Max Steiner and Erich Korngold and wall-to-wall music, insisted on a full score, and the fact that Franz Waxman composed a masterpiece that considerably enhances the film is perhaps an indictment of the director's judgment in this area. But for the ending, according to Zinnemann, Waxman was imposing an interpretation on the film, his exultant music affirming the triumph of individuality. Zinnemann fought against this, or any other, interpretation, and this time he won: the film ends in near silence, with only the sound of a bell (harmonized by strings) summoning Gabrielle back to the world she has abandoned forever. It is the most perfectly poised of all endings and together with the chaste austerity of the entire work makes *The Nun's Story* a transcendent film, comparable more to Bergman or Bresson than to anything in the American cinema. Such transcendence has always made critics uneasy, for what is to be said about a film that has no genre and from which the director has deliberately erased his "personality"? Only that such is the way great movies are sometimes made in America. To have made such a film in 1959 is an achievement beside which questions of personality pale in comparison.

Zinnemann's subsequent career has exhibited a pattern of ambitious, thwarted projects followed by successfully realized pictures on a smaller scale. By 1965 his reputation was at low ebb. *The Sundowners,* a shambling, affable picture about Australian sheepherders, had roused little excitement, though it did contain another earthy performance from Deborah Kerr, an actress who has always responded especially well to Zinnemann's direction. *Behold a Pale Horse,* his symbolic drama of postwar Spain, had been a complete failure, and several years had been wasted on an ambitious project to adapt James Michener's *Hawaii.* (One can see what appealed to Zinnemann about the book, which concerns the conflicting demands of Christian missionaries and native tradition. It was later realized as two separate films, *Hawaii* [George Roy Hill] and *The Hawaiians* [Tom Gries], the former an incomparably meaner-spirited work than anything Fred Zinnemann is likely to have achieved.)

Zinnemann turned to England for the first of his "comeback" films, the screen version of Robert Bolt's *A Man for All Seasons,* which earned him almost as much acclaim as he had enjoyed in the early fifties. Despite all the honors, however, the film must, by the highest standards, be judged a failure. It is another stage adaptation—always an uncongenial form for Zinnemann—and although he and Bolt labored mightily, they failed to come up with a convincing screen equivalent for the Common Man, the chorus figure who, by playing several of the minor, conscienceless characters in the play, insinuates their attitude into the audience, thus setting off Thomas More's integrity all the more sharply.

Without such an intermediary figure, the heroism of More inevitably seems chilly and remote, an effect emphasized by the virtuoso performance of Paul Scofield in the title role. Scofield's More is an infinitely more skillful variation on the type played by Gary Cooper in *High Noon:* the man of conscience who does not desire a confrontation but who faces it squarely when his honor forces it upon him. But Scofield is almost too good in the role. With his weathered face and anguished eyes, he seems too much the ascetic for the family-loving More proposed by history and the script. We never quite believe him when he taps his chest and says, "This is not the stuff of which martyrs are made." (Charlton Heston wanted to play the role, and one can see his point: the film needs a flesh-and-blood hero.)

A Man for All Seasons remains a stirring document with some memorable images: the inexorably flowing river; Orson Welles's monstrous Wolsey, seeming to engulf his chambers in cardinal's red; and Robert Shaw's golden young Henry VIII stepping leonine out of a blazing sun (an image to which the actor's subsequent career, like the monarch's, has added inescapable resonance). Yet the film finally remains stagebound. For all its merits and for all the desperate ploys, such as rapid pans across a tumultuous courtroom, Zinnemann's camera too often remains stationary at that safe middle distance, an approach that is simply not sufficient for this particular drama.

MGM's cancellation of *Man's Fate* in 1970, just as a dream cast (Liv Ullman, Eiji Okada, Peter Finch) was going into production in expensive Oriental locations, was a blow from which some directors might never have recovered. One era of classically crafted movie making was coming to an end in 1970: William Wyler retired in that year, and David Lean has completed no film since. But Zinnemann did bounce back, with a seemingly atypical thriller concerning an attempt to assassinate de Gaulle. *The Day of the Jackal* is a fascinating contrast to Zinnemann's films of conscience, for the plot hinges on the professional killer's complete lack of conscience or other human attributes that would make it possible to trace him. Given such a protagonist, Zinnemann's impersonal style cannot but be an asset.

But such a pat explanation for the film's success would be unfair. The silent, uncommunicative killer—he lacks even a name—is from a technical point of view almost as difficult a character to probe as Sister Luke, and yet (as in *The Nun's Story*) he effectively carries the entire film (for the "police" half is relatively weak and perfunctory). Zinnemann does not really attempt to probe the Jackal's mind. (In the film, those who do usually come to a bad end.) Instead, he falls back on crisp documentary technique, notably in the scenes of de Gaulle's public appearances, an apparent mix of stock and recreated footage. Toward the end, when the Jackal has been "lost," the repeated scanning of boulevard and plaza and cathedral is a tour de force of frustration relieved—for viewers if not for the police—when the camera finally comes to rest on a long street. Slowly we realize that the one-legged man who has been inexorably moving toward us is in fact the Jackal in the last and finest of his disguises. It is a chilling moment, the most convincing demonstration of the film's impossible premise: for an instant we are persuaded against all logic that nothing can stop this killer. Of course the character has not the tragic dimension of Will Kane or Sister Luke; his downfall comes merely through the mechanics of plot. But Zinnemann has visualized him with the same skillful eye.

Julia, though perhaps the clearest treatment in Zinnemann's entire oeuvre of a conscience in formation, is a difficult film to analyze, for it derives from a completed script that had originally been intended for Sidney Pollack, and its romantic color photography has no parallel elsewhere in Zinnemann's work. The moderately complex, Resnais-like memory structure is thus probably irrelevant to Zinnemann's contribution. Alvin Sargent's screenplay, from a brief memoir by Lillian Hellman, is also more uneven than most Zinnemann films. Indeed, parts of the film are well-nigh unbearable: Jane Fonda as Lillian Hellman in How I Became a Great Writer—which turns out to be by chain smoking, heaving typewriters out the window, and seeking the approbation of that other Great Writer, Dashiell Hammett.

Nevertheless, the heart of the story is the awakening of Lillian's social conscience through the inspiration of her friend, and here Zinnemann is firmly on his chosen ground. The casting of Jane Fonda and Vanessa Redgrave is a major coup, for the two women are themselves close personal friends as well as icons of the contemporary Left, and thus direct heirs to Hellman's Hollywood role of forty years earlier. Fonda's blunt stridency makes her the perfect foil for the extravagant Redgrave, whose glowing presence here supplies an inspiration only outlined in the script. (Zinnemann had used Redgrave just so for a key moment in *A Man for All Seasons,* one of her first screen appearances.)

The climax of *Julia*—the two women exchanging the burdens of a lifetime while under observation in a Berlin café—is its most effective scene. The camera is stationary, the cutting merely functional. The tone is guarded, emotions are underplayed. Julia has to maneuver her friend out of danger. She does it quietly, unobtrusively, masterfully. It is one of the most moving scenes in recent films and emblematic of the cinema of Fred Zinnemann at its best.

CONTRIBUTORS

John Belton teaches film at Columbia University. He is the author of two books, *The Hollywood Professionals* and *Robert Mitchum,* and his articles and film reviews have appeared in *The Velvet Light Trap, Film Quarterly, The Village Voice, Rolling Stone,* and other periodicals.

Jean-Loup Bourget was a French Embassy cultural attache in London, Chicago, and New York, and now teaches at the University of Toulouse in France. He is a regular contributor to *Positif* and his book on Robert Altman has been published in France.

Jean-Pierre Coursodon was born near Paris in 1935 and has written on film since he was sixteen. He studied English at the Sorbonne and in England, as well as at the Ecole Normale Supérieure. In 1960, his first book, *Vingt ans de cinéma américain,* was published. A specialist in American film comedy, he subsequently published *Keaton & Co.,* an introduction to silent comedy (1964), monographs on Laurel and Hardy (1966) and W. C. Fields (1968), and *Buster Keaton* (1973), the most comprehensive study of Keaton's work. Equally well received was his 1970 collaboration with critic and film director Bertrand Tavernier, *Trente ans de cinéma américain,* in which he took up and expanded the format devised for the 1960 book. Coursodon moved to the United States in the mid-1960s and has lived in New York City ever since. He has taught French Literature and/or lectured on film at the City College of New York, the State University at New Paltz, and Sarah Lawrence College. He contributes to film magazines on both sides of the Atlantic and frequently writes for the French monthly *Cinéma,* for which he is U.S. correspondent.

John H. Dorr, formerly a movie reviewer/historian for *The Hollywood Reporter, Take One, Millimeter,* and other publications, is now an independent writer/producer/director of movies on videotape. His first three features are: *SudZall Does It All!* (1979), *The Case of the Missing Consciousness* (1980), and *Dorothy and Alan at Norma Place* (1982).

John Fitzpatrick is a free-lance editor for several New York publishing companies and has written extensively on film music. He is editor of *Pro Musica Sana,* a leading journal of comment on film music, and is an associate editor on the *Dictionary of the Middle Ages.*

Barry Gillam is a freelance writer and researcher and is editor of *TV Tout Sheet,* a newsletter devoted to television credits and commentary. His articles have appeared in *SF Commentary* and *Thousand Eyes.*

Michael Henry teaches film at the University of Paris and is a member of the editorial board of *Positif.* He is secretary general of the French Association of Film Producers and the Independent Film Producers International Association. He has also served as a consultant to the production of a number of films, including *In the Realm of the Senses* and *The Tin Drum.* He is currently producing a series of film portraits of leading American filmmakers.

Tim Hunter taught film history at the University of California at Santa Cruz, produced and directed several shorts, and wrote the screenplay for *Over the Edge* before directing his first feature, *Tex* (1982).

Diane Jacobs is the author of two books, *Hollywood Renaissance* and . . . *But We Need the Eggs: The Magic of Woody Allen*. She has written of film for such periodicals as *The New York Times, The Village Voice, Soho News,* and *American Film*.

Mark LeFanu teaches English at Cambridge University and has contributed to *Monogram, Positif,* and *The Monthly Film Bulletin*. He is currently writing a book on the relationship of film to literature and painting.

Alain Masson, who teaches linguistics and literature in France, is a regular contributor to *Positif* as well as various literary journals. He is also the author of a book, *Comédie musicale,* published in Paris.

Myron Meisel is a writer, producer and attorney in Los Angeles. He produced *Final Exam* and *I'm a Stranger Here Myself: A Portrait of Nicholas Ray* and has written on film for numerous periodicals ranging from *Rolling Stone* to *Film Comment* to *The Los Angeles Times*. He is the film critic of the Los Angeles *Reader* and a member of the National Society of Film Critics.

Barry Putterman is a Ph.D. candidate in cinema studies at New York University; from 1971–1977, he wrote for *Audience,* a film criticism magazine, and has completed a critical history of Warner Brothers cartoons.

Pierre Sauvage is an Emmy Award-winning writer/producer/director who learned to appreciate films while working at the Cinémathèque Française in the 1960s. A former writer about the movies, trade paper editor, U.S. correspondent of *Positif,* and staffer at the Academy of Motion Picture Arts and Sciences, he has also served as U.S. director of the Deauville Festival of American Film and as a member of the selection committee for the Los Angeles International Film Exposition. His 1983 production of *Le Chambon: The Village That Defied the Nazis* deals with the heroic actions during the Holocaust of a devoutly Christian community that provided shelter to some five thousand Jewish refugees, including Sauvage himself, who was born there.

Ronnie Sheib teaches film at Barnard College. She has written articles on Hitchcock, Fuller, Tex Avery, and Charles Schnee for *Film Comment* and various publications. She is currently writing a book on William Wellman and one on Ida Lupino.

Eric Sherman is a filmmaker, teacher, and the author of two books, *Directing the Film* and *The Director's Event*.

David Sterritt is the film critic for the *Christian Science Monitor,* where he also writes regularly on music and theater. His criticism has appeared in numerous other publications and can be heard frequently on National Public Radio.

Richard Thompson has taught film at UCLA, the University of California at Riverside and at San Diego, and is currently chairman of the division of Film Studies at La Trobe University in Melbourne, Australia. His articles have appeared in such periodicals as *Film Comment, Velvet Light Trap, American Film,* and *Sight and Sound*.

Yann Tobin is the pen name of N. T. Binh, a French critic of Vietnamese origin who has worked as a technical advisor and assistant director on medical films. He is a frequent contributor to *Positif*.

General Index

Index of Movie Titles